The Lost Light

AN INTERPRETATION OF ANCIENT SCRIPTURES

Alvin Boyd Kuhn

ISBN 1-56459-177-8

To

THE MEMORY OF

DR. ROBERT NORWOOD

WHOSE CHARGE TO ME TO WRITE THIS
BOOK WAS AN IMPELLING AND SUS-
TAINING INSPIRATION TO THE
TASK, THIS WORK IS
AFFECTIONATELY
DEDICATED

CONTENTS

PROLOGUE

COMING forth in a day when theology has long been discredited—even in its own ecclesiastical household—and religion itself is threatened with obliteration by rampant forces hostile to it, this book aims to rehabilitate theology and to stabilize true religion. It must be said at the very outset and with blunt insistence that it is *for* religion and not in any way against it. It is written to establish religion again as the cornerstone of human culture, when civilization has largely turned away from it to seek elsewhere the guiding light. It is designed to redeem Divine Theology from her outcast condition and place her again beside Philosophy and Science on the throne in the kingdom of man's mind.

It needs sharply to be asseverated that the book is for religion because many will pronounce it the most forthright attack on ecclesiastical doctrinism yet presented. It can hardly be denied that it sweeps away almost the entire body of common acceptance of biblical and theological meaning. But it makes no war on anything in religion save the idiocies and falsities that have crept into the general conception of orthodox belief. Finding that the chief enemies of true religion were those within her own gates, the book has had to address itself to the ungenerous task of repudiating the whole untenable structure of accredited interpretation in order to erect on the ground the lovely temple of ancient truth. If theology is to be rescued from its forlorn state of intellectual disrepute into which not its enemies but its friends have precipitated it through an unconscionable perversion of its original significance to gross repulsiveness, the errors and distortions perpetrated upon it by those of its own household must be ruthlessly dismantled. Hence to many the book will seem like a devastating assault on the very citadel of common religious preachment. In the face of all this it must be maintained that the work is written to support and defend religion against all its foes and that it is constructive and not destructive of true religious values at every turn. It was no light or frivol-

I

ous gesture to affront a settled and rooted growth of beliefs and doctrinal statements that have been cherished for centuries around the hearthstone of Christian culture and become hallowed by age-long acceptance and the strong loves and loyalties inbred in sensitive childhood. But it was seen to be a drastic operation quite necessary to save the organism of religion itself from further decay and menacing death. Excrescences of misconception and superstition had to be heroically cut out of the body of theology and the calcareous incrustations of ignorant interpretation dissolved and carried away by the acid stream of living truth flowing forth, after centuries of suppression, from the mighty scriptures of the past.

The Western world has too long and fatuously labored under the delusion that a pious and devout disposition fulfills the whole requirement of true religion. Ancient sagacity knew that piety without intelligence, or religion without philosophy, was insufficient and dangerous. It knew that general good intent was not safe from aberrancy, folly and fanaticism unless it was directed by the highest powers and resources of the mind. And the mind itself had to be fortified with specific knowledge of the nature of the cosmos and of man and the relation between the two. Following the dictum of the sage, Hermes Trismegistus, that "the vice of a soul is ignorance, the virtue of a soul is knowledge," the scriptures of old inculcated the precept that with all man's getting he must first get wisdom and understanding. These were related to his well-being as health to his navel and marrow to his bones, and would alone give him a crown of eternal life. They were pronounced more precious than all the things that he could desire. The council of Illuminati therefore laid down their systems of cosmology and anthropology, which have become by immemorial tradition the Bibles of humanity, universally reverenced. In them were given the ordinances of life, the constitution of the cosmos, the laws governing both nature and mind. They still constitute the Magna Carta of all human action guided by intelligence. For they were the first Institutes embodying the Principia and Fundamenta of all moral behavior, the only true chart and compass to guide human effort in a line of harmony with an overshadowing divine plan of evolution for the Cosmos.

The corruption and final loss of the basic meaning of these scriptures has been, in the whole of time, the greatest tragedy in human history. Like Shakespeare's tide, which, taken at the flood, leads on to fortune, but, omitted, casts all the rest of life in shoals and quicksands, the wreckage of the Esoteric Gnosis in the centuries following Plato's day, culminating in the debacle of all philosophical religion about the third century of Christianity's development and ushering in sixteen centuries of the Dark Ages, has thrown all religion out of basic relation to true understanding and caused it to breed an endless train of evils, fanaticisms, bigotries, idiosyncrasies, superstitions, wars and persecutions that more than anything else blacken the record of man's historic struggle toward the light. The present (1940) most frightful of all historical barbarities owes its incidence directly to the decay of ancient philosophical knowledge and the loss of vision and virtue that would have attended its perpetuation.

What, then, must be the importance of a book which restores to the scriptures of ancient wisdom the lost light of their true original meaning?

In a very real and direct way the salvation of culture and a free spirit in the world is contingent upon this restoration of the ancient intelligence to modernity. For man at this age has had new and mighty powers of nature suddenly placed in his hands, and yet lacks the spiritual poise and sagacity to use them without calamity. Most strangely, the control of the lower physical, natural or brute forces by the mind or reason was the one central situation primarily and fundamentally dealt with in the sage tomes of antiquity. To effect that control in a perfect balance and harmony, and to train the reasoning intellect in the divine art of it, was the aim and end of the Arcane Philosophy. Ideology in the Western world has endlessly vacillated back and forth between the cult of the inner spirit and engrossment in objective materialism. Ancient philosophy taught that the true path of evolutionary growth was to be trodden by an effort that united the forces of the spirit with those of the world, the lower disciplined by the higher. The whole gist of the Esoteric Doctrine was the study and mastery of the powers engaged in working out the evolutionary advance, so that the aspirant might be able to align his cultural effort in consonance with the requirements of the problem and the end to be achieved.

Without this guiding data and this evolutionary perspective modern man is totally at a loss how to focus his endeavor and is unable to point

3

his direction in line with anything more fixed and basic than his next immediate objective of apparent desirability. He has neither a knowledge of his origin, a chart of his path, an inventory of his capacities or a vision of his goal. Hence he travels the long road still a benighted wanderer without compass. He can but recoil from one mistaken plunge after another, learning sporadic lessons from pain and misfortune. The ancient torch that was lighted for his guidance he has let burn out. This lamp was the body of Ancient Philosophy. In this critical epoch in the life of the world this book proclaims afresh the message of lost truth.

Three ancient and long-discredited sciences have had a surprising renaissance in popular fancy and scientific interest: symbolism, alchemy, astrology. The last has particularly come into a general vogue, but on a basis which still inclines conservative positivism in science and scholarship to regard it as allied closely with "popular superstition." In its predictive or "fortune-telling" aspect it is generally looked at askance. But there is another side on which it has pertinence and value that has not been recognized in the modern revival and on which perhaps its most legitimate claim to consideration rests. This is its function as symbolic theology. Unquestionably cosmic operation, cosmic significance, lie behind the twelve constellations of the zodiac and the thirty-six or more other stellar configurations. The planisphere or chart of the heavens was doubtless the first of all Bibles, pictorially edited. Not quite simply and directly but intrinsically, all Bibles are amplifications and elaborations of the original volume of ideography first written on the open face of the sky, charted in the zodiac and heavenly maps, and later transferred to earth and written in scrolls and parchments. Man was instructed to fashion his new body of spiritual glory "after the pattern of things in the heavens," the heavenly or zodiacal man. And a graph of the structure and history of this celestial Personage was sketched by the enlightened sages in the configurated star clusters. Zodiac comes from the Greek word *zodion*, a small living image, signifying that it is a graph of the microcosmic life of man, which is cast in the form of the macrocosmic life of the universe, or of God. Man's own small body is a replica of this body of God, made in its image and likeness. The vast frame of Cosmic Man

4

was outlined in the scroll of the heavens, the solar systems and galaxies being living cell clusters in his immense organism.

A deal of this adumbrative symbology elucidating theological doctrinism is set forth in the body of the present work. But there is a group of its data that strikes so deeply into the heart of general theology that it is given here at the outset for the sake of its overwhelming impressiveness. It must prove to be so conclusive an evidence that Biblical theology rests more solidly than has ever been believed on zodiacal backgrounds that its presentation will be admittedly a matter of great moment. It traces the unsuspected significance of two of the twelve signs, Virgo and Pisces, in the very heart of New Testament narrative. Let the reader picture before him the ordinary zodiac, with the house of Virgo at the western equinox point and that of Pisces directly opposite on the eastern side. The simple fact that they stand six months apart will presently be seen to assume great importance in Gospel determination.

The exposition must begin with the puzzling and hitherto unexplained item of ancient religious myth, that the Christs, the Sun-Gods, the Messiahs, all were depicted as having two mothers. How, one asks, could there possibly be rational significance in this? It has been put aside as just some more of the mythical rubbish and nonsense of early Paganism. The profundity of pagan intelligence, hiding sublime cosmic truth under glyph and symbol, has not been dreamed of.

The depiction should not have created incredulity, seeing that the Gospel Jesus himself, dramatic figure of the divine principle in man, announced it categorically in declaring to Nicodemus that "ye must be born again." Nicodemus asks if this means that we must enter a second time into our mother's body and experience a second birth in the natural manner. Jesus replies that we "must be born of water and the spirit." Attention must be directed a moment to the fact that the Latin word *spiritus,* translated "spirit" in many passages, means as well "air" or "breath." One of the great keys to Bible meaning is the series of the four "elements" of ancient mythicism: earth, water, air and fire. The body of the physical or natural man was conceived as being composed of the two lower, earth and water, while air and fire, representing mind and spirit, commingled to make the higher or spiritual man. Jesus' statement to Nicodemus, then, could have been rendered, "born of water and air." And John the Baptist uses three of the four ele-

5

ments when he states that he, the forerunner of the *Christos,* and therefore a type of the lower natural man, indeed baptizes us with water (omitting earth), but that there cometh after him one higher than himself who shall baptize us with the holy *spiritus* (air) and with fire. Jesus thus affirms that we have two births, necessitating two mothers, and John the Baptist adds that we must have two baptisms.

Since man's spirit is an indestructible fragment of God's own mighty Spirit, truly a tiny spark of that cosmic Intelligence and Love which we call the Mind of God, the ancients typified the divine element in man by fire and in contrast the lower or human element by water. The fiery soul of man *is* housed in a tenement of flesh and matter which is seven-eighths water by actual composition! The crossing of rivers and seas and the immersion of solar heroes in water in olden mythologies, and the rite of baptism in theology, signified nothing beyond the fact of the soul's immersion in a physical body of watery nature in its successive incarnations.

Now man is distinctly a creature compounded of two natures, a higher and a lower, a spiritual and a sensual, a divine and a human, a mortal and an immortal, and finally a fiery and a watery, conjoined in a mutual relationship in the organic body of flesh. Says Heraclitus: "Man is a portion of cosmic fire, imprisoned in a body of earth and water." Speaking of man Plato affirms: "Through body it is an animal; through intellect it is a god." To create man God incarnated the fiery spiritual principle of his life in the watery confines of material bodies. That is the truest basic description of man that anthropology can present. All problems spring from that foundation and are referable for solution back to it.

Man is, then, a natural man and a god, in combination. Our natural body gives the soul of man its baptism by water; our nascent spiritual body is to give us the later baptism by fire! We are born first as the natural man; then as the spiritual. Or we are born first by water and then by fire. Of vital significance at this point are two statements by St. Paul: "That was not first which is spiritual, but that which is natural"; and, "First that which is natural, then that which is spiritual." Again he says: "For the natural man comprehendeth not the things of the spirit of God, neither can he." Of course not; for he is not yet in that higher kingdom of evolution, and he must be transformed, transfigured, lifted up into a superior world of consciousness before

6

he can cognize spiritual things. Evolution will thus transform him, and nothing else will.

Using astrological bases for portraying cosmic truths, the ancients localized the birth of the natural man in the zodical house of Virgo and that of the spiritual man in the opposite house of Pisces. These then were the houses of the two mothers of life. The first was the Virgin Mother (Virgo), the primeval symbol of the Virgin Mary thousands of years B.C. Virgo gave man his natural birth by water and became known as the Water-Mother; Pisces (*the Fishes* by name) gave him his birth by the Fish and was denominated the Fish-Mother. The virgin mothers are all identified with water as symbol and their various names, such as Meri, Mary, Venus (born of the sea-foam), Tiamat, Typhon and Thallath (Greek for "sea") are designations for water. On the other side there are the Fish Avatars of Vishnu, such as the Babylonian Ioannes, or Dagon, and the Assyrian goddess Atergatis was called "the Fish-Mother." Virgo stood as the mother of birth by water, or the birth of man the first, of the earth, earthy; Pisces stood as the mother of birth by spirit or fire, or the birth of man the second, described by St. Paul as "the Lord from heaven." Virgo was the water-mother of the natural man, Pisces the fish-mother of the spiritual man.

There must now be brought out an unrevealed significance of the fish symbol in the zodiac and in mythical religion. It is of astonishing import. Water is the type of natural birth because all natural birth proceeds in and from water. All first life originated in the sea water. The fish is a birth in and from the water, and it stands patently as the generic type of organic life issuing out of inorganic! The fish typifies life embodied in a physical organic structure. Organic life is born out of the water, and is the first birth, child of the water-mother. And if organic life is in turn to become mother, its child will be mind and spiritual consciousness, son of the fish-mother! In brief, water is the mother of natural physical being, and organic structure becomes the later mother of divine mind.

Now, strangely enough, water is the type of another thing which is still more germinal of life, namely, matter. Matter is the virgin mother of all life in the aboriginal genesis. All things are generated in the womb of primordial matter, the "old genetrix" of Egyptian mythology. And it is by a consideration of the nature of matter and its evolution that we are enabled to arrive at last at the true meaning of the double motherhood of life. For oddly enough, matter is seen to exist in two states, in each of which it becomes mother of life, at two different levels. Primordial matter, the sea of (to us) empty space, is the first mother of all living forms. This is the primal "abyss of the waters" in *Genesis*. The Latin word for "mother" is our very word "matter," with one "t" left out—*mater*. And how close to *mater* is *water!* And organic structure is the second mother, parent of spiritual mind.

The ancient books always grouped the two mothers in pairs. They were called "the two mothers" or sometimes the "two divine sisters." Or they were the wife and sister of the God, under the names of Juno, Venus, Isis, Ishtar, Cybele or Mylitta. In old Egypt they were first Apt and Neith; and later Isis and Nephthys. Massey relates Neith to "net," i.e., fish-net! Clues to their functions were picked up in the great *Book of the Dead:* "Isis conceived him; Nephthys gave him birth." Or: "Isis bore him; Nephthys suckled him," or reared him. The full sense of these statements was not discerned until they were scrutinized in the light of another key sentence which matched them: "Heaven conceived him; the Tuat brought him forth." With this came the flash of clear insight into the mystery. For that which is to eventuate in the cycles of evolution as divine mind in an organic creature—man—is aboriginally conceived by divine ideation in the innermost depths of Cosmic Consciousness, or in the purely noumenal world, or again in the bosom of Infinite Spirit, where Spirit is identical with pure undifferentiated matter. This is mirrored in the Egyptian statement that Isis conceived him. Matter in its invisible, inorganic state was the womb of the first conception. Isis is virgin, i.e., pure matter, or matter sublimated to spiritual tenuity. The Tuat, on the other hand, is really earth, as the type of physical matter, or matter organic, aggregated into substantial forms, called by us physical matter. It is matter as substance, constituted and existent in the visible world in structural forms. Isis was matter subsistent as empty space, and Nephthys was atomic matter, constituent of visible structural forms. The physical worlds which we must now think of as floating in the sea of empty space like fish in the water, are the second form of matter, and their organic bodies of substantial matter give birth to the Logoi in the solar systems and to the *Christos* in man. So divine spirit is conceived in the womb of Isis, the first universal mother, and brought to birth in the womb of

8

Nephthys, the second mother, the immediate incubator and gestator of its manifest expression. One might paraphrase this situation by saying that a human child is first conceived in the love, or mind, of its parents, and later born from the womb of its physical mother. Thus life has two births and must of necessity have two mothers. Life is spiritually conceived and materially born. Or, man may be said to be born as a natural creature from spirit into matter, and born later as a spiritual god when he emerges from his baptism in the water of the body and re-enters the bosom of his Father. Or, finally, he is born first as man, by water; and reborn later as god, by fire. And the first birth was depicted as taking place on the western side of the zodiac, in the house or womb of the Virgin Mother, Virgo, because in the west the sun, universal symbol of spiritual fire, descended into organic matter in its setting, or incarnation. So man is born as natural man on the west, to be regenerated as spiritual man on the east. Spirit's descent on the west makes it man; its resurrection on the east, like the summer sunrise, makes it deity again. This is the death and resurrection of the god in all religions. It is incarnation and return to spirit. It is the descent of the Messiah into Egypt and his exodus back to Canaan.

Further scrutiny of such data brings to light links of connection with the Bible. The chief one is found in the symbol of bread in connection with both Virgo and Pisces. Pisces is the house of the Fishes by name, but it is not commonly known that Virgo in astrological symbology was the house of Bread. This is indicated by several items of ancient typology. Many centuries ago in the precession of the equinoxes, the end of the year was marked by the position of the great Dog-Star Sirius, mighty celestial symbol of the divinity in man. Precisely at midnight of December 24 it stood on the meridian line from the zenith to Egypt. At the same moment there arose on the eastern horizon the constellation of the Virgin, bearing in her left arm the Christ child, symbol of the Christhood coming to function in man, and in her right hand the great star Spica (Latin, a head, or "spike" of wheat), symbol of that same divinity coming as celestial food for man. It must ever be remembered that the Gospel Jesus told us we had virtually to eat his body as food, and drink his blood, if we would inherit eternal life. So typism represented him as coming in the form of man, the babe Christ, and as food for man, the wheat. John speaks of the Christ principle in the words: "This is that bread which came

9

down from heaven, that if a man eat of it he shall hunger no more." Jesus broke a loaf into fragments and gave to his disciples, saying that it was his body, broken for them.

We now have Virgo established as the house of Bread and Pisces as the house of Fish. But the characterization of the two houses must be brought along to a more specific evolutionary reference. What are these "houses," thus delineated? They are, as at first, the two states of matter, but now to be taken in immediate reference to the life of man on earth. They are in the final stage of the meaning man's body itself, which consists of matter in both its invisible and its visible forms. For man has a natural body and a spiritual body. Man's body itself houses the two mothers. The body is this double house of Bread and of Fish.

And the next link is seen when it is considered that this physical body is for the soul the house of death and in its regenerative phase, the house of rebirth. It is the house into which the spirit descends to its partial obscuration in the darkness of the grave of matter, into the night of death, or incarnation, out of which it is to arise in a new birth or resurrection on the opposite side of the cycle. A significant passage from the *Book of the Dead* recites: "Who cometh forth from the dusk, and whose birth is in the house of death"—referring to the incarnating soul. In a spiritual sense the soul "dies" on entering the body in incarnation, but has a new birth in it as it later resurrects from it. The body is therefore the house of his death and rebirth, or the place of his crucifixion and resurrection.

And the Egyptians had a name for the body as the locus of these transformations, which carry the central meaning of all theologies. This name now rises out of the dim mists of ancient Egyptian books to enlighten all modern Bible comprehension. This city of the body, where the sun of soul sank to its death on the cross of matter, to re-arise in a new birth, was called the city of the sun, or in Greek, Heliopolis, but in the Egyptian, ANU. The name was given to an actual Egyptian city, where the rites of the death, burial and resurrection of Osiris or Horus were enacted each year; but the name bore a theological significance before it was given to a geographical town.

The name is obviously made up of NU, the name for the mother heaven, or empty space, or abyss of nothingness, and Alpha privative, meaning, as in thousands of words, "not." A-NU would then mean "not-nothingness," or a world of concrete actuality, the world of physical substantial manifestation. Precisely such a world it is in which units of virginal consciousness go to their death and rise again. A-NU is then the physical body of man on earth. The soul descends out of the waters of the abyss of the NUN, or space in its undifferentiated unity, which is the sign and name of all things negative. The NUN is indeed our "none." Life in the completeness of its unity is negative. To become positively manifest it must differentiate itself into duality, establish positive-negative tension, and later split up into untold multiplicity. This brings out the significance of the Biblical word "multiply." Life can not manifest itself in concrete forms until it multiplies itself endlessly. Unit life of deity must break itself up into infinite fragments in order to fill empty space with a multitude of worlds and beings of different natures. The primal Sea or Mother must engender a multitudinous progeny, to spawn the limitless shoals of organic fish-worlds. This is the meaning of the promise given to Abraham, that his seed should *multiply* till it filled the earth with offspring countless as the sands of the seashore. And if life was symboled by bread, as the first birth, and by fish, as the second, then we might expect to find in old religious typology the allegory of a Christ figure *multiplying loaves and fishes!* Are we surprised to find that the Gospel Jesus does this very thing, *multiplying* the five loaves and two small fishes to feed a *multitude!*

This is astonishing enough in all conscience, but it yields in wonder to the next datum of Comparative Religion which came to our notice as a further tie between the Bible and antecedent Egyptian mythology. Who can adequately measure the seriousness of the challenge which this item of scholarship presents to Gospel historicity? For a discovery of sensational interest came to light when a passage was found in the *Book of the Dead* which gave to Anu the characteristic designation, *"the place of multiplying bread"!* Here in the long silent tomes of old Egypt was found the original, the prototype, of the miracle of the loaves and the fishes in the Gospels of Christianity. And a meaning never before apprehended had to be read into this New Testament wonder. At last we were instructed to catch in the miracle the sense that the physical body, as A-NU, was the place where the corpus of the Christ's deific power was broken into an infinite number of fragments and distributed out among a multitude of creatures, enhungered after

II

a three-days' fast, or deprivation of the food of spiritual life in their sojourn in the three kingdoms, the mineral, vegetable and animal, before reaching the plane of mind. Here are all the elements of the inner meaning of the Christian Eucharist: the broken but multiplied fragments of the body of the god, distributed to feed hungry humanity. And as humanity is composed of twelve groups of divine conscious units, there were gathered up twelve baskets of fragments! And this episode of the Christ's ostensible life is found to be Egyptian in origin and meaning and symbolic in character!

But new implications arise and lead us on to more startling disclosures. The Hebrews came along and appropriated Egyptian material. They picked up the name ANU and fitting it back into its zodiacal setting as Virgo, they called it the "house of Bread." This required their adding to ANU their word for "house," which, as anyone knows, is *Beth*. This yields us Beth-Anu. Now it is a fact of common philological knowledge that the ancient Greek and Egyptian "U" is rendered as "Y" when the words are brought over into English. The "U" became a "Y," and Beth-Anu now stands before us as the Bethany of the Gospels! Bethany is thus just the sign of Virgo, as the "house of Bread," the home of the great star Spica, the head of wheat!

But let us say "house of Bread" in ordinary Hebrew. What further astonishment strikes us here, as we find it reads Beth-Lehem (Lechem, Lekhem), for *lechem, lekhem,* is bread in everyday Hebrew. The Christ was born in Bethany or Bethlehem, the astrological "house of Bread." (Later it seems that the two signs, Virgo and Pisces, and their symbols, bread and fish, were almost interchangeably confused or commingled in the symbolic imagery. This was natural, since the two signs represented the same body of man in its two aspects of dying and being reborn, and the two processes are confusedly interblended.)

If Pisces is then the "house" in which the Christ in man comes to his birth, it is pertinent to ask if there are evidences in the Bible or Christianity that Jesus was colored with the fish typology. Here we encounter material enough to provide another nine-days' wonder. For we find the Gospel Jesus marked with many items of the Piscean symbology. He picks his twelve disciples from the ranks of fishermen (in Egypt they were as well carpenters, reapers, harvesters, sailors, rowers, builders, masons, potters, etc.); he told Peter to find the gold in the fish's mouth; he performed the miraculous draught of fishes; he declared that he would make them "fishers of men." In the catacombs under Rome the symbol of the two fishes crossed was displayed on the Christ's forehead, at his feet, or on a plate on the altar before him. And the Romans for several centuries dubbed the early Christians Pisciculi, or "Little Fishes," members of the "fish-cult." And the Greeks denominated the Gospel Jesus as *Ichthys,* the Fish. All this fish symbolism can not be explained away as sheer incidental material. It is the product of ancient custom, which figured the Christs under the symbolism of the reigning sign of the zodiac, according to the precession of the equinoxes.

And yet another surprising correlation comes to view. The Christ, as it has here been delineated, is the offspring or creation of a conception of deific Mind, first in the inner bosom of spiritual matter, then in organic bodily structure. Primeval space, we have seen, was called in Egypt the NUN, or the Waters of the Nun. All Bible students recognize a familiar ring in the phrase "Joshua, Son of Nun." But so far has ignorance and obscurantism gone with its deadly work in Christian literalism that hardly anyone knows with definiteness that Joshua is just a variant name for Jesus. The phrase is actually written in some old documents as "Jesus, Son of Nun." At any rate Joshua is just Jesus, no less. So here is the Christ, called Jesus, son of the aboriginal space, or the NUN. But the wonder increases when we turn to the Hebrew alphabet and find that while "M" is called and spelled "Mem" and means "water," "N" is called and spelled "Nun" and means—of all things— "Fish"! Jesus, then, is son of Pisces, the Fish-sign, as he indeed is in the Gospels themselves.

And Horus, the Egyptian Christ, who is identical with the Jesus of the Gospels in some one hundred and eighty particulars, performed at Anu a great miracle. He raised his father Osiris from the dead, calling unto him in the cave to rise and come forth. Anu, as we have seen, became Bethany of the Gospels; and it was at Bethany that Jesus raised Lazarus from death! And who was Lazarus? Here the greatest of all the marvels in this chain of comparative data unfolds under our eyes. According to Budge and other eminent Egyptologists the ancient designation of Osiris was ASAR. But the Egyptians invariably expressed reverence for deity by prefixing the definite article "the" to the names of their Gods. Just as Christians say, or should say, *the* Christ, they said: *the* Osiris. It will be found that the article connoted deity in ancient usage. Our definite article, "the" is the root of the Greek word *theos,* God; the Spanish article, masculine, *"el,"* is the Hebrew word for God; and the Greek masculine article, *"ho,"* is a Chinese word for deity. To say *the* Osiris was equivalent to saying Lord Osiris. When the Hebrews took up the Egyptian phrases and names they converted the name of "the Osiris" or "Lord Osiris" directly into their own vernacular, and the result was "El-Asar." Later on the Romans, speaking Latin, took up the same material that had come down from revered Egyptian sources and to "El-Asar" they added the common Latin termination of the second declension masculine nouns, in which most men's names ended, namely, *"-us"*; and the result was now "El-Asar-us." In time the initial "E" wore off, as the scholars phrase it, and the "s" in Asar changed into its sister letter "z," leaving us holding in our hands the Lazarus whom Jesus raised at Bethany! To evidence that this derivation is not a fanciful invention or sheer coincidence the Biblical names of High Priests may be cited. We find one with the name of El(e)azar and another by name Azar-iah, "iah" or "jah" being suffixes of great deific connotation, matching "el." And so we are faced with the irrefutable evidence of Comparative Religion that Jesus' raising of Lazarus at Bethany is but a rescript of the old Egyptian dramatic mystery in which Horus, the Christ, raised his "dead" father Osiris, or El-Asar-us from the grave. And the Egyptian recital was in the papyri perhaps 5000 years B.C.

Also at the Egyptian scene were present the two divine sisters, Isis and Nephthys. An old source-name for Isis was *Meri,* basic for the Latin *mare,* the sea. The Egyptian plural of Meri was *Merti.* In Latin feminine form this became *Mertae.* In Hebrew it resolved into what was rendered in English as Martha. So even in the ancient Egyptian transaction there were present the two Maries, or Mary and Martha, the sisters of Lazarus!

All this sets the stage for the crowning item in the correspondence. In the Gospel drama John the Baptist bears the character of the first-born or natural man, coming first to prepare the ground or make straight the path for the advent of the spiritual man or Lord Christ. He would therefore stand as the son of the water-mother, Virgo, and under the astrological symbolism would be born at the autumn equinox, or in his mother's house. On the other side of the cycle of descent and resurrection Jesus, the *Christos,* would be the son of the fish-mother, and would be born in his mother's house, Pisces. These houses are six months apart astrologically. The whole edifice of Gospel historicity trembles under the impact of the strange dramatic circumstance, given in *Luke,* that the annunciation to Mary of her impregnation by the Holy Ghost came when John the Baptist was six months in Elizabeth's womb. The natural man, having covered the "six months" between his birth and the date of his quickening into spiritual status in the evolutionary cycle, was thus quickened, or leaped in his mother's womb, when the time for the birth, or advent, of the spiritual Christ had arrived. The water baptism was to be consummated with the fire baptism. And Justin Martyr adds an item left out of the Gospels, that at the baptism of Jesus by John, a fire was kindled in the waters of the Jordan!

St. Paul declares that we come to birth spiritually only as we die carnally, which means that the quantum of divine character in us grows in proportion as the quantum of raw nature declines. As the spiritual man, Jesus, son of Nun, the fish, increases, the natural man, John, son of Virgo, the Water, must decrease. Astrologically, as a constellation or star sinks below the horizon in the west, its opposite constellation would be rising in the east. As John, type of the natural first birth, went down, Jesus, type of the spiritual second birth, rose on the world. And, says John the Baptist: "I must decrease as he must increase"!

On the analogy, might one venture to predict that a new day of brotherhood in human society may be about to dawn, as the "six months'" reign of a degrading literal interpretation of the Sacred Scriptures goes down to desuetude and the day-star of a transfiguring spiritual interpretation rises in the east?

Chapter I

TRAGEDY DIES IN LAUGHTER

LITTLE could the ancient mythologists and sages have foreseen that the "fabulous narrations" which their genius devised to cloak high truth would end by plaguing the mind of the Western world with sixteen centuries of unconscionable stultification. They could not possibly imagine that their allegorical constructions to dramatize spiritual truth would so miscarry from their hidden intent as to cast the mental life of half the world for ages under the cloud of the most grotesque superstition known to history. Nor could they have dreamed that the gross blindness and obtuseness of later epochs would cite these same marvelously ingenious portrayals as the evidence of childish crudity on the part of their formulators. Who could have suspected that a body of the most signal instrumentalities for conveying and preserving deep knowledge ever devised by man would become the means of centuries of mental enslavement?

Nothing more clearly evidences the present age's loss of fixed moorings in philosophical truth than the inconsistency of its attitudes toward the sacred scriptures of antiquity. The general mind, indoctrinated by priestcraft, regards them as infallible revelations and holds them as fetishes, which it were a sacrilege to challenge; while theological scholarship hedges from pious veneration of them over to outright skepticism of their divine origin, swinging more recently to a view which takes them to be the simple conceptions of men just emerging from cave and forest barbarism. The character of divine dictation and absolute wisdom assigned to them on the one thesis has yielded to that of ignorant speculation of primitive folk on the other. That there is a possible truer characterization of them lying midway between the extravagances of these two extreme views has not seemed to come through to intelligence at any time. It has not occurred to students of religion that ancient scripts are the work neither of Supreme Deity on the one side, nor of groping infantile humanity on the other, but that their production must be sought in a region intermediate between the two. They came neither from supernal Deity nor from *common* humanity, but from humanity divinized! They were the output of normal humans graduated to divine or near-divine status, St. Paul's "just men made perfect." Their divinity is therefore not transcendent and exotic, and their humanity is not crude and doltish. They bear the marks, therefore, of human sagacity exalted to divine mastership.

When a student graduates creditably from a college he is presumed to have acquired a mastery over the field of knowledge covered in his course. Human life is a school, and why should not its graduates be presumed to have gained mastery over the range of knowledge which it covers, and to be able to write authoritatively upon it? Humans must at some time attain the goal, the prize of the high calling of God in Christly illumination, the crown of glorious intelligence. Life's school issues no diploma of graduation without attainment, for the graduation *is* the attainment. We have here the ground for the only sane acceptance of the ancient scriptures as books of accredited wisdom. We are neither asked to believe them inscribed by the finger of omnipotent Deity, nor forced to attribute them to the undeveloped brains of primitives. They can be seen as the products of the sage wisdom garnered by generations of men who had finally risen to clear understanding. They are the literary heritage bequeathed by men grown to the stature of divinity. Their veneration by the world for long centuries, even carried to the extreme of outrageous sycophancy, attests an indestructible tradition of their origination from sources accredited as divine and infallible. Their successful hold on the popular mind for many ages bespeaks also the unshakeable foundations of their wisdom. They have withstood consistently the test of generations of human experience. Their wisdom holds against life; it rings true. And it is all the more precious to us because of its authorship by men of our own evolution, since thereby it does not miss immediate pertinence to our life.

Both the conventional views of Bible authorship have militated against the possible high service of the scriptures to mankind. The theory of their divine dictation to "holy men of old" has led to the abject surrender of the rational mind before their impregnable fortress of direct assertion, its hypnotization by a fetish, and the crippling of its native energies. The theory of their production by early crudity tends to the disparagement of the value and validity of their message. The other view here advanced preserves their venerated authority while it brings their authorship from alleged Cosmic Divinity back to men of earth. It saves us from the fatuous claim that "God" took time out to dictate a volume of absolute verity for the inhabitants of a minor planet amongst millions of trillions of such worlds. Relieving us of the necessity of asserting that Supreme Deity went into the book publishing business on this globe and took advantage of his commanding position to write the planet's "best seller," it preserves mental integrity by enabling us to assign scriptural authorship to human agency, where alone it is acceptable. It is understandable that evolved men, with vision opened to knowledge of the laws of life, would indite sage tomes for the enlightenment of those less advanced. In any case the Bibles are here; they must be accounted for. The phenomenon of their existence among the nations, their hoary age, their escape from destruction through the centuries, the ineradicable tradition of their divine origin and authority, their almost universal veneration, must all find some factual ground of explanation. The theory offered in refutation of the two conventional ones seems the only one that provides such a rational and acceptable basis. And since the belief in their sacredness generally persists, it can not be regarded as less than momentous that the world should know of a surety that, while these revered relics are not the voice of the personified Cosmos, neither are they the mere speculative romancing of cavemen or scholastics. They are the sure word of perfected wisdom.

There was a time, then, in early human history, when enlightened men possessed true knowledge, the passport to wisdom. Clear and concise answers to the profoundest problems of philosophy were known. In so far as the human intellectual faculty is capable of it, an understanding of the mystery and riddle of life itself and the laws of its evolutionary unfolding, was achieved by men who, as Hermes says, had been "reborn in mind." Philosophy was no mere "speculative enterprise," or tilting at logical windmills; it was a statement of the fundamental *archai,* or basic principles, of the science of being. It formed the groundwork for the elevation of theology to its true place as the King of Sciences, or the Kingly Science. Together philosophy and theology held the throne in the mental life of mankind; and justly so, for a reason which modern thought would do well to consider: they must ever be the ultimate science because they motivate finally the use we make of all other sciences! They hold final answers to all life's problems. They are the determiners of all human action in the end. They alone can direct man finally to the path of good, for by no other means can he learn to know what constitutes the good. The sore need of the world today is the restoration of philosophy, to supply the proper motivation and end of action.

Though zealously guarded from the unworthy by its accredited custodians, knowledge was extant in the ancient day. Modern zeal for publicity finds it hard to understand why it was so sedulously kept esoteric. Briefly—for the full reason is a lengthy matter—a thing so precious, the distillation of ages of experience and the deposit of many lives of painful earning, could not be given out loosely to the undisciplined rabble to be violated and despoiled. Yet it was withheld from no worthy aspirant. No bars of bigotry or persecution interdicted its free culture. The Societies in which it was secretly pursued were honored by kings and the populace alike.

That halcyon age passed, that priceless legacy of knowledge was threatened with extinction, its pursuit was forbidden, its devotees assailed and exterminated; and for more than fifteen centuries the Occidental world has muddled through its age-to-age existence in nearly total ignorance of the fact that antiquity held, in its philosophy and theology, an adequate answer to the great interrogatory, the Sphinx riddle of human life.

The gift and then the loss of primal wisdom are the two most momentous events in human history. This age will be spectator to the third most significant event—the Renaissance of Ancient Culture. The plans of demi-gods and divine men, interrupted for fifteen centuries of the Dark Ages, will move forward again toward destined goals.

This age faces the denouement of a drama the like of which has not been unrolled in world history before and will hardly be repeated in aeons. Tragedy and comedy being copiously admixed in mortal existence, the astounding spectacle to which the world will shortly awake will exhibit untold calamity and the ludicrous conjoined in incredible fashion. We are destined soon to pass from a stunning sense of tragic loss to a world-echoing burst of laughter. The sting of our realization of our duo-millennial loss will melt away under the dawning recognition of our previous unbelievable stupidity. We are in a little time to be made acutely aware of a situation that will become the butt of hollow

20

mirth for ages to come. Other egregious follies of history can be accepted or extenuated to the point of being condoned and forgotten. But this colossal ineptitude, prolonged over sixteen centuries, can not escape being laughed at for centuries more. A joke owes its character to the miscarriage of the intended sense into something ludicrously different. This denouement will stand as the historical joke of the ages. No less than this quantity of hilarity can balance the weight of the tragedy which loads the joke at the other end. For the ludicrously different direction in which the intended sense of the great mythical religions and dramatic rituals of the past took its perverted course entailed as a consequence the greatest of all historical tragedies,—the frightful chapter of religious bigotry and persecution. This worst of all forms of man's inhumanity to man was bred out of the miscarriage of the concealed meaning of the ancient spiritual myth. The transaction carried the form of a joke, but it also carried the substance of the most appalling terrorism in history. And this most calamitous of all blunders was the mistaking of religious myth, drama and allegory for veridical history!

The promise of our coming awakening lies in the progress made and to be made in the study of Comparative Religion, Comparative Mythology and Comparative Philology. What they will ere long make clear to us beyond further dispute is the almost unthinkable fact that for sixteen centuries the best intelligence of the West took the ancient sages' Books of Wisdom, which were in all cases the spiritual dramatizations of the experience of the human soul on earth, for objective historical narratives. The spectacle that will soon throw a world first into wonder, confusion and dismay, and then into clownish laughter, is that of a civilization covering one third of the globe, and boasting itself as the highest in culture in the historical period, all the while taking its moral and spiritual guidance for an aeon from a Book or Books, of the true content and meaning of which it never for a moment has had the slightest inkling.

The superior knowledge vouchsafed from early graduates in life's school to disciplined pupils in the Mysteries of old was transmitted from generation to generation by oral teaching and preserved only in memory. But later, lest it be lost or corrupted, it was consigned to writing. Hence came the Sacred Books, Scriptures, Holy Writ, of antiquity. So highly were they held in the esteem of early men that when in later days their true origin and character had been forgotten, they were exalted to the position of veritable fetishes and assigned a quite preternatural source and rating. Regarded as books of superhuman intelligence, men have in face of them practically set in abeyance their human reason and bowed to them as the oracles of absolute Truth. This was natural and to a degree inevitable. But it spelled catastrophe to the general mental life of man by fixing upon him the basest hypnotization in all the annals of record, when a literal and historical, instead of a purely spiritual and typical interpretation of the books was broadcast to general acceptance. The evidence is mountain high that the taking of ancient ritual dramas and scriptural myths for objective history and the figures in them for human persons has been the fountain source of the most abject corruption of man's mental forces since the race began.

In mechanical exploit this is an age of marvel, and credit for this type of achievement should not be withheld. In study of life and its objective powers it has labored with wondrous accomplishment. In psychological delving into deeper phases of consciousness it has begun a pursuit long neglected. But in religion and philosophy it is one of the blindest of ages. It is not overstating the case to say that in these areas of human enterprise the mind of this era still slumbers in a state of ineptitude and gross darkness at least a degree or two below that commonly termed barbaric. At this moment the common mentality of the day, led and fed by a compactly institutionalized ecclesiastical power, stands committed to ideas as to the origin, structure, meaning and destiny of life which have not been surpassed in crudity and chimerical absurdity by the tribes of the forest and the sea isles. Conceptions in theology having to do with basic realities of man's relation to the universe are still presented in pulpits, Sunday Schools and Theological Seminaries which the uncorrupted native intelligence of children of eight and ten years shrinks from or accepts with startled dismay,—to the subsequent confusion of their whole mental integrity. A "scheme" of explanation of cosmic processes and world design, of human and angelic relations, of the plan and purport of life itself, is advanced for popular acceptance, yet is grotesque to common sense and fantastic to rational thought. Philosophy and religion are still propagated on the basis of a theology that is received without understanding by the "common people," entirely repudiated by the intelligentsia and brazenly dissembled by the very priesthood that lips its cantos and its oracles from Sunday to Sunday. In sum it can be said without the remotest possibility of successful dispute that the general grasp of the mind of this age on philosophical verity and the truth of life, as proffered by orthodox religionism, is still steeped in the crassest forms of dark superstition. And this has been due to the miscarriage of ancient symbolism.

History would seem to present a pattern of retrogressive current if it can be shown that this late epoch grovels in a mire of semi-barbaric philosophical grossness from which a former period was free. Degeneracy must have set in at some distant time and swept onward to this day. And such a phenomenon must have had its due cause. A great work of a learned author some years ago pointed to the approaching "decline of the West." What has not been seen, however, is that the West has long been in decline, is at a low stage of decay, and has not risen out of the murks of the Dark Ages. This has come in the wake of causes long operative in the world situation, which have been overlooked or failed of discovery through an egregious obscuration of the vision of scholars since the early centuries. And if this failure of insight is not to be attributed to stupidity that is in itself beyond understanding, then it becomes necessary for the historian of these things to posit for it another cause, one that casts the dark shadow of sinister motive over the whole course of that historical enterprise in which sinister motive is of all places most unpardonable. Corruption in politics or in economic or social life can be understood in relation to the imperfection of human nature, and in a measure pardoned. But designed corruption in religion is shattering to the very foundations of human aspiration. It shocks and paralyzes fundamental urges to sincerity. It weights the human spirit with the hopelessness of its effort to conquer imperfection. Dishonesty and insincerity in worldly dealings may entail disaster of greater or minor degree. In religion they are never less than fatal. There is one domain in which untruth is insupportable, that field of the human soul's endeavor of which Truth is the very substance and being,—religion.

Whether stupidity or sinister design prove to have been the cause of the loss of true original meaning must be left to the historical sequel to disclose. And whether the cause of the perpetuation of rank superstition in the present day of alleged enlightenment is to be laid at the door of ignorance or knavery or a combination of both, must likewise be determined as time moves on. It is certain that both the primal and the present causes of nescience are kindred, if not identical.

It is the purpose of the present volume to set forth to the modern mind the extent of the wreckage which splendid ancient wisdom suffered at the hands of later incompetence. And it is designed to accomplish this by setting up the sharp contrast between the present disfigurement and the past glory of the structure. This purpose entails the task of revealing for the first time the hidden meaning of the body of archaic scriptures by means of a clear and lucid interpretation of their myths and allegories, fables and dramas, astrological pictographs and numerological outlines. It will be at once seen to be a labor of no mean proportions to convert the entire mass of antique mythology and legend, Biblical glyph and cryptogram, from presumed childish nonsense into an organic corpus of transcendent scientific significance. It involves the reversal of that mental process which in the days of early Christianity operated to change myth and allegory in the first instance over to factual history. As third century ignorance converted mythical typology to objective history, the task is now to convert alleged objective history back to mythology, and then to interpret it as enlightened theology. The almost insuperable difficulty of the project will consist in demonstrating to an uncomprehending world, mistaught for centuries and now fixed in weird forms of fantastic belief, that the sacred scriptures of the world are *a thousand times more precious as myths than as alleged history*. It can only be done by showing that as myths they illumine and exalt the mind to unparalleled clarity, while as assumed history they are either nonsensical or inconsequential. But centuries of erroneous indoctrination have so warped and victimized the modern mind that the effort to restore the scriptures to their primal mythical status will be met with the objection that the transaction will wipe the Bible and other sacred literature out of the realm of value altogether. In the common mind this would be to rob them of worth and significance utterly. So wretchedly has the ancient usage of the religious myth been misunderstood that the cry, "the Bible only a myth!", will fall upon the popular ear with all the catastrophic force and finality of the tolling of a death knell. And no statement that words can phrase will stand as a more redoubtable testimony to the correctness of this estimate of the present stupefaction of modern intelligence concerning religious philosophy than just this reaction. Ridicule, contempt and flat rejection will be the greeting accorded the proclamation that Biblical myth is truer and more important than Biblical history. Our book aims at nothing less than the full proof of this contention. It flies directly in the face of the awaiting scorn of common opinion on the point at issue. Yet nothing is easier than to demonstrate that Bible material taken as history is the veriest nonsense. Anyone with an analytic mind and an imagination to convert its narratives into realism can make it a laughing-stock. The Voltaires, Paines, Ingersols and the freethinkers have done this successfully enough. But having disproved it as history, they have not redeemed it as spiritual mythology. The world awaits this work of interpretation, and only when it is supplied will the full force of the tragic humor of mistaking drama for history be grasped.

The loss or corruption of the philosophical interpretation of ancient scriptures precipitated the West into the Dark Ages, and a main factor in this disaster was a general obscuration of intelligence concerning the myth. Catastrophe was made the more readily possible because the rationale of the use of the myth in ancient hands passed from knowledge. When the recondite suggestiveness of the myth was lost, the inner essence of esoteric wisdom was dissipated away. Philosophy died out. And, bereft of its inner soul, the myth came to stand as the mere ghost of itself. With its hidden significance gone, it read nonsense and caricature. And so it has stood till this day. The word connotes in the popular mind of the present something about equivalent to fairy-tale, a fiction little removed from a "hoax." It is something that is sheer fanciful invention. To declare a narrative formerly believed to be true "only a myth" is to toss it out on the rubbish heap as a thing no longer of value. This attitude of mind toward the myth is itself the sign and seal of the decadence of this age. For ancient sagacity could hardly have assumed that any succeeding age would prove so obtuse as to take the outward form of its spiritual allegories for factual occurrence, or suppose that their formulators believed them to be true objectively.

To be sure, they *are* fanciful creations and entirely fictitious. They are fables of events which, as events, never happened. The aim was never at any time to deceive anybody. It was never imagined that anybody would ever "believe" them. Nevertheless the myth was designed to tell truth of the last importance. Its instrument was fancy, but its purpose was not falsehood, but sublime truth. Outwardly it was not true, but at the same time it portrayed full truth. It was not true for its "characters," but was true for all mankind. It was only a myth, but it was a myth *of* something. It used a false story to relate a true one. While it never happened, it is the type of all things that have happened and will happen. It is not objective history, but it embalms the import and substance, the heart's core, of all human history. Such authors as Spengler and Lord Raglan have begun to see that the ancients regarded it of far less importance to catalogue the occurrences of objective history than to dramatize its inner "spirit." The outward actions of humans are in the main trivial, because they constitute in the end only a partial and ephemeral account of whole verity. Ancient literature aimed at something infinitely higher and more universal. It strove to depict in the myths and dramas the eternal norms of life experience, which would stand as truth for all men at any time in evolution. The myths were cryptographs of the great design and pattern of human history, limning in the large the truth that is only in fragmentary fashion brought to living enactment in any given set of historical circumstances. *The myth is always truer than history!* Only in aeons will history have caught up with the myth, when it will have unfolded the entire design of the original mythograph. Hegel indeed essayed to read the features of a grand cosmic design in the straggling line of actual events. But the myth already foreshadows the ultimate meaning of history.

Such being the portentous function of the myth in the early stages of the life of humanity, it becomes in some degree apparent what blindness must have fallen upon the mental eye of practically a whole world to have blotted out in little more than a single century the knowledge of a thing of such vast utility. No matter how conclusively the data may prove the fact, it will probably remain forever incomprehensible to unstudied folk that whole bodies of ancient mythology and spiritual typology suddenly became metamorphosed into alleged history. It is incredible enough, in all conscience. It has been the supreme tragedy of history. And because it ensued through sheer gaucherie and clumsy loutish dumbness, it will, as predicted, rise on our horizon as the supreme folly of the ages. When it is realized that an early gift of divine wisdom, planned to aid the race fight through the exigencies of its historical evolution, totally miscarried into tragic nonsense through the simple mistake of taking spiritual allegory for literal history, a humiliated world will find difficulty in ridding its memory of this preposterous blunder.

Deprived thus of a legacy of transcendent knowledge vouchsafed for its instruction, Western humanity has wound a tortuous path through dangerous terrain that the lost wisdom would have enabled it to avoid. It has been a journey made without the guiding light that had been given to render the road more easily passable. Civilization has floundered in the shoals and quicksands of ignorance. And its contemporary phase presents the strangest of spectacles,—that of a modern culture boasting its superiority over any antecedent one, yet admittedly guided in its ethical life by a Book of which it is now possible to affirm that not the most rudimentary sense of its message has ever been apprehended. The declaration can be made and supported that the Bible is still a sealed book. This study will vindicate that declaration by setting forth the hidden meaning of ancient scripture for the first time. Gross misinterpretation cannot be seen as such until its product has been set down alongside a true rendering. The crudeness and baseness of a literal and historical translation of the sense will only be brought into glaring light by being held up against a background of the clarity and dignity of a true spiritual meaning.

The promised interpretation is not predicated upon the play of a genius superior to that of the accumulated scholarship and acumen of centuries of religious students and theologians in Christendom. It was made possible purely by the discovery of clues and "keys" to the old scriptures hidden deeply in the tomes of ancient literature, which had escaped the notice of the long line of exegetical inquirers. If wonder and skepticism arise over the difficulty of understanding why discovery was made at this epoch and not in so long a time before, the answer is most probably to be found in the fact that the thousands who failed approached the study of ancient treasure-tomes with an attitude of mind that made defeat inevitable, while success came finally through an attitude that, if it did not of itself guarantee victory, at least opened the door to it. This is of immense significance and carries a weighty moral connotation with it. With the scales fallen at last from the eyes of purblind prejudice, it can be patently enough seen that there was little chance of discovery of the cryptic burden of ancient books as long as scholars undertook their study with the ingrained and obstinate assurance that they were the products of primitive infantilism. Ever thus have the archaic volumes been approached by Orientalists and Western savants. It is next to unbelievable to discover in what a rigid posture of predetermined estimate the scrutiny of antique writings has been undertaken by Western Christian scholars. Even when the evidence of sage wisdom was present under the eye, the relentless force of the fixation could never rest content until it had read the imputation of simpleness and crudity into the text. If early literature did not manifestly read as folly, it had to be made to do so. The inviolable presupposition in the case was that by no possibility could it be admitted that the ancients knew a modicum of what we know today. If it was to be granted that the seers of yore knew life truly and profoundly, it would be gall to modern intellectual pride, and the very walls of boasted modern superiority would be breached. The content of old scripts, mysterious and haunting as it often appeared, had to be explained on the basis of primitive naïveté of mind. By no right were the supposed aborigines of remote times entitled to the presumption of high knowledge or a scientific envisagement of the world. No thesis found in modern view could account for the prevalence of developed culture in the early stages of the chart of progressive evolution as at present conceived. The assignment of puerile nescience to the civilizations of even three and four thousand years ago had to be vindicated at all costs. The rating of primitives for early men had to be maintained.

Little wonder, then, that a literature scanned with such a blighting spirit never yielded its buried light. Supercilious contempt blinded the eyes of inquiry and closed the mind to all discovery. Obdurately refusing to admit the possibility of the presence of knowledge, no amount of search would reveal it. All the surer was inquiry doomed to failure in this field, when the most exalted genius the world ever knew had been at pains to disguise the outward appearance of that knowledge. It was only when at last the arcane writings were inspected with the eager spirit of genuine seeking and the reverent assurance of their holding precious mines of instruction, that the open sesame unlocked a hoard of hidden wealth.

If it shatters current orthodoxy in science or philosophy to establish the fact that archaic man possessed supernal sapiency, then shattering there must be. The thing cannot be obviated. It is a fact that out of the night of antiquity looms the giant light of transcendent intelligence on the part of numerous sages. At a period remote enough to be contemporary with the times incorrigibly marked as "primitive" by historians, the ancients possessed books of such exalted spiritual and intellectual content as to lie yet beyond the comprehension of vaunted modern intelligence! Modern pride must face the situation: "primitive" people already possessed books which by no possibility could have been produced by "primitive" mentality. Books which only sages could have written bespeak the presence of sages on the scene.

And sages there were. Popular academic theory must perforce revise its postulates in the case. It has stubbornly refused to admit the operation of a law of life in this situation which it sees at work everywhere else in the realm of genetic procedure. Universal observation yields the truth that infant life is everywhere parented. The period of helpless infancy is safeguarded by parental oversight. The elder generation is at hand to protect, nurture and instruct the young of every kind. Modern theory admits the prevalence of this rule everywhere—except strangely in the biological history of the human race as a unit. Granting the sway of the principle in the case of the individual, animal or human, it has refused to predicate its governance over the early life of humanity as an entity. But the presence of sapient writings, the evidence of great lost arts, and the remains of structures surpassing present achievement, attest incontrovertibly the uniform working of the law of parenthood here as elsewhere. The human race was parented. It was not left to struggle through its helpless infancy without guardianship. Ancient legend in the mass bears this out. Prehistoric lore teems with the stories of heroes and men of divine stature, demi-gods and sons of God who mingled with humanity, and who left codes of laws and manuals of civilization that manifest a mastery not possible of acquirement by primitives. Hermes, Orpheus, Cadmus, Zoroaster, Hammurabi, Manu, Buddha, Laotse, Moses, and even Plato and Pythagoras, hover in the dim light of remote legendary times as figures transcending normal human stature, and leaving behind writings that have been held up as the norm of perfect wisdom and conduct down the centuries. The Laws of Manu have stood for ages as the prototype of all legal and social codes since formulated. Hermes, Orpheus taught the nations agriculture, writing, astronomy, language, religion, philosophy and science, the saga runs.

Hence there is posited for the first time a natural and competent answer to the great and insistent question of the authorship of

29

primeval books overpassing even present capability. The authorship of the sages removes these books at once from the category of merely human speculation and places them securely in the place of authority and authenticity. They were the products, not of early man's groping tentatives to understand life, but of evolved men's sagacious knowledge and matured experience. On no other ground can their perennial durability and universal power be accounted for. The early races obviously received and treasured these documents with the same high reverence with which the human child receives the codes and rules of conduct first handed down to it by its parents, who stand to it *in loco Dei*. If the primal world-reverence is found wanting in certain groups today, it is due not so much to the fact that the books have been proven of unsound merit, but to the failure to know what they actually say. They are uninterpreted to this moment. They could not be scorned if their intrinsic meaning was known. The republication of that lost meaning will restore the bibles to universal veneration, but not as fetishes.

Incidentally all speculation of scholars as to the date of the personal authorship of the Bible books or other ancient documents of the kind must be declared to be pure and simple impertinence. Nobody knows or can know what hand first set these verses to paper, or at what epoch. The books are of unknown antiquity. They were extant thousands of years B.C. When they passed from oral impartation to written form none can say. Hundreds of volumes proclaim Moses to have been the writer of the *Pentateuch*. Yet the last of the five books describes Moses' death and burial, and adds that not in a long cycle since his day (estimated by scholars at six hundred years at least) hath there been found one like unto him in wisdom and piety in all Israel! To ascribe any of the Bible books to any named writer is to trespass on the ground of folly. Indeed it is possible to assert that, in the common meaning of the term, they were never "written" at all. No man sat down and composed them out of his thought or his knowledge. They were the outlines of a great universal tradition formulated by the accumulated wisdom of those first "parents" or "guardians" of infant humanity, and, like the thousands of lines of the great Homeric poems, which had been held purely in the memory of the Hellenes for five hundred years, were finally committed by scribes to written form. Thus came those set formulations of systematic knowledge, cosmic data and moral codes, that have survived the test of time and still stand as sacred commitments. Their material presents the substantial truth of life, and not primitive man's erratic guessings. And sixteen hundred years of the most consecrated effort to study them has left their meaning still unrevealed.

But the Western mind has begun to delve into the fathomless spiritual philosophies of the ancient East. The renaissance of Oriental thought, which was first quickened by Schopenhauer in Europe and by Emerson in America, is now sweeping Occidental religious consciousness to a new and lofty height of vision and uplift. The eminent psychologist, C. G. Jung, declares this movement to be the most significant taking place in the thought life of today. The philosophy that could give an expansive illumination to a brain like Emerson's is proving a fount of light and incentive to millions more at present.

· The mask of literary disguise is being slowly lifted from the face of ancient scripture, and what has been gratuitously assumed to be the product of primitive naïveté and ignorance is now seen to be the many-colored cloak of recondite wisdom. Even so apparently quixotic a construction as the body of Greek myths, which has gained for its originators the imputed status of moronism, bewildering and baffling the world for two millennia, is to be revealed as perhaps the most lucid presentment of philosophical truth ever given to the world. The light so long buried under a bushel of myths is beginning to shine through. Not only do they bear the impress of a genius able to portray mighty truth in fable and fiction, but they register an equal skill in artful concealment. Their employment of the craft of disguise has carried them so far beyond us that we have been gulled into taking the mask for the reality. The devisers of the myths were master dramatists and poets. With such deft touches did they weave the pattern of cosmic, mundane, spiritual and physical truth through their myriad narratives of gods and men, mermaids, harpies, satyrs, centaurs, stags and boars, labyrinths, rivers, trees and stars, that not the most outlandish detail of their fabrications can be ignored without the loss of some signal link of meaning. Generations of scholars, chained in the cave of orthodoxy with their backs to the light, have perennially scoffed at the idea that the myths might be fanciful portrayals of esoteric truth. And we have charged the most enlightened races in history, the Greeks, Chaldeans and Egyptians, with possessing the mentality of immature children.

We accused them of taking their three-headed dogs, their fire-breathing dragons, their griffins, naiads, Cyclops, Circes and Medusas for sure-enough actualities. We were sure we could afford to laugh at the simpleness of a people who ascribed the summer's drought to Phaëthon's losing control of the horses of Apollo's sun-chariot. But modern presumption must brace itself for a rude jolt, when it shortly transpires that not one in a hundred of our population will be able to grasp the involved and profound signification of the Phaëthon myth even when it has been clearly set forth. Face to face with what we could not understand in ancient literature, we assumed that the unintelligibility was due to ancient unintelligence in the construction. That it might be due to *our* unintelligence in the comprehension was unthinkable. We could only hold our ground of supposed enlightenment by shifting our ignorance to the ancients. If the myths made no sense to us, it was proof that there was no sense in them. But history is soon to reverse judgment. The comics in the case will be found to be modern, not ancient. Not they, but we, will be adjudged the simple-minded children lacking insight. And we will see ourselves at last, clowns and buffoons, laughing and grimacing in hideous mockery of a treasure the value of which we cannot grasp.

Perhaps there will be wanting to us the powers of discernment needed to catch the grandeur of arcane systems of philosophy under their covering of allegory. Habits of thought and postures of mind hostile to the presuppositions of the archaic knowledge will not easily adjust themselves to new views. The attempt at a full revelation of buried meaning will come with a shock to current theological vanity, to the pride of present knowledge and to the complacency of the mechanistic cast of modern thought. But the release of the hidden significance of the world scriptures at this epoch may be destined to achieve our salvation from threatened social catastrophe. For the ancient wisdom held the prescription for both individual sanity and a righteous social order. Folly flourished only by grace of its despoliation.

The release of the enlightenment potentially held in the old books will challenge many traditional habitudes of mind and most of the lingering relics of theological inculcation. It will republish the postulates of ancient knowledge that have been lost or discredited and establish them once more as the principia of understanding for both the phenomena of life and the deep lore of the scriptures. Some of these, long without the pale of orthodox acceptance, will strangely have been found corroborated by late scientific discovery. The philosophical method was that of deduction, since it conceived life as unfolding in the outer order the pattern of things innately involved in its inner heart. The conclusion reached by evolutionists in present studies is that "evolution is centrifugal, developing outward from within the geneplasm, rather than centripetal, developing inward from without the geneplasm," in the words of Henry Fairfield Osborn. Another late finding is that "evolution is creational rather than variational. Variation of the species is the result of an original creative pattern within the geneplasm which is there from the very beginning." And a third pronouncement demolishes completely the theories of materialism, affirming that "evolution is prot-empirical rather than meta-empirical; the organs developing before there is any actual need for them rather than after the need for them arises." Nature already carries in her womb the embryo of that which will come to form. Life works ahead to an end premeditated in the beginning, so that Aristotle's scheme of "entelechy" is a sound principle in philosophy. Plato told us twenty-four hundred years ago that life is weaving on the field of manifestation the design of the archetypal ideas in the Cosmic Mind. Modern science and the clear interpretation of the arcane philosophy of the past will together restore Plato to his seat on the throne of mind.

The debate on teleology has been long and acrimonious. Negative conclusions have been fostered and apparently affirmed by the shortness of our perspective. The immensely extended outline of evolution envisioned by the cosmology of old will enable the mind to see the working of design. Mr. Clarence Darrow asks skeptically if the Lisbon earthquake was designed. As well might a colony of ants ask if the destruction of their burrow as we spade our garden was designed. Neither to the citizens of Lisbon nor to the ants in the garden would the philosophy of design be comforting. But we know that the digging was designed, not to destroy the ant-city, but to prepare the garden. So we may equally well know that the processes of world building were designed, not to destroy Lisbon, but to adjust the earth's crust properly about it. The designed activities progressing in two different worlds happened to clash, man being no more intelligent about the plans of cosmic beings than the ant about human intentions. And as man cannot change his larger designs always for the convenience of ants in certain situations, or indeed may not even be aware that his designs jeopardize their lives, so neither presumably can higher beings alter their operations for the temporary advantage of little man. Neither man nor nature has yet learned how to work on in evolution without the element of some sacrifice of life. It does not impugn design in the course and speed of an automobile that a child has been unfortunate enough to drift into its path.

Centuries of world life have been lived all awry because the philosophical insight into the structure of archetypal design has been dulled and obscured. The outlines of the pattern of evolution formulated in the beginning by Cosmic Mind were known of old, but lost in the long interim. The world being the crystallized projection of a divine thought-form and history the slow filling out of the lines of the pattern, what man can know of the structure of the original ideation, or the Great Plan, becomes of incontestable importance. This was the base and content of the Ancient Philosophy. It must be restored to knowledge. Fortunately it has never been lost beyond recovery, merely lost out of common thought. It was safe even while unknown, being preserved in the amber of a subtle cryptography. Ignorance came along and swept out of ken the esoteric purport; but at the same time it perpetuated the myths and allegories, believing them to be history. Deluded piety made a hash of the sense of the scriptures, yet all unwittingly saved them for the advantage of a wiser age.

On the one hand materialism has ignored the spiritual nature and motivation of the universe; on the other, ecclesiastical zealotry, blinded by stupid literalism, has rendered religion ridiculous. The truth must combat untruth on both these fronts, rebuffing a philosophy that denies the ideal frame of things, and rebuking an eccentric religionism that distorts early truth into revolting irrationality. To redeem religion from ignominy it is necessary to stigmatize its historical caricature, ecclesiasticism. War must be declared on its falsities to vindicate its truth. Medieval and modern incrustations, excrescences and abnormalities of a hundred types must be brushed away, if the brilliance of the splendid original creation of supernal genius is to shine forth again. Plato's theology and "divine philosophy" must be vindicated.

Chapter II

ECCE HOMO—ECCE DEUS

THE modern zeal to exploit "the practical" is about one part good philosophy and nine parts sheer fatuity. The whole matter has been involved in the utmost fog and mental haze. The groundlessness of current notions of what constitutes "the practical" is readily disclosed by asking the question: What does modern man do with the gains which his practical effort has brought to him—wealth, comfort, means, freedom, competence? They bring him certain satisfactions, no doubt, and the answer in part is there. But often the satisfactions turn to ashes in his hands, or melt away as he reaches out to grasp them, or prove hollow soon or late. Their inadequacy and shallowness attest their futility and give "practical" philosophy the lie.

The entire question rests on the determination of what constitutes ultimate values in life itself, and this is only fixed by an adequate philosophy. To be sure, a basic ingredient in philosophy is experience, and a philosophy is largely a digest of experience. But philosophy is finally and inexorably the mind's grasp of a set of formulas of meanings which array the data of experience into a meaningful pattern, or structural design, *which design must eventually match the outline of the archetypal noumenal thought form projected by Cosmic Mind for this area of creation.* Harmony with this immanent pattern is the insistent demand, as well as the touchstone and seal of truth. The lower mind in man, being a fragment of cosmic intellect, is by nature keen to recognize and register, by an expansive pleasure, the concord of its ideas with the overshadowing form of truth. Some knowledge of the features of this living mosaic is essential to the final allocation of values, else there will be no criterion other than an unauthoritative sensual hedonism to determine whether an experience or a philosophy is good or detrimental. All actions and opinions rate a final appraisal on the ground of a deposit they leave in consciousness, according as

35

they harmonize or disagree with the cosmic thought structure that is working to manifestation in the process. They accord, or not, with the elemental pattern of creation. Deep within is a sense that registers in the outer mind the thrill of that accord or disagreement. The acuteness of this barometer of values may be viciously blunted, so that its registering sense is sadly vitiated. Yet in the end it speaks in the stern language of pain and discord for violation of its principles, and positive pleasure for virtuous action. And the final definition of "the practical" is that which relates the life of man ever closer to the form and substance of the primordial pattern laid down for human evolution.

Early theology presented the general cast and outline of the great cosmic plan of creation, in the reflected light of which mortal mind could frame the more or less definite graph of the structure of this life on earth. The profound philosophy, then, that rested on this stratum of basic knowledge brought the offices of enlightened intelligence to the aid of the outer and less reliable pragmatic criteria in the ego's effort to direct the evolution of the organism. Philosophical understanding thus in large measure could be made to obviate the toilsome methodology of trial and error, and both conserve available force and save valuable time and much suffering. One of the deep principles of the Buddha's system was that "right knowledge" must come to save the individual from pitiable suffering arising from ignorance. If, as he averred, it is a fundamental truth that ignorance is the cause of sorrow, then knowledge is its antidote. And all the great religions of antiquity make this assertion. Says Hermes: "The vice of a soul is ignorance; the virtue of a soul is knowledge." The *Book of Proverbs* in the Bible enjoins at length the prime necessity of getting wisdom, understanding, knowledge. Its preciousness is set above "all the things that thou canst desire." It is glorified as an ornament of grace and a crown of life unto its possessor. In this document it is not placed second to Love or Christly Charity. By an invincible dialectic Plato and Socrates work out in dialogue after dialogue the proposition that one cannot be good until one *knows* what the good thing is, and even what it is good for. According to Rhys Davids in his *Hibbert Lectures* of 1881 on *The Origin and Growth of Religions: Buddhism* (p. 208), "it is not by chance that the foundation of the higher life, the gate to the heaven that is to be reached on earth, is placed, not in emotion, not in feeling, but in knowledge, in the victory over delusions. The moral progress of the individual depends, according to Buddhism, upon his knowledge. Sin is folly. It is delusion that leads to crime." An editorial in the *New York Times* of June 20, 1938, well says that the hearts of such folks as the German persecutors of Jewry "are bitter only when their minds are dark," and cites Voltaire's trenchant utterance that "men will continue to commit atrocities as long as they continue to believe absurdities." In so far as men act for reasons—instead of sheer brute impulse—the soundness or the imperfection of their "philosophy" in the case determines the good or evil quality of their deeds.

Knowledge has long been apostrophized as a beacon light, a lamp unto the feet. It seems to be an inexpugnable datum of history that fully enlightened sages of the past gave to infant humanity mighty formulations of cosmic truth, evolutionary schematism, wisdom of the last practical utility, and supernal knowledge of the worlds of men and of angels. They placed this torch in the hands of the early races for the advantage and behoof of all succeeding humanity. Precautions of the most extraordinary nature were taken to safeguard the deposit. But, *miserabile dictu,* the doltishness of historical groups at various times so far imperiled the gift that in a long period, roughly from the third century of Christianity until almost the present day, the open promulgation of the high teaching invited the bitterest persecution from the entrenched forces of cruder belief. Esoteric philosophy was forced to hide underground and make its way through the centuries by subterranean channels and covert devices. Barbarism threatened the utter extinction of previous light. Supervening ignorance swooped down upon and buried earlier knowledge. But in one of the resurgent waves of revival, the ancient light is breaking through the incrustation of ignorance once again. Wisdom is having its rebirth.

Obscuration enveloped brighter enlightenment because mankind seems unable to maintain its hold on the golden mean between extreme views. It is constantly following the swing of the pendulum from one movement to violent reaction in an opposite direction. Religious history is in the main a record of oscillation between arrant supernaturalism and soulless naturalism. The group mind bends far over to mystic or spiritistic faith on one side, and then sways equally far over to a dead materialism. It is either believing in angels, ghosts, spirits, saints, virgin births, elementals, divine interventions, miracles, transfigurations, salvations, vicarious atonements; or it is rebounding from these to blank mechanism which rates all such things as delusions. In his revulsion from eccentric mysticism man has sought always the wrong antidote—a barren naturalism. In his revulsion from the latter he has again always gone too far into uncritical mysticism. But there is a middle position that meets the essential truth between both attitudes. And the soul science of old set forth this median position. It presented mystic elements without irrationality, and advanced such knowledge of spiritual experience as to make the negation of such values impossible. Ancient theology was the science that dealt with the more sublimated essences and forces latent in the human endowment, exploiting them for the vast enrichment of the conscious life. It was the science of spiritual growth without mystic extravagance, the science of the dynamically real elements in the psychic constitution of man, the very existence of which mechanistic science has disregarded. What the ancients called esoteric science is but the steady direct penetration of human intelligence into the deeper heart of nature, to manipulate creatively her hidden springs of power. It was based on a knowledge of the laws ruling the higher octaves in the diapason of consciousness. It was firmly grounded on premises which authenticated the existence of the soul as an entity. The soul has ever been the scarecrow in the garden of positive science. But modern science has itself re-established the ground for such a predication in its recent findings with regard to the more sublimated constitution of matter, making a way for the reification of bodies of sub-atomic or ethero-spiritual composition, in which a unit of soul might find subsistence when disengaged from a fully substantial body. Late physics has gone far toward hypostasizing St. Paul's asserted "spiritual body," and his other statement that he knew a man "who was caught up into the third heaven." In the rarer forms of matter now hypothecated by our adventuring science will be found the rarefied physical implementation of whole octaves of "spiritual" phenomena catalogued by ancient psychic discernment, but looked at skeptically by positivism in our day. There is a spiritual evolution proceeding *pari passu* with the physical, and implemented by it. Our late science has only now come into view of nature's sublimated matter of varying gradations of density, enabling it for the first time to give body to the beings of ancient hierarchies and to give veritude to the ancient affirmation of "spiritual bodies." In proportion as the redoubtable solidity of science's basic stuff melts down into mere swirls of force, to that extent can the angels and demons of ancient systems stalk forth in something like veritable substantiality.

A penetrating view of the interior sublimation of matter opened to the eye of antiquity a fuller and more detailed charting of the basic components of man's constitution. Human nature was seen as a compound of at least four segments or strata of being, possessing four bodies of differentiated substance ranging from dense physical coarseness through etheric and mental gradients to spiritual tenuity. In short man has a physical, an emotional, a mental and a spiritual body, each finer one interpenetrating successively its coarser substrate and being held in linkage to it by vital affinities. Hence the deep lore of old dealt with a keen analysis and formulation of the laws of interaction between the several "men" in us and catalogued the extensive schedule of reactions in consciousness in that amplified psychology to a degree that proves astonishing to students of our time. The psychology of past days has names for a host of sharply drawn segmentations of subjective activity that modern probing has never systematically distinguished. *Their "gods" were the living energies of nature and of mind,* realities of the cosmos, and by no means fanciful and fictitious nonentities. They were the personified rays and energies that our science is now discovering. The broad field of what is termed mystical experience was mapped, with every section of its area charted in relation to the economy of the whole. It was no realm of whimsical idiosyncrasy, of sheer feeling. The revelation that the ancient East had perfected the technique of an elaborate spirito-psychological science, surpassing anything yet adduced by modern genius, is a marked denouement of current history. The renaissance of this buried "science of the soul" is giving birth again to the knowledge that man may pass from unconscious drifting with the tide of evolution to a conscious self-directed mastery of his progress. He may step from the status of a victim of evolution's forces, such as he is when without cognizance of its laws, into the ranks of those who work intelligently with its plan. Hence he can advance more smoothly and swiftly with the tide, as Shakespeare asserted, instead of being tossed about by cross and counter currents whose play he does not understand. The vitalizing item of ancient knowledge was the prime datum that man is himself, in his real being, a spark of divine fire struck off like the flint flash from the Eternal

Rock of Being, and buried in the flesh of body to support its existence with an unquenchable radiant energy. On this indestructible fire the organism and its functions were "suspended," as the Orphic theology phrased it, and all their modes and activities were the expression of this ultimate divine principle of spiritual intelligence, energizing in matter. Philosophy so grounded was able to meet the exigetical demands of the "mind-body problem" by its hypothecation of states of rarefied matter mediating between immaterial spirit and gross body and linking them commodiously in one organism. How the gross body holds connection with sheer "anima"—how it holds on to its "ghost"—was readily understood in the terms of their knowledge of intermediate structures which bridge by several steps the wide gap between pure spirit and palpable matter.

At the summit, or in the interior heart, of man's nature was the divine and immortal *Atma* or spirit; on the lower level there was the body, with its twofold equipment for sensation and emotion. Bridging the gap between the two was the principle of conscious mind called *Manas*. It could span the gap between "quickening spirit" and inert matter, because it stood between them and possessed affinities with both of them, which they lacked with each other. It could touch soul above and flesh beneath and pass the lofty motivations of the one across the gulf to the beneficiary below. Modern religious conception faces the absurd situation of envisaging man as obviously physical and animal by virtue of his body, and as obviously intellectual and spiritual through his soul, but with the ancient hierarchical grades of intermediacy torn out of the gap between the two. Early Christian revolt against esotericism threw down the ladder of linkage between man below and his soul above, and now has no resources to diagram the steps of his possible communion with his Emanuel. The gap left vacant had perforce to be filled in by theology with the single figure of the historical Jesus as mediator between man and his God. *A historical personage was called in to implement a function that was originally assigned to one of the principles of man's own constitution.* This was one of those consequences which the little blunder of mistaking myth for history entailed for succeeding ages.

On the strength of the new data furnished by modern science, present thought must orient its attitude toward basic problems, since it must view life as the play of causal forces in consciousness more sublimated and potent than any of the energies so far discerned in matter. It will then be in position to take counsel again with the primeval divine revelation. It will be able to predicate again the human soul and the divine spirit in man. In the ultimate it has been its failure to posit the independent Atmic entity in our life that has blocked its every excursion toward a vital religious philosophy. It has made philosophy the dead speculation it now is and religion both a chimerical and a fruitless enterprise. When theology wisely guided the effort to relate the lower man to the god within, it was the central pursuit in the life of the world and stood at the apex of dignity and importance. But the loss of vital premises of understanding blinded following ages to the value of spiritual culture, and theology and philosophy now go abegging for recognition, bereft of their former kingly renown. And now their continued abeyance threatens civilization itself. No age calls so piteously for the certain knowledge of the science of the soul, since to soul alone can be attached the anchor for all shifting human values. *Without the scientific grounding of an inner principle in man which is itself a portion of Eternal Durability, and which will carry the values built up in life to endless perpetuity, human philosophy must forever lack stability and prime utility.*

Such a carrier and preserver of values was the Atmic spark, described by Heraclitus as "a portion of cosmic Fire, imprisoned in a body of earth and water." It was on earth to trace its line of progress through the ranges of the elements and the kingdoms, harvesting its varied experiences at the end of each cycle. It was described by Greek philosophy as "more ancient than the body," because it had run the cycle of incarnations in many bodies, donning and doffing them as garments of contact with lower worlds, so that it might treasure up the powers of all life garnered in experience in every form of it. The mutual relation of soul to body in each of its incarnate periods is the nub of the ancient philosophy, and the core of all Biblical meaning. As the Egyptian *Book of the Dead* most majestically phrases it, the soul, projecting itself into one physical embodiment after another, "steppeth onward through eternity." No more solid foundation for salutary philosophy can be laid than this rock of knowledge, and civilization will flounder in perilous misadventure until this datum of intellectual certitude is restored to common thought.

The practical service of philosophy is the proper direction of effort.

41

Its function is to furnish guiding intellectual light. Religion is the consecration of purpose to attain the goal indicated as blessed. But *knowledge is the only guarantee of right effort.* Misunderstanding leads the feet into morasses and quicksands. *An errant philosophy is the poison of human endeavor at its source.* Modern psychology loudly asserts that failure of the mind to know the answers to life's riddles breaks down its integrity and racks even the body. Philosophy, reduced now to tedious and jejune speculation, is that very bread of life for which we starve. It was once a body of positive truth. To it the mind could anchor. Only intelligence can save motivation from rank exuberance of eccentricity. Despoiled of the early truth, later ages have been in the position of a person trying to think without true premises. It is the function of science and philosophy to furnish the mind true premises. As Gerald Massey says, thinking is in essence a process of "thinging," since thoughts must rest on the nature of things. And things are themselves God's thoughts in material form.

The one grand premise for constructive thinking is that man is a god functioning in the body of a human animal, and that this situation is typical of all other existent life, and a key to the comprehension of all. Religion is that field of effort in which man strives to relate a divine element, transcending immeasurably his own natural powers, to a lower self in which it is tenanted. In this comparative sense, its true function is and always will be to deal with those three elements which it has so shockingly abused and misapplied, the supernatural, the miraculous and the magical. In any absolute sense, to be sure, these terms are misnomers and can become misleading. But relative to the viewpoint of the merely natural man, the work of the god in his nature is transcendent and is indeed fittingly termed supernatural. For it is the province of religion to transfigure the natural life of man with the irradiance of cosmic romance, magical potency and unearthly splendor. It is designed to refashion the natural man into the likeness of a glorious spiritual being, the cosmical man of the heavens. To lower orders of life the capabilities of beings of a superior kingdom of life are justifiably designated as supernatural. Our brain power is supernatural to the dog.

Even now Socrates' "daimon" (daemon), that hovering presence which guided and warned him constantly throughout his life, is being entified as the "unconscious" mentor of present psychology. The restoration to Western thought of the divine monitorial guardianship of the individual will instigate the mightiest reformation in the history of Occidental religion. It will enforce a drastic alteration in theological dogma. For it will demand a discarding of the conventional form of the God idea and a return to that of learned antiquity.

It flouts current belief most flagrantly to assert that the Christian movement represented a descent from high pagan levels of knowledge and spiritual insight. Not a churchman but harbors the smug assurance that Christianity arose like a stately phoenix out of the ashes of a decadent paganism, to save a benighted world from sinking into a morass of degradation horrendous to contemplate. But current notions, however sanctified by pious belief, must yield before the influx of positive facts and the light of a proper interpretation of revered scriptures. This only means, however, that Christianity must cast off a heavy incrustation of exoteric literalism and reassert its own primal majestic message. No student conversant with the history of early Christianity will for a moment maintain that medieval or modern presentations of theology are identical with those held at the start. One of the most influential and admittedly the most learned of the Church Fathers, whose scholarship had been powerfully instrumental in formulating the early creedology, was excommunicated as a heretic within three hundred years after his death by a Church that had so quickly lost the light of its original inspiration.

"Origen, the pupil of St. Clement of Alexandria, and the best informed and most learned of the Church Fathers, who held the doctrine of rebirth and karma to be Christian, and against whom, 299 years after he was dead, excommunication was decreed by the exoteric Church on account of his beliefs, has said: 'But that there should be certain doctrines not made known to the multitude, which are revealed after the exoteric ones have been taught, is not a peculiarity of Christianity alone, but also of philosophical systems in which certain truths are exoteric and others esoteric.'" [1]

Both Origen's statement and his posthumous discrediting at the hands of the Church Council make it clear that Christianity had been radically transmogrified within a few hundred years after its inception. And every individual or sect in the centuries following the third that endeavored to revive the pristine purity of the original formulations was acrimoniously hounded and persecuted. Paulinism itself, which represents perhaps the clearest stream of high spiritual teaching, was hard put to escape being torn out of the context of scripture or defeated in ecclesiastical controversy.

The issue must be faced and determined now if religion is to live and exalt the race. *The crux of the entire problem is the conception of deity in a form perennially available for man in the heart of his own nature.* This conception is the core of all religious theory, and loss of it has been the cause of doubt, confusion and despair. Light and truth long lost are once more at hand to illumine minds now groping in darkness. False notions of deity have nearly cost mankind the loss of its birthright of knowledge.

The boast of Christianity and Judaism is that they alone have presented to mankind its purest concept of deity in the form of the One God—Monotheism. The claim is by no means true as fact. They may more correctly be said to have been the first to present the One God without the ancient train of the subordinate gods. They boast of having abolished the magnified evils of polytheism. But to the ancient sages the task of handling the Supreme God without his pantheon of lesser divinities was much the same as trying to deal physiologically with a man without consideration of his arms, feet, head and several organs. The gods of primeval religion were the active manifest powers, faculties, organs of God himself. Nature was his body, elemental forces the agents of his operative economy, universal mind his thinking faculty and ultimate beneficence his spiritual heart. The ancient systems of wisdom thought it not blasphemy to delineate the organic structure of deity to explain to human grasp the cause and nature of the world. Reverence was not withheld from even the lowest instrumentalization of Godhood. And God organically apprehended was to be better adored than God as an abstract "nonity."

But some strange quirk of philosophic revulsion against the function and nature of matter militated later to cause theologians to deem it a blasphemy to give God a body, parts and divisions. The mind could only be saved from defiling his purity by keeping him an empty abstraction. Unknowable and Absolute, he was to be kept ineffable. He was not to be dragged into the purlieus of mortal description, degraded into the semblance of a creation of man's low thought.

But the astute Greeks kept the one without foregoing the other. They reverenced the One as beyond the reach of thought, yet portrayed his emanations in the field of manifestation. And they ranked themselves as his sons. They deemed it not dishonoring to deity to recognize his being in all things. They saw him in nature, and not as abstracted from nature. And they studied nature as the living garment of God's immanence.

Therefore, though the monotheistic concept has a place in man's thought problem, it is nevertheless to be appraised in its final utility to religion as practically valueless. The human mind cannot think without the concept of First Cause, and God must stand in the thought problem to fill this need. It has this dialectic utility. But it must ever remain a contentless abstraction. As such it turns out that the chalice of divinity that the Church proffered to benighted nations as the supreme boon of religion, was well-nigh an empty cup. And engrossing the mass mind with a philosophical concept that is unassimilable and must forever remain meaningless, ecclesiasticism perpetrated the far worse crime of condemning to desuetude that more realistic conception of resident deity which alone is fraught with pregnant power to apotheosize human life. Holding out a supreme Ineffability to its followers, it withheld from them at the same time the knowledge of that deity that is lodged immediately within their own selfhood. Giving them a God who is utterly inaccessible, it blocked their approach to the god who was "closer than breathing, nearer than hands and feet."

This is of surpassing importance. It is revolutionary. It is devastating to prevalent orthodoxies. It shocks traditional piety to hear that the concept of the One Supreme can never be of great practical utility to man. But apart from its offices in generating in us perpetual wonder and awe, our dealing with it ends when we have placed it in the thought problem where the mind demands the postulate of First Cause. Beyond that it has little service to render us. Give it form, substance, content, description, we cannot, without destroying its necessary being. Whatever good will flow from our knowing that the Unknowable is back of all phenomena is ours. We can hardly love or worship what we cannot know. The boundary of our reach is wonder and speculation. Our attempts to worship it are the flutterings of a moth about the light we dare not look at. Ancient religion was suspected of having left the monotheistic God out of its picture. It did not leave it out, but it had the discretion to leave it alone! The sage theologists reverenced it by a becoming silence! Communion has never been established be-

45

tween man and an Absolute God in the cosmic heavens. But the pagan world provided a contact with a god dwelling immediately within the human breast. No reaching after the moon of the Absolute diverted conscious purpose from actual touch with the god who stood at one's elbow. The seers of old held it a sacrilege for mortals to worship any power outside themselves. And this implied no spirit of vaunting humanism or affront to deity. It was just the recognition of deity at the point where it was accessible. The real heresy and apostasy, the gross heathenism, is to miss deity where it is to be had in the blind effort to seek it where it is not available.

Deity for man is at home, not afield in distant skies. The kingdom of heaven and the hope of glory are within. They lurk within the unfathomed depths of consciousness. Divinity lies buried under the heavier motions of the sensual nature and the incessant scurrying of the superficial mind. It is the still small voice, drowned out mostly by the raucous clamor of fleshly, material and mental interests. It is a pure, mild Presence, awaiting the day when the outer man will give more heed to its quiet speech. The Supreme God is not available; but within the quietude of his own being every man may find a fragment of that same God, made personal in his own individuality. This is the burden of the lost wisdom of antiquity. Other than potentially, God in his wholeness is not present with man; but he has not left man without that measure of his grace that man can utilize. He has projected into our nature a portion, a ray, of his own life. He has apportioned amongst all his creatures that measure of his ineffable power which each is capable of receiving. Yet potentially he has lodged the whole of himself in every man, for the nucleus of his divinity that he has implanted in every creature is a seed of the whole of his being. In man the divine seed is the *Christos*, the son of the Almighty Father. It is no negative statement, but the glorious affirmation of all attainment, to assert that this germ of divinity within the heart is all of God that man can possibly absorb in the present cycle. The cosmic God is hardly an object of worship by humanity; but that segmented portion of infinite Being that is tabernacled within the flesh of mortals—that is the actual divinity assigned to receive the attention and homage of mankind, and sacrificially to be eaten.

The indwelling god is himself being brought to birth within the womb of humanity. Each individual is gestating a divinity within the deeps of his own nature. Christianity has fervently exhorted us to look into the empyrean to find the unapproachable God. All the while the infant deity slumbers unheeded within the heart. Christianity has largely nullified the force of St. Paul's almost frantic cry to us: "Know ye not your own selves, how that Jesus Christ is within you?"

The seers of old distinguished between the Unknowable God of the thought theorem and the actual Presence in the human constitution by denominating the former "God" and the latter *"the* god." Intermediate deities were called variously "the Gods" and "the gods." The object of most constant attention in philosophy was "the god," the personal daemon of the individual. On the plane of all practical living value, it was useless to look to higher evolutionary forms of deific expression unless and until that was brought from infancy to maturity of function, since its qualities had to be assimilated into human nature before anything higher could be received. It can be stated as a matter beyond controversy that the vital concern of ancient religion was with the god lodged within the human psyche. If man missed contact with deity there, he missed it utterly.

Christianity euhemerized the pagan conception of the germinal deity in us in the historical Jesus. But this has left the rest of mortals unsanctified. The personalized Christ cuts the commonalty of mankind off from its divinity. An "only-begotten son of God," made to carry all the values and meanings in his human person, robs mankind at large of its birthright. The mistranslation of the Greek *"monogenes"* as "only-begotten" was an error fraught with the most terrific consequences for Christendom. It properly means "born of one parent alone" (the Father, Spirit), in contradistinction to the idea of being born of the union of Father and Mother, or spirit and matter. It was a reference in ancient theogony to the descent of the Logos (the cosmic counterpart of the *Christos* in man) from the spiritual side of God's nature alone, as distinct from its progenation from the union of spirit with matter. The doctrine was primordial in the Egyptian conception of the god Kheper or Khepera, symboled by the scarab, which, the Egyptians asserted, produced its young through the male or father alone. If Jesus was the sole epiphany of deity on earth, then the promises of our universal sonship are made nugatory. We are assured again and again that we are all sons of God and sons of the Highest. Christianity not only thrust upon the man Jesus the divinity that was apportioned amongst us all, but also, in its confusion and ignorance, forced upon his mortal person the function, power and office of the Cosmic Logos, which in the carefully graded system of the hierarchies could not conceivably have been embodied in the constitution of a mere man on earth. How could the mighty power that organized and ensouled galaxies of solar systems be confined within the tiny limits of a physical brain and nervous system? The great Christian Fathers, Clement of Alexandria and Origen (and others) expressly repudiated the possibility of the Logos taking flesh in one person of merely human stature. Such a limitation blasphemed Deity.

What has not been recognized is that the solitary exaltation of the man Jesus has inevitably demeaned humanity. His lonely apotheosization has disinherited us. And the general revolt of the intellectualism of this age against the resultant debasement of human nature to the level of the worm of the dust through Augustinian and Calvinistic impositions should stoutly attest the falsity of the orthodox characterization.

The mythical as opposed to the historical interpretation of the Gospels has been presented with some clarity by such men as Dupuis, Drews, Robertson, Smith, Renan, Strauss, Massey, Higgins, Mead and others. The historical view of Jesus' life is stubbornly maintained in spite of the evidence adduced by Comparative Religion and Mythology, which points with steady directness to the fact that the events of the Gospel narrative are matched with surprising fidelity by the *antecedent* careers of such world saviors as Dionysus, Osiris, Sabazius, Tammuz, Adonis, Atys, Orpheus, Mithras, Zoroaster, Krishna, Bala-Rama, Vyasa, Buddha, Hercules, Sargon, Serapis, Horus, Marduk, Izdubar, Witoba, Apollonius of Tyana, Yehoshua ben Pandira, and even Plato and Pythagoras. It is also held in the face of the consideration that the body of the material used in the ceremonial dramas performed by the hierophants in the early Mystery Religions for 1200 years B.C. constitute by and large the series of events narrated as the personal biography of the Galilean. It is worth impressing on all minds that the legend of the historicity of the Gospels is only to be held by ignoring the solid weight of such—and vastly more—significant testimony. Instead of permitting its adherents to move in the freedom of a spiritual interpretation, the ecclesiastical power is holding them rigidly to a doctrinal meaning that is badly vitiated by literalism. In exalting Jesus in unique magnificence, it lets the divinity in every man's heart lie fallow. The deity that needs exaltation is that which is struggling within the breasts of the sons of earth. Theological dogmatism fails utterly to see the ultimate Pyrrhic nature of its victory. Jesus' enthronement is the disinheritance of common man. Taught to look outside ourselves for the source of power and grace, we ignore the real presence within us that pleads for closer recognition. The historical Jesus blocks the way to the spiritual Christ in the chamber of the heart.

All Christian history would have been markedly different had not the historical Jesus been interpolated into the spiritual drama. By this diversion the aims of a true spiritual culture were sentimentally turned outward to the worship of an extraneous but romantic impersonation. The consecrated devotion of hundreds of millions of souls in Christendom for centuries, instead of being focused upon the effort to nurse to life a Christly spirit within the collective body of Western humanity, has been dissipated in almost total fruitlessness upon the figure of an historicized myth. The present demoralized state of civilization in countries most thoroughly saturated with Christian doctrinism confirms the sorry truth of this statement. And the earlier Christian history lends further corroboration in its record of bickering, heretical persecution, violent warfare and ghastly crucifixions that sicken the heart. And all this was perpetrated in the name of the personal Jesus! It could hardly have been done in the name of the spiritual *Christos*.

If it be advanced in rebuttal that the example of the historical Jesus has stood as a loadstone and beacon to inspire and attract the hearts of millions of devotees, and that the contemplation of his excellency will work a miracle of uplift in the believers' nature, this but proves the efficacy of psychology and not a fact of history. Ecclesiastical propaganda has more than once produced psychological hysteria, as witness the Crusades and the Inquisition. And religious hysteria has ever produced its marvels—stigmata, speaking in tongues and healings. Every religious psychologization has run into phenomena and sums its lists of "demonstrations." It is folly to question the psychological power of an example such as the pictured Jesus. Humans are almost helpless in their tendency to ape some paragon. It was precisely because mankind needed to be inspired to idealism that the formulators of the dramas in the Mystery Rituals introduced the Messiah, the Sun-God, the *Christos* as the central character of the piece. But he was there as ensampler and by no means as substitute or scape-goat. Much as man-

49

kind needs to be confronted by the constant presence of a model of its own destined perfection, it needs far more the invincible knowledge that divinity is its own inner possession.

To hold his place in mass reverence, Jesus had to be made matchless, incomparable, unapproachable. No man dared stand beside him. But overpowering splendor only twits and chides mediocrity. It reminds us of our littleness. It leaves us gazing blankly, hopelessly. The higher the elevation of Jesus, the vaster the gulf fixed between the ideal and the adorer. It clips the wings of aspiration. The setting up of a figure of perfection outside is in part psychologically hazardous. To approach him, to match his purity, is to reduce his stature. He must be kept beyond compare, the ever-receding ideal.

Ancient psychology of religion worked on a different principle. The motive to zeal was an ever-present possibility of attainment. Numbers of the sages were men who had gained the sunlit summit. They thought it not robbery to be equal with the god, for he was sent to call them into the mount of fellowship.

To sense poignantly the degradation to which literal caricature of spiritual knowledge has reduced theology, one needs but to point to the picture of millions of votaries gazing into the physical heavens to find God, where Laplace said that no telescope had ever located him, and searching the map of Judea to localize the *Christos*, whose dwelling can be only in the heart and conscience. And the Prince of Peace still awaits to be crowned the King of Glory.

Chapter III

TRUTH CRUSHED TO EARTH

THE resolution of the "birth of Christ" into the delivery of a babe in a localized Bethlehem has kept the race from realizing the true meaning of the Messianic fulfillment. With the third century conversion of the features of the age-old spiritual drama into the alleged biography of a man-savior, the outlines of the great truth that a ray of the solar Logos was incorporated distributively in animal humanity faded out and were obliterated. All sound sense of the inner signification of the Christmas nativity tableau was irrevocably lost. The annual celebration of the advent of deity to earth remains a meaningless travesty to this day.

It becomes necessary, then, to outline the historical trends that led to the obscuration of this central feature of religious cultism. This is in no sense a diversion, but the most direct approach to the correct envisagement of ancient material. It will reveal items of the utmost strategic importance for a true evaluation of archaic structures. The restoration of the lost meaning will be given greater credence if the causes of its decadence are set forth.

The knowledge that a fragment of the spiritual heart of the sun was implanted in the body of each son of man to be his soul and his god was the golden secret imparted by the hierophants in the Mystery Schools to their qualified pupils. It was regarded as such a priceless treasure that these Secret Brotherhoods were organized specifically to guard its esoteric inviolability. From age to age it passed down the stream of oral transmission, now waning in one quarter, but spreading in another, and was revived periodically by messengers who came as the agents of a hierarchy of perfected men. From remote antiquity it was present in China, Tibet, India, Chaldea, Egypt. It was carried by the priests of the Orphic Mysteries over to the Hellenic world.[1] It was disseminated in the Greek areas in the philosophies of Pythagoras, Plato, Heraclitus, Empedocles, Anaxagoras;[2] was embodied in the poetry of Homer, Hesiod, Pindar; in the dramas of Euripides and Aeschylus. From Egypt and Chaldea it emerged in the religion of the Hebrews, who wrought its myths, allegories and symbols obscurely into their Old Testament, but had more authentically kept the deposit in their ancient Kabalah. It was taken up by pre-Christian and early Christian Gnostics, being contained with sufficient clarity in the great Gnostic work, *Pistis Sophia,* a work conjecturally of Basilides or Valentinus. Its Orphic-Platonic rescension was widely republished by the Neo-Platonist school in the second, third and fourth centuries, with ample elucidation, a measure adopted in all likelihood by the spiritual hierarchy to check the growing trend of the nascent Christian movement toward the complete exoterization of its esoteric message. It was reintegrated eclectically around Alexandria by such syncretists as Maximius of Tyre, Ammonias Saccas and Philo Judaeus, powerfully influencing the character of primitive Christianity. It was carried most directly into Christian documentation by St. Paul, whom many scholars claim on evidence to have been himself an Initiate in the Greek Mysteries (as were Clement and Origen in the Egyptian), and also by St. John, whose Bible writings are decidedly more Platonic than distinctively Christian. The visible thread of its transmission runs on to Plutarch, after whom it became more subterranean, being propagated by Hermeticists, Therapeutae, Rosicrucians, Platonists, Mystics, Illuminati, Alchemists, Brothers of various designations and secret fraternities in Europe, out of sight of the jealous eye of the all-powerful Church. At the period of its lowest ebb in Europe it was tided over the danger of total extinction by Arabian and Moorish scholars and Jewish students in Spain. The teaching was preserved and handed on by such associations in Medieval Europe as the Cathedral Builders, the Platonic Academy of Florence, the Alchemists, the "Fire Philosophers," the Troubadours and Minnesingers, by secret printers, among them Aldus Minutius of Venice, who reprinted the classic Greek literature that ushered in the Italian Renaissance. Sporadically, now in one region, now in another, it took form in outward movements in groups of mystic and pietistic tendency of many names. It was the secret spring of motive and meaning in most medieval literature, in the folk-lore, the hero legends, the fairy myths, the Arthurian cycle, the Mabinogian tales, the Peredur stories, the Niebelungenlied, the castle ballads, the Romance of the Rose and many another invention of esoteric skill.

Features of it came to be embodied in a thousand conventional forms of common "superstition." It was pictorially outlined in the set of Tarot Cards of the Bohemians in the twelfth century. Philosophers such as Paracelsus, Raymond Lully, Pletho, Cardano, Philalethes, Robert Fludd (from whose work on Moses Milton is said to have derived his theses on which Paradise Lost was built) and others presented aspects of it in more or less surreptitious fashion. Jacob Boehme's "Theosophical Points" vitally influenced Newton's thought in important directions, as he confesses. Copernicus, Kepler and Galileo acknowledge their debt to the principles of the ancient science. Later came the English Platonists More and Cudworth, and it is alleged that Francis Bacon and the mysterious Count de St. Germain formulated the body of Masonic ritualism upon the old principles.

Coming to the surface again in recent years it is being revived by Rosicrucians, Theosophists, Kabalists, Esotericists, Mystics, Spiritual and Psychic Scientists and Parapsychologists in large numbers, and is perhaps the most vital movement in the thought life of today.

The door to this rejuvenescence of an influence so long buried was opened during the last century by the studies in Comparative Religion and Comparative Mythology assiduously pursued by many scholars. There was needed nothing but a mind free from bias to discern the unity, amounting virtually to identity, underlying all the old systems, which expressed so clearly the characteristic features of what appeared to have been a universal primal world religion, with the solar myth as its corner-stone. Every great historical religion is readily seen to have been, at its start, a pure expression of the basic elements of this outline, and equally readily seen to have badly vitiated the pristine purity of teaching in later decadence. A gross transgressor in this respect is seen to be Christianity, which carried original spiritual meaning further afield than perhaps any other. It is desirable to trace the causes and progress of this corruption.

The blanket assertion that ancient spiritual light was darkly obscured under Christian handling is a challenging statement and must be given the room to vindicate itself. This work in its entirety will amount to a substantiation of that claim. The point can be carried only by an ample reproduction of the substance of the archaic world religion, so that the clear outlines of the great pristine doctrines of theology as they were apprehended in the arcane schools, may by contrast reveal the darkness and vacuity of present readings. Only in the light of the radiant wisdom of the past will the glaring corruption of current interpretation become discernible.

The stream of degradation of originally pure teaching flowed in through the channels of literalism. The simple but still nearly incredible truth of the matter is that elaborate charts of spiritual ideography, devised with poetic genius and analogical skill, were mistaken for literal objective fact. The ancient theologists had sought to portray the essence of deep truth by means of fanciful constructions of many kinds. The whole of early Egyptian and Greek religious literature was a construction commonly termed mythology. What now looms as the consummate catastrophic stupidity of the centuries was the traducing of it into alleged history. This has been perpetrated in spite of the obvious impossibility of explaining how a people that produced Plato, Aristotle, Socrates, Pericles, Heraclitus, Homer, Pindar and Demosthenes could gull itself into taking poetic fiction for objective occurrence on a grand scale. Our explanation of the mythology of the Greeks commits us to accrediting such sages with the minds of children. The myths were the lenses through which the gaze might be focused on the realities of recondite truth. Only to the crudely ignorant were the representations not diaphanous. But, oddly enough, blind misapprehension carried the day, and the transparency of the myths was darkened into solid opaqueness.

Christianity started out as a system closely kindred with the cults environing it, and boasting of conformity with them. The early Church Father, Justin Martyr in particular, is at pains to protest that Christianity in no wise differs from pagan usages. But a strange and curious thing then happened. There came to a head a virulent rebellion of mediocrity and inferiority against the aristocracy of intellect and culture. Christianity carried in large measure the impetuosity of this revolt. It became the embodied expression of a vehement assault on the esotericism of the Mystery Religions. It was evidently motivated by a popular resentment against the exclusiveness and aristocracy of the cults. Only a restricted and tested minority was eligible to admission into the Associations. The hidden teaching was withheld from the populace, under the strictest of secret bans. A wave of hostility to the privileged groups swept over the masses and culminated in an effort to crash through the restrictions of esotericism and bring out the secret doctrine for general behoof. Distrust of the possession of any real truth beyond ordinary grasp and perhaps the degeneracy of the Mysteries themselves to some extent, lent substance to the popular enmity. A movement to spread abroad a plain man's simple enunciation of the truths gained heavy momentum. A definite trend away from esotericism carried the impulse far over into literalism. The genius of culture in mankind has constantly had to contend with this effort of dull mediocrity to tear down its best structures of truth and beauty.[3] The attempt to unmask the myths for commonplace rendering was quite like the present-day demand upon popular publicists for a reduction of their best wisdom to the level of moronic bluntness. But the effort to simplify the esoteric purport was to lose it, to wreck the spiritual edifice altogether. Truth can make no terms with incapacity.

When, later, the headship of the early Church passed out of the hands of the academicians of Athens and Alexandria, of Antioch, Tarsus and Ephesus, and fell into those of the less studied Romans, the trend to literalism had gained such volume that there swept into the movement a spirit of fell vindictiveness against the dominant systems. When the conception of the purely spiritual *Christos* could no longer successfully be imparted to the turbulent masses, who were clamoring for a political savior, it was found necessary, or expedient, to substitute the more concrete idea of a personal Messiah, who would be so obviously factual and realistic as to preclude the possibility of being misconceived by the most doltish. The swell of this tide of force carried the Church Fathers to the limit of recasting the entire Gospel in the terms of a human biography. So that what had been originally in the Mysteries and the sacred scripts a combined astrological and mythical dramatization of man's total experience, was now turned into the story of one character put forth as a "life." In spite of almost insuperable obstacles and the outcropping of endless absurdities and inanities of meaning in the transposition, the undertaking was carried through. The outcome has been that the theology handed down to us by the early reformulators is the crudest, least rational and intellectually most disconcerting rendition of the ancient revelation anywhere extant. Philo, Origen, Clement and Josephus had expressly declared that scripture shielded beneath the literal narrative a secret profundity of meaning, which was its true message. Philo specified four distinct levels in which the sense of scripture was to be apprehended, the purely literal, or physical, the moral or emotional, the allegorical or mental and the anagogical, or lofty spiritual. The later Church discarded or disregarded the two or three more abstruse ones and held only to the lowest and basest.

The drive to convert the highly concentrated "meat" of spiritual truth into "pap" or "milk" for the babes in capacity probably gave to Christianity that volcanic fervor that swept it forward among the lower ranks and shortly enabled it to turn the tide against its chief rival, Mithraism. The masses will always, as they did in Luther's Reformation, seize upon a sweeping current of ideological force and attempt to utilize it as a means of escape from their lowly economic lot. The hopes of the rabble interwove the dream of political liberation with the religious message, adding an extraneous factor to the pressure to translate allegory into a tale of history. Then as now low culture soon turned from the fervor to achieve the slow laborious task of mastering an inner kingdom of spiritual character to eager expectation of a utopian regime in world affairs. In the spiritual drama were many lines which could be so misconstrued.[4]

Thus Christianity lost its *Gnosis;* and all Christendom has since had to suffer the blighting of its best spiritual effort. If by the tactic the Church may be said to have gained the whole world, it lost its own soul in the process.

That Christianity after its inception was a ferment confined largely to the poor and untutored classes is indicated both by the Gospel story itself and by much data of history. Some authentic testimony may be useful in impressing the little-known fact upon general knowledge. The cultured Celsus, writing about 200 A.D., cannot refrain from commenting on the social complexion of the Christians of his day. He wrote:

"It is only the simpletons, the ignoble, the senseless—slaves and womenfolk and children—whom they wish to persuade . . . wool-dressers and cobblers and fullers, the most uneducated and vulgar persons . . . whosoever is a sinner, or unintelligent, or a fool, in a word, whoever is god-forsaken (*kakodaimon*), him the kingdom of God will receive."[5]

Edward Carpenter, an unbiased and kindly student of early Christianity in relation to its contemporary faiths, says:

"The rude and menial masses, who had hitherto been almost beneath the notice of Greek and Roman culture, flocked in; and though this was doubtless, as time went on, a source of weakness to the Church, and a cause of dissension and superstition, yet it was the inevitable line of human evolution, and had a psychological basis." [6]

Many additional statements in the same tenor could be quoted, but it is needless to enforce what is known and indisputable.

But one hears the protestations of Christians that the ministrations of their faith to the simple and the downtrodden was its glory and demonstrated a sounder humanitarianism than the Mystery Schools displayed. Let it have whatever praise goes with this part of its program. It is to the credit of any system that it gives to the lowly the food they need. The default of Christianity is that it gave to one class and withheld from another. Even to that one class it gave the poorest of bread—truth vitiated, devoid of nourishing sense, corrupted and corrupting—as witness its own unconscionable history. It attempted to furnish to the uncultured the easily digested provender they required, but swung with such zeal into this labor that it denied the need of strong meat to more capable digestions. Christianity's culpability was not that it fed the outcast and the sinner, but that it denied the *Gnosis* to the intelligent—or to any. Its Roman revolt against the spiritual esotericism constituted its betrayal of the innermost heart of all religion. It chose to feed the religious hunger of all grades of people with food that was not even wholesome for the simple.

And it must answer for its vicious resentment and unholy violence against the high-minded groups that again and again in the whole course of its history essayed with sincerity to restore to it the lost message of the *Gnosis*. Students of the situation in the early Church will know the factual ground beneath the Emperor Julian's caustic observation that "there is no wild beast like an angry theologian." And the murder of the learned Hypatia and the burning of the priceless books of the Alexandrian library are sufficient attestation of the level of savage ferocity to which the reaction against the lofty wisdom of the past had reduced its uncultured opponents. Christianity now lives to witness a world of more general intelligence, after repression by fiend-like persecution for fifteen centuries, once more and this time with irrepressible purpose, turning with an eagerness born of long denial to the

57

esotericism of revived Oriental philosophies for the deeper nourishment of the human spirit.

Christianity can not shake off its pagan parentage. It must be seen that in spite of the almost complete dismantling of the esoteric interpretation, the system retained practically all the outward vestments of the hidden truth. That Christianity presented to the world a complete new system of high truth unknown before is of course now understood to be an unfounded legend. That it failed to make any single advance from ignorance to wisdom is not so obvious to its partisans or to the general public, but seems nevertheless indisputable on the evidence. It sadly bedimmed the old splendor of knowledge. For it threw away the golden grain and kept only the husk. The legitimacy of such a dogmatic assertion can become evident only in the light of the entire study here undertaken, since such a lengthy scrutiny is required to demonstrate that in dogma after dogma, rite after rite, and parable after parable, Christianity substituted a mean and valueless literal sense for the original inspiring message. If this was the sacrifice it made on behalf of the lowly masses, it wrote off the payment by a total suppression of light for those in higher intellectual brackets. It sealed up the anagogical meaning and hounded to the death the parties that strove for its dissemination.

Devising nothing new and retaining the outward form and dress of pagan systems, Christianity has ever been hard put to explain the undeniable similarity between antecedent religions and its own faith and practice. Intelligent churchmen have seen the futility of denying the fact and have readily admitted the pagan sources of Christianity. But in the third century it was a matter of critical importance to maintain the novel and superior character of the new religion. The device resorted to by numbers of the Fathers bears indisputable testimony to the desperateness of their plight. Church membership today will be loath to credit the reliability of the evidence on this matter, so nearly does it exceed all belief. Confronted from time to time with amazing evidences of identity between their own and pagan material, there was no recourse save to that negation of all logic, that last resort of bigotry and zealotry—the plea of diabolism! Christian pride should blush at the disingenuousness of its founders in this matter. The evidence bearing on the point is neither inconsiderable nor vague. In his excellent work, *Pagan and Christian Creeds,* Edward Carpenter comments at length on the subterfuge, as follows:

"The similarity of these ancient pagan legends and beliefs with Christian traditions was indeed so great that it excited the attention and the undisguised wrath of the early Christian Fathers. They felt no doubt about the similarity, but not knowing how to explain it, fell back upon the innocent theory that the Devil—in order to confound the Christians—had *centuries before,* caused the pagans to adopt certain beliefs and practices! (Very crafty, we may say, of the Devil, but very innocent of the Fathers to believe it!) Justin Martyr, for instance, describes the institution of the Lord's supper as narrated in the Gospels, and then goes on to say: 'Which the wicked devils have *imitated* in the Mysteries of Mithra, commanding the same thing to be done. For that bread and a cup of water are placed with certain incantations in the mystic rites of one who is being initiated you either know or can learn.' Tertullian also says (*De Praescriptione Hereticorum,* C. 30; *De Bapt.,* C. 3; *De Corona,* C. 15) that 'the devil by the mysteries of his idols imitates even the main part of the divine mysteries. . . . He baptizes his worshippers in water and makes them believe that this purifies them from their crimes! . . . Mithra sets his mark on the forehead of his soldiers; he celebrates the oblation of bread; he offers an image of the resurrection and presents at once the crown and the sword; he limits his chief priests to a single marriage; he even has his virgins and ascetics.' Cortez, it will be remembered, complained that the Devil had positively taught to the Mexicans the same things which God had taught to Christendom."

To which may be added the astonishing statement of a modern Catholic priest, quoted by Carpenter (p. 68):

"And the Tartary Father Grüber thus testifies: 'This only do I affirm, that the Devil so mimics the Catholic Church there, that *although no European or Christian has ever been there,* still in all essential things they agree so completely with the Roman Church as even to celebrate the Host with bread and wine; *with my own eyes I have seen it!'*"

There are many accusations against "the devil" in the same strain from Christian apologists. Not only were the theory and practice of the new cult identical in most respects with those of previous systems, but its own central thesis—the divinity of the Savior—had been anticipated by some hundreds of years in other cults.

"If we look close," says Prof. Bousset,[7] "the result emerges with great clearness, that the figure of the Redeemer, as such, did not wait for Christianity to force its way into the religion of Gnosis, but was already present there under various forms."

Discussing the doctrine of a Savior, Carpenter writes:[8]

"Probably the wide range of this doctrine would have been far better and more generally known, had not the Christian Church, all through, made the greatest of efforts and taken the greatest of precautions to extinguish and snuff out all evidence of the pagan claims on the subject. There is much to show that the early Church took this line with regard to pre-Christian Saviors."[9]

Carpenter makes it clear that the coming of a Savior-God was in no sense a belief distinctive of Christianity. He explains that the Messianic prophecies of the Jews and the fifty-third chapter of *Isaiah* infected Christian teaching to some degree with Judaic influence. The Hebrew word Messiah, meaning "The Anointed One," occurs some forty times in the *Old Testament;* and each time in the *Septuagint,* written as early as the third century *before* our era, it is translated *Christos,* which also means "Anointed." It is thus seen, says Carpenter, that the word "the Christ" was in vogue in Alexandria as far back as 280 B.C. In the *Book of Enoch,* written not later than B.C. 170, the Christ is spoken of as already existing in heaven, about to come to earth, and is called "The Son of Man." The *Book of Revelation* is full of passages from *Enoch,* likewise the Epistles of Paul and the Gospels.

These statements are but a suggestion of the full truth in this direction. The Christians were not content to let the matter rest with the explanation that Satan had teased them with some anticipatory resemblances. They resorted to the most violent measures to blot out all links between their body of doctrine and former pagan material. This is a black page in the history of Christianity and a measure of evil policy not easily condoned. They destroyed as far as possible the entire body of pagan record to obliterate, as Carpenter says, "the evidence of their own dishonesty." Porphyry tells of their destruction of elaborate treatises on Mithraism. And his own work on Christianity fell a prey likewise. Their vandal work is of record. The whole matter may be tersely summed up in the words of Sir Gilbert Murray: "The polemic literature of Christianity is loud and triumphant; the books of the pagans have been destroyed."

It is clear, if comment be not superfluous, that Christianity has lost, not gained, by its masking the truth about its origins. Rabid fanaticism and the destruction of literature are always the resort of a bad cause, revealing a want of a good defense on open ground. The frenzy of zeal to wipe out all the testimony that pointed to derivation from pagan forms argues a weak confidence, if not a bad conscience.

It may be said, in partial extenuation of the Fathers' conduct in the second, third and fourth centuries, that their discovery now and again of the startling similarities between their religion and earlier paganism may have come with genuine astonishment. It is commonly believed that the Greeks and Romans of the early Christian days stood far closer to the great Egyptian and Chaldean cultures than we do today. Such is far from the truth. The Egyptian papyri, monuments and tablets were a sealed book to the Christian Fathers, and remained so until Champollion worked out the key to the hieroglyphics from the Rosetta Stone in the early nineteenth century. The connection between the Christian cult and its antecedents in India, Chaldea and Egypt was not seen then as it can be today. We can in a measure understand the indignant surprise of the propagators of the new faith on finding that their alleged novel truth had been copied ahead of them by the heathen!

The crux of present interest in the matter is the consideration that the Christianity of our time is imperiling its own standing and repute by perpetuating a mistake made at its inception. Continuance in a folly so obvious in the face of modern scholarship will henceforth be an open confession of disingenuousness. It will be at the risk of the loss of the last vestige of respect yet accorded to it by studied intellectuals. Its only salvation from neglect and scorn constantly augmenting is a frank admission of its outgrowth from pagan antecedents, and a willingness to reconstruct its interpretation in relation to them. It must manifest a disposition to lift the stigma of "heathenism" from off the ancient faiths and restore them to their high place of nobility and worth. For in elevating its sources it will exalt itself. It thought to win high status by disparaging its parentage. The outcome has been disastrous.

61

The Church might be well advantaged by paying heed to Carpenter's candid conclusions on the subject. He says:

"I have said that out of this World-Religion Christianity really sprang. It is evident that the time has arrived when it must either acknowledge its source and frankly endeavor to affiliate itself to the same, or failing that, must perish. . . . Christianity, therefore, as I say, must either now come frankly forward and, acknowledging its parentage from the great Order of the Past, seek to rehabilitate *that,* and carry mankind one step forward in the path of evolution—or else it must perish. There is no other alternative." [10]

It will be hard for an ingrained devotionalism to turn back and embrace what it had been so long taught to despise. But it must be done, or all pretense at regard for the truth be abandoned. The grand body of ancient teaching should never have been brought into contempt. Convicted of its error the Church must go the whole way in making the correction. No course but that of candor and honesty will now suffice, if indeed it is not too late even now to make amends and save a bad situation. Further concealment and evasion will only prove the more surely disastrous. For the sun of the moral zodiac has swung around into the sign of Libra, where the good and evil of historical action are weighed in the balance, and piled high on the adverse pan are the knavery and ignorance of early policies, the violent treatment of earnest esotericists, the destruction of priceless books and the cruel persecution of sincere sectaries. The way in which ecclesiastical Christianity meets this issue will determine its fate. If it confronts it with honest humility it may rise again in power. For there *is* power in the ancient spiritual science to transfigure Christian nations with the glow of righteousness. Readoption of the pagan wisdom will glorify a movement now sunk in nearly hopeless ineptitude. The Dark Ages are not yet past, and that treasure which slipped away through the fingers of early Christianity has not yet been restored.

Chapter IV

WISDOM HIDDEN IN A MYSTERY

WE have remained stodgily and stupidly impervious to the infiltration of ancient truth because *we have remained blind to the method of its presentation and preservation*. We have lost the power to grasp the premises of true knowledge laid down by sage ancestors because we have been too dull to see through the subtleties of *a methodology different from our own*. These premises for thought will only be regained as the devices resorted to in their statement are comprehended. The very possibility of making the interpretation at all is intimately bound up with the use of abstruse keys to bring to light meanings covered under an adroit strategy of concealment. Modern mentality almost instinctively resents the presumption that sages of old put truth under a mask of subtle disguise. Modern canons of utility can admit no sense or sanity in a procedure of the sort. Truth is for general broadcasting, if only that its discoverer or author may get his financial reward for his contribution. But truth in ancient days was not sold to the public. There were, in the first place, no printing presses to manage its general and quick distribution. Secondly, it had to be safeguarded from the undisciplined who would misuse it. And thirdly, it had to be preserved. To this end it had to be embalmed in the amber of such myths, legends, folk-tales, parables and structures of natural symmetry as would become unforgettable mnemonics through the power of tradition. And finally it had to be expressed in a language that would be universally comprehensible—a language of living symbols. Therefore truth was dramatized and symbolized. The figures in the drama were the elements of divine and human nature; and the symbols were an alphabet of truth because they were phases of truth itself in the world of flesh and matter. They carried to the mind their message of invisible truths because they were those invisible truths themselves appearing in man's cognizable world clothed in a garment

63

of concreteness. Words are themselves but symbols. Objects of living nature are more definite speech to a discerning mind than formal language. It is as if one could throw the ideas of the mind on a screen. And Universal Mind *did* throw its archetypal ideas onto the screen of matter, where mortal man may look at them in their appearance that is not false, as philosophy has so mistakenly alleged, but true.

Unable to decipher the archaic language used, we have made hash of the true meaning of ·sacred lore. The grandest of structures for truth-telling have been made into the grossest of fabrications. What the Bible has been declared to mean is inane nonsense; what it does actually mean is splendid truth. And the gross perversion and loss of its sense have come solely through our unfamiliarity with the special and involved techniques employed in writing the sacred books. Our efforts to read the texts in total ignorance of their art of literary indirection have run into the territory of the ridiculous.

The ancient scribes were, first of all, esotericists and wrote esoterically. All spiritual wisdom was held in secret brotherhoods and rigorously safeguarded from common dissemination. There existed a spiritual aristocracy quite difficult for us to conceive of, based on considerations the force of which we have lost the insight to appreciate. There were intellectual and spiritual castes, and the lower orders of mental capacity were not regarded as fitted to receive information where the qualifications for its social use were not fulfilled. Sheer pious faith could not alone gain one admission into the Mystery Schools. Actual discipline of body and mind, and certain inner unfoldments of faculty were held as requisite for the grasp of deeper truth. Initiation was to some real extent a matter of the mastery of theurgic powers dependent in the main upon purity of life. Esotericism arose primarily from the necessity of safeguarding the use of dynamic knowledge. Religion was far from being the jejune shell of social or mystical sentimentalism that it has so largely come to be at this epoch. It aimed to liberate the powerful forces hidden in the depths of man's psyche. It bore an immediate reference to individual evolution, in the processes of which nature's dynamic energies had to be controlled and intelligently directed. What we have derided as "magic" in the religion of old was just the control of subtle powers which we mostly permit to slumber in dormancy beneath the surface of our superficial life. Religion touched man so deeply in olden times that it awakened the potencies of his godlike endowment, an enterprise which concerns us rather little now. The imputation of sacredness to the rites of religion flowed directly from recognition of the vital issues at stake in the soul's incarnation on earth. And the right to participate in the higher mysteries, of which St. Paul speaks, belonged to those who had won it from nature by the payment of the full price—a life schooled to harmony by intelligent consecration of every personal force.

In spite of the enormous quantity of evidence pointing to the existence of a great body of esoteric teaching in the Mystery Brotherhoods, such a scholar as Renouf asks:[1] "Was there really, as is frequently asserted, an esoteric doctrine known to the scribes and priests alone, as distinct from the popular belief?" And his answer is: "No evidence has yet been produced in favor of this hypothesis." But how can Renouf support so negative a statement in the face of the positive testimony offered by Plato, Porphyry, Apuleius, Herodotus, Plotinus, Proclus, Iamblichus, Euripides and Cicero? He is decisively contradicted also by many modern writers, among them Angus, Kennedy and Halliday, who have undertaken profound and searching studies of the Mysteries. Certainly a man like Cicero can not be scorned when he testifies as follows:

"There is nothing better than those Mysteries by which, from a rough and fierce life, we are polished to gentleness and softened. And *Initia,* as they are called, we have thus known as the *beginnings* of life in truth; not only have we received from them the doctrine of living with happiness, but even of dying with a better hope."[2]

And is such a statement as the following from Plato without weight:

"But it was then lawful to survey the most splendid beauty, when we obtained, together with that blessed choir, this happy vision and contemplation. And we indeed enjoyed this blessed spectacle in conjunction with Jupiter . . . at the same time being initiated in those Mysteries which it is lawful to call the most blessed of all Mysteries. . . . Likewise in consequence of this divine initiation, we became spectators of entire, simple, immovable and blessed visions in the pure light. . . ."[3]

To Renouf's ill-founded assertion it need only be rejoined that, to be sure, there is little or no evidence of esotericism, for the good reason that esotericism is the one thing in the world that is bound by its nature to leave little evidence! Does the scholar expect that the members of the Mysteries would have published their secrets abroad? On the contrary, they were bound to secrecy by the severest of all pledges.

Religious books have been written, if written at all, in cryptic form, with truth heavily veiled under the garb of cipher and symbol. Figures and glyphs had to be devised that would convey meaning to the initiated, but conceal it from the uninstructed. To interpret archaic literature one must learn to discern the intent of truth under the disguise of designed duplicity in the telling.

And it is further absurd for a Christian apologist to protest the fact of ancient esotericism, seeing that Christianity itself perpetuated esoteric distinctions in its own practices for two centuries. To this effect there is a mountain of evidence. Even the Christian Creed was kept largely a secret down to the fifth century. It was to be preserved in memory only. St. Augustine urged that no writing be done about the Creed because God had said that he would write his laws in our hearts and minds. According to J. R. Lumby, in his *History of the Creeds* (pp. 2, 3) there is found no specimen of a Creed until the end of the second century, and the oldest written Creed dates about the end of the third century.

The demands of an esoteric methodology account for the ancient use of *mythopoeia*. Here we encounter that feature of ancient procedure that has bred the prevalent wide confusion with respect to past wisdom, and find the solution of our bewilderment and ineptitude in face of ancient mythology. Our childish misconstruction that has written the record of our dull incomprehension across the scroll of literature for a millennium and a half, comes out in glaring silhouette as we fathom the devices of this cryptic treatment. *We have mistaken symbolic language for direct speech.* We have pitying condescension toward early races who explained the discovery of "fire" by the Promethean legend. We laugh at Hindus for saying that the earth is upheld by an elephant, which stands on a tortoise. We pridefully ask them on what the tortoise stood. Their pertinent answer might well be: "On modern stupidity." Not the ancients, but we, are the puerile party in the case. We, not they, have "believed" their myths. The apparent childishness of the myths is far overmatched by our real childishness in supposing they were taken as factual. One can not read in any modern academic work on ancient culture in Greece, Egypt, Chaldea or India without having to witness the birth anguish of the laboring idea that the myths reveal an inceptive stage of the slow evolution from primitive infantilism to our smug all-knowing wisdom.

We cast in the face of this presupposition the statement that the *mythos* was the designed instrument of consummate poetic and dramatic art!

The stories were devised to convey cosmical history, theogony, anthropogenesis, and finally individual experience of humans in the psycho-physiological development of mortal life. The whole cycle of the history of unfolding divinity in humanity was dramatized for stage enactment in the annual round of Mystery festivals. And portions of this drama have filtered down into the ritualism of practically every religion in the world. The epic of the human soul in earthly embodiment was the theme of every ancient poet and dramatist, and each strove to dress out the elements of the struggle in a new allegorical garb, with a new hero, whether Achilles, Hercules, Horus, Theseus, Aeneas, Orpheus, Jason, Dionysus, Buddha, Ulysses or Jesus, enacting the central role of the divine genius conquering the animal nature. In lieu of love, sex, detective, murder and gangster novels, the writers of the bygone era could deal but with one theme, that of the pilgrimage of the soul through the gamut of the elements. Each work was a Pilgrim's Progress. And novelty could be introduced only by the device of depicting the soul's experiences under a new allegorical situation, symbolizing afresh the old, old story of the immortal spirit's immersion in the sea of matter. In all, combats with dragons, wrestling with serpents, harassments by brute creatures, enchantments by Sirens, plottings of conspirators, imprisonment in dungeons and a struggling through to an ultimate return to the original home of felicity, find their place. In one type of adventure after another the many features of the history of the divine Ego in its progress from earth back to the skies were allegorically portrayed. Every aspect of the experience had its appropriate myth.

Indeed there is every presumption in favor of the belief that the *mythos* was an infinitely more profound instrument in the hands of its inventors than we yet can fathom. It is hardly too much to affirm that it was the echo of the Logos itself carrying the form of the emanational Voice out into the material realm. The *mythos* brought the unseen forms of abstract truth out into physical representation for the grasp of thought. There is warrant for believing that *mutheomai,* the Greek, meaning "to fable," "represent," "invent," is derivable from the Egyptian *mutu,* "quick utterance." It would suggest a form of direct speech to the intuitions. The myth made an outward picture of ideal forms. It dramatized truth. It had the graphic impressiveness of a cinematograph. This view is upheld by a writer who yet refutes at every turn the mythological basis of religion:[4] "It is the property of the mystic to proceed by way of images to the summit of a pure idea and the intellectual vision of the substance." That the myths were thus the vehicles for conveying the realization of abstract truths which could not be presented so forcefully in words alone seems indisputably clear. What is equally clear now is that, in the hands of ignorance, an exoteric rendering has taken the place of the esoteric, depriving the mind of its grasp on the essential truth intended in the adumbration. The danger of such a confusion was seen by Philo, the learned Jew, who when speaking of the Mosaic writings told his countrymen that "the literal statement is a fabulous one, and it is in the mythical that we shall find the true."[5] Philo's statement is not less apt for the present age.

Reluctant as is the modern scholar of repute to assent to the ascription of vital hidden meaning to the ancient legends, the truth in this regard is occasionally seen and admitted. It is refreshing to read such a passage as the following from one of the accredited authorities in the field of Egyptology. Speaking of the Mysteries of Osiris and the dramatic representations enacted each year at Abydos, he says:

"Every act was symbolical in character and represented some ancient belief or tradition. The paste, the mixture of wheat and water, the egg, the naked goddess Shenti, i.e., Isis in her chamber, the placing of the paste on her bed, the kneading of the paste into moulds, etc., represented the great processes of Nature which are set in motion when human beings are begotten and conceived, as well as the inscrutable powers which preside over growth and development. . . . And there was not the smallest action on the part of any member of the band who acted the 'miracle Play' of Osiris, and not a sentence in the Liturgy which did not possess importance and vital significance to the followers of Osiris."[6]

In the light of such true words from one of the most eminent of Egyptologists it becomes next to incomprehensible that modern scholars have so wretchedly misconceived the inner purport of these old Mystery rituals and that the same scholar has himself most ridiculously misconstrued their meaning in many particulars. The broad modern assumption has been that the *mythos* was *in toto* a lot of mummery and that the rituals were a lot of hollow ceremonialism based on superstition. That they shadowed the greatest of spiritual truths has not yet entered the mind of any man highly received in the ranks of orthodox scholarship. No one has yet been able to tell these savants that they have been handling pearls, and not rubbish.

Yet they have been told, and by no one more courageously and vehemently than Gerald Massey, a scholar of surpassing ability whose sterling work has not yet won for him the place of eminence which he deserves. The wrecking of the *mythos* by ignorant literalism stirred Massey to bitter resentment against the perpetrators of the crime. His own words will speak best for him, while they support our own contentions:

"The aborigines did not mistake the facts of nature as we have mistaken the primitive method of representing them. It is we, not they, who are the most deluded victims of false belief. Christian capacity for believing the impossible is unparalleled in any time past amongst the race of men. Christian readers denounce the primitive realities of the mythical representations as puerile indeed, and yet their own realities alleged to be eternal, from the fall of Adam to the redemption by means of a crucified Jew, are little or nothing more than the shadows of these primitive simplicities of an earlier time. It will yet be seen that the culmination of credulity, the meanest emasculation of mental manhood, the densest obscuration of the inward light of nature, the completest imbecility of shut-eye belief, the nearest approach to a total and eternal eclipse of common sense, has been attained beyond all chance of competition by the victims of the Christian creeds. The genesis of delusive superstition is late, not early. It is not the direct work of nature herself. Nature was not the mother who began her work of development by nursing her child in all sorts of illusions concerning things in general. . . . Primitive man was not a metaphysician, but a man of common sense. . . . The realities without and around him were too pressing for the senses to allow him to play the fool with delusive idealities. . . . *Modern ignorance of the mythical mode of representation* has led to the ascribing of innumerable false beliefs not only to primitive men and present-day savages, but also to the most learned and highly civilized people of antiquity, the Egyptians." [7]

He asserts again that the Egyptians "knew, more or less, that their own legends were mythical, whereas the Christians were vouching for *their Mythos* being historical." Concerning symbolism and mythical representation he emphasizes that "the insanity lies in mistaking it for human history or Divine Revelation." Mythology, he avers, is the repository of man's most ancient science, and *"when truly interpreted once more, it is destined to be the death of those false theologies to which it has unwittingly given birth."* Holding that all mythologizing originated in Egypt, he fights the conclusion of Renouf that "neither Hebrews nor Greeks borrowed any of their ideas from Egypt." The eminent scholar could not have known of Herodotus' statement that it was Melampus, the son of Amytheon, who introduced into Greece the name of Dionysus (Bacchus) and the ceremonial of his worship, having become acquainted with these and other practices in Egypt. Herodotus concludes:

"For I can by no means allow that it is by mere coincidence that the Bacchic ceremonies in Greece are so nearly the same as the Egyptian." [8]

Elsewhere (II, 81) he repeats:

". . . the rites called Orphic or Bacchic are in reality Egyptian and Pythagorean."

Massey claims that modern misinterpretation of ancient typology has made a terrible tyranny in the mental domain, much of our folklore and most of our popular beliefs being fossilized symbolism. "Misinterpreted mythology has so profoundly infected religion, poetry, art and criticism that it has created a cult of the unreal." He asserts that "a great deal of what has been imposed upon us as God's direct, true and sole revelation to man is a mass of inverted myths."

Massey insists that theology is a diseased state of primitive mythology, contradicting the renowned Max Müller, who has stated the contrary—that mythology was a disease of theology. Elsewhere he says that the *Märchen* are not reflections, but refractions, of the ancient myths. The *mythos* passed over into the folk-tale, not the folk-tale into the *mythos*. He contends that in truth the myths were the earliest forms taken by primitive thought in formulating representations of reality. Simple-minded early man saw life pictured by the living processes under his observation. Our own opinion diverges considerably from

Massey's at this point, since there is massive evidence, of the general type adduced in this work, to show that the myths were not the product of "primitive" simplicity, but on the contrary were devised by the highest mythopoetic genius. They were the output of a line of sages who *knew* the truth of what Paul has told us, that the inner world of ideality is understood by those things which are made, in the outer world of *physis*. They traced a marvelous series of parallels, correspondences, analogies between things seen and things unseen, the better to illustrate the latter. They knew that physical nature typed spiritual reality, and used the outlines of the former to pictorialize the latter. They took the tadpole or the serpent as the type of resurrected life, because they saw the spiritual process exemplified in these creatures. They took the hawk as the symbol of the risen soul because they saw the bird soar into the airy heights. They found in the mole a fit symbol of the soul immersed in the dark underworld of flesh, because the analogy was evident and under their eye. Nature supplied the suggestive identity, and they used it to teach subjective truths. Primitive man may well know the simple processes of nature from first-hand contact; but he will not know that they bespeak a spiritual counterpart of themselves in the interior life of man unless the sages so inform him. Massey's view was not well considered in this regard. Whole generations of civilized folks have gazed upon the phenomena of nature and failed to be instructed spiritually by the spectacle. One must ask Massey if primitive fancy could construct allegories so profoundly elaborated that the united intelligence of the world for centuries has been unable to fathom their hidden significance. Millions of intelligent persons today have looked upon sun and moon throughout the whole of their lives and have never yet discerned in their movements and phases an iota of the astonishing spiritual drama which the two heavenly bodies enact each month, a drama disclosed to our own astonished comprehension only by the books of ancient Egypt. Hundreds of celebrities in the field of Egyptology have mulled over the same material and have not yet lifted as much as a corner of the veil of Isis. Primitive simplicity could not have concocted what the age-long study of an intelligent world could not fathom. Not aboriginal naïveté, but exalted spiritual and intellectual acumen, formulated the myths. Reflection of the realities of a higher world in the phenomena of a lower world could not be detected when only the one world, the lower, was known. You can not see that nature reflects spiritual truth unless you know the form of spiritual truth. And such knowledge would be an *a priori* requirement to making the comparison at all! Did primitive man possess such profound knowledge of subjective truth?

But whence, it will be asked, came such exalted intelligence amongst the early undeveloped races? This question has been answered by the earlier statement that graduates of this or other cycles of growth had parented and tutored early mankind. A parent or guardian gives to the immature child a set of high maxims into the practical wisdom of which he is to grow in the course of his later development. Humanity was the ward of the demi-gods in remote times. And none but an intelligence beyond Shakespeare's, beyond Plato's, could have framed so marvelous a quiver of myths, the interior purport of which cannot even now be grasped save by the help of most recondite keys, themselves the distillation of a whole course of philosophical education. We have not read into the myths, as Massey claims, an unwarranted implication; we are only now, all too belatedly, drawing out of them some portion of a meaning deep as life itself, which they were from the first designed to embody. We do not have to superimpose extraneous meaning upon them. We find them already pregnant with truth. They shine with the flashing light of an inner connotation which they were intended to reflect. They were themselves the shadow in objective form of the substance of truth, and Massey must not object to our working from the shadow, as Plato suggested in the "cave allegory," back to the substance. It is the only method operable by men in the "cave."

The religious texts of old are at least one thing that did *not* arise from "primitive" ignorance. Says Budge, in speaking of the Egyptian *Book of the Dead:* "They can't be the literary product of savages or negroes." [9] He adds elsewhere:

"The descriptions of the heaven of the Egyptian depicted in the *Pyramid Texts* represent the conceptions of countless generations of theologians." [10]

Yet he refers to these Egyptian people as primitives. He reveals his mental obfuscation again in speaking of the Egyptian judgment:

"The pictorial form of the Judgment Scene cannot fail to strike us as belonging to a primitive period, when the Egyptians believed that hearts were actually weighed in the Balance before Osiris, while the words of the

72

texts . . . suggest a development of ethics which we are accustomed to associate with the most civilized nations in the world." [11]

Apart from the fact that almost certainly no age of Egyptian history was so stupid as to believe that a living Osiris ever observed the weighing of physical hearts in an actual Judgment Scene—it being all a symbolical depiction—the passage discloses the confusion of the scholastic mind at the contemporaneous presence of elevated spirituality or ethics with alleged primitive culture. We see the same inadequacy of the "primitive" theory to meet the facts again in the following quotation from Budge:

"Mr. Dennett, after a long study of the religions of many tribes in Western Africa, says that the Bavili conception of God is so spiritual, or abstract, that he fears the reader will think him mad to suppose that so evidently degenerate a race can have formed so logical an idea of God." [12]

It seems never to have occurred to either Budge or Mr. Dennett or others that some saner age might some time pass upon our scholars the judgment of madness in thinking that the sublime spiritual conceptions of the *Book of the Dead*, the *Chaldean Oracles*, the *Orphic Hymns*, could have been the product of primitive peoples.

In discussing the (figurative) partaking by the ancient votaries of the bodies of their gods in the Eucharistic festival, which he mistakes for a literal eating (!), Budge traces the practice to a savage custom of cutting out and eating the vital organs of the bodies of captives in order to imbibe their courage, and says that "it is hard to understand the retention of such a notion in a text filled with sublime thoughts and ideas." Could not this distinguished scholar see that the sole difficulty in the matter was caused by the foolish attempt to read poetry and allegory as objective occurrence?

It is perhaps permissible to interject here an instance of the incapacity of modern academicians to interpret the ancient use of symbols. Says Budge again:

"The Egyptian Christians also associated the frog with new birth and on a Christian lamp described by Lauzone, Is a figure of a frog surrounded by the legend '*Ego eimi Anastasis,*' 'I am the Resurrection.' It is not easy at first sight to understand why the frog should have been a symbol of new life to the Egyptian any more than the beetle. . . ." [13]

73

He finally arrives at the solution: "The frog appears with the coming of the rain, just as the beetle appears with the rising of the Nile, and so the ideas of new life and fertility became associated with them." That so eminent a scholar as Budge should admit the difficulty of understanding why the frog—which transforms from the tadpole—and the beetle—which goes into the ground only to reissue after an incubation of twenty-eight days as a new generation of himself—should have been taken as apt symbols of the resurrection is a sufficiently striking demonstration of the blindness with which modern presumption has approached the study of the lore of antiquity. The frog, the beetle, the snake, the worm becoming the chrysalis, were the obvious visible types of transfiguration and regeneration, the outward mark of the spiritual idea. Massey states that the Christian Fathers, with the exception perhaps of Clement of Alexandria, "had scarcely enough knowledge of the ancient symbolism to put any perceptible boundary to their ignorance." [14] They did not know that their Gospels were old Egyptian myths ignorantly literalized. Massey notes that Celsus "asked concerning the Christian legends, made false to fact by the ignorant literalization of the Gnosis,—'What nurse would not be ashamed to tell such fables to a child?'" One might paraphrase Celsus' question today by asking: "What age would not be ashamed to confess that it could not tell the difference between myths and actual history?"

Every religion apparently has begun at a high level and become corrupted until it stood in need of reformation and purification. Religions decay through atrophy of spiritual vision. Their course is marked by a blurring of the original light. Their fiery motivating spirit ever tends to become static. Early passion for radical regeneration of the life dwindles into a conservative tendency. The early dynamic symbols and slogans after a time lose their pristine significance. Hence the traditions, legends and rites found to be cherished by many semi-civilized tribes of our day are doubtless the decadent remnants or mere husks of former grand representations of spiritual truth. They do not represent the *beginnings* of crude religious apprehension; they are the crumbling ruins of once noble structures of wisdom and genius. Modern insight has entirely failed to sense this status of the religious material in anthropological study, in consequence of which the handling of religion as a sociological investigation has been marked by the grossest misconception, bewilderment and confusion. Academic opinion is that the myths and folk-tales are the groping efforts of undeveloped mind to interpret nature. But, on the contrary, they are the floating debris of splendid old formulations that once brimmed with the golden wine of high meaning. They are the wrack of mythology. "Whoever begins with the myths as a product of the 'savage' mind as savages are known today is fatally in error." [15] Years of study convinced Massey that all the *Märchen* were the flotsam of old Egyptian wisdom-structures. He avers:

"We must go back to the Proto-Aryan beginnings which are Egyptian and Kamite. In Africa we find those things next to Nature where we can go no further back in search of origins. Egypt alone goes back far enough to touch Nature in these beginnings, and . . . Egypt alone has faithfully and intelligently kept the record." [16]

In Budge's *Osiris and the Egyptian Resurrection* (Vol. I, p. 365) the author writes of the people of West Africa in relation to the assertion that they were primitive savages:

"This is a great mistake, for they possess the *remnants of a noble and sublime religion,* the precepts of which they have forgotten and the ceremonies of which they have debased."

Here for once the scholar glimpsed the truth of the anthropological situation as regards religious origins and subsequent decadence, and had he followed the light which here shone in his mind for the moment, he would have been spared the floundering in bogs and swamps of misconception which makes his treatises so nearly worthless in the end. In treating of that supposedly most debased of African religious customs, fetishism, he writes:

"Wherever we find fetishism it seems to be a corruption or modification of some *former* system of worship rather than the *result* of a *primitive* faith."

"All this is only theory as far as the Egyptians are concerned, but authorities on modern African religions tell us that this is exactly what has taken place among the peoples of West Africa. Thus Col. Ellis says that there is more fetishism among the negroes of the West Indies, who have been Christianized for more than half a century, than amongst those of West Africa; for side by side with the new religion have lingered the old superstitions, whose true import has been *forgotten or corrupted.*" [17]

It served partisan ecclesiastical purposes in early times to weave some history into the texture of the allegory or to use certain bold historical events as the frame for the allegorical depiction. And this mixture has made the determination difficult in places. It is not an overstatement of truth to aver that the systems of mythology have served little better purpose in the Christian era than to derail the entire train of meaning. They have proved to be insoluble puzzles and enigmas. Our inability to make sense of them has totally distorted our estimate of Greek, Egyptian, Hindu and Chinese mentality, causing us to belittle their product most egregiously. Evidences of our erroneous estimates of their work are abundant. Lewis Spence quotes Budge (*Egyptian Magic*) as asserting that the Egyptians believed the gods could assume at will the forms of animals, and that this belief was the origin of the sacred position accorded to animals in Kamite religion.

"This was the fundamental idea of the so-called 'Egyptian animal-worship' which provoked the merriment of the cultured Greeks and drew down upon the Egyptians the ridicule and abuse of the early Christian writers." [18]

Budge is of record in a statement that

"it is doubtful if the Egyptian, at that time, had developed any spiritual conceptions, in our sense of the word; for although his ideas were very definite as to the reality of a future existence, I think that he had formulated few details about it, and that he had no idea as to where or how it was to be enjoyed."

Such a quotation provokes the comment that it might be heartily agreed that the Egyptians had no "spiritual conceptions in our sense of the word," for their understanding of eschatology far transcended ours in definiteness and lucidity, being both scientific and consistent, while ours is hazy and conjectural. And again, one could ask Budge just where in modern life the details as to the future state have been so expressly "formulated" on an accepted basis, and where one can gain explicit information nowadays as to "where and how it is to be enjoyed." For the Spiritualists are the only ones who have tried to set forth these matters with definiteness, and are we to understand that Budge regards their theories as the accepted knowledge of our brilliant era? Have not both science and the academic world scoffed at Spiritualistic offerings? Budge goes on to say that the student who views Egyptian religion "from the lofty standpoint of Christianity only," will regard it as gross polytheism or pantheism, expressed through rites that were cruel, bloodthirsty and savage, embellished with legends of the gods that are childish, the outcome of debased minds and imaginations, featuring a story of the resurrection of Osiris that is a farrago of nonsense in which absurd magical ceremonies play an impossible part, and a conception of heaven that bespeaks the imagination of a half-savage people. Yet he has more than once expressed his surprise at the sublimity and lofty purity of their presentments!

In his sorry effort at interpretation of the *Egyptian Myths and Legends* Lewis Spence adds clinching evidence of the utter incapacity of academic brains to discern in the least degree what the sages of old were laboring to do, when he permits himself to place the following shameful appraisal upon archaic intelligence:

"Again, to the Egyptian mind, *incapable of abstract thought,* an immaterial and intangible deity was an impossible conception. A god, and more so by reason of his godhead, must manifest and function in an actual body. . . . As the Egyptian everywhere craved the manifestation of and communion with his gods, it thus came about that incarnations of deity and its many attributes were multiplied." [19]

The consummate obtuseness that could prompt the ascription to the ancient Egyptian seers of the flat incapacity for abstract thought may not be comprehended in its bald grossness until the reader has finished the perusal of the present volume. We have not hitherto had the presentation of the lucid meaning of Egypt's religion to enable us to gauge the amazing injustice, as well as the crass stupidity, of so rank a judgment pronounced by ignorance against wisdom. In spiritual science *we* are still the barbarians.

· Further comment would call attention to the sagacity of the Egyptians in refraining from doing the very thing of which Spence accused them,—of actualizing their deities as persons. Not the Egyptians but the Christians did this, in the person of Jesus. Personal gods were precisely the kind they did *not* have. What they had was *representations* of the gods, which is a whole kingdom's length away from the other conception. Their "gods" were in reality the actual energies of nature, of matter and of mind in the universe, graded in a wonderful hierarchy. These are intangible powers, and what can puny man do other than *represent* them by one or another type of image? The Egyptians had quite unaccountable knowledge of these sublimer forces, with some of which, as the ethers and the rays, modern science is now slowly becoming acquainted, and they poetically imaged them under deific names, as Thoth, Anup, Kheper, Khnum, Osiris, Horus, Ptah, Set, Isis, Nephthys and Ra. But gods in human flesh (except by personation) they expressly did not have. Budge wastes pages over the discussion as to whether Osiris was a living character; and decided that his tomb, with his actual bodily remains, was at Abydos. The time has come to cry out against such incompetent muddling and to bend ourselves with what capacity we have to unravel the golden threads of supernal wisdom running their magnificent design through the old books of Egypt.

Budge was a few times astute and fair enough to admit that injustice had been done to pagans by Christian aspersions as to their addiction to idol-worship and fetishism. He well recalls that the Portuguese Christian explorers adjudged the African tribes to be practitioners of witchcraft and sorcery simply because they were themselves familiar with it and gratuitously translated observed African ceremonies as such. He is good enough to say that "neither the Egyptian nor the modern African ever believed in the divinity of their amulets or fetishes, and they never considered them to represent deities." He quotes Dr. Nassau as a final authority in stating that "the thing itself, the material itself, is not worshiped. . . . Low as is fetishism, it nevertheless has its philosophy, a philosophy that is the same in kind as that of the higher forms of worship." The apex of fairness is reached in Budge's statement in the *Osiris and the Egyptian Resurrection,* Vol. I, p. 198:

"From first to last there is *no evidence whatever* that the Egyptians worshipped a figure or symbol, whether made of metal or wood, stone, porcelain or any other substance, unless they believed it to be the abode of a spirit of some kind. So far from fetishism being peculiarly characteristic of Egyptian religion, it seems to me that this religion, at all events in its oldest forms, was *remarkably free from it.*"

Chapter V

LOOSING THE SEVEN SEALS

IF the mythologies of the early nations have been a source of perplexity and bafflement to students, no less so has been the Christian Bible itself. Not even the most rabid Christian partisan could claim that the book has throughout a clear message, clearly to be apprehended. Outside of much simple homiletic truth which has yielded comfort to troubled hearts, the Bible is as yet practically a sealed book. Its meaning is not known at the present day. Nothing but the thinnest shadow of the truth that the book portrays has yet fallen across the threshold of modern understanding. No suspicion of the grand completeness of its message has yet dawned upon us. Nineteen hundred years of theological digging has not unearthed the treasure buried under its allegorical profundities. And this failure has been due to our stubborn refusal to reject the Bible as history, and to accept it as cryptic typology. From beginning to end the Bible is nothing but a series of spiritual allegories traduced to history or interwoven with some history.

A further startling discovery along this line is that the series of myths deals not with a wide variety of spiritual or cosmical situations, but only with the same one situation in endless repetition! There is but one story to religion and its Bibles, only one basic event from which spring all the motivations of loyalty and morality that stir the human heart. The myth-makers had but one narrative to relate, one fundamental mystery of life to dilate upon. All phases of spiritual life arise out of the elements of the one cosmic and racial situation in which the human group is involved; and all scriptural allegory has reference to this basic datum, and meaning only in relation to it. The myths are all designed to keep mankind apprised of this central predicament. It is the key to the Bible. And it is the loss of this key situation that has caused the Book to be sealed against the age-long assaults of our curious prying and delving. The restoration of this key to our hands will be seen at once to open the doors to a vision of clear meaning, where now stalks dark incomprehensibility. Cosmology has been almost wholly discarded from religion since Milton's day, yet a cosmical situation provides the ground for all adequate interpretation of Bible representation. *The one central theme is the incarnation.*

Beside esotericism and allegorism the Bible composers had recourse to another method which is less readily demonstrable and which has caused the confusion incident to mistaking myth for history to be far worse confounded. It was the method of uranography. The uranograph was the chart of the heavens with the constellated pictography. From remote times the ancients dealt with a celestial chart or map, on which their earliest teachers had essayed to depict the features of the soul's experience in the scenes which their enlightend imaginations had traced about the star clusters. The stellar zodiacs left at Denderah, Pylae and elsewhere are impressive reminders of the influence of this heavenly scenograph. The discovery in quite recent years of the Somerset zodiac in England, a giant zodiac wrought, it is calculated, 2700 B.C. in the natural features of the countryside covering one hundred square miles, with the figure of Leo, the Lion, four miles from nose to tail-tip, is another most authentic attestation to the basic significance which symbolical astrology has held in ancient religious formulations. Present students have as yet little conception of how generally this graph was employed in spiritual ideography and how pervasively it colored the composition of the scriptural writings. It is next to impossible to grasp subtle references in the Bible and other archaic literature without a knowledge of the features of this planisphere. Bibles are in fact, in a broad general sense, just the literary extension and amplification of the symbology of the zodiac! The sages had first written the history of the human soul upon the starry skies.

If we hold them guilty of having thus perpetrated what seems to us pure whimsicality, we are convicted of ignorance on another count. They were depicting history in that sphere where it had first occurred, before it began with man on earth. Spiritual history had been enacted on a cosmic scale in the heavens, in higher ranges of cosmic life, before it was repeated and copied in the human drama on this globe. The heavenly man, in whose image and likeness earthly man is made, and in whose body the suns and planets are but cells and organs, was the prototype of man himself. And so it comes that humanity was in primordial times instructed to build its life "after the pattern of things in the heavens." The planisphere was the historical and anatomical graph of the Divine Cosmical Man, and it became at once a secret glyph for the behoof of mundane humanity.

In the spirit of this understanding the religious teachers of yore ever sought to write into human, racial, national and individual history the reflection or pattern of the uranograph. *This effort was the secret motif back of all national epics!* The epic was an attempt to fashion national history in the similitude of the structural unity of the divine plan for macrocosmic, and by reflection, microcosmic, man. This is in general the theme of such an esoteric work as the Jewish *Kabalah*.

The distinctive features of the cosmograph are in evidence in every case. In every religious epic there is first and centrally a Holy City, a "Jerusalem," residence of the king and the eventual home of all the elect. There is next an Upper and a Lower Land, typifying the dual segmentation of heaven and earth, or spirit and body, in man's nature, which was, in all systems held to be the union of a divine with an animal principle. The two sections were always connected by a river, rising in the higher mountainous sources in the Upper Kingdom and flowing thence, carrying its blessings of fertility, down into the Lower Kingdom, which is thus nourished by the living water from above. Then there was always a bordering sea, symbolical in every case of the stormy ephemeral scene of the mortal life. No less was there a smaller water, a lake, Sea of Galilee, Dead Sea, Black Sea, Red Sea, Jordan River, Styx River, or the marshes or fens, which were to be crossed by the voyaging soul to reach the more blessed isles, or farther shore of spiritual bliss. Strangely enough there, was a further division of the land into seven tribal provinces, a heptarchy or heptanomis, as in Egypt, Judea, England and elsewhere. This division was representative of the seven kingdoms of nature, the seven stages of unfoldment through which life must pass in the completion of every cycle. At other times the division was a decad, after the pattern of the Sephirothal Tree of the *Kabalah,* but eventually redistributed in twelve sections, as in the case of the Hebrews, Athens, Afghanistan and some others, reflecting the twelvefold segmentation of the zodiac, which in turn typified the twelve levels of man's evolutionary attainment, or "twelve manner of fruits" on the branches of the Tree of Life, the twelve divine elements of man's perfected being. Likewise there was always a definite locality designated as the birthplace of the god, which was in many instances also his place of death and burial and following resurrection. Other centers marked the scene of his initiations, temptations, baptisms, trials, crucifixion and transfiguration, every stage of his evolutionary experience, in fact. Then there were cities dedicated to the special cult of the sun, the moon, and even such stars as Orion, the stellar symbol of the *Christos;* or of Sirius, the great Dog-Star, symbol of the advent. The four cardinal points were featured, as emblematic of the four pillars of man's constitution, his physical, emotional, mental and spiritual bodies and natures. A warfare between the Upper and Lower Lands and their kings was generally a part of the "history," ending in the conquest of the Lower by the Higher and the union of the two under the crown of dual sovereignty. This drama was enacted so often in the "history" of so many kings of Egypt that even a scholar of the eminence of the late William H. Breasted, in his *History of Egypt,* expresses his puzzlement over the fact that nearly every Pharaoh of the dynasties had to conquer Lower Egypt afresh and unite the two halves of the country under a common hegemony! In all likelihood the physiography and organic structure of the heavenly man was to some extent copied in the distribution and construction of pyramids, tombs, temples and other sanctuaries, and the pyramids themselves were quite obviously astronomical graphs with ceremonial design and conformations. There was a mountain or holy hill of the Lord, and there were points of entrance and exit from and to the lower world of Amenta.

The celestial typology having been engrafted on the topography of the country itself, the next measure was to weave the dramatic features into the national history. Egypt and the Hebrew tribes are perhaps the most outstanding examples of the operation of this methodology on an extensive scale, how extensive the general student of the present age is unprepared to believe. Thus the names associated for ages with cosmic and spiritual typism were spread out over the maps of the different lands; and the national kings, heroes, warriors, sages became titular characters in the immemorial heavenly drama. In the light of this custom we are in a position to reach a conclusion of the very greatest importance for research, affecting the entire view of scripture as history. For we are confronted with the inexpugnable fact that the names and events in religious scripts were for the greater part not the products of objective history in the first place, but on the contrary the names and events in assumed history were a deposit from the religious books! The names of kings, heroes, cities, lakes, rivers and mountains were on the uranograph long before they appeared on national maps! They were transferred from the uranograph to the maps! The occurrences of Bible "history" had been enacted annually or nightly among the stars of the sky long before they became incorporated in the epics of religion. And they had been in the epics before they became assigned to actual localities and personages. Heavenly regions and spiritual transactions were finally brought to earth and given a local habitation on land and in history. In short, the naming of geographical features was done by the sacerdotal castes in each country, in which task they simply sought to pattern their country and its history after the scheme of the uranograph! Their map and their history were cast as far as could be done in the mold of the cosmic chart. Each nation designed to make its configuration and history *reflect* and *fulfill* the heavenly model!

A partial exemplification of the same tendency can be seen even in our own American history, where the priestly class gave religious names to the earliest settlements and geographical features. The practice is attested by such names as Salem, Providence, New Haven, Newark, New Canaan, Bethlehem, Nazareth (Pennsylvania), Santa Fe, Sacramento, Corpus Christi, Los Angeles, Vera Cruz, San Salvador, San Domingo and a list of saints' names and holy appellations. The Puritans from England and Holland emigrated to New England actuated powerfully by the assurance that they were going to fulfill in the new continent the ancient Covenant between Jehovah and the Israelites. The *Mayflower* was part of the religious epic. The Anglo-Israel movement of the present day manifests largely the same tendencies.

The theory here advanced is not without support from other authorities. The following brings the weight of a very venerable document to the endorsement of the idea:

"It has already been suggested that the mapping out of localities was celestial before the chart was geographically applied and that all common naming on earth came from one common naming of the heavens, commencing with the Great Bear and the Dog. The mapping out of Egyptian localities according to the celestial Nomes and scenery is described in the inscription of Khnum-hept, who is said to have 'established the landmark of the south, and sculptured the northern—*like the heaven*. He stretched the Great Bear on its back. He made the district *in its two parts,* setting up their landmarks, *like the heaven.*'" (*Records of the Past,* XII, 68.)

An evident additional corroboration of the theory is contained in the injunction given to Moses in the Bible:

"See that thou make all things after the pattern shown thee in the Mount . . . the pattern of the heavens."

"Jerusalem, the Mount of Peace, the Nabhi-Yoni of the Earth, was one of these sacred cities that were mapped out according to the Kamite model in the heavens." [1]

"The pattern of things in the Mount," "the pattern of the heavens," has not hitherto been seen to be the Biblical analogue and symbol of Plato's ideal forms. The Mount, the heavens, are of course the heights of divine ideation, whereon God projected his new world in thought forms before he impressed them upon matter. The heavens are the uplands of consciousness, or spheres of being, not physical localities. God formed his mental models on the Mount of Vision and Imagination before he cast them into concretion.

So far from grasping the uranographic art as the key to the historical problem in all scriptures, late writers vent their skepticism on this point in passages such as this:

"What proof is there—we ask once more—that the people, the mystics even, of two thousand or more years ago, read all this into the heavens; that they regarded the various divisions and towns, and the river and name of Galilee, as mystical and earthly reflexes of these celestial phenomena!" [2]

There is proof enough in the very fact that the ancient seers were poets and allegorists, and not historians. Practically conclusive evidence that Bible names are not objective or historical (in the first place) is to be found in the fact that there are in the Bible some scores of allusions to such local names as Egypt, Jerusalem, Nineveh, Babylon, Tyre, Sidon, Gilead, Assyria, Galilee, Ethiopia and others which, if taken in the earthly geographical sense, yield no intelligible meaning whatever. Further evidence is to be found in the notable fact that the divisions and localities on mundane maps do in the main largely match the celestial features. Charts of the "Holy Land of Canaan" have been found extant in early Egypt as much as three hundred years before the alleged Israelite exodus, whence it is to be presumed that this promised land of peace and plenty was *allegorical before it was historical*. Massey states that an entablature on the wall of an Egyptian temple bore a list of some hundred and twenty place names afterwards localized in Palestine, at a date at least one hundred and fifty years before there could possibly have been an exodus of Israelites from Egypt. It requires little "proof" to ascertain that "Egypt" as used throughout the Bible has the meaning of the lower self or animal-human personality, indeed the physical body of man itself. Jerusalem means the "holy city" or the heavenly realms, which are in consciousness, not on the map.

"The picture of this paradise in the Hebrew writings, the *Psalms*, the *Books of Isaiah, Ezekiel, Zechariah* and *Revelation*, were pre-extant long ages earlier as Egyptian. What the so-called 'prophets' of the Jews did was to make sublunary the vision of the good time in another life. There were always two Jerusalems from the time when Judea and Palestine were appenages of Egypt. Two Jerusalems were recognized by Paul, one terrestrial, one celestial. The name of Jerusalem we read as the Aarru-salem or fields of peace in the heaven of the never-setting stars. The burden of Jewish prophecy, which turned out so terribly misleading for those who were ignorant of the secret wisdom, is that the vision of this glorious future should be attained on earth; whereas it never had that meaning. . . . Thus Jerusalem on earth was to take the place of Jerusalem above and the Aarru-hetep became Jerusalem simply as a mundane locality." [3]

From numberless texts in the Bible itself which point to the correctness of the uranographic interpretation of names we take one alone, which by itself is enough to substantiate the claim made in this connection. In *Revelation* (11:8), speaking of the two witnesses whom it is said the dragon will rise up and slay, the apocalyptic writer says:

"And their dead bodies shall lie in the street of the great city, which *spiritually* is called Sodom and Egypt, *where also our Lord was crucified.*"

There is enough in this verse to confound the entire schematism of Christian theology as historically based. It implies a clear refutation of the whole Passion Week and Good Friday ritual, as commemorative of "history." Jesus, so it says, was not crucified in an earthly Jerusalem, but only in a spiritual one, the name of which is indifferently Sodom or Egypt, the latter not even the name of an earthly city, but of a country! Jesus crucified in Egypt! And what becomes of the Gospel "history"? It is left to take its only true place, which is among the sacred myths! The crucifixion was, on the authority of the Bible itself, a spiritual and not a historical transaction.

T. J. Thorburn, author of a work aiming to invalidate the mythical nature of the Gospels, reveals the perplexity as well as the ineptitude of orthodox scholars in the face of the ancient trick of uranography and allegory:

"And if their statements are not to be taken in their natural and historical sense, then we must hold that in ancient literature it is more than doubtful whether writers ever mean precisely what they say." [4]

They surely never dreamed that an age would come, so far lost to the mythical intent of their writings as to suppose they ever meant *literally* what they said. They could not know that the wisest savants of a distant epoch would be so blinded by the forces of obscurantism as not to realize that the old books spoke only in the terms of those earthly forms that adumbrate spiritual realities. The old masters of religious science were not in the habit of speaking "precisely"; they spoke under the forms of figure always. They could not suspect that their indirect poetical method would so outrageously befuddle modern "intelligence."

Ancient philosophy was intensely responsive to the conception that all things mundane were a lower copy of things empyrean. On the theory that all forms of life were typical of the one basic nature of all life everywhere, the sages read into earthly things the reflection of things celestial. Jesus said he could not tell the disciples of heavenly things unless they had first believed in earthly things. The sea of earth life reflected heavenly life in its bosom. The seers who knew that nature was a dramatization of cosmic *archai,* sought for the evidence of the archetypal design in every phenomenon on earth. With what remarkable nicety they traced higher truth in the mirror of nature we shall see clearly as the story unfolds. So, in the end, in their religious life they labored to represent their history as conforming to the primordial type. To this end they resorted to a measure which has caught and deceived purblind scholarship since that time.

From the general thesis that their national history reflected God's plan for the world, it was an easy step to the more explicit assumption that their national life *embodied* the divine plan. They threw about themselves the aureole of divinely constituted agency to fulfill the cosmic plan. They therefore arrogated to themselves the title of "God's chosen people," and took the names allotted only to the spiritualized humans, the men evolved to divinity! This tack will not appear either unlikely or outlandish when we ponder the disposition of nations in our own day to put forth blatant claims to be the chosen agents of Providence for the cultural rulership of the world.

Even if there seems to be veridical history in the Bible, it can be viewed properly as a setting for the spiritual dramatization, or as the clothing in which the drama was garbed. At times, perhaps, the writers appear to have utilized the data of actual history to stage the symbolic figurations. To this task the religious poets dedicated their ingenuity.

It becomes evident on this thesis that the historical element of scripture is of far less significance than has been supposed. It is the philosophy of history and not the data of history that is of foremost concern. As exhibiting providential design in world life it becomes of epic moment. The Hebrew race has exploited this phase of the old methodology to its highest possibility, only, however, as Egypt had done before it; and has been so successful that it has left the impression of a unique and exalted hierarchical status for the Jewish race. The outcome of our correction of vision will be that we shall for the first time properly regard the *Old Testament* books as, in the main, the universal drama of the spiritual life masquerading in the disguise of Hebrew history subtly woven into the great cosmic epic! The Biblical title *Israelites* is a spiritual designation purely, and is wrongly taken in the sense of the name of an ethnic group. "My people Israel" or "the children of Israel" of the Hebrew deity are just the divinized humans, mortals who have put on the immortal spiritual nature, men graduated into Christhood, a spiritual group in the early Mysteries. Gentiles were those who were not yet spiritually reborn. The word comes from the Latin and Greek roots, *"gen," "gent,"* meaning simply "to be born." They were those born as the first or natural man, but not yet reborn as the spiritual Christ. It can be given no ethnic reference. The name "Israelite" is obviously compounded of "Is," abbreviation of Isis, or Eve's original name, Issa (See Josephus); "Ra," the great Egyptian solar god, male and spiritual; and the Hebrew "El," God. It would then read, Father-Mother-God, making his "children" the sons of God, i.e., Christs. Likewise the name "Hebrews" means "those beyond" (the merely human state), and therefore is practically identical with "Israelites." Finally the term "Jews" (from the plural of the Egyptian *IU*—Latin *JU*) refers to the "male-female divinities," a title given in the Mysteries to men made gods and thus restored to androgyne, or male-female, condition. The national Jews thus adopted for their historical name all three of the exalted spiritual designations conferred in the Mysteries on the *Epoptae* or completely divinized candidates.

It was hardly expected that any positive documentary evidence could be found in support of the evident fact that these names had simply been appropriated by the race using them as illustrious titles abstracted from the uranograph. But a direct statement to that precise effect was found in the Hebrew Grammar of Gesenius, a learned German scholar, (on p. 6):

"Of the names Hebrews . . . and Israelites . . . the latter was more a national name of honor and *was applied by the people to themselves* with a patriotic reference to their descent from illustrious ancestors; . . ."

This is of vast significance as affecting the historical view of the Bible, with possible extremely severe repercussions on world history of the present.

The fourth consideration found essential to a grasp of archaic meaning is the knowledge that religion was an outgrowth from a specific situation involving the human race at its beginning. Religion is commonly assigned to a category under the head of psychology. It is a matter of mind and emotion.

But the roots of religion are found to go deeper than any mere inclination of the psyche. Eventually religion took psychological forms of expression, but it was originally not mere psychology. *It was an outgrowth of anthropology.* It took its rise out of the racial or evolutionary beginnings and bore an immediate relation thereto. Every feature of it was engendered out of the interrelation of the several elements entering into the compound of man's constitution.

Human nature was composed of more than one element. There were the physical, the emotional, the mental and the spiritual. More

88

compactly viewed, there are the human-animal and the divine. Religion is just the play of the factors of the interrelationship subsisting between these several natures in man. Or it is the relation between man and his god, the latter being universally existent primarily within him, secondarily without. It details the history of the soul or divine spark of spirit in its cyclical incorporation in human bodies. Its central fact is the incarnation, the relation of soul to body, God to man, man to God.

According to Plato's *Timaeus* and other archaic documents a group of twelve legions of "junior gods," who were sparks of the eternal Flame of cosmic mind, were ordered, as their assignment in the co-operative work of creation with Deity, to descend to earth and elevate the races of the highest animal development by linking their own mental capacity with the organisms thus far developed by the evolution of form. They were to lift the animals across the gulf between the summit of instinct and the beginnings of reason. These angels were devas, "bright" or "shining" emanations of divine intelligence, but were not exempt from the "cycle of necessity," or periodical immersion in forms of physical embodiment on a planet for purposes of their own further self-evolution. It subserved both the interests of their own progress and that of the animals they were to uplift, that the two races, the one germinally conscious and immortal, the other dumbly brutish and mortal, should be periodically joined together, the higher to be the king and ruler of the lower. The procedure thus adopted by life gave to the animal the possibility of evolving a mind through association with a mental nature, and to the intelligent spirits the physical bodies that were their particular requirement for contacting the type of experience they were destined to undergo. If this seems bizarre, it must be remembered that all living entities are the result of the linkage of a spiritual nucleus with a material organism. No creature lives but what is compounded of "soul" and body.

In conformity with evolutionary law these legions of devas or angels, we are told, descended to earth, took lodgment in the bodies of higher animals and began their career of redeeming the lower creatures to mental status. In the *Timaeus* these "junior gods" are addressed by the Demiurgus (the creative Logos, Jupiter) and are told to descend and "convert yourselves according to your natures to the fabrication of animals," the gist of their mission being summed up in the command to "weave together mortal and immortal natures." This is one of the most important utterances of ancient scripture, because it announces the character of our constitution and sets forth plainly our evolutionary commission. It tells us that we are both animal-human and divine at once, animal as to our bodies, divine as to our intellects. For Plato says: "According to body it is an animal, but according to intellect a god." Our earthly task, according to St. Paul, is to link together the two natures in "one new man," bringing to an end in a final "reconciliation" "the battle of Armageddon," the aeonial warfare between the "carnal mind" of the animal and the spiritual mind of the god. This warfare is also Plato's strife between *noēsis*, the spiritual intelligence, and *doxa*, the motions of the sense nature. The soul is here in body to discipline the latter by the inculcation of habits of rectitude until the animal learns to use the powers of mind. Tutoring the animal, the soul at the same time achieved its own higher schooling in deific unfoldment. This interlocking of the two grades of life in one organism must be constantly kept in view if the proper study of religion is to be made. No organic evolution can proceed from one kingdom to another without the deploying of the mental resources of a superior kingdom in aid of the level below it. And each kingdom profits by the act of brotherhood. The god achieves his own further apotheosis by reaching down to raise the animal to human estate.

It must be noted that when the intelligence of the god is joined to the life of the animal, it communicates but a fragment of its power to the organism, remaining for the larger part of its conscious being hidden on its own spiritual plane. It thus becomes an invisible guardian, or what the ancients called the "daimon." Lurking in the background of consciousness, it is what modern psychology has lately discovered and named the "collective unconscious." From behind the curtain, as it were, it directs the animal with only a tentacle of its power. It can not incorporate in the animal a greater measure of its capacity than the latter can suitably accommodate and carry. It will push down into expression more and more of itself as the refinement of the coarse body goes on apace. Like a radio, the mechanism must be tuned up higher to register finer vibrations. In the Greek theosophy it is stated that "the gods distribute divinity" to the grades of being below them, which "participate according to their capacity."

In briefest summary (to be amplified to greater elaboration in the sequel) this is the basic cosmological and racial datum of every old religion. Together with its implications it is the basis of every religious interpretation ever made or to be made. Every problem of ethics, devotion, discipline and intellect receives its full complement of value and meaning only in reference to this fundamentum. Religion is far more than a posture of mystic feeling; it was in origin a series of codes, principles and practices given by the demi-gods to early mankind to awaken the torpid genius of our actual divinity. In a true sense it was designed to wield a semi-magical influence to transform animal man into the divinized human! Its rites were formulated with a view to bestirring man's memory of his essential deific character. It was in no sense merely worship. It was the most intensely practical and utilitarian culture the world has ever known. It was designed to prevent the utter loss of purpose and failure of effort in the cosmical task to which man, as a celestial intelligent spirit, had pledged himself under the *Old Testament* covenant and "the broad oaths fast sealed" of Greek theology. In coming to earth to help turn the tide of evolution past one of its most critical passages, he bound himself to do the work and return without sinking into the mire of animal sensuality. We must henceforth approach religion with the realization that it is the psychic instrumentality designed for the use of humanity in charting its way through the shoals of the particular racial and evolutionary crisis in which it was involved. All the stupendous knowledge relating to the entire cosmic chapter was once available, given by the gods to the sages. We have nearly lost it beyond recovery because the ignorance of an early age closed the Academies and crushed every attempt to revive the teaching. The prodigious folly of the modern essay to vitalize religion through piety alone will be more fully seen as the ancient picture takes form in the delineation. Our present business is to struggle to regain that lost paradise of intelligence. We must work again to the recognition of our high cosmic mission, and revivify the decadent forms of a once potent religious practique, based on knowledge. For spiritual cultism was once vitally related to our evolutionary security, which stands jeopardized by present religious desuetude.

The nature of the material to be presented in volume will enforce by the sheer illuminative power of the interpretation itself the necessity for this extended introduction. It was quite impossible to undertake the exegesis of recondite scriptures long misinterpreted or never interpreted at all, without providing a rationale of ancient literary methodology and setting up a background of philosophical light. The erection of this background was made all the more necessary by the inveterate recalcitrancy of modern scholarship to recognize the applicability of the methods and principles outlined. Their validation by the substance and meaning of the larger presentment now to be made involves nothing less than the complete revision of all our interpretative norms in religious study.

Chapter VI

THE DESCENT TO AVERNUS

THE rectification of misguided rendering of holy writ in its entirety is a work of great magnitude and will tax severely the capacity of a single book. Particularly in regard to the traditional dogmas of theology, where misconception has become embedded in set habitudes of mind, the reinterpretation can be established only by the presentation of material in overwhelming quantity. The bare statement of the main theses of the venerable philosophy would be met with contempt or arrogant rejection. The claims must therefore be buttressed by a mass of irrefutable data. This material has not been marshaled for this use before in anything like organic array.

The story most properly begins with what is called in theology "the descent of the gods." Traditional lore is replete with legends of the "expulsion of the angels," "the fall of Lucifer and his hosts," "the fall from heaven," and the more philosophical "descent of the soul." These phrase-titles relate to the first step in the series of pre-historical and even pre-mundane episodes which culminated in the establishment of humanity on earth and the fabrication of human nature combining both a natural and a supernatural element. The substrate datum in religion is that man is an animal and a god in union. There were animals on earth and angels in heaven; and the counsels of cosmic intelligence decreed that the angels should join forces with the animals and be their gods. The conjunctive experience would educate both parties. The effort to overcome matter's inertia and the sense urge of the flesh would develop more dynamic spiritual initiative for the gods. They would be forced to deploy more of their potential and as yet static divine power to gain mastery over the elementary forces of the physical world.

Hints are not wanting in the old scripts to show that their obligation to leave their home of blissful rest in dreamy sub-consciousness in the ethereal spheres and suffer the hardships of earth life in gross animal bodies was in some part at least a measure of karmic retribution for past dereliction elsewhere. Pride and insolence are ascribed to them by Greek theology. Violated oaths and "Moira's bounds transgressed" are alluded to by the philosophic poets. As evolution links penalty with readjustment and forward progress, it is not difficult to admit the play of both retributive and normal procedure in the enforced descent of minor deities to our globe. It is the expulsion of Satan and his hosts from heaven in *Paradise Lost* and *Revelation*. So presented, it has been taken either as a mythical unreality or an inscrutable chapter of celestial history, and discarded from serious consideration in religious systematism. It is, however, the central situation and must be restored to its pivotal place of consequence in the picture. The doctrine of the "descent" is crucial for the interpretation. True or false, it is what the scriptures are building their narratives upon.

Of the original twelve legions of deities, ten have plunged into the stream of incarnation and are now passing through the experiences incident thereto. At the conclusion of the venture, after many incarnations for each individual member, they will return to their celestial abodes, transfigured and further divinized. The allegory of the Prodigal Son is a short glyph or graph of this evolutionary descent and return. There is hardly a religious book of any ancient nation that does not deal more or less directly with that event.

To see the "descent" as an integral function of cosmic process and not as a calamitous "fall," it is quite necessary to expound a portion of Orphic-Platonic cosmogony.

The beginning must be made where creation itself begins. It starts from Unity. All things proceed from what was aboriginally and ever ultimately is, the One Life. The pagan name for the Supreme Power was commonly The One. All things ultimately resolve into the primordial One, since they emanate from that One in the beginning. Before manifestation takes place, Being is homogeneous, undifferentiated. It is uniform similitude and excludes dissimilitude. It is all One Essence, alike in every part, if parts there are.

But in such state it is unmanifest, and from our point of view unconscious, asleep, inert. The Hindu term is *Pralaya*. And out of *Pralaya* it must awake, for it sleeps only in alternate turn with waking

94

activity, as do all its creatures made in its likeness. It passes, like them, from death to life and back again, in eternal routine.

To awake and come into being it must by force of logic perform an operation upon its own nature which is the first ground of manifestation. It can not create a universe in which to live and suffer experience without breaking its Unity apart into duality. For it must become Consciousness on the one side, in order to *know* what and how to create, and Matter on the other, if it is to have material with which to create! So it must split its primal Oneness into a dualism which however is still subsumed under the unity. It becomes two in one or the One in two. The One has not become Two, but a twoness.

It virtually can not create without throwing itself into the condition of being at a tension between two aspects of itself, on the strength of which tension it can exert its inchoate energies. It must therefore manifest itself as the two ends of a polarity, positive and negative. It must become polarized in relation to itself; and so it takes on the double-aspected characterization of spirit and matter, male and female, consciousness and vehicle, function and instrument, attraction and repulsion, visible and invisible, real and actual. Positively, like the proton of the atom, it must stand stably in the center, governing, holding, regulating the cyclical whirl of negative force about its eternal rock of durability. Negatively, like the electrons, it must revolve in the periodic swing of active life. It must provide the dual grounds for living existence, a conscious nucleus presiding at the heart of moving, changing embodiments. It must become, out of itself, subject, knowing, and object, to be known. Its entire purpose is obviously to arise out of unconscious slumber and become ever more awake and more concretely conscious. Since there is nothing of which it can be conscious save itself, the aim of Life is thus ever to become more Self-conscious! Therefore it must, so to speak, set itself as object over against itself as subject, and down the ages and the cycles ever thus contemplate itself. It is the seeing eye and the thing seen, as all profound esoteric philosophy asserts.

As *Genesis* puts it, God effected his creation, gazed upon it with gratification and pronounced it good. To see his creation he had to objectify, hypostasize, reify his thoughts, the radiations of his subjective aspect. For he creates by thoughts. He must see his ideas form in

95

concretion before him, take on material body and come to visible manifestation for himself and his creatures.

So his expression proceeds from unity to duality, and from duality it runs further outward to infinite multiplicity. Multiple manifestation is achieved by the operation of a principle which is easily comprehended. As life has split into spirit and matter, the one mobile, the other inert, the unity of the mobile is broken up into multitude as it moves against the immobile. The lighter essence, spirit, is broken and divided as it moves outward against the resistance of matter. A suggestive illustration is the infinite division of a body of water dropped as one unit from a height as it falls against the resistance of the air. Its sheer motion and speed throws it apart. The circulation of the blood from the central heart, dividing endlessly till it reaches the periphery in numberless streamlets, is a similar reflection of the universal law. Outward bound, it divides; on the return it reunites! Life descends, "falls," from the summit of its primal unity down into the arms of matter, dividing as it goes. Division is a logical necessity if it is to multiply itself, for unity can not multiply out of itself without first dividing itself. And it can not divide itself unless it falls or descends against resistance. The importance of this determination for clear grasp of basic theology can not be overstressed. Angels "fall" by divine ordinance, and not by literal folly of rebellion against deity. Evolutionary gravity brings them down from heaven to earth.

The wind does not commonly blow a steady gale, but comes in rhythmic puffs. Creative impulse acts similarly. Every cycle of energization of the universe finishes its work in seven waves or impulses, and the sub-cycles have also seven waves. Life projects its formative energies outward, or matterward, in surge after surge. Each one carries the impulse as far as it will go under its original force, or until the wave is brought to a dead standstill by the inertia of matter, the carrying and resisting medium. Each propulsion of power comes to a stop, locked in the embrace of matter. In this embrace the capacities of the two nodes of being interplay, fecundate each other, generate a growth of new life, and build up what is termed a plane or level or kingdom of nature, with creatures embodying the type of life there engendered. Thus there are terrestrial and celestial worlds (as Paul says), noumenal and phenomenal realms, physical and ethereal planes, material and spiritual bodies, heavens, fairy-lands, underworlds, hells, limbos, Isles of the Blessed, Elysian Fields, the meadows of Aarru-Hetep and homes on high. And the beings on the ranges from high divinity down to man are the gods of ancient mythology.

The capacities of life on each level are expressed and given play by the organic beings built up thereon. Thus each kingdom has its own specific nature and determinations. But life is not static; it is generative, reproductive, forward-moving. It creates anew, in its turn, at its level, and passes the stream of creative force on down the line. Thus the succession of waves of projection runs down the scale, each one carrying the formative force one surge farther out. On and on it goes, establishing the kingdoms of nature and the living citizens on them. The contiguous planes form a link of connection from top to bottom of the series, and this is the golden chain of life. And each level bears a definite relation to its neighbor on either side.

The explication of this relationship involves a law that is basic for all evolution. Its statement will render understandable the constitution of man. It tells why he is a soul and a body linked together. It may be called the great Law of Incubation.

Under its terms each plane is mother to the life on the plane above it and father to that of the plane below it. It *receives* from above the seed germs of higher life and harbors them in the womb of its soil, or matter, gestates them and eventually gives them their new birth. This is the function of motherhood. And matter (Latin *mater*, mother) is the universal mother. But, having received from above, it also *gives* the impulse to the order below; and as giver it is active, aggressive, generative—the father function. Feminine to life above, masculine to life beneath, it is the link and bridge between two worlds.

But at each step of transmission the primal impulse suffers a diminution of its impetus, a weakening of its force, and in consequence a further and further fragmentation. The matter of each plane on the downward or involutionary track being more dense in atomic structure than that of its superior, the living bodies it provides can not bear as heavy a life charge as the beings above can support, and the voltage of power must be stepped down if it is to be incorporated fittingly in the less capacious bodies of a lower kingdom. To effect this reduction in dynamism the bodies carrying the life of each plane act as electric transformers, changing a high current into numerous lesser currents to be accommodated to the lower carrying capabilities of bodies on the

97

plane beneath. Hence the unit charge received from the plane above by each life structure on any plane must, in falling one step further downward, be again broken up into a large number of fragments, each of which will become the energizing soul of a lower body. The Greek philosophers say in this connection that "the gods distribute divinity," scattering its higher units abroad from plane to plane, the units multiplying in number, but diminishing in power, as the stream flows on. This is what ancient theology connotes by "the river of life." The Orphic system speaks of "rivers of vivification," which, they say, "proceed from on high as far as to the last of things," or to the lowest stratum of the mineral kingdom. And as the gods distribute divinity, the secondary ranks in each case are said to "participate according to their capacity." The gods pour out their life for the vivifying of all lower beings, and the latter partake of this bounty or "grace" to the measure of their receptivity. Nothing other than this is meant by the "shed blood" of the gods, given for the life of the worlds. All old theologies aver that the blood of the gods, or of God, mixed with the clay of earth, makes the "red earth" which is given as the etymological signification of Adam in Hebrew, i.e., man. Man is compounded of the red life-blood of deity and the dust of the ground, which in Hebrew is *Adamah,* purely the feminine or material aspect of *Adam,* spirit, itself. Deity mixed together spirit and matter to make man.

One more step in the analysis yields the final phase of the Law of Incubation. If life is to be propagated in eternal renewal, in multiplied individualization, it becomes necessary for any living creature on each plane to produce a multiple progeny of the seeds of its own life and "plant" or bury them in the soil of the kingdom immediately below it. There they go first to their "death," after which they are reborn or resurrected in the sprouting of the seeds and their growth back to maturity. Each generation lives anew in its regeneration, but multiplied by as many times itself as the number of seeds it produced and successfully germinated in the plane below.

The vegetable buries its seeds in the soil of the kingdom beneath it, the mineral. The animal's life is embodied in a corpus built up of vegetable material taken in each day as food. The human is rooted in an animal body. And now comes the pivotal fact in theology. The lowest ranks of gods, in their position just above humanity, must, by the Law of Incubation, send down their seeds, plant (incarnate) them in the bodies of humans, and win their next cyclical generation of divine life in that ground! Centuries of theological maundering have not told the millions of hungry sheep this plain truth as to why man nurtures a winged spirit of intelligence—a soul—in his physical body. The soul of man is in his body as a seed of divinity planted, buried, gone to its "death" in the soil of the human kingdom, and bears the same relation to that soil as does any seed to its bed. The greatest truth that can be told to mortals is that their bodies are each the gestating womb of a god. As said St. Paul, the Christ is being "formed within" each mortal body. Man has a soul because his physical human self is the nursery or breeding ground of the seeds of divinity. And man's divinity is, or begins as, a seed. His duty is to cultivate the growth of that deific embryo. It is gestating in the womb of his physical body, and he must, as said Socrates, become a philosophic "midwife" and aid in its birth. Plato reports the Demiurgus in the notable speech to the legions of devas in the *Timaeus* as saying that "whatever is immortal and divine" in the human makeup, "of that I will furnish *the seed and the beginning*. It is your business to do the rest; to weave together mortal and immortal natures." The upper plane furnishes the seeds of godhood, the lower furnishes the soil or garden. Divinity is planted in "the garden of the world." It is the seminal soul of divine mind, destined to germinate and eventually blossom in the ground of humanity.

If, in sum, God is to multiply himself, his tree of life must reproduce on its branches a numerous progeny, each child bearing the potentiality of renewing the parent life in its fullness, and of *carrying its eternal unfoldment one step ahead*. As no living thing can subsist save as a result of a linking together of spirit and matter, a germinal unit of spirit must be incubated as the god in a body of material structure. This divine economy gives every creature its soul, which is its god. In the long chain of linked lives, from God down to mineral crystal, no being is deprived of its possibility of immediate communion with deity, up to the border of its capacity. But the "arm of the Lord" that is potent to bless and to save is within, not without. It is Emanuel, God with us, the hope of our glory. God is everywhere, within and without; but his son, the *Christos*, is only within. If he is not sought there, he will not be found. His inner presence is the provision of life that no entity should be bereft of instant contact with its parent god, who dwells on the plane just over its head, though rooted in its very

99

body. Man's deity is not a personage in a distant land and time, but, as an Eastern saga puts it, "closer is he than breathing, nearer than hands and feet." No man can fail of touching his divinity, but failure of his knowledge that his deity is *in* himself may palsy his effort to arouse its latent faculties.

A legend of India tells of a council of the gods at which it was purposed to invest man with deity. A debate arose as to how it might be entrusted to him without his misusing it. One suggested that it be buried in the depths of the sea, so that he would not easily find and abuse it. Another advised placing it on the most inaccessible mountain top. Finally the supreme head of the assembly declared he had thought of a place where no man would ever think of looking for it,—in the deepmost chambers of man's own heart!

The basal truth that every living thing is a union of spirit and matter, soul and body, was put in a graph by the Egyptians. It is perhaps the oldest and most meaningful of signs. The great symbol carried in the hands of the gods was the Ankh, or *crux ansata* (ansated cross), a "T" topped with the circle. The circle is the female symbol, the boundless infinite matter, the mother of all things in endless round. The vertical line is the male symbol, a ray of intelligence that goes out from the heart of the universe to impregnate the worlds. The horizontal line is the line of division between the two, at the point where they are joined. It is the cross-line between them. The word Ankh means three most significant things: *love, life* and *tie*. It is a formula of all life, signifying that *life* is the resultant of a *tying* together of two things, spirit and matter, by the force of an attraction, which is *love*.

The great doctrine of the "descent" or "fall" can now be clearly envisaged. Deity, in the form of its seed potency, must descend from its own plane into the soil of the plane below it and be incubated there. It must leave its own home, its father's house, and go out into another country, where it will be an exile and a stranger. And like the youth going out from home into a rough world to make a fight of it under temptation and gross influences, he must undergo a long toilsome trial and testing and crucifixion to become an eventual victor and return with laurels. Said Jesus: "I came forth from the Father and am come into the world."

Additional elucidation of basic meaning flows from the consideration of the great doctrine of the Trinity in theology. One is not too bold in asserting that this formula of ancient truth is not comprehended in its clear and profound significance by the Church which still blindly offers it. Once a year the pew occupants listen to a sermon on the Trinity, but go away unenlightened. Yet it is the heart of the mystery of life, the base of theology, and—easily comprehensible.

Plotinus, the Neo-Platonist of the third century, who gave the doctrine to Christianity through Augustine, has given us an analogy with a natural phenomenon by which it is possible, with the additional link of a finding of modern science, to see the simple meaning of a doctrine that has baffled comprehension for sixteen centuries. He said that we can understand how one deity can have three aspects if we think of the sun, its light and its active energy. The sun in heaven is comparable to the Father of the Trinity. It is a glowing globe of *fire*. The fire of the sun does not go forth into the ends of space, but abides at home. Like a match which you strike in a dark room, the *fire* stays on the match; it does not leave it. The *fire* stays; but it generates and sends forth its son,—the *light*. This is the second aspect or "person." It is of the same essence with the Father, yet not he. And the Psalmist sings: "Send out thy light"!

Now a flood of clear light is released on the problem by following the implications as to the identity of the third "person," the Holy Spirit. But here it is necessary to adduce some pertinent data which is given to us by modern physical science to round out our analogy. We are told that a ray of the sun's light out in the void of space (not near a planet) is inert. It is both cold and dark. If one could reduce one's body to the size of a pin-point, one would be in total darkness and the intensest cold, though the sun be glaring overhead. The ray is impotent, inactive, uncreative and can generate no life until—and here is the nub of all philosophy—it falls upon a surface of a material body, a globe or planet! Only by incidence upon its opposite pole, matter, can the light of spirit come to its creative function. There is required the interplay of its rays with a resistant surface to bring out its own powers from latency to potency. Matter is, as already shown, the "mother" of life, while spirit (God) is its father. And, as everywhere, father spirit can not become creative until it unites with and fecundates mother matter! His ray of power, his son, is in a sense the phallic emanation of his seed, and the seed must become coefficient with the unfructified egg of life in matter's bosom to bring a new birth to pass. Almost it might be said,—here is all truth in a nutshell. The light of God would remain uncreative unless it entered the body or womb of mother life and aroused the slumbering potentialities therein. And here is the solution of a riddle of mythology which has baffled and horrified Christian moralists no end. The fables of the gods represent the son of deity as turning about and creating upon his own mother. Horus is called "the Bull of his Mother"—Isis. The sons of God marry their own mothers! Horrible! Detestable! shout the offended Church Fathers. Yet the son of present life marries and impregnates his own mother every time an acorn or grain of wheat falls into the ground and germinates! It is discernible at last why the letter H comes a second time into the form of the sacred tetragrammaton, or four-letter name of Jehovah, the Ineffable Name of ancient Kabalism—JHVH. "J" is the Father God, the line that comes down from on high, goes deep into the heart of matter and then turns upward to return to deity. The H represents by its two vertical lines life divided into its two aspects, spirit and matter, joined by the cross line, and so brings its activity into the realm of the mother, matter. The V is their son, who goes down in his turn into matter and returns. Now, why does the mother H come into the formula of creation a second time? The J H V would be a formula covering one—the first—generation of life. It would take it through one cycle. But that would not be a glyph that would represent life as perpetuating itself through endless cycles of renewal. It would end there. The graph must carry it on. As, then, the son must take up the line and become father in his turn, he must unite his productive fecundation with his old mother, matter. And so the H, or mother, must be brought into the picture once more. And the holy name becomes thus a descriptive form for all creation. For spirit is creatively helpless, like the sunlight, without the co-operation of its opposite, matter, which is dramatized as its wife and sister. Hence every mythological deity was linked with his *shakti* or spouse, his creative potency, without whom he would remain forever ungenerative. The implications of this determination are tremendous, for if spirit can not give birth to its archetypal conceptions without the implementation of matter in actual creation, neither can it function apart from matter in philosophy! And a thousand fantastic "spiritual" cult systems that have deluded uncritical minds in every age by a denial of the utility of matter, are at one stroke given the *coup de grâce* as illogical fallacies.

Reverting to the Trinity, it is desirable to go further with the Greek elaborators of the Orphic wisdom in delineating the aspects of divine activity.

Of the Father they assert that he "abides." A Hindu script has the passage in which Lord Krishna says: "Having impregnated the universe with a *portion* of myself, I yet remain." He remains on his own plane. He is the unmoved Mover and the uncaused Cause. He is without experience himself, delegating the function of acquiring it to his Son. He is unaffected, undivided, unchanging and undiminished.

Of the Son they say that he "proceeds." He bears the Father's potentialities out into all the universe. He is the radiating arm of his Father's power. He goes out to do the will of his parent and become his vicegerent in the worlds. He becomes God's spoken Word. He conveys the Logoic ideas out upon the bosom of his Father's emanations to stamp them upon plastic matter. And proceeding from the bosom of the Father, he goes forth into every condition which is precisely the opposite of that of the Father. He will become subject to experience and suffer all things, while the Father abides unmoved. He will be affected, divided, changed and be sadly diminished, suffering the loss of all that he enjoyed with the Father. He will endure all experience in every kingdom, will be fragmented into "partial natures," will enter a moving stream of endless change, and will be reduced to a minimum of his glory on the cross of suffering.

Of the Holy Spirit they say that it "converts" matter to its own likeness; "is converted" by matter to its next higher estate; and finally "returns."

What, then, is the Holy Spirit, the Third Person? It is the first Ray of divine life, undergoing its final conversion into active creative agency. It is latent power of God's mind, transformed into working efficacy. It is static divinity become kinetic. It is God's Logos, or Word, carrying the command of his creative Voice, now converted into an energy that moves matter and builds worlds. It is, finally, God's spirit at work; no longer static, or merely potential, but released upon matter in moving force—*kinesis*.

It may be helpful to present a diagrammatic sketch of this formulation, as it is a brief but complete graph of the entire rationale of all incarnation, or involution of life in matter, and its evolution back to spirit. It is thus a concise formula comprehending all that ancient scriptures have been designed to elucidate.

SUN .... FATHER .... ABIDES.

LIGHT .... SON .... PROCEEDS.

EARTH .... HOLY SPIRIT... { { CONVERTS (Matter).
IS CONVERTED (By Matter). }
RETURNS }

All "history" takes place at the point where the light, or latent radiation of divine force, comes in contact with matter, earth, the mother. For there involution is brought to a halt and, spirit being implanted within the heart of matter and awakening its slumbering potencies, there is begun at that point a new growth of life, actuated by the union of intelligence with sheer energy. And this new growth begins the *evolutionary* stage, or the return unto the father, or parent, status.

When Trinities are given as Father, Mother and Son, the aspect here characterized as the Holy Spirit is the "Son," the product of the union of Father and Mother. When given as Father, Son and Holy Spirit, the Mother is implicit, being the material element necessary at all times.

The Son's, or the ray's, impregnation of Mother matter begins a new process of growth from seed to adulthood, which through a cycle of "conversion" and "being converted" lifts up the new form of Sonship of deity to the stage which the Father had reached in its last previous cycle. The cycle is completed with the "return"; but after aeonial rest life gets ready to make its next rhythmic movement outward to unite again with the Mother.

Having set forth in the most compact form the outline of the structure of ancient evolutionary knowledge, it is incumbent on us now to trace the origin and fix the place of every single doctrine of theology in the draft. It is requisite also that sufficient space be granted to present as much as is permissible of the vast body of data supporting each phase of the exegesis. The "descent" is the first feature of the chart that relates heavenly creation to earthly life, and is logically the first aspect of divine activity to be taken up. Its groundwork and presuppositions having been laid down, its presence in ancient religion must be demonstrated with sufficient fullness.

Chapter VII

COLONISTS FROM HEAVEN

To begin with there is that vast mass of Medieval legend that became focused in Milton's grand epic. The tradition of man's having lost a Paradise, having been cast out of heaven and thrown into a prison, a dungeon, a pit, a lake of pitch, a dark cavernous underground where suffering was intensified by fire, was almost universal in the background of theological belief over a long period. This wide possession might have remained highly instructive had not Milton, in common with all save isolated groups of Hermeticists in Europe, lost the signal knowledge that the fallen angels, the rebel hosts, the armies of Satan-Lucifer were, collectively, *man himself,* and that the fiery lake into which they were hurled was just our good earth! This tradition was the far-trailing descendant of the ancient Mysteries, in which the entire drama of man's evolution was enacted at the great annual festivals. Says Thomas Taylor, perhaps the most understanding of all Plato's interpreters:

"I now proceed to prove that the dramatic spectacles of the Lesser Mysteries were designed by the ancient theologists, their founders, to signify occultly the condition of the unpurified soul invested with the earthly body, and enveloped in a material and physical nature: . . ." [1]

Cocker in his *Greek Philosophy* says that Plato in the *Phaedrus,* under the allegory of the chariot and the winged steeds, represents the lower or inferior part of man's nature as dragging the soul down to earth and subjecting it to a slavery under corporeal conditions. Taylor says [2] that

"the descent of the superior intellect [3] into the realms of generated existence becomes, indeed, the greatest benefit and ornament which a material nature is capable of receiving; for without this participation of intellect in the lowest department of corporeal life, nothing but the irrational soul and a brutal life would subsist in the dark and fluctuating abode of the body."

The whole design of the Mysteries, according to the great Plato himself, was "to lead us back to the perfection from which, as our beginning, we first made our descent." One of the mysterious significations of the Thyrsus or reed used in the Mysteries was connected with the descent of the soul, for, "as it was a reed full of knots," it became "an apt symbol of the diffusion of the higher nature into the sensible world." Bacchus (the divine self) carried a reed instead of a scepter, and it betokened the god's "descent into our partial nature." "Indeed the Titans are Thyrsus-bearers; and Prometheus concealed fire in a Thyrsus or reed; after which he is considered as bringing celestial light into generation, or leading the soul into the body."

The Greeks allegorized the descent of the soul again in the fable of Ceres and Proserpine. Ceres is the higher intellect, Proserpina being her daughter, the soul. Edward Carpenter says

"that there were ritual dramas or passion plays [in the Mysteries], of which an important one dealt with the descent of Kore or Proserpine into the underworld, as in the Eleusinian representations, and her redemption and restoration to the upper world in spring." [4]

No less applicable to the same fundamental situation is the Greek fable of Eros and Psyche. Love, the divine Eros, descends into the mortal sphere to redeem the human soul, or Psyche, from suffering in its animal habitat by marrying her. In the Mystery celebrations lasting nine days, Taylor tells us that on the eighth day the "fall of the soul into the lunar orb" was commemorated,

"because the soul in this situation is about to bid adieu to everything of a celestial nature; to sink into a perfect oblivion of her divine origin and pristine felicity; and to rush profoundly into the region of dissimilitude, ignorance and error. And lastly, on the ninth day, when the soul falls into the sublunary world and becomes *united with a terrestrial body*, a libation was performed such as is usual in the sacred rites." [5]

Proclus, the great Neo-Platonist of the fourth century, expounding Plato's theology, says that it is the peculiar function of "heroic souls" (an order above daemons) to express "magnitude of operation, elevation and magnificence," but that this order "descends indeed for the benefit of the life of man, as partaking of a destiny inclining downwards." [6]

Iamblichus corroborates Plato as to these grades of the hierarchy:

"Angels above dissolve the bonds of generation. Daemons draw souls down into nature; but heroes lead them to a providential attention to sensible works." [7]

Iamblichus makes an unequivocal statement of the descent when he says:

"But from the first, divinity sent souls hither in order that they might again return to him." [8]

He reiterates the idea (p. 68) when speaking of the gods:

"These, therefore, descend with invariable sameness for the salvation of the universe, and connectedly contain the whole of generation after the same manner."

He utters a strange sentiment when he affirms (p. 89) that the

"magnitude of the epiphanies [or manifestations] in the Gods, indeed, is so great as sometimes to conceal all heaven, the sun and the moon; and the earth itself, *as the Gods descend,* is no longer able to stand still."

Greek philosophy, as we have seen, embodies the traditions of the descent in several molds. In the cycle of the twelve mystic operations of Hercules, the hero is ordered to go down into Hades (our world) and bring up the three-headed Cerberus. His journey is a symbolic tracing of the experiences undergone by the soul on earth, not in some mysterious underworld below it. Orpheus descends to the underworld to recover his lost Eurydice, the soul. In Virgil's epic Aeneas finds the gate to Avernus and descends for the inspection of the Tartarian regions. It is instructive to note the etymology of this word "Avernus." It is the Greek *ornos,* a bird, and alpha (α) privative, meaning "un-" or "not" or "-less." The "v" is thrown in for euphony between the two vowels, and the "o" is shortened to "e." It would therefore read "not birds" or "no birds," with the implication of "not a good place for birds." When it is known that in all arcane systems the bird was the universal symbol for the soul, the meaning comes clear that this earth was regarded as the place where souls were poisoned by the noxious fumes arising from the carnal life, since the birds were lethalized by the vapor rising from the mouth of the pit of Avernus, became stupefied and fell into the underworld. The allegory tells the story of our descent with a force that no philosophical descanting could match. So deftly has ancient philological skill woven a theosophical meaning into the structure of language.

Dante's tour of Purgatory and the deeper Inferno is a treatment of the old myth, with political and other connotations. Ulysses' visit to the cave of Polyphemus is again a form of the representation, and Theseus and his labyrinthine adventure underground is another rendering of it. From Herodotus we have an account (II, 122) of the descent into Hades of King Rhampsinitus, in whose honor the priests of Egypt instituted a rebirth festival. The *Rig Veda* parallels this story with an account of the boy Nachiketas, who descended into the realm of Yama, the deity of the earthly underworld, in Yama-Loka, the kingdom of the dead, and then returned to the world of life. Needless to say, neither Egyptians nor Hindus took their theological myths for history.

A number of utterances in the *Chaldean Oracles* point to a quite complete harmony with Orphic Platonism and Neo-Platonism. Indeed opinion veers strongly to the conclusion that Pythagorean, Platonic and Greek philosophy generally was formulated out of the principles of theology promulgated through the powerful agency of the Orphic Mysteries, and that those principles were brought by the Orphics into Greece from Chaldean sources. The *Oracles* agree with Greek doctrine that higher deific energies emanated outward from a spiritual focus into the material worlds. One of them runs: "For all things thence begin to extend their admirable rays downwards." The life of the gods rays outward into corporeal beings and becomes the animating principle or soul of living things.

A passage from the *Tibetan Book of the Dead* (p. 130) warns devotees to "be not attracted towards the dull blue light of the brute world," under penalty of falling into that kingdom of nature. It asserts (p. 125) that the predilection of our immortal nature toward animal grossness will cause it to "stray downwards." The text represents the human soul as beseeching the "Knowledge-Holding Deities" not to let it drift further down, but to lead it to the holy paradise. The soul exults that "These Knowledge-Holding Deities, the Heroes and the Dakinis have come from the holy paradise realms to receive me." The text traces the descent of these divinities who, *false to their oaths,* fall

108

from lower to still lower stages of the Bardo, or world of dark embodiment.

A cuneiform tablet in the British Museum holds a legend of the rebellious angels who broke into the Lord's song with impious shouts, destroying the harmony, and who, for punishment, were cast down out of heaven. They are referred to in the *Book of Jude* (Ch. 6) in the line: "They kept not their own habitations." These in the *Book of Enoch* are the seven stars which "transgressed the commandment of God and came not in their proper season" (*Enoch* 18, 21, 22). It is said in the cuneiform text, "May the God of divine speech expel from his five thousand those who in the midst of his heavenly song shouted evil blasphemies."

Of tremendous significance to the thesis that early Christian doctrine was intimately allied with and influenced by the prevalent esoteric wisdom of environing cults, is a fragment called the *Naasène Hymn*, preserved by Hippolytus (*Haer.* V. 5). After describing the woes and sufferings of the human soul during its wanderings on earth, the hymn continues:

> But Jesus said: Father, Behold
> A war of evils has arisen upon earth;
> It comes from thy breath and ever works;
> Man strives to shun this bitter chaos,
> But knows not how he may pass (safely) through it;
> Therefore, do thou, O Father, send me;
> Bearing thy seals *I will descend* (to earth);
> Throughout the ages I will pass;
> All mysteries I will unfold,
> All·forms of Godhead I will unveil,
> All secrets of thy holy path
> Styled Gnosis (knowledge) I will impart (to man).

The Jesus character alluded to here is, it seems certain, the Gnostic Jesus, or Ieou, whom we shall see is traceable to Egyptian origins many centuries B.C. Scholars will haggle over the question of the date of the hymn, whether A.D. or B.C. The possibility that it dates B.C. has already been repudiated with great speciousness.[9] The name Naasene, of apparently Ophite connection, seems to have etymological relation to both the names Essene and Nazarene. If an Essene production it could readily be given a B.C. placing without violent improbability. There is evidence that cults of Nazarenes (*Nararaioi*) teaching Egypto-Gnostic Christolatry antedated the coming of the Gospel Jesus. The Ophites (serpent-symbolizers, not serpent-worshipers) were a Gnostic sect of early Christianity, later persecuted as heretics, who believed in a spiritual Christ-Aeon that descended into the material chaos to assist Sophia (Wisdom) in her efforts to emancipate the soul from the bondage of the flesh.

Turning to the material of Egypt we find the descent traced unmistakably in a thousand references. The conception is so pervading that all three persons of the Egyptian Trinity, Isis, Osiris and Horus, are represented as descending to the nether earth. Osiris, the Father God, descends, is cut to pieces by Sut (Satan) and the fragments of his body scattered over the earth. Isis, the Mother, descends to earth to search for the fragments. Horus, the Son, comes down in the identical character of the Christian Jesus in the advent at Christmas as the bringer of peace. As Jesus descends into hell (*Apostles' Creed*), so Horus descends into Amenta, the dark underworld (our earth). Horus came from heaven into the realm of darkness as the light of the world. It is said that he descends into the funeral land, the abode of darkness and of death. The Speaker in the Egyptian *Ritual* (representing always the human soul) says: "I have come upon this earth, and I take possession of it with my two feet." It is said that Osiris goes down into Tattu (another name for Amenta) and finds there the soul of the sun, and is united thereto. The Manes (again the human soul) says: "I am he that cometh forth by day . . . I descend upon earth and mine eye maketh me to walk thereon." It is said of him: "Thou enterest in to the place where thy Father is, where Keb [Seb, the god of earth] is." Again: "Thou descendest under protection. Ra ferries thee to Amenta." In the *Ritual* (the *Book of the Dead*) it is said: "This is he who in his resurrection says, 'I am the Lord on high and I descend to the earth of Seb that I may put a stop to evil.'"

Such references to the advent of divinity in the scripts of Egypt could be multiplied to great length. Likewise the religious lore of scores of aboriginal tribes in all continents hold multitudinous corroboration of the fact and confirm its status as the basic datum of all religious construction. A hundred folk-tales begin with the coming of some hero from heaven to earth, or with the flinging down of some object emblematic of divinity. The variety of symbols used is wide, and to one lacking the keys of interpretation, bewildering. It is enough to say that in all such legends the idea of the descent is central.

Looking now at the Christian Bible we shall find in plenty the features of the same myth. Bible students are not generally aware of the directness with which the descent of the gods to earth is there told. There is first the well-known declaration of God himself (distorted into a reference to the historical Jesus) that he sent his only-begotten son into the world that all believers might have everlasting life. Then there is the remarkable pronouncement in the *Gospel of John* (3): "No man ascendeth into heaven but he that cometh down from heaven." From *Luke* (19:10) we have: "The Son of Man is come to seek and to save that which is lost." Then there is Jesus' direct statement to his disciples: "Ye are from beneath; I am from above." The Lord's affirmation that he laid down his life for his sheep surely means not that he was immolated on a wooden cross, but that he resigned his celestial life to endure the burden of the cross (of flesh and matter). The Apocalyptist's vision of the New Jerusalem coming down from God out of heaven is a reference to the descent of divinity in its fragmented form. The line that follows—"Behold the tabernacle of God is with men, and he shall dwell with them . . . and God himself shall be with them· and he shall be their God" (*Rev.* 21:1), is to the same effect. Jesus declares that he came from the Father into the earth.

Lifting from the term *Christos* the Christian limitation of its personification in the body of the historical Jesus, and reading for this distorted meaning the idea of the gods incarnated distributively in all men, it is possible to discern allusions to the descent all through the Bible. Though not so immediately obvious, the Lukan account which states that Jesus came down from the mount and "stood on a level place" (Ch. 6:17) before he delivered the Sermon, is another indirect allusion to the same fact. For the *Pistis Sophia,* the Gnostic Gospel, states that Jesus preached his discourse to his disciples "in the midst of Amenta"! Later comparison of many texts discloses the surprising fact that both the mount and the level plain, whereon the Sermon was delivered in the Gospels, are diverse forms of the same symbolism! Both refer to our earth, under the terms of equinoctial symbolism. The "mount" in the *mythos* was never in any sense an earthly elevation. Paul in one passage propounds the logical problem, which should have been given consideration, analogically, by our scientists,—how we can envisage the resurrection without the postulation of a previous *descent* from heaven. He asks (*Ephesians* 4:9): "(Now he that ascended, what is it but that he also descended first into the lower parts of the earth? He that descended is the same also that ascended far above all heavens. . . .") The pertinence of this material for science is that science has studied life as in evolution without having postulated a necessary *involution* antecedently! Science must meet Paul's significant query. Likewise must theology restore to its high place the doctrine of the descent.

Symbolizing the divine nature as bread for man, John gives Jesus' announcement of his descent (6:47, 48): "I am the bread of life . . . such is the bread that *came down from heaven,* that a man shall eat of it and shall not die." The general allegorism of scattering or sowing seed is employed to depict the Platonic "distribution of divinity" among men. In the parable of the sower we have a portraiture of the partitive incarnation of divine natures in mortal bodies. The falling of the seed into various types of soil is a natural version of the diversified embodiments the descending souls might have apportioned to them. This interpretation raises the parable to infinite heights of dignity and meaning above the feeble and ineffective rendering of uncomprehending thought, which is able to see in the figured situation nothing higher than the sowing of the "word," that is, the Sabbath droning from pulpits, impinging upon different grades of mental acumen or moral character! The "Word" is in no case the written Bible, even, but the Logos, or form of divine ideation, powerfully stamped upon the physical universe by the deific utterance. No student is in position to grasp the significance of the Logos doctrine until he has mastered the principles of Platonic theology, as outlined by Proclus[10] or Plotinus. Christian interpretation has merely shuffled along in the darkness without a light. "Like the streams in the circle of heaven I besprinkle the seeds of men," runs a text in the *Records of the Past* (Vol. III, 129).

The angels in *Revelation* pour out the contents of their censers over the earth, granting a nucleus of solar "fire" to each mortal to divinize him. As the *Timaeus* of Plato reports, the deity was to furnish the collective seed of what was to be immortal in humanity.

In *Old Testament* allegorism the doctrine is found most unexpectedly to be the core of meaning in the Abraham story. Like the Prodigal

Son of the *New Testamant* he was sent out from his home, country and kinsfolk (in the heavenly Eden) to go to a strange land (incidentally to the West, where was the Tuat, or gate of entry to the earth!). There his seed was to multiply until it filled the earth with his children, the heirs of supernal grace.

But the hidden sense of the name Abraham or Abram has escaped notice, and it is of great moment, as are all Bible names. Scholars may protest, but it seems obvious that the word is simply A-Brahm, (Hindu), meaning "not-Brahm." Abraham, the Patriarch or oldest of the aeons or emanations, was not Brahm, the Absolute, but the first emanation from Brahm. He was the first manifestation of the Not-Self of Brahm; the first ray, the first God, perhaps equivalent to Ishwara of the Hindus. He was the first life that was not Absolute, yet from the Absolute. He was to go forth into the realms of matter, divide and multiply, and fill the world with his fragmented units. To return to Abraham's bosom would be just to complete the cycle of outgoing and return, to rest in the bosom of the highest divinity close to the Absolute. Also he came out of Ur, of the Chaldees (or Kasadim), which is another key word, since Ur is the Chaldean word for "fire," the celestial empyrean, out of which all souls, as fiery sparks, are emanated. Kasadim, or Kasdim, was a term given to the highest celestial spirits, who fathered the production of the divine sparks of soul. It is practically equivalent to "Archangels."

Then Abraham went straight to Egypt from the land of Canaan, and his descendants were to suffer bondage in that lower country. It is a crushing blow to the historical rendering of Bible narrative to declare, on evidence that is incontrovertible, that the "Egypt" of the scriptures is not the country on the map. It is the term used in the allegories to designate the plane, state or "land" of embodied life, life on earth. "Egypt" is just this earth, or the state or locale of bodily life on it. It even at times connotes the physical body itself, as in "the flesh pots of Egypt." Hence the descent of Abraham, and later of the twelve sons of Jacob, into "Egypt" are again the fable of the soul's adventure here. If the term Egypt is taken as the geographical unit, many passages in which it occurs will be found to read as sheer nonsense. Had theology known that "the strange land" and "the far country" were glyphs for this earth of ours, greater sanity would have marked the counsels of ecclesiasticism down the centuries. If the "bondage in

113

Egypt, that slave pen," as the Eternal repeatedly calls it (in the Moffatt translation), has been in some way interlocked with an historical servitude (as may have been the case), it still does not prove that the allegory intended to recount the bondage of a nation. It was a bondage of spirit under sense that was thus portrayed. Many passages from the *Old Testament* books refer to the Israelites as captives, outcasts, expatriates and exiles, matching Greek, Egyptian and Gnostic terminology, and alluding of course to the expulsion of the angelic hosts from a celestial Paradise to a bleak earthly exile. The sons of God had to go to Egypt also in order that fulfillment might be given to the hoary scriptural line from the Mystery drama: "Out of Egypt have I called my Son." For resurgent deity in the wandering exiles would eventually lead them back to their home on high.

In *Luke* (10:18) Jesus says that he "beheld Satan as lightning fall from heaven." As Satan is identical with Lucifer, the bringer of deific light, or the god (collectively), and the hosts of angelic souls (distributively), Jesus' utterance is readily seen as another affirmation of the descent of the spiritual principle, eternally symboled by "fire" from heaven. Again, in the resurrection scene "an angel of the Lord descended from heaven." Once more this is not a fragment of veridical history, but another brief figuration of the descent. In an Egypto-Gnostic fragment the same ideograph is repeated under the double representation,[11] when "the heavens opened and two men descended thence with great radiance," and both the young men entered the tomb. The seer in *Revelation* descries an angel in flight toward the earth and also sees the holy city of Zion, radiant with the glory of God, descending from the skies.

One of the *Old Testament* allegories has to do with the Lord's reminding Israel that he had "opened the doors of heaven" and "rained down manna upon them to eat." As bread is the Johannine symbol of divine nature on which the mortal race was to feed, so manna in the Mosaic narrative stands in the same usage. There is reason also to suppose that manna is cognate by derivation with the Sanskrit *"manas,"* the principle of intelligence, which was the gift of deity to "man." Its distribution over the ground in a thin layer like frost and glistening white is a symbolism of the spirit, which comes to us in the form of a distillation over the ground of our concrete experience out of the brooding atmosphere of divine super-intelligence. And all deity is described as shining with radiance.

A frequent figure for the descending spirits of light is the falling star. In the Egyptian *Records of the Past* (Vol. II, p. 16) the Speaker says: "The place is empty into which the starry ones fall down headlong upon their faces and find nothing by which they can raise themselves up." In the same thought the Chinese have a venerable proverb which runs: "The stars ceased shining in heaven and fell upon earth, where they became men." That the star as an emblem of the divine soul is not altogether a sheer poetic fancy, is shown by the fact that, as Massey points out,

"The Elementaries or brute forces of nature may be said to have obtained their souls in the stars. Hence, as Plutarch says, the Dog-Star is the soul of Isis, Orion is the soul of Horus, and the Bear is the soul of Typhon,—Soul and Star being synonymous in the Egyptian word Seb." [12]

In one of the addresses to King Pepi it is said to him: "Thy soul is a living star at the head of his brethren." [13] In the texts of Egypt the evil crocodile, typifying Paul's "carnal nature," is said to "swallow the sinking stars," the souls that fall into the darkness of incarnation. Among the ancients the stars that dipped beneath the horizon were emblematic of souls in physical incarnation, in contradistinction to those that never set, which typed the non-incarnating gods. Souls in incarnation were dubbed by the Greeks "moist souls," since they were immersed in the body, which is seven-eighths water by composition. The redeemed souls rejoiced in the Egyptian *Ritual* (Ch. 44) at being lifted up "among the stars that never set." Those condemned to descend were represented as falling stars in danger of being devoured by the open jaws of the dragon (of mortal life). This reptile lurked in the "bight of Amenta" or the bend of the river "where the starry procession dipped down below the horizon." The Swabian "Lindwurm" was another form of the dragon that "swallowed the setting stars." Indeed the entire myth of the casting down of Satan and his hosts was figured under the symbolism of falling stars. The dragon that "made war with the woman drew down into his kingdom many of the stars of heaven." One of the phenomena of the Crucifixion mentioned in *Revelation* along with the darkness over the earth, the veiled sun, the blood-stained moon, is that "the stars from the heavens fell." In the same place we read that "when the message of the third angel was sounded forth, a great star went down from heaven and it fell upon the earth." Another star fell at the sounding of the trumpet of the fifth angel. The various legends, then, of falling stars become invested with unexpected significance as being disguised allusions to the descent of the angelic myriads to our shores,—to become our souls.

But nowhere is the statement of the descent of soul made more explicitly than in the very Creed of the Christian Church, wherein the second person of the Trinity is described as he "who for us men and for our salvation *came down from heaven . . .* and was made man." Our material will show that the idea was common to many early nations, in whose literature it is stated with more definiteness than in the Christian.

If the descent was in partial degree a karmic punishment for sin, an enforced expiation of evolutionary dereliction in past cycles, as is hinted in Greek philosophy, it was also pictured as a seeking of refuge or a hiding for safety. Some contingency or crisis in celestial affairs, not fully divulged, made it both obligatory and advantageous for the angel hosts to flee heaven and find on earth, or in "Egypt," an escape from danger involved in some evolutionary impasse. It is not customary to think of hell as a haven, but certain implications in the old theology require us to do just that. At all events the legend of the hiding away of the young divine heroes is too general to be without deep significance. Adam hid himself when the Eternal walked in the garden. Moses as an infant was hidden in the papyrus swamps of "Egypt"; later he was hidden by the Eternal in a cleft of the rock as the majesty of the Lord swept by. Jonah ran and hid from the Eternal when first commanded to execute a mission to the Ninevites. The child Jesus had to be hidden away from danger in "Egypt"! The *Old Testament* Joseph went down to "Egypt" to be saved from danger. Jotham preserved his life from his murderous brother Abimelech by hiding. Saul was found in hiding among the baggage when he was chosen to be king in Israel. In Egypt, Buto, the nurse, concealed Horus, the analogue of Jesus, in Sekhem, "the hidden shrine and shut place,"—our earth. Horus' birth was in a secret place. A similar legend is related of the mythical Sargon in the cuneiform tablets. He says: "My mother, the Princess, conceived me; in a secret place she brought me forth." The supreme Egyptian Sun-God, the mighty spiritual divinity Ra, says to the earth: "I have hidden you." [14] He says that in the "Egypt" of this lower world he had prepared a secret and mysterious dwelling for his children. This divine dwelling created by Ra as the place of protection for the elect, is called "the Retreat." Amen, an aspect of Ra, was termed "The Master of the Hidden Spheres"; and Amen itself means "the hidden god." In the *Ritual* (Ch. 22) Osiris cries: "I rise out of the egg in the hidden land." Under another name, Qem-Ur, he addresses the earth (Aukert, the underworld) as the land "which hidest thy companion who is in thee." The god again speaks of "hiding himself to cast light upon his hidden place." This is the typical Lucifer character of the descending god, the Light-Bringer. He hides himself in order, it is said, to perform there the "mysteries of the underworld." "These things shall be done secretly in the underworld." (Rubric to Ch. 137A of the *Ritual*.) Under the title of Unas he "gathers together his members which are in the hidden place." He says that he has "made Horus enter into the Hidden Shrine to vivify the heart of the god."

It is desirable to search a little more closely for the rationale of this hiding in the secret place of earth, as the bases of the whole theological situation are involved in this dark background. Two causes can be assigned for the descent, a normal evolutionary one, and another rising out of the motives of karmic punishment for error, stubbornness, pride or wrong. As to the first, the Greeks postulated the Cycle of Necessity, which required that all souls or fragments of divine being must pass through the round of all the elements, in order to embody in their finished perfection the qualities of every modification of life. The second cause is less philosophically rationalized and—hints are given us—grew out of a special situation involving the recalcitrant behavior of twelve legions of angels, who, in retribution for evolutionary irregularities on their part, were forced into an earthly incarnation distasteful to them. In the character of King Teta, Osiris is made to say: "This Teta hath detestation of the earth, and he will not enter into Seb" (god of earth). There are also references to the anger of the higher gods, enkindled against them. Plato (*Phaedrus*) speaks of those souls who were "subject through the ancient indignation of the Gods in consequence of former guilt" to severe penalties on earth. In the *Cratylus* he concurs with the doctrine of the Orphics that the soul is punished through its union with body. Iamblichus (*Mysteries of the*

117

Egyptians, Chaldeans and Assyrians, p. 133) states that a partial motive in the celebration of the Mysteries of Sabazius was the appeasing of "the ancient divine anger." Clement of Alexandria (*Stromata,* III) preserves a passage from a celebrated Pythagorean, Philolaus, which runs: "The ancient theologists and priests also testify that the soul is united with body as if for the sake of punishment." The *Book of Enoch* points to a motive for this punishment in that the deities "came not in their proper season." It is given that they were ordered to incarnate at an earlier period, when the bodies of the animal race were of a requisite preparedness to receive the principle of intelligence, but that they refused and in consequence were forced to descend much later, when the animal vehicles were far gone in a state of degeneracy. Proclus in his *Hymn to Minerva* prays to the goddess:

> "Nor let these horrid punishments be mine,
> Which guilty souls in Tartarus confine,
> With fetters fastened to its broken floors,
> And locked by hell's tremendous iron doors."

Dante in the *Inferno* alludes to the souls in bondage:

> "Hither for failure of their vows exiled."

There is ground for connecting all this allusion to the penal character of our adventure on earth with the oft-cited "rebellion of the angels." Theological students should be more familiar with Plato's version of the Demiurgic speech to the hosts about to incarnate, the "junior gods," in the *Timaeus.* The Creator covenants with them to insure their immortality, to support them with his power; and then charges them to come to earth and "weave together mortal and immortal natures." It is said they rebelled, procrastinated and, when finally forced to descend by virtue of karma, missed the crest of a wave of evolution that would have carried them more smoothly forward past a crucial point. As it eventuated, their delay brought them to the earth when the lower race they were to uplift had sunk back into brutal degradation, and their penal infliction became the greater by the enhanced grossness of the bodies they were to inhabit. Their proper season had passed, as say *Jude* and *Enoch.*

Strangely we find in an old Egyptian inscription called "The Destruction of Mankind" a parallel to this somewhat anomalous situation in Platonic systematism. There is a rebellion against Ra, the Sun-God, followed by a great destruction and a deluge. Atum-Ra had been established as the king of gods and men, the God alone. There is a revolt against his supremacy. He calls the elder gods around him for consultation and says to them:

"You ancient gods, behold the beings who are born of myself; they utter words against me. Tell me, what would you do in these circumstances? Behold, I have waited and I have not destroyed them until I should hear what you have to say." [15]

The elder gods advise that he permit them to go and smite the enemies who plot evil against Ra, and let none remain alive. The rebels are then destroyed by being cast down *for three days*. Here is the distinct clue to true meaning, for the three days are a glyph for the time spent by evolutionary consciousness in the three lower kingdoms beneath man, the mineral, vegetable and animal. And "destruction" in this usage can not be taken as equivalent to actual annihilation or extirpation. This latter point is an extremely important one, as it saves many a Biblical allegory from utter perversion of meaning. After the exaction of the penalty, the "majesty of Ra" declares that he will now protect men on this account. "I raise my hand (in token) that I shall not again destroy men." The similarity of this description to more than a score of such narratives of the almighty anger against "a stiff-necked and rebellious people," their being cast out from celestial court and favor, and the eventual divine relenting and restoration of them to his providential care, must strike any fair-minded student who has read the *Old Testament*.

It is charged that Job, when cause is sought for his trial, had added "rebellion unto his sin." [16] It does not seem to be well known that the *Old Testament* contains an account of the "rebellion of the angels" in the guise of alleged Hebrew history. It is the rebellion of the "Sons of Korah," given in the Mosaic books, and recalled to the attention of the Israelites several times by the Eternal. It is told that at the rebellion the Lord caused the earth to open and swallow them up. It should be noticed that they were engulfed by the *earth*. It is known that two different groups of *Psalms,* thirteen to forty-nine, and eighty-four to eighty-eight, are specialized as "Psalms of the Sons of Korah." It is to be remarked as significant also that while swallowed up by earth, they were not destroyed! The rebel hosts, cast out of heaven, were not annihilated! What can this mean but that the term "destruction" is purely a glyph for the enforced descent to earth? Here they could expiate their contumely by sojourning in the untoward conditions of animal embodiment. Milton in the *Paradise Lost*, expresses Adam's surprise to find that his sentence of "death" for disobedience is a long, living death, not extinction. The account of the Korahitic rebellion expressly states that they were swallowed alive.

Happily Chaldean as well as Hindu records reaffirm the correctness of our interpretation, for Massey says:

"The Chaldean and Hindu legends know nothing of a *human* sin as a cause of the deluge. The sin against the gods, however, is described as the cause of the deluge in the so-called 'destruction of men.' . . . But these beings in the case were elemental, not mortal, and the sin was not human." [17]

This is quite important. The beings were pre-human and angelic, not elemental in the theological sense. Their rebellion, in short, occurred in heaven, not on earth, though indeed it has been prolonged into the earthly life. They carried their rebellious attitude down with them and exhibit phases of it to the present!

An Egyptian text says of the god Anhur that he had seen the malice of these *gods* who "deserted their allegiance to raise a rebellion," and "he refused to go forth with them." Other texts contain references to "the children of impotent revolt," and tell of their "inroad into the Eastern part of heaven, whereupon there arose a battle in heaven and in all the earth." And another passage alludes to the "carrying out of the sentence upon those who are to die," and says it is "the withholding of that which is so needful to the souls of the children of impotent revolt." The meaning here is obviously their expatriation and consequent cutting off from participation in the life of their celestial estate.

In general summary of this point, it may be said that the implications and the moral of these traditions of rebellious and outcast angels are these: our divine souls (for *we* are those rebellious deities) fled under karmic pressure from heaven to earth, and we have carried the same refractoriness down in our racial history. We refused at first to incarnate in the animal forms, and we still are rebellious in our refusal to take full charge and assume complete mastery over the "animal" segment of our composite nature. Hence the frequent injunctions in old scriptures to "kill out" the lower elements in us, and such a statement as that in the Egyptian text of Unas to "slay the rebel" in consummating our work of redemption.[18] Angels indeed were despatched to this realm, and their presence in the human constitution accounts for the divine element apostrophized in all religion. In the *Epistle to the Hebrews* (1:14) it is asked: "Are they not all ministering spirits sent forth to minister for them who should be heirs of salvation?"

The next step in the unfoldment of the theme is to establish beyond dispute that it was to our earth that the descent was made. This is tremendously vital to true interpretation.

In Egyptian scriptures we encounter the promise that "if Pepi falleth on to the earth, Keb [Seb] will lift him up." Pepi here stands for the divinity in man, the god come to earth. To him in another place it is said: "Thou plowest the earth . . . Thou journeyest on the road whereon the gods journeyed." Here is identification of the earth as the place to which the gods were sent to travel the road of evolution.

One of the most conclusive statements of this fact in Christian scriptures is that memorable passage in *Revelation* (12:7-9), where we have a succinct rehearsal of the "war in heaven" and the casting down of the angel hosts in the character of Satan, as the dragon or serpent.

"There was war in heaven. Michael and his angels went forth to war with the dragon; and the dragon warred and his angels; and they prevailed not, neither was their place found any more in heaven. And the great dragon was cast down, the old serpent, he that is called the Devil and Satan, which deceiveth the whole world; he was cast down *into the earth* and his angels were cast out with him."

It is of prime interest to note that the war in heaven was continued on earth, as has been intimated before. For *after* the dragon had been cast down to earth, he "waxed wroth with the woman and went away to make war with the rest of her seed."

This can be seen as the confirmation of the narrative in *Genesis*, wherein the Lord swore to place enmity between the serpent, or dragon, and the seed of the woman.

In the Egyptian *Ritual*, in the "chapter by which one cometh forth by day," the spirit of the descending god pleads:

"Let me have possession of all things soever which were offered ritualistically for me in the nether world. Let me have possession of the table of offerings which was heaped up for me *on earth*." He asks "that he may feed upon the bread of Seb [the earth god] or *the food of earth*." Proceeding he urges: "Let the Tuat be opened for me. Here am I."

This is an announcement of his advent upon earth, for the Tuat is the gate of entrance to Amenta. He is coming to this world to feed upon that type of concrete experience which the conditions here alone afford, under the name of "the bread of Seb." Later, *following* his resurrection, he says: "The tunnels of earth have given me birth." "I rise as a god among men," he exclaims. If there are men elsewhere than on earth, they are not those referred to in the old scriptures. He is described again as "Thou who givest light to the earth" (*Rit.*, Ch. 15). Again he says: "I come that I may overthrow my adversaries upon earth." It is on earth that his opposition is to be met and hither he must come to conquer it, for his undeveloped divinity must grow by overcoming opposition. He is spoken of again as "he who has caused the authority of his father to be recognized in the great dwelling of Seb,"—earth. Another passage (Ch. 64) describes the lower self in man as saying: "I draw near to the god whose words were heard by me in the lower earth." As the god-soul descends he says: "My body shall be established and it shall neither fall into decay *nor be destroyed* upon this earth." His mission to earth is proclaimed as being to "vivify every human being that walketh upon the regions which are upon the earth." In another place we have a combined reference to the earth both as the "hidden place" and as the globe where the young gods came to progress. It is said of Isis that "she suckled the child in solitariness, and none knew where his place was, and he grew in strength and his arm increased in strength in the house of Keb," or the earth. Egypt will offer us in later connections a superabundance of testimony to the thesis under discussion, the relevance of which can not be so well appreciated until other phases of the mundane journey of the god can be presented. The localization of the place where the gods fell when ejected from heaven in the *mythos* as being *our earth* is one of the three or four major postulates of the ancient theology which this work is undertaken to establish, and its implications must alter all religious construction drastically.

122

The point was once known, but was obscured by ignorant handling of the Gnosis and was lost. It is almost unthinkable that it could have met such a fate when the Church had constantly before its eyes the legend of Christmas, with its clear imputation of the incarnation of the children of spiritual skies on earth. But the distributive nature of the Christhood had been submerged, and the tradition of the fall of the angels had been wrenched out of all relation to the Nativity at the winter solstice.

The passage in *Revelation* (22: 16) that has left theological thought in such deep obscurity, may find acceptable rendition of its meaning in the light of the thesis of the descent: "I, Jesus, have sent mine angel to testify unto you these things in the churches." To apprehend the statement clearly we are required to read the name "Jesus" in the light of its Gnostic meaning as an Aeon, or emanation of divine spirit, an interpretation that is not at odds with its usage in the *Book of Revelation*. Students have been impressed with the evident resemblance of the Apocalypse to Gnostic literature, and one writer has ventured the opinion that it could have been written only by a Platonist versed in Mystery and Magian symbology. It bears quite pointed resemblances to such a Hermetic book as the *Enoch*. The Jesus referred to in it obviously has no identic relation to the Jesus personalized in the Gospels. His figure here is of cosmic proportions and equates the stature of the Logos. His dispatching of his angels to testify unto the churches can mean only that the Demiurgus, or Cosmic Intelligence embodied in an exalted being of the hierarchy, ordered the incarnation of the legionary hosts in the interests of the human evolution on earth. The "churches" can by no possible sophistry be distorted into a reference to the early Christian congregations. This would be to bring the dignity of cosmic operations down almost to the level of the monthly meeting of the Ladies' Auxiliary! The "churches" were groupings or gradations of spiritual beings at or near the completed state of human development, if not the *"ecclesia"* or "assembly" of the divinized mortals.

Theology has never adequately traced the course of the evolutionary processes by which the simple fact of the descent of the angels for incarnation took on the character of a "fall," with the implication of disaster. Says Cocker: "The present life is a fall and a punishment." [19] Many passages from the Bible could be adduced to show that the incarnation was held to have resulted in a fall or debasement of pristine angelic virtue. The *Revelation* apostrophe to the fallen Babylon, the mighty, whose ancient glory had departed, giving place to the glory of the Beast, whose courts had become the habitation of devils, and whose fornicatory wines had made the nations drunk, is doubtless an allusion to the situation here envisaged. To what else could St. Paul conceivably be referring when, speaking of the Gentiles, he says:

"And they changed the glory of the incorruptible God into the likeness of the image of a corruptible man, and of birds, and of four-footed beasts, and of creeping things."

An earlier paragraph has corrected the miscomprehension of the meaning of the term "Gentiles," which has beset the theological mind for centuries. It would be illogical to ascribe so dire an evolutionary degeneration to the mere accident of non-membership in a religious caste, or nation of allegedly "chosen" people. The Gentiles were the as yet undivinized "sons of men," as distinct from the "Sons of God," or Israelites, and it was their unpurified natures that dragged down the gods who incarnated in their bodies and dimmed their glory. The Gentile is the man "from beneath"; the Israelite is "from above," as Jesus affirmed. "The first man is of the earth, earthy; the second is the Lord from heaven," says St. Paul. The immersion of the latter in the bodies of the former reduced their originally vivid intelligence to such a point of stultification that they sank by degrees under the dominance of the sensual disposition. And here is found the conversion of the evolutionary "descent" into the theological "fall." The two terms Gentiles and Israelites can not be attached to any historical nationals. Their employment by several nations was at first only an allegorical flourish. The Greek use of the term "barbarians" and our own recent literary use of the word "Philistines" somewhat parallel this treatment of the word "Gentiles." The Gentiles were the party of the first part in evolution, who drew down the gods and changed their glory into the semblance of grinning hyenas, chattering apes, braying asses and rapacious wolves, in spite of "broad oaths fast sealed" and a covenant with deity.

The advent of the Prometheans to earth was the oblation, the divine sacrifice, the sacrifice "for sin." Yet it is only a perverted connotation of the word "sacrifice" that has caused this act of cosmic policy to be taken in the light of a self-privation on the part of the Luciferian hosts. Few words of noble meaning have not been touched by the disfiguring hand of low human understanding. Sacrifice (Latin: *sacra* and *facio*) means "to make sacred," and has no immediate correlation with the denial to oneself of benefits. If privation came in the process of incarnation, it was incidental, not inherent. The angel legions descended to make a lower order of life holy—"to adorn what was below them," as Plotinus puts it. Their labor was to the end of "sacrifying" a merely natural kingdom of life. It was to sanctify with the gift of divinity the mortal race, and make it immortal and divine.

This is not to assert that the enterprise did not entail hardship. The labor of evolution especially when self-consciousness had been awakened and the Ego became aware of his failures, and knew that he bore responsibility for his conduct, is more likely to be a *Via Dolorosa* than a path of roses. The reason for the accentuation of the denial aspect of the sacrifice is to be found in the fact that the upliftment of the lower grade entailed a long relinquishment of paradisiacal blessedness for the spirits of light, and a quenching of their deific fire in the moist humors, or "water," of the body. The adventure brought privation, torture, woe. It was an exile from a home of beatific happiness. To be plunged from a state of dreamy blissfulness into a state of dull realism and concrete objectivity, where the golden glow of idealism faded from every sight, was for them a dimming of the bright lamp of life. It was indeed a plunge from lively consciousness into partial unconsciousness. It was an ostracism from heaven into a long, hard and unattractive migration. They were to become colonists of a strange, distant land, if not castaways on its unfriendly shores. Cocker, already quoted, comments, in reference to Plato's Cave Allegory: "Their sojourn on earth is . . . a dreary exile from their proper home." Earth life is only a shadow of reality. In Egyptian scriptures the holy city of Aarru-Hetep (Salem) was to be built up by "the outcasts or the colonists from Egypt." St. Paul states that *we are a colony of heaven* (Moffatt translation). This is a clear Biblical intimation that we are expatriates from a higher world. Greek philosophy and mythology are replete with allusions to souls wandering on earth, exiles from a diviner sphere. Most of the semi-divine heroes had long journeys and crusades assigned to them. And the Prodigal Son is of course the unquestioned representative of the exile's role in Bible lore. From the

Greek philosopher Empedocles comes the echo of the sentiment that the soul has migrated to a foreign country:

"For this I weep, for this indulge my woe,
That e'er my soul such novel realms should know."

Moses' son was Gershom, which the Moffatt translation gives as meaning "Stranger," with the parenthetical explanation: "For I have been a stranger in a foreign land."

In this connection there is the possibility of a rational solution of the meaning of a text in the Bible which, in its conventional reading, has proven a perplexity and a "hard saying." It appears to be a stroke at the fundamental integrity of human kinship, family affection. In *Luke* (14:26) Jesus tells the multitude that no one can be his disciple unless one hate father, mother, brother, sister and all kin. In the great Gnostic-Christian work, the *Pistis Sophia* (Bk. 2, p. 341) a text runs to nearly the same effect:

"For this cause have I said unto you aforetime, 'he who shall not leave father and mother to follow after me is not worthy of me.' What I said then was, ye shall leave your parents, the rulers, that ye may all be children of the first, everlasting mystery."

In the light of the additional explanatory material given in the *Pistis Sophia* and omitted from the Gospel account, it is possible to see that this necessity of the disciple's leaving father, mother and kin and breaking all home ties in an apparently ruthless disruption of the most commendable of earthly loves, bore no original reference to human parents and kindred, but was another of the many allusions to the expatriation of the angelic orders. This breaking of home ties occurred in the celestial paradise, which in all portrayal is called "the Homeland." To be a follower of Jesus in his mission to a submerged humanity was to accompany him in his descent to earth from heavenly Father and empyrean home. If religion had kept its original knowledge of our cosmic errand, we could have been saved the perennial perplexity of wondering why the Lord's disciples are commanded to flout the tenderest of human ties.

Many of the allusions to the children of Israel as exiles, captives in a foreign land, hostages and outcasts, are made during periods when the historical Hebrews were not in either the Egyptian or the Babylonian or Assyrian captivities, and were not in any mundane sense exiles. Empedocles describes mortals as "Heaven's exiles straying from the orb of light." In line with our thought are the words of the Christian Advent hymn:

> O come, O come, Emmanuel,
> And ransom captive Israel,
> That mourns in lonely exile here,
> Until the Son of God appear.

Nor less grandly true are the lines of the "Gospel" hymn:

> I'm but a stranger here;
> Heaven is my home.

The various exiles, captivities and wanderings of the children of Israel were not historical. They were symbolic accounts of the descent of the twelve "tribes" of angelic spirits, "chosen" by the higher Lords in heaven to come to earth and divinize incipient humanity.

Chapter VIII

IN DURANCE VILE

HAVING established the place of the soul's fall or descent as our earth, the next task is to present the teaching of ancient philosophy as to the character of the soul's actual experience in the dismal habitat of the animal bodies. Christian theology makes much of the doctrine of the Incarnation, but a vast amount of primary knowledge that would enlighten the mind with reference to this cardinal item has been lost by the Church's flouting of the early Gnosis. The doctrine has been to ecclesiasticism such a baffling conundrum that it was shelved to a place of happy security in the person of the historical Jesus. Indeed the evidence grows stronger, as study proceeds, that the theory of a carnalized or personalized Savior, comprehending in himself every divine attribute, became established in early polity from the sheer fact of its serviceableness, it being found an easy solution of many a knotty problem of exegesis to ascribe every aspect of Godhood to the man Jesus. All divinity once safely localized in his person, a hundred confusing questions arising from the entanglement of deity with mortal flesh in all humanity could be summarily disposed of. Pagan philosophy required the presence of divinity in every son of earth. But a decadent religionism found the rationale of the situation too difficult to purvey to its ignorant following, and the euhemerized Jesus proved an easy evasion. Was not Jesus the only-begotten son of God? Insecure as this left the hierarchical status of every other Christian, it was sufficient for pious zealotry. The Incarnation was condensed in Jesus, touchingly born in a stable amid all the snowy pageantry of a region almost in the climate of tropical Egypt, and heralded by a star which in any astronomical view whatever becomes a natural monstrosity. All things considered it was a device of consummate utility to consign the whole matter of the Incarnation to the distant and sacrosanct person of the Nazarene. Beside bearing in his body the sins of the world, he has borne also in his frail person the unsolved problems of a blind and errant theology! The Jesus of Christianity was as much an intellectual necessity to a befuddled ecclesiasticism as Voltaire's God has been to a humanity trying to rationalize the universe. To a theology plunged into dialectical difficulties by its rejection of esotericism, a Jesus who "paid it all" has indeed been "a very present help in trouble." By cramming all the essence of divinity that came to earth into the sainted confines of Jesus' body and life, all qualms concerning the neglected "Christ in you" could be overborne by a wave of the hand toward the picture of the man of Galilee on the cross.

But pagan thought faced the implications and the data of the incarnation problem squarely. A fragment of deity was brought and lodged within the breast of every animal form evolved to the verge of the human kingdom. The animal race awaited the implantation of the divine spark, as their hope of a link with the order of responsible free agency and self-conscious intelligence. They stood at the point at which physical evolution could take them no farther toward mentality without the endowment of a nucleus or seed of potential mind from the plane above. They awaited the incubation of divine intelligence in their physical forms. The agents of such a blessing were at hand in the legions of Asuras, who had evolved the desired element of mind in former cycles elsewhere, but yet required some rounds of incarnate experience to, complete the perfection of their divinity. After rebellion and delay they came to fulfill their cosmic destiny. *We* are those "unwilling Nirvanees," those "junior gods," those angelic hosts! By our coming and sharing our nature with the lesser creatures, they, too, become the heirs of immortality; for the essence of which our higher nature was nucleated is imperishable. If the animal could append it to his being, he would be immortalized also. The Demiurgus in charging us with the commission, assured us that we "should never be dissolved" (*Timaeus*). The gist of Plato's, as of Paul's, writings is that man is a being compounded of a lower perishable and a higher indestructible vesture, the two linked by an intermediate principle which may be inclined to a union with either, and which therefore stands at the place of the balance in human destiny. The fleshly form was contributed by physical evolution on earth, but it was molded upon the matrix of an emotional body of finer etheric substance supplied by the men of the previous Moon race,

129

or the Lunar Pitris, at the end of their life period on our satellite.[1] A higher race, concluding a course of incarnations upon another planet of our system, Venus or Mercury, contributed the mental or *manasic* principle, which was to control emotion and sensation. And the highest spiritual node of being was the gift of entities embodying the soul of the sun. We can see now why in ancient legends of the formulation of mankind, the various gods are said to contribute each a bit of his own nature to compile the final product, as in the Pandora myth. *Manas* or mind was the intermediary between emotion and spirit. Spirit was to control mind as mind controlled emotion. With the descending Asuras [2] came potential mind and the germ of undying spirit.

To present briefly the archaic legend of the advent, the accounts relate that of the twelve legions chosen to undertake the adventure in the far country, two were lost and had to find their place again in evolution later. Of the remaining ten, one group of five responded willingly to the order. They were therefore known as the *Suras,* or "willing Nirvanees." They are the *obedient elder brother* of the Prodigal Son allegory! But in their effort they did not descend to full incarnation in animal bodies, but remained suspended, so to say, over the earthly scene in what might be called spiritual bodies. They never reached the flesh, never became the souls of fleshly creatures. They were obedient, but never fully executed their commission. The remaining group of five legions, profiting by their example, at first refused to run the risk of the same abortive effort, and were known as the *Asuras,* or "unwilling ones." (Syrians and Assyrians became their earthly counterparts in the handling of the uranograph, the ancient "u" changing always to a "y" when Anglicized.) However, they could not avert their destiny, and reluctantly obeying, they succeeded in linking their divine principle of intelligence to the mortal forms of the animal-men awaiting them. "The underworld awaits your coming" is a statement made to them in one of the prophetic books of the *Old Testament.* They were the younger and wayward son in the Prodigal Son allegory! But they did go out from home, as the elder brother did not. Therefore they were worthy of the fatted calf and the shining robe on their return, victorious. The elder brother, though obedient, had not earned the reward. This is the solution of the difficult situation in the allegory, in which the sulkiness and apparent neglect of the obedient son who had remained faithfully at home, have *so* universally defeated the exigetical efforts of the theologians. The parable of the five wise and five foolish virgins is likewise a glyph of this same cosmic predicament. For one of the names of the Asuras was *Kumaras*, meaning "celibate young men," or "spiritual virgins." They are the "Innocents" of the Gospel story and the *Hamemmet Beings* of the *Book of the Dead*. Their virginity is by virtue of the fact that they were entities of pure spiritual nature, radiations of basic Spirit, who had not yet had full incarnation, which was ever symbolized as a "marriage" of spirit with flesh! They were cosmically unmarried, hence "virgin" young men.

We have here a new intimation of profound meaning back of the feature of the "virgin birth" and the "immaculate conception." The virginity pertained to both sides, the spiritual as well as the material. If the matter that was to give birth to spiritual mind was hitherto unwedded to spirit, never impregnated by spirit, so likewise were the spiritual units who were sent to be the "Bridegroom" of *New Testament* dramatism to wed these immaculate virgins of the material nature. They were yet "innocent" of copulation with matter. They were the ones chosen to descend to earth and wed material forms, inoculating virgin matter with the principle of immortal mind. They were "young men" and "celibate." Beside *Hamemmet Beings* the Egyptians termed them "younglings in the egg" and the "younglings of Shu," the god. And they dramatized them as birds' (souls') eggs in the nest in the tree of life in danger of being devoured by the serpent— of the lower nature! One Egyptian name given, in addition to Apap or Apep, or Apepi, to the great Hydra serpent that lay in wait to devour the Manes in the "bight of Amenta" was Herut or Herrut. Evidence that is not lightly to be brushed aside in derision can be adduced in support of the suggestion that the name Herod, foisted on this serpent character in the myth when drama was historicized, is just a cover for the Herut reptile that threatens the Innocents! The historical Herod, tetrarch of Galilee, was dead at the year 4 B.C. Christian chronology has had to shift the "date" of Christ's "birth" to the year 4 B.C. in order to be able to include Herod in the story. But Cyrenius (Quirinus), the "Governor in Syria" at the time of Jesus' birth according to the Gospel account, reigned from 13 to 11 B.C. Will another shift of seven to nine years be made to include him?

The Kumaras in the Egyptian books exult in their escape from the serpent threat with the cry: "Apap hath not found my nest. My egg has not been cracked!" The infant Hercules in his cradle strangled the two great snakes that crept up to devour him, and both Horus and his cat symbol stand with feet upon the giant serpent's neck, the cat severing its head with a knife.

Thomas Taylor, the discerning Platonist, states that we mortal men are composed of the "fragments" of the Titans. In Platonism generally the Titans were styled Thyrsus-bearers, as having "led the soul into the body," or "brought ungenerated into generated existence." Their part in implanting the seed of intelligence in man is poetically set forth in Proclus' *Hymn to Minerva:*

> "Invigorated hence by thee we find
> A demiurgic impulse in the mind."

Massey tells us that

"in the *Latita-Vistara* eight heavenly beings are enumerated as *the* Gods or Devas. They are the Nagas, Yakshas, Gandharvas, Asuras, Garudas, Kumaras and Mahorgas." [3]

They are the gods who (collectively) in *Leviticus* (26) say to the Israelites:

"I will ratify my compact with you; I will pitch my tent among you and never abhor you. I will *live among you* and *be your God,* and you shall be my people."

In this great enterprise of leading whole and impartible natures into the realm of division and darkness they were said to have established "the garden of the Asuras" about the South Pole of the heavens, the Paradise of Yama, Lord of the region of death, whilst the Suras, or unfragmented deities, are said to have dwelt in the locality of the North Polar region, the fabled Mt. Meru, or Paradise of Indra. This opposition of the two races of divinities, termed the War in Heaven, was the celestial counterpart and prototypal aspect of the later struggle inaugurated between the heavenly and the earthly elements in human nature when the Asuras descended to assume physical vestures. It was the pattern in the heavens of the war between the first Adam, or natural man, and the second Adam, or the man regenerated by the infusion of a spiritual consciousness.

The point now to be demonstrated beyond cavil is that the incarnation was localized in the bodies of a race that at the beginning was animal and in the end was to be human. The "tabernacling with men" which the deities undertook consisted in effecting the incorporation of their subtler faculties and capacities in bodies originally animal. The ancient apothegm of the sages—"Nature unaided fails"—must be given due consideration in the scheme of things and accepted as one of the canons of understanding. It seems to introduce into the system of evolution a bizarre and unaccountable factor. It appears to thrust the causative principle of mind, intelligence, into the order of natural unfoldment in a purely arbitrary way, such as science can not countenance. It appears to make evolution jump over the gap between beast and human, and suddenly presents man endowed with self-determinative intelligence with no provision made for his having earned it in orderly development. But the ancient wisdom does supply the link that to science *is* missing. It reveals the irrationality of science's attempt to account for the presence and growth of a plant without permitting the assumption that its seed was first planted in the soil. Science has been straining to explain the presence of mind in man without knowledge of the ancient theorem that each kingdom serves as the seed-bed for the generation of life of the kingdom above it. It has been searching for formulae of explanation in total want of the understanding that

"one long immortal chain, whose sequence is never-ending, reaches by impact with that immediately above and by contact with that immediately below, from the very lowest to the very highest." [4]

It is possible to discern a replica of this same linkage of principles in the functioning of our bodily organism, reaching from spirit at the top to flesh and bone at the bottom. Spirit touches and influences mind, mind touches emotion, emotion modifies nerve impulse, which affects the composition of the blood, and blood builds cell structure, eventuating in actual flesh and bone. The spirit in the human body is like a power current in a dynamo, motivating a dynamic impulse which reaches to the utmost bounds of the organism. But man, like nature, is composed of a series of structures of different tenuity, and each member of the series is a link in the chain, bound above and below to the contiguous links. The interrelation of the links is governed by the Law of Incubation, by which the seed germ of life on the level above is deposited in the soil of the level below, there to be hatched to new generation. In the Egyptian *Ritual* (Ch. 85) the incarnating Ego says: "I am the soul, the Creator of the god Nu, who maketh his habitation in the underworld; my *place of incubation* is unseen and *my egg is not cracked*." And in the resurrection scene in the *Ritual* the revivified Ego, figured as a dove, exclaims: "I am the Dove; I am the Dove,"! as he rises from the realm of darkness wherein the "egg of his future being was hatched by the *divine incubator*" (Ch. 86).

In the *Pistis Sophia* of the Gnostics the doctrine of the incubation finds clear expression when Jesus says:

"I found Mary, who is called my mother, after the material body; I implanted in her the first power which I had received from the hands of Barbelo, and I planted in her the power which I had received from the hands of the great, the good Sabaoth" (Mead's Trans., Bk. I, 13).

It is of transcendent importance to note that the Greek (Gnostic) work directly identifies Mary, the mother of divinity, with the physical body! Let Christian theology be advised of the long-lost truth of this matter. The mother in all ancient allegories typifies nothing more than the physical body which in man becomes the womb or matrix in which the radiant Christ-body of spirit is brought to birth. Is Christianity to fall below heathenism in its inability to rise above the level of the symbols to the discernment of the abstract truth behind them?

Proclus speaks of the soul having fallen *like seed* into the realms of generation.[5] Paul's characterization of the nature of man as *sown* in corruption is a resort again to the imagery of incubation. The "junior gods," potentially if not yet actually divine, were sown, planted in a soil prepared by evolution to nourish their latent fires to expansion and full function, and this was the incarnation. The "fleshly" connotation of the word leaves no doubt as to the full reality of the process; the ground prepared was the physical body of animal-men. The entry of these divine seeds of life and mind into each animal form made possible for those creatures their transition across the gap of the "missing link" to the plane of humanhood. The link between brute beast and thinking man *is* missing on earth; for it was forged by evolutionary process in another realm, on another planet, and transferred to earth at a given critical epoch in mundane history. As Plutarch tells us, only one fourth of man, his physical body, is derived directly from the earth; the other three parts are brought here and linked to his material frame by appropriate affinities. That this may not remain an insoluble enigma to modern skepticism about such things, it may be said that each of these principles intermixed in man's constitution was the product of an evolution on its particular globe, and that, since these globes themselves are but cells or organs in a larger composite living stellar *being,* the possibility of their sustaining vital relations or co-operative linkage in a common creative work is far from an unnatural presupposition. Science must go several steps deeper than it has yet gone into the secret workshop of nature before it can admit the legitimacy of such predications. Yet ancient psycho-physics faced the problems of life with the knowledge that all living organisms are concocted of a perishable material element and an imperishable subjective element bound together in temporary union. When the corruptible sheath fades away the imperishable nucleus floats free, persists and may later be embodied in another form. Science is to be reminded that substances are the more enduring in proportion to their tenuity, that "soul," as the Greeks affirmed, is far more lasting than body. Hence impressions made upon it are a more ineradicable book of life than any cemetery epitaph. Our emotional body, our mental vehicle and our immortal spiritual vesture each brings the record of its past indelibly imprinted upon the underlying etheric substance of its composition.

From Greek Platonism we draw some of the most direct and dialectically essential support for the thesis of the bodily incarnation. From Olympiodorus' *Commentary* on the *Phaedo* of Plato we take the following:

"It is necessary, first of all, for the soul to place a likeness of herself in the body. This is to ensoul the body. Secondly, it is necessary for her to sympathize with the image, as being of like idea. For every eternal form or substance is wrought into an identity with its interior substance, through an integrated tendency thereto."

We are here enlightened about the interior affinities which the two partners to the union manifest toward each other, the bonds that draw and hold and eventually weld them together.

Another pointed assertion comes from the *Chaldean Oracles:*

"For the Father of Gods and men placed our intellect in soul, but soul he deposited in sluggish body."

Perhaps we shall find nowhere else so detailed and analytic a statement of the principles on which life and nature regulate the metamorphoses which divine consciousness undergoes as it descends the Jacob's ladder from spirit heights to mortal sense on coming into incarnation, as in a paragraph from Proclus in the quaint style of Thomas Taylor's rendering:

"In order likewise that this may become manifest and also the arrangement, let us survey from on high the descent, as Plato says, and defluxion of the wings of the soul. From the beginning, therefore, and at first the soul was united to the Gods, and its unity to their one. But afterwards, the soul, departing from this divine union, descended into intellect, and no longer possessed real being unitedly and in one, but apprehended and surveyed them by simple projections and, as it were, contacts of its intellect. In the next place, departing from intellect, and descending into reason and *dianoia,* it no longer apprehended real being by simple intuitions, but syllogistically and transitively, proceeding from one thing to another, from propositions to conclusions. Afterwards, abandoning true reasoning and the dissolving peculiarity [analysis], it descended into generation, and became filled with much irrationality and perturbation. It is necessary, therefore, that it should recur to its proper principles and again return to the place from whence it came." [6]

Nothing would so quickly aid modern psychology to work for fruitful results in understanding as to adopt this table of the successive "defluxions of the wings of the soul" in Plato's magnificent analysis. Surely the present status and modus of the psyche's operation are to be better envisaged if they are known to be the lowest and most darkened activity of a spiritual intelligence that on the heights above functioned by flashing intuition. Clearly outlined are the several steps which the soul takes from piercing light into murky darkness as it descends into body: first from identity with reality and direct inclusion of consciousness in it; then the plunge downward into that form of intellect which apprehends by immediate intuition; again the dip into the more sluggish processes of logical reasoning, in which, the inner relations of things being lost, the mind must establish them slowly by syllogistic process; and finally the dropping altogether from rational procedure into following the lead of sheer sense and impulse of the lower nature. With mighty realizations we are now able to see what St. Paul meant in saying, "Now we see through a glass darkly."

From a dissertation on *Theurgy* translated by the Renaissance Platonist, Ficinus, we take the following clear statement of the gradations in the chain of the descent:

"So that all things are full of divine natures; terrestrial natures receiving the plenitude of such as are celestial, but celestial of supercelestial essences; while every order of things proceeds gradually, in a beautiful descent, from the highest to the lowest. For whatever particulars are collected into one above the order of things, are afterwards dilated in descending, various souls being distributed under their various ruling divinities." [7]

From the grand master of divine knowledge himself, Plato (*Timaeus,* xliv), comes the remarkable declaration:

"The Deity (Demiurgus) himself formed the *divine;* and then delivered over to his celestial offspring (the subordinate or generated gods), the task of creating the *mortal*. These subordinate deities, copying the example of their parent, and receiving from his hands the *immortal principles* of the human soul, fashioned after this the mortal body, which was consigned to the soul as a vehicle, and in which they placed also another kind of soul, which is mortal and is the seat of violent and fatal passions."

For sheer enlightenment these passages are worth whole libraries of modern speculation. The lower soul spoken of is the one which emanated from the moon race, and is, strictly speaking, the soul of the animal, not the god-soul of the man. It is this lower soul, called often the "elemental," the seat of the animal's instincts, that the god has come to educate, and in the same body with which it has come to dwell. When Plato describes it as "the seat of violent and fatal passions," he is definitely identifying our mortal tenement with the body of an animal. This conclusion is strengthened by one of the Zoroastrian Oracles, which declares: "The wild beasts of the earth shall inhabit thy vessel." [8]

Edward Carpenter, in reviewing the multifarious forms of the "sacrifice" doctrine in religions, says that "Brahma, . . . Indra, Soma, Hari and other gods, became incarnate *in animals*." [9] And it is not without extreme significance that we have such a statement as the following from a scholarly authority:

"The sense of an absolute psychical distinction between man and beast, so prevalent in the civilized world, is hardly to be found among lower races." [10]

Naturally so, because the gap between man and animal there *is* less wide than it now is in cultured races. The animal did not at one jump land into full manhood. He was given the as yet ungerminated seed of divinity to nurse within the depths of his own nature. Only a tiny segment of the god's life was in conscious manifestation in and through the lower mentality of the beast at the start. The god could put little of his full power and capacity into expression through the imperfect brain of the animal. For a long time, or until the angel's presence in the brute body could refine the latter's impulses and proclivities and increase brain expansion, the deity could only lurk in the background of consciousness, becoming what we now so ignorantly term "the subconscious mind." There was obviously little difference between the first humans and the nearest animals. The difference did not assume marked proportions until ages had rolled by and the slow march of development had enabled the god to project more and more of his innate endowment into the sluggish nature of the beast he was tutoring. We have here, systematically propounded for the first time, the basic criterion for evaluating the progress of human culture. Culture is essentially nothing but the gradual modification of crude animal impulses into the gentler motions of the higher self. Modernity has never concisely known the cosmic or evolutionary foundations of this transaction. These lay hidden under the rejected esotericism of Platonic and other arcane teachings.

The Bible sets forth the implications of the incarnation in sensationally direct form in the *Book of Daniel*. Addressing the king (always a figure for the god) Daniel tells him that he will be taken away from human beings to dwell with the wild animals; and he condenses volumes of Platonic philosophy dealing with the obscuration of deific intellect in the descent, into the pithy statement, repeated three times in the first five chapters, that "you shall be given the mind of an animal"! "An animal's mind was given unto him and his dwelling was with the wild beasts." Also: "He ate grass like cattle, and his nails grew like the claws of a bird." (Incidentally, here is positive proof of the non-historicity of Bible narrative, since these things did *not* happen to the historical King, Nebuchadnezzar!) But the Paradise lost in the incarnation was regained in the end, for finally, "When the time was over, I, Nebuchadnezzar, lifted up my eyes unto heaven; *my reason returned unto me,* and I blessed the Lord, praising him and honoring him forever." The period of the duress in animal habitat is given as "seven years," each cycle of incarnate life being completed in seven ages! And all the mighty meaning of this grand allegory was missed because Nebuchadnezzar was taken for an historical personage, instead of a figure for the god in man.

Egypt furnishes us with one of the most direct and indubitable bits of testimony to the animal incarnation of the soul in one of the numberless prayers addressed to Osiris:

"Hail, Osiris Khenti-Amentiu (Lord of Amenta)! Thou art the Lord of millions of years, the *lifter-up of wild animals,* the Lord of cattle; . . ."

As Amenta is the region in which the Osiris-soul contacts the body, the verse is of surpassing meaning in this connection.

Massey writes in *The Natural Genesis* (Vol. I, p. 71):

"A very comprehensive designation for the divinities of all kinds, says Gill (*Myths and Songs,* p. 34), is the Mangaian *'te anau tuarangi,'* the heavenly family. This 'celestial race includes rats, lizards, beetles, sharks and several kinds of birds. The supposition was that the heavenly family had *taken up their abode* in these birds and fishes.'"

"Plutarch refers to the idea 'that the Gods, being afraid of Typhon, did, as it were, hide themselves in the bodies of ibises, dogs and hawks,' and repudiated it as 'foolery beyond belief.' This, however, is a matter of interpretation. We know that *such representations were part of the drama of the Mysteries.* Many descriptions might be quoted to show that in their religious ceremonies, the actors performed their masquerade in the guise of animals."

We have here a sterling clue to the lost meaning of most of the weird ritualism still carried out in our celebration of Hallowe'en. The importance and gripping significance of this remnant of ancient symbolic dramatism is not dreamed of today. The masks worn were originally those of animal faces or hides. The festival, coming at the time of the September equinox (with a forty-days' interval), when the sun, eternal symbol of the divine soul, was descending across the line which marked the boundary between disembodied spirit and soul embodied, dramatized the entry of the god into the animal body. "Mask" is in Latin *"persona."* The god was then putting on the mask of his *personal*ity; and all the weird capers, grimaces, horseplay and general buffoonery of the Hallowe'en revelry most piquantly prefigure the deity's ungainly animalish behavior when cavorting behind the outward mask of the animal's nature! The moon being the parent of the mortal body, lunar symbolism was prominently introduced into the portrayal. And all this is another strong proof that it was the primal religious ritual drama that gave rise to social tradition and celebratory custom, and not folk-practice that gave rise to the myth, as scholars have always so erroneously contended.[11]

A patent hint of strong esoteric significance is found in the following:

"Diodorus has it that the gods were at one time hard pressed by the giants, and compelled to *conceal* themselves for a while under the form of animals, which in consequence became sacred." [12]

Here is straight anthropology hidden under semi-fable. It is the true explanation of a vast amount of tribal custom that has perplexed the learned world no end. Whole chapters of Frazer's *Golden Bough* and similar works, of which the authors have offered no rational interpretation and believed none possible, become intelligible at one stroke, and such a cultured people as the ancient Egyptians are exculpated from the charge of crude animism and fetishism in "worshiping animals."

The incarnation was incontestably the most fateful event that had ever taken place in the evolutionary career of animal-man, giving him a status far above that of his former condition. It was the far-away beginning of his apotheosis. It was his passport of entry into the kingdom of mind. The folk-lore and *Märchen* of the nations carry the story of this mighty crisis in evolution in an apparent *mélange* of childish fancy, flippant caprice of invention and forms of the grossest imagery. These seeming qualities have been the means of derailing the train of our understanding of the hidden purport of the relics. We have but to use our imagination constructively to see how mythography passed first into the realism of dramatic representation, then into legend lacking the original spiritual meaning, and finally into a sadly distorted and barren folk-tale.

"Herodotus was told that the Neurian wizards among the Scythians, settled about the Black Sea, became each of them a wolf for a few days once a year. The Texan tribe of the Tonkaways did the same, when, clothed in wolf-skins, they celebrated the resurrection of the wolf from the Hades. The head of a wolf was worn in the Mysteries of Isis; because the wolf (Anup) was her warder and guardian during the search for Osiris in the underworld. . . . The candidate as the Loveteau of French Masonry still enters as a young wolf." [13]

A Chinese remnant relates that a maid conceived by air (the Holy Spirit!) and brought forth a child, which the father then threw into the *pig-yard!* "It was the rightful heir, who lived to become the monarch." If this seems tawdry and profane, let the reader note the obvious resemblance to the Prodigal Son allegory and the conception story of Mary.

The Shilluks have a tradition that "Nyakang then created men and women out of the animals he found in the country." The promise to mankind in the *Genesis* account, that the human should be lord of the animal creation, ruler of the beasts of the field, has obvious reference to the headship of the mental man over the body itself, which would be assumed by the soul or god upon his entry therein, under the terms of his covenant with Deity. His task in the incarnational assignment was to tame, subdue, discipline and finally exalt the lower personality, which was the depository of all animal experience in *its* soul,—our sub-conscious mind. Passages in the *Book of Enoch* state that man shall dwell with the wild beasts and shall subdue and overcome them. A verse in Ezekiel declares to the soul: "I shall fill the wild beasts of the earth with thee." But one of the most straightforward figurations of the incarnation in all religious literature is found in the *Epistle of Ignatius to the Romans,* an apocryphal *New Testament* Gospel, when the soul, speaking as one of the characters in the drama, most beautifully poetizes his nature and mission in this remarkable utterance: "Suffer me to be food to the wild beasts, by whom I shall attain unto God. For I am the wheat of God, and I shall be ground between the teeth of the wild animals that I may be found the pure bread of Christ." The crushing of wheat into flour for bread was a widely used symbol of the fragmentation of unitary deity consequent upon his descent into bodies. The statement here that the crushing was done by the teeth of the wild beasts is beyond cavil a positive reference to the animal embodiment. And the added information that by such lowly incarnation the soul shall attain unto God should restore to theology the lost conception of the importance of the bodily life.

The Bible's declaration that we "shall be as sheep among wolves" is a slanting hint at the picture of the gentle Christ spirit tenanting the bodies of the wild beasts of earth! And the scene of Daniel, the man of God, in the lions' den, is another suggestion that the soul may safely reside in the animal's body or "den," if it holds true to its divine ideal.

An Egyptian text addresses Thoth as "he who sendeth forth his heart to dwell in his body." Another presents us with a definite corroboration of the incarnation thesis. It speaks of Annu (in this case our earth) as "the land wherein souls are joined unto their bodies even in thousands."

An Arunta legend describes the animistic powers attributed to beings as the "ancestors who reproduce themselves by incorporation in the life on earth in the course of becoming men or animal."

It was the fundamental Egyptian conception that the god, on descending to earth, became "fleshed." The word *Karas*, which was used to designate the mummy, is traced to the Greek *kreas,* flesh. The taking on of a carnal form was in its true connotation the mummification of the Osiris or spirit.[14] An Egyptian text asserts most positively the union of soul and body. Chapter 163 of the *Ritual* says: "Let his soul have its being within his body, and let his body have its being within his soul." And another chapter (89) is entitled "the chapter by which the soul is united to the body." This can not mean the dead body, since obviously the soul is separated from, not united with, the cadaver. It can mean nothing but the conjunction of the incoming soul with the body at birth or a little later.

The amassing of so much data in support of the Incarnation, a doctrine of theology that is still included in ecclesiastical acceptance, may appear a labor of supererogation. Far from it. The data presented have been assembled with the purpose of restoring the dogma to its pivotal place of importance in the theological temple. It has been so viciously emasculated that a mass of testimony as to its original cardinal utility had to be adduced, if it is to be re-established in its rugged pristine meaning. Mankind works blindly at the main problem confronting it so long as this doctrine is obscured. It was never intended to mean that the whole of the power of the Logos was crowded into the admittedly limited area of a single personality. It was not accepted in this light by the intelligent Fathers of the early Church, such as Clement and Origen; for they are on record as expressly repudiating such an eventuality. They regarded a personalized embodiment of deity as infinitely degrading to the Logos, verily a blasphemy.

Furthermore how can we understand Paul's preachment of the warfare between carnal and spiritual natures unless we are assured that soul and flesh were conjoined in intimate and affective relationship? If theology is to rise again to benignant influence, it must be mounted again upon its ancient bases of anthropology. If the advent, the incarnation, the birth, the temptation, the baptism, transfiguration, crucifixion and resurrection can not be shown to be the type of our own actual experience in present living, the temple of theology can not be expected to be rebuilt on a foundation of mystical sentiment alone. If the cosmological and anthropological aspects of the original esotericism had not been disdained, theology would not now stand in such forlorn case before a world styling itself intelligent. Thrown down from her pedestal of ancient dignity, she lies prostrate in the courtyard of the Church, and the busy populace hurrying by on worldly bent mocks her or heeds her not. She has no place in the hall of science, no true home in the human heart. Hardly even in the somber pulpit does she stand in honor. Her only place is in the dim and darksome alcoves of the ecclesiastic's library; and priestly zeal essays in vain to win back for her the departed power.

On this score it is desirable to give assent to one or two of Massey's discerning judgments before passing on to the corollaries of the doctrine:

"The doctrine of the incarnation had been evolved and established in the Osirian religion at least four thousand years, and possibly ten thousand years, before it was purloined and perverted in Christianity." [15]

"The legend of the voluntary victim who in a passion of divinest pity became incarnate and was clothed in human form and feature for the salvation of the world, did not originate in a belief that God had manifested once for all as an historic personage. It has its roots in the remotest past. The same legend was repeated in many lands with a change of name, and at times of sex, for the sufferer, but none of the initiated in the esoteric wisdom ever looked upon the Kamite [Egyptian] Iusa, or Gnostic Horus, Jesus, Tammuz, Krishna, Buddha, Witoba, or any other of the many saviors as historic in personality, for the simple reason that they had been more truly taught." [16]

The incarnation, however, only begins the impartation of deity to the human race. It inaugurated on the planet a chain of events, the circumstances and trend of which must now be outlined. All of these involvements are profoundly relevant to the system of theology.

Greek philosophy viewed the descent and incarnation of the gods as entailing upon these exalted beings an almost total loss of their pristine glory and felicity, and a devastating reduction of their coefficient of consciousness. The soul became "cribbed, cabined and confined" in the sorry limitations of the carnal body, as it lost a dimension of consciousness at each step on the downward path. It becomes bound to the sensual and the palpable, after having been able to range at will throughout the limitless spaces of universal thought. It is impossible to surpass in lucidity the language of Greek philosophy in delineating these matters. Proclus, as reported by Iamblichus, avers that [17]

"the soul by descending into the realms of generation, resembles a thing broken and relaxed. . . . Hence the soul energizes partially and not according to the whole of itself . . . the intellectual part of it is fettered . . . but the doxastic [18] sustains many fractures and turnings."

Proclus elucidates Plato's findings to the effect that

"it is impossible while here, to lead a theoretic life in perfection, as is evident from the causes which are enumerated in the *Phaedo,* viz., the occupations and molestations of the body, which do not suffer us to energize theoretically without impediment and disturbance." [19]

And his fellow-Platonist, the learned Iamblichus, adds a forceful assertion of the same idea:

"For the human soul is contained by one form and is on all sides darkened by body, which he who denominates the River of Negligence or the Water of Oblivion, or ignorance and delirium, or a bond through passions, will not by such appellations sufficiently express its turpitude. How therefore is it possible that the soul which is detained by so many evils can ever become sufficient to an energy of this kind?" [20]

Empedocles, evidently drawing his philosophical ideas from Orphic Mystery cultism, has a poem, a fragment of which speaks of the "joyless region" in which the souls on earth

"Through Ate's meads and dreadful darkness stray."

The soul descends from the realms of light to the region of gloom:

"She flies from deity and heavenly light
To serve mad Discord in the realms of night."

A dialectical echo of Plato's Cave Myth is heard seven centuries after the *Republic* was written, in the language of the great Plotinus, mystic Neo-Platonist of the third century. Dealing with the fable of Narcissus and elucidating its hidden purport, he says:

"Hence, as Narcissus, by catching at the shadow, plunged in the stream and disappeared, so he who is captivated by beautiful bodies, and does not depart from their embrace, is precipitated, not with the body, but with his soul, into a darkness profound and repugnant to intellect, through which, remaining blind both here and in Hades, he associates with shadows." [21]

In the *Phaedrus* Plato, in the beautiful allegory of the Chariot and the Winged Steeds, portrays the soul as being dragged down by the lower elements in man's nature and subjected to a slavery incident to corporeal embodiment. Out of these conditions he traces the rise of numerous evils that disorder the mind and becloud the reason. Indeed he shows with convincing dialectic that evil is just this breaking up of the vision of whole natures into distracted particulars where the interconnection of part with part is lost sight of. Evil is seen to be due to the condition of partiality and multiformity inseparable from the incarnate state, "into which we have fallen by our own fault." The rational element, formerly in full function, now falls asleep. Life is thereupon more generally swayed by the inclinations of the sensual part. Man becomes the slave of sense, the sport of phantoms and illusions. This is the realm in which Plato's *noesis,* or godlike intellect, ceases to operate for our guidance and we are dominated by *doxa,* or "opinion." [22] This state of mental dimness is the true "subterranean cave" of the Platonic myth, in which we see only shadows, mistaking them for reality.

Thomas Taylor's clear language enforces these ideas for our benefit:

"Such indeed is the wretched situation of the soul when profoundly merged in a corporeal nature. She not only becomes captive and fettered, but loses all her original splendor; she is defiled with the impurity of matter; and the sharpness of her rational sight is blunted and dimmed through the thick darkness of a material night." [23]

Proclus, an expounder of Plato rated nearly equal with his great inspirer, writes:

"When it [the soul] energizes according to nature, it is superior to the influence of Fate, but when it falls into sense and becomes irrational and corporeal, it follows the natures that are beneath it, and living with them as with intoxicated neighbors, is held in subjection by a cause that has dominion over things that are different from the rational essence." [24]

Indeed we have here the Greek philosophical root of one of the pivotal phases of Pauline doctrine. It was the descent and mooring of the soul "to the ruinous bonds of the body" that brought the spirit of man under the dominion of what Paul calls "the law"—of Fate, Karma and Necessity. This, too, was "the bondage in Egypt" of the *Old Testament*. On her own high plane the soul was in a state of liberty, "the glorious liberty of the sons of God." Only by her incarceration in a vessel whose constitutional functions were under the laws of physics and chemistry was she subjected to the rule of matter. The Greek philosophers declared that her release from this bondage was to be won only through the discipline of "philosophy." It taught the earnest man to abjure the motions of the flesh and to rise to the delight and freedom of the noetic consciousness. Paul couched the process in the language of religion, and called it spirituality or "grace."

"The dark night of the soul," no less than the *Götterdämmerung*, was, in the ancient mind, just the condition of the soul's embodiment in physical forms. Taylor reasons that Minerva (the rational faculty, as Goddess of Wisdom) was by her attachment to body given wholly "to the dangerous employment and abandons the proper characteristics of her nature for the destructive revels of desire." All this is the dialectic statement of the main theme of ancient theology—the incarnation of the godlike intellect and divine soul in the darksome conditions of animal bodies.

The modern student must adjust his mind to the olden conception—

renewed again by Spinoza—of all life as subsisting in one or another modification of one primordial essence, called by the Hindus *Mulaprakriti.* This basic substance was held to make a transit from its most rarefied form to the grossest state of material objectivity and back again, in ceaseless round. Darkness was the only fit symbol to give to the mind any suggestive realization of the condition of living intellectual energy when reduced in potential under the inertia of matter.

So severely curtailed were the soul's powers in bodily life that it was denominated her incarceration. The soul was a captive, caught in a prison, the doors of which were clamped fast upon it. Its jailer was the body with its sensuous nature. And like Paul in prison at Philippi, the soul would have to convert her jailer and transform his nature to the likeness of her own, to gain her release.

The implications of this cardinal item for ethics, pietism and spirituality are of the highest moment. For all such philosophies as Buddhism, Christian Science and Spiritualism (of certain forms), which seek escape from the rigors of incarnation by a sheer fiat of philosophical thought, and look to a disembodied state for immediate bliss, this principle is very directly an antidote and corrective. It points clearly to the false premises of all philosophies of "escape." We can not escape our obligation to the animal who is lending us his body for our own advancement. We came hither to transfigure these brute bodies, and such a miracle demands the exercise of the highest philosophical virtues and the fixed habits of theoretic contemplation of the beautiful and the good. Job asks if the days of man on earth "are not the days of an hireling," and declares that he has "found a ransom."

The Greeks believed "that human souls were confined in the body as in a prison, a condition which they denominated generation; from which Dionysus would liberate them." Their sufferings, their progress through the ascending stages of being, their *catharsis* or purification, and their enlightenment constituted the theme of the Orphic writers and the groundwork of the mystical rites.

We have Proclus declaring that Plato in the *Phaedo*

"venerates with a becoming silence the assertion delivered in the arcane discourses, that men are placed in the body as in a prison, secured by a guard, and testifies, according to the mystic ceremonies, the different allotments of purified and unpurified souls in Hades." [25]

147

Here is evidence that the Mystery Plays were dramatic representations of our earthly imprisonment, with all that was corollary to it.

Of our condition of bondage Plato speaks in the following manner: ". . . liberated from this surrounding vestment, which we denominate body, and to which we are now bound like an oyster in its shell." It is Plato who states that the function of philosophy is to "disenthrall the soul from the bondage of sense." We are "captives chained to sense."

It seems never to have occurred to modern classical students that the many descriptions scattered through the *Aeneid* of Virgil, of shadowy groves, vales and caves, are allegoric of the gloomy conditions the soul encounters in her residence in bodies. The woods whose bristling shades terrify the hero (the soul) are the dismal murks of physical incarceration. Physical imagery must be translated over into spiritual or psychic realities. For of such matters only were the early sages discoursing. Speaking of the removal of the junior deities from heaven to earth, the poet writes in the *Aeneid:* "Nor do they, thus enclosed in darkness and the gloomy prison, behold the heavenly air."

One of the Egyptian texts says that it is impossible for the shade (soul) to leave the body on earth until the latter is raised up. After the telestic or perfecting work is finished, it is shown (*Rit.,* Ch. 91) that the soul "does not [any longer] suffer imprisonment at any door in Amenta," this lower earth, "either in coming in or going out."

David echoes the Egyptian idea when *in the cave* (*Ps.* 142) he cries to the Lord: "Bring my soul out of prison." In the great Kamite religion Horus, exactly as the Christian Jesus, comes to "the spirits in prison" to set them free from bondage and darkness and lead them to the land of light. The Manes, or soul in the body, cries to the keepers. "Imprison not my soul, keep not in custody my shade. Let the path be open to my soul. Let it not be made captive by those who imprison the shades of the dead. O keep not captive my soul, O keep not ward over my shadow" (*Rit.,* Ch. 92). Says Massey:

"Horus is the Kamite prototype of the chosen one, called the servant by Isaiah, who came 'for a light to the Gentiles,[26] to open blind eyes, to bring out prisoners from the dungeons, and them that sit in darkness out of the prison-house.'" (*Isaiah* 42: 7.) [27]

An allied appellation of the "spirits in prison" is "those who are in their cells." Horus comes to wake "those who sleep in their cells."

148

Again the Manes in the prison of Osiris cries: "Let not the Osiris enter into the dungeon of the captives." "Let not Osiris advance into the valley of darkness." Osiris says to the warders of the prisons: "May I not sit within your dungeons, may I not fall into your pits." (Ch. 17.) Osiris elsewhere asks to be delivered from "this land of bondage." Sut, the personified evil one as opponent of the deliverer Horus, is called "the keeper of the prison-house for death," to which Horus comes as the lord of life and freedom. Horus, as deliverer, is said to come "to those who are in their prison cells," held captive by Sut. An interesting sidelight is thrown on one aspect of the function of the Goddess Hathor, who was the "habitation of the hawk, or the *birdcage of the soul*"! Hathor was the goddess of material creation, to which the body belonged, and the hawk represented the soul. The soul is caged in the body. The latter is even called "the chamber of torture" in the title to Ch. 85 of the *Ritual*. In Ch. 164 it is promised that the soul "shall not be shut in along with the souls that are fettered," and the prayer is uttered: "Let him escape from the evil chamber and let him not be imprisoned therein." The title of Ch. 91 of the *Ritual* is: "The chapter of not letting the soul of Nu . . . be captive in the underworld." In Ch. 130 there is a prayer: "Let not the Osiris-Nu fall headlong among those who would lead him captive."

In the Egyptian fable of the lion and the mouse, the mouse, a symbol of the quick energic life that descends into the underground and lives in subterranean darkness, comes like Jesus and Horus to gnaw the bonds of the great lion, here seemingly standing for the animal soul in the toils of flesh and matter.

In the Egypto-Gnostic text, the *Pistis Sophia,* there were twelve dungeons of infernal torment, in which the twelve legions of angels were imprisoned. The souls could only escape by pronouncing the name of the god who guarded each dungeon door. To pronounce a god's name was to become equal to him in nature.

In the Bible *Exodus* recounts that the children of Israel, who are figured as these twelve legions of devas "chosen" for the specific work of incarnation, "were groaning under their bondage, and the wail of their cries for help came up to God." The land to which they had been sent to work their redemptive errand in bondage to the flesh was "Egypt, that slave pen." In *Leviticus* (16) he admonishes them: "Remember, you were once a slave in Egypt."

149

A passage from the *Logia,* or recovered "sayings of the Lord," declares that "Whosoever followeth the Beast, into captivity he goeth; for the Beast maketh captive all who so will to follow him."

Beside Plato's immortal allegory, there are many uses of the cave as emblem of the dark chambers of the body. David's pleading in the cave to be delivered from his prison is paralleled by Osiris' crying for deliverance in the cavern of Sut in Amenta.

Thomas Taylor expressly says that the cavern was used to "signify union with the terrestrial body."

In the fables of the Hercules cycle the hero (the soul, as always) tracks the Nemean lion into a cave where its capture is effected. As it was in the body that the divine nature in man was to "capture" or embrace the animal soul to lift it up, the cave symbolism for the body is again indicated.

In the Egyptian *Ritual* (Ch. 28) the soul affirms: "This whole heart of mine is laid upon the tablets of Tum, who guideth me to the caverns of Sut," or through the dark passages of Amenta. The tablets of Tum are records of the law, or Maat. They are kept by Taht, the divine scribe, in the Hall of Judgment. Thus to come under the law (St. Paul) brings the deity to the caverns of Sut, the physical body. Of Horus it is written again that he comes to awaken the "prisoners in their cells, the sleepers in their caves."

As ancient burial places were frequently caves in the hillside, we shall have little difficulty in tracing the symbolic meaning of the cave in both the birth and the resurrection scenes, not less than in the raising of Lazarus at Bethany, in Palestine, and of El-Asar(us) at Beth-Anu in Egypt.

Another direct employment of the cave emblem in Egyptian scripture is in Ch. 182 of the *Ritual:* "Taht says: 'I gave Ra to enter the mysterious cave in order that he may revive the heart of him whose heart is motionless.'" As Ra is always the divinest spirit, there is again a clear allusion to the god descending into the cave of the body. In the Egyptian Bethany scene the "dead" soul is called aloud nine times to come forth from "the mysterious cave." Massey traces the word "cave" to the Egyptian *Kep,* which he says means a secret dwelling. It is obvious that, whether this etymology stand the scrutiny of linguistic scholarship or not, the mythologists of old did at any rate conceive the body to be that mysterious hidden dwelling, that shadowy cavern into which the legionaries of heaven were obliged to plunge for added physical experience. With this point established beyond cavil, one of the great stones in the arch of ancient interpretation will have been put in place and one of the supports of the structure of a correct theology will have been set up.

From the idea of a cave it was but a short step to that of a pit. In *Job* a remarkable verse adduces the theory that in sleep, when the lower mind is in abeyance, the inner soul, the god, speaks to Job and admonishes him as to the fluctuating issue of his battle with the flesh: "He keepeth back his soul from the pit." "The Lord is gracious unto him and saith, deliver him from going down into the pit." [28]

In the Biblical account of the rebellion of the sons of Korah, already noticed, it is said that they went down into the pit in death, but lived on, as did the Manes in the Egyptian Amenta. As the earth opened to swallow these rebels (ourselves), the pit is equated with our mundane home. In the Hebrew writings the pit is identical with the region known as Sheol, equivalent to the Greek Hades and the Egyptian Amenta. Horus is cast into the mire of the pit.

Jonah, upon being saved from the sea-monster, exclaims: "Yet thou hast brought up my life from the pit, O Lord, my God." *Ezekiel* contributes a reference both to the pit and to Egypt in a passage which appears to be beyond question a replica of the myth of Joseph in Egypt. The prophet says (19:1-5):

As "a lioness she couched among lions and she brought up one of her whelps; he became a young lion"—Jesus as lion of the house of Judah— "nations also heard of him; he was taken in their pit, and they brought him with hooks into the land of Egypt."

On this portion of Bible text Massey comments as follows:

"The descent of the sun-god into the lower Egypt of Amenta is portrayed in the *Märchen* as the casting of Joseph into the pit, and the ascent therefrom in his glory by the coat of many colors," adding: "in an exodus from Egypt which can no longer be considered historical." [29]

In the *Book of Hades* (10th division) there is a scene "of making fast the dragon in the pit," which is preparatory to the rising of Ra, or the birth of the divine in and from the human.

In *Revelation* (20:2, 3) the seer visioned an angel coming down out

151

of heaven, having the keys of the abyss, or pit, and a great chain in his hand, with which he bound the dragon, the devil or Satan, for a thousand years, and sealed him fast in the pit. Horus makes war on the powers of evil for what they have done to his father Osiris, and calls to the gods to strike them and "punish them in your pits." To them he says: "Your particular duties in Amenta are to keep the pits of fire in accordance with Ra's command, which I made known to you."

Let the reader estimate how far theology has departed from understanding that these "evil spirits" that were cast down and bound for a thousand years, or a long series of incarnations, were the angels of light, denominated Satan because of their rebellious and recalcitrant behavior under the hard decree of incorporation in beastly bodies, and that these fiery pits are none other than our very physical bodies. Is not Satan equated with Lucifer, and is he not the Promethean Light-Bringer?

In Budge's account of the functions of the *ba*-soul in Egyptian spiritism, he states that in the *Papyrus of Nebqet* the *ba* is seen, depicted as a human-headed hawk, flying down the funeral pit, bearing air and food to the mutilated body lying in the mummy-chamber. Here is additional confirmation that the pit designates the human body. Another Egyptian text, the *Book of Am-Tuat* (Division 20) describes the mutilation of the gods and their being cast down into pits of fire. *Revelation* tells of the horsemen, ten thousand times ten thousand, going forth to battle with those forms which had come up out of the smoke that ascended from the pit of the abyss, emitting fire. These may be taken as the forms of evil generated in the struggle between the gods and the animals whose natures are long in combat with each other.

Massey links the Egyptian *Tepht*, the abyss, with our "depth." He equates it also with *Tevthe*, and that with the Babylonian *Tiamat*, as well as the old Egyptian underworld monster, *Typhon*, the Dragon of the Deep. As such it figured the original birthplace of creation, and in a more human application it meant the human body as the seat or birth-place of the spiritual life. For the body is composed of matter, the infinite abysmal mother of all things. *Typhon*, who brought forth her brood of chaos in the abyss, later brings forth the young Sun-god, the divine immortal soul. The figure in this connection is common, we are told, in Akkad, China, Egypt and inner Africa. It is but a step in etymology from *Tepht* to the Hebrew *Tophet,* the dark pit.

There were said to be "seven sons of the Abyss,"[30] or the seven powers generated in nature, to be matched later by seven phases of growth in the human constitution—the ubiquitous seven in archaic literature.

The universal religious myth of the descent of the solar hero, ever typical of deity, into some dark abysmal region, emerging from it after ordeals of suffering, can have but one explanation: the incarnation of the hosts of light in the dense physical body.

Another earthly figure much used to type the dreary existence in the flesh was that of the "wilderness." A variation of it was the "desert." The people in the Typhonian darkness of Amenta were furnished a guide "through this wilderness." The Quiché *Popul Vuh* portrays the ancestors of the race as wanderers in a wilderness upon their way to their final homestead. A Hawaiian legend has it that the progenitors "wandered in a desert wilderness until at last they reached the promised land of Kane"—Canaan!

Numbers (14:33, 34) reads: "Your children shall be wanderers in this wilderness even forty days, for every day a year." The same book supplies another highly elucidative text (14:31, 32) which says: "Your little ones will I bring in, but as for you, your carcasses shall fall in this wilderness." The spiritual meaning here adumbrated is that the earthly or carnal nature in which the gods took residence would be conquered and disintegrated, or die, as the substance of the old seed dies in the ground in generating its offspring, while only the new-born god, the "little ones," the resurrected sons of dying fatherhood, would achieve the spiritual homeland of Canaan.

Elsewhere the term "desert in the Amenta of Egypt" is used to name the locality of bodily life. The people there are said to "dwell in darkness and black night."

The wanderings of the Biblical Israelites are a symbolic graph of this spiritual and racial experience, and have no other meaning, historical or literal, whatever. Hagar's fleeing into the wilderness under the compulsion of her situation, is but another similar picture of the same truth.

The hiding of the various Sons of God in a mysterious cave or secret earth of Amenta is but the mundane segment of a drama, the full action of which is involved in the grand play of forces and sweep of relations in higher spheres, as to the complete outline and significance of which we have not been fully informed by the archaic writers. Earth, it is clear, is but an appanage of heaven, and our history here is without full meaning when detached from its celestial base. The old books of Greece, Egypt, Chaldea, Persia, India are priceless for what they give us of this material.

It has been impossible in these excerpts entirely to avoid anticipation of the next symbol of earthly life, darkness. The body was pictured as the abode of night and gloomy shadows.

We have noticed Plotinus' statement that in her descent the "soul was precipitated into a darkness profound and repugnant to the intellect," which was obscured by it. The body is "night's dark region" and the soul's "sojourn on earth is thus a dark imprisonment in the body."

One of the riddles of Greek mythology—why so intelligent a people as the Greeks symbolized deity as Bacchus, the god of intoxication—is solved by the keys here presented. Intoxication was used to image the befuddlement and mental darkness, the scattering of the god's high intellectual powers in mundane life. Says Thomas Taylor:

"For Bacchus is the evident symbol of the imperfect energies of intellect, and its scattering into the obscure and lamentable dominions of sense." [31]

And *Revelation* declares that even the Saints (the gods) have been made drunken with the power of the lower contacts. Soul had been intoxicated with the wine of sense.

The body is thought of as actually seizing souls. The Speaker in the *Ritual* cries to Ra:

"O deliver me from the god who seizes souls. The darkness in which Sekari dwells is terrifying to the weak." [32]

In this darkness Osiris suffers, supplicating Ra for light. Ajax cries for light. Horus in his resurrection rises "from the house of darkness." Sut (Satan), the twin of Horus, is portrayed imprisoning his brother, the soul of light, in the realm of darkness. He is called "the power of darkness." A dozen sections of the *Pyramid Texts* and the *Records of the Past* describe the journey of the soul through a "valley of darkness." The place to which the soul in the Egyptian scripts was conducted was termed "An-ar-ef, the house of obscurity, the city of dreadful night." The mole or shrewmouse was the animal symbol used by them to depict the god groping his earthly way in an underworld region of darkness. Horus, coming as deliverer, says: "I have sung praises unto those that dwell in darkness." The chapter in which this occurs is entitled "the chapter of making the transformation into the god who giveth light in the darkness." He comes to set prisoners free, and also, it is said, "to dissipate darkness." Incarnation being necessary for the higher birth of the soul, an Egyptian text reads: "The soul is brought forth through the embrace of the Lord of Darkness. He is Babi, the Lord of Darkness." In Ch. 175 "saith Osiris, the scribe Ani: Hail, Tmu! What manner (of land) is this into which I have come? . . . it is black as blackest night, and men wander helplessly therein. In it a man may not live in quietness of heart, nor may the longings of love be satisfied therein."

The very name of the great Egyptian script, the *Book of the Dead,* hints at the realm of darkness from which the soul emerges in its resurrection; for the title, translated, means "The Coming Forth by Day," —or into the daylight, ostensibly from some region of darkness.

Our Hebrew and Christian scriptures provide a multitude of fitting texts which might be used to enlarge vastly this résumé of the old material that points to the earthly body of man as the theological world of darkness. Notably there is that in *Matthew* (4:16) which recites:

"The people which sat in darkness saw a great light; and to them that sat in the shadow . . . did the light spring up."

And is it not the universal prayer of Christendom each Sabbath that the deific power should "enlighten our darkness"?

Chapter IX

ALIVE IN DEATH

SUCH then was the archaic view of the origin of the soul from on high, its fall into the darkness and distractions of the body and its consequent submergence in carnal sense. And, drastic as is seen to be the necessary rehabilitation of all scripture on the basis of this revised understanding, it will be far overshadowed in theological importance by a still more radical reconstruction arising from the ancient use of the figure under which life in the body was mythically represented. For everywhere throughout antiquity *earthly life was depicted as our death!* It is of little avail that the portraiture be uproariously protested as not befitting such a condition of vivid life as is ours in the body. We may indignantly cast back upon ancient heads the obloquy of such an inappropriate metaphor. But our repudiation of their choice of figure falls entirely wide of the mark as affecting the meaning of ancient texts. The fact stands that they did call our life here *death,* and that when they spoke of "the dead" in sacred books, it is indubitable that they meant the living humans. The words "death" and "the dead" are used in the old scriptures to refer to living humanity in earthly embodiment. We scurrying mortals are "the dead" of the Bible and other sacred books, and the "death" spoken of there is our living existence here. We may reject the aptness of their symbolism, but it is past our prerogative to read a meaning into their books other than the one they intended; or to read out of them a meaning they consistently deposited therein. The astonishing point, of revolutionary significance for all religion, will receive textual treatment in the present chapter, and a later one will further vindicate the correctness of the thesis. It is perhaps the cardinal item of the whole theological corpus, the real "lost key" to a correct reading of subterranean meaning in esoteric literature. In ancient theology "death" means our life on earth.

Be the figure apt or be it considered unthinkable—as it will be at first by many—the texts of scripture will yield their cryptic meaning on no other terms. And the Bible is a sealed book mostly because these two words, "death" and "the dead," have not been read as covers of a far profounder sense than the superficial one.

To be sure, it is death in a sense to be understood as dramatic and relative only. And it pertains to the soul in man, not to the body. Life and death are ever as the two end seats on a "see-saw." As the one end goes to death the other rises to life. The death of the body releases the soul to a higher life; conversely, the "death" of the soul as it sinks in body opens the day of life to that body. The theological death of the soul in incarnation is a death that does not kill it in any final sense. It is a death from which it rises again at the cycle's end into a grander rebirth. It is a death that ends in resurrection. And sixteen centuries of inane misconception of the resplendent glory of the greatest of all doctrines, the resurrection from the dead, will be resolved at long last into the bursting light of its true meaning when the dust of ignorance is brushed away.

For animal man the advent of the gods was propitious; indeed it was the very antithesis of death. The plunge into carnality that brought "death and all our woe" to the soul, brought life to the lower man. That was part of its purpose. The gods came to "die" that we mortals might "live." They came that both they and we might have life more abundantly, but at what a cost to themselves—a long "walk through the valley of the shadow of death." Theirs was the death on the cross of flesh and matter.

The use of the term "death" must be in any case a comparative one, for there strictly is no death, in the form of total extinction of being, for any part of real being. All death, so called, is but a transition from state to state, a change of form, of that which is and can not cease to be. Life and death are eternally locked in each other's arms, for as Thales says, "Air lives the death of water; fire lives the death of air," and so on. So body lives the death of the soul, and soul lives the death of the body. It thrives by virtue of that death. The germ and young shoot of any seed live the death of the body of the seed. The law of incubation brings high deities into their Hades, into Pluto's dark kingdom. For the gods the cycle of incarnations was the descent into hell—their crucifixion, death and burial, in all archaic literature!

The material demonstrating this proposition must be of sufficient

157

volume to obviate all doubt as to its validity. Upon its successful vindication hinges the final determination of meaning for hundreds of passages, and the ultimate interpretation of the main theses of all theologies. As will be shown later, it carries with it the purport of the resurrection doctrine, the cornerstone of religions. When we come to that climactic doctrine, it will be possible to locate with exactness what and where that tomb was whose gates and bars were rent asunder by the resurgent Lord. Modern theology little dreams, to this day, the truth back of its own mishandled, but still grandiose, symbols.

The incarnation, for the soul, was its death and burial. But it was a living death and a burial alive. It was an entombment that carried life on, but under conditions that could be poetically dramatized as "death." Our inability to comprehend any but a physical sense of the word "burial" has left us easy victims of ancient poetic fancy, and led to the foisting upon ourselves perhaps the most degraded interpretation of the crucifixion, death and resurrection of deity in mortal life ever to be held by any religious group. Not even woodland tribes have so wretchedly missed the true sense of the great doctrines. Literalism in this instance has debased the human mind more atrociously than fetishism or totemism.

The textual testimony supporting the thesis is so voluminous that practical considerations forbid its full amassing. Nothing less, however, than the serried marshaling of much material will avail to carry conviction to minds unalterably set to opposing views.

Proclus advises us that the incarnating Egos were forewarned that their venture into flesh would be successful on condition that they achieved it "without merging themselves in the darkness of body." They were to make a magnetic connection with the animal body by means of a linkage of their currents of higher life with the forces playing through the nervous system of the animal. They were thus to be in position to pour down streams of vital power into the body, but were not to sink their total quantum of divine intellection into the sense life of the beast. They were to hover over the physical life of the body, touch it with divine flame, but not be drawn down into it. To fall into this dereliction would be to sin, to lose a measure of their vivific life and eventually to die. For there were always two deaths spoken of in the books of the past. It was death, in the first place, for them to come under the heavy depression of fleshly existence. This was the first death. But to sink farther down and be lost in the murks of animal sensualism to a degree that made a return to their heavenly state next to impossible, was to suffer the "second death," of which the soul ever stood in fear and terror in the old texts. The first death was the incarnation; the second was failure to rise and "return unto the Father."

As Apuleius says, the soul, then, approached the "confines of death." And on her approach, and at the moment of her divulsion from her seat on high, there ensued an intermediate or preparatory stage, a partial loss of consciousness termed by the writers a "swoon." Corroboration of this experience is found in a very old document known as the *Tibetan Book of the Dead* (44):

"In the Bardo Thödul the deceased [1] is represented as retrograding step by step into the lower and lower states of consciousness. Each step downward is *preceded by a swooning* into unconsciousness; and possibly that which constitutes his mentality on the lower levels of the Bardo is some mental element or compound of mental elements . . . separated during the swooning from higher and more spiritually enlightened elements. . . ."

This swooning on the downward path to earthly death is likened to a falling asleep. Jesus' assertion that Lazarus was not dead but only sleeping, and needed only to be awakened, is a picturing of the same condition. Incidentally the same thing is said of the earth-bound Osiris in Egypt. "That is Osiris, who is not dead but sleeping in Annu, the place of his repose, awaiting the call that bids him come forth to day." Massey comments:

"Osiris in Annu, like Lazarus in Bethany, was not dead but sleeping. In the text of Har-Hetep (*Rit.*, Ch. 99), the Speaker, who personates Horus, is he who comes to awaken Asar (Osiris) out of his sleep. Also in one of the earlier funeral texts it is said of the sleeping Asar: 'The Great One waketh, the Great One riseth . . .' The Manes in Amenta were not looked upon as *dead*, but sleeping, breathless of body, motionless of heart. Hence Horus comes to awaken the sleepers in their *coffins*." [2]

Horus says (*Rit.*, Ch. 64): "I go to give movement to the Manes; I go to comfort him who is *in a swoon*,"—showing the perfect matching of Egyptian and Tibetan "necrological" science.

The swoon attending each further step matterward deepens by degrees until it amounts to the full "sleep" or "dream" of mortal existence, induced by the incubus of body upon spirits of light. It is the Oriental *Maya*. The vivid awareness of existence which we feel so indubitably is to the ancient sages only a dull slumber and stupor in comparison with that life of ecstatic realism from which we were divulsed by the decree of our Fate.

Thomas Taylor expounds Greek Platonism as holding that the soul "in the present life might be said to die, as far as it is possible for a soul to die." He asserts directly that the soul, until purified by "philosophy," "suffers death through this union with the body."

We have the whole idea most tersely expressed in the *Gorgias* of Plato:

"But indeed, as you say also, life is a grievous thing. For I should not wonder if Euripides spoke the truth when he says: 'Who knows whether to live is not to die, and to die is not to live?' And we perhaps are in reality *dead*. For I have heard from one of the wise that we are now dead; and that the body is our sepulchre; but that the part of the soul in which the desires are contained is of such a nature that it can be persuaded and hurled upward and downwards."

If incarnate life is the burden of this death, then release from it must presuppose a liberation from the thralling "dead weight." Our work aims to correct the misconceptions that have vitiated previous studies in eschatology. Reputed savants in the field give no evidence of having the remotest apprehension of textual meanings pertaining to this phase of theology. Even Massey and Taylor have fallen just short of that final step in comprehension which would have taken them into the temple of truth, the threshold of which they never quite crossed. They knew that the ancients styled this life "death," but they were unable, apparently, to apply the connotations to the Bible and theology. The obsessions of current thought were too strong for them, and overrode the logic of their own premises.

The great Plotinus (*Enneads* I, lviii) gives us a clear presentment of the Greek conception:

"When the soul had descended into generation (from this first divine condition) she partakes of evil and is carried a great way into a state the opposite of her first purity and integrity, to be entirely merged in it . . . and death to her is, while baptized or immersed in the present body, to descend into matter and be wholly subjected to it. . . . This is what is meant by the *falling asleep in Hades,* of those who have come there."

It is worth noting that he uses the word "baptized" to describe incarnation. To incarnate was to be plunged into the watery condition of the body! This is the whole of the meaning of the baptism in ancient theology!

To the above may be added a supplement from Pythagoras, according to Clement, "that whatever we see *when awake* is death; and when asleep a dream."

It is sometimes true that archaic usage of the word "death" makes it cover the period following the occurrence of death in its common meaning, the demise of the body. Incarnation was regarded as a continuing experience, the periodical rhythm of release from the body no more breaking the sequence of lives than does our nightly sleep break the continuity of the experience of the days. But as our waking days are the important parts of our earthly activity, the nights being but interludes of repose and renewals of strength, so the positive incarnate periods of our larger lives are the primarily significant phases of our mundane history. The ancient seers both knew more about the subjective experiences of the soul when out of the body and were less concerned with them than modern Spiritualists. They regarded the phenomena of discarnate manifestation as but the more or less automatic reaction of the soul to the sum of its impressions in its last incarnation, a kind of reflex, threshing over the events of the life just closed. They would have regarded it as preposterous to use the vaporings of the spirits for the tenets of a religion. They were but the products of a mental automatism set up by the engrossments of the last life. The *post mortem* existence of the soul was only the hidden side of the life on earth, and regarded as comparatively inconsequential to the larger processes of conscious living. Theologically, "death" was the bodily life on earth, but comprising its two aspects of sleeping and waking, living and dying, in its comprehensive unity. Activity in the body during the waking phase of the "death" was alone determinative of destiny. By unfortunate diversion of the original cryptic sense, the unimportant portion of the experience, the interlude between lives, became the locale to which practically all religious values were shunted when esoteric knowledge was lost. The meaning of all religion has in consequence fled from earth, where it properly belongs and where alone its true value is realized, to heaven, where present focusing of meaning has little utility for man.

Taylor quotes the priests as testifying "that the soul is buried in body as in a sepulchre." [8] Alexander Wilder, in a note to Taylor's *Eleusinian and Bacchic Mysteries* (p. 31), comments:

"Hades . . . supposed by classical students to be the region or estate of departed souls, . . . is regarded by Mr. Taylor and other Platonists as the human body, which they consider to be the grave and place of punishment for the soul."

Virgil adds significant testimony. In the *Aeneid,* writing of that "interior spirit" which sustains the heavens and earth, men and beasts, "the vital souls of birds and the brutes," he continues:

"In whom all is a potency . . . and a celestial origin as the rudimentary principles, so far as they are not clogged by noxious bodies. They are *deadened* by *earthly forms* and *members* subject to *death;* hence they fear and desire, grieve and rejoice."

Plato's able expounder Proclus, writing that the soul brings life to the body, says that

"she becomes herself situated in darkness; and by giving life to the body, destroys both herself and her own intellect (in as great a degree as these are capable of receiving destruction). For thus the mortal nature participates of intellect, but the intellectual part, of *death,* and the whole, as Plato observes in the *Laws,* becomes a prodigy composed of the mortal and the immortal, of the intellectual and that which is deprived of intellect. For this physical law which binds the soul to the body *is the death of the immortal life,* but vivifies the mortal body."

Wilder in his Introduction to Taylor's *Eleusinian and Bacchic Mysteries* comments again:

"The soul was believed (by the Greeks) to be a composite nature, linked on the one side to the eternal world, emanating from God, and so partaking of Divinity. On the other hand, it was also allied to the phenomenal and external world, and so liable to be subjected to passion, lust and the bondage of evils. This condition is denominated generation; and is supposed to be a kind of *death* to the higher form of life. Evil is inherent in this condition; and the soul dwells in the body as in a prison or a *grave*."

It has been claimed in some quarters that the death here mentioned is simply Greek tropology for a state of spiritual decay into which mortal man sinks. But a proper view sees such degeneracy as the result of the incarnation, which was the occasion of it. The concrete and the moral situations do image each other; but it is a matter of vast importance which one is primary and casts the reflection. There was a descent in historical fact. From it flowed the moral delinquency.

Having seen the lucid presentation of the "death" philosophy in Greek systems, we turn to Egypt. Does the wisdom of this venerable nation support that of Greece? With such fullness and positiveness does it agree with Greek conception that dispute as to the legitimacy of the interpretation must henceforth be silenced forever. It is from these unfathomable wells of Kamite knowledge that we draw the water which nourishes our intellectual life. Again the volume of material is prodigious.

It must be prefaced that the Egyptian writings use more than one character to personate the incarnating god. We may find Osiris, or Ra himself, or Tum, Atum or Horus taking the role. Then there are the two characters which we meet most often, the "Speaker" and the Manes in the *Ritual*. These appear to be distinctly the human soul. Sometimes again it is represented as the "deceased," again as the "Osirified deceased." Besides, the names of four or more kings are used to stand for deity: Unas, Ani, Pepi and Teta, frequently with "the" prefixed.

It is definitely corroborative of the thesis here defended that the central god figure in Egyptian religion, Osiris, the Father, in distinction from Horus, the Son, is consistently assigned the functions, prerogatives and sovereignty of the "king of the dead." He is hailed in a hundred passages as the Ruler of the Underworld, or as Lord of Amenta (Amenti, Amentiu), the Egyptian Hades, the correct locating of which region in theology is one of the major aims of this work. He is assimilable to the Greek Pluto, ruler of Hades, the dark underworld. That this dismal limbo of theology is actually our earth is a fact which has never once dawned upon the intellectual horizon of any modern savant, however high his name. Osiris, the "Speaker," the "Manes," the incarnating deity, is indeed the king in the realm of the dead. For we are those dead, and the god within us came to rule this

163

kingdom, according to the arcane meaning of every religion. For the Egyptians called the coffin "the chest of the living." [4]

A passage from Budge is of importance here:

"About the middle of the Ptolemaic period the attributes of Osiris were changed, and after his identification with Serapis, i.e., Pluto, the god of death, his power and influence declined rapidly, for he was no longer the god of life. In the final state of the cult of Osiris and Isis, the former was the symbol of death and the latter the symbol of life." [5]

This change does not betoken what Budge supposes, but quite the contrary. It hints at the fact that the Egyptian conception of the character of Osiris as Lord of the Underworld of death began to weaken in the later days, as foreign influences crept in, and the profound esoteric meaning of "death" became obscured. The god's influence as Lord of Death declined rapidly at this epoch, not because of the ascription to him of a new and untrue character, but because of the decay of the true comprehension of his place and function in the pantheon. His influence in his perennial office decayed because knowledge of him in that role had decayed. With many such misapprehensions must the battle for a sane grasp of the ancient wisdom contend. The actual issue has been beclouded at almost every turn.

In confirmation of our claim that death in the ancient usage did not imply extinction, the Manes in the *Ritual* (Ch. 30 A) says: "After being buried on earth, I am not dead in Amenta." Horus knows that though he enters the realm of the dead, he does not suffer annihilation. He knows that he *is* that which survives all overthrow. Even though, as he adds, he is "buried in the deep, deep grave," he will not be destroyed there. He will rise out of the grave of the (living) body in his final resurrection.

Such a passage as the following carries in its natural sense the allocation of the term "dead" to living inhabitants on earth, not to spirits of the deceased: "The peoples that have long been dead (?) come forth with cries of joy to see thy beauties every day." [6] It pertains to the resurrection. Another text says: "Tanenet is the burial-place of Osiris." Tanenet, along with Aukert, Shekhem, Abydos, Tattu, Amenta and half a dozen others, is a designation for the earth as the place of burial for the soul living in death.

Cognate with the idea of death is the presumption of burial in a tomb, grave, coffin or sepulcher. Evidence of the prominence of these terms in relation to the descent into earth life is not wanting in the old texts. The matter is not left in any state of doubt or confusion. A sentence from Cocker's *Greek Philosophy* speaks in terms of unmistakable directness: "The soul is now dwelling in 'the grave which we call the body.'" [7] Here is indeed the undebatable clarification of that poetic imagery, the confusion of which with the natural fact of bodily decease has cost Christianity its heritage of wisdom.

In the Egyptian records we have Osiris as the god who "descended into Hades, was dead and buried" in Amenta. Massey's succinct statement covering the point is: "The buried Osiris represented the god in matter,"—not in a hillside grave. The hillside grave, however, was the typograph used to designate the non-historical burial in the body. What could be more pointed and conclusive than Massey's other declaration: "In the astronomical mythology the earth was the coffin of Osiris, the coffin of Amenta, which Sut, the power of darkness, closed upon his brother when he betrayed him to his death"? [8] "The coffin of Osiris is the earth of Amenta," he says again. [9] It is worthy of note that the shrine in the Egyptian temples, representing the vessel of salvation, was in the form of a funeral chest, the front side of which was removed so that the god might be seen. Chapter 39 of the *Ritual* contains a plea for the welfare of the incarnated soul: "Let not the Osiris-Ani, triumphant, lie down in death among those who lie down in Annu, *the land wherein souls are joined unto their bodies.*" So that it is quite apparent that the land in which souls lie down in "death" is this old earth of ours. For nowhere else are souls joined unto their bodies! This is the only sphere in the range of cosmic activity where this transaction is possible, and this fact is sufficient warrant for focusing upon it all that mass of vague meaning for which theologians have been forced to seek a locale in various subterranean worlds whose place is found at last only in their own imaginations.

Horus says in one text: "I directed the ways of the god to his tomb in Peqar . . . and I caused gladness to be in the dwellers in Amentet when they saw the Beauty as it landed at Abydos." [10] Abydos was claimed to be the place of entry to the lower world where the "dead" lived, but in this use it was another of those transfers of uranographic locality to a town on the map in some way appropriately symbolizing the spiritual idea involved. There was no actual entrance to an actual underworld at Abydos (or anywhere else), but to complete the astral typology a temple, tomb and deep well (of great symbolic value) had been constructed there to the god Osiris. It was mythically and poetically the door of entry to the lower world, or realm of death, Amenta. Budge does not realize that he is writing only of the historical adaptation of a spiritual allegory when he says:

"But about Osiris' burial-place there is no doubt, for all tradition, both Egyptian and Greek, states that his grave was at Abydos (Abtu) in upper Egypt." [11]

He argues that Osiris must have been a living king, who was later deified. This is not likely, as there is little to indicate that the Egyptian gods were other than abstract personifications of the powers of nature and intelligence. The legend that his body was cut into fourteen pieces, scattered over the land and then reassembled for the resurrection could have no rational application to the life of an actual king. Myth has been taken for history on a vast scale.

Another text carries straightforward information of decided value: "In the text of Teta the *dead* king is thus addressed: 'Hail! hail! thou Teta! Rise up, thou Teta! . . . thou art not a dead thing." [12] What can be the resolution of so evident a contradiction of terms—telling a dead king he is not dead—unless the new interpretation of "death" as herein advanced and supported be applicable? [13] The souls as deities entered the realm of death, our world, but were not dead; philosophy dramatized them as such, however.

In a different symbolism the Eye of Horus, an emblem typifying his life and said to contain his soul, was stolen and carried off by Sut, the evil twin. Of this Budge says that "during the period when Horus' Eye was in the hands of Sut, he was a dead god." His regaining possession of his Eye symbolized the recovery of his buried divinity and his restoration to his original godhood. Horus elsewhere (*Rit.*, Ch. 85) says: "I come that I may overthrow my adversaries upon earth, though my dead body be buried." If such a declaration is not to be taken for a species of after-death spiritism, it can have logical meaning only in reference to the contention that the buried god is the soul in the fleshly body.

It is imperative to look next at the conceptions of the sphere of death that were expressed through the use of the term "underworld." This

166

region of partial death in which the outcast angels were imprisoned was styled the dark "underworld." A variant name was "the nether earth." It is often actually pictured as a subterranean cavern. It may be asked if it has ever occurred to any scholar of our time that "the underworld" was but another figurative appellation for the condition of life in the human body. Again a mass of data is available.

All nations of antiquity show in their literature traces of a legend in which the soul makes a journey through a dark underworld. The vagueness of its location, however, has failed to give any scholar an illuminating suggestion as to its totally figurative and unreal character. Nobody has ever seriously presumed to locate this dreary region, in spite of the fact that it was childishly regarded as an actual place. It .was hazily associated with the grave or assumed to lie in some dim region into which the soul passed after death, somehow, somewhere "under," but under what, it was not apparently ever determined. The cause of bafflement was the ineradicable assumption that its "underness" was to be oriented in relation to the earth! No one has caught the idea that its location was *under the heavens,* and hence that it was our own earth itself! The surface of the earth, man's world, was assumed to be obviously not an "underworld." But the problem of locating another limbo beneath *it* baffled theological speculation through the ages. The outcome is that the locale of Pluto's shadowy kingdom has been hung indeterminately between the surface of the ground and the dubious dim region of after-death spheres. All the while a thousand texts point to its location in the physical body!

Lewis Spence cautiously admits that the court of the Mayan underworld seems to have been conducted on the principles of a secret society with a definite form of initiation, and that the Mysteries of Eleusis and others in Greece were concerned with the life of an underworld, especially dramatized in the story of Demeter and Kore.[14] He admits that the Greek deities were gods of the dead. But he mars his tentative approach to the truth by advancing the conjecture that the *Book of the Dead* may have been the work of prehistoric Neolithic savages! We refrain from caustic comment, save to aver that if the Egyptian *Book of the Dead* was the product of Neolithic savages, the status of modern mentality which is as yet totally incapable of understanding its high message, must by inference lie a stratum or two below that level.

The Mystery Rituals did dramatize the life of an underworld, but the gods, as kings of this nether realm, were not subterranean deities. The gnomes and other nature sprites were the only "deities" that were believed to subsist beneath the surface of the physical earth. The gods of the underworld were always the gods of the dead. And as the souls of deceased mortals were in all religions asserted to ascend to heaven and never to remain in the burial ground with the corpse, it was again impossible to place the underworld down with the gnomes. But it seems next to incredible that academic diligence should have missed the plain correlation which would have made the descent of spirits from heaven equate the descent of all the divine heroes and sun-gods into the dark underworld—of earth.

From the great Egyptian *Ritual*, which so cryptically allegorizes this earthly death, we learn that the mystery of the Sphinx originated with the conception of the earth as the place of passage, of burial and re-birth, for the humanized deities. An ancient Egyptian name for the Sphinx was *Akar*.[15] This was also the name for the tunnel through the underworld. And it is said that the very bones of the deities quake as the stars go on their triumphant courses through the tunnels of *Akar* (*Pyramid Texts: Teta*, 319). As the stars were the descending deities, the metaphor of stars passing through the underworld tunnels is entirely clear in its implication. The riddle of the Sphinx is but the riddle of mankind on this earth. The terms of the riddle at least become clearly defined if we know that the mystery pertains to this our mortal life, above ground, and not to our existence in some unlocalized underworld of theological fiction.

The entrance to Amenta, with its twelve dungeons, consisted of a blind doorway which neither Manes nor mortal knew the secret of and none but the god could open. Hence the need of a deity who should come to unlock the portals and unbar the gates of hell, and be "the door" and "the way." The god came not only to unlock the door of divinity to human nature, but to be himself that door. The giving of the keys to bolt and unbolt the doors of the underworld was but the allegory of this evolutionary reinforcement of the human by the divine nature.

Descriptions of this dark realm of our present state are given in the texts. "It is a land without an exit, through which no passage has been made; from whose visitants, the dead, the light was shut out." "The light they beheld not; in darkness they dwell." Massey ventures the assertion that "the inferno, the purgatory and the paradise of Dante Alighieri are extant recognizably in the *Book of the Dead* as the domains of Amenta."[16]

The first chapter of the *Book of the Dead* was repeated in the Mystery festivals on the day when Osiris was buried. His entrance into the underworld as a Manes corresponds to that of Osiris the corpse in Amenta, who represents the god rendered lifeless by his suffocation in the body of matter. The dead Osiris is said to enter the place of his burial called the Kasu. In this low domain of the dead there was nought but darkness; the upper light had been shut out. But Horus, Ptah, Anup, Ra and others of the savior gods would come in due time to awaken the sleepers "in their sepulchres," open the gates and guide the souls out into the light of the upper regions once more. One of the sayings of the soul contemplating its plight in the underworld is: "I do not rot. I do not putrefy. I do not turn to worms. My flesh is firm; it shall not be destroyed; it shall not perish in the earth forever" (Ch. 154). Inasmuch as the flesh of the physical body most certainly *will* perish, rot, putrefy, and turn to food for worms in the only grave that Christian theology has been able to tell us of, the term "flesh" in the excerpt can not be taken as that of the human body. And that it is not to be so taken is obvious from other passages. It refers to the substance of another body which does not rot away.

The same sense may distinctly be caught in the term "body" as used in the prayer uttered by the soul in the body when it says: "May my body neither perish nor suffer corruption forever." Such a prayer directed to the physical body would be obviously irrelevant, expecting the impossible. Horus, on his way to earth to ransom the captives, says: "I pilot myself towards the darkness and the sufferings of the deceased ones of Osiris" (Ch. 78). Massey sums the discussion:

"The wilderness of the nether earth, being a land of graves, where the dead awaited the coming of Horus, Shu, Apuat (Anup), the guide, and Taht . . . as servants of Ra, the supreme one god, to wake them in their coffins and lead them forth from the land of darkness to the land of day."[17]

Analysis of other types of representation will disclose the fact that the Egyptians, in their lavish use of animals as symbols, filled the underworld with a menagerie of mythical monsters. Without trespassing on the ground of later discussion, it may be briefly said that a number of animals—dragons, serpents, crocodiles, dogs, lions, bears, etc.—lay in wait in the underworld to devour the luckless Manes. What is the significance of this? Patently it figures the menace to the soul of its subjection to the constant beat upon it of the animal propensities, since it had taken residence in the very bodies of the lower creatures. In a measure detached, it was yet not immune to being drawn down into ever deeper alliance with the carnal nature. Ever to be remembered is Daniel's statement that "his mind was made like the mind of an animal."

Etymology supplies a sensational suggestion of the soundness of the present thesis in the similarity of the two words "tomb" and "womb," which Massey avers rise from the same root. At all events it is rigorously in accord with the Greek theory that the body, as the tomb of the soul, is at the same time the womb of its new birth. In the Egyptian *Ritual* the soul is addressed as he "who cometh forth from the dusk, and whose birth is in the house of death." This was Anu, Abydos, On (Heliopolis), or other uranographic center localized on the map, or the zodiacal signs of Virgo and Pisces. The Greek language bears striking testimony to the same kinship of the two words, as Plato points out in the *Cratylus,* in the practical identity of *soma,* body, and *sema,* tomb.

In the Christian Bible the textual evidence is multitudinous. A few excerpts only can be culled. First is St. Paul's clarion cry to us ringing down through nineteen centuries: "Awake thou that sleepest and arise from the *dead,* and Christ will shine upon thee." Job, combining his death with its correlative resurrection, exclaims: "I laid me down in death and slept; I awaked, for the Lord sustaineth me." Paul cries in the anguish of the fleshly duress, "Who shall deliver me from the body of this death?" And it is an open question whether the final phrase might not as well have been rendered "this death in the body." And Jonah, correlative name with Jesus, cries from the allegorical whale's belly: "Out of the belly of death have I cried unto thee, O God." Paul again pronounces us "dead" in our trespasses and sins, adding that "the wages of sin is death" and "to be carnally minded is death." It is sin that brings us back again and again into this "death" until we learn better. And the Apostle affirms that we are dead and that our life is hid with Christ in God. Our true life is as yet undeveloped, buried down in the depths of the latent capacities of being. The *Psalms* say that we "like sheep are laid in the grave," though "God will redeem my soul from the power of the grave." The death spoken of is at one place defined as "even the death of the cross," when spirit is bound to the cross of matter and the flesh. Isaiah declares that "we live in darkness like the dead." And Jesus broadcasts the promise that whosoever believeth on him, "though he were dead, yet shall he live." Assurance is given (*Peter* 4:6) that the Gospel is preached "to them that are dead." Would not such addresses to the dead, as noted in several of these passages, be absurd if not referable to the living on earth?

Then there is that ringing declaration of the Father God in the Prodigal Son allegory, rebuking the churlish jealousy of the obedient elder brother at the rejoicing over the wastrel's return: "This my son was *dead* and is alive again." The thing described here as death was just the sojourn in that "far country"—earth.

A most direct and unequivocal declaration, however, is found in the first verse of chapter three of *Revelation:* "Ye have the name of being alive, but ye are dead." And this is at once followed by the adjuration to "Wake up; rally what is still left to you, though it is on the very point of death." This is again a strong hint of the danger that the soul might be so far submerged under sense as to fail to rise again, and sink down into the dreaded "second death."

But the most astonishing material corroborative of the thesis here propounded is found in St. Paul's discussion of the problem of sin and death in the seventh chapter of *Romans*. The statements made can be rendered intelligible and enlightening only by reading the term "death" in the sense here analyzed. He says first that "the interests of the flesh meant death; the interests of the spirit meant life and peace." And then he says: "For when we were *in the flesh,* the motions of sins, which were by the law, did work *in our members* to bring forth fruit unto death."

In this chapter Paul concatenates the steps of a dialectical process which has not been understood in its deep meaning for theology. It is concerned with the relation of the three things: the law, sin and death. He asks: "Is the Law equivalent to sin?" And he replies that sin developed in us "under the Law." What is this mysterious Law that the Apostle harps on with such frequency? Theology has not possessed the resources for a capable answer, beyond the mere statement that it is the power of the carnal nature in man. It is that, in part; but the profounder meaning could not be gained without the esoteric wisdom —which had been discarded. This Law—St. Paul's *bête noir*—is that cosmic impulsion which draws all spiritual entities down from the heights into the coils of matter in incarnation. It is the ever-revolving Wheel of Birth and Death, the Cyclic Law, the Cycle of Necessity. As every cycle of embodiment runs through seven sub-cycles or stages, it is the seven-coiled serpent of Genesis that encircles man in its folds.

Now, says the Mystery initiate, by the Law came sin, and by sin came death. Here is the iron chain that binds man on the cross. The Law brings the soul to the place where it sins and sin condemns it to death. Death here *must* mean something other than the natural demise of the body, for *that* comes to *all* men be they pure or be they sinful. Reserving a more recondite elaboration of the doctrine of sin for a later place, it may be asserted here that the great theological bugaboo, sin, will be found to take its place close along the side of "death" as the natural involvement of the incarnation itself. Sin is just the soul's condition of immersion or entanglement in the nature of the flesh. And happily much of its gruesome and morbid taint by the theological mind can be dismissed as a mistaken and needless gesture of ignorant pietism.

Neither as animal below our status nor as angel above it can man sin. For the animal is not spiritually conscious and hence not morally culpable. And the angel is under no temptation or motivation from the sensual nature, which alone urges to "sin." Only when the Law links the soul to animal flesh does sin become possible. *Romans* (7:7) expressly declares: "Nay, I had not known sin, but by the law . . . For without the law sin was dead." Paul even says that at one time he lived without the law himself; this was before "the command" came to him. And what was this command? Again theology has missed rational sense because it has lost ancient cosmologies and anthropologies. *The "command" was the Demiurgus' order to incarnate*. It is found in the *Timaeus* of Plato and Proclus' work on Plato's theology. Then the Apostle states the entire case with such clarity that only purblind benightedness of mind could miss it: "When the command came home to me, *sin sprang to life,* and I *died; . . .*" He means to say that sin sprang to life *as* he died, i.e., incarnated. And then he adds the crowning utterance on this matter to be found in all sacred literature:

"the command that meant life proved death to me." He explains further: "The command gave an impulse to sin, sin beguiled me and used the command to *kill me."* And he proceeds to defend the entire procedure of nature and life against the unwarranted imputations of its being all an evil miscarriage of beneficence: "So the Law at any rate is holy, the command is holy, just and for our good. Then did what was meant for my good prove fatal to me? Never. It was sin; sin resulted in death for me *to make use of this good thing."* [18]

The clarifying and sanifying corollaries of this explication and St. Paul's material are so expansive that pause should be made to consider them. In this light it may be seen that the whole of the negative and lugubrious posture of theology as to "sin," and "death" as its penalty, might be metamorphosed into an understanding of the natural and beneficent character of all such things in the drama. Ancient meaning has miscarried, with crushing weight upon the happy spirit of humanity; and rectification of such misconstruction is urgently needed.

In *I Samuel* (2:6) it is written: "The Eternal kills, the Eternal life bestows; he lowers to death and he lifts up." Job says: "I shall die in my nest, and I shall renew my youth like the eagle."

And a most significant verse from *Isaiah* (53) can be rescued from mutilation and sheer nonsense only by the application of the new meaning of "death." Speaking of the divinity, it says that "He hath made his grave with the wicked and the rich in his *death."* A marginal note is honest enough to tell us that the word "death" here used was in the *plural* number—"deaths"—in the original manuscripts. Here is invincible evidence that the word carries the connotation of "incarnations," for in no other possible sense can "death" be rationally considered in the plural number. In one incarnation the Christ soul is cast among the wicked; in another among the rich. This is a common affirmation of most Oriental religious texts. And his body is his grave.

St. Paul says some man will ask how the dead are raised and in what body do they come. And Christian theology has stultified the sanity of its millions of devotees by giving the answer in the words of the Creed: "The resurrection of the body"—leaving untutored minds to understand the physical body, or the corpse. The only comment provoked is to say that the picture of the cemetery graves being opened at the last trump, and the "dead" (cadavers) arising to array themselves in line before the tribunal of the judgment, has turned millions in disgust and revulsion away from the fold of orthodoxy. Paul states in the verses immediately following that the dead will rise in a *spiritual* body.

And then we face that climactic assurance that "the last enemy to be overcome is death." In lack of the covert intent of the word, Christian thought has ever believed that in some way this promise meant we should overcome the incidence of bodily decease, and live on in the physical vessel indefinitely. This would paralyze evolution. It would wreck the Cyclical Law. The Trinity is the Creator, the Preserver *and* the Destroyer. Without the periodic destruction of form there could be no renewal of life in higher and better forms. Life would be imprisoned forever in matter, and choked to its real death. Its charter of liberty is its periodical release from forms that while they enable, they also limit. What, then, means the passage? If death is the incarnation, the significance is found in the assurance that at the conclusion of the cycle, when the spirit has mastered all its mundane instruction, it will be made a "pillar in the house of God and shall go no more out." Its descents into the tombs of bodies will be at an end at last. "Death" will then be finally overcome.

In the Egyptian *Ritual* the soul rejoices in life, shouting, "He hath given me the *beautiful* Amenta, through which *the living* pass from *death* to life." Amenta is this world, and the soul is pictured as running through cycles of descent from life to "death" and back again. The same sequence is set forth in the third chapter of *Revelation:* "I am he that *liveth* and was *dead,* and behold I am *alive* for evermore!" The Law precipitates us from the life above to the "death" down here, but lifts us up again.

There is no sublimer chapter in the entire Bible than the fifteenth of *I Corinthians.* And perhaps this treatment could not possibly be more fittingly concluded than with some of St. Paul's magnificent utterances therein. It may give us at last the thrilling realization of their grandeur when grasped in the majestic sense of their restored original meaning. Need we be reminded that these words of the Apostle will ring from our own throats in ecstatic jubilee, when, victorious at last over "death" and the "grave," we arise out of our final imprisonment in body and wing our flight like the skylark back to celestial mansions?

"So when this corruptible shall have put on incorruption, and this mortal shall have put on immortality, then shall be brought to pass the saying that is written: Death is swallowed up in victory."

"O death, where is thy sting? O grave, where is thy victory?"

· · · · · · · · ·

We have drawn enough material from the ancient fund now to have bountifully supplied the demand for "evidence" that in archaic philosophy the field of our life here is depicted as the dark cavern, the pit, the abyss, the bleak desert, the wilderness, the grave, the tomb, the underworld and hell of a life that migrated here from the skies. "We are a colony of heaven." Our deific souls are at the very bottom of the arc of death, and can never be as dead again as they are now, and have been.

But stranger revelations await us still.

Chapter X

THE MUMMY IN AMENTA

WE now approach a phase of the general theme, the correction of popular misconception about which will be attended with the most momentous consequences for the whole of world religion. Only one or two other items of our revision of current belief will prove to be of more sensational interest. The matter that promises so largely .is the Egyptian mummy and the practice of mummification. When the true signification of this mysterious custom of a sage race begins to dawn in clear light, it will assuredly seem as if modern appreciation of a great deposit of ancient knowledge could hardly have suffered so utter a rout, so total a wreckage.

General opinion, expressed and shared by the most learned of the Egyptologists, holds that the Egyptians mummified their dead for the reason that, believing in reincarnation or forms of transmigration, they desired the physical body to be preserved intact for the reoccupancy of the Ego or soul upon its return to earth. Common belief asserts that they hoped by this provision to make reincarnation easier for the returning soul, inasmuch as he would find his former body ready for him, and would not have to build a new one or enter the body of some animal. The quantity of "explanation" of this sort that one reads in the works of reputed scholars is indeed enough to drive any astute reasoner *ad nauseam*. Nothing betrays the shallow insufficiency of our knowledge so flagrantly as does this matter.

It would seem as if it should be unnecessary to issue a denial of the correctness of the popular theories just indicated. The truth of the matter should be evident to anyone who can frame a syllogism. One fact alone should have been sufficient to forestall the arrant blunder in misconceiving the mummification motive. An act performed for the alleged purpose of preservation began with a gross mutilation! The viscera, the whole of the organs of the chest and abdominal cavity were first removed, and the entrails placed in the Canopic jars at the four corners of the coffin. One does not mutilate that which one wishes to preserve. If this be not conclusive, let us add that at times both the head and the feet were cut off! Could the returning soul profitably use this old shriveled, leathery and mutilated shell as its next living tenement? Our idea has been a tacit insult to Egyptian intelligence. Surely we might have credited them from the start with being no such fools. Because we believed, under the lashing of medieval theologians, that Christ rose in his flesh and that we should do likewise at the last trump, we assumed that the Egyptians indulged their credulity in the same weird fashion. We are yet as children essaying to frame an explanation of the most profoundly symbolic act of the most illumined race of history.

It is the declaration drawn from our studies and supported by the evidence to be submitted, that the practice of embalmment was nothing more than a mighty rite of symbolism! One immediate item of confirmation is the fact that it was performed for only a relatively few of Egypt's deceased, notably kings and functionaries. It was costly, required a hundred days, and so was indulged in only in the case of those who could afford such an elaborate funeral ritual. If the motive for mummification had been one arising out of universal philosophy or accepted religious theory, it would have been practiced generally, with rich and poor alike. Not all Catholic Christians can afford elaborate masses. No enlightened nation would countenance for centuries a practice based on a theory which made the difference in worldly wealth critical for the whole future destiny of the great mass of its inhabitants. If the hope of future evolutionary welfare depended on this performance with the cadaver, then Egypt was guilty of a felonious neglect of her general population in favor of her overlords. And we know that early nations were, as we like to say, superstitious in the extreme about the punctilious observance of funeral rites. Virgil tells of the dread of the heroes of having their dead bodies lie unburied on the sand (*inhumatus arena*). Egypt could not have given the benefit of a vital ceremony to only a limited class.

The effort is here made for the first time in our day to set forth the inner spiritual significance of this great rite. Our development of the obsolete meaning of "death" in primal theology has led us right up

177

to the threshold of the denouement. One further step will take us into the heart of the age-old mystery.

In the esoteric doctrine which regarded the present life as death, and the living body as the soul's tomb, we have the necessary background for adequate elucidation of the matter. The body was mummified to serve as a powerful moving symbol of the death of the soul in matter, and the various features of the meaning of this mundane life! Nothing more. But this far transcended in graphic impressiveness and cathartic virtue any theoretic dramatization of the philosophy of life made by any people since the days of Egypt's glory. The mummy was designed to point the whole moral of human life in a form of overwhelming psychological power. To a deeply philosophical people the lifeless body became at once the most impressive symbol of the entire import of life itself. The preserved corpse became the mute but grandiloquent reminder of life and death, mortality and immortality, in one mighty emblem.

The custom was an attempt to utilize the cadaver as the central object in a ritual designed to incorporate the essential features of their entire philosophy of life. The import of a ceremony based on the ostensible preservation of a thing which obviously could not be preserved for living purposes, was the enforcement upon all minds of the truth that the mortal part of man could be immortalized! Concomitant with this, the ritual bore the message that the divine part of man, the immortal soul, though in this body it has gone to its "death," is immortal still. It will defy death and corruption, as will the mummy.

The mummy was the cardinal object in a grandiose ritual precisely because it was a dead thing! It prefigured the nature of this life, which was, philosophically, death. The dead thing thus became the emblem of immortal life itself. The "dead" shall live forever. The mummy symboled life as death, and death as the gate to immortal life. And the preservation or immortalizing of the dead mortal by the infusion of spiritous oils, balsams, ichors, was to emblem the raising of this mortal to immortality through the adoption by the lower man of the spirit of eternal life from the injected Christ nature. By the infusion of the mind of Christ into the dead Adamic nature, born to sin, it could be raised to eternal life out of the realm of decay. To associate ritualistically the idea of undying existence with the defunct relic was to impress the lesson of the burial in matter of that divine fragment whose attribute is "life and everlastingness." Under the garb and swathings of death, its mission was to bring life and immortality to light.

The embalming was not the enactment of a vague spiritual ideal. Every detail of the process, as Budge has testified, was a typical performance with specific relevance. The injection of preservatives was designed to do for the corpse symbolically what the putting on of the Christ spirit would do for "the body of this death."

An elaborate ritual was built up about the mummy. There were the mutilations and exsections, symbolizing the dismemberment or fragmentation of the divine intellect when cast into the distracting turmoil of sense life. The facial mask carried the implication of the "false" nature of the physical man, the personality, which was the mask (Latin: *persona,* a mask) the soul donned over its true self. The bound legs and arms symboled the limitation and motionlessness which matter ever imposes upon active spirit. The four Canopic jars at the corners of the coffin stood for the physical world, which is ever four-square as the base that upholds all higher life. The mummy case itself signified the body or earth, the physical house and habitat of the soul. The coffin lid served as the table for the mortuary meal, or the partaking of the "bread of Seb" or food of earth. The bandages were emblematic of the material vestures or bodies which enwrapped the soul, for on coming to earth it was "all meanly wrapped in swaddling clothes," the "coats of skin" that God gave to Adam and Eve in *Genesis.* Then there was the light, signifying of course the presence of the glowing power of deity within the fleshly house. When darkness was over the land of Egypt, "the Israelites had light in their dwellings." More meaningful still was the image of the hawk, or the hawk-headed Horus, which hovered over the mummy; for this was the figure of the resurrection, the soul as a bird leaving the body to return to the upper air of heaven. The ankh-cross, symbol of life when spirit and matter are tied together, the ankham-flower of immortality, the Tat cross, symbol of eternal stability, the level of Amenu, symbol of the balance of nature's forces, the scarab, symbol of the resurrection, the vulture, the greenstone tablet of resin, all shadowed in one way or another the immortality of the spiritual principle lodged within the mortal vehicle. The spices and balsams were preservatives, sweet of savor. And the fluids that did so marvelously work their miracle of preservation upon the substance of decay, were as "the Amrit juice of immortality." In many countries a liquor called Soma (the Greek word, incidentally, for the "spiritual" body) was considered to bestow immortality. A tribal chant runs, in one verse:

> "We've quaffed the soma bright
> And are immortal grown;
> We've entered into light
> And all the gods have known."

The lower man's immediate relation to his soul permits him to drink of that immortalizing nectar, and as it was always Eve, or Hathor, or Ishtar, a goddess, a woman, who offers to man the tempting cup, the inference is that mundane experience with matter, the mother of life, is the brimming chalice for our deification.

The mummy thus stood for the soul buried in body, or sometimes perhaps for the body itself. By its descent the soul had become, as it were, the mummy. It became the Manes, or shade of a dead person, in the depiction.

Massey comes very close in one place to sensing that the mummy must be given a spiritual significance:

"Hence the chapter of 'introducing the mummy into the Tuat [underworld] on the day of burial' deals not with the earthly mummy, but the mummy of the *dramatic mysteries* as a *figure of the living personality*." [1]

This is the truth; but having seen the mummy in its true light for a moment, Massey still adheres to his precarious endeavor to read "the mummy in Amenta" into the life *after* (bodily) death, instead of allocating it to its relationship to earth, where only the living personality was in function. His phrase—"the mummy of the dramatic mysteries" —to all intents and purposes concedes the legitimacy of our thesis as to the mummy's true function.

But this scholar's study is so splendid in the main that we will be enlightened by looking at portions of his material:

"Amenta as the place of graves is frequently indicated in the Hebrew scriptures, as in the description of the great typical burial-place in the valley of Hamon-Gog. This was in the Egypt described in the *Book of Revelation* as the city of dead carcasses, where also their Lord was crucified as Ptah-Sekari or Osiris-Tat. Amenta had been converted into a cemetery by the death and burial of the *solar god,* who was *represented as the mummy* in the lower Egypt of the nether earth. The *Manes were likewise imaged as mummies* in their coffins. They also rose again in the mummy-likeness of their Lord, and went up out of Egypt in the constellation of the Mummy (Sahu-Orion), or in the coffin of Osiris that was imaged in the Great Bear." [2]

Can we miss the plain evidence here presented? The Manes were imaged as mummies in their coffins! Amenta (this earth) converted into a *cemetery* by the advent of the gods, our souls! We, the living on earth, figured unmistakably as mummies in our sarcophagi! Hence the grave and tomb of all ancient theology is the living physical body of man!

There will be profit in considering another Massey statement, since it reveals how he stumbled and fell at the very door of the truth:

"There is no possibility of the Manes coming back to earth for a new body or for a *re-entry into the old mummy*. As the Manes says, 'his soul is not bound to his old body at the gates of Amenta'" (Chs. 26, 6). [3]

That the soul would not re-enter the old mummy is a vital point of truth, and Massey deserves all credit for discerning it. But that it would not return to enter a *new* body flies in the face of all ancient and universal belief in reincarnation. This is just the point of issue to be clarified. The soul returns from life to life to be re-clothed in new garments, since it assuredly does not take up life again in the mutilated and decomposed old hulk. The Manes positively states that he is not bound to the old body; but a score of times he says he will construct, or reappear in, a glorious new vesture. This of course is the spiritual body of the resurrection. But it is not built up in one brief life on earth. It is the product of many successive lives, each in a *new* physical body. There is no room for confusion or dispute on this matter.

Ptah, Atum and finally Osiris are described at different stages as the solar god in mummified form in Amenta.

"He was the buried life on earth, and hence the god in matter, *imaged in the likeness of the mummy*. . . . Such was the physical basis of the mythos of the mystery that is spiritual in the eschatology." [4]

And we find desirable explicitness in the following passages:

"In the Osirian mythos, when the sun-god enters the underworld, it is as a mummy or 'coffined one' upon his way to the great resting place."

181

"The mummy-Osiris in Amenta is the figure of the sleeping deity. He is the *god inert in matter,* the sleeping or resting divinity." [5]

Another most pertinent corroboration of our thesis that the mummy was but a ritualistic figure for the human soul "dead" in the body, is found in the following from Massey: [6]

"And just as Ra, the holy spirit, descends in Tattu on the mummy Osiris, and as Horus places his hands behind Osiris in the resurrection, so Iu [7] comes to his body, the mummy in Amenta. Those who tow Ra along say, 'The god comes to his body; the god is towed along toward his mummy.' (*Records,* Vol. X, p. 132.) The sun-god, whether as Atum-Iu (Aiu or Aai) or Osiris-Ra, is a mummy in Amenta and a soul in heaven. Atum or Osiris, as the sun in Amenta, is the mummy buried down in Khebt,[8] or lower Egypt." [9]

These passages conclusively indicate that the mummy was the type of the god in the body.

Conquest of the carnal nature and escape from it is in another place called the "overthrowal of your coffins." (*Book of Hades,* Fifth Division, Legend D.) Again, the earth is denominated "the coffin of Osiris, the coffin of Amenta."

In his descent to open the tombs for the release of the sleeping captives Horus says: "I am come as the mummified one," that is, in fleshly embodiment. It should be noted that this explicit statement of the god himself that he comes in the character of the mummy, taken with his other assurances that he comes *to* "those in their coffins," must be admitted to certify the truth of our contention throughout—that it is the god who comes to be buried in the matter of a lower kingdom, from which burial both he and the lower entity will be raised again to higher estate. When the sun-god entered "the ark of earth, which is called his coffin or sarcophagus," he was buried in obscurity and shorn of his power. In a sculptured sarcophagus of the fourth century the three Magi are offering gifts to the divine infant, a mummied child! Here the mummy is a figure of the divine nature circumscribed tightly by the garment of flesh. Need we remind the student that numberless images of the mummied Child-Jesus were found in Christian catacombs, tombs and chapels in the early centuries? At first view the linkage of the idea of death, as suggested by the mummy, with the infant figure, rather than with the more appropriate stage of senility, seems an ineptitude. In early Christian and pre-Christian iconography Jesus was indeed often figured as an aged one, about to enter the grave. It only requires that we move the symbolic hint one short step forward to see the pertinence of the mummified child, called by the Egyptians the *Khart*. For the buried god was to have his rebirth in matter and to begin life anew as an infant. The deceased father-god was to metamorphose into the new form of himself as his own child, as God the Son. While yet a baby-god, beginning his new career, he was cramped by the limitations of matter and the undeveloped stage of his own powers. He was the new god, who had not yet broken his bonds or risen from the limitations of his new incarnate situation.

It is evident that Hebraic development of archaic typology did not carry the figure of the mummy into Biblical literature. Yet a cognate symbolism is expressed through the word "flesh" mainly. Where the Kamite *Ritual* says: "My dead body shall not rot in the grave," the Hebrew Psalmist writes: "My flesh shall dwell in safety. For thou wilt not leave my soul to Sheol; [10] neither wilt thou suffer thine holy one to see corruption."

But occasionally an original Egyptian term has been retained in Hebrew transcription. Such a term is Sekhem, one of the names of the burial-place of the Osiris-mummy in the *Ritual*. The deceased is buried as a mummy in Sekhem. Also the well of Jacob near Sechem answers to the well of Osiris at Abydos, and the oak or terebinth in Sechem to the tree of life in the Pool of Persea. The fields of Sechem correspond to the Sekhet-Hetep or fields of peace and plenty in the Kamite original.

Also the incident of Joseph carrying Jacob's coffin matches Horus' carrying the Osiris-mummy.

The word mummy is perhaps derived from the Egyptian *mum,* to "initiate into the mysteries." This origin would suggest that the elaborate procedure of mummification was inaugurated to typify the whole broad meaning of the incarnation, as a submerging of high spirit in the dense state of mortal matter. For such a downward sweep through the world of material inertia was, as we shall see, the only, if fateful, path leading to the "initiation" of the spirits into the higher mysteries that lurk in the depths of life. The Sphinx riddle of life can be solved only by a living experience in all worlds from the lowest to the highest. Life's own justification of its processes is the *raison d'être* of our mum-

183

mification in gross earthly bodies, and the great Nilitic rite was designed to express nothing more.

Attention must now be given to the Egyptian word which was used to designate the mummy. It was usually marked upon the coffin lid. It may offer a connection of great potential fruitfulness for knowledge. It consisted of the consonants K R S with a suffix T, giving K R S T. The voweling is indeterminate, as it always was in ancient writing. Scholars have introduced an A before the R and another after it, making the word K A R A S T as generally written. There is probably no authoritative warrant for this spelling, but there has ever been a stout resistance to all suggestions that the alternative vowels, E, I, O or U be used in the form. Yet scholarship would be hard put to substantiate any objection to the spellings Karist, Karest, Kerast, Kerist or Krist. Indeed, as the root is very likely a cognate form with the Greek *kreas,* flesh, there would be more warrant for writing it Krast, Krest or Krist than the usual Karast. If we know how easily a "Kr" consonant metamorphoses into the Greek Chr, we can not dismiss the suggested closeness of the word to the Greek *Chrestos* or *Christos* as an absurd improbability. This may indeed be the Kamite origin of our name Christ, whatever be the outcry against such a conclusion.

There are presented some other extremely interesting possibilities in this etymological situation, for by the use of another vowel we stand very close to the Latin *crux,* cross, the Middle English *cros* (cross) and our own word *crust.* For indeed the ground meaning of the entire incarnation story might well be expressed in the grouping of these very terms: The Christ on the cross is the en*crust*ing of the divinity with flesh (Greek *kreas*). Not far away also is our word *crystal,* which contains the root meaning of any process of in*crust*ation, or the precipitation of spirit energies into forms of solidification around an actuating nucleus of force. The large idea behind all these forms that stand so closely related in spelling is just that of spirit crystallizing and forming a crust about a spiritual node of life. And then the Greek word *chruseos,* golden, points to the end of the process to be consummated by the spirit in matter, when, metaphorically speaking, all baser forms of the encrusted covering or mummy will be transmuted by the divinity's glowing fire into the purest spiritual "gold." The "crystal sea" that is to receive all back into its depths links the two ends of the chemicalization, first downward, then upward, together in one coherence. Our *kreas* or mummy case, that becomes but the *crust* of our life here on the *cross* of flesh, *kreas*, will be translated into *crystals* of pure gold, *chrysos*, by undergoing the *chrys*alis transformation into full deification. Still within the circle of these meanings we have *chrism, cruse* (of ointment), *chrisom, charism,* an anointing oil (our *cream*—French *cresme,* with the "s" dropped out, being a derivative of this stem), and finally within the glow of its influence comes the bright outline of the meaning of the great sacrament of the Eu*charist.* If all this etymological flourish appears to be highly fanciful, let the reader be assured that not a single term of the interwoven ideas in this chain is missing from the ancient symbolism. If it is a delightful play of fancy, its poetic originators were the sages of old.

When, then, Osiris is called the Karast-mummy, the meaning is doubtless that of spirit "fleshed" or incarnate. The flesh was the crust crystallized about the soul and as such became not only the cross, but the cruet or cruse containing the golden liquor of life. The partaking of it was our Eucharist, and our final transfiguration will be the putting on of the golden hues of immortality, symboled by the insect chrysalis operation.[11] "O thou who risest out of the golden" is an address to the soul in the *Ritual.*

Finally, then, we have Massey breaking through the philological defenses thrown up by the alarmed orthodox scholars and openly connecting the Egyptian Karast with the Greek *Christos* or Christ. He announces the derivation dogmatically:

"Say what you will or believe what you may, there is no other origin for Christ the Anointed than for Horus the karast or anointed son of God the Father. . . . Finally, then, the mystery of the mummy is the mystery of Christ. As Christian it is allowed to be forever inexplicable. As Osirian the mystery can be explained. It is one of the mysteries of Amenta, with a more primitive origin in the rites of Totemism."[12]

He adds that Osiris as the Karast-mummy was the prototypal *Corpus Christi.* As Osiris-Sekari he was the coffined one. Aseris, or the Osiris, represented the god in the anguish of his burial in the cerements of the mortal body, whose cries and ejaculations are to be heard ascending from Amenta in many a page of the *Ritual,* or from Sheol in the Hebrew scriptures. Massey states what has not been readily acceptable to Christian apologists hitherto when he writes:

185

"Indeed the total paraphernalia of the Christian mysteries had been made use of in Egyptian temples . . . Osiris in the monstrance should of itself suffice to show that the Egyptian Karast is the original Christ, and that the Egyptian mysteries were continued by the Gnostics and Christianized in Rome." [13]

Immediately connected with the *Christos* is the term *Messiah*, since both terms, the one Greek, the other Egypto-Hebraic, mean "the anointed." The word *Messiah* is traced to the Egyptian *mes* or *mas*, to steep, to anoint, as also to be born. *Messu* was the Egyptian word for "the anointed" initiate in the Mystery rites. The "*-iah*" was a quite significant suffix added by the Hebrews, meaning, like the ubiquitous suffix "*el*," deity or God. As "*-iah*" or "*-jah*," it occurs in many Hebrew sacred names, sometimes as a prefix, as in *Jah*weh, but mostly as a suffix, as in Eli*jah*, Hallelu*iah*, Mess*iah*, Zechar*iah*, Abi*jah*, Nehem*iah*, Obed*iah*, Isa*iah*, Hezek*iah* and a long list more. The name *Messiah* then denotes the "divinely anointed" one or the "born (reborn) deity." When the first or natural man was anointed with the chrism of Christly grace, he was reborn as the *Christos*.

An item of great importance in this ritual was its performance always previous to the burial. It was a rite preparatory to the interment. Said Jesus himself of Mary: "In that she poured this ointment upon my body, she did it to prepare me for my burial" (*Matt.* 26: 12). She was symbolically enacting the Mystery rite of the chrism, and her performance quite definitely matched the previous practices of the Egyptians, from whom it was doubtless derived. But what does such an act denote in the larger interpretation here formulated? If the burial was the descent of the gods into bodily forms, then the anointing must have been enacted immediately antecedent to it or in direct conjunction with it. The etymology of the word sheds much light upon this whole confused matter. The "*oint*" portion of it is of course the French softening of the Latin "*unct*" stem; and this, whether philologists have yet discovered the connection or not, is derived from that mighty symbol of mingled divinity and humanity of ancient Egypt—the A N K H cross. The word Ankh, meaning *love, life* and *tie,* or life as the result of tying together by attraction or love the two nodes of life's polarity, spirit and matter, suggests always and fundamentally the incarnation. For this is the "*ankh-ing*" of the two poles of being everywhere basic to life. The "unction" of the sacrament is really just the "junction" of

186

the two life energies, with the "j" left off the word. Therefore the "anointing" is the pouring of the "oil of gladness," the spiritual nature, upon the mortal nature of living man. The "unguents" of the mummification were the types of the shining higher infusion, and they prepared the soul for, or were integrally a part of, its burial in the grave of mortality. And the Messiah was then crucified in the flesh. On this point Massey speaks clearly:

"In preparation of Osiris for his burial, the ointment or unguents were compounded and applied by Neith. It was these that were to preserve the mummy from decay and dissolution." [14]

Neith applies the preservatives in Egypt; Mary in the Gospels. And as the feminine figures emblem matter, we must take the ritual as dramatizing the anointing of divinity with materiality, rather than just the anointing of the physical man with divinity. The same situation is found in the baptism allegory, where the lower man, John the Baptist, anoints with his element, water, the very deity, Christ, himself. In that close conjunction and interrelation of the two natures which the great Ankh symbol connotes, each nature "anoints" the other, and it matters little for final outcomes of meaning which is considered. All ancient symbols denoting the two elements in life are not only dual in themselves, but may generally be interchanged without damage to the ground signification. This strange—and practically unknown—aspect of the science of typology merits a full chapter in itself; but perhaps it will be enough to point out its application in specific situations where it will clarify the exegesis. Since the soul's burial in body is the cause and occasion of the release of its own higher potencies, its being anointed or baptized by matter (or "water") is thus both its active and its passive anointing. Let it be remembered, it both converts matter and is converted by matter. This is ever the basic formula. The anointing thus becomes kindred with the embalming. The chrismatic ceremony was the "ankh-ing" or tying together of soul and flesh for fuller outflow, giving in the outcome the Karast or Christ. In man the angel and the animal-human anoint each other.

As the climactic step in a series of benefits which Horus, the deliverer and reconstituter of his father Osiris, enumerates in an address to the latter, he likens the anointing to the gift of grace and spiritual unction:

"I have strengthened thine existence upon earth. I have given thee thy soul, thy strength, thy power. I have given thee thy victory. I have anointed thee with offerings of holy oil." [15]

The whole procedure of incarnation from its inception to the Prodigal's return, is to be seen as an anointing, first of spirit with flesh, then of flesh with spirit. Massey says that anointing was the mode of showing the glory of the Father in the person of his Son, and that Horus was anointed when he transformed from Horus the mortal to Horus the divine man.

The usual material for anointing was oil, but at least one other comes in as symbol. We are familiar with Jesus' mixing his spittle with a little earth to anoint the eyes of the blind man in the Gospels. A Hawaiian legend also has it that the first man was created from red earth (the meaning of "Adam") mixed with the spittle of the gods, and the triadic god then blew into his nose and bade him rise a living human being. Egyptian ideography pictures that the primeval god Tum conceived within himself, then spat, the spittle becoming the gods Shu and Tefnut, whose union as male and female produced the world. Another Kamite construction holds that the Eye of Ra (symbol of divine intelligence), being injured by the violent assault of Sut, was restored when anointed with spittle by Thoth.

In many more legends the gods are said to have mixed mortal clay with their blood, emblematic of their living power. The early mythmakers were adept at variation of the symbols. Horus, representing the god in man, says:

"He anointed my forehead as Lord of men, creating me as chief of mortals. He placed me in a palace as a youth, not yet come forth from my mother's womb."

This is a reference to the god's burial in matter, where life was a process of gestation for a new birth in spirit. The mortal man has not yet resurrected, not yet come forth from mother nature's womb! The spirit entombed is like Joseph in "Egypt" and Daniel in "Babylon" before they rose from out their "prisons" to become the rulers of the kingdom. We are still to have our birth out of matter into spirit. Our incarnation is our birth *into* body; our resurrection is to be our second birth, this time *out of* body.

Isaiah (61:1, 2) emphasizes the anointing in a famous verse:

"The spirit of the Lord is upon me, because the Lord hath anointed me to preach good tidings unto the poor. He hath sent me to bind up the broken-hearted,[16] to proclaim liberty to the captives. . . ."

The "poor," it is to be recalled, are equivalent to the Gentiles, the unregenerate natural man. They were the ones for whom the message of the Messiah was intended. The announcement from heaven to earth that a race of deities was about to descend to lift animal life into the kingdom of reason and articulate speech was verily "the good tidings of great joy which shall be to all people," the best news ever wafted to the denizens of the planet up to that period. "Thou hast anointed my head with oil, my cup runneth over," echoes the immortal Psalm (23). "Having had my flesh embalmed," says the Osirified deceased in the *Ritual* (Ch. 64), "my body does not decay." Hence flesh, inoculated with spirit, or the mummy embalmed, becomes immortal. And the Word *was* made flesh! And flesh will be immortalized!

But the Egyptians had a correlative phrase with "the Word made flesh." It was "the Word made Truth." The Logos or spirit made flesh produced the first birth, the natural man, the first Adam. This was not the true Word, for it was falsified by the admixture of the earthly, natural element, by which it voiced the animal note. As the boy's voice at the age of manhood changes from a feminine to a masculine timbre, so the speech of the mortal had to swing away from the tones of its mother nature and issue as the voice of the spiritual Self. Figuratively at the human race's age of twelve, always the number marking our spiritual perfecting, the Christ within us has to abandon the concerns of the maternal physical life and "be about his *Father's* business,"— the spiritual life. The race must turn from Mother Nature to Father God at its spiritual puberty.

It is quite noteworthy in this connection that one of the most eminent of modern psychologists, C. G. Jung, has divided human life into two periods, which he calls the forenoon and afternoon of life, the boundary line being placed at the age of thirty-five. He says that in the forenoon mankind lives the life of "nature," but turns in the "afternoon" to a life of "culture." So that we find even the span of mortal life epitomizing the larger scheme, in that we begin the "day" of life by living under nature, and turn in the afternoon to the concerns of the spirit and the mind. "First that which is natural, then that which is spiritual," St. Paul has reminded us.

The world took form upon the model of divine ideas, Plato affirms. In us men a god is striving to stamp his lines of beauty and grace upon the features of an animal! The God-word was fleshed so that it could preserve and finally transfigure the mummy with its splendor. But— and let ultra-idealists be advised!—spirit had to have plastic matter upon which to imprint its form and comeliness, else it would have remained forever unknown. The visible manifestation of latent wisdom, power and love could be achieved only by the spirit's encasement in a body. Matter, so derided by extreme "spiritual" theory, is the womb in which alone divine conceptions can be brought to birth. So that the fleshing of soul works the miracle of its own anointing. Flesh is the way and the means by which man, the divine thought, is christened with an ever fuller measure of the oil of beatification.

Carried some distance afield by certain involvements of the mummy discussion, we return to that aspect of it suggested by the mythical underworld. It has been already hinted that this nether world is our earth itself. But readers may not be fully aware that this assertion is here made directly in the face of all previous and present scholarship, and that it flouts all scholastic opinion. So open a challenge to world scholarship must summon additional proof to its support. The substantiation of the point is pivotal to the entire interpretation here advanced. The case wins or loses on the determination of this issue. Likewise the correct understanding of all theology hinges upon the outcome. As the many transactions involving the experience of the human soul in the body were enacted in Amenta, the underworld, the final meaning of the whole structure of theology is bound up with the correct location of this realm of gloomy shade. It is believed that the correction of the error under which the academic world has labored for centuries with regard to this region will necessitate the most sweeping alterations in religious and philosophical ideology, nothing short, in fact, of a total recasting of all meanings and values.

Amenta, the Egyptian term for this underworld, is given as a compound of the Egyptian *"Amen,"* meaning "secret," "hidden"; and *"ta,"* "earth" or "land." In this formation it becomes "the hidden earth" or "secret, hidden land." It is the land where the divine sons were hidden away in "Egypt" till the "wrath" of the Karmic Lords should be appeased. "Amen" was the "hidden deity," "the god in hiding." His hieroglyph pictures him as kneeling under a canopy. The "wrath" of

God, be it proclaimed at last, is no divine "anger," in any human sense of the word, but the universally burning, consuming, transforming, building and destroying energy of Life itself, always anciently characterized as a "fire." And the word seems derivative from *"Ur-ath,"* the original fiery force in matter, as *"Ur"* is "fire" and *"-ath"* is the feminine, that is, material classification. It therefore connotes the cosmical transforming energies locked up in the bosom of matter! This is of consummate importance. And all this complex ancient indirection of description is just to carry the idea that the soul must be tied down in its linkage with the deeply hidden energies of matter and body until the fiery potencies burning at that level refine and purify its grosser elements. A Biblical text speaks of its being "thrice refined in the fire," and Egyptian scripts abound with statements of its purification "in the crucible of the great house of flame." Maintaining the revolutionary thesis that Amenta is this earth, and not some realm elsewhere into which men relapse *after* earthly demise, the exposition will establish the fact that all the typology referring to it pertains to our own world. In every ancient system of cosmology this globe is the lowest of all planetary spheres. There can be no other hell, Tartarus, Avernus or Orcus, Sheol or Tophet below it. It is that darksome limbo where the Styx, the Phlegethon, the river of Lethe and other murky streams run their sluggish courses through the life of mortals.

Very apt, then, is the story of Isis and Osiris. Their infant, Horus, was suckled by Isis in solitude. She reared him in secret, and his limbs grew strong in the hidden land. None knew the hiding place, but it was somewhere in the marshes of Amenta, the lower Egypt of the *mythos*. This is matched *in toto* by the story of the birth of the mythical Sargon of Assyria. Likewise it is the background of the "flight into Egypt" of Jesus in the Gospels. The divine child had to be taken down into "Egypt" until the Herut menace was passed and in order that the son of God might be brought up out of it. As the angel of the Lord says to Joseph, "Arise and take the young child and his mother and flee into Egypt," so at the birth of Horus the god Taht says to the mother, "Come, thou goddess Isis, hide thyself with thy child." She is bidden to take him down into the marshes of Lower Egypt, called Kheb or Khebt. But the Egyptian version gives us more ground for understanding the maneuver as a cosmographic symbol, because Taht tells Osiris that there "these things shall befall: his limbs will grow, he will wax entirely strong, he will attain the dignity of Prince . . . and sit upon the throne of his father." This is highly important, since it makes the hiding away a part of the cosmic process and not a mere incredible incident in Gospel "narrative." In the mutilated Gospel account the sojourn in Egypt is left as if it were a matter of brief duration, followed by the child's return. In the fuller Egyptian record it is seen that the dip into Lower Egypt is that necessary incubation in matter that must continue until it has brought the infant potentialities to actualization and function. As the seed in the soil, so the god in the earthly body and the "child" in "Lower Egypt"—all are hidden away for the growth that only thus could be attained. The secreting of the child is no more than the planting on earth of the divine seed in its appropriate soil—humanity.

In the *Ritual* the Manes, or Osiris-Nu, says: "I am he whose stream is secret." Of Ptah it is also said: "Thy secret dwelling is in the depths (or the deep) of the secret waters and unknown" (Renouf: *Hibbert Lectures,* p. 321).

The presentation of the evidence supporting the mundane location of Amenta takes on from this point largely the semblance of a debate with Massey. If our study seems overburdened with his material, apology may be found in the explanation that, in the first place, he has fairly earned this amount of recognition, and secondly that his presentations focus the issues at stake with more definiteness than those of any other scholar. Though he missed the golden truth of this matter in the end, he still comes so close to it that he at times almost states it in spite of himself. The truth can hardly be better expounded than as the correction of his error, which proved so fatal at last to his work. No one has ever put more succinctly and clearly the nature of the experience of the soul or divine child in Amenta than he has done in the following excerpt:

"In the eschatology Horus, the child, is typical of the human soul which was incarnated in the blood of Isis, the immaculate virgin, *to be made flesh,* and to be born in mortal guise on earth as the son of Seb (god of earth) and to suffer all the afflictions of mortality. *He descended to Amenta* as the soul sinking in the dark of death. . . ." [17]

Everything in this passage points to the identity of Amenta with earth. Clearly as Massey saw through the thousand disguises of ancient method, he was tricked at last by the arcane ruse of presenting earth experience under the mask of a ritual for the dead. He could hardly bring himself to believe, sharp as was his break with orthodoxy, that the miscarriage of esoteric sense had gone so utterly awry as to misplace all religious values finally in a wrong world. The enormity of cleric aberrancy was already so shocking to him that he can be pardoned for failing to perceive that it was indeed still seven leagues worse.

He fought his way through by what seemed the only device which would enable him to keep the judgment, hell, purgatory and the underworld in the after-death realm. He was forced to split the term "earth," so frequently used with Amenta, into two parts, distinguishing an "earth of time" from an "earth of eternity." He took Amenta to be this fancied "earth of eternity" beyond the grave or death. He located it vaguely in the *post mortem* state, and segregated it from the earth of time, or the earth we know. But a little reflection on his part would have told him that the term "earth" has no possible appropriateness to a non-physical existence in spiritual areas. The designations "land," "country," so often applied to the heavenly state of being, are used only by grace of euphemism or figure. Massey must have felt this, but it permitted him to use the word "earth" in reference to a purely celestial locale. This could not have been other than a bit disingenuous; and it cost him his place in renown and kept us an additional forty or fifty years in bondage to religious superstition.

He rightly insists that "not until we have mastered the wisdom of Egypt as recorded in Amenta shall we be enabled to read it on the surface of the earth." This is precisely what should be said, but where do we have access to "wisdom recorded in Amenta" (considered as his spirit world) if not on this earth, either in books or in experience? Can we go to (his) heaven and read records left there? He speaks of a first paradise as being celestial and a second one as "sub-terrestrial," and says that the latter is "the earthly paradise of legendary lore." But, as has been shown, a "sub-terrestrial" residence for man is meaningless verbiage, imagery without possible counterpart in actuality. The "sub-" was to be taken as subsolary and perhaps sublunary, at any rate sub-celestial, but never—really—sub-terrestrial. If it was used for poetic figure, there need be no quarrel. The ancients did use subterranean caverns as *types* of our life in Amenta, but only as *types*. Of a surety we shall not read old Egypt's mighty wisdom aright until we read it on the surface of this earth, for the inexpugnable reason that the "wisdom recorded in Amenta" is the wisdom pertaining to this earth! *Amenta and this earth are one and the same place.* Religion must bring back to this earth the core of all those meanings which took their flight from this sphere on the wings of scholarship's egregious mislocation of the mythical region of Amenta.

His mistake, as that of all other scholars, was occasioned by loss of the archaic signification of "death." Books of the dead, forsooth, must inescapably apply to deceased humans, and hence their rituals must be designed for the spirits of the departed on "that other shore." It was thus not possible for anyone under this persuasion to discern that the Biblical phrase "after death" could mean its precise antithesis, as commonly viewed; that is, after *entry* into this life. It could not be seen that the phrase "deceased in their graves" had already been appropriated by the sages of Egypt to type the living denizens here on the globe.

Nevertheless the identification of Amenta with a *post mortem* state should have been seen at one glance as inadmissible in the light of a single consideration. Amenta, Hades, Sheol are always portrayed as the land of gloom, darkness and misery. These terms are often translated "hell" in the Bible and elsewhere. They are the dismal underworld. In it souls are imprisoned, captive, cut to pieces, mutilated, buried. Exactly opposite in description in every religion is the state of life after decease! It matches the Amenta characterization in no particular, but is its exact opposite. In it the soul finds release from the dark, heavy, dreary, wretched conditions that are descriptive of Amenta. It is the land of light, bliss, surcease from distress, rest and peace! The two portraitures will not mix! The Amenta of misery and gloom can not be at the same time the Happy Isles, the Aarru-Hetep and the asphodel meads! If to enter the body is to undergo captivity, then to leave it is to regain freedom, not to enter Amenta. Surely in this confusion of two worlds of diametrically opposite classification our savants are convicted of the most amazing want of acumen in reaching conclusions preposterously out of line with the data of scholarship. Massey should have been enlightened by what he wrote in this passage:

194

"Except when lighted up by the sun of night, Amenta was the land of darkness and the valley of the shadow of death. It remained thus, as it was at first, to those who could not escape the custody of Seb, the god of earth, 'the great annihilator who resideth in the valley.' "

If Amenta was the place where the god of earth detained souls in darkness, its localization on earth would seem to be incontrovertibly indicated. Or was not the god of earth on earth? We might expect a god to inhabit his own kingdom, the one over which he ruled.

Osiris, king of the land of the dead, is denominated "lord of the shrine which standeth at the center of the earth." (*Rit.*, Ch. 64.) Massey speaks of "the human Horus"—and Horus was in Amenta. Humans exist only on the earth. The earth must be Amenta, then. He writes again that the drama "from which scenes are given in the Hebrew writings, as if these things occurred or would occur upon the earth, belongs to the mysteries of the Egyptian Amenta, and only as Egyptian could its characters ever be understood." The scenes in Hebrew scriptures *are* drawn largely from the early Egyptian Mysteries, which typified cosmic and racial history under the forms of dramatic ritual. But they were not events of either Egyptian or Hebrew *objective* history. They did not "occur" anywhere on earth, but they portrayed the interior meaning of all that did occur on earth. The events were not here, but their meaning was. They were not occurrence factually, but the key to all occurrence. Massey thought the myths must be veridically true in (his) Amenta, since they were not objectively true on earth. He caught half the truth only. The myths were only symbolic language telling human dullness of mind what life meant. The moment the myths are alleged to have taken place in heaven or anywhere else, that moment superstition begins to stalk into the counsels of religion. Nothing could occur in Amenta as a place distinct from this earth, since it was a mythopoetic name for earth itself.

But the sad part of Massey's story and the reason it is important for us to scrutinize his mistake is that it is the story of a whole race's deception for sixteen centuries! The localization of Amenta in heaven instead of on earth has defeated the whole purpose of religion for ages. And no pen or tongue will ever record the monstrous fatuity involved in the spectacle of a race looking into the wrong world and waiting with sanctified stupidity for the fulfillment of values that have slipped by them ungrasped all the while! When religion gave up its effort to realize values in the life here and fixed despairing eyes on heaven, it betokened the decay of primal human virtue and a sinking back into mystical fetishism. Came the Greek "loss of nerve" and the turning from earth to heaven for the realization of hopes ground to dust on earth. And this shift of philosophical view left the ground of culture lie fallow, and bred the rank growth that covered the whole terrain of the Dark Ages. There is needed no other warrant for the extension of the material of this chapter to some length. As things have turned out, it may well be that the true location of the Egyptian Amenta, instead of being a mere point in academic scholarship, is the critical item in the life of culture today. *The collapse of true religion is ever marked by its turning for its real experience from earth to mystical heavens.*

Scholars have not sufficiently or capably reflected on the significant fact that ancient sacred books or Bibles have been largely Books of the *Dead.* The obvious glaring peculiarity of this fact has never seemed to occur to students. It should from the first have provoked wonder and curiosity that the sages of antiquity would have indited their great tomes of wisdom in such a form as to serve as manuals *in the life to come,* and not as *guides for the life lived in the sphere in which the books were available!* Only the heavy tradition that religion was a preparation for a life to come, instead of a way of life here, could have stifled this natural reaction to a situation that is odd enough in all conscience. It is no slight or inconsequential thing that Budge writes in one sentence of ". . . religious texts written *for the benefit of the dead* in all periods . . ." (of Egyptian history), without the least suspicion that he was penning an astonishing thing. It had been ponderously assumed by scholarship that the ancient sages were more concerned with the hereafter and the next world than with life down here. How the march of history would have swung into different highways had the world known that we living men were those "dead" for whom the sagas were inscribed by the masters of knowledge! And what must be the sobering realization for present reflection of the fact that the primeval revelation given to early races for the guidance and instruction of all humanity has missed entirely the world for which it was intended!

The scene of critical spiritual transactions is not "over there" in spirit land, but here in the inner arena of man's consciousness. Life's accounts do not remain suspended during our active experience on earth, to be closed and settled when the exertion is over. We are weaving the fabric and pattern of our creation of ourselves when we are awake on earth, not when we are at repose in ethereal heavens. The droning cry of lugubrious religionism for centuries has been to live life on earth merely as the preparation for heaven. But there is no logic in the idea of making preparation for rest! It is the other way around: rest is a preparation for more work. The positive expression of life is the exertion of effort to achieve progress. Rest is just the cessation of the effort, and needs no preparation. The character of our effort may, to be sure, determine the nature of our rest, yet one should say, rather, its completeness. Rest is in some degree correlative with the effort. Still the logic is indefeasible, that we work to achieve our purposes, and not to gain rest. The presumption that this life is of minor consequence and has value only as the stepping-stone to another where true being is alone achieved, is one facet of that enormous fatuity of which we are holding orthodox indoctrination guilty. It is the last mark of the miscarriage of primal truth in the scriptures that its meaning and application have been diverted from that world it was intended to instruct, and projected over into another where its code can have no utility whatever. The offices of religion have fled to heaven, and must be brought back to earth. This return can be effected only by the right interpretation of the term "the dead" and the true location of Amenta, the scene of the judgment, hell, purgatory and the resurrection, and the seat of all evolutionary experience.

Massey asserts that "the nether earth was the other half of this" and that the "Gospel history has been based upon that other earth of the Manes being mistaken for the earth of mortals." But he errs on both counts. For the "other half of this" life is lived in a sphere which all faiths have located *above* this one, and not nether to it. The spirit world can in no way be localized as *under* our world. His second statement misses truth through the fact that the events in the life of the Manes are not, as he supposes, actual transactions in the after-death life of the spirit, but are only allegorical depictions of the soul's history in this life.

But he makes a point of great moment, worthy of transcription, when he states that the miracles of Jesus were not possible as objective events:

"They are historically impossible because they were pre-extant as *mythical representations* . . . in the drama of the Mysteries, that was as non-historical as the Christmas pantomime. The miracles ascribed to Jesus on earth had been previously assigned to Iusa, the divine healer, who was non-historical in the pre-Christian religion. Horus, whose other name is Jesus, is the performer of the 'miracles' which are repeated in the Gospels; and which were first performed as the mysteries in the divine nether-world. But if Horus or Iusa be made human on earth, as a Jew in Judea, we are suddenly hemmed in by the miraculous, at the center of a maze with nothing antecedent for a clue; no path that leads to the heart of the mystery, and no visible means of exit therefrom. With the introduction of the human personage on mundane ground, the *mythical inevitably becomes the miraculous;* thus the history was founded on the miracles, *which are perversions of the mythology* that was provably pre-extant."

It was in these discernments that Massey rose to heights of clear vision and made a contribution to the cause of religious sanity that can not be rated too highly. This passage is a clear and courageous declaration of the long-lost truth of the matter. He performed a great service in discrediting the myths as history; but by thrusting them over into a purely suppositious world as alleged realities in the "eschatology," he committed his costly blunder.

It was into Amenta that both Horus and Jesus descended to preach to the souls in prison. Horus' object in making the descent was to utter the words of his father to the lifeless ones. So in the *Pistis Sophia* Jesus passed into Amenta as the teacher of the great mysteries. It is said in this Gnostic work: "Jesus spake these words unto his disciples *in the midst of Amenta.*" [18] Moreover a special title is assigned to Jesus in Amenta. He is called *Aber-Amentho;* "Jesus, that is to say, *Aber-Amentho,*" is a formula several times repeated. *Aber* means lord or ruler; so that again Jesus and Horus are exactly matched in title.

If Jesus delivered his discourses to his disciples "in Amenta," all question of where this hidden land is located should be settled forever. For unless all Gospels are accounts of the doings of wraiths in a spectral underworld, as even Massey suggests, we are bound to suppose that their transactions, historical or mythical, transpired on earth.

The hazy character of current Egyptological scholarship is notably manifest in a passage from Budge dealing with the location of the *Tuat.* It is clearly given in the *Ritual* as the gate of entry to the underworld. But Budge gives it as "the name of a district or region, *neither in heaven nor upon earth,* where *the dead dwelt* and through which the sun passed during the night." Where else the *Tuat* might be, if neither in heaven nor on earth, deponent saith not. In another place (*Egyptian Literature,* Vol. I) he defines the *Tuat* once more. "Tuat is a very ancient name for the Other World, which was situated either parallel to Egypt, or across the celestial ocean which surrounded the world." This goes far to prove that the science of Egyptology has been but a blind groping amid ideas utterly uncomprehended by the "learned" men in the field. Indeed Budge himself has penned what may be called his own "confession" on this score. For its downright candor and its general importance, it is quite worthy of insertion:

"Is it true that the more the subject of Egyptian religion and mythology is studied the less is known about them? The question is, however, *thoroughly justified* and every honest worker will admit that there are at the present time scores of passages even in such a comparatively well-known compilation as the *Book of the Dead* which are inexplicable, and scores of allusions to a fundamentally important mythological character of which the meanings are still unknown." (*Gods of the Egyptians,* Vol. I.)

The sun passing through the *Tuat* depicted the divine soul as passing through its incarnation, which being in the darkness of the body was charactered as the "dark night of the soul." As it entered the gate of Amenta, called the *Tuat,* it crossed the horizon line dividing the region of spirit or heaven from earth or embodiment, and there it stood in the twilight. Budge says that "the *Tuat* was a duplicate of Egypt," laid out in nomes, with a river valley and other similar features. This should further identify it with our earth.

In Amenta the soul was said to receive a new heart shaped "by certain gods in the nether world according to the deeds done in the body whilst the person was living on earth." Here again is confusion and a missing of the intent. The award of a new heart is not made like that of a prize on graduation day. The larger meaning is that the whole long experience of many lives creates a new heart, which is the resultant of the transformation of nature that is gradually accomplished by the whole process. *It is quite impossible to draw intelligible meaning from the scriptures if we limit our survey to a single span of earth life as a prelude to an infinite "eternity" in its wake. Reason forbids our conceding to the actions of a single life on earth sufficient moment to fix the destiny of a soul forever.* Ancient theology rested on no such irrational presumption.

Many statements aver that the soul passes into Amenta at death. Massey felt sure that this clinched his location of Amenta in the ghost world. He did not dream that the "death" the ancients spoke of brought the soul here instead of taking it away. The soul's statement that it came "to overthrow mine adversaries upon the earth" should have enlightened him. The soul descends here to battle the lower nature, the only adversary contemplated in the whole range of holy writ.

The attendants of the soul in its incarnational descent say to it (Ch. 128): "We put an end to thy ills through thy being smitten to earth"— "in death," Massey himself adds. But not even this brought discovery to his mind. The following is highly indicative also:

"From beginning to end of the *Ritual* we see that it is a being once human, man or woman, who is the traveler through the underworld. . . ."[19]

Even though the *Ritual* assigned to this underworld pilgrim all human characteristics, scholars still have missed the hint that he *was* the human. Later texts give to the Manes in Amenta all the traits and features of the earth mortal.

The solar god in Amenta is addressed as "thou who givest light to the earth." This again is definite localization on earth. It was the sun-god who "tunneled the mount of earth and hollowed out Amenta,"— mistaken for two operations when they are of course one and the same. The sun-god's "boring through the earth" was one of the tropes.

Instruction is derived from noting how Massey's erroneous idea entangled him in the following passage:

"The lower paradise of two is in the mount of earth, also called the funeral mount of Amenta. [Identification again.] The departed are not born immortals in that land; immortality is conditional. They have to fight and strive and wrestle with the powers of evil to compass it."[20]

His own exegesis convicts him of shallow thinking here. For he has stated repeatedly that the soul enters *his* spectral Amenta with character already formed by "the deeds done in the body." *His* Amenta could not be the arena of moral conflict or fight to win immortality.

He has indeed called it "the earth of eternity." It is too late to writhe and wrestle for moral victory when *that* "Amenta" is entered. The earth is the one and only theater of spiritual struggle. So he errs in reiterating:

"The world-to-be in the upper paradise was what they made it by hard labor and by purification in Amenta." [21]

Massey's mistake, in common with that of much general religious opinion on these matters, lies in his affirming that after the termination of life in the body the soul first *descends* into Amenta, then later rises into Paradise. This flies in the face of all basic postulation of theology itself. The soul *descends* in coming to earth, and there is no lower region left into which it can *further* descend on quitting the body. Its incarnation in flesh drags it down, its release at decease lets it free to return upward. The false *downward* direction assigned to the soul on leaving earth is a perversion of true original conception due to the loss of the meaning of the term "death" in world religion. Profound philosophical insight corroborates the instinctive unconditioned idea which rises in connection with physical death, that the soul when released begins its *ascent* to celestial habitat. Only perverted theology inculcated the thought of further descent when the war between flesh and mind is over. The dissipation of that idea is ample justification for this chapter. Another sentence pictures his entanglement in the net:

"The sub-terrestrial paradise was mapped out for the Manes to work in, and work out their salvation from the ills of the flesh and the blemishes of the life on earth."

But how can he call this dark, murky, dismal underworld of subterrestrial life a "paradise"? In no religion is paradise pictured as a gloomy and forbidding place. This obsession of his, that the soul must first go down into a region of agony and bloody sweat and fiery torture after separation from the body and be purged of its earthly sins before it can rise into paradise, warrants all this dissertation upon it because it is the delusion of millions.

It is conceivable and admissible that the soul upon release from body may need a period of time to throw off some heavier portions of its clinging earthly mires, before it can return to the highest place of purity. But in all reason it must be contended that the locale of such a stage must be *above,* not *below,* the earth life. If the soul lingers a while on a level of purgation after life here, it is at least on a plane one step higher than this.

The general commitments of this whole discussion are of sufficient importance to excuse a general critique of the pious theory that life equalizes the balance of her forces by having us commit error in one world and do penance or make atonement in another. Almost universal as is the idea, there is little foundation for it in the great systems of early racial instruction. It is an excrescence on the body of saner teaching.

We must reap *as* we sow. "He that soweth to the flesh shall *of the flesh* reap corruption." Half the world has been hypnotized with the belief that mankind can atone in an ethereal world for "deeds done in the body." Perfect justice would obviously require that we return to the same world in which acts were committed to square the Karmic accounts engendered by them. To work out our salvation from the ills of the flesh, the soul must at least be where flesh is! If we are to erase the blemishes of earth life, we must return to those conditions which constituted the nature of the problem in the first instance. In spirit world the problem is no longer present; it has been dissolved with matter. If we break the dishes in the kitchen we can hardly atone by singing in the parlor. How it is presumed by an eccentric theology that we can work out concrete problems in a world where concreteness has been dissolved, is not at all easy to see. Those who plan to win the unfought battles of spiritual life from a bower in Paradise had better take counsel with the ancient wisdom. There is no heavenly "peace without victory," or a victory without St. Paul's long fight. The arcane science tells modern ignorance why we are on earth. If there was some sufficient primal necessity for our coming to wrestle with flesh and sense in the first instance, then it must be essential that we continue to come until these forces and natures are overcome and raised. The wisdom of civilizations already hoary in Egypt's time is back of that pronouncement, and it is back of no other. The static angelic immortality of the Christians, the "eternal spiritual progress in heaven" of the Christian Scientists, Spiritualists and other cultists, find their rebuke and their correction in the venerable knowledge of the ancient sages.

The divine word or the Logos "is to be made truth in the life *lived on earth,* so that the spirit when it entered the hall of judgment, was, as it were, its own book of life, written for the all-seeing eye." This is magnificent truth that Massey states; but how infinitely more meaningful it becomes when it is known that the hall of judgment entered by the spirit to reap the fruits of former action and amend its ways, is not a spirit plane after death, but this present "underworld," to which it will return, after a rest, to face the further issues involved in its evolution. Returning here again and again, the soul brings its own record book of life with it, written in its own character. Character can be built nowhere else than on earth. No religion has ever said that we would be judged for deeds done in the spirit world! We are asleep then and inactive, and making no Karma, as the East phrases it. As St. Paul says, sin is lying dormant until incarnation again brings the moral agent, the soul, into subjection to the body of sense, when "sin springs to life."

The title of one of the chapters of the *Ritual* is: "Of introducing the mummy into the Tuat on the day of burial." This becomes absurd if the mummy is the corpse and the Tuat a spectral realm of wraiths. No more than that a man can take his gold watch with him to heaven could a mummy be introduced into Massey's and Budge's Tuat! The burial is the advent of the "mummified" soul or Karast into its coffin-case of the physical body.

Elsewhere Massey equates "the pillar of earth" with "the Tat of Amenta" and still fails to see identification. In another connection he writes:

"Thus we can identify Eve or Chavvak, as Kefa or Kep, the Great Mother, with Adam or Atum in the Garden of Amenta." [22]

Were not Adam and Eve on earth?

A striking pronouncement in the *Papyrus of Ani* should have awakened true intelligence in his mind: "The soul, or Manes, makes the journey through Amenta in the two halves of sex." Where are there male and female sex distinctions save on earth? And one wonders how the scholar could have written the following and failed to see the basis of identity suggested:

"The mortal on earth was made up of seven constituent parts. The Osiris in Amenta had seven souls, which were collected, put together and unified to become the ever-living one."

But all students of ancient literature are aware that earth was the place where the collecting and unifying of the seven constituent souls of man were accomplished. Again a most direct hint of the truth was ignored by the savants. Also Greek metaphysical science asserts that the soul came down through nine stages "and became connected with the sublunary world and a terrene body, as the ninth and most abject gradation of her descent." [23] Here is philosophical testimony that negates the existence of any hell or underworld *below* life in the body. Any observer of human life knows that it is possible for the soul to fall to the most abject baseness while *in* the body. We are in the lowest of the hells—Amenta.

Again and again the texts say that Amenta is the dwelling of Seb, the god of earth.

Massey states that in the resurrection "man ascended from the earth below, or from below the earth." The first point of departure is correctly placed; but the alternative, meant to be an appositive, is ruled out of court. Man was never below the earth.

In the Jewish scriptures twelve sons of Jacob go down into Egypt for corn; in the *Book of Amenta* twelve sons of Ra make a journey toward the entrance to Amenta, represented as a gorge between two mountains, heaven and earth, and they go down into the lower Egypt of the *mythos*. All this is figurative for the descent of the twelve legions of angels of light (sons of Ra, the Light-God) upon this planet. These are the true prototypes of the twelve tribes of Israel, to whom the Eternal as recorded in one of the prophetic books of the *Old Testament,* before their descent, calls: "The underworld awaits you with eager joy. It watches with open jaws to receive you." (Moffatt Trans.) In the Egyptian this is matched by the statement that "the reptile, or dragon, 'eternal devourer' is his name (Ch. 17), lurks and watches in the 'bight of Amenta' for its prey." The "bight of Amenta" accurately matches the "recess of earth" in the Greek terminology. In another form of typology the twelve are called "the twelve reapers of the harvest on earth, which was reaped in Amenta by Horus and the twelve." [24] If the spiritual harvest was reaped "on earth" and "in Amenta," earth and Amenta must be the same place.

Massey places the habitat of those "people that sat in darkness" and who saw a great light, in Amenta. When Horus descends to them to bring the divine light, he is declared to "descend from heaven to the darkness of Amenta as the Light of the World." How could he be the light of the world if he did not come to the world? It is our earth, surely, and this is once more equated with Amenta.

When Satan takes Jesus into a high mountain for his trial (against the powers of matter) it was a place whence "all the kingdoms of the earth could be seen."

Horus in his coming is said to kindle a light in the dark of death for the soul "or spiritual image in Amenta." But he came to earth to bring light. When he arrived at the outer door of Amenta in his rising Horus says: "I arrive at the confines of earth." Says Massey himself: "He was to be the light of the world in the mortal sphere." And when Horus comes to give the breath of life to the inert Manes in Amenta and delivers his message, it is declared in the Rubric (to Ch. 70): "If this scripture is known upon earth, he (the Osiris) will have power to come forth to day and walk upon the earth among the living."

An important link in the chain of evidence is the statement that the seven principles or vehicles that were integrated in one organism to form perfect man "were all believed to come into existence after death." [25] But as the *khat* or physical body was one of them, and it was incontestably dropped from association with the others after death, the phrase "after death" must here be taken in the peculiar theological sense delineated in this analysis. For only after the death and burial *in* body could the god begin the work of welding the seven principles into an aggregate harmony. We are now put in position to grasp the true import of all those religious phrases which speak of the various works that take place "after death." For in the light of the new-old meaning of "death" all the experiences dramatized as occurring after bodily demise can be seen as falling within, not outside of, the limits of earthly life. Physical birth here is the beginning of that "death" and the events of life thus come "after (the beginning of) death." Even that redoubtable verse in the Bible, "It is given unto man once to die, and after that the judgment," does not overrule the exegesis here advanced. The integration of the seven constituent principles in man can not be carried on without the *khat* in a spirit-Amenta.

In describing the judgment of Ani (the Manes-soul) in Amenta, Budge writes: "Ani is here depicted in human form and wearing garments and ornaments similar to those which he wore on earth." To

205

explain this, to him, odd phenomenon, Budge weaves an intricate conjecture that

"the body which he has in this hall of judgment can not be the body with which he had been endowed on earth, and we can probably understand that it is his spiritual body, wearing the white robes of the beatified dead in the world beyond the grave, that we see."

But what more natural than that the hierophants should portray the personage in the drama representing the human in the likeness of the human? The scrolls of old Egypt depicted Ani in human form and dress because it was to him as a human being that the meaning of the drama applied. Budge (and all others) first allocates the trial of the deceased to the nondescript astral world and then wonders why the human character in it is represented as human! If the pundits will have it that the Amenta in which the judgment trial takes place is the realm of flitting specters, they will have to contrive as best they can to solve the perplexities of Egyptian procedure created by their own preconceptions. But if they will follow the indicated guidance of the symbology employed, they will find their difficulties obviated as if by a touch of magic. For if Amenta is our earth, then Ani may be expected to appear as the typical human, with flesh, complexion and ornaments to match, and a little clothing if needed!

The text says of Teta: "This Teta hath broken forever his sleep in his dwelling which is upon earth." This assures us that the Amenta sleep takes place upon our earth.

Using "day" in the sense of incarnation, another text reads: "Thou appearest upon the earth each day," under the figure of the rising sun, of course.

Another chapter title (132) in the *Book of the Dead* gives a clue that is inerrant: "The chapter of causing a man to come back to see his house upon earth." And in the Saitic Recension the "house" is said to be in the underworld. The two are then equated.

Another chapter (152) gives a quite illuminative title: "Of building a house upon the earth." As this "house" is the temple which Jesus said he would re-erect "in three days," and is the central structure of all Masonry, it is important to note that its erection takes place on earth.

"I died yesterday, but I come today," exclaims the Manes (Ch. 179).

"He sitteth as a living being in Amenta," affirms another verse. These do not sound like the expressions of the real defunct.

Budge tells us that the duty of supplying meat, drink and apparel to the "dead" was deputed to Anup, Keb and Osiris. Anup was the guide of souls in the underworld; Keb (Seb) was the god of earth; Osiris was the ruler of the kingdom of the dead. All three distinctly locate the region of death on this globe.

The following from Budge is noteworthy: [26]

"For the goddess (Taht-I-em-hetep) adds, Amenti is a place of stupor and darkness, and death calleth every one to him, gods and men, and great and little are all one to him; he seizeth the babe as well as the old man. Yet [Budge adds] the Egyptians did *not* [27] live wantonly, as if this life were a preparation for a gloomy death. They lived in expectation of passing into a region of light and glory."

Here is powerful confirmation of the contention that the Egyptians could not have regarded the gloomy and darksome Amenta as the region of life after death, and that the soul ascended to realms of glory and brightness on leaving the body instead of descending into the scholars' purgatory—Amenta. The Egyptians were taught in the Mysteries that this life *was* that Amenti of stupor and darkness, and out of it they would pass to rest and brighter scenes in the empyrean. Budge supposes the call of "death" to be from the earth to heaven, when it is from heaven to earth, on the thesis here established. The call of death was the summons to bright angelic spirits to enter the life in body. It was St. Paul's "command." No wonder the noted Egyptologist has to register some incomprehension over the fact that the Egyptians were cheery in the face of passing at death into what he supposed was the fearsome Amenta. Pluto's rape of Proserpine should have enlightened him. The Grim Reaper calls all souls, when ready for the human trial, into the kingdom of "death." The other Egyptian designation for death is notable: "'Devourer of Millions of Years' is his name." This would indicate the total cycle of incarnations to be of great duration, which indeed all esoteric teaching asserts it to be. And still more significant is another title given him: "His name is either Suti (Sut) or Smam-ur, the Earth-soul." There is no escaping the invincible evidence: to die is to live on earth.

There are not wanting forthright statements from the Egyptians themselves which should prove conclusive as to the point under discussion. Massey himself gives one of them:

"In the inscriptions on the sarcophagus of Seti the earth is used as *equivalent to Amenti* and opposed to heaven." [28]

Yet he did not see that this inscription was destructive of his own interpretation. He says further:

"Also the sun descending into the underworld is thus addressed: 'Open the Earth! traverse the Hades and the Sky! Ra, come to us!'"

If now mundane life be found to be the seat of all human experience and human meaning, what must be made of the Biblical adjuration not to lay up treasures on earth? If this life is the scene and theater of destiny, why should it be ignored and scorned?

A part of the answer is that, to be sure, values are not held here in permanency. Obviously they could not be, if the bodies through which they are implemented disappear. But neither are they enjoyed forever in the spiritual existence which the soul has in the interim between lives. But the great and momentous question then arises: if they abide in perpetuity neither on earth nor in heaven, where *are* they preserved? The answer is: in the inner spiritual entity of the man wherever he is, be it on earth or in heaven. It appertains to him wherever he goes; it is his permanent possession and he takes it with him always. It is his, whether in or out of the body, as St. Paul says. But—and this is the item of final import for man—though the gains of evolving life are not held on earth in perpetuity, *it is on earth that they are won!* And this knowledge is the sum and substance of philosophy. The soul comes to earth to win its pearl of great price in the depths of what is called the great sea of mortal life.

The scholars' thesis that religious texts were written for the benefit of the dead is the dire result of the complete reversal of the meaning of ancient typology. All the offices of poetry vindicate the claim that imagery uses the less real to depict the more real; a natural process to depict a spiritual one; a fairy tale to portray the deepest living realities. But a perverted theology used the real to depict the unreal. As to the mummy, current misconception holds that its preservation was to suggest an absolutely unreal future for the defunct body that could have no future and for the soul that as certainly could not return to it. On

208

the contrary, the symbolism centering about the mummy, an entirely insignificant and unreal thing, was an elaborate device to impress on living humanity the far more real experience of the immortal self interred in the coffin of the fleshly body, but immortalized there.

The Books of the Dead should be pondered by the Western world with a new intensity. For with the new canon of interpretation laid down in the present work to guide our thinking, the title will yield a stunning realization of the catastrophic blunder of sixteen centuries of theological blindness. And flashing through awakened intelligence will dawn that benign understanding that religious scripts were meant for human guidance through *this* benighted land of the dead, the only Amenta, Sheol, Hades, Tophet or underworld ever contemplated by the original framers of the grand *mythos*. And not the less impressive will be that philosophical reognition, at last as at first, that man is himself the mummy, "dead" on earth, but preserved to immortality by the injection of the Amrit or Soma juice of the Christ nature.

Chapter XI

DISMEMBERMENT AND DISFIGUREMENT

THE answer to the riddle of the generally feeble pulse of religion in the modern age has been compounded out of the material adduced in the preceding chapters. But there are many distinct doctrinal items the corruption of the significance of which is a strong ancillary cause of the reduced power of ancient faith, and one of these can now be enunciated. In the light of extended exposition we shall be able to see why it was that the gods' descent into our realm, heralded by angel hosts as the event of supreme omen thus far in the history of the globe, has failed to bring to every mortal the climactic joy it was designed to release. It will be seen why the celestial tidings proclaimed of old to bring an era of peace and good-will to all men have stirred us so faintly. A false theology has stepped in between the supernal messengers and the minds of the sons of earth to dull the thrill of the "good news." On the day of the Advent heaven's arches rang with the proclamation of peace and amity among men on the basis of the fact that a fragment of divinity had been lodged in the holy of holies of the temple of each human body. Emanuel had come to dwell with man. But the exuberant joyousness of all mortal hearts over the event has been clogged. No longer the substance but only the shadow of the truth remains to kindle Yuletide ecstasy. The allegory of the birth in the stable or cave was devised to keep mankind in exultant memory of its divinity. Alas! It speaks no more of *our* divinity. It extols the godly nature of but one. The paeans of sacred hilarity that are raised for the birth of our Savior are appropriate and efficacious only as that Savior stands as symbol of the glorious birth within ourselves. Long ago Angelus Silesius, a Christian mystic, admonished Christendom:

> "Though Christ a thousand times in Bethlehem be born,
> But not within thyself, thy soul will be forlorn;

> The cross on Golgotha thou lookest to in vain
> Unless within thyself it be set up again."

If the birth of the god in each individual heart is not the interior meaning of the Nativity, then we celebrate the event to no purpose. No amount of adoration accorded to a newborn king in Judea will avail to redeem a single wayward heart if the Christ Child is not eventually domiciled in the breast of the individual. The King of Righteousness must be cradled in the manger of each human self ere the myth can work its magic in the world.

This miscarriage of the vital significance of the event has come about entirely through the desuetude of the doctrine that may be denominated by the Greeks' philosophical term, the god's *dismemberment*. The reconstruction of pristine wisdom can not be encompassed without the rehabilitation of this great doctrine. Sunk entirely out of sight, its restoration to its integral office in the body of theology will enable that science to function again with the semblance of its former power.

For the god came to earth not in his entirety, not in his single deific unity, but torn into hosts of fragments, grouped in twelve principal divisions. How could he hope to enter every mortal life, to tabernacle in every breast, if he came as one unit? This is just the mistake that Christian doctrinism made, fatal to humanity at large. It is a matter of simple logic. To be the divine guest in every human life he had to suffer fragmentation into as many portions as there were to be mortal children for him to father, in order that each might possess a share of his nature. This procedure was necessitated by the conditions extant. The terms under which the law of incubation operates require that the forces of life on any plane must take rootage in the soil of the kingdom below, as the sheer seeds of their own capabilities, and fragment their unity by division to accommodate their higher potencies to the lesser capacities of the lower organisms. These could not carry the heavier voltage of life in its unitary volume on the plane above. Man on earth could never implement and incorporate the full power of heaven. The embodiment of superior force in less capacious vehicles is accomplished by the partition of that upper unity into fragments, after the analogy of the oak tree in its annual production of a thousand embryonic units of its potential nature, each of which, when incubated in the mothering womb of the soil below it, is capable of regenerating its dying

211

parent. And so every divine son of God raises his Father from the dead, as did Jesus and Horus. The god in man can not move across the dividing line between the kingdoms, stepping from the divine level down into the human, without suffering a dismantling of his integrity and a partitioning of his "body" into a multitude. He must experience a diminution of his intellectual genius analogous to what a human mind would suffer if it was to be incorporated in the brain of a dog. And *Daniel* does say this very thing! "An animal's mind shall be given unto him." Only a portion of the god's intellectual light, and that reduced in strength and luminosity, could function in the brain mechanism of animal man. In short, the gods could not transplant their full and mature selfhood into man, but *only the seeds of its next cycle of growth.* Indeed *all projection of deity outward into matter is in embryonic form.* Divine thought is sent out to take root in matter, there to have its cycle of new growth. The analogy of the oak and its acorns leaves nothing wanting for understanding of the evolutionary method. And it clarifies for us the incarnation, as being the planting, germinating, budding and flowering in mortal life, of the seed-germ of divinity. Jesus is the embryonic deity, born in the crib or crypt of man's mortal nature.

Clement of Alexandria, describing the *sacra* of the Mysteries, speaks of those who ignorantly worship "a boy torn to pieces by the Titans." This was Bacchus, in a part of whose Mystery ritual the body of the god was represented as torn into pieces by the Titans and *scattered over the earth!* It is significant that in the drama the god is cut into pieces while enticed into contemplating his image in a mirror. Greek philosophy spoke of the soul's projecting a similitude of herself into matter. She was to reproduce a likeness of herself in flesh, for the lower must be formed in the image of the higher. Man is to reproduce, as the acorn the oak, the image of his maker. This detail is an intimation that it was the god's inclination toward a life of sense, depicted by his bending down (Cf. the fable of Narcissus) to gaze delightedly at his reflection in the water of generation, that preceded his fall and divulsion into fragments. Jupiter, hurling his thunderbolts at the Titans, the forces of elementary nature, committed the members of Bacchus to Apollo, the Sun-god, that he might properly *inter* them. The god's heart, which had been snatched away by Pallas (the higher mind) during the laceration, and preserved for a new generation, emerges, and about it as a nucleus the scattered members are reassembled, and he is restored to his pristine integrity!

Turning to Egypt there is found an exactly parallel *mythos,* which has the god Osiris in place of the Greek Dionysus. Says Budge:

"Throughout the Egyptian texts it is assumed that the god suffered death and *mutilation* at the hands of his enemies; that various members of his body were scattered about the land of Egypt; that his sister-wife Isis 'sought him sorrowing' and at length found him; that she fanned him with her wings and gave him air; that she raised up his body and was reunited with him; that she conceived and brought forth a child (Horus); and that he (Osiris) became the god and king of the *underworld.* In the legend of Osiris as given by Plutarch (*De Iside et Osiride*) it is said that he was murdered at the instigation of Typhon or Set, who tore the body into fourteen pieces, which he scattered throughout the land; Isis collected these pieces. . . ." [1]

It is hard to think that this legend or glyph of our evolutionary history has stood in the books for five thousand years and failed eventually to illuminate the race's understanding of its own cosmic situation.

Osiris was not the only sun-deity whose body suffered dismemberment in the Egyptian pantheon, for Ptah, an earlier god, shared the same mythic fate. Under his name of Ptah-Sekari he underwent fragmentation as did Osiris. For "Sekari is the title of the suffering Ptah, and *sekar* means to cut; cut in pieces; sacrifice; or, as we have the word in English, to *score* or *scarify.*" [2] Ptah was said to be the earliest form of God the Father, who became a voluntary sacrifice in "Egypt," and who, in the name of Sekari, was the silent sufferer, the coffined one, the deity that opened the nether world for the Manes. As a solar god he went down into Amenta. There he died and rose again. Atum, son of Ptah, also became the voluntary sacrifice as the source of life to mortals. As the "silent Sekari" Ptah was an earlier type of the figure of Jesus, who was as a lamb dumb before his shearers, and opened not his mouth against his accusers. The title of Sekari is in fact added to Osiris, as well as to Ptah, and as Osiris-Sekari he is the dismembered and mutilated mummy in his coffin. The Speaker in the *Ritual* cries: "The darkness in which Sekari dwells is terrifying to the weak." The Egyptian festival of the resurrection, celebrated every year in the month Choiak (Nov. 27 to Dec. 26, Alexandrian year) was devoted to the god Osiris-Ptah-Sekari, "who had been dead and was alive again; *cut to pieces* and reconstituted with his vertebrae sound and not a bone of his body found to be broken or missing." (Cf. the Gospels: "And they brake all his bones." This was the form of the dismemberment, to be followed by the reconstitution.)

That which applied to the Osiris-god also applied to "the dead in Osiris." (Cf. the Gospels: "Dead in Christ.") "They were figuratively cut in pieces as the tangible image of abstract death."[3] "When the mortal entered Amenta it was in the likeness of Osiris, who had been bodily *dismembered* in his death, and who had to be reconstituted to rise again as the spirit that never died."[4] It is certain that the Manes was considered to have suffered dismemberment like his ensampler Osiris, because it is written that before the mortal Manes could attain the ultimate state of spirit in the image of Horus the immortal, he must be put together part by part like Osiris, the dismembered god. From a divided being he had to be made whole again as Neb-er-ter, "the god entire." In one phase of the drama the deceased is put together bone by bone after the model of the backbone of Osiris. The backbone was an emblem of sustaining power, matching indeed the Tat cross of stability. In the *Ritual* (Ch. 102) Horus says: "I have come myself and delivered the god in his dismembered condition. I have healed the trunk and fastened the shoulder and made firm the leg." Horus, entering the lower world to seek and to save that which is lost in the obscurity of matter, says (Ch. 78): "I advance whithersoever there lieth a *wreck* in the field of eternity." On their drop into matter, the first episode in the gods' multilation was the loss of their intellectual unity, typified by the figurative cutting off of their heads. "And the god Horus shall cut off their heads in heaven (where they are) in the form of feathered fowl, and their hind parts shall be on the earth *in the form of animals*. . . ." It is even directly stated that "Ra mutilates his own person" for the benefit of mortals. Thoth later came and healed the mutilations. As Thoth was the god of knowledge, it can be seen on what plane of comprehension the mutilation and healing are to be given meaning. The dismemberment was only the division of unified intellect into partial vision. The reconstitution of the torn divinity is referred to in the address to Teta, the "dead" king on earth: "Hail, hail! Rise up, thou Teta! Thou hast received thy head,

214

thou hast embraced thy bones, thou hast gathered together thy flesh."

In far India the Lord of Creation, Prajapati, was represented as having undergone dismemberment. Likewise Sarasvati. There is no question as to the wide prevalence of the symbol.

Nothing is more shattering to our modern sense of superiority and condescension with regard to early nations believed to have been "primitive" and ignorant, than to find in their literary relics the outlines of some of the grandest conceptions of Platonic or other high philosophic theory. In a Mexican legend we come upon the idea of the god's dismemberment in a striking form. A story portrayed the union of physical man with a higher spirit under the imagery of mixing a bone with blood. The tale runs to the effect that the Great Mother of the gods instructs them, in the creation of man, to go down to Mistlanteuctli, the Lord of Hades, and beg him to give them a bone or some ashes of the dead, who are with him. These would represent the lower natural body. Having received this, they were told to sacrifice over it, sprinkling the blood from their own bodies upon it. This would typify the impartation of their own divine natures to the mortals. After consultation they dispatched one of their number, Xolotl, down to Hades. He succeeded in procuring a bone *six feet long* (a certain identification with the human body) from Mistlanteuctli and started off with it at full speed. Wroth at this, the infernal chief gave chase, causing Xolotl a hasty fall, in which the *bone was broken in pieces*. The messenger gathered up in all haste what he could, and despite the stumble made his escape. Reaching the earth he put the fragments of bone into a basin and all the gods drew blood from their bodies and sprinkled it into the vessel. *On the fourth day* there was a movement among the wetted bones and a boy lay there before all, and in four days more of blood-letting and sprinkling, a girl came to life. If the Bible student is inclined to disdain this myth as profitless, let him turn to *Ezekiel* (37) and reflect on what he finds there. For the Biblical fable of the valley of dry bones contains five or six distinct points of identity with this legend: the operation of the gods upon the lifeless bones, a noise, a stirring and movement among the bones, a coming together and eventual constitution of them into living bodies, with flesh and sinew, and their creation as humans, male and female, as in *Genesis*.

The early Egyptians laconically dramatized the doctrine of dismemberment, but the intellectual Greeks wrote elaborate disquisitions upon its import. It is set forth by the Platonists with dialectical precision. The doctrine grows out of the very laws of thought. It is no whimsical speculative fancy. It rests on a logical necessity. For if life is to proceed from primal unity to manifest multiplicity and diversity, there is no way for the One to *multiply* itself save by an initial *division* of itself. Life proceeds from oneness and identity of nature into number and differentiation, and the structure of thought requires that multiformity arise from unity by partition of that unity. The One must break himself into pieces, tear himself apart, and this is the meaning of the mutilations and exsections of the gods. The One must give himself to division. And with division comes addition of forms, multiplication of units and combinations, but subtraction of deific power in the divided parts.

Each wave of creative impulse quivered outward from the central heart of being and, like falling water, body-blood and tree-sap, was fragmented by the resistance of matter. From plane to plane the dispersion continued. Wholes were broken into parts, which as wholes on their own plane went into further partition to plant the field of the next lower level. With his own inseparable being torn into multiple division, and each part an integral unit of the total, his life is seminally distributed in each. He lives in the parts and the parts live in him. The fragments are the cells of his body. "We are all members of one body, and Christ is the head." So Greek philosophy states that "each superior divinity becomes the leader of a multitude, generated from himself." And at last there is the basis for comprehensible sense in the phrase "the Lord of Hosts." Each deity is the lord of a host, who are the fragmented children of his own body.

Each unit of division, when incubated in the lower realm, begins to renew its father's life. It must arise and return unto the father's estate. The son must restore the parent who has died in him to his former greatness, with something added. He must raise that which has fallen and redeem that which has been lost. No one shall see the father save him to whom the son revealeth him. This was the typical function of Horus in relation to Osiris in Egypt, as it was that of Jesus to God his Father in the Gospels.

Buried within the heart of each fragment, then, is the hidden lord of divine life, and from no one is he absent. He dwells there to be the guide, the guardian, the comforter and informing intelligence of the organism. He is the holy spirit, the flame, the ray, the lamp unto our feet. Says St. Paul (*I Cor.* 4:7): "For God, who commanded the light to shine out of darkness, hath shined in our hearts . . . but *we have this treasure in earthen vessels.*" The ancients oft termed this presence the daemon or guardian angel, as in the famous case of Socrates. He is that attendant monitor who stands behind the scenes of the outer life, instant to bless, ready to save, a never-failing help in trouble. His counsel is never lacking, if one seeks it or has not previously stilled its small voice. It reasons with us until many times seven. It abides within our inner shrine, patiently awaiting the hour of our discovery and recognition of its presence.

We must take time to hear the voice of Greek wisdom anent the dismemberment:

"In the first place, then, we are made up from fragments (says Olympiodorus), because, through falling into generation, our life has proceeded into the most distant and extreme division; and from Titanic fragments, because the Titans are the ultimate artificers of things, and stand immediately next to whatever is constituted from them. But furthermore, our irrational life is Titanic, by which the rational and higher life is torn in pieces. Hence when we disperse the Dionysus, or intuitive intellect contained in the secret recesses of our nature, *breaking in pieces* the kindred and divine form of our essence, and which communicates, as it were, both with things subordinate and supreme, then we become the Titans (or apostates); but when we establish ourselves in union with this Dionysiacal or kindred form, then we become Bacchuses, or perfect guardians and keepers of our irrational life; for Dionysus, whom in this respect we resemble, is himself an *ephorus* or guardian deity; dissolving at his pleasure the bonds by which the soul is united to the body, since he is the cause of a parted life. But it is necessary that the passive or feminine nature of our irrational part, through which we are bound to body, and which is nothing more than the resounding echo, as it were, of soul, should suffer the punishment incurred by descent; for when the soul casts aside the (divine) peculiarity of her nature, she requires her own, but at the same time, a multiform body, that she may again become in need of a common form, which she has lost through Titanic dispersion in matter."[5]

"Now we know in part and we prophesy in part, but when that which is perfect is come, then that which is in part shall be done

217

away." Had we held our culture closer to the heart of Greek philosophy we should have seen the whole of things more clearly. We are the Titans who tore the divine philosophical fire away from the central altar in the empyrean and scattered it like sparks amongst the race of mortals. And these Titans, or Satanic hosts, were those apostates who compounded the felony of stealing the divine fire by further carrying its dispersion into remote depths of matter. Yet they were the agents of deity to bring salvation, or the purifying, cleansing fire, to man on earth. They distributed the divine life in fragments among mortals, administering the cosmic Eucharist of the broken body and shed blood of the gods for a benison to all humanity. The divine intellectual power, the mind of the god, was divided amongst us, not, however, with the loss of the total unity of the godhead on his own plane. Only his lower fragments in body felt their reduction to poverty. Says Taylor:

"And thus much for the mysteries of Bacchus, which, as well as those of Ceres, relate in one part to the descent of a partial intellect into matter, and its condition while united with the dark tenement of body; but there appears to be this difference between the two, that in the fable of Ceres and Proserpina, the descent of the whole rational soul is considered; and in that of Bacchus the *scattering* and going forth of that supreme part alone of our nature which we properly characterize by the appellation of intellect." [6]

In Proclus' *Hymn to Minerva* we have a spirited statement of the unified god-mind, Bacchus, fragmented:

"The Titans fell against his life conspired;
And with relentless rage and thirst for gore,
Their hands his members into fragments tore."

Olympiodorus unfolds the dialectical thesis in three propositions: (1). It is necessary that soul place a likeness of herself in body. (2). It is essential that she should sympathize with this image of herself, as it tends to seek integration with its parent. (3). "Being situated in a divided nature, it is necessary that she should be torn in pieces and fall into a last separation," after which she shall free herself from the simulacrum and rise again to unity. The gods impart their divided essence to mortals and then the fragments seek to rejoin their parents and be united again with them in nature. Bacchus pursued his image,

218

formed in the mirror of matter, and thus was carried downward and scattered into fragments. But Apollo collected the fragments and restored them to union in the heavens.

If the Bible student judges all this to be foreign to his interpretation of his Book of Wisdom, let him consult the nineteenth chapter of *Judges,* and read the story of the rape and destruction of the concubine of a man whose name is not given, but described as "a Levite . . . in the remote highlands of Ephraim," which would seem to identify him with some higher spiritual principle. The concubine, who left for her father's house in a fit of rage, would perhaps correspond to Proserpina, the detached incarnating soul. The man sought her, and after long dallying with her reluctant father, started home with her, "from Bethlehem to the remote highlands of Ephraim." At Gibeah, among the Banjaminites, they lodged over night, and there the unruly citizens, "certain sons of Belial" (our lower propensities) attacked the house, forcing the man finally to send out his host's virgin daughter and his own concubine to be ravished by the crowd. In the morning he lifted the concubine's body on his ass and took her home. Here "he took a knife and *cut up* the concubine's body, limb by limb, *into twelve pieces,* which he sent all over the country of Israel, telling his messengers to ask all the inhabitants, 'Was ever such a crime committed since the Israelites left Egypt?'" Twelve baskets of *fragments* in the *New Testament* miracle; twelve legions of angels ready to come to Jesus' assistance in the garden of Gethsemane; twelve stones set in the midst of the Jordan when Joshua led the Israelites from Amenta into the Promised Land; twelve fragments of the soul's dismembered life in the story in *Judges!* If the literalist insists that *Judges* is talking about a concubine in the flesh, and not a principle of divided intellect in Greek philosophy, the all-sufficient answer is that he thus keeps the incidents of his Book on a level where they mean nothing and hold no instruction or appeal for the mind of man. And the proof of this is that on the level on which he keeps them nobody pays any attention to them. Only through Greek philosophy can we lift such neglected allegories to a height of impressive significance.

In the "miracle" of the Lord's feeding the five thousand with the loaves and fishes in the Gospel narrative we have a repetition of the dramatization of the Eucharistic rite minus only the accompanying statement from the Christ himself that the loaves were his own body, broken for the multitude of humans. We have set the stage certainly, however, for the first full and clear comprehension of the meaning of the disciples' "gathering up" (the Egyptian reconstitution) *twelve* baskets of *fragments*. In *multiplying* the bread, he dramatized the doctrine of the dismemberment, which was in twelve main sections or groups.

But Christian intelligence is not aware that in the very heart of its own chief rite of formalism this great doctrine lives in unsuspected completeness. St. Paul makes a specific announcement of it in *I Corinthians* (11:23):

"I pass on to you what I received from the Lord himself, namely, that on the night he was betrayed the Lord Jesus took a loaf, and after thanking God he broke it, saying, 'This means my body *broken* for you; do this in memory of me.'"

Here is the fragmentation of the god announced at the heart of the Christian Eucharist! The body of the Messiah *broken* for us! The main symbol in all Christian ritual is the *breaking* of a piece of bread into fragments and distributing them out among the communicants! And all theological acumen has missed the relation of this to Greek Platonism just because the recital was not explicit enough to state that the Lord's body was broken into pieces.

Scholars have long quarreled over the word translated "broken," and will do so again, doubtless more violently than before, when the attempt is made to relate its meaning to the Greek doctrine of dismemberment here suggested. But the quarrel is gratuitous. There may be dispute about the word, but there can be no dispute about the *act* of *breaking* the bread, which dramatizes the meaning. For Jesus dismembered the bread as the indisputable outward symbol of the cosmic truth of his fragmented body of spirit; and to avoid the use of the participle "broken" in the verse would be a faithless betrayal of the obvious meaning of the text. Here then is Greek esoteric philosophy functioning on the innermost altar of the Christian faith!

The entire temple of Christian theology would be beautified and strengthened if this cardinal doctrine could once more be adequately envisaged and included in living presentation. But, the true meaning lost, and the spiritual signification deeply buried under the outer debris of the myths, the Church has nothing more sublime to offer its devotees than the picture of a physical body suffering alleged laceration on a wooden cross! *Such* a body could *not* rise and be reconstituted. But the unit body of deific virtue, distributed out into myriad earthly vessels of human life, broken thus and buried piecemeal in the soil of mortal flesh, *could* be reassembled and reunited in the increasing brotherhood of humanity. There is no truth in ancient scripture outside of a spiritual rendering of the material. As soon as the Church returns to the true original meaning of the "broken body of our Lord," it may take up again its prime function as nourisher of the souls of men.

Incarnation brought dismemberment; but this was not the only form of diminished power and beauty incurred in the process. The god also suffered many kinds of *disfigurement*. Dead and buried in matter, he was typed under a variety of figures representing his suffering and deformity. The depictions included those of a decrepit old man, a wizened babe (the mummy-Christ), a maimed, crippled, wounded, impotent, halt, lame, inert, motionless, breathless, speechless, blind, dumb, deformed, disfigured, demoniac, deaf, naked and ugly little child! He was bereft in every particular. Several of the early Church Fathers, misled by the change from drama to alleged history, actually described the person of Jesus as not comely and radiant, but ugly and deformed! This is but one of the many absurdities that came to light when allegorism was converted over into realism. Some of the disfigurement material from the Scriptures must be presented here briefly:

"In the Egyptian mysteries, all who enter the nether world as Manes to rise again as spirits, are blind and deaf and dumb and maimed and impotent because they are the dead. Their condition is typified by that of the mortal Horus who is portrayed as blind and maimed, deaf and dumb, in *An-ar-ef,* the *abode of occultation,* the house of obscurity . . . where all the citizens were deaf and dumb, maimed and blind, awaiting the cure that only came with the divine healer, who is Horus of the resurrection in the *Ritual,* or Khnum, the caster out of demons, or Iu-em-hetep, the healer, or Jesus in the Gospels, gnostic or agnostic. This restoring of sight to the blind man, or the two blind men, was one of the mysteries of Amenta that is reproduced amongst the miracles in the canonical Gospels." [7]

When Horus, the deliverer, descends into Amenta he is hailed as the Prince in the City of the Blind; that is, of the dead who are sleeping in their prison cells. He comes to shine into their sepulchers and to restore spiritual sight to the blind on earth. Horus is designated "he who dissipates the darkness and *gives eyes to the gods* in obscurity."[8]

"The typical blind man in Amenta is Horus in the gloom of his sightless condition, as the *human soul obscured in matter,* or groping in the darkness of the *grave.* Sut has deprived him of his faculties. This is Horus *An-ar-ef* in the city of the blind."

What becomes of the Gospel healings and miraculous cures in the light of this *antecedent* material in the Egyptian scripts? It is a question momentous for the future of orthodoxy. There seems to be but one answer open to sincerity: the *New Testament* "miracles" are the reproductions of ancient Egyptian religious dramatizations in the Mysteries, and not actual occurrences.

Horus, prince in the city of blindness, as his father was king in the realm of the dead, comes to reconstitute his father whole and entire, and to give lost sight to all those dead as and in Osiris. The Manes were all blind, and the god had to work a magical operation on them to restore their sight. We have the Gospels dramatizing the god's opening up of intellectual faculty when at the typical age of twelve years he makes his transformation into the adult. The Egyptian emblem of the hawk's head given him at that epoch betokens his restored sight. His eye, stolen from him by Sut, is then restored. Under the astrological sign of Orion Horus was typed as the god of the night or dark, the blind god who received sight at dawn. He describes himself as the mortal born blind and dumb in *An-ar-ef,* the abode of occultation, but who in regaining his own sight will likewise open the eyes of the prisoners in their cells. The circle of the gods rejoices at seeing Horus take his father's throne and scepter and rule over the earth, replacing blindness with spiritual sight.

A most suggestive portrayal of this condition was hinted at in a calendar published in 1878 at Alexandria, in which there is recited a tradition that on December 19 "serpents become blind," and that on March 24 they "open their eyes." (A. Nourse, p. 24). As the serpent typed here the divine soul, the imagery is readily grasped. One must connect the story with the yearly astrology to see its full appropriateness. We read that three months of the year were assigned to the blind serpent or dragon in the abyss. The three months, as elsewhere three

222

days and the three kingdoms below the human, figured the period of the god's burial in the material worlds. "As Jonas was three days in the whale's belly, so must the Son of Man be three days in the bowels of the earth."

Jesus after his baptism announces his messianic commission to preach "recovery of sight to the blind," and healing to them that are bruised. And St. Paul writes that we wait for the coming of the Lord Jesus Christ, "who shall fashion anew the body of our humiliation." Of Jesus it is written that "to many blind he gave sight," not physical but spiritual.

The story of Samson, the luni-solar hero, does not omit the feature of loss of sight, when, as the god in incarnation, he is shorn of his power and bound helpless. He is eyeless in Gaza, pitiful and forlorn, like "the blind Orion hungering for the morn"—the return of the lost light. The Hebrews have a Talmudic tradition that Samson was lame in both his feet, which was also the status of the child-Horus, who was pictured as maimed and halt in his lower members, the crippled deity, as he is called by Plutarch.

Isaiah's chapter (61) in which the Manes announces that the Lord has sent him to bind up the *broken-hearted* and to open blind eyes, has been noted. But *Isaiah* has a far more touching portraiture of the suffering servant in reference to his disfigurement in chapter 53:

"His visage was so marred, more than any man, and his form more than
    the sons of men.
Disfigured till he seemed a man no more,
Deformed out of the semblance of a man."

Horus bewails the loss of his eye to Sut who has pierced it, or stolen it. He cries: "I am Horus. I come to search for mine eyes." In the spring Sut restores the god's sight.

The mouse, the mole and the shrewmouse were all employed as symbols of the soul shut up in darkness, in the crypt of the body. Yet only by such burrowing in the dark underworld could the soul be transformed into a new and higher stage of life.

Harpocrates, the Greek-Egyptian god of healing, is traceable to the Egyptian Har-p-khart, who as a crippled deity was said to be begotten in the dark. The term "khart" signifies a deformed child, and includes also the idea of speechless. It should not be overlooked that our own word "infant," from the Latin, means "speechless!" Har(Horus) -p (the) -khart(speechless child) was the character depicting the god just born into matter, and not yet able to manifest or utter "the Word made Truth." One of the supreme features of Horus' mission was to open dumb mouths, or to give mouths to the dumb. This was to cause their lives to express the words of power and truth. *Isaiah* sings that "the dumb are to break forth into singing and the lame to leap for joy." Jesus was silent when accused. This is all to typify the infant god in the flesh, who has not yet learned to articulate the living reality of spiritual truth. As the human infant is speechless for an initial period of some two years, so the god is silent in the expression of his divine nature for a corresponding period at the beginning of his incarnate sojourn. At the judgment trial vindication for the Manes was assured if he could assert that he had given bread to the hungry, *speech to the speechless,* drink to the thirsty, clothes to the naked and a boat to him that had suffered *shipwreck* on the Nile—of life.

A further anthropological reference of great importance is suggested by the typology of the dawn of speech, in that it carries an allusion to the opening up of the faculty of speech by the race with the coming of the gods. Psychology reveals that speech was necessary for the development of thought. But it is just as rational to say that the power to think made speech possible.

Deprivation of breath was another form of typology for "the dead." And with breathing stopped, there was also the motionless heart. The Osiris says:

"I am motionless in the fields of those who are dumb in death. But I shall wake, and my soul shall *speak* in the dwelling of Tum, the Lord of Annu."

For it was in Beth-Annu (Bethany) in Egypt, the place of weeping, that Osiris lay in his coffin inert and motionless. Hence Osiris is portrayed in the likeness of the mummy called "the breathless one"; also "the god with the non-beating heart." Mummification set the seal of indestructibility on the soul. The god in his advent announces:

"I utter Ra's words to the men of the present generation, and I repeat his words to him who is deprived of breath"—the Manes in Amenta. (*Rit.,* Ch. 36).

224

Multitudes of crippled people followed Jesus into the mountains and cast themselves at his feet to be healed. "And he healed them; insomuch that the multitude wondered when they saw the dumb speaking, the maimed whole, the lame walking and the blind seeing." (*Matt.* 15:29 ff.).

A festival known as the *Hakera* was celebrated in Egypt. The name means "fasting" and the festival terminated the fasting with a feast. It was for the benefit of those who had been deprived of breath, who were dumb and blind, motionless and inert—in·short, the deceased lying helpless like "wrecks" in the fields of Amenta.

Upon the Gnostic monuments in the Roman catacombs Jesus is portrayed in one of his two characters, matching Horus, as the little, old and ugly Jesus; in the other he corresponds to Horus of the beautiful face. The first is the suffering infant Messiah, the man of sorrows and acquainted with grief, the despised and afflicted one. As Jesus in this character was never more than twelve years of age, "Old Child was his name." In the *Pistis Sophia* Jesus is again pictured in his two characters, the first being that of the puny child, the mortal Horus, born of the virgin mother (nature) as her blind and deaf, her dumb and impubescent child. It was the human Horus again who was pierced and tortured by Sut in death until the day of his triumph, when he rose to become king and conqueror in his turn. We are by this exposition permitted to see the mythical character of Job, the assailed one, subjected to the assaults of Sut (Satan). Practically all the central figures·of the *Old Testament* enact the role of the Manes, the soul of buried deity.

In the *Orphic Tablets* the dead person is thus addressed: "Hail, thou who hast endured the suffering, such as thou hadst never suffered before; thou hast become god from man!" One portion of the Mystery ritual recited the sufferings of Psyche in the underworld of Pluto and her rescue by Eros, as described by Apuleius (*The Golden Ass*), in the cult of Isis. "Almost always," says Dr. Cheetham, speaking of the Mysteries, "the suffering of a god—suffering followed by triumph—seems to have been the subject of the sacred drama."[9] The minds of the neophytes were prepared for the glorious breaking of the light by the preliminary ordeal of darkness, fatigue and terrors, typical of this earth life. Carpenter[10] compares with the wounding of the side of Jesus an Aztec ceremonial of lighting a holy fire and communicating

225

it to the multitude from the wounded breast of a human victim, celebrated every fifty-two years, when the constellation of the Pleiades is at the zenith. (Prescott, *Conquest of Mexico*, Bk. I, Ch. 4).

In the *Ritual* the Manes cries: "Decree this, O Atum, that if I see thy face, I shall not be pained by the signs of thy sufferings." In *Luke* (24:26) it is asked: "Ought not Christ to have suffered these things and enter into his glory?" And John declares that in the world we shall have tribulation.

Budge describes a form of the suffering Messiah:

"Thus the great god Ra, when bitten by the adder which Isis made, suffered violent pains in his body, and the *sweat of agony* rolled down his face, and he would have died if Isis had not treated him after he revealed to her his hidden name." [11]

The serpent formed by the goddess is the lower nature which is made to sting the life of the god into a coma upon his incarnation. A prayer in the *Ritual* pleads that the divine beings do away with the sorrow of the Osiris-Nu, his sufferings and his pains, and that his ills be removed. Massey draws a composite picture of the god beset with material limitation:

"This was the Horus of the incarnation, the god made flesh in the imperfect human form, the type of voluntary sacrifice, the image of suffering; being an innocent little child, maimed in his lower members, marred in his visage, lame and blind and dumb and altogether imperfect." [12]

But the most appealing portrayal of this phase of the Christ experience, save that of the crucifixion of Jesus, is the picture of the "suffering servant" in *Isaiah* (Ch. 53). It is so striking that we must make space for it, in the beautiful language of the Moffatt translation:

"He was despised and shunned by men,
   A man of pain who knew what sickness was;
   like one from whom men turn with shuddering,
      he was despised, we took no heed of him.
And yet ours was the pain he bore,
      the sorrow he endured!
We thought him suffering from a stroke
      at God's own hand;

yet he was wounded because we had sinned;
    'twas our misdeeds that crushed him;
'twas for our welfare that he was chastised;
    the blows that fell to him
    have brought us healing.

And the Eternal laid on him
    the guilt of all of us.
He was ill-treated, yet he bore it humbly,
    he never would complain;
Dumb as a sheep led to the slaughter,
    dumb as a ewe before the shearers.
They did away with him unjustly;
    and who heeded how he fell,
torn from the land of the living,
    struck down for sins of ours?
They laid him in a felon's grave,
    and buried him with criminals,
    though he was guilty of no violence
    nor had he uttered a false word.

he shall succeed triumphantly,
since he has shed his life-blood,
and let himself be numbered *among rebels,*
    bearing the great world's sins
    and interposing for rebellious men."

This is a graphic depiction of the nature and office of the *Christos,* and written long before the appearance of any historical Jesus! The Gospel "life" of Jesus, *Isaiah's* account of the suffering servant, the chronicle of Job's afflictions, the pre-Christian Gnostic story of the suffering Christ-Aeon and the description of the pierced, wounded, crucified Horus of antique Egyptian records, match each other with unmistakable fidelity.

The diminished glory of descending godhood is also portrayed under the figure of disrobing. As the soul descends from one plane to another she is represented as being divested of one of her robes of glory at each step. The student of esotericism will see at once the meaning of this. Each plane clothes the soul with a body of its proper matter, *pneumatikon, psychikon, physikon,* or spiritual, psychic, physical. As the soul steps down the grades of being she takes on a coarser body, which is equivalent to her losing a more ethereal one, at each landing. And the incubus of each heavier one yields her a less and less vivid contact with reality. At last she descends virtually disrobed into the prison and tomb of the gross body.

In the *Ritual* (Ch. 71) we are told that in his incarnation Horus, or Iu, the Su, (Iusu, Jesu, or Jesus) "disrobes himself" to "reveal himself" when he "presents himself to the earth." The Babylonian goddess Ishtar is said to have made her descent through seven gates, at each of which she was stripped of one of her robes of glory.[18] Massey gives us an important point in Comparative Religion in the following:

"The mutilation of Osiris in his coffin, the stripping of his corpse and tearing it asunder by Sut, who scattered it piecemeal, is represented by the stripping of the dead body of Jesus whilst it still hung on the cross, and parting his garments among the spoilers. 'For they stripped him and put on him a scarlet robe.'"[14]

The god sinking into earthly embodiment is stripped of his finer robes and covered with the scarlet, red-blooded body of flesh!

In the *Ritual* (Ch. 172) the text runs:

"Thou puttest on the pure garment and thou divestest thyself of the apron when thou stretchest thyself upon the funeral bed. Thou receivest a bandage of the finest linen."

Which is to say, that on the return, the coarse bodies are thrown off and the robes of radiant light resumed. And what more apt symbol of the fleshly body than an apron? It is a garment put on to fend off the grime of earth, to hang between the purity of spirit and the smudginess of matter!

It is of the utmost significance that in the *Genesis* account it is twice said that Adam and Eve knew they were naked, and that they felt no shame the first time, but were overcome with shame after their fall into nakedness. The sense is that their first nakedness came while they were still in the "garden," the celestial paradise, and probably intimates their freedom from coarse garments of the lower natures. Their later nakedness came when they had been spiritually stripped, though clothed with coats of skin, or fleshly vestures. The "shame" arose from the god's recognition of his having fallen into a state of comparative

228

degradation in which he would have to resort to sexual methods of procreation, when hitherto his life had been renewed by the sheer force of divine will, called *kriyashakti* in the East. Paul speaks of this body of our shame, as do Plotinus and the Neo-Platonists generally. It is the main basis of the widespread ascetic inclination in history. And the Jesus of the *Pistis Sophia* tells Salome that his kingdom shall come when "thou hast trampled under foot the garment of shame" and restored the soul, split into male and female segments here on earth, to its pristine whole, or androgyne condition.

In the *Ritual* the judgment is designated as that of the clothed and the naked. If the Manes appeared naked before the judges, it meant that he had not overcome the grossness of his physical nature and robed himself in more radiant spiritual garb. To appear clothed was to have resumed the shining vestments of light. There is comment on this in *Revelation* (16:15): "Blessed is he that watcheth and keepeth his garments lest he walk naked and see his shame." The seductions of earth and flesh were strong enough to cause many of the Manes to lose the luster of their inner vestures. Thus disrobed of their finer garments, they presented the evidence of their poor condition to pass the ordeals of the judgment. What further light do we need to interpret Jesus' parable of the man ejected from the marriage feast because he came in without a wedding garment? Massey comments:

"The Manes in the *Ritual* consist of the clothed and the naked. Those who pass the judgment hall become the clothed. The beatified spirits are invested with the robe of the righteous, the stole of Ra, in the garden." [16]

In the resurrection ceremony of Osiris, the god is divested of his funerary garment and receives a bandage of the finest linen from the attendants of Ra (*Rit.*, Ch. 172).

It is notable in this light that in *Revelation* the angel discerned in flight toward the earth came with outstretched wings "and veiled face." And what *Exodus* says of Moses has meaning in this connection (Ch. 34):

"Whenever he went into the presence of the Eternal to speak to him, he took the veil off, till he came out again; and when he came out and gave the Israelites the orders he had received, the Israelites would notice that the face of Moses was in a glow; whereupon Moses drew the veil over his face again till he went into the presence of the Eternal."

In this symbolic fashion the wise seers of old represented the incarnational going in and out before the Lord, the adventuring of the immortal soul out into body where it put on the veils of matter and flesh, and its retiring again into the holiest shrine of spirit where it dropped its heavier outer bodies and again became "clothed in light as with a garment."

In the Hindu, Egyptian and Greek Mystery rites the ceremony of indicating the soul's pilgrimage round the Cycle of Necessity was performed over what was called the "Snake's Hole," and the "Inevitable Circle." It was imaged by a coiled snake. A part of the rite was to strip the snake in token of its sloughing, a symbol of the divestiture of the soul to be clothed anew in bright raiment. Proclus states that in the most holy Mysteries the *mystae* were divested of their garments to receive a new divine nature, or vestment of salvation.

Horus covers the naked body of Osiris with a white robe when he comes to raise the inert one. This act is paralleled in the Hebrew scriptures when Shem and Japheth go in backward to cover the nakedness of their father Noah. The drunkenness of Noah here betokens the swooning which accompanies the descent, as already set forth.

A number of verses in the Bible yield new and impressive evidence if read in the sense here indicated. The "coats of skin" made for Adam and Eve by God would be taken as the outer physical vehicles. The *Psalms* entreat that "thy priests be clothed with righteousness." *Proverbs* states that "drowsiness shall clothe a man with rags." *Isaiah* speaks of the joyful ones being clothed with the garments of salvation and the robe of righteousness. Jesus' declaration that he was naked and "ye clothed me" would be inconsequential if taken as a historical fact. But in *II Corinthians* (Ch. 5) Paul gives strong confirmation of the higher sense:

"(For in this we groan, earnestly desiring to be clothed upon with our house which is from heaven. If so be that being clothed we shall not be found naked. For we that are in this tabernacle do groan, being burdened; not for that we should be unclothed, but clothed upon, that mortality might be swallowed up of life)."

"It makes me sigh, indeed, this yearning to be under the cover of my heavenly habitation, since I am sure that once so covered I shall not be 'naked' at the hour of death. I do sigh within this tent of mine with heavy anxiety—not that I want to be stripped, no, but to be under cover of the other, to have my mortal element absorbed by life . . . Come what may, then, I am confident; I know that while I reside in the body I am away from the Lord (for I have to lead my life in faith without seeing him); and in this confidence I would fain get away from the body and reside with the Lord."

This is direct and eloquent confirmation of Greek and Egyptian philosophy in the Christian Book. Here is the soul conscious of its alienation from heaven, miserably exiled in the flesh, made poor in spirit, yet striving resolutely to carry the mortal burden up the hill to its summit. *Revelation* (3:17) has a passage hardly less germane:

"Thou knowest not that thou art wretched and miserable and poor and blind and naked; I counsel thee to buy from me gold refined in the fire, that thou may be rich, white raiment to clothe you and prevent the shame of your nakedness from being seen, and salve to rub on your eyes that you may see."

Revelation (19:8) gives a definition of our spiritual clothing, when referring to the soul, the bride: "And to her was granted that she should be arrayed in fine linen, dazzling white; (the white linen is the righteousness of saints)." For those who rebel stubbornly against the mythical interpretation of the Bible, let it be noted that here the writer of holy gospel positively states that a physical thing, linen, *is* a spiritual quality.

And he that rode on the white horse is described as "clothed with a vesture dipped in blood; (his name is called THE LOGOS of God)." And here a Bible personage is merely a figure for an item of Greek philosophy! Will we not be instructed by such things?

It needs but to make the transfer in meaning from material to ethereal or spiritual clothing to discern the depth of practical significance in these allusions. The revelation will be lost only for those who persist in the assumption that Oriental imagery was so much fanciful froth, and not an endeavor to delineate by poetic figure a veridical basis of fact and phenomena. Instead of vaunting ourselves in superiority over presumed primitive crudity, we may have to demonstrate even our own good rating as pupils of sage wisdom when that is presented. The ancients had more to conceal than we yet seem capable of grasping.

Chapter XII

AMBROSIA AND NECTAR

THEOLOGICAL confusion over the ancient use of bread and wine and various foods as types of spiritual nourishment makes necessary a chapter to clarify these matters. All such figures—heavenly manna, bread, wheat, ambrosia, nectar, meat, corn, wine, honey, barley—are forms of typology suggestive of the deific life offered to mortals for their immortal nutriment. The body of spiritual intellect, Ceres, which was the true "cereal" food for man, was crushed into bits and then welded into cake so that it might be "eaten" by mortals. The body of Christ was the intellectual bread broken to be made edible and assimilable by our lower range of digestive capacity. We could not eat the god in his wholeness, or his rawness. The golden grain of life-giving wheat had to be crushed, ground, lacerated, before it could be rendered fit food for our consumption, in the Eucharistic cake and the sacrificial meal on the altar. Jesus says that we must "eat" his body, and the *Epistle of Ignatius to the Romans* (Apocryphal) says that the wheat of God must be ground between the teeth of wild animals, our animal bodies, to be made the pure bread of Christ.

The breaking of the bread and the libation of the wine are now clearly seen to be emblematic of the partition of the unified energy of the god's life for distribution to the races of men. The banquets of the gods, the Passover feasts, the funerary meals, the last suppers and the Totemic repasts were all forms of a primary Eucharist. Man was given the transcendent privilege of feeding upon the life of the gods! And it can be freely admitted that nowhere is the necessity of transferring a literal physical meaning over to a spiritual one more definitely apparent than here.

The final definitive meaning of the great Eucharistic rite is bound up in the reconstruction of lost significance in this doctrine. The entire debate as to the matter of transubstantiation, transfusion, the partaking of the material body and blood or their inner essence, finds its resolution in the premises of this interpretation. Strangely enough it is now seen to be possible to give up the physical meaning of the sacrament and yet take it as a thing of literal reality. Man is literally to eat his Lord's body; only it is not a physical body. The eating is literal and real enough, but neither it nor the body eaten is physical. Stout human good sense has revolted at a rite of swallowing a *physical* body, but theology has failed to picture how we can partake of a spiritual essence or body of divinity. The absorption and transmutation of currents of deific life in our own nature is as possible as our digestion of food. The physical rite was only a symbol and, its higher meaning once apprehended, its efficacy is secured. The eating of bread and drinking of wine outwardly dramatize the inner reality, a transubstantiation which can be literally, though not physically, true.

Says St. Paul:

> "shun idolatry, then, my beloved [doubtless the material sense of the symbols.]
> I am speaking to sensible people: weigh my words for yourselves.
> The cup of blessing which we bless,
>   is that not participating in the blood of Christ?
> The bread we break,
>   is that not participating in the body of Christ?
> (for many as we are, we are one Bread, one Body, since we all partake of the one Bread)." [1]

But the nauseous ecclesiastical wrangling over whether the bread and wine *were* the body and blood of a historical Jesus, or merely symbols of them, points to the frightful desecration of the wholly spiritual and figurative nature of the drama. The inner sense of this mighty typology passed out of ken with the submergence of Greek wisdom under canonical literalism. The body of Christ, emblemed by bread, wheat, ambrosia, meat, flesh or other forms of solid food, can mean nothing but the substantial essence of divine nature; the blood, wine, nectar, ichor, honey and liquid forms of nourishment can mean only that same divinity when liquefied to be poured out in streams of nourishment for man. The cutting of meat is to render it macerable; the grinding of grain is to render it edible; the crushing of the grape for wine is to liquefy it for drinking. In every case there is the destruction of the bodily integrity of the food, and a fragmentation for better assimilation. The ritualism of Christianity thus still dramatizes the principles of Greek spiritual philosophy, which it persists in denying as part of a true religious system. If we were to eat the body of *Christos* and drink his blood, the first had to be macerated and the second liquefied.

Briefly, solid food typified divine essence on its own high plane, the more ethereal states being the more substantial! Liquid forms emblemed the same divine nature poured out in streams, "rivers of vivification," for the feeding of "secondary natures." Also in its descent godhood became admixed with the "watery" elements of the life down here and were further liquefied thereby. Solid food was the emblem of stability; liquid food the sign of that mobile essence which was to run out in blessing.

The several symbols must be looked at more minutely, for they cover deep suggestions of vital meaning. We take first that of bread. There is in all literature no more direct and compelling statement of the spiritual significance of bread than the verses of John's Gospel (6:47 ff). Says Jesus:

"I am the bread of life. Your fathers did eat Manna in the wilderness and have died; such is the bread that *comes down from heaven,* that a man shall eat of it and shall not die.

"And in truth the bread which I shall give for the life of the world *is my flesh.*

"Verily, verily I say unto you, Unless you eat the flesh and drink the blood of the Son of Man, you have not life in you. He that eateth my flesh and drinketh my blood hath eternal life, and I will raise him up at the last day.

"For my flesh is food indeed and my blood is drink indeed. He that eateth my flesh and drinketh my blood abideth in me and I in him." [2]

The bread is, then, the radiant divine principle of light and life. The blood is the pledge of the same life poured out for man's behoof. But Jesus was not the only divine personage who offered his body and blood for the nourishment of mortals. Says Massey:

"Horus was not only the bread of life derived from heaven and the producer of bread in the character of Amsu, the husbandman; he also gave his flesh for food and his blood for drink." [3]

234

Horus says (*Rit.*, Ch. 53A): "I am the possessor of bread in Annu. I have bread in heaven with Ra." Again the deceased says: "I am the lord of cakes in Annu; and my bread is in heaven with Ra, and my cakes are on the earth with the god Seb." The distinction here between bread in heaven and cakes on earth is perhaps of vast significance, matching, as it does, many assertions that the soul is in heaven and the body on earth. The cake form of the divine pastry must have been regarded as a state of soul more highly advanced or refined by organic evolution. Many texts carry out the two types. The soul continues: "I eat of what they [the gods] eat there; and I eat of the cakes which are in the hall of the lord of sepulchral offerings"—or bread with the gods in heaven and cakes with the "dead" on earth. And in the Rubric to the 71st chapter of the *Ritual* this meaning is confirmed: "Sepulchural bread shall be given to him and he shall come forth into the presence of Ra day by day, and every day, regularly and continually." Sepulchral bread, like the funerary meals, undoubtedly refers to the "bread of Seb," or food of earth, earth and body being the sepulcher of the soul.

Wheat is much employed as a symbol. The law of divine incubation in matter is expressly intimated in Budge's account of the Resurrection in Egypt:

"The grain which is put into the ground is the dead Osiris, and the grain which has germinated is the Osiris who has once again renewed his life." [4]

The resurrection of Osiris is closely interwoven with the germination of wheat. Jesus announces: "My father giveth you the true bread out of heaven: For the bread of God is that which cometh down out of heaven and giveth life unto the world." And as Jesus was the divine bread out of heaven, the consubstantial essence with the Father, so Horus: "He is Horus, he is the flesh and blood of his father Osiris." Horus in his Christological character says: "I am a soul and my soul is divine. I am he who produceth food. I am the food that perisheth not—in my name of self-originating force, together with Nu"—the Mother Heaven. (*Rit.*, Ch. 85).

The body of Christ could not be mystically eaten in its wholeness and unreduced power. It had to be crushed and bruised, broken and mutilated, so that from its deep gashes would flow out the living streams. If taken literally and materially, the wounded side is not only gruesome, but carries only a feeble suggestion of its grand meaning. And herein lies the spiritual meaning of all blood sacrifice and "shed blood." There is no truth found in it until for "blood" (of the gods) we read "divine intellect." Had early theology made it clear, in a word, that the "shed blood" of God connoted spiritual force, which we must embody in our lives, there would have been a vastly less amount of actual "bloodshed" in European history! The god shed his life essence for us out of his earth-bruised body of deific mind.

On this divine wheat, it is said, Osiris and his followers lived. It was a form of Osiris himself, as the god who brought it from heaven, and those who ate it and lived upon it nourished themselves upon their god. As he came to feed them, he is declared to have "provided them with food and drink as he passed through the Tuat." How the partaking of the divine body would affect man is set forth by Budge:

"Eating and drinking with the spirits raised man's nature and 'made his spirit divine,' and destroyed the feeling of separation which came with the appearance of death . . . And it must always be remembered that the altar was the place to possess the power of transmuting the offerings which were laid upon it and of turning them into spiritual entities of such a nature that they became suitable food for the god Osiris and his spirits." [5]

But we are those spirits, the living men or Manes in this underworld. The recovered Logia, or "sayings of the Lord," give a most direct allusion to the dismemberment doctrine of the Eucharist in the line: "the flesh of the Son of God, broken for all souls."

By a slight shifting of the symbol, the ceremony performed in the rites of many lands, of eating the serpent and drinking the dragon's blood, was a replica of the Eucharistic festival. For the serpent was universally a type of supernal wisdom—"wise as serpents"—or the intellectual nature of the gods.

Horus, we find, was the Kamite prototype of Bacchus, Lord of Wine. Like Bacchus and Jesus, Horus is the vine, whose season was celebrated at the Uaka festival, with prodigious rejoicing and a deluge of drink. The divine mania, declared by Plato to be better than laborious reason, was the heady transport resulting from the imbibing of the spiritual liquor of life. The Bacchic feast of intoxication was, however sensual in later performance, a token of the legitimate and blessed ecstasy of the soul upon partaking of the heavenly wine. The vine and the mixing bowl were constellated as celestial symbols, the latter as the cluster called the Crater (Latin: bowl) or the Goblet, the sacramental cup or grail. The juice of the grape was the blood of Horus or Osiris, in the Egyptian Eucharist.

The Manes in one of the chapters in the *Ritual* prays that he may have possession of all things whatsoever that were offered ritualistically for him in the nether world, the "table of offerings which was heaped" for him on earth, "the solicitations that were uttered" for him, "that he may feed upon the bread of Seb," or food of earth experience. "Let me have possession of my funeral meals." A fact that should loom large in any valuation of Eucharistic meaning is that the flat surface of the coffin lid of the mummified Osiris constituted the table of the Egyptian Last Supper. It was the board whereon were served the mortuary meals. This unmistakable connection of the Eucharist with the burial, which is only the passing of the god into the mummy or incarnate form, speaks volubly as to the hidden relation of the two symbolic operations. For the god, about to be buried in body, was to be *eaten* by the mortal nature.

Ancient tribes indulged in the rite of a symbolic feeding upon the body of their god. At times when spiritual symbology had passed into the literalism of ignorance and barbarity, a living victim was cut to pieces and actually eaten by the celebrants. In very early periods of the matriarchate, when the mother was the only known giver and fount of life, a living mother was dedicated to the office of *hostia* or victim, and her body cut up and eaten as a token of the distribution of her fecund life. "The primordial Eucharist was eating the Mother's flesh and drinking her blood!" [6] A converted phase of this custom exhibits the idea of the "disrobing" combined with the Eucharistic rite:

"A young girl called (significantly) the Meriah, was stripped stark naked and bound with cords to a maypole crowned with flowers, and ultimately put to death . . . torn in pieces and partly eaten." [7]

Human sacrifices were later commuted to animal offerings. And when crude natural instincts were softened by humane ideals, bread and wine were substituted. Thus one can see how an original spiritual conception, passing from hand to hand in the lapse of time and changing *mores*, reverts at one time to a brutal literalism amongst untamed peoples, and again rises to symbolism in more cultured races. Through all stages, however, can be seen the lineaments of the germinal high spiritual idea back of each rite.

One of the Egyptian texts reads: "Shesmu cuts them in pieces and cooks them in his fiery cauldrons." Another line runs: "O, Osiris-Pepi, the Sma-Bull is brought to thee cut in pieces."

Expressing a phallic significance to the ritual, it is of interest to note that in very remote tribal celebrations of the Eucharist the female participants invited the fecundating offices of the males. The two sisters, or wife and sister, of Horus plead with the still recumbent god to arise and come and embrace them. There are two women in the Biblical resurrection scene. And when Isis and Nephthys invite the young lord to come to them, Isis says: "Thou comest to us from thy retreat to . . . *distribute the bread of thy being,* that the gods may live and men also." This is of transcendent importance as pointing to the verification of the basic thesis of our study, that the dip into incarnation is an avenue of evolutionary advance for both the god and the animal-human in their linked lives. It is striking that in this context both Jesus and Horus are themselves raised up from death, and both raise up in turn those below. Two far separate streams of evolution are confluent in man, and both are going onward as the result of their co-operative life in one body. The Manes pleads:

"May I go in and come out without repulse at the pylons of the lords of the underworld; may there be given unto me loaves of bread in the house of coolness, and offerings of food in Annu (Heliopolis) and a homestead forever in Sekhet-Aarru (paradise), with wheat and barley therefor." [8]

And the Rubric to this chapter recites that if the chapter be known by the Manes he shall come forth in Sekhet-Aarru, "and he shall eat of that wheat and barley and his limbs shall be nourished therewith, and his body shall be like unto the bodies of the gods." Here is perfect matching of Egyptian script with Paul's statement that Christ shall "change our vile body into the likeness of his glorious body."

Holy Thursday was especially consecrated by the Roman Church to a commemoration of the Last Supper, and the institution of the Eucharistic meal was fixed, at which the corpus of the Christ, already dead, was laid out to be eaten sacramentally. In the Gospels the Last

Supper, with Jesus present, is eaten *before* the crucifixion has occurred. There is obviously confusion of ancient ritualistic practice here, yet strangely enough no grave violence is done to the inner significance either way, since the Christ was "dead" in the one sense, and alive in the other. The whole of incarnation is the "crucifixion, death and burial" of the Lord.

After the raising of Osiris Taht says: "I have celebrated the festival of Eve's provender," or the meal which came to be called the Last Supper. The raising of Lazarus is likewise commemorated by a supper. "So they made him a supper there" (*John* 12:2).

In the Greek Mystery play the candidate for initiation underwent the *taurobolium* or bull's-blood bath. He stood under a grating and received upon his naked body the dripping blood of the sacrificial bull, in token that his nature was being suffused with the shed blood of the god emblemed by the astrological sign of Taurus, as in Christian practice it was the blood of the ram or lamb, the zodiacal Aries. The sign of the sun in the spring equinox determined the zodiacal type under which the *Christos* was figured. Elsewhere animal blood was actually drunk as a more literal partaking of the emblem of divine life.

In the *Ritual* the evening meal depicted the absorption of the higher nature into and by the lower, and the occasion was called the "Night of Laying Provision on the Altar." Not in a given moment of time, but in the total course of the cycle, each physical body was to be transubstantiated into spirit. The whole round of human incarnations was provided to this end. As the physical was converted into sublimated essence, we have an explanation of the strange disappearance of the physical body in all resurrection scenes. In one of the texts cited by Birch concerning the burial of Osiris at Abydos, it is said that the sepulchral chamber was searched, but the body was not found. "The 'Shade' it was found." [9] In Marcion's account of the resurrection no body is found in the tomb; only the phantom or shade was visible there. So in the Johannine version (Ch. 20:17) the body of Jesus is missing; the "Shade" is present in the tomb. But this was of a texture which forbade its being touched.

The night of the evening meal was called also "the night of *hiding* him who is supreme of attributes" (*Rit.*, Ch. 18). We have seen that

239

the descent into the tomb of body was considered a hiding, and the period of incarnation was called the night of the soul.

The Eucharistic emblems are many and varied. The deceased in the *Ritual* prays: "Grant unto me ale, and let me cleanse myself by means of the haunch and by the offerings of cakes." In Chapter 65 cakes of white grain and ale of red grain are mentioned. The juxtaposition of the statements in the following citation is noteworthy, as identifying the emblems with their non-material references: "Thou descendest under protection; are given unto thee bread, wine and cakes . . . thou art endowed with a soul, with power and with will." "He hungers not, for he eats bread-cakes made of fine flour . . . He lives on the daily bread which comes in this season"—of incarnation. "He shall have offered wine and cakes and roasted fowl for the journey . . ." The bird was a universal symbol of the soul, and its descent into the lower fires of earth and hell provided the basis of the allegory of "roasting." In Chapter 106 the Manes says: "Give me bread and beer. Let me be made pure by the sacrificial joint, together with white bread." Horus is both the bread of life and the divine corn (*Rit.*, Ch. 83). In *I Corinthians* (37:38) Paul has a remarkable imagery of divine food:

"And that which thou sowest, thou sowest not that body that shall be, but bare grain, it may chance of wheat, or of some other grain. But God giveth it a body as it hath pleased him, and to every seed his own body."

The remarkable passage from the Apocryphal *Epistle of Ignatius to the Romans,* already quoted, should be recalled at this point, as it definitely states that the soul comes to be food to the wild beasts, by whom it will attain its new godhood. The figure of the soul as wheat, ground between the teeth of the wild animals to be made the pure bread of Christ, is a most pungent typograph,—of the incarnation. And this passage prepares the ground for understanding the relevance of the manger symbolism in the Nativity scene. The Christ, at birth, was laid in a manger, the place where animals eat! He came to be eaten by the lower, animal nature.

In the *Ritual* the soul entreats: "Give thou bread to this Pepi, give thou beer to him, of the bread of eternity, and of the beer of everlastingness." "This bread which can not go mouldy is brought to Pepi, and this wine which can not go sour." What sublime imagery for states of spiritual immortality, and natures that change not!

A special feature in connection with the Eucharistic bread is seen in several passages from the *Ritual*, which are of great weight in stabilizing the general position of the purely figurative nature of the symbols. It is found in the chapter "of not eating filth in the underworld":

"Let food come unto me *from the place whither thou wilt bring food,* and let me live upon the *seven* loaves of bread, which shall be brought as food before Horus, and upon bread which is brought before Thoth . . . Let me not eat filth and let me not trip up and fall in the underworld."

Again in the "chapter of not letting a man perform a journey being hungry" we read:

"Let me live upon the *seven* cakes which shall be brought unto me, four cakes before Horus, and three cakes before Thoth."

Four is the number of the lower physical world of the body, three the number of the soul as the triad of mind, soul, spirit. Horus was the soul in matter, Thoth the cosmic spirit.

Massey writes that a three-days fast was ended by the feeding of the multitude on what the *Ritual* terms "celestial diet," i.e., the "seven loaves" of heavenly bread that were supplied as sustenance for the risen dead in Annu, *"the place of multiplying bread."* In this phrase descriptive of Annu (Anu), one of the cities named as both the place of death and resurrection of the sun-god, we find the open sesame to the *New Testament* "miracle" of Jesus feeding the multitude. But in the Gospel "miracle," instead of the seven loaves we have the five loaves and the two small fishes, the latter being introduced evidently to bring in the Piscean house along with Virgo, the house of bread.

Hebrew symbology closely matches Egyptian. In *Exodus* (29) one reads that

"With the former lamb you must offer about *seven* pints of fine flour mixed with nearly three pints of beaten oil, and nearly three pints of wine as a libation . . . This is to be a regular burnt-offering made, age after age, at the entrance of the Trysting-Tent before the Eternal, where I meet you and speak to you."

If it was known that this Trysting-Tent is the human body, where alone God can meet man and speak to him, and that the three pints of oil and wine stand for the three elements of divine consciousness that are to be mixed with the seven elementary powers of nature or *physis*, the brotherhood of man might not so fearfully have miscarried. The human body is the place where the two lovers, spirit and matter, or body and soul, make their tryst, and that they are to make their libation to the Eternal before the entrance to the tent indicates that the higher and lower partners to the coming marriage compound their elements as they enter into incarnation. One stroke of symbolism tells us more than volumes of theology.

Divine food is called sometimes simply "meat." "Thou hast in great abundance in the Fields of the Gods the meat and drink which the gods live upon therein."

Even butter comes in as a type of representation, and coming from a female source, indicates the material foundation of life. The seven cows of Hathor produce the divine butter. As the formation of primal matter out of the primeval undifferentiated essence was pictured as a kind of curdling, the butter symbolism has a profound cosmical significance.

The Manes' life is fed upon divine food throughout its sojourn in Amenta; Horus and Jesus, Jonah and Ioannes of Babylonia, all came as the zodiacal Pisces, or the Fish, offering themselves as food for man while he is immersed in the *sea* of generation! The Egyptians saw in the tortoise, which lived half in water and half on land, the sign of Libra, the Balance, and took it as another type of divine nourishment, when the two natures, divine and human, are in equilibration in the body.

When the Manes have sufficiently cultivated the fields of Aarru, Ra says to them: "Your own possessions, gods, and your own domains, elect, are yours. Now eat. Ra . . . appoints you your food." They have labored at cultivation and at last they collect their harvest of corn. Their seeds are warmed into germination by the sunlight of Ra at his appearance. The radiance of the god in human life causes the divine seed buried in us to sprout and grow as the sun fructifies plants in any earthly garden. The elect, enveloped in light, are fed mysteriously with food from heaven. Milk is one of the types used and is called "the white liquor which the glorified ones love," and it was supplied by the seven cows, providers of plenty in the meadows of Aarru. The seven cows, of course, emblem the seven modifications of cosmic energy which create and sustain the worlds of life, the appropriate counterparts of which irradiate man's being and formulate his basic constitution. The uplifted Manes says: "I eat of the food of Sekhet-Hetep and I go onward to the domain of the starry gods." The zodiacal twelve supply food to the gods and the elect in two groups, seven reapers and five collectors of corn (*Book of Hades*). The spiritualized Manes live on the food of Ra, "and the meats belong to the inhabitants of Amenta," a possible reference to the animal bodies on earth. The divine food is apparently repeated in the quails and manna that were sent from heaven in the Biblical account. The Osiris-Nu asserts: "I am the divine soul of Ra proceeding from the god Nu; that divine soul which is God. I am the creator of the divine food . . . which is not corrupted in my name of Soul." This soul "comes to him and brings him abundance of celestial food, and what the god lives on he also lives on, and he partakes of the food and drink and offerings of the god." At another place we are told that the Manes "maketh his purificatory substances with figs and wine from the vineyard of the god."

As the living rivers flow forth out of the heart of eternal matter, the womb of all life, the godly nutriment is again proffered to man streaming from the breast of the Mother Isis or Hathor. "She giveth him her breast and he suckleth thereat." Paul (*I Corinthians* 10:1, 2) writes that all those in Christ have eaten "the same supernatural food and all drank the same supernatural drink (drinking from the supernatural Rock which accompanied them—and that Rock was Christ)." *Revelation* (2:17) enlightens us with the following: "To him that overcometh, to him will I give of the hidden manna." When the deceased is making his way through Amenta, Hathor, the Egyptian Venus, goddess of Love, emerges from the trees and offers him a drink of fruit juice, which she prepared to woo him with. By accepting this gift he is bound to remain the guest of the goddess and return no more to the world of the living, unless by her permission. This fruit is not that which is sent down gratuitously from heaven, but the fruit of the soul's living experience on earth, yet it is the same thing in the end. For it is sent down as seed, and bears its fruit on the ends of the branches of the Tree of Life and Knowledge, of the taste of good and evil here on earth. And this is the same tree which in the *last* chapter in the Bible is declared to bear twelve fruits upon its branches. These twelve fruits are the completed unfoldment of the twelve original types of Kumaric infant deity that will be brought to their maturity by cultivation on this planet. The bread of Seb becomes metamorphosed eventually into the divine food. Eve and Hathor are identical figures. They offer to virgin spiritual units and to animal man the opportunity to live, grow and create, out of which cycle they will emerge as gods, through knowledge of good and evil. And the temptation is baited with the promise, "yet shall not surely die." The fruit of earthly life is divinization. Says Massey:

"Hathor was the goddess draped in golden vesture, who drew men with the cords of a love that was irresistible."

"Instead of being damned eternally through eating the fruit of the tree, the Manes in Amenta are divinized piecemeal as the result of eating it." (*Rit.*, Ch. 82).[10]

Again pause must be made to reflect that had these two items of theology been known in clear light, as here presented, whole centuries of human bigotry and hate might have been painted in brighter colors.

Red as the color of blood, and white, the color of milk, emblem the two natures of man, his bodily birth through the mother's blood, and his later nourishment through her milk. Red is connected closely with the first Adam, whose name means in one interpretation, Red Earth, that is, physical matter mixed with red blood. In this character he would be the answer to the Bible's query, "Who is this that comes from Edom, with his *garments crimson* from Bozrah?" Edom was this man Adam, red earth, mortal clay mixed with the life essence of divinity typed by the blood, in which the *Old Testament* affirms several times the life of the soul is to be found. And he who comes out of Edom may be taken as the Christ, the Son of Man. For the first Adam is to give birth to the second Adam. Blood here types the divine part of man, as contrasted with earth or with water. Jesus emblems the two births as those of "water and the blood." But when the blood is used to typify the lower natural man then it is contrasted with the white essence, the mother's milk, a higher nutriment than her blood, or with the father's seminal essence. White universally types that which is spiritually highest, up to the shining white raiment of the redeemed. Perfection being the synthesis of all lower or divided natures in original unity, white represents that perfection, as it is the synthesis of the

244

colors. Ra says to the god: "Light the earth up bright! My benefits are for you who are in the light." The food he promised them is itself of the nature of intellectual light. "The immortal liquor is the Solar Light." [11] No utterance surpasses this for sublime import. A *Chaldean Oracle* asserts that "the Intelligible is food to that which understands." And the solar light *is* intelligence, shining abroad.

Looking now at wine, many phases of meaning not commonly considered are brought to view. The grape and the vine share in the symbolism. There is first the significant detail, brought out by Massey, that the Egyptian Garden of Aarru, or Allu (the Islamic Garden of Allah!) has in the *Ritual* the same name as the grape, the vine-branch and the wine. The import of this is that the heavenly impartation of life typified by the wine is of the same essence as the substance of that celestial life itself in the Paradise above. The wine offered by the gods for man's uplift is their celestial nature.

Horus came as the lord of wine and is said to be "full of wine" at the Uaka festival. The old "festival of intoxication" is the prototype of all later communal rites that celebrate the outpouring of lofty deity. The form of this festival has become universally popular, but as usual its interior meaning has been lost. The Christian Agape and Eucharist are moderate demonstrations of the same old effort to commemorate the perpetual gift of divine afflatus to mankind. Horus achieved the sub-title of "the Jocund" when he rose up "full of wine," and was astrologically typed as Orion, with the constellation of the Crater or bowl for his cup. The fable said that this cup held seven thousand gallons of intoxicating drink and that Horus brought the grapes to make the wine. "Thou didst put grapes in the water that cometh forth from Edfu." The seven thousand had no explicit numerical significance beyond the number seven itself, the thousands only adding the idea of multiple division and diffusion. Horus came to distribute to the thousands of mortals the divine essence in its seven-fold expression in the full gamut of its nature. Who shall prove that the Jesus of the canonical Gospels, who gained notoriety as a wine-bibber and came eating and drinking, is not a frayed copy of this Kamite original? For Greece in her Bacchus repeated the same type. Christ came to intoxicate man with the divine wine.

In the Assyrian account of the Deluge those who came out of the ark poured out a libation of *seven* jugs of wine. And they built an

245

altar on the peak of the mountain, or set up contact between man and god at the summit of man's spiritual being. Likewise after the Deluge Noah planted the vine and became intoxicated. This vine may be seen in the decans of Virgo, where the star Vindemeatrix denotes the time of the vintage in Egypt, a symbol of the infusion of the higher nature into the lower.

The Christ treading the grapes in the winepress is all very like the portrait of Har-Tema (Horus), the mighty avenger of his despoiled father, and he came at the end and the re-beginning of the cycle of incarnation, which is called the year of redemption. Careful research discloses that Edom is another name for Esau, the Red; he had asked to be fed with pottage, translated in one text "red." Edom, not identical with Eden, seems to refer to earth as the "red land." In all its Biblical usages Edom refers to the lower kingdom of human nature, not the celestial sphere in any case. Edom was heavily punished by the Eternal, David put garrisons in it and reduced its people to servants, and they later revolted. It refused passage to the Israelites, as the lower nature refused entry to the godly part. In *Obadiah* (I:6) we read: "But what a ransacking of Edom! What a rifling of her treasures!" Edmonites were Esau's descendants. The avenging god's anger (dramatization merely, of course) is apparently vented upon the lower propensities of human nature, which are the foes of his incarnating enterprise, the obstructors of his path and mutilators of his father Osiris. The figure of treading the winevat is a noble one and definitely points to the earth as the great winepress wherein the essence of the mortal nature is crushed and trampled by deity into a liquor to reinforce the god's dying life. That the god trod the winepress alone is evidence of the loneliness of his mission. Jesus' loneliness is accentuated in the Gospel drama. That the god comes from the underworld stained with the blood of his foes is an allegorical way of saying that he had not kept himself entirely "unspotted from the world" in his wrestling with the flesh. Greek philosophy asserts that his garments were badly stained by terrene contacts.

Plutarch tells us that the Egyptian priests conceived vines to have sprung from the blood of those fallen deities mixed with the earth. A Babylonian legend sets forth that the blood of the god Belus was mixed with the earth in the same way. Man is compounded of the mud of earth for his body, and the blood of the gods for his animating soul. He is Adam, red earth.

Hathor, the great mother of the living in Egyptian mythology, pours out the heavenly drink made from the fruit of the sycamore-fig tree, a most prominent ancient form of the tree of life. Hathor was the Shekhem, or shrine of the child, figured as the bearing tree, the genetrix, the womb, bird-cage and significantly the tomb, not that of final death, but of buried life about to germinate. The word Shekhem, hidden shrine, is from *sekh*, "liquid," "drink." *Teka* means "to supply with drink." The fig, like the pomegranate, is an emblem of the womb. The Persea fruit is the fruit of the sycamore-fig tree. Sycamore is from *sykos* (*sukos*), the Greek for the fig-tree, from the fruit of which a powerful beverage was made. The root means latent power unfolded, as by fermentation; to fill with aeriform spirit force, as by the bubbles of air in fermentation. It becomes possible now to sense the meaning of Jesus' pronouncement (*Luke* 17:6):

"If ye have faith as a grain of mustard seed ye would say unto this sycamore tree [Moffatt: 'mulberry'], Be thou rooted up and be thou planted in the sea; and it would have obeyed you."

As *Revelation* and the *Book of the Dead* both describe the entry of divine fire into the "sea," causing a fermentation in it to *spirit*ualize or divinize it, the sycamore's removal into the sea to lodge inspiriting power in it at last comes to clear significance. To have faith as a grain of mustard seed, so tiny, is for the soul, buried in the deep soil of the mortal self, to have an instinctive assurance that, like the life in any seed, it will rise out of death to live again.

Who can fail to trace the *Genesis* story in the following legend preserved among the Hottentots? The deity, Heitsi Eibib, tells his son Urisip, the whitish one, not to eat of the raisin trees in the valley. Heitsi Eibib in his travels came to a valley (the earth) in which the raisin trees were ripe. There he was attacked by a severe illness. Then his young second wife (Eve is often called Adam's second wife, Lilith being the first) said: "This brave one is taken ill on account of these raisins; death is here at the place." The old man told his son: "I shall not live, I feel it." And he spoke further: "This is the thing which I order you not to do: Of the raisin trees of this valley ye shall not eat, for if ye eat of them I shall infect you; and ye shall surely die in a similar way." So he died. When they moved to another place, they heard always from the side whence they had come a noise as of people eating raisins and singing. The song ran:

> "I, father of Urisip,
> Father of this unclean one;
> I, who had to eat these raisins and died,
> *And dying, live.*"

The raisin tree gave dysentery, and this natural detail was used to prefigure the sickness, swooning, distress and intoxication that came over the gods upon their plunge into this life, or their eating of the fruit of the tree whose juice made them drunk with a mixture of spiritous and sensuous ingredients. This is, in short, to type the effect of incarnation upon the god as a bewildering, befuddling, stupefying drunkenness, as from a semi-poison injected into his blood; and such indeed the Platonists have ever described it.

"Heaven is pregnant with wine" is an Egyptian fragment.

In the *Book of Judges* (Ch. 6) Gideon, the son of Joash, is found beating out some wheat *inside the winepress* to save it from Midian, when the angel of the Lord comes down to entrust him with the commission to redeem Israel. What appears here like a mixed metaphor is perhaps only a close mingling of several customary symbols. Beating out the chaff was a kindred figure with that of stamping out the wine.

Greek philosophy, rising sphinxlike out of the Orphic Mysteries, proclaims a hidden meaning of the grapes in the winepress. Thomas Taylor says that the pressing of grapes is as evident a symbol of the dispersion of divine energy into humanity as could well be devised.[12] The grape was for this reason consecrated to Bacchus, who personalized empyreal intelligence flowing out in divided streams. Previous to its pressing it aptly represented that which is collected into one; when pressed into juice it aptly represented the diffusion of the same. Hence wine-pressing symbols the crushing and division of unity to flow into multiplicity and spiritize divided creatural life. What is most singular is that Taylor likens this process to another oft-used typology, that of fleece, stating that the Greek word for "wool," *lēnos,* is practically identical with that for a "winepress," *lēnôs.* The tearing and carding of wool matches the liquidation of the grape for purposes of typism. Should it be deemed strange, then, that Gideon, found threshing wheat in the winepress, should immediately ask the Eternal to authenticate his commission to him by the test of the dew on the fleece? It need hardly be pointed out what strength these symbols of wine and fleece, along with flour, bring to the theory of dismemberment. And there is also the obvious suggestion of the fruitful rendering of the symbolism of the mythological Golden Fleece (Aries of the zodiac), as typing the Christ avatar who came under that sign. Fleece, says Taylor, is the symbol of laceration or distribution of intellect, or Dionysus, into matter; and he adds that Isidorus traces *lana* (Latin: "wool") from *laniando*, "tearing," as *vellus* (Latin: "fleece") from *vellendo*, also "tearing." *"Delano,"* "to tear asunder," he uses "in relation to Bacchic discerption." So succinctly and integrally is the history of ideas preserved in the amber of words.

Massey explains:

"The typical tree of life in an Egyptian-Greek planisphere is the grapevine. This is the tree still represented by the female vine-dresser and the male grape-gatherer in the decans of Virgo [W. H. Higgins, *Arabic Names of the Stars*]. Orion rose up when the grapes were ripe to represent the deliverer who was coming 'full of wine.'" [13]

The birthplace of the grapes was figured in or near the sign of Virgo, the mother of the child who was to rise up out of death to bring salvation to lower man under the symbol of the vine. He was also typed as the rising Nile, bringing a new birth to the parched land of Egypt. And the grape ripened with the rising inundation! In ways that astonish us with the fidelity of the parallelism, both natural and astronomical phenomena reflect man's inner history.

The vine and sycamore tree were two types of producing life in the Kamite Paradise. In the *Papyrus of Nu* the Manes prays that he may sit under his own vine and also beneath the refreshing foliage of the sycamore-fig tree of Hathor. The Garden of Aarru is the garden of the grape, and the god Osiris is sometimes seated in a Naos, under the vine, from which branches of grapes are hanging. Moreover Osiris was characerered as the vine and his son Horus the *unbu* or Branch. Need we pause to point out the identity of this with the Biblical sentence (*I Kings* 4:25): "And Judah and Israel dwelt safely, every man under his vine and under his fig-tree"?

Jesus was the true vine of the Logos and we are his branches, destined to bear the fruit. Horus bore the same representative character in Egypt. The American Indians have traditions of tribes climbing to safety across the Mississippi, or up out of the interior of mother earth to the land of light, by means of trees with overhanging branches and grapevines. (Schoolcraft: VI, 14). Jack climbing the bean stalk to overcome the ogre is a variant of the aboriginal type-legend.

The Eucharist easily lends itself to characterization as a festival of intoxication if it is viewed in the light of the following lines from the *Ritual:* "Are not all hearts drunk through love of thee, O Un-Nefer (Osiris), triumphant?" The entire body of mystic testimony from St. Augustine to St. Francis of Assizi and on through to the modern revivalist, is to the effect of the spiritual intoxication of the supreme love frenzy or mania, as Plato terms it. It needs no descanting to enhance it further. There is every warrant for the ancient imagery. Only it must be seen as working at both ends of the gamut. The meaning covered by intoxication is dual, good and (relatively) bad. The god suffered an evil intoxication, a swooning and giddy stupefaction after his entry into mortal body; while mortal man undergoes a more positive intoxication, an exaltation and marvelous giddy expansion of his faculties when he becomes filled with the power of divine intellect and begins to feel its influence expanding the whole range and vividness of his consciousness. The one is to be thought of as a scattering of wits, the other as an overpowering afflatus. Yet incarnation is the open doör to both god and animal for the advance into higher life, and their opposite elements finally so merge in the new expansion that the intoxication is the same for both in the end. The god, drunk with animal sensual enjoyment, and the animal mind, intoxicated with undreamed-of delirium, reel onward together in the dance of life, and who shall sharply distinguish where intoxication ends and ecstasy begins? All this is germane to the understanding of the symbolism and the irrefragible factuality behind it.

The Delaware Indians put into effect an outward demonstration of the intoxicating imagery when in one of their festivals an old man threw handfuls of tobacco on heated stones in a tent, and the sitters, narcotized by the fumes, were carried out in a swoon. The ceremony typed the inhalation of spirit, producing a delirious rapture. Vapor has ever been a mode of representing spirit, and the smoke of the Indian's

250

pipe was suggestive of allaying the fierce nature of rude forest children to mildness and *peace*.

The Egyptian typology placed a Lake of Sa in the northern heavens. Sa was the name of a sort of ichor that circulated in the veins of the gods and perfected mortals. This they could communicate to men on earth and give them health, vigor and new life. This datum will be of significance when we come to study the Egyptian spirit body, the Sahu.

Honey, as symbol, shared place with the Greek nectar served at the tables of the Olympian gods. Its plain suggestion is of the sweetness of the divine life as sustenance for starving mortals, and as bestowing immortality. Some of its relevance of course can be traced to its origin from the bee. There is a tradition that bees alone of all animals descended from Paradise. Virgil (*Georgics* IV) celebrates the never-dying bee that ascends alive into heaven. The faithful diligent insect is thus an image of the immortal soul, or the god. Egyptian typology makes the Abait, or bird-fly, the guide of the souls of the dead on their way to the fields of Aarru, the land of celestial honey. The "bee-line" directness of travel betokens the unerring sense of the soul, lost afar in Amenta's fields, to go straight home. This Aarru is, of course, "Jerusalem the Golden, with milk and *honey* blest" of the Christian hymn. The *"ba"* name of the astral or ethereal body of man in Egypt may be related to "bee." For *ba* is also a word for "honey." Honey was used in embalming. It is suggestively entwined with the imagery of the "meads of amaranth." The soul is as the bee gathering sweet honey of immortality from the flowers of life experience on earth. Also the bee reproduces the new life in plants by acting as the intermediator between male and female flower elements; and the divine soul likewise links male spirit and female body and marries them in man.

The myth represents the sun, eternal type of divine generative source, as "letting water fall from his eyes; it is changed into working bees; they work in the flowers of each kind, and honey and wax are produced instead of water." Shu and Tefnut give honey to the living members. Divine emanations, falling as tear drops, diffuse their power of blessing over the earth, like Shakespeare's "gentle rain from heaven."

The Samson story in *Judges* bears on the meaning of honey. "Out

251

of the strong came forth honey." The honey was found by the solar god (Samson means "solar") in the decaying carcass of the lion upon his return. The return types evolution, as the outward journey, involution. The god, as the lion, is "slain" on the outward arc or descent, overcome by matter. But in evolution, the bees (the soul) have built their nest of sweet honey in the very midst of the old decay, in the very body of corruption. In the Persian myth we see the lion depicted with a bee in his mouth.

There are, however, intimations of involved astrological reference in the linking together of the bee and the lion. Massey thinks that the bee typifies the sweet refreshing waters of the inundation in Egypt, which came to its fullest outpouring in the month of July, the sign of the lion. His elaboration of the point is lengthy and the reader is referred to his *Lecture on Luniolatry*. The lion, or lioness, he claims, types the fiery solar heat (Cf. the lioness in heat) and the bee the cooling influence of the waters. For the hero, Samson, fairly immersed in symbols of the number thirty, obviously is a soli-lunar character, and the full moon in the lion sign rose in conjunction with the sign of Aquarius, the Waterman. The moon brought the cool waters that conquered the solar heat. The application of the typism may hint at the god's bringing the force of cool intellectual judgment to allay the fierce heat of sensual passion of the lower self. The types of divinity in the summer season are the reverse of those appropriate to the winter. Salvation comes to man in the heat of summer in the form of shade, coolness and water. Earth and water type the lower self and the evil side under winter's symbolism. But they spell salvation under reversed conditions. The duality and reversibility of the symbols must be constantly borne in mind.

The most meaningful aspect of the wine symbolism is perhaps that of fermentation. This arises from the development in the liquid of a potent energy at first latent. Hidden and buried, silent and inert, the dynamic fiery spirit rises to activity and exerts an influence that yields to mortals a semblance of divine inspiration and glorious liberty. As a symbol it is far-reaching and vivid. The "spirit" in wine and the spirit in man are not inaptly related even as a pun. The Greeks indulged in such puns, as in the *Cratylus* of Plato, and yet have covered the most majestic significations under these light touches. The "spirit" in wine is a graphic figure of the other spirit. Wine is water that has in it the fire of spirit, and in American pioneer days it was often called "fire-water." Fire universally typed spirit. Grape juice is just water of earth that has had injected in it a power engendered by the sun, again the type of spirit, as it passed through the length of the vine to be deposited in the berry at the end. The sun, like the Christ it symboled in his "miracle" at Cana, turns water into wine in any vineyard!

The Egyptian goddess who represented the "spirit" of alcoholic fermentation was Sekhet, and her pictures show her carrying the sun-disk on the head of a lioness. Her name is also, says Massey, the name for the Bee. As a goddess Sekhet is the fiery energy of Mother Nature, which engenders the ferment out of which comes the soul, the bee. For she is also the goddess of sweetness or pleasure, literally "goddess of the honeymoon." She is designated the "force or energy of the gods, astonisher of mankind." (Birch, *Gallery,* p. 17.) She was the inspirer of the male, his Sakti, or creative force. The Egyptian *sakh* means "to inflame," "to inspire," and Sekhet is the double force personified as female. This *sakh* brings us close again to the *syc-* of the sycamore fig, whose juice bred spirit intoxication, and the Greek *psyche* hovers close in the background of this etymology. The soul is, or causes, the divine ferment in the body of life, developed there, as in the vine, by the sun of man's spiritual self. Drink and divinity are thus found under one name, as were fleece and grape, seven and peace, star and soul.

Isis, whose original variant names were Hes, Hesit, Sesit, Sesh, etc., also carries this element of Sekhet's function. Sesh means primarily "breath," which is the inspirer (Latin: *spiro,* I breathe) in the sense of imparting the gift of higher life of spirit to a creature "dead" in matter. Man was not finished until God had breathed into him divine breath. Ses, Sesh is "breath," "flame," "combustion"; also "the spirit of wine." From it Massey traces the *"svas"* from which we have the Swastika, the sign of vivifying fire,—*"tika"* meaning "cross."

Another root yields meaning along the same line. *Kep* means "to light," "kindle," "heat," "cause a ferment." And from it Massey derives the Greek fire-forger of the gods, Vulcan or Hephaestus, who is *Kep* and the Greek root of the Latin *aestas,* summer heat. He forges for the gods whatever needs to be shaped by fire. Vapor produced from water by heat was the primitive illustration for breath which gave a creature its soul. It was a natural marvel, this emergence of a principle of fiery

253

energy in vapor form, so likely a type of soul engendered in man out of the mixture of his lower earth and water elements.

Horus and Jesus, both turning water into wine, represented this transforming power of the god, maturing the inert elements of sense and feeling into spiritual character. Horus put grapes into the water, and "the water of Teta is as wine even as that of Ra." The Jewish Feast of the Tent or Tabernacle was a ceremony embodying the turning of water into wine.

There are many instances of rivers and seas being turned into blood. *Revelation* reports that at the sound of the angel's trumpet a mountain, around which lightning played (symbol of the divine emanations, Jove's thunderbolts), went down into the sea and changed its waters into blood. As the first forms of life were generated in sea water, their initial body plasms were just that water. In eras of evolution this primitive life fluid was gradually transmuted, by the operation upon it of ever higher voltages of life force, into that which eventually in man became human blood! Sea water has been turned into blood in man's constitution! Blood is the fluid containing the living dynamic, and the Bible states that the soul dwells in the blood. Now, astonishingly, chemical analysis reveals that sea water and human blood are identical in elementary composition. It has remained for science and ancient symbolism to combine in this latter day to tell us the hidden meaning of one of the great spiritual allegories that theology failed to interpret for eighteen centuries.

Blood is the last of the Eucharistic signs to be dealt with. Few Christians can tell capably why it was that the human race had to be redeemed by the blood of an innocent victim poured out for its guilt. There is so glaring an inference of vicariousness here that common sense has halted long before giving credence to this dogma. It seems to contravene all natural justice and leaves an unstudied laity incredulous and unconvinced. There could be found no ground of fitness in the necessity that made a being of a higher rank, a god, come down and suffer gratuitously for sins of ours. With its linkage to evolution and anthropology cut totally away from it, there was no way to connect the doctrine with elucidative reference. Even Massey revolts in horror from the Biblical verse, in the words of the Son: "My father! This day shalt thou refresh thyself in blood." The picture of a bloodlustful deity terrifies us. But such revulsion is gratuitous. The primal

254

implications hold nothing to cause us horror. The Son is only reminding the Father that the descent of his germinal essence into the blood of this human body would give him his next cycle of rebirth and renewal. "Day" is one of the glyphs for cycle, aeon, round of incarnation, as in *Genesis* with its seven "days" of creation. The god finds fresh experience and new conquest in each life; he renews himself like the phoenix or the eagle, when bathed in new blood-bodies in incarnation. In our cycle he does this in the blood of man. But what might well cause Massey and the whole world abhorrence is that blood as symbol should have been taken for blood as substance, and that a whole millennium and a half of alleged civilized history has been deluded with the picture of a human personage buying unearned redemption for a race by the gruesome act of pouring out the blood of his physical body on a wooden cross! Rational reaction from religion is largely, if not overwhelmingly, justified. To a degree distressing to contemplate religion has befogged the mind of the world by converting the forms of ancient tropism into a sense repugnant even to the intelligence of children.

The entire theological theme of blood sacrifice, so literalized in the *Old Testament* rites, reduces itself to the one simple meaning of divine life poured out to circulate vitally through the mental and spiritual veins of man on earth. Mortal man underwent a transfusion of deific "blood." Divine energies of consciousness course and thrill through our life. This higher infusion regenerates us, makes us new. The lamb slain on the altar was but the ceremonial token of this meaning. The bull-bath of Mithraic rites was the washing away of sin in the blood of the Tauric emanation of deity. On the other side, however, the consuming of the animal on the altar by fire that flashed down from heaven was the token of the transfiguration of the animal nature in man into immortal purity by the aeonial "burning" of the godly fire in life after life. Man was nourished in the blood of the gods; but the god was refreshed and nourished in the substance of animal life, as the candle flame feeds upon the animal tallow below it, converting it from gross substance into divine flame. That a race of people could for centuries believe that God demanded the killing and burning of actual animals on actual altars for his sensuous delight of sniffing the odors of roasting flesh—a sweet savor unto his nostrils—well nigh destroys faith in human intelligence. The imputation of gory sensualism to

255

supreme deity, the unconscionable assumption that he would delight in the slaughter of billions of his own creatures, and that he would discharge man's sins by accepting the suffering of a lower order of his creatures as yet incapable of sin, form a list of theological aberrations that have gone far to throw the general mind into nearly barbarian besottedness.

The cleansing power of the blood was in part at least borrowed from the fact of the menstrual process. The ancient allegorists did not hesitate to employ the generative functions in the way of cosmic analogues. It is outwardly easy to fasten the charge of phallicism on the symbolic religion of the past. But man's creative processes *are* typical of *all* creative process, and the sages did not scruple to use the known functionism to depict the unknown cosmic procedures. There is no taint of ill in this until sordid sensuality invades the realm of pure depiction. Each incarnation in earthly bodies subjected the soul to a sort of menstrual purification, working, so to say, a lot of bad blood out of the system of god-man. It linked him with a body of flesh which came "under the law" of periodicity and purgation. Books on primeval religious customs tell of men dressing as women and laboring to manifest the menstrualia, in token of the entry of the god into his feminine phase, becoming a child of Mother Nature. In Egypt Tefnut (the Greek Daphne) was a name formed from the root *tefn, tebn,* "to shed, drip, drop." The same root means also to "rise up, spread, illumine," as the dawn. The dawn of womanhood came with the cleansing by blood.

However theology might like to disown the connection, this background looms as essential for our interpretation of the Gospel "bloody sweat" of the savior in the Garden of Gethsemane. The menstrual purification of the god in Egypt was in *Smen!* Legends of Tem, Atum and Ra portray them as shedding drops of their blood, under male symbolism, to fall on the earth and create mankind, or man and woman, Shu and Tefnut, Hu and Sa. The relation of Smen to the essence of the male blood is obvious. The gods poured out their vital life to fecundate matter, their mother and sister, to give creation a new birth. This general typism is all that could ever have been hinted at under the figure of the bloody sweat. The emission of life-fluid is accompanied by sweating. The male and female aspects of the meaning enter side by side. Smen, says Massey, was the place appointed for the purging, purifying and cleansing of souls. It is the place of pain and torment, the birthplace of the new moon, symbol of the infant birth of solar light in humanity. *Hesmen* is the Egyptian name for the rhythmic purgation. It is the voice of matter, the woman, saying in the *Ritual*: "I am the woman, the orb in the darkness; I have brought my orb to darkness where it is changed to light." The bloody sweat of the god in Smen is described as *"the flux emanating from Osiris,"* when Osiris is the god in his feminine or material expression. It is the divine "shedding of blood," without which humanity would have no cosmic opportunity to escape the eternal weight of karmic "sin."

Where the outpouring of deific power was not as yet linked with Mother Nature's body, was not yet implemented by its proper Shakti, or force in matter, the god was figured as "masturbating." Kheper-Ra was the Egyptian deity fulfilling this function. His type was the beetle or scarabaeus, which, according to Egyptian belief, created its young by itself alone, without the female. There was hidden in this symbolism the truth that would have settled the famous *"filioque"* dispute that split the early Church into Greek and Roman Catholicism.

Chapter 17 of the *Ritual* runs:

"O ye gods who are in the presence of Osiris, grant me your arms, for I am the god who shall come into being among you. Who then are these? They are the drops of blood which came forth from the phallus of Ra when he went forth to perform mutilation upon himself. They sprang into being as the gods Hu and Sa." [In another legend Shu and Tefnut.]

The *Ritual* states that "the sun mutilates himself, and from the streams of blood all things come into existence." Here is so-called phallicism, yet with sublimity.

Matching the Assyrian and Egyptian jugs of wine and pitchers of mixed drink, the Hebrews (*Leviticus* 4) were ordered to sprinkle some blood seven times before the Eternal in front of the curtain of the inner sanctuary. This was for a sweet savor and soothing fragrance to deity. In their sacrifices they were instructed never to consume the blood of any animal: "The soul of any creature lies in its blood . . . blood expiates by reason of the soul in it."

Esau was called "red" because he sucked his mother's blood before his birth. He is said to have sold his birthright for a mess of "red." Tradition shows him to have been a divinity imaged by the solar hawk, which symbolized blood "because they say that this bird does not drink water but blood, by which the soul is nourished" (Hor-Apollo, Bk. I, 6). The soul lives on natural forces, its Mother's blood, before it is born into Christhood in man.

One of the marvels in *Exodus* that were to persuade the reluctant Egyptians to let the Israelites go was the turning into blood some water that Moses poured on the ground. The pouring it *on the ground* would point to the necessity of making the transformation *on earth*. A Mexican legend sets forth the vivification of the dead remains of former races by the blood of the gods.

As the sun of spirit descending into the darkness of matter, in the evening or autumn, the god was suggestively depicted as the woman, suffering, becoming ill, wasting her substance unproductively. The god linked with Mother Nature was as a woman not yet impregnated by spirit. It required the passage of "virtue" from the Christ to stop her wastage.

A further aspect of the red-and-white symbolism comes to view here. If the red types the mother's blood giving generation, the white types the seminal life of spirit. The union of the white of divinity with the red of nature produces the new birth. Nor did the sages overlook the meaningful fact that it is the white creative essence of the father's blood that releases the stream of the mother's white nourishment for the new child. So the first or natural man, born of the blood, the first Adam or "red earth," is raised to his status of spiritual new birth by "the white liquor which the glorified ones love." And both the mother's and the father's condensation of white creative and sustaining essence is distilled out of the natural red blood. *Our divinization turns us from red to white.* Under Christmas tropism, the red stands for the divine; the green—universal color of nature—for the physical.

The red color of the evening sun, sinking into his feminine phase, and the red color of the morning sun, when for a brief space of his infancy he is still close to his Mother Earth, like the human child tied through the first years to his mother, again beautifully adumbrate the feminine connotation of red; while the white blaze of the sun throughout the day suggests the male or spiritual power.

In the *Ritual* (Ch. 37A) the Speaker is told he shall make four troughs of clay and shall "fill them with milk of a white cow." The four containers of the divine ichor are the physical, etheric, emotional

258

and concrete mental natures in man's lower self. An instructive picturing of the human creation is given in this Kamite description: the basis of the oblation in the Egyptian sacrifice is "the blood of beings that have been destroyed."

"Said by the majesty of the god, Let them begin with Elephantine and bring to me the fruits in quantity. And when the fruits had been brought they were given . . . (Lacuna).

"The Sekti (miller) of Annu was grinding the fruits, while the priestesses poured the juices into vases; and those fruits were put into vessels *with the blood of the beings,* and there were seven thousand pitchers of drink.

"And there came the majesty of the king of Upper and Lower Egypt, with the gods, to see the drink after he had ordered the goddess to destroy the beings in *three days of navigation.*"

The Assyrian seven jugs and the Egyptian seven thousand pitchers of drink are brewed from the blood of the massacred beings (the dismembered incarnating gods) mingled with the juice of the fruits of earth. This is vastly significant. Massey comments instructively:

"Blood and the fruit of earth were the two primitive forms of the offering, and these are blended together in a deluge of intoxicating drink." [14]

The plain inference here is that the mingling in one drink of the juices of the fruits of earth and the blood of the "beings," is a type of the blending in one composite nature of the life of the gods and that of animal-man—the base of all religion.

An exactly similar depiction is found in the Berosan account of the Babylonian creation. The deity Belus cut off his own head; whereupon the other gods mixed the blood as it gushed out with the earth, and from the mixture men were formed. "On this account it is that men are rational and partake of divine knowledge."

The Beast in *Revelation* is to be overcome by the blood of the Lamb. The lower sense creature in us is to be raised up by the infusion of godlike quality from above.

We are now in possession of much of the multifarious data which will enable proper judgment to be exercised in interpreting the central significance of the Eucharistic meal. We commemorate our partaking of the Lord's body and blood to remind our sluggish sense that there dwells in us a god, whose nature is compounded with that of a beast.

In the drama the Lord assigned immediately a pointed reason for his institution of the rite. And in this reason we come upon one of the pivotal elements of the Platonic philosophy, the loss of which out of Christian theology has contributed to our generally palsied grasp of fundamental truth. Little is it dreamed that the Lord himself announced the great Platonic doctrine of "reminiscence" in the midst of his ordination of the Eucharist. The world's astutest students have been puzzled and perplexed over the great Academician's principle of regained memory for the soul, and they have labeled it a philosophical fantasy, a finely spun poetization. That it bears direct relation to our earthly history has not been discerned by scholars.

When the *Christos* concluded his injunction to eat the broken fragments of his body and to drink the flowing stream of his life-blood with the command: "Do this in memory of me," he set Plato's great doctrine at the very heart of Christianity. But Christianity could not catch the relevance of the statement because it did not have the correlative tenets of the dismemberment and disfigurement. The restoration of memory can have understanding only in relation to a previous loss of it. Paradise regained must follow Paradise lost. So "rememberment" is the repairing of the dismemberment. Reminiscence is the recuperation of shattered memory. Death must have its resurrection. Divine intellect, dispersed into all forms of divulsion and enfeeblement, torn into fragments, with the links of connection lost, condemned to wander blindly in murks and shadows, must be reintegrated in the end. "My reason returned unto me," says the reconstituted Nebuchadnezzar. The Prodigal Son *remembered* his forgotten Father's house on high. Away off in that "far country," the Vale of Lethe and Land of Oblivion, the exiled soul begins to recover from its amnesia, and the divine nostalgia sets in to lead it back home.

A *Chaldean Oracle* states that the "paternal principle" of higher intellect "will not receive the will of the soul till she has departed from *oblivion;* and has spoken the word, assuming the *memory* of her paternal sacred impression." Immersed in scattered and partial images of reality, the soul can not regain her former unity of vision until she has restored some semblance of her former integrity of intellection. She must weave the tangled strands of mental fleece again into a garment with pattern matching archetypal ideals.

The figures of both Jesus and Jonah, fast asleep in the holds of their

260

respective ships in the storm are variant types of this oblivion of the god in his mundane journey. In a similar episode in the career of Horus, "there was deep slumber within the ship."

Iamblichus paints a beautiful picture of the gods gathering up the loose shreds of memory and weaving them again into the design of original loveliness, to escape their dire condition of forgetfulness:

"Neither is it proper to say that the soul primarily consists of harmony and rhythm. For thus enthusiasm would be adapted to the soul alone. It is better . . . to assert that the soul, before she gave herself to body, was the auditor of divine harmony; and that hence, when she proceeded into body and heard melodies of such a kind as especially preserve the divine vestiges of memory, she embraced these, from them recollected divine harmony, and tends and is allied to it, and as much as possible participates of it." [15]

Amid her distraction the soul catches faint and feeble glimpses of former felicity and these stir her latent recollection of harmonies known before. Through them she strives to integrate her former bliss and grandeur. And this states the whole office of ritual religion!

Plato's esoteric principle, grounded in segments of recondite anthropology lost out of modern consideration, is one vital to all theory and practique of education. Subtle principles of cultural technique are involved in the incarnational situation which make learning not at all the acquiring of something new and alien to the soul, but the remembering or re*collect*ing of scattered fragments of things inherently kin to consciousness itself. Culture is reintegration, not the acquiring of a collection.

Of the nine Muses of classical mythology Mnemosyne is the goddess of memory, and memory is thus indicated as one of the nine paths by which we return to our divinity. Mercury also shared the function of rehabilitating the memory. A note by Thomas Taylor reads:

"Hermes disperses the sleep and oblivion with which the different herds of souls are oppressed. He is likewise the supplier of recollection, the end of which is a genuine intellectual apprehension of divine natures." [16]

As man is a rational soul thrust into an irrational life, the province of Mercury is to impress upon the mind, distracted by the shifting flux of this world's dream images, the beauty of the stable principles of Universal Mind that were visioned by the soul in her own world.

Chapter 90 of the *Ritual* gives a prayer in these words:

"O thou who restorest memory in the mouth of the dead through the words of power which they possess, let my mouth be opened through the words of power which I possess."

The title of Chapter 25 is itself convincing: "The chapter of making a man possess memory in the underworld." This again is the whole office of religion. Of what, be it asked, could a man on earth be expected to have memory, if not of a former life which he had forgotten?

If religion is to be animated and inspired by its most forceful significance, it must be practiced with a view to awakening in earth-bound souls lost divine memories. This is the import of all its song, its ritual, its rhythms and prayers. A powerful reinforcement of spiritual unction and dynamic life would well up out of its decadent forms if this motif were revived. Salvation, the aim of religion, is by way of rekindled memory of slumbering divinity.

In an address to Pepi it is written that the god "setteth his remembrance upon men and his love before the gods." Indeed the *Ritual* records the fact that the deceased in Amenta was shown his Ka (higher soul body) and assured that it accompanied him through the lower earth in order that he might not utterly forget his divine moorings, or as he says, "that he might not suffer loss of identity by forgetting his name." Man is on earth like one stricken with amnesia. Showing him his Ka bestirs the Manes to recall his divine name and nature. Also the passage of Osiris through the underworld is effected only by means of his preserving all the mystical names in memory. Ra has 75 names, Osiris 153. As the "name" stood for one of the higher spiritual principles, to call upon the name of the Lord, or to know the deity's name, was to have come *en rapport* with his higher nature. This presupposed the restoration of all the soul's higher metaphysical faculties. This is given elsewhere as knowing the names of all the gates and their god keepers, past whom the voyaging soul had to go.

In the Orphic Mysteries of Greece the phrase occurs more than once: "I am a child of earth and the starry sky, but my race is of heaven alone." The "dead" man is instructed to address these words to the guardian of the Lake of Memory, while he asks for a drink of water from the lake. In our highest flights toward divine consciousness we drink from that Lake of Memory and regale ourselves anew with aboriginal harmonies. If it holds true to its prime purpose the persistent vogue of religion in human society is abundantly warranted.

Max Müller gives an important link of philology when he derives the Sanskrit word *Smara*, "love," from *Smar*, "to recollect"! [17] He states that the German *Schmerz*, "pain," and the English "smart," come from this root. Love, then, like learning, is only the memory of former transports and ecstasies of the glory the soul once had with the Father before the worlds.

When, therefore, Jesus breaks the bread and sips the wine in token of his death till he come—his discerption and dismantling—he is dramatizing the necessity of their "remembering" his scattered self-hood in their lives. The *Ritual* of Egypt assigns a name to the ship of Horus as it passes across the sea of this lower life, which name shows the archaic origin of the sage philosophy of Greece: "Collector of souls is the name of my barque"! Recollection is the soul's office on earth. We are to gather up in the boat of our life the twelve baskets of scattered fragments and restore the broken body of our Lord "whole and entire."

Out of the dissertation on divine food here elaborated there should accrue to the modern mind a new and grander sense of the Christ's ordinance: "Do this in memory of me." And an elevated consciousness arising from the double sense of the word "remember" should lift humanity once more to an awareness of its mission, which is to bind up the broken and dismembered body of the Lord of Hosts, by welding together the nations in the spirit of a lofty fraternity. In the light of restored sublimity to the doctrine, every individual will know that the appeal to remember his deity comes not from an isolated figure in ancient Judea, but from the living god within, begging all to drink the cup of communion with him and thus hasten to forge that recollection of him which alone will effect his release from the dreary grave of the body.

Chapter XIII

EARTH, WATER, AIR, FIRE

THE possibility of making an effective interpretation of arcane scriptures will be seen to be closely interwoven with the part played in symbolic structure by the four elements, earth, water, air and fire. Grasp of the ideas hidden under the use of these four emblems comes close to putting one in possession of the key to most of the mystery. The revelation of the full force of their application will prove astonishing.

Much absurdity has found expression in common belief as to their significance. It has everywhere been asserted that the ancients conceived all substances to be composed of these four primary and irreducible constituents, instead of the ninety-two mineral elements of modern chemistry. This is folly. What they were dealing with is a vastly different formula. They were not asserting that man's physical body, with all other things, was compounded of only four elements. They held man's total constitution to be compounded of four distinct grades or modifications of original essence, each of which gave him a body, by virtue of which his life effected its conscious expression in four different worlds at the same time. Each of the bodies was charactered and symboled by one of the four elements, and the more sublimated ones interpenetrated the coarser, localizing the functionism of all four in the lower one, man's physical body. Occult view held that man possessed a physical body, symboled by the earth; an emotional body, of which water was the suggestive emblem; a mental body, with air as its sign; and a spiritual body, typed by fire or the sun. A fifth, not yet evolved to function in humanity and beyond the ken of mortal knowledge, was predicated as the development of a distant future. It was called a body of aether, the fifth element, called by Aristotle a term equivalent to "quintessence." It yet lies latent and undifferentiated in the inner core of the element of fire.

The Bibles of antiquity can not be understood unless this basic predication be made, that man lives not alone on one plane of nature, but on four, and that he makes contact with the realities of each of them by means of a body composed of the matter indigenous to that realm. His focus of consciousness may pass from one to the other of the four bodies under pressure of the swing of his interests. When we grandiloquently speak of living within the whole range of our being, we are unwittingly repeating a conception of ancient theory, the literal truth of which we have lost the data to comprehend.

Of an eventual septenary constitution man has as yet progressed only so far as to have deployed into function the lower quaternary of powers. Plato in the *Timaeus* says that "three genera of mortals yet await to be created." Each emanation of energic force brings to manifestation one of the bodies of our composite mechanism, as it does one of the planes of nature. We are now in the fourth of such rounds or cycles, and have therefore developed four of the ultimate seven bodies of our equipment for contacting the reality of all worlds. And these four bodies are typed by earth, water, air and fire, symbolically.

The matter of the contemporary existence of these four (or five) bodies within the single space of the physical may occasion some incredulity as to the ancient theory. But modern science has itself opened the door of explanation here. It is a matter of the fineness of molecular particles and interstitial spaces. Certain rays can be passed through "solid" substances, because their electrons swing in minute orbits amid vaster ones. It is declared esoterically that the atomic matter of which each of man's four bodies is composed is in structural essence a sevenfold attenuation or sublimation of the one which it interpenetrates. Each one interpenetrates its coarser neighbor, and at the same time is interpenetrated by its next finer associate. So the four dwell together, occupying the same three-dimensional area, yet with a "great gulf" fixed between each pair, the abyss of difference of electronic vibration, wave length, frequency and radial orbit. This is the great gulf that divides each world from all others. It is not a chasm of spacial distance, but a hiatus between vibrational frequencies, wave length and other forms of potency. To bridge the abyss and step from one world to another, it is requisite that man should be able to tune up, or down, the mathematical "pitch" of his consciousness, as exemplified by the "tuning in" process of the radio. Two discordant tones of consciousness are not on the same plane, or in the same world. Their failure to harmonize puts them into different areas of the field of life.

The five planes were represented by the five geometric figures, the cube for earth, the sphere for water, the triangle for fire, the crescent for air, and the candle-flame tip for aether. Certain significations of the figure-symbols will be presented in the sequel, but it is doubtful if anyone at present knows authoritatively the full range of meaning attached to them. In some drawings of the series, air, the third, and fire, the fourth, are reversed in position. Their relative place in the order is doubtless of vital importance, but for the ends of religious symbolism, it seems not to be a question of critical value. After examination of many applications of the typing it has been found advantageous to make a more condensed grouping of the four under the two heads of fire and water, as these two appear to do double duty in carrying the burden of the symbolism.

This reduces the fourfold nature of man to the broad generality of the dualism, or the compound of two elements, the divine and the earthly, in one body.

This will be found to serve the readiest purposes of interpreting the many myths, for there appears to be a vast preponderance of the dual representation in the scriptures and folk-lore of the world, under the wide imagery of fire and water.

The two most distinctive symbols, then, are fire and water, and their proper interpretation almost alone gives a key to the religious texts. Let fire be taken to refer undeviatingly to our higher or divine segment, and water to our lower or animal-human portion; or fire to connote the god from heaven, and water the earthly man, the first Adam. In an even more condensed form, fire may type the soul and water the body. Classifications so general are not to be taken as scientifically precise; but they will be seen to be systematically applicable, without loss of explicit meaning. The fifth element, aether, may profitably be ignored, as it stands for the innermost essence of all manifest life, and humanity is not in conscious relation to its high mode of activity.

Oddly enough, by one of those inversions to which the imagery is susceptible, the serpent has become a symbol of both the fire and the water elements, and hence types both our divine and our sensual natures. "When above it was the serpent of air and fire, and when below the serpent of water and earth."[1] There was the fiery serpent

266

that Moses lifted up, and the water dragon of *Revelation,* of the *Aeneid* and other classical works. There is the Good Serpent, *Agathodaemon,* and the Evil Serpent, *Kakodaemon,* symbol of Satan. Water, too, became a dual sign, with a higher and lower translation. As the first it was an emblem of the outpourings of divinity, the water of life that Jesus promised to the woman at the well; as the second, it typed the fluctuating, restless, sensual nature in which the divine fire was so nearly drowned out. Even fire shares the dual meaning, for it symbols the celestial life, the fire of Prometheus, Jove's thunderbolt, as well as the fires of the torture and hell of earthly existence. The *Ritual* speaks of our baptism on earth "in the Pool of the Double Fire." This is easily comprehensible because of the shifting of the divine beings from the empyrean to the mundane sphere of activity. In heaven it was a pure and clear flame; on earth it was fed with damp, coarse fuel, and became lurid in hue and charged with noxious, sulphurous gases, and turned to steam and smoke. A large part of the whole significance of the incarnation can be seen reflected in the imagery of fire introduced into a semi-watery condition. Our work will be wasted effort if it does not succeed in imprinting on every imagination the indelible suggestion that our earthly history is adumbrated by the picture of an imperishable and unquenchable spark of divine fire struggling to live and expand its power in a moist environment. Our inmost essence is as a central nucleus of fire striving valiantly to light a mass of damp green wood—the animal nature. The resultant smoke and smudge is the perfect type of our life here, intellectually and spiritually. These were the very symbols of our terrene existence employed in Greek philosophy.

This peculiar duality of the symbols, discerned throughout, is itself a reflection of the twofold movement, or double status, of the soul in incarnation. For that which began as heavenly passed into earthly embodiment, and the pertinence of the symbols had to change with the change of milieu. All the heavenly symbols became inwrought with earthly reference and imperfection, and thus picked up the implication of evil. On earth, then, we may expect to find the celestial symbols with meanings almost completely reversed, or with their purity besmirched, so to say. It is not surprising that the wise Egyptians should have given us a picture of this very reversal in one of their typical vignettes. For, says Massey:

"The god advancing in a reversed position is the sun [the god, soul] in the underworld. The image accords exactly with an Egyptian scene of the sun passing through the Hades, where we see the twelve gods of the earth, or the lower domain of night, marching towards a mountain turned upside down, and two typical personages are also turned upside down. This is an illustration of the passage of the sun through the underworld. The reversed (people) on the same monument are the dead. Thus the Osirified deceased who had attained the second life, in the *Ritual* says exultingly, 'I do not walk on my head.' The dead, as the Akhu, are the spirits, and the Atua is a spirit who comes walking upside down." (*Book of Hades.*) [2]

One of the rites of the resurrection was the "erecting of the Tat," or setting the Tat cross or the mummy upright on its feet. In addition to the imagery of death in all its forms to type our spiritually defunct condition here, there was employed also the idea of an entire reversal of position to portray the true state of the soul in its untoward predicament. We are heavenly spirits turned upside down on earth! Earth reverses heavenly lines of motion. It reflects the pattern of things in the mount, but inverted. The highest symbols of heaven therefore fall at the very bottom of earthly tracing. And the very spirit of the god who came to earth, renouncing his bliss on high to bring immortal gifts to man, was himself later inverted into the personification of evil! We have, then, the angels of light turned into demons, the bright flame of divinity metamorphosed into the lurid fire of hell, the waters of life becoming the raging seas that engulfed the boats of Jonah and Jesus, the serpent of wisdom becoming the dragon of evil.

With the four basic elements now established, it is interesting to note the curious typical results obtained when any two are brought together, as the fact of incarnation does bring all four together in man. Some remarkable and surprising combinations are produced, both in symbol and in actuality.

Man's lower nature, as seen in any diagram, is composed of the elements of earth and water, his higher nature of fire and air. Any time either of the two upper is crossed with either of the two lower, there is a rough symbol of incarnation, or combination of the divine with the human. But the two that together comprise either our lower or higher nature may also be found in correlation. This is admirably seen in the two lower, where the mixture of earth and water produces, as any child can tell, mud or mire. At once we have a key to translate the significance of the papyrus swamps of Egyptian legends, the "miry clay" of Plato and the Bible, and the celebrated Reed (not Red) Sea of *Exodus* (see Moffatt Translation). The marshes of Lower Egypt in which Horus and Jesus and Sargon were all secreted can be taken now as the glyphs of the human physical body, compounded of earth and water. The body is itself about seven-eighths water and the remainder earth. The lotus, papyrus or reed has a number of meanings, but in the main they typify the new life springing up out of the mud and water, to flower out in the air and the fire of the sun. The risen Horus is figured seated on a lotus pad above the water.

Mud, as the type of matter (and matter, mud, and mother all come from the same linguistic root), is dialectically analyzed in the Greek philosophy:

"Matter," says Simplicius in his commentary on the first book of Aristotle's *Physics,* "is nothing else than mutation of sensibles, with respect to intelligibles, deviating from thence and carried down to non-being. These things, indeed, which are the properties of sensibles are irrational, corporeal, distributed into parts, and passing into bulk and divulsion through an ultimate progression into generation, viz., into matter; for matter is always truly the last sediment. Hence also the Egyptians call the dregs of the first (or highest) life, which they symbolically denominate water, matter, being, as it were, a certain *mire.*"

What Simplicius is quaintly telling us in terms of reasoned analysis of the elements of being which are quite "Greek" to us moderns, is that matter is to be thought of as a kind of sediment deposited on the lowest levels of inert life by the crystallization of ethereal forces, precisely as snow is the sedimentary deposit of vaporous states of water, subjected to a reduction of temperature. Nature furnishes a perfect analogy for every truth.

A common ancient symbolic term for our life here is the "sea of generation." Iamblichus joins Heraclitus in likening generation to a water symbol, that of a river, as being always in flux. It is the river of Lethe, flowing through the dark meadows of Ate, as Empedocles says. It represents in its swirling currents the voracity of matter and the light-hating world, as the gods say, and the winding streams under which many are drawn down, as the *Chaldean Oracles* assert. The fitness of the meadow to stand for this life is seen in its lying always in a low marshy place contiguous to a stream. It tells of land and water in juxtaposition and therefore matches mire in its suggestiveness.

Plotinus in a passage already quoted has called our descent a fall into dark mire. The Hebrew Psalmist, in the words of the incarnated deity, cries:

"Save me, O God! for the waters are come in unto my soul. I sink in deep *mire*, where there is no standing. I am come in unto deep waters where the floods overwhelm me."

Without the skill of the Greeks in dealing with abstruse facts of cosmology under symbolic typism we are hardly prepared to catch the aptness of the figure of water for the creeping inroads of sensual impulse upon the divine purity. But the god cries that the waters of animal passion have come in to inundate his soul. Again he prays:

"Deliver me out of the *mire*, and let me not sink. Let me be delivered from them that hate me. Let not the water-floods overwhelm me, neither let the deep swallow me up."

His gratitude for eventual deliverance takes the form (*Ps.* 40):

"He brought me up also out of an horrible pit, out of the *miry clay*, and set my feet upon a rock, and established my goings."

Yet—"he hath founded the earth upon the waters and established it upon the floods" (*Ps.* 24), because out of the water and the mud of mortal life was to come the new generation, the son, Jesus or Horus, as the young shoot of the papyrus reed of divine life.

The mire and filth of the Augean stables cleansed by Hercules is another form of this imagery, for the solar hero turns into them the waters of two rivers. The two streams represent those of spirit and matter, generally, and only out of the interworking of the two does eventual purgation come.

A vivid light can now be thrown on such a fiction as this: Horus was mutilated and his members cast into the water. To find them Isis invoked the aid of Sebek, or Sevekh, the crocodile-god, an ancient solar deity, who, having examined the banks of the swamps with his claws, took his net and fished out the pieces. Sebek then reconstituted the god whole and entire. The significance of Sebek's participation is in his name, which means "seven," intimating that a septenary development was entailed in the perfective process. Man is perfected always in a cycle of seven stages.

Water and earth yield another deposit than that of mud or mire, a very curious one. Water, depositing particles of mineral earth, petrifies a piece of wood, a combination of water, earth and air. Not even such a symbol is irrelevant, since it speaks in loudest tones of the hardening influence of the lower nature upon the higher, and images the Gorgon shield, turning all softer natures to stone.

Air and water in conjunction provide much matter for symbology. In the first place there is air in water, and it needs only the application of the still more energic element fire to beget life and engender most of the other forms of living symbolism. In ice or cold water the energies of life remain inert; let fire be applied and the resultant energization gives us a faint suggestion of the whole meaning of the entry of the gods into the province of less active substances. Fire plunged into water most pointedly dramatizes the basic import of the whole incarnation procedure. The soul, a fiery nucleus of noetic intelligence, is plunged into the watery habitat of the fleshly body. The moral fight is a combat between the fire of spirit and the water of emotion and desire; and fire must win the victory by eventually drying up and converting into steam the heavy humid nature of animal-man. Fire must dry out a path across the sea of generation, so that it may cross this Reed (Red) Sea out of Egypt, as also the Jordan River, into the Holy Land, without wetting its feet! Fire enters the watery realm of body, already permeated by air in hidden form. Heat raises the water into vapor, which, being an airy form of water, suggests the birth of mind out of emotion. We read in the *Ritual* (Ch. 164): "Oh, the Being dormant within his body, making his burning in flame, glowing within the sea by his vapor. Come, give the fire, transport [perhaps better, "transform"] the vapor of the Being." The vapor was a type of the breath of life, air containing moisture, symbol of the soul that was linked with emotion. It was a plea for the god to come and sublimate the emotional element of the lower self, water, by unifying it with air, mind. Each higher element is able to raise the potential of the one below it and refine it. So earth (sense) is raised and purified by water (emotion); water (emotion) by air (mind); and air (mind) by fire (spirit). This gives us the key table of values. By their simple application in various combinations a hundred intimate meanings of ancient scriptures may be resolved into comprehensible reading.

A common form of air and water mixed is foam or bubbles. Froth arises when air becomes violently active in water. Fire, spirit, quickens and intensifies the process. We have here the ground for the solution of that riddle of Greek mythology which makes Venus to be born from the sea-foam, produced by the energy of the great God Jupiter striding through the sea. It is a beautiful allegory, hinting that the goddess of Love is born in the evolutionary process when air, mind, is injected into the field of the animal impulses and passions. This came when the god, descending, brought air and fire to energize the elements in the sea water (of the body). Froth would intimate the elevation of emotion to the plane of thought, or the thorough mixing of thought with emotion,—perhaps also the emotionalizing of thought. Bubbles rising to the surface suggest the evolution of thought out of the very depths of the physical and emotional departments of man. The Egyptian image of the water-cow indicated life emanating from the primordial waters. And the rising of Aphrodite into breathing life and beauty out of the foam marks this idea as Egyptian in origin. *Nu-ti,* "froth," is the same word as Neith, who was one of the early Kamite personifications of the first life rising from the waters. Neith is Hathor, the Egyptian Venus, the mother of life, twofold in character as liquid and aeriform. Her celestial representative was Ursa Major, the Great Bear (or Bearer, suggests Massey), the great dipper in which the water of life was held, and from which, as it turned around the pole, it was periodically poured out and again dipped up! In early times its orbit dipped down into the sub-horizonal sea. So this great sidereal directory of the heavens became the greatest of astronomical symbols to the ancients, dramatizing the seven great elementary mother powers of nature that periodically arose out of the waters of life. Operated by its handle of three stars, typing the solar triad of mind, soul and spirit, it caught up the living waters in its four-starred cup, the fourfold physical basis of all things.

The Egyptian male-female pair of Shu and Tefnut personify the dual subsistence of breath and moisture. "These in one form may be the breath of life and its dew, as *Tef* is to drip or drop." [3] Air and moisture are combined in the breath of mortals. The creative breath of mortal life is emaned and drips its moisture upon the earth in rain, fog or dew. The spirit of God outbreathed as air or breath, from which was precipitated the water of life on earth. Rain is distilled out of the bosom of the air. In the form of vapor, visible or invisible, the upper heaven holds the celestial water, the type of divine life embosomed in air—emotions germinally latent in thoughts. And when this water has fallen to earth, it takes the action of fiery spirit to convert it back again to heavenly state, and this can only be done by the superior energy transmuting its nature from liquid to vapor or "spirit" form.

The deceased, awaiting his resurrection, cries to Nu: "Give me water and the breath of life!" The reply comes: "I bring thee the vase containing the abundant water for rejoicing the heart by its effusion, that thou mayest breathe the breath of life resulting from it." Water, though not in its liquid form, is the first aspect of matter in all the oldest mythologies and cosmologies. It is indeed the primal substance of the universal mother. In the Berosan account of creation the primal mother is called Thallath, which is the Greek *thallassa,* "the sea." Tiamat and Typhon are equivalent to Tefnut (Greek Daphne), the Great Depth, or *Tepht* (also Tophet). Basically, mother, matter and water are one. Plato speaks of water as "the liquid of the whole vivification." Again he alludes to it mystically as "a certain fountain."

The interpenetration of the gross bodies by the subtler ones in man may perhaps be realistically depicted by the relations subsisting between the four elements in the outer world. Living physical bodies of earthly constituency hold water, the water embosoms air, and in the air is the hidden potency of fire. The elements consistently interpenetrate each other, the finer in the coarser. We have already traced the vivid symbolism of fermentation, or the generation of air in water, type of the enkindling of spirit. At the baptism of Jesus by John, according to Justin Martyr, "a fire was kindled in the waters of the Jordan." This matches the Egyptian "a burning within the sea." Spirit sets its ferment and its blaze a-going amid the watery elements of the body.

Seeking in the heights and depths of the natural creation for symbols of truth, the mythographers could not miss so patent a type as that of the fish leaping out of the water. It was a vivid suggestion of the soul in matter leaping in aspiration for short breaths of air in the kingdom above it. Whether it be seeking a moment's breath of a diviner air in the kingdom above, or only a fly as food, it projects itself from the lower to a higher plane, prefiguring the sallies of the human soul—often otherwise represented by *ichthys,* the fish—from its mortal habitat into the purer realms of spirit. The soul, like the fish, must occasionally clutch at a morsel of more heavenly food. The fish stood for the immortal soul as breather in the water of mundane existence.

A Norse myth tells of the division of a single primal world into two halves, or the separation of the two waters of the firmament, as in *Genesis.* The one was a world of water, the other of air, and the beings in the lower water ascend by night to breathe the pure air of the upper half; and it is said the sun consumes them like vapor. This would restate the Assumption of the Virgin, the festival of the old astronomical phenomenon of August and early September, when the sun absorbs the constellation of the Virgin, emblematic of the dissolution of all physical worlds in the bosom of the Absolute. It might be said that after every day and every incarnation man ascends to inhale refreshing draughts of spiritual air on an upper plane. Without this frequent release and relief he could not support prolonged existence in the denser world below.

The "secret of Horus in An" is the mystery of how his mother caught him in the water. Neith, given by Massey as equivalent to "net," fished him out. Cosmically he typified the first life emanating from the water; humanly the god coming to birth in the water of the body. Many of the symbols can be worked on two or even more planes of explanation. Every cosmic process has its reflection in the natural world, again in the spiritual life of man, and lastly in the very physiology of the body. Nature is meaningless nowhere.

The perch on the head of Neith or Hathor is a badge of the birth from water. Neith also carries the shuttle or knitter for her net, wherewith she becomes a catcher of men out of the waters, and draws them up into the world of air and spirit.

The East has always portrayed true being as an escape from the waters of life. Hence the widespread use of the fisherman's net as an emblem of salvation. Jesus did not startle his disciples with a new metaphor when he called them to be "fishers of men." Two *Ritual* chapters furnish suggestion here. Chapter 153A is entitled "of coming forth from the net," and 153B "of coming forth from the Catcher of Fish." Water so obviously presented a menace to life by drowning that it becomes the focus of ideas emphasizing an escape from evil. As such it is not the water of life, but the water of death. It signified the lower life of generation, or life in "death." Water stops our breathing and perils the air-sustained life of deity. An oyster that could keep shut up and safe under water was one of the figures of spiritual security.

Nun in the Chaldean is the Great Fish; Nuna in Syriac is the constellation Cetus, the Whale. Nun of the Hebrew alphabet is the fish, as Mem is water. The picture of a great fish "breathing out" water caused it to be personified as the mother heaven that poured forth water and the breath of life. The Egyptians also made the lotus, ascending from the water, a symbol of breath, and the Egyptian *Seshin* for "lotus" is from *ses,* "breath."

The close philosophical relation of water and air is shown in a number of languages by the identical derivation of the words "to swim" and "to be born." Birth and swimming in or on water are practically synonymous. It is best seen in the Latin. The same root, *na,* means both "to be born" and "to swim." Being born of water, avers Massey, is but to be borne upon it. As man was not able to live under water, life was pictured as a coming out of it or a floating upon it. To be born into life, therefore, was to escape from the water, and come up where breath was obtainable. The very first act of the babe new-born out of the water of the womb is to catch its first breath! Immersed in the waters of generation, of sense and desire, man can not come to his real life, or second birth, until he can rise out of the "water" to breathe the more vivifying air of the heaven of mind and spirit. The power of the sun (god) to stimulate life and growth could not reach him effectively in the kingdom of water (nature); he had first to lift his head out of the water into the kingdom of air (mind) before the rays of the god could breed spirituality within him.

From the *na* stem we trace both "naval" and "navel," relating birth and sailing. *Nef,* says Massey, means in Egyptian both "sailor" and "to breathe." The navel was one of the earliest doorways between the two worlds (of water and air), and as such it maintained its symbolic value. The navel was an image of breath in the waters of the womb. It was the channel by which the breath of life passed into the soul in the water. The god, through whom we partake of the breath of life from a higher plane, is spiritually our navel, located at the very center of our being.

In the ideography the female came to be regarded as the furnisher of water, and the male as the supplier of breath, the combination yielding life. These were Tefnut and Shu. He became the inspirer of soul, she the former of flesh. It was the god, masculine, who breathed the breath of life into the nostrils. In the *Ritual* the Speaker, coming to his new life, says he has been "snatched from the waters of his Mother" and "emaned from the nostrils of his Father Osiris." The Chinese matched this with their Ying and Yin, the male and female, or breath and water sources.

The water and the lotus were both female emblems at first. The papyrus-scepter of Uat is the express sign of the feminine nature of Uati, who represented the features of both wet and heat, water and breath, or body and soul, heat being necessary to turn water into vapor or breath.

A simple yet strong ideograph of the unified action of water and air is a ship driven by the wind. The wind (intellect) imparts motion to that which navigates the waters. The body is driven by the mind! Mind and wind, both unseen, energize the visible.

Very suggestive is the request in the *Ritual* (Ch. 55): "May air be given unto these young divine beings," a reference to the Kumaras or Innocents when first plunged into their material baptism. And even more directly pertinent is the chapter title (56): "Of sniffing air in the waters of the underworld." And another title (Ch. 54) is: "Of giving air to the overseer of the palace . . . Nu, triumphant, in the underworld." And again Chapter 57 is that "of breathing the air and having dominion over the waters of the underworld." When Horus rises he is exultingly welcomed as escaping from the dark lower region, "without water and without air," as the conditon of soul in matter.

In Africa and Central America the god Houragan (Hurricane) was the personification of the mingled power of water and air. *Hurakan* in Quiché means a stream of water that pours straight down. In the hieroglyphics *Hura* is heaven (Greek: *oura*-nos), "over," "above." *Khan* is a watery tempest. Typhon, the abyss of primordial heaven, is identical with typhoon. Mixcohuatl, the "cloud serpent," the chief of the Mexican gods, bears the name of the tropical whirlwind.

The flying fish came in for its share of appropriate suggestiveness, and another bird, the hissing widgeon, which issued from the waters to fly along the surface, became a symbol of the soaring free soul, which was nearly always pictured as winged or feathered.

Naturally all species of aero-aquatic birds came under the scope of this typology. The bird that could rise off the water and soar away was inescapably a type of the rising soul. But the ancients joined the two kinds of life in one creature which became one of the most universal of all symbols, the winged serpent or feathered snake. Recent researches in Central America have brought to light the wide prevalence of this emblem in the Mayan and other civilizations on the American continent. And since it was general in Asia and Africa in remote times, the question of intercommunication or separate origin is once more pertinently raised. The snake that could fly is the incontrovertible evidence of ancient knowledge of the union of divinity and earthiness in man's organic life. Man that is born of water and the spirit (air) should once again become wise as to his dual origin. And modern man should cease to belittle the mythopoetic genius of his ancestors who endeavored, with almost incredible sagacity, to embody important knowledge of cosmic facts in imperishable glyphs. In the terms of evolutionary biology the swan *is* the feathered snake, and Hansa, the bird of primordial life and intelligence that floats above the waters of the abyss, is the eternal emblem of that spiritual life that has stepped into our fluctuating sea of natural impulse to bring order, harmony and beauty into the realm of nescience and chaos.

The Akhekh gryphon is a dragon with wings. Wings and feathers supply the type of air and fire in the later Bird of the Sun. The bird symbolized the swift-darting and lofty-soaring motion of divine intelligence. The French Swan-Dragon unites the bird's head with the serpent's tail. An ancient Greek work makes the first godly nature a serpent which later transmuted into a hawk. One form of the gryphon was the body of a beast, the tail of a serpent and the head of a peacock. This is the mythical cockatrice. It was so named because of its origin from the egg of a cock hatched by a serpent. The divine is hatched and nurtured in the body of nature.

Earth with water yielded mire, or sensuousness; water with air suggested mingled emotion and dawning thought; spiritous wine hinted at a fiery element in water, or "fire-water." Beside Isis, whose name derives from stems meaning to breathe and ferment, there is the goddess Uati, a name congenital perhaps with our "wet" and "heat," if not the basis of "water" itself. She was the genetrix, and signified wet and heat in conjunction; and her function suggests the conversion of water into breathing life by the mother in heat, or gestating! Unleavened bread would represent the natural man unspiritualized by the ferment of divine efficacies. It would show the first Adam, the man unregenerate, born of water, the natural body, but not of the spirit. Leavened bread was "spiritualized" bread. And oddly enough the little leaven that leaveneth the whole lump does indeed generate by its ferment a sort of breathing in the dough, for the latter becomes permeated with air bubbles which work to the surface. Bring the god of fire into matter and the latter begins to manifest the breath of life. Fire rises, and is the ultimate type of evolution, in which life sparks ascend to the empyrean. Water falls, and is the type of involution, or life descending to incubate in matter. But water below, acted upon by fire, is transformed into a sublimated state in which it can effect its return to the empyrean. The gist of the story of religion is here. Fire had to be brought down from heaven to convert fallen water into spiritous vapor, to enable it to rise again.

Physical nature presents a notable exemplification of the fourfold elemental typology in the phenomenon of a thunderstorm. Our universal mother has set the advertising sign of her modes and configurations all about us, but only the ancients heeded her message or read her language. The upper air, or heaven, surcharged with electricity, discharges its pent energies above the earth in flashes of fire. The mighty potency performs a sort of electrolysis upon the constituent elements of the air, dismembering, so to say, the unit mass of embosomed moisture held in suspension in the atmosphere and sending it in fragments to the earth to nourish the life of man and beast. Not an item or detail of the theological typism is lacking in the phenomenon. As the fire emanation from heaven operated to precipiate its latent forces in the broken globules of water to the earth to fructify its life, so the fiery nature of deity came potentially to earth in fragments to liberate its powers in new growth. The celestial energy of pure spirit runs down the gamut of fire, air, water and earth. In man likewise a flash of the fire of spirit darts out of the surcharged bosom of the upper aether of consciousness, agitates the elements of the plane of mind next below it, these in turn release emotions on the plane below, and they deposit a final influence upon the very material of the earthy body. Each plane in succession receives the effects of the outrush of life from above. A breeze ruffling the surface of a pond is a vivid symbol of a thought stirring the emotions, the type of which is water. And the waves washing the shores portray in a measure the emotional wear and tear on the body. "Let nature be your teacher," says Wordsworth.

But a still more eloquent symbol comes to view to edify the mind of man at the end of the shower: the rainbow! In its sevenfold coloration we read again the septenary design of all natural constitution, including the life of man. The one divine essence of white light, shining out through the descending waters, is broken into its seven constituent rays. All manifest form must therefore be septenary in structure. Every cycle runs its course and comes to its perfection in seven sub-cycles. Hence the Eternal placed the rainbow in the heavens, *at the end* of the rain, in token that "never again will he destroy mankind." For man, at the end of his sojourn in the watery habitat of body, will have completed his perfection in seven stages and will not need further immersion in the sea of generation. As the rainbow disappears with the last rain, the sun reigns alone again in its one white light.

A unitary ray of light, passed through a three-faced glass prism and breaking into its seven colors, is a memorable certification of cosmic creational method. Man actually presents a three-faced transparent medium for the first light in the upper levels of his nature to provide the requisite condition for this phenomenon in his life. The immortal unit of spirit itself has segmented already into a triad which hovers in the upper sphere of consciousness. It is the great solar triad of Mind-Soul-Spirit, the reflection in human make-up of the cosmic Trinity of Will-Wisdom-Activity. It is man's triangle of conscious faculty and it is of bright essence. Through it shines the one unbroken ray of Intelligence from the primal fount of light to be reflected on the physical screen of human life on earth, in a final sevenfold differentiation.

Still another phase of portrayal meets us in nature when we consider the change from a watery beginning to a fiery heyday in the progress of each day's summer sun. The dewy freshness of dawn (water) and the burning heat of mid-day (fire) are personalized in Egypt by the goddesses Tefnut and Sekhet respectively. *Tef(n)* connotes the meaning of "dew" and "moisture" from its primary signification of "to drip, or drop." Then the watery phase of the goddess is superseded by the fiery one, and Tefnut becomes Sekhet, the heat principle which engenders ferment and new life. This is the transformation of Daphne (Tefnut) dawn, into the laurel or wood of fire, in the Greek poetization.

Another *Ritual* title (Ch. 163) is deeply suggestive: "Of not allowing the body of a man to molder away in the underworld." (The spiritual body is meant here, as the physical body *does* molder away.) The Manes is addressed:

"Hail, thou who art lying prostrate within thy body, whose flame cometh into being from out of the fire that blazeth within the sea (or water) in such wise that the sea (or water) is raised up on high out of the fire thereof."

If there are still any who dispute the mythical nature of ancient constructions, let them demonstrate how a fire blazing in the midst of a sea could be spoken of otherwise than allegorically. But when one knows that a universal code of symbol language made fire represent spiritual mind, and water flesh and carnality, then it can be seen how the poets speak rationally of a fire blazing in the sea and trying to raise it up again in vapor or spirit.

Another strong confirmation of the analysis is found in the *Ritual* (Ch. 176). In comment on it Budge writes: "As fire and boiling water existed in the underworld, he hastened to protect himself from burns and scalds by the use of chapters 63A and 63B." For the titles of these two chapters are: "Of drinking water and not being burnt by fire in the underworld," and "Of not being scalded with water." How squarely this is matched in the Bible (*Is.* 43):

"When thou passest through the waters I shall be with thee; and through the rivers, they shall not overflow thee; when thou walkest through the fire thou shalt not be burned; neither shall the flame kindle on thee."

The underworld, then, is the place where fire and water are joined in affective relation; and where could this conjunction take place other than in the physical body?

And what pithy moral corollaries are discerned in the analogies if they are carried into particulars! The god (fire) stood in danger, as the Greeks clearly intimate, of suffering from the exhalations arising from its contact with the humors of the carnal body. It must be seen that the god's entry into the body of an inferior being would result in the injection of an increased voltage, as it were, in the activities of all its forces. Animality would be more keenly energized as the transforming ferment began its work. The god stood in danger of being "burned," "scalded" by the "steam" engendered by the heightening of all lower psycho-chemical powers. The enhanced potential of the sense and emotion functionism provided by his own alliance with them, might overpower him.

One of the phallic renderings of the rainbow symbolism is curiously interesting. It is made to allegorize the prohibition of the male from union with the female during menstruation. Erymanthus, the son of Apollo, was said to have been struck blind because he looked on Venus when she was bathing. Acteon, seeing Diana at her bath, was turned into a stag. David was punished for his relations with Bathsheba, whom he saw bathing. What is the significance of the punishment of all these solar heroes for contacting the woman during her period? It is but one of the forms of cryptic typology under which ancient sagacity limned in outline the "fall" of the god when he linked his life with the feminine or material powers in a cycle of manifestation. He is dramatized as contaminating himself by his union with the wasting expenditure of natural force. He looks upon mother nature when she is shedding her life-blood fruitlessly. The glance of his eye, the sun, through her shower fixes the sevenfold division of physical nature in the sky. But the rainbow comes at the end of the rainstorm, and union of spirit with matter at the end of its outpouring is the time propitious for fecundation and the new birth. At any rate the punishment allotted to deity for intercourse with the flowing stream of the natural physical order, typed as feminine, is his being reduced to imprisonment in the animal body of man! Like the rainbow, this is sevenfold in organization. The sun, peeking out and beholding nature dripping, projects the sign of his intercourse with matter upon the opposite side of heaven in his septenary dismemberment. The sevenfold fission of his primal unity shows the disruption of his integrity in the sight of all the earth!

This is not empty imagery. It has had historical actualization in a strange way. It is related in *Genesis* (6) and in other racial epics that the sons of God had untimely intercourse with the females of the more advanced animal species, breeding the races of half-human, half-animal types. Early connection with the female animals instituted the miscegenation that so nearly thwarted the cosmic plan. As a result of the unleashing of powerful procreative forces in the animal world there ensued an unnatural production of hybrid monsters and prodigies of lust, which, the books hint, had to be expunged from evolution by the sinking of continents. One of the backgrounds of the "deluge" is thus erected. Procreation in the Golden Age or Edenic state was by *kriyashakti,* exercised by the will and the mind. This was possible because incarnation had not yet been fully achieved, and the forms of flesh were of ethereal tenuity. But miscegenation began prematurely and bred misshapen monsters. The enhancing of the keen powers of sense by the entry of the gods intensified the carnal mind, and a more or less promiscuous generation ran riot. This is the meaning of the harlotry or whoredom against which the Eternal vents his displeasure so vehemently throughout the prophetic books of the *Old Testament.* It is also allegorized by the various tempests on the sea into which the solar heroes must be cast, after being awakened, to still the raging waters of animal lust. This is the meaning of Jonah's being cast into the waters after the casting of lots showing him responsible for the tempest. As the belly is the seat of the sexual and animal nature, the solar god is appropriately placed in the fish's belly. And that neither Jonah's venture nor Jesus' burial is historical is indicated by the fact that both were held captive in this cavern of death for three days!

In the Eternal's promise to Noah that the rainbow after every storm would remind him of his compact not to bring further destruction on the earth, he concludes with: "and the waters shall never again become a deluge to destroy every creature." The structure of this sentence is enlightening; for it is to be noted that the Eternal does not say that there shall be no waters to cover the earth, but that the waters of living force released for evolutionary purposes shall not again get out of hand and "become a deluge."

Of great value in this connection is the latter part of an Egyptian inscription called the Destruction of Mankind, dealing with the rebellion and fall of the angels. It ends similarly to that of Noah:

"When the deluge of blood is over, it is stated by the majesty of Ra: 'I shall now protect men on this account. I raise my hand (in token) that I shall not again destroy men.'"

282

Here it is distinctly called a deluge of blood, not of water, signifying that the fiery nature of deity was drowned in the blood of incarnation. This points clearly to the racial biological nature of the deluge and away from any historical imputation whatever. Cosmology, biology, racial origin and individual spiritual history are all woven together in the skein of both the rainbow and the deluge symbolism. The thread that is missing is objective history!

The four elemental symbols are found to suggest these interesting correlations when two or more are seen in interplay. But there is almost no end of allusions to each of them separately in the tomes of the old wisdom. Much of this material is too valuable to be passed by. We begin with earth at the bottom.

This element need not be dealt with at great length. It is readily seen for what it truly is, the nethermost stratum of matter to which intelligence descends to manifest. The mineral kingdom of earth, the physical base of man's body, marks the nadir of the downward sweep and the turning point or pivot. On its descending arc life undergoes a subjection of its finer forces to sluggish inert matter, on the analogy of a fire being reduced in burning potency. The earth is thus the opposite pole to heaven, as matter is the opposite node to spirit. And forever between these two extremes of positive and negative being plies the tireless shuttle of life. From spirit to matter and back again is the schedule of life's endless journey. The ultimate significance of this is the profound mystery of all being. But Life *is;* and one of its activities is the cyclical periodicity of its creative function, its circulation around the wheel of birth, growth and death. It rhythmically institutes a progressive order, runs its course, perfects its products and then annihilates these products (to outward sense), leaving their seeds of new life, however, to flower in the next cycle.

Archaic wisdom expounds more intricate cosmic and evolutionary data than modern science has yet picked up. It asserts that the stars and planets are living beings, like humans. If a mortal-immortal man has four distinct bodies appertaining to his entire being, so does a planet. The ancient science says that each globe physically discernible is but one of a chain of seven bodies existing, like man's vestures, in four types of matter symboled, again like man's bodies, by earth, water, air and fire. A life wave emanating from the Father darts outward and courses around this chain of seven globes, organizing them in fact, and creating a kingdom of kindred matter on each plane. The direction is downward or matterward for the first four globes, after which it turns again spiritward and sweeps upward through the last three. That is, the life wave builds a planetary spirit body on the plane of spirit (fire), a more material body on the plane of mind (air), a still more dense one on the plane of emotion (water), and finally an entirely material globe on the plane of mineral earth. Then it turns upward in its swing, rebuilding new globe bodies on the subtler planes through which it descended till it rests at last in the glorious new spirit body on the plane of the empyreal fire. On the fourth or lowest plane it builds up, lives in and then retires from, the dense physical globe which is the earth.

The earth is thus the place of critical interest in the whole cycle. The life wave is sent forth to return with a harvest of more abundant life. Now it is only as spirit contacts and overcomes the inertia of matter that it brings its own potentialities to birth. Abiding eternally on its own plane, as Platonic philosophy says, it remains non-productive. It must go forth, seek adventure, meet with opposition, wrestle with the powers that would choke it, and achieve its new cyclical victory in a world of adversity. As Plotinus writes, "It is not enough for the soul merely to exist; she must show what she is capable of begetting." Here is the model and the genius of all romance, all drama. And the earth is the scene of this conflict between the embryonic immortal and the titanic mortal forces. And where the earth stands in the chain of planetary bodies, the physical body of man stands in the chain of vehicles or vestures which compose each individual. The human body is the seat and arena of the great conflict of personal destiny. Without dwelling in and mastering the body of flesh, the individual soul, as says Plotinus, would never know her powers. She would be spiritual, as she was from the start; but she would dream her existence away without ever becoming consciously aware of her latent creative capabilities, if she did not incarnate. Incarnation is evolution's method of setting the seal of reality upon conscious life. This is the office of earth-life in the cycle and of incarnation for the individual soul. And it is the crucial point in all philosophy, as it is the critical point in individual destiny. As for the soul her pathway to heaven runs through the earth, and on it she goes to her "death" to be born anew.

284

In the *Ritual* (Ch. 19) the chapter of the Crown of Triumph shows the meaning of placing a floral wreath or crown upon the mummy in the *sheta* or coffin. It was to depict that the "garland of earth in the nether world becomes the crown of triumph for eternal wear." The crown of life was given to those who had suffered on earth. Earth and the body were the double arena in which the soul wrought out its perfection. Untried, untested in the fires of bodily experience, its faculties could not have been forged into strength, power and beauty. The soul comes into the underworld of darkness to win the immortal crown of light and glory, for only by victory over the powers of darkness can the light be brought to shining.

The *Ritual* makes it clear that the underworld of the earth is the realm to which the father Osiris, or Amen-Ra, or other deity pictured as aged, comes to regain his youth. "The old man (Amen-Ra) shineth in the form of one that is young"; "the old man that maketh himself young again"; "the unknown one who hideth himself from that which cometh forth from him"; and finally the one who is "deified in the underworld." In the *Book of Breathings* the Manes is told:

"Then doth thy soul breathe forever and ever, and thy form is made anew with thy life *upon earth;* thou art made divine along with the souls of the gods, thy heart is the heart of Ra, and thy members are the members of the great god."

Again:

"And the god Ap-uat (i.e., the Opener of the Ways) hath opened up for thee a prosperous path."

The Manes cries to Ra, his divinity:

"Make thou thy roads glad for me; and make broad for me thy paths when I shall set out from earth for the life in the celestial regions."

Saying that the divine speech of Ra is in his ears in the Tuat (underworld) the Manes prays that "no defects *of my mother* be imputed to me." This is to say: let no stains from my contacts with mother earth adhere to me. Yet to the unit of undivinized spirit it is told· "Through Keb (Seb) thou dost become a spirit." Apotheosis is on earth. The swamps of earth are the miry path to the Aarru-Hetep at the summit of the mount.

We meet in the *Ritual* the statement that "Earth opens to Ra! Earth closes to Apap!" It is the story of the Reed (Red) Sea over again. The physical domain opens as the soul learns the keys of magic power that part the waters. These keys are virtue, discipline, wisdom. But earth closes to block the way to Apap, or evil and ignorance. Earth provides the conditions that induce every quality of spirit to burgeon in beauty; but it brings to nought the counsels of the ungodly through karmic law. To live in the lower, sensual, grasping nature is to plunge into the waters and be overwhelmed; to aspire after fervent righteousness is to find that dry land between the parted waters.

The next element is water, and this is a more pertinent symbol of the lower self in man even than earth. It stands in two senses, first, for the primordial essence of all substance, the water of the abyss, the mother principle of all things; secondly for the higher water of life. The first is called in Egypt the water of the Nun, or of Nu (Nnu, equated with Noah by Massey). The Greek *Nux* (*Nyx*), Latin *Nox*, perhaps matches this goddess of the infinite void, in whom there is nothing but the sheer potentiality of life. As this is the primal darkness and the void, Nu, Nun, Nyx, is apparently the linguistic original of all things negative in speech, as "no," "none," "not," "nought," "never," "negative," German "nichts." But out of it flashed the first ray of light. It was the water of source, and life is born out of water.

But the primal abyss splits into two firmaments, and there is the water above to match the water below. So secondly there is the water of life, the higher firmament. This is practically equivalent to spirit and is another but less used form of the fire symbol itself. The rain that falls from the skies, and not the flowing water below, would be its type.

Closer to man, however, there is a third application of the water symbol. The element is made to stand for the second of his constituent principles, the emotional nature, which is so closely inwrought with his physical body as generally to include the latter in its reference. This is the most suggestive and fruitful use of water as symbol. It is the water of earth, of sense, of generation, that holds the threat of drowning the god. It is the water in which he has to learn to walk without sinking! It is the water that he has to transmute into wine as spirit. Water is the aptest symbol of the lower life because of its fluid nature and its constant motion and fluctuation, picturing sense and emotion.

Life cast amid the senses and the feelings is in unceasing flux, as Heraclitus said. Like the restless throb of ocean, it is never still. No figure could better portray the dual sense-emotion life of mortals than the heaving bosom of the sea, or the moving current of a river or brook.

Nature indeed holds before us a marvelous textual illustration of the whole cyclical life process in her water-circulation system. We have the ocean as the source of all rising water emanations. The sun elevates great masses of moisture into the skies by its power; and a reduction of temperature causes this water vapor to condense and fall upon the land. From remote highlands it trickles into the brooks, streams, rivers and bays, and finally rejoins its primal sea of source. The circuit bristles with analogies to the life cycle at every turn. The sun's function in lifting masses of vapor invisibly to heaven types the spirit's power to refine the unseen elements of consciousness and elevate the substance of life. The reduction in temperature symbolizes a procedure in evolution which leads souls back to earth. The condensation of the vapor mass into individual drops symbols the dismemberment of deity. The fall to earth matches the descent of the gods. The beneficent agency of the rain in uplifting natural growth is evident as a parallel with the work of the god in uplifting the human. Without water from heaven sterile earth would produce no life! Without deity from heaven humanity would be equally sterile, spiritually, as are the animals. The return to primal unity in the sea is manifest in the conversion of individual selfishness back to social and spiritual solidarity. Then comes a step in the cycle that yields the utmost of instruction for thought. Every phase of the round is visible except that in which the water is lifted from the sea again into heaven. The entire cycle is perceptible except the one arc in which matter is returned to spirit (vapor) form. In every visible round of life process there is always the one stage that is invisible!

This observation holds a pointed moral for science and truth-seeking generally. It has been the unwillingness to recognize the reality of the process of life in its invisible stage that has kept science from discerning full truth. For human life runs a similar cycle, issuing from the subjective or spirit world into the objective palpable life of body, and retiring again. But, like the vapor rising from the ocean, its return to heaven and its positive existence there is unseen. Science stands on its firm denial of the soul's subsistence after death on the sheer ground of its disappearance. Nature's typology intimates that, like the vapor that has risen to the skies, it will return again to earth, and that it must therefore be subsistent in the interim. As the water cycle is complete in spite of one invisible segment, so the natural cycle of life is complete, with no arc missing. The apparently missing link is found in the unseen world. But is not science itself finding that the most vital and dynamic realities are in the unseen world?

The sally of the gods into nature's realm is imaged as a welling forth of water from a living rock or secret source. Ihuh (Jehovah), the Lord, is described in Egypt as "the fountain of living waters" (*Psalms,* 29:10). *Revelation* speaks similarly (Ch. 22:1): "And he showed me a river of water of life bright as crystal, proceeding out of the throne of God." And in *Isaiah* when it is said that the dumb shall break forth into singing, it is added: "Waters are to well forth in the wilderness, streams in the desert." Jesus cried:

"If any man thirst, let me come unto me and drink. He that believeth on me, as the scripture hath said, out of his belly shall flow rivers of living water." (*John* 7:37).

In the *Ritual* the god says: "I flood the land with water." There were various pools and lakes which the Manes was to cross on his journey through the underworld. Pepi, the soul, is called "the efflux of the celestial water, and he appeared when Nu came into being." For the Manes the promise is made: "He shall quaff water at the fountain head." In an Irish myth seven streams flowed forth from "Counla's Well" into the River Shannon. All cosmic effluence is in seven rays or streams. The Egyptian text says of the Manes: "He gulpeth down seven cubits of the great waters." The *Rig-Veda* (10:8, 3) gives us a similar hint, though it has several loftier interpretations: "When the sun flew up, the (seven) Arushis refreshed their bodies in the water." The disappearance by day of the seven stars of the Great Bear, which always typed these seven creative emanations, is probably the natural basis of this poetization. The water issuing from the base of a rock is typical of godly life emanating from the eternal rock of being. In the *Ritual* we meet with the hero who, like Moses, causes water to gush from the rock. He says: "I make the water to issue forth." Of this water the children of light "drink abundantly." The water of dawn, the dew, symbolizing the first outpouring, is called "the water of

288

Tefnut," twin sister of Shu, god of life by air. And it is notable that in the Hebrew version the first to make the water come forth by miracle for the people to drink is Miriam, whose relation to Moses is identical with that of Tefnut to Shu. This Shu, as the son of Nun, the firmamental water, is the life in breath; and almost unquestionably furnishes the prototypal character for Jo*shua*, the son of Nun in the Hebrew book. And Joshua is identical by name with Jesus. The text pictures the goddess Nut standing beneath her sycamore tree, from which she pours out the water of life, as Hathor offers her fruit juice from the tree.

The Hawaiian *mythoi* have a rock that yields water on being struck with a rod.

Heaven as the source of celestial water is indicated in the derivation of the Greek *Ouranos,* "heaven," from the Egyptian *Urnas,* which is the celestial water (probably giving the root of our "urn"). It is the blood of *Ouranos* that gives birth to Aphrodite.

Neptune is traced to the Egyptian *nef,* "sailor," and this god was the sun over the waters, the god who completed the circuit round or over the waters.

Water was the first creation, and up out of its depths came the emanating gods to get the breath of life. Could one find a more astonishing replica of this cosmic situation than that furnished by the modus of human birth? Every child who in this life is to travel from nature to God issues into life out of a sack of water, and the first thing done by the attendant is to stimulate the latent breathing power. "Tefnut bears him, Shu gives him life."

The gods who brought the water of life down to mortals had thereafter to endure the drenching by this same elements in its earthly form. Says *Daniel:* "He shall be drenched with the dews of heaven." As the original cosmic water was the Nun, or the negation of all positive life, so the earthly shadow of water, that is, matter, is similarly a type of the negation of life. It is inert. The Egyptian ideograph of privation, negation, is a wave of water! And many Indian languages have a similar term for "he dies" and "water." This indicates the idea of death by drowning, the paraphrase of incarnation. The gods descend to drink of the waters of carnal life at the peril of their immortal souls. The dead beneath the waters, says Massey, are the Manes in Amenta, where the waters are an image of the lower Nun, the water not above, but below, the horizon. Isis sought her drowned son Horus in the waters of the underworld, from which he was fished out by Sevekh. Bacchus, lord of the humid nature, in being raised again, ascends from the water, enters the air and comes then as the Fanman or Winnower, the purifier by air (mind). (Plutarch: *De Iside et Oside*) This marks once more the evolution of natural man over into the kingdom of spirit, the transition from water to air, or from emotion to mind, from Tefnut to Sekhet, or from Tefnut to Shu. Jonah, the personification of the god in matter, cried from "the belly of death":

"For thou didst cast me into the depth, in the heart of the seas, and the flood was round about me; all thy waves and thy billows passed over me . . . The waters compassed me about, *even to the soul*. The deep was round about me; the weeds were wrapped about my head."

Job (26) cries that "the dead tremble beneath the waves . . . He stilleth the sea by his power," as did Jonah and Jesus, Horus and Tammuz and others. "He turneth back the waterflood which is over the thigh of the goddess Nut . . ." The Manes in dread of the deluge prays to "have power over the water and not be drowned" (*Rit.*, Ch. 57). Glimpsing his coming earthly victory, he cries: "I am the being who is never overwhelmed in the waters."

Herod in attempting to kill Jesus by a slaughter of the innocents is paralleled by the Pharaoh. He attempted to blot out the menace of the Israelites by ordering the Hebrew midwives to kill all the *male* children at the time of birth *by drowning* (*Exod.* 1:22). This is a depiction of the general danger menacing the god during his incarnation in the watery realm of the body. The *Psalms* express it indirectly (74): "Thou breakest the heads of the dragons in the waters." The gods had to break the power of the elementary lives engendered in the lower or water kingdoms. Sargon says that his mother gave him to the river, "which drowned me not."

"He drew me out of great waters," sings the Psalmist. Moses is water-born. Josephus explains the name as signifying "one who was taken out of the water." Moffatt translates it as "removed" (from the water). Pharaoh's daughter called the name of the child Mosheh, and said "because I drew him out of the water." (*Exod.* 11:10). Maui, of New Zealand legend, like Moses and Sargon, was drawn out of the water at birth. And the floating ark was the coffin. The Speaker says: "I am coffined in an ark like Horus, to whom his cradle is brought." This cradle is often represented as a nest of *papyrus reeds,* equated thus with the ark of bulrushes. Thor in the Norse *mythos* had to wade through the waters, there being no bridge for him, as he fares to the Doomstead under the Ygdrasil. The root of this great Norse tree of life was beneath the water, its stem and branches above, like the lotus. The Ygdrasil ash stands in the well of the Urdar fountain. The Egyptian Pool of Persea nourished the roots of "the two divine sycamore trees of earth and heaven." In *Revelation* the tree of life is planted on both sides of the river of waters.

It was in the storm on the sea that the distressed sailors in the gray light of dawn saw Jesus walking upon the troubled waters, drawing nigh to them. In quieting the storm he played the part of Horus in the *Ritual,* of whom it is written: "He hath destroyed the water-flood of his mother"—nature. In another form this stands: "He hath broken the power of the raging rain-storm." And again: "He hath dispersed for thee the rain-storm, he hath driven away for thee the water-flood, he hath broken for thee the tempests." All this prefigures the stilling of the strong restless power of the natural elements in man's lower life, the mother-material nature, symboled by water. The god descending into the sphere of "water" was imaged by the duck, goose or swan, who all dive for food under the water. In a beautiful myth of the island of Celebes, *seven* celestial nymphs descend from the sky *to bathe.* They are seen by Kasimbaha, who stole the robes of one of them named Utahagi. These robes gave her the power of flying, and without them she was caught. She became his wife and bore him a son. Here we find ignorant primitives, according to scholastic rating, preserving a definite legend of the highest spiritual truth. For the robe stolen by the man on earth was her divine vesture, the immortal spiritual body.

The *Ritual* speaks eloquently again in one of its chapter titles: "Of drinking water in the underworld." And in this chapter the Manes prays: "May there be granted to me mastery over the water courses as over the members of Set (Sut)."

One of the Chinese Trinity of gods "showed the people how to cultivate the ground which had been reclaimed from the waters" (Shu-King).

We have in this imagery the meaning of "casting bread upon the waters." It is the going out into incarnation of that "bread" which cometh down out of heaven for the life of the world. As the life in generation is distressful for the god, one of the promises pertaining to final release from the ordeal emphasizes that "there shall be no more night, no more *sea*" in the blessed homeland of the father. But the bread cast out is multiplied and returns a sevenfold increase.

The zodiacal sign of Aquarius is the Waterman pouring from an urn the water of life in a double stream. The sacred literature is filled with references to the two waters, or the water of the double source. In many myths there are two streams, two springs, two wells, two lakes. Cosmically the two indicate the original fission of God's being into the two poles of positive and negative life, or spirit and matter. This was the divine life that emanated in two streams to fructify creation. In the lower world it is reflected in the division between the water of the air above and on the earth below, vapor and liquid, cloud on high and stream on the ground. Sometimes the goddesses representing primal fecundity are cut in two, as Tiamat, Isis, Neith, Hathor, Apt, Rerit. Thus Nut was the goddess of celestial water and Apt of the terrestrial; Isis of the heavenly, Nephthys of the earthly. These were pictured as the two cows or two groups of seven cows (as in Pharaoh's dream) or a cow of two colors, fore and hind. The cow, as productive source of life-food, was paired into the water-cow of earth and the milch-cow of heaven. The water-cow symboled Mother Nature alone, before the advent of divine spirit, the masculine bull, into creation—matter unfructified by intelligence. The seven cows betoken the seven creative Elohim, the living energies of matter. The two living streams of water were put in the uranograph in the form of a water-course with two branches, one of which was the Iarutana (Egy.), Eridanus (Greek), Jordan (Hebrew); and the other the milk stream, the Milky Way, Via Lactea. The Eridanus, or earth water, was the stream that had to be passed over in incarnation; the Milky Way was the water course by which the soul ascended again into the heavens of spirit. The cow of earth was constellated in the seven stars of the Great Bear, the Milch-cow of heaven in Cassiopeia.

The Hindu Aditi, as the Great Mother of the Gods, becomes twain. She yields milk for the gods, and is identical with the heaven cow in Egypt. Aditi was the primal form of Dyaus (Zeus), the sky divinity.

She alternates with Diti as mother of the embryo that was divided into seven parts, the seven Elohim. As Aditi she was the undivided Absolute; as Diti she was the divided one, mother of the two streams of outpoured life.

Of Ra it is written: "Thou bringest the milk of Isis to him and the water-flood of Nephthys." Or again: "Thou hast brought the milk of Isis to Teta, and the water of the celestial stream of Nephthys."

The Egyptians figured the two waters in the Nile, with its two arms, the Blue Nile and the White Nile. In the planispheres the south was the region of source, and the Nile rose in the highlands of the south, Upper Egypt (by elevation); so the heavenly chart depicts the celestial Nile or Eridanus (Jordan) as pouring forth its divine stream from the southern sky, rising from the star Achernar in Eridanus constellation, and traveling northward to Orion's foot, or where Orion rises up as Horus, the lord of the fertilizing inundation. Horus' representative in the planisphere is Orion. In the celestial chart Orion is found standing, club in hand, the mighty hunter, with one foot on the water of the River Eridanus. By this it is depicted that the young solar god, our divinity, rises up where the stream of natural evolution ends and stands over it invested with the majesty and power of the lord of the lower waters of sense and emotion. Also in the case of the Nile there were two sources of its water, one earthly, the Lake Nyanza, the other celestial, or the rain and snow from heaven in the highlands of source.

The Persian *Bundahish* details the two waters of origin as female and male seed. "All milk arises from the seed of the males and the blood is that of the females." The two waters, or blood and milk, were both typed as feminine at first, to represent nature as productive without spiritual fecundation. To symbol the latter, the one was afterwards made masculine. The first pair was the mother's blood and milk; the second, blood and seminally-engendered milk, or milk treated as of male generation.

As in the cosmos, matter, the virgin mother of life, was evolving her forms without the visible presence of animating divine intelligence, that is, before a creature embodying intelligence had been evolved, so in human racial history the body of man was built up by nature without the ensouling presence of mind. Matter and its inherent force, the feminine aspect of life, alone occupied the field. Marvelously this phase is paralleled not only in some aspects of biology but in early racial --

293

history itself. Following upon Totemic social organization there was the Matriarchate, when the woman was head and ruler, because she was the only known producer of life. The function of fatherhood was obscurely known. The mother and later the daughter, or the mother and her sister, were the only known bonds of blood relation for the children. As in the cosmos, so in human society, the male element, while operative, was hidden out of sight and knowledge. A child was related only through two women, mother and daughter, or mother and aunt. Massey asserts in a hundred pages that these two are the archetypal forms of the two wives, or two women who are *dramatis personae* in nearly every religious myth of origin. Adam, Abraham, Jacob, Laban, David, Moses, Samson had two wives, and the *Old Testament* is replete with stories of two women, who are sisters, as Aholah and Aholibah, in *Ezekiel*. Two Meris figure in the story of Osiris, and the two Maries in that of Jesus.

Two pools were pictured in the *Ritual*, the Pool of Natron and the Pool of Salt. Also the Pool of the North and the Pool of the South.

The male or seminal element, then, marked the introduction of spiritual vivification into the natural order. A new birth ensued for nature, new powers were released for her creatures, and they sprang forward to attain a new status in conscious being. The element injected into nature to produce this regeneration was typified, both by the Gnostics and by Jesus, as "the salt of the earth" and the "light of the world." The sowing of the spiritual seed, or the potentiality of the god, was the earnest of man's redemption from animal status. The effort to fix the character of our "salvation" without knowing specifically the nature of our "fall"—without definite knowledge of what we were to be saved from—has held the human mind for centuries captive to a vague dread, a bogie apprehension, that has been a vast discredit to theology. Salt is the figure of preservation. As in the case of the mummy unguents, salt was to preserve the lower nature of man from decay.

Curiously the two Pools are elsewhere called the Pool of the Moon and the Pool of the Sun. In the Pool of Natron, or Hesmen, or Smen, the bloody sweat of menstruation, we have the feminine, that is, material aspect of life, for which the moon ever stands, in opposition to the sun, which is masculine, life-generative and vivifying. The moon in its phase unlighted by the sun represented the woman, nature, in her unproductive stage. She was in her virgin state, unwedded to male spirit, unfecundated by mind. Impregnation by Intelligence would make her productive and take her out from under her subjection "to the law" of periodicity and matter.

And this alone is the meaning of the "miracle" in which Jesus heals the woman with an issue of blood from her youth, who touched the hem of his robe and received the perceptible discharge of his power. The incident is just one of the old mythic depictions, using the sexual procreative functionism as a weather-vane of spiritual meaning. When matter, the virgin mother, received the impregnation of spirit, the periodic course of nature was interrupted and a miraculous new birth of life was inaugurated. The stoppage of her issue of blood was but the sign of the entrance of deity into humanity. For the ceasing of the natural flow is the sure index of the ensuing advent of a higher birth. Nature, running to waste without fruitage, was healed by divine impregnation or vivification. Christianity has been content to take from this incident the meager wealth of a physical "cure"; ancient poetic genius deposited in it a mine of inexhaustible cosmic suggestiveness, a source of great moral enrichment for all.

That antique document, the *Book of Enoch,* comments directly upon the point under discussion (80: 7-10):

"The water which is above shall be the agent (male) and the water which is under the earth shall be the recipient, and all shall be destroyed."

Jesus said that he was from above and natural man from beneath. It is found in the *Ritual* that in the Pool of Natron and the Pool of Salt the sun was reborn each day and the moon each night. The circuit of experience each day, or each life, for both the divine man (sun) and the animal man (moon) amounted to a rebaptism and renewal of life. "I grow young each day," exults the soul in the *Ritual.*

The constellation of the Great Bear was called "The Well of the Seven Stars." The Hebrew Beer-Sheba (Sheba meaning obviously "seven") was an early form of the primordial water. Beer-Sheba in the *Septuagint* is given as *"Phrear Horkou"* (Greek), meaning: "The well of the oath." What can this strange name connote, save that it is a subtle designation for this life in watery body, to which the soul descended under the karmic "command" or covenant, or oath, which binds it to return to this living well of life?

The twin pools were located in Anu, the white water being southward, the red northward. In the *Ritual* one name for it is the "Well of Sem-Sem." Sem-Sem denotes regenesis. The *Ritual* says: "Inexplicable is the Sem-Sem, which is the greatest of all secrets." It was the place where sun and moon were renewed. In consequence it was a place where the deceased seeks the waters of regeneration, or fount of youth. He says (Ch. 97): "I wash in the Pool of Peace. I draw water from the Divine Pool under the two Sycamores of heaven and earth. All justification is redoubled on my behalf." "Osiris is pure by the Well of the South and the North."

In plain language all this metaphorization means simply that man, a biune being, strides forward in his evolution by dipping in the experiences of both the carnal embodiment, the Pool of Natron, the "Nature" Pool, and in the god's divine essence, the Pool of Salt, the "Spirit" Pool.

The water of life is sometimes said to be concealed between two lofty mountains which stand close together. But for two or three minutes each day they move apart, and the seeker of the healing and vivifying water must be ready on the instant to dart through, fill his two flasks and instantly rush back. *Zechariah* (14:4) hints at this:

"And the Mount of Olives shall cleave in the midst thereof towards the East and towards the West, and half of the mountain shall remove toward the North and half toward the South."

"Day" is a glyph for a cycle of any length, here an incarnation. The period of openness between the two mountains is just the time between birth and death in this life, during which brief moment, the soul must fall speedily to work to wrest all it can from this opportunity for contact between the two natures, animal and divine. It must strive quickly to fill its cup of experience from the flowing waters. The night cometh when no man can work. For this is the only time in its evolution when it can drink from the double spring, the two pools. The two or three minutes coincide with the two (or three) days in the tomb.

And by the shifting of the earth's axis the east-west relation was supplanted by the north-south one, as referred to by *Zechariah*.

The Egyptian god Hapi, being of both sexes, denotes the eunuch in whom the two were united. He is the epicene personification, androgyne. From the mouth of Hapi issues the one stream which enters two other figures from whose two mouths it is emaned in a double stream. This is the one water dividing into two in the mythology. In the astrograph this is Aquarius.

In Egyptian and Hebrew traditions the deity is represented as shedding two creative tears, a poetic version of the two waters.

In the Hindu picture of Mahadeva and Parvati the waters of Soma are seen issuing from the head of the male deity and from the mouth of the cow, the feminine emblem. Siva is the mouth of the male source and Parvati, the Great Mother, is that of the feminine source. "He who knows the golden reed standing in the midst of the waters is the mysterious Prajapati, the generator."

Milk from the body signified the female water, while Soma juice figured the male element, the wine that went to the *head!*

The ancient mother source was portrayed as twofold, a breathing land-animal in front, a water-animal behind, typing the elements of water and air. This is seen in the zodiacal Capricorn, the sea-goat, land-goat in front, sea animal in the rear. The Hindu goddess Maya hovers over the waters, and presses her two breasts with both hands, ejecting the twofold stream of living nutriment. The Hermaean Zodiac shows the Great Bear with streaming breasts, and the zodiacal Virgin is represented by the Bear as unproductive in Virgo, but the "bearer" in the sign of Pisces, where she is half fish and half human. Ishtar, another personification of the genetrix, was dual. One of her names was Semiramis, the daughter of Atergatis. The latter has the tail of a fish, but the daughter was wholly human. The fish denoted water, and the dove on Ishtar's head signified air, again throwing sense and soul into relation.

Since the Eridanus is the Jordan, the word merits closer attention. It came from the Egyptian *Iarutana. Eri*, later *Uri*, was an Egyptian name for the inundation, meaning "great, mighty," whilst *tun* or *tana* signified "that which rises up and bursts its bonds." In *Eritanu*, or *Iarutana*, we then have the mighty river rising to overflow its banks. Astrologically it was placed in the heavenly chart as issuing from the mouth of the constellation of the Southern Fish, type of life source, and flowing north to the foot of Orion.

It is of note that in *Joshua* (22) it is said the Eternal made the Jordan the boundary between the main body of the Israelites and the Reubenites and Gadites, who had not been permitted to cross into the Promised Land because, as it is put, "you have no share in the Eternal." Naturally this stream of life force sweeping mankind onward marks the boundary between the animal and the spiritual kingdoms. Animal man can not cross it until he has been bathed in its waters and been purified and transformed. We are crossing this boundary line between our lower and higher natures.

There is plentiful use of the water symbol under the special form of the sea. "The angel descended until he reached the *sea of the earth,* and he stood with his right foot upon it." This matches Horus-Orion in the starry chart standing with his foot upon the end of the Jordan River. The Dragon poured forth the water flood to overwhelm the Woman cast out of heaven. This points to the release of the surging forces of the carnal nature upon the soul after incarnation. But the earth opened to swallow up the released waters and helped the Woman, at which the Beast waxed more wroth; "and he waged war against them *upon the borders of the sea which encompassed the earth.*" This is Paul's war of the carnal mind against the spirit on the rim or boundary between earth and sea, our two natures!

The watery field of life is pictured as a "crystal sea wherein the *fire was reflected,* and upon it there stood those who had overcome the influence of the Beast, who had not worshiped his image nor borne upon them the mark of his number."

Ra brings to Teta "the power to journey over the Great Green Sea." The Manes (Teta) "goes round about the Lake and on the flood of the Great Green Sea." Again: "Thou sailest over the Lake of Kha, in the north of heaven, like a star passing over the Great Green Sea . . . as far as the place where is the star Seh (Orion)." This matches the location of the Eridanus. Hawaiian tradition says that the voyaging souls "waded safely through the sea."

One of the most specific corroborations of the meaning of the water symbol is found in *Revelation* in the expression that when the books of life were opened, "the sea gave up its dead, for Death and Hades found no more any place, because they were judged and cast down." Orthodox typology presents two varying symbols of what takes place "when the dead are raised." One says the *graves* were opened; the other that the *sea* gave up its dead. Here is a land and water conflict, only resolvable by symbolism, which may use many figures to picture one truth. But literal history falls meaningless between two varying statements of fact. The grave and the sea both refer to mortal life, which under any figure yields up its living "dead" at the end of the accomplished cycle. Then the seer "beheld the fashioning of the earth anew; for the sea out of which the Beast had risen was now no more." "There shall be . . . no more sea."

It is necessary to give some space to the symbolism of the fish, for it carries part of the imputation of the water element. For practical purposes it is possible to equate the four terms, fish, sea, matter and mother, in significance. The fish denotes, first, life in submergence, or the god in matter, who yet does not die, who can still breathe under the elements. But more specifically it intimates the source of life flowing outward toward matter. It is the outrance, not the entrance, of life. The whale spouting out its water stream is suggestive. The Eridanus poured forth from the mouth of the Southern Fish. The *os tincae,* or tench's mouth, was one of the religious symbols of frequent occurrence. Watching a fish, one notes an apparent expulsion of water from the mouth with the semblance of chewing. It is the door of life's emanation, and it is the denizen of the waters out of which life streams. The zodiacal Pisces is the sign of the birth of saviors. Jesus, Horus, Ioannes and others came as Ichthys (*Ichthus*), "fish" in Greek. And we have the fish-avatar of Vishnu. The door of life is figured in the shape of a fish-mouth at the western or feminine end of a church. The Pope's miter is the mouth of a fish. The soul of life comes by way of the water.

The *Vesica Piscis* or fish's bladder denoted the presence of air in the water, and the bubbles rising from the fish's mouth double this hint as to the presence of mind in matter. The fish was a lower symbol than the swan or duck, for it must swim *in* the water; the other can float on the surface. In this sense it types the god caught, trapped in water; also likely to be caught in a net. It is said that cynocephali, who lay in wait to seize fish, "were allowed to catch them because of their ignorance." It is the soul's lack of full knowledge that causes it to be caught again and again in the meshes of carnality.

The fish zodiacally stands for the feet of the man. The mermaid with tail of fish represented the body as partaking in its nether half of the lower forces of life. Man's feet are in the water of life. Ishtar-Semiramis was given the tail of a fish. The tail also portrays the, as yet, non-dual character of life, creative power not yet bifrond. It shows

299

the non-division of the legs. The mummied Christ figure in the Catacombs, with legs bound helplessly together, depicts the god strapped in the bonds of the natural elements, not yet having manifested the duality. He can not use his two legs and walk, like a god. He is only the first, natural man, not man and god conjoined.

Semiramis' brother was Ichthys in the statue at Ascalon. Ichthys was a title of Bacchus. In the Hermaean Zodiac Pisces is named Ichthon, and the fish is the female goddess who brought forth the young sun-god as her Piscean offspring, whether called Horus in Egypt, Jesus in Palestine and Rome, or Marduk, the fish of Hea, in Assyria. Christ was Ichthys the Fish from 255 B.C. until about 1900 A.D., or for the period of the Piscean era in the precession. Previous to that he was Aries, the Lamb of God. Who will figure him now as the Waterman?

An old Egyptian story, the tale of Setnau, written by Taht himself, and alleged to be so potent that two pages of it, when recited, would open the secrets of nature and unlock all mysteries, says: "The divine power will raise fishes to the surface of the water." Metaphorically this refers to the power of the god to lift the natural man, immersed in the sea of material life, to mastery over his lower self, and bring him to the top or surface of his fleshly nature from out the depths of it.

The *Ritual* reports the god as declaring: "I am the great and mighty Fish which is in the city of Qem-Ur." This is the god in matter. But it is promised that Ra "shall be separated from the Egg and from the Abtu Fish." Abtu is a form of Abydos, the place of burial of the god. Ra shall be freed from the fish or submerged state. Two chapter titles tell of "coming forth from the net" and from "the catcher of the fish." The swampy region from which Sevekh, solar deity, recovered the mutilated limbs of Horus, was called Ta-Remu, "the land of the Fish," a name given it by Ra.

Gathering up some scattered fragments of the water emblem, we note Homer describing the river Titaresius flowing from the Styx as pure and unmixed with the taint of death and gliding like oil over the surface of the water by which the gods made their covenant. Oil on troubled waters may be seen to be a profounder symbolism than was conceived before. For the god, oil is no chance symbol, as it was regularly employed in the anointing to type celestial radiance, the sheen of the divine glory. To pour oil on the waters is indeed to quiet the storms of raging animality by the calm of reason and the gentleness of love.

In the Hebrew the water of life flows from the rock Tser till the time of Miriam's passing away. This represents the female source. The change to the masculine phase occurs when the water gushes forth for the first time from the rock Seba (Beer-Sheba) by the command of Moses. This was the water of Meribah, and in the Egyptian *Meri* is water, and *Bah* is the male.

In *Judges* (30) God split the rock as sign of the dual nature, and water flowed forth to quench Samson's thirst, as in the case of Moses.

The throne on which Osiris is seated is sometimes placed, in the vignettes to the *Ritual,* on water, still or running. This is to say that the god is seated above the unstable foundation of the changing earth life. But life is to be established through its experience here, and so "he hath established it upon the floods."

When the god had been transformed he is said to "have gained power over fresh water." As salt typed the saving grace of divinity, the fresh water would point to the new and as yet unsaved natural creature. "Moisture," says the *Chaldean Oracles,* "is a symbol of life, and hence both Plato and, prior to Plato, the gods call the soul at one time a drop from the whole of vivification; and at another time a certain fountain of it."

The chapter can be brought to a close with a few intimations of the air symbolism. It is much less general than those of water and fire. The Sanskrit *"Asu,"* meaning "vital breath" is of great importance because it is the base of *Asura* (Persian: *Ahura,* surname of Ahura-Mazda), one of the specific names of the hosts of incarnating gods.

Both Horus and Jesus came forth with a *fan* in their hands, as the Winnower. This emblem is a clear glyph for the principle of mind. Intellect is to sweep out the chaff of sensuality and free the golden grain. Those initiated into the Greater Mysteries were washed with water and then breathed upon, fanned and winnowed by the purifying spirit. This was the dual baptism of water and the spirit, or fire. One of the two great symbols held in the hands of the Gods in Egypt was a fan called the Khi, the sign of air, breath and spirit. The other was the Hck, or Aut-crook, which denoted laying hold, in the downward direction, of matter by spirit; in the reversed direction, of spirit by the lower personality.

Lack of air, or smothering, was a twin type with drowning for the limitations of incarnation. A phrase of the *Ritual* indicates this: "whose throat stinketh for lack of air." In descending to seek her lost brother and husband Osiris, Isis is claimed to have "made light appear from her feathers; she made air to come into being by means of her two wings,"—another personation of the fanner or winnower. The god fans the mortal to keep him from being suffocated for lack of air, mind. The god brings us intellect, which indeed keeps us from being smothered by the intolerable life of sense. The cogency of leaven as a symbol lies in its generating air within the material mass. The raising of dough is synonymous with the resurrection of mortality. In the *Ritual* there is a "chapter of giving air to the soul in the underworld." Mind came as our savior.

Chapter XIV

FIRE ON HEAVEN'S HEARTH

The way is now cleared for the majestic sweep of the fire symbolism. It rises above the other elements in grandeur and impressiveness. The full implication of its meaning lifts the mind into reaches of luminous suggestiveness as to the splendor of the experience awaiting us in future arcs of our unfoldment. Fire is the emblem of our highest nobility, and even as a mere figure it has a certain power to stir dim intimations of the magnificence of that reality which it hints at. There is in nature hardly a phenomenon more wonderful than the eating away of a stick of wood by a flame. The mystery of all life is back of that energic display. And the mystery becomes awesome when we realize that our own life is more than analogous to fire; it is of kindred nature with it. The soul within us is a spark of divine flame.

The origin of the word is of interest. It goes back to the Greek *pur(pyr)*. Massey traces the word "pyramid" from the stem, plus the Egyptian *met*, meaning "ten" or "a measure," giving us *pyramet*. He asserts that it stands thus for the ten original measures or arcs traced by the god of fire, the sun, through the zodiacal circuit. As the great pyramid at Gizeh, and others, seem to have been intimately related to sidereal measurements, this theory of origin is plausible. The word would then mean "a ten-form measure of fire," a figure for manifest life.

But the Greek *pur* itself traces back to the Chaldean *ur*, primitive word for "fire." To this the Egyptians added their article "the" as prefix, in the form of *p-*, making the word *p-ur* or *pur*. The first emanation, Abraham, came out from *ur*, the primal fire of creation.

The Sanskrit *Agni*, god of fire, is traced by Massey to the general root, *ag*, meaning "to move quickly," as in the Latin *ago*, "to go," *agile* (Lat.), "active," our "agitate" and others. As this derivation links it closely to the Greek *theos*, "god," who by etymology is the "swift runner," "the swift goer," Agni, god of fire, may well be connected with the *theos,* the god whose symbol everywhere is the swift-darting shaft of fire, whether in the heavens or in the uplands of reason and intelligence. The "flash of intelligence" is the exact sign and token of the swift activity of the god within us.

That the soul is a spark from the celestial fire is attested by the words of the Speaker in the *Ritual* (Ch. 97): "Lo I come from the lake of flame, from the lake of fire, and from the field of flame, and I live."

In the *Vision of Scipio* Cicero has preserved some of the ancient doctrine concerning the derivation of souls from the empyrean. The spirit of Africanus tells his son that souls were supplied to men from the eternal fires, which are constellations and stars. Virgil says that in souls there is a potency like fire. In the *Hymn to Minerva* of Proclus, souls originate

> "From the great father's fount, supremely bright,
> Like fire resounding, leaping into light."

One of the *Chaldean Oracles* runs as follows:

"The soul being a splendid fire, through the power of the Father remains immortal, is the mistress of life . . . *the soul extends vital illumination to body.*"

And again most succinctly:

"All things are the progeny of one fire."

The first *Oracle of Zoroaster* tells of a ladder which reached from Tartarus to the first or highest fire. This was the gamut of stages between the lowest levels of material life and the highest spiritual. The principle of soul, says the Oracle, is the operator and giver of life-bearing fire. It fills the vivific bosom of Hecate (the lower nature) and pours on the linked natures of matter and spirit the fertile strength of a fire endued with mighty power. Concerning divine Love the Oracle speaks:

"Who first leaped forth from intellect, clothing fire bound together with fire, that he might govern the fiery cratera (bowls), restraining the flower of his own fire."

When Ceres delivered up the government to Proserpina, her daughter (intellect to soul), she instructed her to have conjugal relation with Apollo, the sun-god, as thus the god would beget "famed off-spring, with faces glowing with refulgent fire."

The upper fire, the *Oracles* affirm, did not shut up its power in matter, nor in works, but in intellect. *"For the artificer of the fiery world is an intellect of intellect."* Saturn, who in the *Oracles* is the first fountain, the strong spirit which is beyond the fiery poles, endues all the lower principles with his essence. These, through his pervading might, "become refulgent with the furrows of inflexible and implacable fire." They "are the intellectual conceptions from the paternal fountain, plucking abundantly the flower of the fire of ceaseless time." And that our progress upward is a return to a fiery nature is shown by these excerpts:

"A fire-heated conception has the first order. For the mortal who approaches to fire will receive a light from divinity; . . ."

"A singular fire extends itself by leaps through the waves of air; or an infigured fire, whence a voice runs before; or a light beheld near, every way splendid, resounding and convolved. But also behold a horse full of refulgent light; or a boy carried on a swift horse—a boy fiery or clothed with gold."

"Rivers being mingled, perfect the works of incorruptible fire."

It was the statement of Greek philosophy that "from the exhalations arising from the burning bodies of the Titans, mankind were produced." [1]

An echo of this abstrusity of esoteric lore is heard in the accounts of the Wiradthuri tribe of Western Australia. One of their initiations is apparently the analogue of the whole basic structure of religion, represented in a fire drama. In the puberty initiations the lads were frightened by a large fire lighted near them, being told that the Dhur-Moolan was about to burn them. This god was supposed to take them into the bush and instruct them in all the traditional customs. So he went through a pretended killing of the boys, *cutting them up* and burning the pieces to ashes, after which he molded the ashes into human shape and restored them to life as new beings. [2] Primitive ignorance may be the nursery of superstition, but much alleged primitive ignorance is old wisdom surviving in ruinous grandeur by the implacable power of tradition.

In the *Clementine Homilies* (8:18) the offspring of the unnatural and untimely union between the sons of God and the daughters of men described in *Genesis* are declared to be "bastards, begotten of the *fire* of angels and the *blood* of women." The gods are rebuked for polluting themselves with women, "as the sons of men do," and for creating a hybrid and unworthy progeny whose destruction they would in the future lament. (*Enoch*·12.)

Many tribes held the fire-fly, which thrives in moist grasses, to be a typical emblem of our divinity. Its periodical flashing in the dark is suggestive.

The *Logia* and *Revelation* both yield data on the theme of fire. At the first angel's trumpet message there ascended on the earth a hail of fire which was scattered from the Altar of Fire before the throne. "And the hail of the fire was mingled with the blood of the Lamb; these were cast upon earth to consume away its evil." Horus had said that he came to put an end to evil. At the second angel's blast lightning flashed forth and *went down into the sea,* which it changed into blood. We have seen that a hail of stars or sparks over the earth was the typical figuration of the descent of the bright deities. The Egyptian ceremony of flinging a blazing cross into the Nile conveys the same connotation. The deities in incarnation were styled by the Greeks water-nymphs. A cross on fire thrust into water carried the purport of the sacrificial act of incarnation. A fiery serpent on the cross is a kindred emblem. The Targum commands: "Make thee a burning." In India the swastika cross was a special emblem of fire, the god Agni. In the early Church the cross of fire was adored on a Friday, when a lighted cross was suspended from the dome of St. Peter's, the cross being covered with lamps in a fire-traced figure. Dante describes the souls in Paradise as praying inside a cross of fire, which is their world. The hawk is a symbol of solar fire, and Horus arose hawk-headed or divinized with fire.

When Lucifer fell upon the earth and with his key unlocked the pit of the abyss, there issued from it clouds of smoke like that which proceeds from a great furnace, and it obscured the light of the sun! That is to say, the mingled steam and exhalation from electrolyzed "water" and "burning flesh," or the carnal nature vivified by currents of deific potency, rose all around the god and well nigh obscured his inner glow. And out of the smoke came forth locusts and scorpions, having power to sting and poison. And these went forth to torment all the dwellers on earth; only they could not harm those who had not the mark of the Beast on them. The army of horsemen that came forth to battle these forms of evil coming out of the smoke appeared as if "emitting fire." This fire scorched those who love to do wickedness, and drove them back into the pit. This denotes the burning out of those strong animal propensities in the fiery furnace of human experience. Proclus in his *Timaeus* (Lib. V) observes concerning the telestic art that "it obliterates through divine fire all the stains produced by generation." This is the true and only meaning of purgatory.

Another angel descended with a rainbow on his head, his face was as the sun for brightness and his feet were resting upon pillars of fire. This lower fire searched the lives of all on earth and filled with pain those who bore the mark of the Beast.

In the *Book of Overthrowing Apap* this arch-fiend and his associates, the Sami and the Sebau (minions of Seb), are burnt up by the flames of the sun-god. In the *Book of Am-Tuat* the bodies, souls, shadows and heads of the enemies of Ra are burnt and consumed daily in pits of fire. In the eighth section of the *Book of Gates* a picture is drawn of a monster speckled serpent called "Kheti," with seven folds, in each one of which stands a god. The open mouth of the serpent belches a stream of fire into the faces of the enemies of Ra, whose arms are tied behind their backs in agonized helplessness. Horus stands by, urging the reptile to consume the enemies of his father. In the *Book of Am-Tuat* there is also a group of twelve serpents, whose work was to pour fire from their bodies "which was to light the dead sun-god on his way." The soul of the god, typed often as "the Eye of Ra," is described as "the flame which followeth after Osiris to burn up the souls of his enemies." "Uatchet, the Lady of Flames, is the Eye of Ra." Ra is addressed as "Thou who givest blasts of fire from thy mouth, (who makest the two lands bright with thy radiance)." The Manes who come out of Amenta pure "shall have burnt incense before Ra."

The inner idea of burning animal flesh on a physical altar was the consuming by divine fire of the dross that emanated from the carnal segment in man. The god came into the natural man to transfigure him. To achieve this aeonial labor his fire had to burn out slowly the grosser elements, earthy and moist, by spiritual alchemy and replace them by subtle and pure essence akin to its own diviner substance. A Buddhist phrase, "the gross purgations of the celestial fire," attests the

307

nature of the chemistry that must take place. The burning up of dross to refine pure metal is a glib poetic shibboleth in philosophy, but few know that it is a description of an actual bio-chemical process taking place in human life. All our lower emotionalism and heavier sensualism is as fuel for the burning. The lurid flare of such a combustion is only turned to pure clear flame by pain and defeat. Animal sacrifice on an altar was only to dramatize the conversion of lower man to higher under the action of fiery spiritual energies. And it is significant that the ancients swore, not by the altar, but by the fire which was on the altar. One would not swear by the impermanent part of his nature, but by the stable and abiding. This was the fire of soul and conscience. The inner fire, imprisoned in body, strives to burn its way into flame. But its fuel is moist and damp—green wood—and it must first slowly dry out the resistant mass. The grossly misunderstood phrase, "the wrath of God," is just this steady consuming of obstructing material.

Says the Eternal, then, in *Deuteronomy* (32), when he notes that his sons have sacrificed to "demons, to no-gods, to gods who are utter strangers, to new-comers of gods":

> "For a self-willed race are they,
>   Children devoid of loyalty.
> My wrath has flared up,
>   flaming *to the nether world* itself,
> burning up earth and all it bears,
>   setting the roots of the hills ablaze.
>
> From Sinai came the Eternal,
>   from Seir he dawned on us;
> from Paran's range he rayed out,
>   blazing in fire from the south.

It is given in the *Ritual* (Ch. 108) that "the Osiris, triumphant, knoweth the name of this serpent. . . . 'Dweller in his fire' is his name."

The Manes "opens the doors of heaven by the flames which are about the abode of the gods; he advances through the fire which is about the home of the gods, who make a way for him, to make him pass onwards, for he is Horus."

According to another text, "Horus led the deceased through the abode of the gods situated among the flames of fire."

Sut and Horus are the representatives of the dual life of man, and are the divine twins, the first of whom, Sut, brings the water of the inundation to submerge the fire of deity in the sea of generation; and the second, Horus, brings the rebirth of the fire within the very borders of the sea of life. Both were astrologically united in the star Sut-Canopus. In an Australian myth the hawk brought the fire to the aborigines.

A typical mythical account of the war in heaven and descent of the fire-devas to earth is found in another Australian legend of the bandicoot who had a firebrand, but refused to share it. This was the rebellion. The hawk and the pigeon were deputed to get it. The pigeon made a lunge for it, whereupon the bandicoot desperately hurled it toward the water to put it out. But the hawk deflected it into the grass over the sea, which caught fire. The hawk and pigeon (dove) are birds of soul-fire, the bandicoot the bird of darkness, a type of the water that put out the solar fire.

All through the world's Märchen one finds that fire is often dual, the first being the natural fire, as of lightning, flint-fire and other forms; the second is a fire that is human in origin, requiring mind to achieve it.

Sut and Horus, as the human duality, are typed in the two phases, light and dark, of the moon. Sut is the black vulture (which lives on blood) and Horus the golden hawk. The lunar ibis, bird of Ptah, is black and white, and portrays the two natures in one creature. There is a legend of a black raven that once was white. In a Thlinkeet tradition the white bird is represented as becoming black in passing up the flue of Kanukh's *fire-place*. This is a form of the phoenix which transforms from black to white (or into the golden hawk) and from white to black in its passage to and from the underworld, which is called Kanukh's flue.

A prayer in the *Ritual* (Ch. 163) begs the god to "grant that the flame may leave the fire, wherever it may be, to raise up the hands of Osiris," which were bandaged to the sides of his inert body in the mummy case. Osiris is himself appealed to, as the Governor of Amenta, to "grant light and fire to the happy soul which is in Sutenkhenen (Heracleopolis)," the underworld. Samson's bound arms were freed by the burning away of his flaxen bonds. The soul (in Ch. 63B) says that Ra has "lifted up the moist emanations of Osiris from the

Lake of Fire and he was not burned." "A fire was kindled for thee in the hands of the goddess Rerit [the hippopotamus goddess of the Nile, i.e., the virgin mother]; she performeth acts of protection for thee every day." The Manes is exhorted to "kindle the fire in order that the flame may rise up; and throw incense upon it in order that the smell of incense may rise up." A chapter (137A) deals with the four blazing flames which are made for the Khu or spirit. The flame riseth, it is said, in Abtu (Abydos) and it cometh to the Eye of Horus. It is set in order on the brow of Osiris and on his breast, and is fixed within his shrine. The Rubric specifies that this chapter shall be recited over the four fires made of anointed *atma*[3] cloth, and the fires shall be placed in the hands of four men who shall have the names of the four pillars of Horus written on their shoulders. It is promised that the soul that undertakes to perform the offices of this chapter of the Four Blazing Fires each day shall find release from every hall in the underworld and from the seven halls of Osiris. The four men are the four guardians of the cardinal points, upholding man at the four corners of his being, or in his four bodies.

The Manes says again: "I am the Great One, son of the Great One; I am Fire, son of Fire, to whom was given his head after it was cut off." The descent was symbolized as a cutting off of the head, since intellect was lost.

The genetrix of the seven stars is called the keeper of fire, the spark-holder.

Sut signifies "Fire-stone," according to Massey. Oddly enough, lightning was anciently regarded as the dart of a fiery stone, and it has the name of fire-stone widely attached to it among many peoples. So we have Jesus saying, "I beheld Satan as lightning fall from heaven." But the name likely has also a reference to the flint-stone fire, as potential fire locked up in stone. Indeed flint was a frequent symbol of the buried deific potency. One of the Mexican legends reports the Mother-Creatrix as having given birth to a flint knife, which fell on earth and became the origin of men. The flint is a graphic symbol of the presence of hidden fire in the physical world. In the same fashion a god (fire) is buried invisibly within the body of physical humanity. Flint nurses the potentiality of the birth of fire within it! "When the Serpent-lightning darted out of the cloud it buried itself in the earth, leaving its stone-head in the aerolith of smelted sand." It was called the Thunder-hatchet. (*Records of the Past.*)

The element of fire was regarded as latent in both wood and stone, needing effort, force, a blow or heat to bring it forth. Fire, with its eternal intimation of spirit, was regarded as the divine inner essence of these materials, a conception now endorsed by late science.

When the Mystery candidate came forth from the examination he was asked what the judges have awarded him and he replies: "A flame of fire and a pillar of crystal." (Ch. 125.)

The Quiché name for lightnnig is Cak-ul-ha, that is, "fire coming from water"; and the serpent of fire and the serpent of water are one, ultimately. The winged serpent signified winged lightning.

The *Old Testament* (*Exod.* 24:12) declares that the glory of the Lord was in appearance like a devouring fire on top of the mount. The *Psalms* (18) say that he "thundered in the heavens. He made darkness his secret place; a smoke issued from his nostrils and devouring fire out of his mouth . . . and he hurtled stones and coals of fire." He is called the "Lightning-sender." In *Exodus* (20) the Eternal descended in fire upon a cloud. Here is the mingling of fire and water again. "Smoke rose like steam from a kiln, till the people all trembled terribly." The lightning only flashed on the third day, a significant fact explained later.

In most of these illustrations the fire alluded to is that of upper intelligence flashing forth to enlighten the natural order. But this fire, in its contact with the watery and earthy elements of the carnal self, stirs up steam, sulphurous exhalations, fumes, noxious gases and dust, and in this transformation it becomes truly a fire of Tophet and Hades! Nevertheless it is still the purifying fire. As washing by water was an emblem of purgation, so fumigation was a companion type. Says Massey:

"Amenta was the land of precious metals and the furnace of solar fire. Hence Ptah, the miner, became the blacksmith of the gods, the Kamite Vulcan." [4]

If, then, the earth is the furnace of fire, there can be no quibbling about the meaning of the vivid narrative of Shadrach, Meshach and Abednego, the three who were cast into the fiery furnace, in *Daniel.* It is only another allegory of the solar triadic god, in his three principles of mind-soul-spirit, embodied in the sphere of flesh, typed now as a fiery furnace. The Manes, who is spirit *in* this furnace, is shown his Ka, his pure higher soul, as a means of aiding him to remember his name in the great house, *"in the crucible of the great house of flame."* One of the chapters is designed to be read so that its magical potency may enable the Manes to "escape from every fire." In another the soul prays (Ch. 17) to be "delivered from the god who liveth upon the damned, whose face is that of a *hound*, but whose skin is that of a *man*," "at the angle of the pool of fire." Here is the man and animal combined, another of the oft-recurring glyphs of our duality. And where the man and the animal are united, where they meet, is the pool of fire!

In the *Psalms* it is said, "They go through fire and through water" and are "brought out into a place of abundance." "So," says Edward Carpenter, "was the Greek Hercules, who overcame death though his body was consumed in the *burning* garment of mortality out of which he rose to heaven." [5]

The *Book of Judges* (6) recounts how at the sacrifices for the Eternal, the meat and the unleavened bread which the angel had commanded Gideon to "put on the rock yonder," were touched by the tip of the wand in the angel's hand, at which "fire spurted out of the rock and burned up the meat and the cakes. So Gideon realized it was an angel of the Eternal."

In *Exodus* (12) the directions from the Eternal to the Israelites were that the meat of the sacrificial offering was "not to be eaten raw or boiled in water, but roasted in fire, head and legs and all." The true food for man to consume is not that immersed in his lower watery nature, but that transformed into suitable spiritual nourishment by the fire of spirit alone. It is to be recalled that the Titans first boiled the members of Bacchus in water and afterwards roasted them in fire. The fiery force of deity had caused the lower elements to seethe and boil; when the moisture (carnality) was all dried out, the remainder of the process was a "roasting."

The immolation of Jephthah's daughter as a burnt sacrifice appears to be another figuration of the divinization of the mortal (feminine) nature after two and a fraction aeons. For she asked permission to bewail her unfruitfulness for two months in the hills. Hill or hills is a frequent glyph for earth. To burn her up was not to destroy her, so we can save our tears. It was to set her on fire with a brighter purer flame.

Gideon's routing of the Midianites "in the valley below" by the smashing of the clay pitchers in which were lighted torches, is of extremely apt relevance in the terms of the symbology of fire and water. A pitcher is a water container, but these were empty. The water had been dried up, and the fire burned unquenched. The water of sense burned out, the only remaining task for the spirit, to consummate its full release from its prison, was to rend asunder the veil of flesh, the body. This was achieved in the shattering of the clay pitchers. The Midianites are the multitude of lower impulses, ever the adversaries, the enemies. They flee and vanish the moment they see the divine fire glow forth in its full release of hidden power!

The story of Samson, a typical solar hero, provides splendid exemplification of the fire symbology. When he was delivered over to the Philistines (the lower propensities again) he was bound with two new ropes. But when the Philistines were about to punish him, "the spirit of the Eternal inspired him mightily, the ropes around his arms became like flax that *has caught fire,* the bonds melted off his hands." The god within burned away his bonds. A whole chapter of exposition could not add force to the sublime meaning here pictured.

It is appropriate to consider the beautiful emblemism of the "pillar of cloud by day and of fire by night," whereby the Eternal manifested his guiding presence with his children on their mundane journey. In the full glare of the blinding light of divinity, some watery veil is necessary to intervene between us and the overpowering glory. The Eternal put his hand over Moses' eyes while his glory passed by. Man's face must be veiled in the presence of deity. God interposes the veil of matter between us and his hidden spirit. This is the cloud by day. But in the evolutionary night time, when the soul is deeply submerged in material darkness, there is needed the shining of the pillar of fire. It is the moon by night. In the Elysian or paradisaical realms the angels are represented as refreshing themselves in bowers of shade or cloud. Shade is grateful in the summer. But on earth the buried god needs light. The gross physical sense of the moving pillars is impossible. A marching column of some two million people, and some twenty miles long, would need to rest at night, whereas the literal translation would presuppose their needing a light to guide their nocturnal march.

313

Then there is that other great religious usage, the significance of which no mind can fail to sense in all its dynamic admonition for humanity. Many nations felt it incumbent, under the strength of the most powerful obligations, to maintain a fire perpetually burning on the central hearth of the nation. In Rome a class of virgins, chosen for physical and spiritual purity, were put in charge of the Vestal Fire, and death was the penalty for letting it die out. Likewise, as is not so generally known, death by burial alive was the penalty for sexual intercourse, inflicted remorselessly upon these maidens. This, too, was regarded as a letting of the spiritual fire on the hearth of life go out. The ancients knew that if once the spark of empyreal fire kindled in the moist nature of the earthy man was permitted to die out, it was the second and irretrievable death to the soul. That portion or fragment of deity that was sent into the flesh *could* be divulsed entirely from its linkage to heaven—the silver cord could be cut—and the soul lost, for the rest of the aeonial cycle. The 64th chapter of the *Ritual* is to be recited in order that the person may not die a second time, "but may come forth and escape from the fire." To escape the second death the Manes had to keep the sacred fire aglow.

In the elaborate ceremony conducted over the mummy, there was one act which stands out in the sharp forcefulness of its meaning. The Rubric to the 137th chapter says that the figure of the mummy was to be smeared with bitumen (the same substance was used to calk the wicker boat in which Moses and Sargon floated among the reeds) and *set fire to*. This was to figure the lower nature being lighted up by the fire of the higher. The life of the god, says Budge naively, "sometimes takes the form of a flame of fire." Budge adds: "These ceremonies are said to be 'an exceedingly great mystery of Amenta and a type of the hidden things of the other world.'" [6] Again we see the scholar's mind stultified by want of that one key to ancient books: that this world *is* Amenta. For the mystery pertains to the hidden things of no other world than this one we know. But it is, of course, a *type* of the mysteries of all other cosmic worlds.

Then there is the "burning bush" of Moses. "When he looked there was the thorn-bush ablaze with fire, yet not consumed" (*Ex.* 2). "The angel of the Eternal appeared to him in a flame of fire rising out of the thorn-bush." To be sure, the fire rises out of the natural order, symboled by a bush. The figure of the burning bush seems to offer no more significance than the "golden bough" of classical lore, or the branch of the sycamore-fig that burns with fire but is not consumed. Horus indeed was typed as the "golden *unbu*" (branch) from his mother's tree. No fact in nature lends itself with more felicity to the idea of new life from old than that of the bright new shoot (as of the pine) at the end of last season's more darkly colored growth. Its lighter color is significant of new glory. As Jesus was the shoot of the vine (also Horus), his Egyptian mythical designation would have been the "golden *unbu*." In the texts the *unbu* is the symbol of the son reborn from the dead father. There is a figure of the disk of light raying all ablaze from the summit of the sycamore-fig, which thus appears to burn with fire, but is not burned. The Manes approaches the holy emblem without shoes, salutes the tree and addresses the god in the solar fire: "Shine on me, O unknown soul. I draw near to the god whose words were heard by me *in the lower earth*" (Ch. 64). One is now prepared to sense the meaning of the bright-spangled star that tops our Christmas pine tree. And by the same token one can know the cryptic meaning of the Star of Bethlehem. Need it be added that the burning bush is just the symbol of nature's "green" product, the first Adam, being divinized to golden splendor by the touch of the god's spiritual fire? Any green tree or stalk or stem, tipped at its summit by the bright-hued flower, furnishes the same moral. Human life is to flower out at its summit in radiant colors. And we set fire to the Yule log.

An old English legend identifies the golden bough of Horus with the bush that flowered at Christmas, the Glastonbury thorn. The flowering at Christmas depicts the birth of the solar god at the solstice, the application of which to individual spiritual history will be examined later. Says Horus (Ch. 42): "I am Unbu, who proceedeth from Nu, and my mother is Nut." Again: "I am Unbu of An-ar-ef, the *flower* in the abode of occultation," or in the fleshly world of hiding. Possession of the golden bough in classical mythology was the passport of release from the underworld.

There is, also, the flaming two-edged sword of the angel set to guard the tree of life in the garden. Origen says that the Gnostic diagram of this symbol was as follows: "The flaming sword was depicted as the diameter of a flaming circle, and as if mounting guard over

315

the tree of knowledge and of life." There is doubtless much mystical, astrological and other occult symbolism in the sign; but in relation to the human situation its meaning seems to be simpler. Man's life here is cast between the two fires of heaven and earth, the bright fire of celestial splendor and the lurid one of earth. They are of course two aspects or modifications of the same one fire. Hence his life is cut by the fire that catches him on both sides, upper and lower. The fire of life consumes in both directions. It lights and it also burns. It glows in beauteous glory; it painfully consumes the lower self. Heaven is fiery; so is hell. As the waters were sundered, so was the divine fire. The flaming sword is the eternal reminder of the two-edgedness of our nature. The doubleness of the fire that has come to deify us is announced in the line in the *Ritual:* "Pepi is the country (or the god) Setit, the conqueror of the Two Lands, *whose flame receives its two portions.*" We are bathed in "the Pool of *the Double Fire.*" The Two Lands are the two areas or fields of our dual selfhood. Man is to conquer the twoness of his being, merging the two portions into one new creation. The *Ritual* says that "he cultivates the Two Lands, he pacifies the Two Lands, he unites the Two Lands." It says also that "he cultivates the crops on both sides of the horizon."

John Baptist's statement in the *New Testament* is a mighty affirmation of the truth of what is here presented. He represented the lower man, antecedent and preparatory to the spiritual self. He bears the symbolism of water (if not of earth), as Jesus does that of fire and air. For his statement yet rings down the centuries of Christian theology: "I indeed baptize you with *water,* but he that cometh after me shall baptize you with the Holy Spirit [Latin: *spiritus,* "air"!] *and with fire.*" The man born of the natural or maternal order (man born of woman) alone, preceded him that was born of the Father's divine spirit. Again our thesis is dramatically vindicated by "scripture."

Iamblichus tells us that the three golden apples of Hesperides are: (1), Illumination; (2), A communion of operation; and, (3), A perfect plenitude of Divine Fire.[7]

A mass of testimony could be drawn from the Bible to stress the prominence of the fire typology. *Isaiah* strongly enjoins us (1:11): "Behold all ye that kindle a fire, that compass yourselves about with sparks: walk in the light of your fire, and in the sparks that ye have kindled." Job admonishes evildoers (18:5): "Yea, the light of the wicked shall be put out and the spark of his fire shall not shine. The light shall be dark in his tabernacle, and his candle shall be put out with him." Paul says that if we awake "from the dead," "Christ will shine upon" us. *Isaiah* says that we wait for the light, and exhorts us to "arise, shine, for thy light is come." *John* says that "light is come into the world" and "that was the true light" when the *Christos* arrived. He declares that the only condemnation was the world's rejection of the light when it came. The Psalmist says that the Lord is his light and his salvation and that "light is sown for the righteous." "In thy light shall we see light." Jesus said: "When I am in the world I am the light of the world." He assured the righteous that they were the light of the world, that indeed they needed no other light to lighten their path, as they had light in themselves. The Lord made his ministers a flame of fire. "The Lord God *is a sun* and a shield"—the pillar and the cloud, the meaning of which, clear at last, is simply spirit and matter. When there was darkness over the land of Egypt, "the Israelites had light in their dwellings." And this is not speaking of rush lights in Egyptian huts, but spiritual light in physical bodies. Jesus was "the *sun* of righteousness" and at the end of human evolution "the righteous shall shine *like the sun*." And if there is needed a point-blank utterance from the Bible to cover our claim, it might be found in the line from the *Psalms:* "Our God is a living fire." For a long series of generations Christendom has set fire to the Yule log and lighted candles on the Christmas tree. Yet there is hardly a child in the West that could give a reason for these rites that would convey a modicum of the truth. For the venerable teaching that nature put forth on its topmost bough a bright effulgence of deity, a bright flower at the top of the green stem, a shining god at the summit of elemental creation, has long been lost. Yet the Christ has come, bringing and distributing "that light that lighteth every man that cometh into the world."

The fire emblem has become involved in a host of combinations with other types, and its play in all mythology is extensive. Many of these references to it carry valuable implications.

The ancient Apt, mother of the world, is called "the kindler of sparks," the "kindler of light for the deceased in the dark of death" (*Rit.*, Ch. 137: Vign: *Papyrus of Nebseni*). Thus the old first bringer of rebirth is the kindler of light in the sepulcher—of earth. Mary Magdalene who is her counterpart in the Gospel version, comes to the tomb "early, while it is yet dark," and finds the stone moved away and light kindled at the tomb sufficient to see by. Chapter 137B is entitled: "Of kindling a flame by Nebseni, the scribe in the temple of Ptah."

The great classical fable of Prometheus bears relations to the fire sign. The myth is not entirely unique. There is, for instance, the Hindu tale of the monster (Titan) Rahu, who smuggled himself into the presence of the Gods of light and drank the Amrit-juice of immortality. He was *cut in two,* but could not be destroyed, by Indra, and the two halves were set as signs in the heavens at the places of the lunar eclipses.

That the Promethean myth is not entirely to be dissociated from the story of the Galilean savior is shown by the fact that, according to Carpenter, "Prometheus, the greatest and earliest benefactor of the human race, was nailed by hands and feet, and with arms extended, to the rocks of Mt. Caucasus." [8] When one knows that this figure fastened to a cross or rock is but the outward dramatization of the truth of the god's impalement on the stake of matter, all historical realism connected with it becomes revolting.

The Titans were styled in the Mysteries "Thyrsus-bearers, and Prometheus concealed fire in a thyrsus or reed; after which he was considered as bringing celestial light into generation or leading soul into body, or calling forth the divine illumination." [9] The natural order harbors in it the seeds of spiritual growth.

Massey quite plausibly allocates to the word "Teitan" the "number of the Beast" given in *Revelation* as 666. He argues that the triple "S" on the Gnostic stones, represents this number, "S" equaling 6. SSS then equals 666. It was a sign of the six elementary creations that prepare the way for the seventh. He traces the value of the letters as follows:

T	300
E	5
I	10
T	300
A	50
N	1
	666

The statement that the Beast lost one of its heads, which was afterwards restored and healed (Cf. a similar case in the Egyptian *mythos*) is interpreted by him to mean that the descent of the Titanic hosts was the figurative equivalent of the loss of the head or intellect to be regained in the evolutionary sequel. The sevenfold corpus of deity,

318

minus one of its heads, was thus numerically reduced from seven to six. Man, then, is to be regarded as a sevenfold being suffering the temporary loss of his (divine) intellect, or head, which he is striving to restore or heal. We must round out the Beast in us by giving him a head of intelligence. There is still more to this typology of seven minus one. The fabled Mt. Meru "is also described as being intersected by six parallel ranges running east and west. Six is typed by the hexagon or space in six directions"—a symbol of our life in this three-dimensional world, where the cube of six sides is the typical shape of any existential object. The six parallel ranges are the six planes beneath the topmost level, where the "heart of Bacchus" was preserved when the mental body was dismembered. Says Proclus in the *Timaeus:* "The Framer made the heavens six in number, and for the seventh he cast into the midst the fire of the sun." This was the crowning of nature's six elementary kingdoms with the element of mind, or the first injection of intellect into the evolutionary creation in and through the person of man, Atum-Ra, the first god-born race. Nature struggles upward through six degrees of material coarseness, till her product, animal-man, is sufficiently sensitized to be made the vehicle of Manas, or Mind.

Job (5:19) relates six and seven mysteriously in a remarkable statement: "He shall deliver thee in six troubles: yea, in seven, there shall no evil touch thee." Trouble is associated with six and deliverance from it with seven. Life is captive and harassed during its long peregrinations upward through the three sub-atomic "elemental kingdoms" in the invisible world, the preliminary stages in the formation of matter out of empty space, and the mineral, vegetable and animal kingdoms in the visible atomic world; and intelligence comes in the seventh kingdom to release it from its sub-conscious captivity. Life is in "Egyptian" bondage to nature through six aeons. The seventh—and seven times seven—brings the glorious "year of jubilee," when all captives and prisoners are set free. In *Numbers* a Hebrew slave was to serve six years and go free in the seventh without paying a ransom. The fields were to be cultivated for six years and to lie fallow the seventh. But when the Messiah came—and his Egyptian name Iu-em-hetep means "he who comes seventh"—he was allegorized as coming under the dominance of the six lower forces; and so the number seven later took on in the texts the evil implications of the number six and is the numerical type of servitude. Jacob is made to serve seven years for Leah and an added seven for Rachel. In some old texts the ten plagues of Egypt were originally seven.

The profounder significance of the first "miracle" of Jesus in turning water into wine at the marriage feast of Cana hinges upon the fact, hardly ever commented on, that the *servants* set out for the transformation *six* pots of water in *earthen* vessels! Jesus, embodying the seventh or transmuting power, came to convert that nature that had been constituted by the first six outpourings of primal life into higher spiritual status. The Christ has the task of transfiguring six lower elemental powers into divinity. And in the Gospel story he went up into the mount for the transfiguration "after six days"! Spiritual "wine" was to be made out of the six types of elemental "water" in man's constitution. And man, physically, comes close to being six-sevenths water in composition!

The "year of the Lord" was divided into six (double) signs of the zodiac. The sun passes annually through these six signs, and man's soul, *his* sun, also passes through six levels of being in attaining self-conscious freedom. It makes the round of the elements of earth, water, air and fire in twelve subdivisions. These elements being embodied in his own constitution, the sun-soul in man passes through them to achieve its mastery of all life. His victory in the seventh kingdom regains for him all that was lost in the beginning. The Christ adds the seventh head to the decapitated natural order. The seventh and "lost" Pleiad will be recaptured by Orion, the mighty hunter, Egypt's astrological figure for Horus. The Christ will restore the lost light.

The Titans, of whom Prometheus was one, appear in a dual and somewhat confusing character in the mythology. They are both man's good angel and his devil. The solution of this enigma of theology will be fully expounded in the next chapter. But, briefly, it can be said that the Titans of mythology match the Lucifer character of theology.

"Hesiod says the Father called the Revolters by an opprobrious name, Teitans, when he cursed them. And they were cast down into Tartarus and bound in chains and darkness in the abyss." (*Theogony* I, 207; II, 717).

The god, the Titan, Prometheus, Lucifer, who brought us our divine fire from the empyrean, was in part converted into the Beast when his

Titanic intellect was linked with the six elementary forces. He mingled his life-blood with theirs, and the contagion of elementary impulse went to his head! Certain of the myths tend to align the Titans *with* the six elementary powers; and this is a natural confusion since the higher mentality did commingle with the lower instincts. The god who was angelic, because untested, in heaven, became demoniacal on earth, and the coloring of every attribute is altered as he indeed "suffers a sea change" in plunging into the lower waters.

The myth of the Greek Saturn, who was overthrown and despoiled of his genitals, or creative power, by Jupiter, who was in turn worsted by the Titans in that heavenly warfare, is read as planetary cosmology by Massey and others. The meaning is that each lower grade of life organized in the progressive outpourings "steals" away the higher creative force to use on its own plane. The functions and the glory of Saturn were alleged to have been transferred to the sun, who became the new lord of the six. Saturn is identical with the Egyptian Sebek (Sevekh) whose name is "seven," and in the early *mythos* he was the deity who crowned the six elementary forces with completion, as their ruler and governor. Says Massey:

"The sun and Saturn both became the lord of the seventh day, the Sabbath, the day of rest and peace, which is Hept, [Hetep] the name of No. 7. But in the cult of Sebek . . . the original of the solar Sabazius, son of . . . Kubele, the sun and Saturn were combined as Sabat, Sabaoth, or Sapt, which, read as Sebti, shows the dual form of Seb, for the sun and Saturn . . . Sabazius was reported to have been torn into seven parts by the Titans, corresponding to the seven days of the week and the seven planets to which they were dedicated." [10]

That is to say, our number "seven" (Latin: *septem*) is derived from Saturn and the sun combined in their two names of Seb and Hept, compounded into *sept*. Seb, as we have seen, covers the dual meaning of "star" and "soul," both suggesting fire. As the coming of the god of intellect and reason, the seventh element, crowned the long elemental warfare of cosmic creation with the peace and rest of intellectual control, order and harmony, so the deific principle gives its name to the day of peace that follows the hurly-burly of the six secular days. In general we devote six days to bodily interests; the seventh should go to the interests of the soul. Ancient discernment of primary creational verities gave us our week of seven days, to stand as an eternal reminder of the sevenfold cosmic order, of which our own basic constitution is itself a reflection and a miniature. And old Egypt gives us the philological demonstration of all this in the dual meaning of the word *Hept*, which is both "seven" and "peace." The seventh element is that noetic intellect which stills the storm on the passional waters and brings peace to chaotic nature, based on its six lower mindless energies. Iu-em-hetep (Imhotep of the Greeks) is he who comes to bring peace as number seven.

In *Exodus* (23) it is written:

"The radiance of the Eternal rested on the mountain of Sinai; for six days the cloud covered it, and on the seventh day he called from the cloud to Moses (the Eternal's radiance looked to the Israelites like blazing fire on the top of the mountain.)"

It is in a verse from this same chapter that a very noteworthy statement is made:

"For six years you may sow your land and gather in your crops, but every seventh year you must let the land alone, so the poor people may pick up something; anything they leave the wild animals can eat, for if you worship their gods it will endanger you."

There is ample warrant for a moment's digression from the main theme of the chapter to follow out several implications of this astonishing passage. The injunction not to cultivate the fields every seventh year, so that the "poor" might have some "pickings," is on the face of it impossible physically. For if the land was left alone, there would be no planting and hence no picking. How could the earthly poor profit from unplanted fields?

The command has nothing to do with agriculture or charity, except that which is cosmic and spiritual. It is one of those ingenious "parables" by which ancient sagacity embodied great evolutionary truth in pictorial representation. It concerns in this case a most recondite fact of esoteric knowledge. Bizarre as it may sound to modern ears, it was the teaching of the abstruse biological science of old that at the dissolution of the several component principles of the multiple human constitution at the completion of the cycle (the seventh day), one of these bodies of etheric material (of types now predicated by science),

322

the "astral," called the "chhaya" in India, floated free as an independent entity, possessing both sufficient vitality to preserve it from disintegration, and a semblance of mental automatism. In this condition it was utilized by nature for a peculiar purpose. It was made the matrix or mold about which was aggregated coarser matter, as a magnetic field organizes iron filings, which matter gave it a body and localized it on earth as a living creature. Both the Bible and other esoteric writings have mysterious sayings about the lower orders of life feeding upon the lees or dregs of the orders above them, even in some cases excrementitious matter. The meaning is approached along the line of a peculiar emblemism. Man's discarded "astral" shells, so the doctrine teaches, serve as the models and the animating principles of lower forms of life. Our "astral" leavings, cast-off clothing, are made to serve as the feeling souls of inferior creatures. The animal picks up our emotion body and builds his physical body over it as a model. Man's part in creative evolution is far more direct than he imagines. Every phase or grade of life is creative, to its degree. If this item seems strange, it assuredly is no more so than many of the almost unbelievable phenomena of physical biology in general in animal and insect life. Nature has a bigger bag of tricks than we realize. She employs a vast range of unsuspected and startling methods in the endless repertoire of her ingenuity. At any rate the fact was so taught in the arcane schools of occultism, and here in *Exodus* is a passage directly pointing to it, since the text can mean nothing intelligible in its literal sense. The seventh round in all cycles of life in nature is always the epoch at which soul consummates its work in an organism and retires to its proper level above, leaving the physical bases of life to stand without further cultivation until the beginning of the next series of seven rounds. During the retirement the lower animal self, the "poor," reaps the harvest of its previous attachment to the higher entity. The ethereal vestures survive, for they are enduring in proportion to their atomic fineness. We have already equated "the poor" and also "the people" with the Gentiles, who were the "sons of men" in contrast to the "Sons of God"; the humans in whom the Christ principle has not yet been made consciously the ruler.

And the second startling item of this excerpt asserts that what those "poor" semi-humans leave may be picked up, in a third order of gradation, by the wild animals. This is informative indeed. The process of divinization begins with the highest God and is relayed, in ever diminishing power, from rank to rank, down to the animal. Only by living on the lees of the superior order can each kingdom link itself to its appropriate measure of divine vivification.

By such occult analysis is it possible to see the meaning of the final hint of danger expressed by the line: "for if you worship their gods it will endanger you." This work has already set forth the peril involved for the heavenly visitant in taking residence in animal forms, if it permitted itself to "worship their gods" of sensuality and beastliness. A number of passages of scripture admonish the children of light to "make no compact" with the "natives" of that realm to which they were sent, nor to marry their "women"!

The sum of this material which shows the world to be figuratively "at sixes and sevens" is that conscious life was in servitude and bondage to blind unintelligent elemental forces for six aeons, three in the invisible and three in the visible worlds, and was only lifted up to the liberty of the sons of God when the spiritual fire of the spiritual sun, the second Adam or the Christ, was set in the heavens of man's conscious being as the ruler of the six sub-mental powers. In *Galatians* (4) Paul clearly states that when we were children in evolution "we were in bondage to them that by nature are no gods." We were in slavery to the elementals of the earth and of the air, as he distinctly says! He warns his brethren not to come under the power of these elementals, as it would endanger their spiritual integrity.

Stars are closely intermingled with the fire symbolism. They are themselves fiery in constitution, blazing suns or their planets. Stars were considered the children of Ra, the great lord of the spiritual sun, who emaned them like tears from his eyes. Souls were his offspring, centrally nucleated by his solar fire. He was the parent of the Kumaras. Stars were held to be a race of higher beings, having souls of the essence of light coming from the sun. "I have shed my seed (of light) abroad for you," he says to his sons.[11] In the *Book of Adam and Eve*, translated from the Ethiopic by Malan, God says: "I made thee of the light, and I wished to bring out children of the light from thee." The sun's children were called Ruti, or men of excellence. Under the name of Khabsu the stars are synonymous with souls, as also in the name of Seb. Souls in Amenta were represented by stars. As the souls arose in their resurrection they appeared above the horizon on the eastern side of heaven. This is why the rising star of the solar deity born in mankind was seen "in the east" in the Gospel story. It dies in the west, like the sun, and has its new birth in the house of bread (Bethlehem) in the east. The god Shu-Anhur was called the "lifter up of the sky," together with its inhabitants, the stars. Ra addresses Shu: "Be the guardian of the multitudes that live in the nocturnal sky," or sky of the Lower Egypt of Amenta. "Put them on thy head and be their fosterer," or sustainer. Spiritually this betokens the elevation of our elemental nature by the shifting of the center of intellectual and spiritual gravity above the horizon in the heaven of consciousness. The stars were in fact the bodies of gods, and the lucent fragment of deity in man is his star.

The Great Bear of seven stars drew the first circle or cycle of time in the abyss of chaos, and gave definite law, order and periodicity to the primary creation. From primal elemental disorder, nature settled down to rhythmic regularity as the beginning of stable order in her worlds. From blind erratic struggle the elements fell into order in a septenary mechanism. This was imaged first in the Great Bear, the mother of the first cycle of regular time and fixed revolutions. This primary cluster in the sky should never cease to speak to our imagination of the heptarchy of forces in nature, which are the bases of our lives as well. This mighty fact of creation was in the mind of the sage who wrote that at the dawn of creation all the sons of the Elohim shouted for joy and "the Morning Stars sang together" (*Job* 38). The music of the spheres began with the first swing into symmetrical order and balanced harmony between centripetal and centrifugal energies that had been jangling in confusion and dissonance before the seventh element, the sun or spirit, gave the six a king. But Plato strangely tells us that "with the sixth creation ended the order of song." (*Philebus*, 66.) Coincident with this we are also told that the sixth pole star in succession passed from the constellation of Lyra, the Harp, to that of Hercules, the man-god. All these veiled hints have tremendous meaning, for this would seem to indicate that the soul comes into the order of nature bringing a power of independent will, which may contravene the mechanical automatism of nature, break into the rhythm and mar the music—until it learns of itself anew to fix the measure to a higher harmony. Man's free agency *does* inject either a reasoned or an unreasoned self-initiative into that which was automatically rhythmic

325

before. In a former reference we have heard the great Lord himself complain of the spirits who had broken in upon his celestial music and marred the harmony, for which he threw them down into incarnation.

The Rubric to chapter 129 of the *Ritual* says of the Manes: "And he shall be established as a star face to face with Septet [Sirius, Sothis, the Dog-Star] and his corruptible body shall be as a god . . . forever." To deify the human is to make a star of him. The Manes himself prays (Ch. 102): "Let me be among the stars that never rest." It is promised (Ch. 164) that "he shall become a star of heaven." Has orthodoxy held out to its votaries any such thrilling cosmic view of their future? The Osiris-Nu pleads (Ch. 188): "May I enter into the house of his body, which, behold, hath become one of the starry gods!" This would be the higher spiritual body, not the corporeal. It is said to the soul: "Thou art purified with the libation of the stars. The stars that never set bear thee up; thou enterest in the place where thy father is, where Keb [Seb] is . . . thou becomest a soul therein." The soul (Pepi) pleads: "Make thou this Pepi to be an imperishable star before thee." The acme of directness is attained in the next statement: "Pepi *is* a star." To Teta, the soul, it is said: "Thou seizest the hands of the imperishable stars . . . for behold thou art one of the gods." "The imperishable stars follow and minister unto thee." Pepi is addressed: "Thou art the Great Star; Orion beareth thee on his shoulder. Thou traversest heaven with Orion, thou sailest through the Tuat with Osiris." Again: "Pepi takes his seat among you, O ye star gods of the Tuat." And finally in grand simplicity stands the categorical pronouncement: "Thy soul is a living star at the head of his brethren." For the six elementary powers were his natural brothers, of whom he, like Joseph and like Jesus, was made the chief or head. From brethren they were reduced to children when the god principle took charge and synthesized their functions. The fiery soul of intellect became king of the lower six elementary powers in man's make-up. The *Christos* came as the Prince of Peace to rise to kingship over nature's six divisions of force. "Unto you a king is given . . . and his name shall be called . . . the Prince of Peace."

But the soul is specifically typed by that great and brilliant emblem of our divinity, the Morning Star. The Titan who came hurtling to earth still clinging to his stolen possession, the spiritual fire, was Lucifer, "the bright and morning star."

The significance of this emblem is in its heralding the approach of day. "The day star is rising." It is the harbinger of the coming of the great Lord of Day. As the announcer it becomes identical in function with Anup, the fiery ape in Egypt, Mercury in Greek mythology, and John Baptist in Christianity. Anup is the way-opener for the advent of Horus, who, though coming after him, was before him in stature and authority (*Rit.*, Ch. 44). Anup abode in the dark and empty reaches of the desert of Amenta until the day of his manifestation in the heliacal rising of the star Sothis (Sirius), the morning star of the year in Egypt, which heralded the birth of Horus, as the opening of the year. John dwelt in the wilderness until the time of his theophany or "showing forth in Israel" (*Luke* 1:80). The soul was held out in the wilderness of the six elemental energies until the arrival of the Christ. Anup was only a star god, but as such he was the precursor of the greater solar light. As the sun in its splendor far outshines the total galaxy of the stars, so the deity whose association with man was presaged by the star-god, was far to surpass in glory any product of the natural series. And this is made clear by the Gospel statement that the least in the kingdom of the god is greater than the highest of those born of woman, that is, nature.

The stars typed one of the elementary creations, of which there seem to have been three, the first being cosmic and universal, offering a sevenfold differentiation in primal substance; the second stellar and planetary; the third racial and individual in mankind. Much of the endless confusion in the interpretation of creation legends has arisen because of failure to distinguish which of these creations was being dealt with. What is fundamental, however, to all understanding is that all of nature's cyclic processes are typical of each other. So that cosmogenesis adumbrates the planetary formation, which in turn is an enlarged picture of the anthropogenesis. As man was formed in the image and likeness of the Elohim, the seven-rayed creative Logoi, the septenary constitution pictured in the first and second creations appertains to him by reflection. All ancient philosophy referable to man was built upon the human constitution as a septenate of powers. We see the first creation in the hebdomadal formation of all physical creation; the second in the septenary solar systems; the third in the human formed of seven principles or natures. Of the first the Mother alone, the Virgin, Achamoth, Typhon, Apt, Nut, Neith, Isis, Hathor, Rerit,

Ishtar, Tiamat, Semiramis, Cybele and other primary feminine deities, become the bearer and producer. Of the second Sevekh (Sebek, Seb), Saturn, and the Sun, as the leader of the seven Rishis, Archangels, Elohim, Kabiri, were the progenitors. Of the third the twelve legions of Asuras, Kumaras, Titans, Deva-Angels, Rudras, Adityas, who came collectively as Prometheus and Lucifer, individually as sons of the solar radiance, sons of Ra, or sparks of the divine fire, were the chief agents. They still supervise their continuing creation from their citadel deep within the shrine of man's life. In one form or another, solar light, essence, power is centered in every manifestation. In the innermost sanctuary of life dwells the spark, the ray, the flame of solar glory. The sun is the central type and embodiment of the highest divinity. The Christs were all sun-gods.

In the Kabalah the vital statement is found that in each solar system the soul in its aeonial round dwells successively on six planets and spends its seventh aeon on the sun of that system. This is after the analogy of the soul in the human body, for there it successively energizes, from lowest to highest, the six elemental physical ranges of power, and six sub-spiritual psychic centers, before it ascends into the supreme flowering of the solar fire in the head.

Sirius, otherwise Sothis and Septet, being the morning star in the *mythos,* etymologically supplies another significant link in the story. Septet is another form of the word "seven." The six natural forces were completed and synthesized by the coming of the seventh. The morning star heralded the perfection of the sevenfold creation as it announced the coming of the crowning glory. This Sirius, the Dog-Star, was the type of Anup, the dog or jackal god, as the guide of souls in the dark of night, or incarnation. "The star Sept (Sothis) with long strides leads on the celestial path of Ra each day, and the blessed one rises as a star." The star precedes Ra, the sun in man. Of Pepi it is written: "His sister is Sept (Sothis), he is born as the Morning Star (Venus)." And again: "His sister, the star Sept (Sothis), his guide, the Morning Star, takes him by the hand to Sekhet-Hetep." Usually women, the two women, are the guides, protectors and watchers of the sun-god in the mythology, as they are the natural bearers, rearers and watchers of the human infant, until his own divinity arises. As the feminine always types the natural as distinct from the spiritual, the religious myth depicts the youthful solar god as being born of woman, cradled, watched and nourished by women, type of the elementary forces. The god comes to be born, nursed and nurtured in the lap of Mother Nature. But he must leave her at twelve!

In one place the text of the *Ritual* says, as to Pepi: "The Morning Star giveth birth to him." In another it says: "Pepi giveth birth to the Morning Star." The apparent contradiction is a matter of viewpoint, or a matter like the priority of hen or egg. Did John the Baptist bring Jesus, or Jesus John? John himself solves the riddle by saying: "He who cometh after me is preferred before me." The star brings the dawn, but the dawn also brings the star. Of the coming god, as of the Christ, the *Ritual* says: "His light appeareth in the sky like that of a great star in the East." *There,* in finale, is our Star of Bethlehem! The soul is told: "Anup . . . hath decreed that thou shouldst descend like a star, the Morning Star." And again: "Thou revolvest about Ra, near the Morning Star." The Manes is instructed: "Command thou that he is to sit by thee, on the shoulders of the Morning Star on the horizon." Following the statement that heaven is pregnant with wine, it is said that "Nut maketh herself to give birth to her daughter, the Morning Star." And immediately follows the exhortation to the soul: "Rise up thou, then, O Pepi, thou third Septet (Sothis), whose seats are purified." Calling Pepi the "third Septet" bears out fully what has just been expounded as to the three creations, each sevenfold in organization, the last being that of septenary man. That the god in his coming was to enter the waters of incarnation and the mires of earth is betokened by the following: "He places thee like the Morning Star in the fields of Reeds (Sekhet-Aarru)."

Numbers (24:17) predicts that "there shall come a star out of Jacob." As the Gnostic Jesus of *Revelation* (22:16) himself declares: "I am the root and the offspring of David, and the bright and Morning Star." And the angel promises in *Revelation* (2:28), to him that overcometh "I will give the Morning Star." This comes as the seventh of a series of promises "to him that overcometh."

. The frequent use of the censer in *Revelation* is to be noticed. Seven angels had given to them seven censers, containing the fire from the altar of God within the innermost place, which the seven were to cast upon the earth! Here is the basic allegory again in small compass. In the *Logia* these details are preceded by the announcement: "And I beheld yet another sign in the heavens, which was marvelous in its meaning and great in its issues!" Surely; for it was the story of the deification of the human race. The burning of incense, a very general custom in religious observance in the world, runs parallel in meaning to keeping alive the Vestal Fire. In the *Old Testament* all cereal was to be mixed with oil and sprinkled with incense—a double seal of divinity. The Manes is addressed in the *Ritual:* "Thou art pure with the incense of Horus." Again we read: "Incense is presented unto thee, thou becomest God." One becomes a god only by the gift of that higher fire that purges the lower nature and refines it to true gold. And this gold is the immortal solar light. The words for gold, light and deity all derive from the same original root, "ar," "aur," "or."

Lightning, a great sacred symbol of the outflashing of the power of God on earth, was often pictured as seven-barbed. This usage establishes it definitely as a figure for the seven-forked emanation that engendered the creation. It is the type of a fiery power resident in latent form in the air and water elements. So the god is latent in the water of physical nature. The swift power of the fiery dart was typical of the "swift-running" power of deity, for the Greek word for god, *theos,* means the "swift-darter." In Assyria Tiamat, mother of "seven sons of the abyss," wielded a seven-speared thunderbolt, typifying her children, as powers. The highest of the seven is lightning by name. In Africa some tribes have a word for divinity which translates "lightning." Many peoples had thunder-gods, and the Bible is full of allusions to thunder. The fiery dart of Intelligence into the bosom of the worlds produces or carries the Voice of the Logos out into nature, in seven primary tones. The Hebrew male god of thunder, Kak, or Iach, probably equates with the Hindu Vach, the Word. As the forerunner and prophet of rain, the thunder held the office of Mercury and Anup, the announcers of divine advent.

Even embers and sparks are not slighted in the typism. We have the ancient Egyptian tale of Cinderella, the "sitter in the ashes," embers or cinders. Sitting in her lonely hutch on earth by the dead embers of the fire, she is the soul come to desolation on earth, stripped of her fire. But she surpasses her sisters and fits herself to be dight with radiance again. The flame that ramifies out in seven tongues is the original figure of the seven-branched candlestick. Deity comes to earth to manifest himself in seven flaming aspects of his being. And still stand the great ancient pyramids, the word by etymology reading "a measure of. (creative) fire," with square base and triangular upper faces, the four and the three united to constitute the sevenfold physical structure of the worlds and man, and multiplied to constitute the twelve deific powers to be unfolded by spiritual humanity.

Chapter XV

NOXIOUS FUMES AND LURID FLARES

It has been necessary to anticipate the substance of this chapter in one or two places in the preceding one, because many important statements so closely link the two fires, the supernal and the infernal, that it was impossible to present the one in entire disseverance from the other. The background for the clarification of this aspect of the interpretation has therefore already been set up. Yet the whole doctrine of "hell-fire" has fallen so infinitely remote from even the outskirts of true understanding that it must be grappled with in good earnest. The deplorable state of modern exegesis in this segment of theology impels one to a vehement expression of that disgust at the harrowing grotesquerie of rendering which a comparison of ancient esoteric meaning with current superstition so readily excites. But this situation must be evident by now as a general matter, and should need but little reinforcement beyond the continued revelation of gaping chasms of difference between the old and the present readings. Yet this theology of a hell of fiery torment has suffered such an unconscionable distortion from its primary bearing, and has afflicted the mind of mankind with so outrageous a delusion, that every consideration points to the necessity of a vigorous handling in the interests of sanity and social benefit. The perversion of original teaching regarding the lower fire has cast over the collective mind of the Western world the foulest hypnotic obsession which it has ever suffered. The strangling tentacles of this theological devil-fish have spread over the whole of Christendom and have compressed the spiritual genius of that segment of mankind into the coldest and most inhuman bigotry known to history. For ages the doctrine in its misconceived form has deprived the Christianized world of its reason, and opened doors to the entry of every superstition. It has snuffed out the native spark of human brotherhood and brought between man and man the lurid glare of its own devilish mischief.

For the fiercest fires of persecution and fiendish cruelty ever lighted upon earth flared out under the impulsion of the fantastic theological teaching that the acts of one's brother may be the impious machination of "the devil." It is too gruesome and ghoulish a chapter of horrors to linger upon; yet the same philosophical benightedness out of which this atrocious monster of diabolism and demonism has emerged has never to this day been dispelled by the light of wisdom. A more sensitive humanity of the present, sickened by the ghastly spectacle of past tortures and holocausts inspired by fiendish zeal, has tried to drop the subject as far as possible out of sight, and has imposed a taboo upon its exploitation in religious quarters. But the darkness has not been dissipated, and the monster is still capable, on provocation, of glaring fiercely out of the murks. The light that would have enabled the Christian world to descry the Beast in his true outlines and character has never been rekindled since it was extinguished about the third century. Had that light been available it would have revealed that the fiery dragon of the pit was none other than the god himself, his face begrimed with smoke, his features distorted by the grimaces of the Beast through whose eyes he looked out upon this strange world, and his countenance luridly alight with the smudgy flare of the earthly furnace. Milton's lakes of seething fire in *Paradise Lost* are a travesty of truth, unless taken purely as the symbology they are. *For Satan is the god himself—on earth!* This broad assertion is incontestable. It is proven by the very name. The descending god was the Light-bringer, Lucifer, the bright and morning star, which is precisely the character assumed by the Jesus of the Biblical *Revelation!* The Christian devil, the hated serpent of evil, Satan, is Lucifer, the god of light on earth, Prometheus, the "benefactor of mankind,"—"the god" himself.

Indoctrinated orthodoxy may rise to protest the identification. Some ghastly mistake will be alleged in the philology. It will be in vain. Erudite theology has at times perhaps known the truth, but has kept an advised silence. The general mind has lost the key to the mystery. By dropping the name Lucifer and clinging to that of Satan alone, the mischief has been bred and perpetuated. That Satan and Jesus are identical is as true as that Sut and Horus in Egypt are twins! The god and devil are kindred. They are full brothers. Their mother is one. They are the two aspects or manifestations of the same force. It may be said that the evil character is the good seen in reversed reflec-

333

tion on earth. For an ancient esoteric adage in Latin ran: DEMON EST DEUS INVERSUS, "the devil is the god turned upside down." Satan is the god in incarnation; or he is the god as he appears after his nature has been diffracted in its passage through the blurred medium of earth life. The devil is the god transformed into a being of reduced power, blunted moral sense, befogged intellect and forgotten glory. He is the god bemired with the slime of carnal generation, beset with the strong sensuous and sexual urge of the brute. In short, he is the divine soul entangled in the bestial nature and himself lending more fiery intensity to the impulses of the body by his vitalizing presence!

The genesis of what is called "evil" may perhaps be dialectically derivable from the fundamental premises of thought. But the origin of evil in reference to man's specific cosmic situation is a particular problem, only to be determined by full knowledge of this situation. As the world does not possess such knowledge in full measure, the great problem is enveloped in some obscurity.

But the sages of the early dawn vouchsafed a portion of this knowledge deemed sufficient to yield to reflection an intelligent comprehension of the issues involved and a philosophic attitude toward them. The rank of the gods sent to earth, their endowments and capabilities, their attitude toward their mission, their obligation in relation to past dereliction, and the implications of their tenanting the animal bodies assigned to them, were broadly revealed to the initiates and *theodidaktoi* of an early period. With all these interests and relations the connotations of the term "evil" are intimately concatinated. This knowledge, elaborated to much detail, was the treasure of the Mystery Societies and Brotherhoods, and formed the esoteric motivation of their regimes of discipline, instruction and consecration. The modern revival of interest in this mine of truth has not yet recovered all that has slipped away. The uncertainty about some of the major premises is supplemented by the additional difficulty of determining which of the two phases of the representative figures, Satan, Lucifer, Apap, Sut, Typhon, the serpent, the dragon, the beast, is being emphasized in the numberless myths and legends. And there is the ever-present doubleness of the meaning of the symbols, making it difficult to know whether the higher or the lower aspect is meant. But enough hints are provided usually to enable scholarship to work with intelligence upon the material.

The origin of evil is indeed the mystery of our life. It is inwrought with the key situation of humanity. The arising of evil in a system of total and absolute good is indeed a riddle that taxes the best effort of brain and heart. The difficulty, however, has been made by the mistaken common assumption that Good is absolute, that is, good as conceived in human ideation, good in its specific human relevance. The Supreme God has been called the Good, and this has been misleading. Good can only be absolute if evil is also absolute, and this can not be, since there can not be two different and opposing absolutes. The absolute is beyond good and evil alike. There is an abstract and detached conception of good which the mind can predicate of the entire scheme of things, to posit which, however, would require our saying that that which is beyond both good and evil is the good. Doubtless the finality of all things must be thought of by us as good. Yet such a declaration is dialectically impossible, because that which we would characterize as good is beyond all character. Descriptive statements about it are empty sound. It is not within the scope of any predication whatever. The ultimate is neutral to us always.

It only becomes either good or bad to us when it ceases to be absolute and relates itself to itself as spirit and matter, positive and negative, male and female, light and dark. And, be it proclaimed in clarion tones, the whole matter of the theological bogie of the devil, or incarnate evil, arose solely from the miscarriage of the dramatic necessity of ascribing an adverse, opposing and *relatively* evil character to the negative or material pole of life force! The bifurcation of the Unmanifest into the two nodes of being to become manifest threw both poles in contrariety and opposition to each other. The spiritual, or active and conscious end came to be represented as the "good" and the inert and negative material end carried the dramatic imputation of the "evil." The two can never step out of their poised interrelation with each other, since they have existence only in the terms of such relation. They are only and always relative to each other. Good and evil have no human meaning outside the terms of a counterpoise with each other. Each gets its characterization by virtue of its being not what the other is, being its diametric opposite. Each gains what it possesses of substantiality and character from being the reflex of the other. Good is Not-evil and evil is the Not-good.

Manifestation of life comes only through the tension between the

335

two modalities, because it requires just such a stress to awaken latent consciousness to open awareness. Actuality comes to birth only at the central point of contact between the subjective and the objective worlds. If life does not establish the countervalence between its two opposite aspects, it remains unconscious. The friction between spirit and matter is the ground of life's ultimate or at least increased self-consciousness. So the soul comes to this earth to partake of the fruit of the tree of the knowledge of good *and* evil. Evil is therefore one of its two essential conditions for normal growth and expansion. A sagacious view of philosophical *archai,* therefore, perceives "evil" in its true light, and once and forever lifts from off its imputed entifications in religion all stigma and bad odor. At the same time it apprehends its role in the drama, in which it plays the part of the "adversary," "the opposer," of the active building power of life. This is the role that has all too easily become misunderstood for one of absolute evil, when it should have been judiciously envisaged as but relative, and as conducive to the awakening of the positive energies of life itself. For without the necessity of exerting itself and deploying its as yet unawakened powers to overcome the opponent's resistance and inertia, the divine seed would continue to slumber on in unconscious ignorance of its own capabilities. It awakes its dormant giant potentialities by "overcoming the adversary."

This is the heavy role of the villain in every play. He is the foil. He acts as the stepping-stone over which the hero strides to victory. His dark designs make the hero's virtue shine out the brighter by contrast. He furnishes the dark background against which the conqueror's exploits stand out in relief.

Hence that which in human and worldly affairs wears all the outward appearance of evil—defeat, disaster, loss, crime, treachery—is to be seen only as good under a disguise. It subserves a karmic purpose,—the challenging of some hidden power to come awake and rouse itself to function. Later on, its hidden beneficence is seen, and we say: Now I know why that happened; without it I would never have gained what I now possess. So "evil" is good under a mask. The villain is our other self in masquerade. If we could at the moment tear off his false face, we would see him as the lovely fairy, ready to transform us into something nobler.

It is the antithesis of good and evil, our experience with both wings

336

of the bird of life, and the resultant deposit of wisdom in our own interior vehicle of consciousness, that gives us ultimately our cognition of values. And in the finale this valuation overleaps mere characterization as either good or bad. We are balanced between the two in order to transcend them both. The child unites characteristics of both its parents and carries life forward one step higher.

The gist of the matter is that value—which should not be thought of as good in contradistinction to evil, but as evolutionary gain—can not be brought to birth unless good is opposed by evil; and evil is just this opposition. It is in every sense except that of immediate human estimate of it entirely necessary, salutary and beneficent. But no one can calculate the untold volume of wretchedness that has been heaped up in world history by the frightful miscarriage of this basic understanding. For the mass mind was overridden by the assignment to "evil" of a positive character, reifying it into a living bogie, and was in the last stage of gross literalization devastated by its personification in an actual "devil." The transmogrification of this dramatic personage into the realistic bogieman to harass millions of earth's simple-minded children by Christendom is perhaps the crowning disservice which a distorted theology has rendered its unenlightened devotees.

Our sense of evil only arises because of our imperfect vision. As Paul said, we now see life in part and through a glass darkly. If we could see it whole, we would see all things in their proper place in the large picture, and hence in their beneficence. More piercing vision would penetrate the mask of evil and reveal it as good. But our sense of evil, and our reactions to it, are part of the cost of our growth. They are the terms and conditions under which we advance to larger appreciations. The apparent evil is part of the path we must tread to reach values beyond. Evil may be said to be episodical, an incident along the way, as life marches on. Seen out of proportion and relation it assumes its grim aspect.

And what is sin? Again has a baleful theology terrorized the minds of millions with an apparition that is as unsubstantial as the bugaboo of evil. Again it is a normal and natural phase of the evolutionary situation which has been wrested from its balanced meaning in the dramatic typology and turned into a thing of psychological terrorism. Sin is in brief nothing but the "lust for life" itself, and the appetency and zest of the higher soul for the life of flesh and sense, through

337

which alone it can become creative in new generations. Sin is the entangling of the entified spirits in the laws and nature and motivations of the flesh, not to add the world and "the devil," and its free indulgence in the play of its creative powers through and upon these elementary forces. Sin is the spirit's subjection of itself to the dominance of these proclivities to an inordinate or disproportionate degree. The Cycle of Necessity draws it down into their domain and makes it for a time and in a measure subject to their sway. Whether duly or unduly influenced by them, its submergence under their power is what the ancient drama pictured as sin.

At least one philosopher has kept his vision of this portrayal true and steady. Plotinus declares that if the soul keeps her eye fixed steadily on the star of her higher self, "she need not regret having become acquainted with evil or knowing the nature of vice," and having had the opportunity of manifesting her creative faculties through her conjunction with the body. This is grandly refreshing amid the welter of corrupted philosophies berating and belaboring the life of sense with the stigma of evil and the curse. The latter have grown up in the wake of a morbid religionism turned ascetic when the lighter play of drama was burdened with the lugubrious weight of misconceived ideas of sin and the devil.

A portion or degree of cosmic divine spirit was to become creative in man, and was sent here to try its intellectual powers upon a formative work. It had thence to show its lordship over the elements and the matter with which creative intelligence had to work. It had to be thrown in strategic relation to the world of matter at its appropriate place and station. Like both Jesus and Jonah, it had to be thrown into the "sea," to subdue its ungoverned raging. It had then to take charge of the seven lower furies and range them under its higher command. The unregulated play of these subordinate and irrational forces of sense in the field of life, once the god had plunged into their milieu, is sin. It is powerful at first and for a long time, until the soul gradually rises to assert its kingship over the seven heads of the Beast. It is only admissibly evil—and then still in a relative sense—when it usurps the prerogatives of the lord, unhinges the balance between the two forces, and becomes grossly immoderate and libertine. Only when the soul, still not wide awake and vigilantly in control, permits the

338

lower animality to rule inordinately, is it sin in the mawkish theological sense of shame and remorsefulness.

To help a world lift itself out from under the darksome shadow of gloomy moroseness, induced by twisted theologies, into the brighter day of clearer comprehension, it may be said that the general mind · must grasp once again the basic deific motif in creation, to begin with. As set forth just now, "sin" has its rise in the desire of life to become parent of each new cycle of recurrent creation. Spirit and matter must woo, win and wed each other; and their copulation, envisaged through the medium of a diseased human view of sexual relation, became tinged with the stains of moral baseness. This is the psychological genesis of the interpretation so long foisted upon the "fall" of Adam and Eve "into carnal sin." Physical parenthood has long borne the stigma of some remote spiritual transgression, and still the shadow of social and universal shame clings to it. A great modern cult, and some of its offshoots, have expressly stressed the possibility of regaining the Edenic spiritual creation of human beings without resort to the physical mode of procreation. And of course the Immaculate Conception and Virgin Birth doctrines have been haloed about with intimations of the same sort. This is all, however, the result of incomprehension turning charming and luminously suggestive typology into crass realism.

Why does God create? Why is he not content to enjoy his exalted position in endless contemplation of his own perfection? As far as human cognition can rise to conceive of it, God's motive in creation announced in the old books, is *Lila,* translated "the sport of the gods," "the delight of God." The highest joy and sweetest preoccupation of mortals springs from the expression of one's power in some creative work. As man reflects deity, it may be known from this datum that God's highest pleasure comes from *his* creative labors. He creates for the sport and the joy of it. He first thinks out (in Plato's "archetypal ideas") what sort of universe he will build, and then proceeds to reap the delight of seeing it grow under his hands. "The sea is his for he made it, and his hands formed the dry land." His reveling in creation does not stop at his ideal conception of prospective worlds; like the true artisan, he must realize the satisfaction of seeing them take form in the concrete. Plastic matter, susceptible to every breath of creative impulse, is his potter's clay. God comes out of his noumenal world

339

to enjoy a period of activity in the realm of sense. Having thought long enough of his projected creation, he now wills to emerge onto the field of physical activity and bring it into substantial reality. He longs to feel the play of elemental energies through his vast physical frame. Any man yearning to rise from sedentary occupation and brain work to experience the "feel" of muscular activity outdoors, is a sufficient analogue. The opposition, tension and zest for the game are provided by the playing forces on the two teams of matter and spirit. The game or battle will yield him adequate thrills, since in it he will find coming to function still unevolved latencies of his own measureless being. Each act will enhance his sense of power and glory. That he may live again and enjoy a new joust with matter he must plunge his nucleated units of consciousness into a state of "death" and burial in material inertia. Paul asks if this is evil; and his own answer, overlooked and never understood, must become the keynote of a new world attitude to life: "Never! The law was holy, just and altogether righteous."

There is evidence that the word "sin" has derivations and connections of the most momentous import. Some of these are astonishing. In the first place "Sin" was a name for "the mount of the moon." Arcane books speak of the incarnating souls as having fallen into the moon, and earth is still called the "sublunary sphere." This has immediate links with pertinent meaning, since the lower aspects of man's nature, his two lower bodies, the "astral" and physical, have been built up over the "astral" molds left by the retreating race of men on the moon chain of evolution. Since the spirit plunges into the lower man, the *belly* of death, it may aptly be said to fall into the mount of the moon. The soul fell into "Sin" or landed on "Mt. Sin."

But another etymology falls in here with unexpected force. The lower physical and emotional half of man's constitution is, in its relation to physical nature, typed in ancient tomes by "the woman." The lower nature, that holds the soul in material bondage, is specifically dramatized by the character of Hagar, the concubine of Abraham, significantly dubbed "the bond-woman." To "her" we are in bondage. There is very definite connection between this name Hagar and the Agar, or Akar, or Aker, which was the name for the tunnel of the underworld through which incarnating souls had to pass from the rear (material) end of the Sphinx forward to the front (spiritual) end or

340

head. The materials are now ready for St. Paul to use in making for us a startling weaving of the several etymological strands into a thread of great strength. For in *Galatians* (4:24 ff) he makes a positive identification of Mt. Sinai with Hagar (Agar): *"Which things are an allegory:* for these are the two covenants; the one from the mount Sinai, which gendereth to bondage, which is Agar. For *this Agar is mount Sinai in Arabia,* and answereth to Jerusalem which now is, and is in bondage with her children." To call a woman a mountain, and that localized in a specific country on the map, for once clearly shatters all possible literalism or historicism in the verse. But beyond that it throws into relation, likely that of identity, the two mountains Sin and Sin-ai. Sinai is derived (by Massey) from the Egyptian *senai, sheni,* meaning "point of turning and returning," and almost surely refers to that point where life strikes a balance between the forces of involution and evolution in the cosmic "solstice." In its descent spirit reaches the nadir point in the depths of matter, is held in a state of exact equilibrium with it—the "pool of equipoise" of the Egyptians— experiences its new birth of life from this relation, and then turns to return to the Father above. The name Sinai, then, is most revelatory. All communication with deity, all revelation of deity to man, must occur on this Mount Sinai, when the feet of the woman clothed with the sun rest upon the moon, or lower part of man's organic structure. So Moses (man) ascends into the mount to receive the commandments of the law and the dicta of the Lord. And Jesus ascends into the same Mount to deliver his sermon unto mortal men. This whole situation is of strategic importance for the entire theme and must be unfolded at length in later connections.

Evil and sin must be cleared of their theological accretions of grue- someness and morbid sentimentalism. They were involvements of the evolutionary predicament which, under the ruses and resources of dramatic representation, became tinged with darksome psychological hues and inspired a volume of unnatural effort to mortify the human part of our nature. Whole generations of children, taught by literal- minded parents and tutors, imbibed the idea that in the universe there was a deity, dividing power equally with God, who was wholly bent on defeating the good, and who must be resisted, if life is to be "saved." Back of this miscarriage, as back of all absurd popular religious no- tions, lurks the great truth, that Life has divided its powers between

·spirit and matter, and that all growth is the outcome of the "war" between these two energies. Clearly apprehended in a philosophical view, this is knowledge of high verity, knowledge that stabilizes the mind with a grasp on the ultimate beneficence of the scheme. On the other hand the popular distortion of it is a horrendous fallacy, devastating to faith in the salutary operation of cosmic law. Between the two there is the whole vast gulf of the difference between sanity and composure and the practical certainty of a monstrous dementia.

The devil is just the god on earth; and how the radiant son of the morning, bright angelic Lucifer, became transmogrified into the dour person of Satan is a matter of deepest concern for religion and for humanity. This problem could have been solved readily enough if the Western mind had not lost the data for thinking. Logic can not proceed when the due premises are wanting. These lie buried in forgotten books dealing with cosmology and anthropology. To supply them again to modern reflection is a major purpose of this work.

The basic item is the duality of man as the result of the incarnation. Evil arises from the union in one organism of brute and god. When the god stepped in, the potentiality of evil was engendered. Evil could not arise from animal alone; paradoxically, it awaited the coming of the god. The animal is unmoral, incapable of either morality or immorality. He has no sense of good and evil. He has not eaten of the fruit of the tree of good and evil. The "god" in man is the first being in evolution who steps out from under the law of natural automatism and periodical regularity, and assumes his training in the art of balancing consciously discerned forces of evil and good. He came into the flesh for the very purpose of opening his eyes (Cf.: "and their eyes were opened" in *Genesis*) and seeing consciously how to weigh his action in the balance between the two poles of life. He came to eat of the fruit of the tree. While the beast was unmoral, the god was morally capable, but innocent. He had to learn grace by contacting guilt. He had to win his right to the enjoyment of good by overcoming evil. "To him that overcometh shall all things be given," but not to divine souls that would rather dream away their existence in mystical bliss in the empyrean. Without warfare with evil the soul would never come into cognition of its own capacities. As Plotinus affirms, "she would not know what she possesses," and her faculties would never receive their development. Nature could not become productive until it had thrown its opposing forces into the duality of spirit and matter, positive and negative, and provided thus the basis for experience. Consciousness can not come to self-consciousness unless the subjective aspect is confronted with the objective. Spirit and matter are helpless, or rather, as Plotinus adds, are really non-existent, until they interact in "opposition." It is this "opposition" that stabilizes them in relation to each other. Monism is a true philosophy applicable only before and after the worlds are! It takes both *Nux* and *Lux* to make life conscious. And virtue can not be won except as the laurel wreath for victory over vice.

The opening of the eyes in the creation allegory is the dramatic typing of man's awakening to his first glimpse of self-consciousness. It marks the distinguishing insignium of man's superior position above the beast. It marks the line of his evolutionary passover. At this point man stepped over the greatest boundary line in all the universe of life. He passed out of the sway of the unconscious mindless energies of nature, the "sub-conscious mind" of cosmic deity, and became, albeit at the lowest level, a sharer with God in his conscious creative intelligence. He stepped across the line from the kingdom of bondage to the natural mindless forces into potential rulership of them. He ceased being the son of Hagar, the bond-woman, and became the son of Sarah, the free-woman. He became, collectively, children of the promise and of the adoption, sons and heirs of the Father. He stepped from bondage under the law to the possible "liberty of the sons of God." Liberty! The animal can not sin; man can. He has this freedom! He may choose—good or evil. But he must face the consequences. These are the terms of his evolutionary education. The good or evil consequences would instruct him. Choose he well or badly, karmic compensation would advise. But his new freedom was his highest prerogative, his badge of incipient divinity. That he was prone, of necessity, to make many bad choices until his karmic education had sobered and enlightened him is indicated from a most significant passage from Plotinus:

"They began to revel in free will; they indulged in their own movement; they took the wrong path. Then it was that they lost the knowledge that they sprang from that divine order. They no longer had a true vision of the Supreme or of themselves. Smitten with longing for the lower, rapt in

343

love of it, they grew to depend upon it; so they broke away as far as they were able."

This tells the whole story of whatever there is intrinsic in the perverted idea of the "fall." It was just the fall of the child learning to walk! It was nothing but the floundering of ignorant innocence before it has grown wise through trial and error. It was inherent in the very conditions of the evolutionary situation. It was more or less inevitable. And its "evil" consequences were to be absorbed in the vicissitudes of later experience, as the follies of youth are ironed out in subsequent larger vision and more steady conduct.

The god brought the possibility of "evil" with him on his arrival. He came to suffer many things, because his coming threw a stable and orderly evolution temporarily into an unstable one. The animal was bound to a fixed order in nature, whose unvarying laws left him no choice, no freedom to deviate. The god came to get practice in the use of freedom to break through this order and win independent creative facility for himself. And he was incidentally to impart to the animal in whose body he lived that part of his new found knowledge that he managed to make habitual, or transferred by the force of repetition over to the sub-conscious, which is *the animal's* highest conscious self. For he was, along with his own education, to help the animal bridge the gulf between its kingdom and the human.

But he threw a disturbance into a condition that had previously been equilibrated and stable. He introduced free choice and variant procedure into the hitherto inerrant course of the animal's behavior. He could break natural routine, initiate new tentative and note the result. A god who could not do evil is a marionette, not a god. There is no merit in compulsory good. Reward must come with victory. Trial and error was to result in knowledge, which therefore could not be its antecedent or concomitant at the start.

Wisdom is a resultant, a deposit, a crystallization of fluid elements. Freedom began with ignorance in order to end in wisdom. Freedom and ignorance are the two ingredients in the problem of evil. Error and blunder were means to an end. The smooth harmony of natural law was bound to be thrown, for a time, into discord. This is the meaning behind the rebel angels' breaking in upon the harmony of the great God's festival song with raucous shouts, which may be seen

344

possibly as their riotous exultation at the prospect of a new freedom never enjoyed before, like schoolboys let out for a holiday, as Plotinus paints it.

While the god was thus to be buried in the very belly of the great Abtu fish, his immunity from complete drowning and loss of his deific life was provided for. It is hinted at in various typographs. He was to be protected, as Plato says, like an oyster in its shell. He was as the fish in the water, that would be able to breathe even under the water. Again he was shown as learning to walk on the water without sinking into its depths. The *Ritual* of Egypt speaks of his being immersed in the water of the underworld, but not drowned thereby. Other types portray him as not actually in, but hovering over, the water; or in it as to his body, but aloof from it as to his soul. The latter is especially prominent in the *Ritual* for the "dead." More than one passage repeats that while "my dead body lies in the grave, my soul is in heaven." "Thy material body liveth in Tattu and in Nif-urtet, and thy soul liveth in heaven each day." "Heaven holdeth thy soul, O Osiris Auf-ankh, and earth holdeth thy form" (Ch. 163). "Thy soul is in heaven, and thy body is under ground" (Ch. 169). "Ra grasps his hands, a spirit in heaven, a body on earth." "Thy water is in heaven; thy solid parts are on the earth." "The Sun-god," writes Massey, "whether as Atum-Iu or Osiris-Ra, is a mummy in Amenta and a soul in heaven."

These passages are of great value. Particularly should the one be noted which says that "thy material body *liveth* in Tattu" while the soul lives in heaven. This forestalls the likely argument that these passages refer to the ordinarily deceased person, whose body is in the ground (if not cremated) while his soul has gone to heaven. The deeper meaning here is that man actually inhabits two worlds at once. He is in heaven by virtue of his divine consciousness; he is on earth through his physical body.

All this situation was part of a larger divine plan. The god was to touch the tip of the head or inchoate mental faculty of the animal with the flame of his intellect, but not further embrace the animal's life. He was to light the wick of intelligence for the lower being. He was to kindle a fire in the body, but not be burned thereby. But it is said that the waywardness of the gods pretty badly marred the progress of the work. As a group they had bound themselves under a covenant to do the work promptly and return. But earth currents overwhelmed them, swept them into forgetfulness, and they truly lost their divine heads and were carried down into sensuous life and sexual procreation. The passage from Plotinus tells why the first essay of Phaëthon to drive the chariot of the Sun resulted in a wild orgy of uncontrolled movement. The seven chargers drawing the chariot proved unmanageable for the untested powers of the young god. He gave himself to the delight of a wild revel in the sensual enjoyment of life, and the thrill of adventure tingled through his blood as he indulged his fancy in free creational direction of energies. His drive was outward, and he threw himself into the interests of the lower vehicle. And here lurks the rationale of his changed character from Lucifer to Satan. In drama he was pictured as in part the author of evil when he lent his own superior forces and faculties to the virile energies of the beast. He threw the added power of his own dynamism into the life of animal man. This is the evil aspect of his kindling a fire on earth, or in the sea around the earth. He in fact kindled a fiercer fire under the caldron containing the water of life and the animal ingredients of the lower human constitution, and raised the potentials of all the elemental appetencies. Into the hellish brew went the qualities of the creatures of earth, of the water and of night—the bat, the owl, the toad, the lizard, the newt, the snake; of herbs gathered under the light of waning moon; of every noxious and venomous thing; and under it all burned the fire of the god! Around flitted the three witches, the masquerading earthly forms, feminine and material, of the three divine principles of mind-soul-spirit, the solar triad, poking the fire. And as they revel around the eerie scene, the fire burns and the caldron bubbles, brewing the double toil and trouble for god and man; but all the while the broth is being transformed into its spiritual sublimation, so that it returns to heaven as vapor, in the midst of which the geni can be seen taking form. So the animal ingredients are transformed and lifted up in the burning lake.

In mutual interplay god and animal accentuate each other's potential energies. In a sense the god makes a worse hell of this nether pit of Tophet, for he plays a part in the degradation of the beast. An excerpt from the *Codex Nazareus* seems to confirm this delineation:

"He himself will captivate the sons of men by the allurements of cunning delusions and will imbrue them with blood and monthly pollution."

Yet both parties find an enhancement of their range and powers of consciousness through the struggle. But traditional figures of the Satanic personage have taken form and clung to popular fancy out of the allegorical depictions of the cosmic scene. The god, plunged into the hell of body, was painted as plying his fierce labor in mingling his higher fire with the lower elementary fury, stoking the furnace with the fuel of his pride, rebellion and lust for sense, and enjoying with the animal the mutual exchange of their polarized forces. Fantasy sets up the portrait—his body reeking with sweat (Cf. the bloody sweat of Gethsemane), his countenance grimy and lurid in the glare of the fire made murky with the commingled smoke, steam, ashes and soot (Sut) arising from his effort to "burn" the damp green material. *This is the ancient picture drawn by high poetic fancy to convey the recondite philosophical principles actually involved; and the failure of heavy ignorant zealotry to catch its fanciful import has cost a crass civilization centuries of woe.* The *Logia* speak in no uncertain terms of this tradition:

"There was one who reigned over them all, even the Star of the Morning, which had fallen upon the earth, Lucifer, but they named him Abaddon, for he was the Destroyer."

Here was in fact proud Lucifer, rebel against the too long protracted passivity of life in the higher worlds, come to earth, baptized in the waters of the Jordan River on the boundary between the two kingdoms, kindling a fire in the water itself, throwing his reed or rod into the Nile of earth and turning it into blood, injecting his own fiery energies into the sluggish life of the beast, himself torn and distracted, abased and crucified, disfigured out of all semblance of his divinity. Let us recall here Isaiah's account: "How was his visage marred, more than any man!" The figure of intoxication used by the mythicists to betoken this phase of the god's condition is by no means inapt. This was indeed the "riotous living" in which the Prodigal Son spent his substance. And St. Paul helps us understand the depth of degradation into which the innocent souls fell by his statement that the sweep of lower motivation caused them to change "the glory of the incorruptible God into an image made like to corruptible man, and to birds and fourfooted beasts, and creeping things. Wherefore God also gave them up to uncleanness through the lusts of their own

347

hearts, to dishonor their own bodies between themselves: Who changed the truth of God into a lie, and worshipped and served the creature more than the Creator . . ." This is also the story of Ichabod, from whom "the glory" had departed.

With its roots winding deeply into the heart of this theological depiction, there has sprung up the growth of a gigantic excrescence on the psychological life of mankind that has found no explanation, and can find none, outside the purview of the background just presented. Here lies the key to one of the most inexplicable and redoubtable phenomena in the domain of sociology, for which sociological science can provide no material for a formula of understanding,—the sense of shame appertaining to the sexual organs and functions. From instantaneous creation in the noumenal world by projection of thought energies, the god found himself thrust into lowly physical bodies and reduced to the sensuous procedure of sexual progenation. Swooning into the "deep sleep" that attended his descent from the higher planes, he awoke on the plane of earth to find himself forced to procreate physically like the animals. From deep within his most real self sprang that sense of revulsion at the change, the shadow of which has clung to his consciousness in spite of all rationalization or sophistication. The soul sensed its degradation. Ancient scriptures reflected this feeling in their naming the physical body, as the agent of this debasement, "the garment of shame." In the *Pistis Sophia* Jesus tells Salome, in answer to her question, that his kingdom shall come "when you shall have trampled underfoot the garment of shame" and returned from the divided life of sex to androgyneity.

If the sense of shame was not inherent in the anthropological situation at the beginning, it was developed and strengthened by the wild license or "Harlotry" in which the first groups of the Sons of God indulged with the females of the higher animal species after reaching earth. There seems to have been a long period of sexual miscegenation, the experience of which would have imprinted the reaction of shame lastingly upon the sub-conscious psyche of early humanity. This is perhaps the "evil concupiscence" against which Paul crusades in his Epistles. And it is significant that in a later passage in the first chapter of *Romans,* in which Paul states that God gave them up to a reprobate mind to do the things "which are not convenient," he adds as their final description that they were "covenant-breakers." We protest that this takes his preachment out of the rank of mere pious homiletics and makes it referable to the racial predicament we are dealing with. Greek philosophy speaks of the violation of "broad oaths fast sealed."

Reverting for a moment to the philosophic analysis of evil, it is highly desirable that the view of Platonic systematism should be gleaned from a few pointed excerpts. Near the end of his two great volumes on the theology of Plato Proclus dilates at length upon the nature of evil in grand fashion. There is not such a thing, he says, as

"unmixed evil or evil itself, or an eternal idea, form and essence of evil; but moral evil is mixed with good, and so far as it is good, *it subsists from divinity;* but so far as it is evil, it is derived from another cause which is impotent. For evil is nothing else than a greater or less declination, departure, defect and privation from the good itself . . . in the same manner as darkness from (want of) the sun. It is debility and absence of power. And that which is evil to partial natures, is not evil to the universe."

Christian aberrancy from high philosophy can be seen in the erection of evil into a positive, active force and personifying it in a semi-deity.

Evil is only a by-product of the good on its march to full development. Proclus has further enlightenment for us, which should not be missed:

"Evil in souls is a debility of not always and uniformly adhering to better natures and to the good. Hence arises their descent to things subordinate, their oblivion, their malefic inclination to things conversant with body, and their discord with reason. According to some, matter is that which is primarily evil, and is evil itself, and the debility of souls arises from their lapse into matter."

But we owe to Thomas Taylor a reminder that it is error to impute evil gratuitously to matter:

"This Proclus denies and says that both body and matter originate from deity and that both are the progeny of divinity. He adds . . . that souls sinned before they were thrust into matter; that there are not two principles (matter and deity); and that matter is neither good nor evil, but a thing necessary, and distant in the last degree from the good itself."

Here is balance and sanity, so sorely needed in an age overrun with cults of the "spiritual" raving against the "evil" nature of matter, making it a theological "devil." This declaration should be advanced to prominence in the philosophic treatment of the place and function of matter in evolution and systematic thought. Modern spiritual cultism needs to be enlightened with the assurance that matter is in itself neither good nor evil, but neutral. It has no moral quality in itself, but receives such from the good or evil use made of it, as any mechanical invention. It is to become the implementation of the good, and is therefore vitally necessary, as Proclus declares. Cult diatribes against matter as evil are at last seen to be beyond the mark, and the orthodox hypostasization and personification of evil is discovered to be equally inane.

Whatever seems evil exists indeed for the sake of the good:

"To divinity, therefore, nothing is evil, not even of the things which are called evil. For he uses these also to a good purpose . . . For he [the demiurgus] concealed evil in the use of good." Evil "consists in the privation of symmetry between form and matter."

The last statement is a detail which is doubtless most relevant. The god and the animal being conjoined in one organism, evil arose from the want of harmony between them. This is at the base of those Platonic discussions on harmony and symmetrical allotment of function in the Greek thought. Two widely diverse and in a sense antagonistic elements were thrust into a marriage in one body. A conflict was inevitable. Paul's war of the flesh against the soul was on. The animal could no longer drift in his course of unintelligent natural instinct; and on his part the god was erratic in his incipient lordship over lower forces. What measure of human wretchedness, instability and recklessness does not flow from these factors operative in the situation?

Hence Lucifer became transformed into Satan. Without his intrusion the animal would have known no evil, no aberrancy, no contravention of cyclic order, with consequent pain and distress. But he would have purchased the continuance of his halcyon blissfulness at the cost of—remaining an animal! He could not step across the gap between beast and sentient man without awakening the knowledge of good and evil. The god stepped into the beast's own province and brought that disturbing influence that began the harrowing process, for both, of learning through suffering. By the god's stripes we are healed, and both he and his pupil suffer many an anguish before the healing is effected. Fittingly the *Logia* are found saying: "The Beast that was, that is, and that is soon to be cast down into the bottomless pit, is the mystery of iniquity by whose power the world hath been made full of sorrow."

The Beast that was chained in prison or cast down into the lake of fire that burned with brimstone is to be found, along with the lake, in the *Ritual* (Ch. 17). He is called Baba, the eternal devourer, whose dwelling is in the lake of fire, the red lake, the pool of the damned, in the fiery pit of the recess or "bight" of Amenta. It is to be pointed out that this Baba, called "the lord of gore," extracts the hearts and viscera from the corpses doomed to be consumed at his banquet and "eats the livers of the princes." This personation is identical with that of the Beast in *Revelation* (10) who makes war on the "Logos of God," but is defeated and cast into the lake that blazes with brimstone. The angel invites all the "birds that fly in mid-heaven to gather for the great banquet of God," at which "the flesh of kings" was devoured. In the Promethean myth the bird, vulture or eagle, comes daily to consume the liver of the king of heaven, bound helpless to the rock, or the cross. The bird typifying generally the soul, coming to devour the liver of the god, unquestionably has some reference to the purificatory offices of the spiritual nature in the evolutionary process, though a more subtle knowledge of the function of the liver in vital economy would probably enable us to read further astonishing significance in the symbology. The myth may perhaps simply signify the soul's periodical visitation to earth to pluck the fruits of the purgative and purificatory experience, by which through bodily suffering evil is transmuted into good, as the liver cleanses impurities of the body.

Paul in *Ephesians* (2) and elsewhere sets forth the forces in conflict in the arena of the human breast:

"You were dead in the trespasses and sins in which you moved as you followed the course of this world . . . when we obeyed the passions of our flesh, carrying out the dictates of the flesh and its impulses, when we were objects of God's anger like the rest of men."

Again this use of the word "anger," often elsewhere "ire" or "wrath," must be carefully delimited in meaning, since it refers to nothing like human vindictiveness, but just the "fire" of deity working its natural

351

efficacy in and upon the elements of the body. "Ire" is "fire" with the Greek *digamma* dropped off, and "wrath" is the original fire of creative force.

Paul's admonition was to "abstain from fleshly lusts which war against the soul." He speaks of the deadly enmity between the two natures, as does Plato, and pleads with the disciples to strive for the victory of the spiritual man over the carnal. He puts sexual vice at the head of a list of corrupt practices, and sexual continence at the head of a list of virtues.

Through the diversion of dramatic meaning into false channels, the god, then, became regarded as the instigator of all evil in the moral situation. It is noteworthy that in the Jonah legend, the god, asleep in the hold of the storm-tossed vessel, is found, by casting lots, to be responsible for the storm. Two features here deserve elucidation. He was asleep. The god, who should have been awake and alert to control the sweeping surges of sensual thought (water agitated by air, mind, symbolically) was asleep. While he lay inert the storm of air and water raged. He was thus responsible, for he was sent to be the master of these very elements. He waked in time and his destiny demanded that he be thrown into the midst of the waters, to take charge and still them. The storm then quieted.

Next, he lay in the hold. This was called Akar (Agar, Hagar), a region of Amenta. It types the lower self, the lower part of the organism, the natural, carnal man. He had been captivated and his divine genius and memory were narcotized by the oblivion-producing influences of incarnation. He lay in a torpor in the hold of the ship, the belly of the mortal man.

So the god, rendered at first sluggish, beastly, brutalized, became the evil one. And the alteration of character from benefactor to demon, has wrought ghastly mischief in religious machination. Spurred on by the imaginary hypostasization of an Evil Spirit in the world, men have by the very force and contagion of a fixed obsession wrought themselves into the likeness of this malignant demon and dramatized in actual history their conception of his diabolical role. Swept on by the inculcated theory of his presence in personal form in the world, bigots everywhere found in the assumption a ready subterfuge for persecution and cruelty. Since embodiment had to be found for the Evil

Spirit, every unacceptable act or idea of one's brother or one's enemy could be charged to demoniac possession. Thus there was provided an easy channel for a terrible outpouring of man's inhumanity to man, and there was let loose an orgy of vicious despotism in religion that has stained the record of Christianity almost past repair. Nothing but philosophical understanding of the real issues involved will clarify the error in religious attitude on this matter. Nothing but the realization that Satan was and is himself the angel of light, our heavenly benefactor, will restore sober sanity to a race rendered next to demoniacal by an infernal theology.

There is documentary evidence to indicate that this figure was not at first regarded as the evil genius of man at all, but was rated as the *Agathodaemon,* or Guardian Spirit. On Massey's authority it may be stated that "the Serpent in Egypt, Chaldea, India, America and Europe is the Good Serpent generally, the *Agathodaemon.*" The *Ritual* (Ch. 83) affirms that "The Great One shining with his body as a God is Sut." Sut was strictly not the evil one. He was the seven-headed serpent or dragon. And the seven Uraei, or serpent-headed gods, are typical not of death, but of life. Another voice concurs in this estimate.

"Like Satan himself, even as the Rev. Dunbar Heath has shown (*The Fallen Angels*), the serpent had not, indeed, a wholly evil character among the early Hebrews." [1]

The same authority (p. 57) goes further:

"Whatever may be the explanation of the fact, it is understood that, notwithstanding the hatred with which he was afterwards regarded, this god Seth, or Set, was at one time highly venerated in Egypt. Bunsen says that up to the thirteenth century before Christ, Set 'was a great god universally adored throughout Egypt, who confers on the sovereigns of the eighteenth and nineteenth dynasties the symbols of life and power.' He adds: 'But subsequently, in the course of the twentieth dynasty he is suddenly treated as an evil demon, inasmuch as his effigies and name are obliterated on all the monuments and inscriptions that could be reached.' Moreover, according to Bunsen, Seth 'appears gradually among the Semites as the background of their religious consciousness'; and not merely was he 'the primitive god of Northern Egypt and Palestine,' but his genealogy as 'the Seth of *Genesis,* the father of Enoch (the man), must be considered as originally running parallel with that derived from the Elohim, Adam's father.'"

353

This is effective corroboration of the claim advanced herein that the father of intelligent man was the Titanic host, typified by the fiery serpent. Once revered by infant humanity as the bestower of light and life, this collective being later suffered a transformation of imputed character and became thought of as the father of all ill. Some of the dramatic implications worked over into popular belief, and the dramatic character of the Adversary overbore the true understanding of the hidden beneficence of the son of the morning.

The doctrine of hell-fire has drifted from original connotation far away from intelligible meaning. It must be reduced again to rational sense.

Chemically all life processes are a burning. Oxidation is a slower burning, as in rust. All decomposition is a burning. Disintegration of a composite by operation of a superior potency is a burning. Hence all energic activity among the elements of life is thought of as the work of fire. Man's whole life, then, is cast in the midst of a veritable welter of fiery forces, and so Egypt described the world as the lake of fire, or again "the crucible of the great house of flame" and "the Pool of the Double Fire." "Higher" fires and "lower" fires, or the rays of cosmic thought and the purely chemical energies embosomed in matter, called by the Egyptians "the seven Uraeus divinities," unite on earth in a combat and interfusion which constitutes indeed "the fiery furnace" of theological myth. The god came here, to transmute both himself and his animal protégé into higher natures. He was to burn out the dross and refine the material of the coarser sheaths, those of "earth" and "water," to make possible the unfoldment to function of the principle of mind. This type of spiritual combustion is all that was originally meant by the purging by fire and the winnowing by air. To *purify* is to make clean by *fire*. Burning out, or blowing out, the chaff of the animal compound in us by the divine fire of soul, or the divine afflatus of spirit, was the universal mythical symbol of our divinization. Coming with his fan in his hand "he will thoroughly purge his floor." The floor is the physical base of life. The higher potency will cleanse the lowest. More than once the Egyptian *Ritual* harps on the soul's "acquiring dominion over his feet." The rite of feet-washing can be immediately divined as a type of cleansing the lowest nature. Texts in the *Ritual* state that he who has won control over his feet has done all he needs to do to insure salvation.

354

Says *Isaiah* (1:25): "And I will turn my hand upon thee and purely purge away thy dross and take away thy tin." After purging his floor, "he will gather his wheat into the garner; but the chaff he will burn will fire unquenchable" (*Matt., Luke*). We are in hell because the lower segment of us needed the burning, and the upper segment the winnowing, or both segments needed both operations, according to the application of the figure.

To be consumed in the lake, or the furnace, of fire, then, is not, as theology has mistaught a harrowed world, to writhe in flames of torment plied by a vengeful god to satiate a thwarted wrath. There are seven-league-boot strides of distance and difference between this insufferable product of a fiendish theology and the august philosophical conception of primal wisdom. The latter is instinct with dignity and truth; the other a frenzy of inhuman weakness goaded by ignorant fear. Some semblance at least of the hidden truth should have been conceived from the fact that even in the distorted rendering, the souls in hell burn, but do not burn up. Their torment, says orthodoxy, is eternal; and the true and sane original meaning of this whole doctrine went awry because "eternal" was substituted in the translation for "aeonial." The stress and anguish of the fiery experience was to last through the aeon or cycle of incarnation. This rendering yields instruction and intelligence; the other mocks the reason.

The souls burn, but are not extirpated. They die, but live on, eventually transfigured. "I died yesterday, but I am alive today," cries the Manes. "In one of the hells the shades (Manes) are seen burning, but they were able to resist the fire, and consequently it is said: 'The shades live; they *have raised their powers.*'"

The lower fires burn with smudge and murk; they must be transmuted to pure flame. Fire there will be; its quality is the vital concern. Says *Isaiah* (9:17):

"For wickedness burneth as a fire. It shall devour the briars and thorns, and shall kindle in the thickets of the forests."

The briars, thorns and thickets are the dense undergrowth of coarse sensualism, which will burn themselves out, by conversion into gentler flames.

In Egypt the goddess Sekhet is made to play the part of the avenger of the wicked with hell fire. She is the fiery energies latent in matter, generating the various forms of burning and purification to which the Kumaras will be subjected. The release of her powers upon the god will search and purge his nature. She is typed by the lioness, material consort and counterpart of Shu, the lion-god, astrologically the hot July sun of the lion sign. Nature's typology is most striking in this relation. In the incarnation cycle, symboled as well by winter as by night, the fire of soul immersed in earthy and watery body, absorbs, as it were, an excess of the two lower elements. In the inter-life periods, when the soul is out of body, and figuratively in its summer time, the heat of July drives out the water and its earthy admixture in sweat! But life in the empyrean then runs to an excess of fire and heated air, and the soul has to escape from this menace by a retreat again to earth and water—incarnation. Even this intimation has its appropriate and very suggestive summer emblemism; for, as in winter fire and heated air stand as the types of salvation for man from menace of earth and water, in the summer water and earth, and even darkness (shade), offer salvation from the menace of air and fire. The seasonal swing, with all its concomitant conditions, can be taken as an exact duplication of the evolutionary pendulum, which swings the soul from an excess of mind and spirit over to the opposite excess of sense and feeling, and back again. In embodiment the water struggles to quench the fire; in heaven the fire expunges the water. It is an axiom of occult and esoteric study that the world shall be alternately destroyed by fire and water. This has been accepted in a literal way, so that the legend is that the continent of Lemuria some millions of years ago was destroyed by fiery convulsions and the later continent of Atlantis submerged by water. If continents sink both fire and water must of necessity play a part in the development. It is true that living factual history, of men and of universes and planets, does in general carry out the outline of symbolism. Yet it may be suggested that perhaps in this instance it is possible that sheer typology became once more too directly historicized. As Horus and Sut alternately vanquish each other in endless repetition, so fire and water eternally dominate in turn.

As Sekhet is linked with the Lion sign, so Serkh, or Heh, is instructively seen as related to Scorpio. We can see this better through Massey's studies:

"The serpent-goddess Heh especially represents the element of Fire that was first symbolized by the lightning of the serpent's sting. But the serpent itself was recognized before the goddess of fire or heat was personified. She is called the 'Maker of Invisible Existence Apparent.' But it was the serpent that first revealed and made manifest in pain and death the fiery power that existed invisibly. The fury of the solar fire suggested the fang-sting. The name of the Sirocco, the very breath of fire, identifies itself with Serkh, the (Egyptian) name of the Scorpion, which further shows the hard form of Serf, the blast of burning breath." [2]

Before dilating upon the Scorpion typology, a moment's attention must be paid to the remarkable name given to the serpent-goddess of fire: The Maker of Invisible Existence Apparent. The whole program of incarnation is designed to enable incipient divinity to bring out into manifestation all its latent powers. All manifestation is to effect an Epiphany. There is nothing hidden that shall not be revealed, as evolution throws out upon the screen of concrete existence the deeper things of God. And the sculpturing tool that molds in matter the forms of archetypal conception is the burning flame of material energy in the veins of substance, guided by intelligence. To impale a cosmic thought in a fixed structure of matter, to imprison it in inert substance, required the deadly sting of the Scorpion-goddess Serkh, which threw the invisible existence into motionless stability in the arms of matter.

The allegorical function of the sign of Scorpio is most impressive. The god in his autumn descent into body to make his hidden existence visible is stung into lethal sleep by the Scorpion-goddess. This is a most striking natural emblem of the swooning noted in connection with the downward march toward body. God caused a *deep sleep* to fall upon Adam when he was to be bifurcated into duality in earthly life. The entire progression into flesh involved the soul's "death," as from a sting of poison. The baser fires of sense, permeating his more ethereal bodies, injected noxious elements into it, rendering it lethal and sluggish. The foreign substances of the lower man poisoned the god. He was stung to death as he descended. This is in keeping with the position of Scorpio in the zodiac, which falls in the October-November date, when the sun likewise is going to its death in winter. He comes with power to tread on serpents and scorpions and put all things under his feet; but his victory is not won at the start; it will

357

come at the end. Like Jesus, Job and Samson, he must first come under the power of the adversary. He first becomes the helpless infant attacked by the serpent, the Herut menace; he becomes Sekari, the silent sufferer. The Scorpion sign in the autumn of the year is the intimation of the fatal sting of spirit by the serpent of the lower nature, the asp or Uraeus of Egypt, "a serpent of fire."

The sense is more directly to be apprehended in connection with several myths that represent Isis (nature) as scheming to extract from Ra his mighty secret of wisdom. She arranges to have Ra pass a certain place at which he would be bitten by a snake or scorpion. In the ensuing coma the secret could be wrested from him. This is a mighty glyph of incarnational truth. It is only when the god is bound in oblivion in the lap of matter that he imparts to matter (Isis) the qualities of his mind. She must reduce him and his intellectual fire to inertness so that she may abstract from him his living intellectual essence and impregnate her body with the seed of his mind after his death, which is exactly the substance and gist of another of the great Egyptian myths of the gods. This one has given ignorant Christian scholars and priests paroxysms of affected revulsion against the imputed sacrilege and obscenity of pagan "beliefs." So Serkh, a form of Isis characterized as the Scorpion-goddess, causes the descending god of pure intellect to be struck and paralyzed by the sting of bodily sense.

It is hardly less than astonishing that one can turn to the field of natural phenomena and find there a living duplication of the death of the *Christos* on the cross of matter. A number of species of insects resort to a stinging of the *male* by the *female,* as the result of which the former is thrown into a state of coma, and the mother takes advantage of his helplessness to deposit her eggs in the fleshly portion of his body, so that when they shortly come into larva form they may have his body to feed upon until able to find food elsewhere. Jesus commanded us to eat his body. He was laid in the manger, where the animals eat. The god goes to his death, and from his dying body and shed blood the young generation draws the nutriment that sustains life. *Job* and *Isaiah* refer to the sting that poisons the god.

Budge seems to have become so entangled in the dual relevance of the serpent symbol that he gave up the effort to grapple with it in despair:

358

"In short, the serpent was either a power for good or the incarnation of diabolical cunning and wickedness." [3]

He did not know it was both. But the matter *is* complicated and his distress is easily comprehended. There is the dragon of wisdom guarding the tree of knowledge, and there is the Apap monster, the crocodile of the waters. The latter is the "villain" of the play. But there is light in many statements that the serpent of evil is to be transformed into the serpent of good. There is the "lifting up of the serpent," which, however, again may have a twofold interpretation, denoting either the lifting up of the elementary powers (the lower serpent) to a higher condition through transformation; or the lifting up of the fiery serpent of the god-nature, after it has fallen into degradation. When Moses lifted up the brazen serpent on the cross in the wilderness, it can mean either that the Israelites should lift up the fallen god to his fiery purity, or that they should raise up the baser nature to a higher place through linkage with their exalted status. Both meanings at any rate eventually merge into one. For as the higher self had intertwined his nature with that of the lower self, the lifting up of the one must involve the redemption of the other. In the famed *caduceus* of Mercury the two serpents intertwined around the staff or wand are united at the bottom, because spirit and matter are joined in man's physical life.

Moses' raising the serpent is paralleled in Egyptian lore by the saying of the Speaker: "I am raised up to (or as) the serpent of the sun." The influence of the Christly deity lifts up the lower self. Moses stands for man, and Jehovah ordered Moses to build a tabernacle in which he (Jehovah) should be raised up. It may fall with surprise and incredulity upon most readers to be told that the Jehovah character of the creation legend is by no means the Supreme Lord, but merely one of the seven Elohim, or builders of the physical universe. He is one of the seven Uraeus "deities"; another one of the seven bears the name of Oreus, which is a form of Uraeus. So man is to raise up the natural order to the spiritual, and he is to do it in the "tabernacle" which he is engaged in building. This is that body of spiritual radiance which every man is steadily formulating out of the fiery essence of the very matter of his body, as lower fires are transmuted to higher. This transformation is made by man here on the cross of material life. The seven

Uraeus deities, of whom Jehovah was one, were the powers that lay embosomed in matter, the forces that built the physical universe, all below the level of mind. They were the Apap or Hydra monster swimming in the water of the lower Nun; and man had to transmute them into solar fires. Uraeus, the name, evidently derives from *Ur,* the original creative fire, and *aei,* meaning in Greek "ever, always." They were the "eternal fires" that forged the various creations. They create life below the level of mind, but must be lifted up to be changed into spiritual intelligences. They begin around the feet of the gods and goddesses, and end on their foreheads. In man physiologically they are brought up from the base of the spine and crown the human development by opening up the latent faculties of divine intelligence locked up in the pineal gland and pituitary body in the head. A line from the *Ritual* dispels all doubt as to their higher or lower rating and nature. It reads: "The seven Uraeus divinities are my body." They are the fiery formative energies of matter, not of mind. They are the energy in the atom, seven blind forces, which, however, draw the chariot of creation and must therefore be directed by intelligence.

One form of the serpent of the water is the great Hydra monster of the uranograph, Apap or Herut. He swims alongside the ship of Horus crossing the Lake of Putrata, or water of the bodily life, ready to devour any careless sailor who may fall overboard. In the planispheres his elongated body stretches across *seven* signs of the zodiac, and his head, with open mouth, comes directly under the feet of the Virgin. Her feet are over his head, fulfilling the Biblical promise that her heel should bruise his head. He is the serpent or dragon of many myths.

The manner in which this monster is to be overcome or beaten off is of great interest. The Speaker (Ch. 108) exclaims triumphantly: "I understand the mystical representation of things and by that means I repulse Apap." By "mystical representations of things" is meant something that modern insight does not discern and with which it is not conversant. It indicates the ancient use of spiritual typology, carried to a high degree of subtlety and artistry that engendered dynamic forms of psychological reaction. The cathartic virtue of Greek drama has been fairly well envisaged by students. But the practice of handling *symbolic formulae* of profound truth was in olden time a high art, used as a means of exalting and purifying the entire life. We note this often in the directions appended to the *Ritual* chapters as Rubrics. To put it tersely for modern skepticism, symbols can be used aright to exert a positive and salutary magic. Certain potencies in nature are released to play in the individual by the habitual contemplation of truth on the analogy of natural and other images. Much ancient ceremonial in religion was repetition of magical formulae of the sort. In the mind's grasp of subtle correspondence between physical phenomena and hidden truth there was liberated a psychic dynamism which was cathartic of the whole nature. To repulse Apap, to transform bestial desire into love and brotherhood, demands the skillful handling of subtle forces. Thought, will and feeling must be harmonized in a delicate balance. Theurgic magic and spiritual therapy were closely bound up with "the mystical representations of things."

To prevent the serpent from stinging, to meet this massive brute force of primal instinct and tame it to reason, required that the god-soul should learn to "charm the serpent." The significance of this "charming" is profound. "These are the gods who charm for Har-Khuti (Horus) in Amenta. They, the masters of their nets, charm those who are in the nets." In the scene portrayed in this chapter of the *Ritual* men walk before Ra to charm Apap for him. They chant: "O impious Apap, thou art charmed by us through the means of what is in our hands!" The first star in Ophiuchus is called "the head of the Serpent-Charmer."

"Who is Manitou?" an Algonquin chant asks. "He that goeth with the Serpent"—the god who lives with and tames the lower self. The widespread use of such terms as Manitou, Mana and Manna to indicate a spirit power in man and things is indicative of much. The words connote "magical power" as believed to be possessed by every tribal medicine-man. The probability is that the term is of kindred root with the word "man" itself, and *Manas* (Sanskrit), "mind." For mind constitutes man what he is, and it is the mind principle in man that was sent precisely for the purpose of charming the animal propensities into culture. A "mantram" is a Vedic word for a magical incantation. The god's action upon the brute self was likened to a charming, and the word "charm" is itself from the stem that gives us "Christ" and "Eucharist" and "charity." For the god to "charm" the beast was to lull the animal nature to docility, the while it lent ear to the sweet strains of a higher melody which transformed it magically.

361

The great potent serpent-charmer is mind, thought. Man is the thinking magician, rendering impotent the baleful sting of the serpent. The *Christos* tramples underfoot the serpents and scorpions, whose lethal sting endangers him.

Singular verification of these interpretations is found in the mythical episodes of Orpheus, the Greek hero-god. He is shown seated amidst eight animals (the elementary seven powers, counted as eight with their Lord) playing upon his lyre of seven strings. Massey traces the name Orpheus to the Egyptian *Uarp*, "the harper." The word is from the root signifying "to delight, charm or be charmed." He enchants the wild beasts and overcomes with the charms of his music all the powers of Hades. Circe's charming was at once followed by a transformation, but in this case from men into beasts, marking the god in his descent charmed by matter, and it had to be followed by a counter-transformation back to men. In most legends of classical mythology in which the solar hero faces the task of rescuing a maiden (the soul) from the cave in which she is guarded by a dragon, he is represented as first lulling the dragon to sleep or charming him by some potent talisman.

Immediately after Jesus said to his disciples that he beheld Satan as lightning fall from heaven he subjoined: "Behold I give unto you power to tread on serpents and scorpions and over all the power of the enemy." And when the seventy returned with joy from their mission, they exclaimed: "Lord, even the devils are subject unto us in thy name." The power to tread on serpents and scorpions was the power to rule—not necessarily to crush—the elementary nature. They were in Egypt the Sami and the Sebau and the minions of Sut. The latter was assigned the scorpion as the type of evil.

The power to charm a dangerous serpent by silent concentration was so evidently a demonstration of the efficacy of some invisible magic that mind, thought and magic were named after the serpent. It, too, was seen to possess this strange power. And the (higher) serpent became the type of occult control, wisdom, sagacity, for this reason. It even was one of the chief symbols of deity itself. The Greek *drakon*, "dragon," denotes the keen-eyed seer, as does the Sanskrit *Naga*, "serpent."

The dual aspect of the serpent symbol is graphed in the heavens in an ancient Egyptian planisphere. The great crocodile (dragon, serpent) appears at the place of the autumn equinox, close to the Scorpion, yet stretches across six signs to the spring equinox. It is the power that reaches from sense to soul. Likewise there is found in the northern sky the (former) pole star Alpha Draconis, and in the southern heavens the star Eta Hydri. On this dual pivot of the dragons the starry skies revolved. As in the uranograph between the two Dragons was run the line of the axis of stability for the planet, so the axis of stability in man's life is the line of force running between the upper serpent of spiritual wisdom and the lower one of animality. All cosmic stability is fixed upon a line of force plying between the two poles of vital affinity, positive and negative, the two serpent fires. Man exists only because spirit and body were united in one organism and the reciprocal play of currents of force between them sustains his life. The seers of old wrote the signs of this relationship in the skies. There was the serpent of heaven and the snake of earth. And man is the compound of their two energies.

Apap, the water monster, grasps at souls to devour them. The souls on board Horus' ship exult at having escaped his jaws. Appropriately he is also called the "eater of the heads" of the dead in Amenta. He subverts the intellect in man. But even his nature is finally changed and exalted, and he, along with the seven Uraei, is lifted up. They all become the servants of the god of light in the sun-cults. They at first war in fierce opposition to man as the Seven Adversaries; later they fight *for* Ra against every manifestation of evil. The Scorpion eventually stings *"on behalf of* gods and men." Serkh, Scorpion-goddess, becomes the guardian of the sun and keeper of the chained Apap. "I have come," says the Manes, "like the sun through the gates of the Sun-goer, otherwise called the Scorpion." (*Rit.,* Ch. 147.) This puts Scorpio at the place of the autumn equinox, where it was in remote times,—the eagle, one of the four cardinal guardians.

When the seven Uraei were raised to be worn on the foreheads of the gods, that which had been most deadly was transformed into that which was divine. It is said of each serpent emitting jets of fire in Hades, "Its flame is for Ra." The death-darting dragons became the watchers of the gates of heaven and guardians of the tree of knowledge, the three golden apples (mind-soul-spirit) and every treasure of light. The seven elementary powers first described as Wicked Spirits are promoted from that character to become the "Seven Great Spirits in the service of their Lord," and the seven attendants of the solar Ra in Egypt. This transformation is matched in Persia and India. In the planisphere they stand behind the constellation of the Thigh or Meskhen, Ursa Major, in the north. They are called "the Followers of Osiris," who "burn the wicked souls of his enemies," and "the givers of blows for sins." Four of these are Amsta, Hapi, Tuamutef and Kabhsenuf, prominent in Egyptian lore as the "Four Chieftains of the Four Corners," and Sons of Horus. They were emblemed by the four Canopic jars at the corners of the mummy-case.

The gist of all this is that the first seven-ply creation was elementary and chaotic, and that the advent of mind in creation in the person of man put these wild forces for the first time under rational control in an organic being. From the status of enemies and opponents, the first principles were tamed to man's service. As a reward of service they will be lifted up to partake of man's higher nature. The text (Ch. 85) has the Osirified dead saying: "I pass through substance. I pierce the darkness. Hidden reptile is my name. The soul of my body is a serpent of life." Chapter 87 of the *Ritual* carries the expressive title "of making the transformation into the serpent Sata." Allusion to the danger encountered by the god in the underworld is found in the "chapter by which a person is not devoured or bitten by the eater of the head, which is a snake."

The frequent early figure of a serpent coiled seven times round the summit of a hill or a cone (seen in the serpent mounds of America) types the fiery energy of life circling the round of the seven cycles in all creations. There was a sevenfold movement in each of the creations, the stellar, the solar or planetary, and the human, both racial and individual. The Beast had seven heads. The *Ritual* gives: "O the very high hill in Hades! the heavens rest upon it. There is a snake on it, Sati is his name. He is about twenty cubits in his coil." He is also called "the Serpent of Millions of Years," which indicates that he is a type of the cyclic revolutions of life force about the globes. The crocodile-god Sevekh (seven) is said to be on the hill of the Lord of Bata.

The serpent laying its eggs and coiling about them for incubation was the true type of natural gestation, which brought forth fixed cycles of revolving life arising out of the primal chaos. By shape the egg itself is a symbol of revolution. Each seven coils or revolutions of the mother life engender a new creation. The seven non-intelligent powers

—monsters, giants, blind adversaries—are the breeding force of a new life that is intelligent. The powers that swirled and swarmed in the abyss of darkness become the nursery of the sun of intellect in the kingdom of man, who is so far the crown of earthly life. The great old giant dragon was simply a type of primordial darkness and chaos. It gave birth to seven powers which fought blindly until they were subdued and synthesized under the last and highest of them, the Christ mind. This great dragon was pictured with its tail in its mouth. The figure betokened the cycle returning into itself or back to source, or the parent life reabsorbing its own products. Kronos, Father Time, in the great myths devoured his own children. The Oriental expects his individual consciousness to be drawn back into the universal Nirvana. The dragon of the original abyss later came to be the dragon of mother earth herself, who swallowed up her children one by one as the grave closed over them. Also she swallowed the sun each evening and the stars as they set.

Sut, as a later representative of evil, became the opponent of the god both in the physical and the moral order. He waged war with the sun-god and was defeated, but never slain. Horus attacked him and fought with him *for three days,* and though wounded, he escaped with his life. He suffered rout periodically and perpetually, but was not destroyed, or only figuratively so. He lived to fight again. The sun-god cast a spell on him every day and rendered him powerless for evil. He was chained down for the aeon. All this was the natural expression of the moral conflict in man's soul, as it is of all other conflict, for life subsists in manifestation only by virtue of the pull, tension or struggle between the two nodal forces. Now one, now the other, is conqueror. The original mother of life, represented variously as the crocodile dragon, the hippopotamus, cow, sow, lioness, water-horse and finally woman, "the great harlot," who all meet in Kep, or Kefa (Heva, Chavvak, Eve), "the mother of the living," was the gestator of Sut and Horus, who are born twins! They typify the two aspects of life's expression, activity and passivity, positive and negative force, light and darkness. The story of life is a story of unending conflict between the two "hostile" powers. The legends paint but a single cycle of growth, but the cycles repeat themselves endlessly. Any cycle is emblematic of every other one, and hence of all movement or all truth. If man knows his own life in its cycle, he knows all. The arcane wisdom exhorted man to know himself.

In Egypt the conflict was first waged between the sun-god Ra and Apap. It was symboled variously by the death and rebirth of sunshine daily and seasonally, by the waxing and waning moon, and by the setting and rising stars. In the realm of spiritual activity it was carried on by Sut and Horus. Astrologically the Dragon in the northern sky was the good serpent of Ra, or Horus, while the elongated Hydra was the evil serpent of Sut or Satan. Lastly the two were depicted as twin brothers fighting over their birthright! Their conflict took place, be it noted, in Amenta, where they fought upon the mount and were constellated as the Twins contending in Gemini. We shall see them as Cain and Abel, Jacob and Esau and other pairs.

The Bible offers first the warfare between Cain and Abel, the first two sons of Adam (Atum). Research brings to light the little-known fact that Abel is feminine in gender! This would seem to put Cain in the role of the conqueror of material nature and darkness. Massey states that Abel represents the waning light of evening or autumn, the god descending into incarnation or entering upon his "feminine phase." Cain then would be the one who puts an end to this cycle, and rises to victory in a new birth. Cain may be a type of Khunsu, Egyptian god, son of Atum-Ra, but Khunsu obtains his victory under the typology of the moon's phases, rather than those of the sun. He is the lunar light, victorious over the dark phase.

In the struggle between Horus and Sut over the succession the two were parted by the intervention of Taht, the moon-god, who assigns each to his domain, the one north, the other south. This marks the bifurcation into spirit and matter, or male and female potency, by the instrumentality of matter, represented by the moon. It is allegorized in the fairy princess stories by the awarding of one half of the father's kingdom to the hero-rescuer of the king's daughter who had been captured by the dragon. In the kingdom of man it meant the placing of the god's intelligence in the upper portion of the body and the animal soul or Sut below the diaphragm, in Jonah's "belly of death." The significance of Taht's mediatorship is that the moon is the agency of effecting an intermediate relation between the hidden solar light and the dark power of night, by its reflection of the sun-god's rays in the darkness. The moon is thus the perfect type of the mediatorial function

366

of that principle in Plato's philosophy which stands midway between the higher *Nous,* or spiritual intelligence, and the *doxa,* or sense mind of the animal self. The bee gets some of its character as type of soul because it is the active agent of marrying the male and female elements of the flower. In Roman religion this principle was the Pontifex or Bridge-builder between the two natures, since it spans the gap between them and makes communication possible. And in human history it grandly types the situation in which, when the soul in body is quite cut off, like the earth at night, from the direct rays of heavenly light, and gropes in darkness, there comes to its aid the principle of *Manas,* the hidden intellect, to intervene, like the moon that relays light from an unseen source, between man and the god who seems to have deserted him. The moonlight is the symbol of that spiritual light that shines not directly in full power, but refracted through intervening media, into our prison of darkness. Cut off from our full solar light in the darkness of incarnation, we still have the divine light by reflection upon our physical lives. The moonlight is not that true light, but it bears witness to that light.

Beside the pairs of contending brothers, mythology presents the many pairs of the two women, whose representative functions are somewhat more difficult to discern. The solar heroes have ever two mothers, a heavenly and an earthly one. The one conceives the son, the other bears him. "The Two Daughters of the king of the north gave birth to thee, the great ladies of his head." It is added, significantly: "Heaven beareth thee up on thy right side, earth on thy left side." The intent here is to tell us that we are upheld by the opposite action of the positive and negative strands of primal force, the powers of "heaven" and "earth," or, for the individual, mind and body. The two women are elsewhere described as the "Two Goddesses who conceive and do not breed"—until fructified by the germ of mind.

But it is said that Sut opens and Horus closes up the two mothers. There is abstruse meaning hidden under this typing. It seems to use the imagery of opening and closing the womb in impregnation and childbirth. The opening was ascribed to Sut because it signals the coming forth of conscious life into and under his domain, matter. As St. Paul has told us, sin and evil sprang to life when the soul came into incarnation. Sut opened the womb of being and began the phase of manifestation in all the lower realms. Horus, spirit force, led the life of nature back from matter to the noumenal worlds, and thus closed the womb of the universal mother. As the "Bull of his Mother," he impregnated her again and again, closing her womb until the birth. The sons of intelligence must reproduce through union with natural and material forms in each generation. Matter, the mother of life, is that Great Harlot, ever fecund, yielding her bosom to spirit to embody its forms. Horus closes the womb with fertile seed; Sut opens it again to let the new birth escape into darkness and death. If this is not the sense of the typology, it hides something else profound indeed.

The two brothers were typed by white and black birds, respectively. The golden hawk pictured Horus, the black vulture Sut. Eagle and crow, dove and raven, hawk and blackbird, pigeon and bandicoot are often paired. The stars Sothis (Sirius) and Canopus likewise carry the characters in the sky. In India Krishna and Bala-Rama do the impersonation. Krishna asks the other: "Do you know that you and I are alike the origin of the world?" Krishna came from the black hair of Vishnu and Bala-Rama from the white. Krishna comes (Massey) from a word meaning "waning moon"; Bala means virile male force. There are the two brothers in the Babylonian books, the one ousting the other each night. It is the younger of the twins that always slays the dragon with seven heads, rescuing the soul. Ultimately he marries the princess, which is to say that the two natures merge into one; and he inherits half the paternal kingdom.

On one occasion when Horus and Sut were battling, Sut cast filth in the face of Horus and blinded him; Horus retaliated by tearing away Sut's genitals. If incarnation entails the god's being blinded by having the "mire" of earth cast in his face, he at least wins the use of the procreative powers of matter for the time. His release finally from the dominance of carnal instincts and his graduation from sexual generation back to spiritual creation would be the general significance of his circumcision.

In the resurrection of the dismembered Osiris, "Horus, who loves him, brings him his Eye; Set, *who loves him,* brings him his testicles, and Thoth, who loves him, brings him his arm and shoulder." Set (Sut) is here painted in friendly colors. So in another text: "Nut gives thee to be a god unto Set in thy name of God. . . . Horus seizes Set, he places him under thee; Set bears thee up, he is beneath thee as earth is beneath thee. Rule thou him, therefore, in thy name of Ta-tcheser.

Horus makes thee to grasp Set by his middle; he shall not get out of thy hand." Here is evidence that the elementary powers were to be taken in hand by the god and utilized in support of his life. The subordination of the beast under divine faculty is surely indicated in this material. The eye definitely identifies Horus as the deity of spiritual vision, the testicles relate Sut to the realm of generation, or flesh.

Sut is definitely made the upholder and servant of Horus in some passages. "Hail, Osiris (deceased), wake up! Horus hath made Thoth to bring thine enemy to thee. *He places thee on his back;* he cannot throw thee off. Thou makest thy seat upon him. Come forth, sit upon him, he escapes not from thy hand. Hail, be thou master of him."

"He sets thee on thy throne; Horus makes thine enemy to bow beneath thee. When he would have union with thee, thou escapest his member."

Here is further and unquestioned confirmation of the claim that the seven lower powers are later drawn into the service of the soul. The god was to "put all things under his feet," to have dominion over the beast, bird and fish of the worlds lying below his plane. The allusion to escaping Sut's member bent on intercourse would dramatize the idea of the soul's escape from being drawn into defilement and pollution by full immersion in the animal nature on its low plane.

Roman classicism presents the fable of Romulus and Remus, and again one kills the other. A common early tradition in the world is the founding of a city by a fratricide.

A Greek version of the twins is seen in Eros, Love, and Ant-Eros, the latter being the opposing phase. He avenged unrequited love and contended with Cupid (Eros).

The natural man and the spiritual son were charactered most peculiarly by another set of symbols. The former became the uncouth "lad from the country," *au naturel,* and the latter the "gilded youth from the town." Grotesque as this may seem, it attests the invincible studiousness of the ancients for suggestive symbols borrowed from nature and life. A companion pair was the King in the city and the Chief in the bush.

Astrally the twins are given places in opposite quarters of the sky, as gods of the north and south. Then they are distinguished as the setting and rising sun, waning and waxing moon. Sometimes the character of Sut is assigned to a double of Horus, who is the ugly old man, fading in his dotage, or the crippled deity, or the immature and impubescent child. He is being worsted and supplanted by the young solar Horus, born anew and come to pubescence (type of the rebirth of his lost power) at the age of twelve, when his wisdom confounds the old men and he leaves his mother. This second and virile character is also taken by Jesus, as the Christ of the catacombs, the "blooming boy" Bacchus of the Greek Mysteries, the youthful Mithras of the Persians, and the fair Apollo of Greece. Also there was an elder and a younger Horus, the one born to suffer and die ignominiously, the other to rise crowned with light. So the Hindu Prajapati was one-half mortal, the other half immortal, and in his mortal life he feared death. There was a double Horus, a biune Bacchus, a two-faced Janus and the two-sided Jesus, the little mummied child and suffering servant, as well as the risen and glorified Lord.

A very important facet of the myth of the Two Brothers is to be envisaged through the story of another pair of twins, Jacob and Esau. They struggle for supremacy in the mother's womb. In the womb of the abyss of matter the two forces struggle before they come to manifestation. We have seen that hair, as in Samson's case, stands as the type of solar radiance or power. Esau is the "red, hairy one." Jacob (Egyptian Hak, Hakh, or Hakekh) is the dark twin. When Rebecca found that "twins were struggling in her womb," she was terrified and consulted the Eternal. She was told:

> "In your limbs lie nations twain,
>   rival races from their birth;
> one the mastery shall gain,
>   the younger o'er the elder reign."

Esau emerged first and Jacob came out grasping the other's *heel*. Much the same story comes to light in the delivery of the twins of Tamar, who had been impregnated by Judah, her father-in-law. During labor a hand appeared, and the midwife tied a red thread around it. But the hand drew back and the other babe was born first. The first-born was Perez (Breach: his untimely birth a breach of order). The brother's name was Zerah (Scarlet).

It is, however, in a well-preserved tradition of the Rabbins that we find the pointed significance of the Jacob and Esau birth. The grasping of Esau's heel by Jacob can not be seen in its full import without completing the story by means of the tradition. It says that on Esau's heel there was the likeness of a serpent! Again we have the heel of the god treading the head of the serpent and being marked with its imprint. If the two natures, one higher, one below it, are conjoined in man, obviously the foot, or heel, of the upper man will be just over the head of the lower, and *vice versa*. And at the point where the two contact there would be localized the whole friction and alternate bruising between them. The god would trample on and eventually crush out the nature, the head, of the brute elementary forces; but he would not come off unscathed. He would bear the mark of the beast on his heel. Esau is thus identified as the higher or spiritual twin.

The vulnerability of the gods in one point, the heel, was not confined to Hebrew literature. Osiris was wounded in the feet and had to recover the use of them. The classical example of Achilles, whose mother Metis held him by the heel while she dipped him in the waters of the Styx, leaving him vulnerable in the heel which was untouched by the water, occurs to every mind. The mother, nature, holds the god in her realm with her grasp only on his lowest part, the heel. If he is stung, it must be there. We are dipped in the river Styx of this life to render us invulnerable to further attack.

The serpent fulfilled his prophesied mission of enmity against the woman's seed, the Christ nature in man. He pursued the woman clothed with the sun, with the moon under her feet, and with twelve stars in her diadem, down to earth and went away to make war with her offspring on the border of the sea that encompassed the earth. The divine sun pours its rays upon the soul and "clothes it with light as with a garment." The moon is the generator of the forces that constitute the nature below, and so the moon is under her feet. And the topmost output of the whole cycle will be the twelve shining powers of intellectual light that man is to evolve. Every impact of the carnal nature of man against the rule of pure intellect in his mundane life is a skirmish in the serpent's warfare against the soul. The war in heaven was transferred to earth and is still going on. It is the Battle of Armageddon. The two wings of a great eagle that were given the woman to transport her to a place prepared by God, where she should be nourished for three and a half cycles, until the time of her delivery of the Christ child, very probably refer to the sign of Scorpio, coming in the late autumn, the time of the soul's descent. For the Scorpion

371

was in its higher of two aspects the eagle, and it is still taken in that character by astrologers. The waterflood poured out by the Dragon to overwhelm her evidently types the release of the strong sweep of karmic and evolutionary forces which drives about one-third of the "stars of heaven" into incarnation. But earth helped the woman and swallowed up this flood. This is our assurance that mundane life is beneficent. The hard experience on earth tamed and subdued the wild energies of elementary nature and became indeed a place of refuge and safety. And here in the crypt of earth, the "bight of Amenta," mother nature brings up her Man-child.

But finally at the judgment, which is held on the highest mount of resurrection glory, the great old Mother and her seven earth-born spirits are judged, rejected and cast down out of heaven. Apt, as the primordial mother of life, is succeeded by Hathor, and the Sevekh dragon by Horus. What this sheaf of events seems to imply is that the powers that had at first functioned cosmically, came in the course of aeons to operate in the building of physical man, a miniature replica of the cosmos, and when finally converted to a higher level, received a new name and nature. The harshness of the details of being judged and cast out is purely a dramatic blind to cover the fine meaning astutely. Deity works out of its system in the fires of earth life the debilitating and paralyzing effect of its initial poisoning by the seven influences of Seb. The text of *Revelation* says that "fire descended from heaven and consumed them"; but consumption must be read as conversion into natures of finer purity. The Christ then moves out of the control of his mother nature and seeks the things of his father, spirit, at the perfection of his twelve facets of intelligence.

It is of the utmost significance that the new heaven and new earth, in which the tree of life was to bear twelve fruits upon its branches. was to be formed according to "the measure of a man." Man means "thinker," fundamentally; and so thought, intelligent mind, was to rule the new dispensation. It would establish life finally in its spiritual kingdom of twelve divisions, superseding the natural order which was founded on a basis of seven divisions. The mother's number, seven, was to be supplanted by the father's number, twelve. Man was to go on to evolve his twelve divine faculties. The twelve signs of the zodiac depict the twelve segments of the nature of man when all have been perfected. No ancient religion can be understood without reference to them. The coming of the twelvefold spiritual hierarchy ended the reign of the seven elementary powers, from bondage to which Paul says we must be freed. The Dragon of seven heads is overthrown, and on the head of the Woman, *saved by earth experience,* is placed the diadem of divinized humanity, studded with twelve stars, or spiritual fires.

. The statement in *Revelation* is that the fifth angel poured out his bowl upon the throne of the Beast in his kingdom of darkness, overthrowing the reign of that power which had filled many with sore disease and made them cry out against the Most High. Occult books reveal that we are now in the fifth race of the fourth round of life energy on this globe, and are developing the fifth principle, *Manas,* the intellect. The reasoning mind, then, is destined to put an end to the reign of bestiality.

When the seven angels had poured out upon the earth the *fires* of "the seven bowls of the judgment of him that lives for ever," it is said that the temple (St. Paul assures us that the temple is the body) became filled with the smoke from the seven bowls, so that the power and the glory of God could no more be seen, nor could anyone enter the temple again until the seven angels had poured out the fires of judgment upon the earth. This is clearly an occult reference to what we have described as the smudge, smoke, vapors, soot and murk arising when the powers of god and beast first mingled in the body. It may also cover the unnatural intermixture and miscegenation of godmen and animals that seems to have been a fact of history. The "temple" had of course to be purified before the true Ego of the individual could enter and rule. Hence the whole earthly experience is the purgation, beyond question.

Matching the splendid imagery of *Revelation,* the *Ritual* of Egypt presents "the woman clothed with the sun," who says: "I am the Woman, an *orb of light in the darkness;* I have brought my orb to the darkness; it is changed into light. I overthrow the extinguishers of flame. I have stood. The fiends have hidden their faces." The seven elements were the powers of material darkness; the Christ power was that of light. The darkness of the seven "woman" powers was changed into light. The unevolved soul goes into darkness to become irradiated with light. The lower passions would extinguish the flames of deity and must be overthrown. They are the fiends, the minions of Sut and

Satan, who turn and flee as the light of virtue shines forth, like the host of Midianites when Gideon's three hundred broke their clay pitchers and revealed the lights hidden within.

In the *Arabic Gospel of the Infancy*, when the boy had been bitten by the serpent, the Lord Jesus says to his playmates, "Boys, let us go and kill the serpent." He proves his power over the reptile by making it suck the venom from the wound. Earthly and Satanic influences poison the descending soul; yet experience in overcoming their power in the milling grind of life extracts the poison in the end. "God sends down to death; he also lifts up," says the *New Testament*. In the same Gospel it is related that a damsel was afflicted by Satan, the cursed one, in the form of a huge dragon which from time to time appeared to her and prepared to swallow her up. He also sucked out all her blood, so that she remained like a corpse. She is cured by a strip of clothing from a garment worn by the child Jesus (Ch. 33). This is obviously another form of the story of the woman with an issue of blood who touches the fringe of Jesus' garment. In the Gnostic version it is Sophia who suffers from an issue of blood, and is sustained by Horus when her life is flowing away. The Christ principle fecundates Nature and closes her unfruitful womb to make her give birth to the glory of an intellectual delivery.

As Joseph takes charge of the virgin mother and the infant fleeing to Egypt for safety, so in the Egyptian *mythos* the earth-god Seb becomes the protector of Isis and the foster-father of the child Horus when they are forced to hide in the marshes till the threat of Herut is passed. And as "the earth helped the Woman" in the *Revelation* version, so Seb, the earth deity, helped the woman and child in Egypt. The dragons issue from a cave on the roadside, but Jesus appears, according to the Gnostic story, and they adore him. So the demons cringe before him in the *New Testament*. In the *Ritual* Horus saves his father from the four crocodiles. "I am the Son," he says, "who saves the great one from the four crocodiles." He orders them to go back one by one and they obey him. For Ra has given him sovereignty over Lower Egypt, with power to tread down serpents, scorpions and dragons. But there is much hidden value in the legend that the serpent stings the child on its way into "Egypt," and that the earth-god heals the wound. It is a mighty item of philosophy, this assurance that mundane experience for the god-soul is the only antidote for certain imperfections inhering even in celestial beings. It is evolution's cure for lack of development, the prime cause of all that is named evil. The god needed further tempering and purification in "the crucible of the great house of flame" of flesh and sense. He was carried far down toward dissolution in the fiery test, but was re-welded into finer temper by the ordeals of earth, water, air and fire, and rebuilt to more perfect wholeness. The goose portrayed on the head of Seb in an Egyptian planisphere (according to Kircher) types the earth as "the goose that laid the golden egg daily." If this be but a poetograph for the new-born daily sun of golden light, that sun in turn is the everlasting symbol of the rise of a golden egg of new divinity from out the confines of earth or the "sea." The god is the divine egg laid in humanity, for he is the heavenly foetus in the womb of the body. As he is destined to burgeon out, like the flower, into a burst of golden glory, it is by no means mere poetic fiction to call him the golden egg. And earth lays this golden nugget. The earth being our common mother, we have before us the Egyptian source of "Mother Goose," and the mysterious sagacity concealed in her catchy jingles.

The Goliath story is but an embellishing of the original glyph of a dragon in its conflict with the young deity in man. A dragon is always exchangeable with a giant. The fabled giants and those mentioned in the sixth chapter of *Genesis*, the Nephilim (the "fallen ones," by etymology) were early beings produced by the intermixture of the Titans with the largest animals in the miscegenation, and are therefore the most literal or historical embodiments of the dragon-monster idea, and they were the prototypes of the ogres of children's books. Egypt shows us fables, more than one, in which the giant-ogre was killed by the blow of a small egg (of the pigeon, dove or other bird) in the middle of the forehead. The significance of slaying the beast or dragon of mental darkness by sinking the symbol of incipient mind and light into its forehead should need little elaboration. The elemental giant or ogre in us is killed when the egg or pebble of intellect (the white stone of *Revelation*) is implanted in the citadel of reason. The egg or pebble can undoubtedly be taken to stand for the pineal gland in the middle of the skull, the opening of which to function brings the full light of deific consciousness into manifestation, and slays the giant or ogre. The germ of mind, reason, intellect will charm and "kill" the Goliath in us. David is proven to be another figure of the solar god.

375

Horus, too, pierces the Apap-dragon in the eye with his lance and pins him to earth. The lance was a figure for the sun-ray tipped with red flame for effective piercing power. The tree we have seen used as the paramount symbol of living force, and the Christmas tree tipped with the blazing star, or the main stem of the pine made red hot at the top, was an instrument in the hands of the sun-heroes. There is outside of Egyptian sources a most famous instance of the occurrence of this emblem. Ulysses bores out the single eye of the massive Cyclopean giant Polyphemus with a great pine stake fired at the tip. And this operation takes place in a cave, which had become the prison of death for the hero and his men—the underworld. The solar hero wounds the giant of darkness by the injection of fire into his head! And fire signifies intellect. Horus at one time fights Sut with the branch of a palm. This weapon matches the golden bough and is a particularly pertinent solar symbol, being a product of torrid lands, and also, according to Massey, putting forth a new branch on its trunk every thirty days, thirty being the number of days in a solar, twenty-eight in a lunar, month.

These seven mighty engines of creative force, presumably the seven great spirits before the throne of God, were indeed the seven creative Logoi, Elohim, Kabiri, Ali, Baalim, Rishis, Cosmocratores, Sephiroth, Aeons. Enoch gives their names: Azazzel, Amazarak, Armers, Barkayel, Akabeel, Tamiel and Asaradel. In the ancient Hebrew version they are: Ildabaoth, Jehovah, Sabaoth, Adonai, Eloeus, Oreus and Astanphaios. Again in Chaldean they are: Bel, Ea, Rimmon, Nebo, Marduk, Nerra and Ninib. They were typified by the seven stars of the Great ·Bear. By some they are taken to be the powers that ruled the seven successive pole stars, which fixed the earth's axial position from age to age. For in one rendering of the *mythos* the seven giants bore the world of the heptanomis, or cosmos of seven divisions, upon their backs, each standing at his station as one of the seven great guardians of stability. It is said that when the Demiurgus asked their help in the work of creation, they meditated and forgot. They slumbered and fell from their posts one by one. The seven sleepers of the myth, and those specifically in the cave at Ephesus, with their dog, answer to the seven sleepers with Anup and his jackal at the pole in the Egyptian portrayal.

In its human application the myth is reflected in the seven elementaries, which, being the original founders of man's constitution, fell from their status as rulers of his life when the crowning principle of conscious intelligence placed mind on the throne and superseded the reign of the seven. The seven giants that have been "slain" by the young solar power, Jack the Giant Killer, were subdued, like wild horses, until they bore the spiritual ruler on their backs. All domestication of wild animals to serve man is a type of the conversion of natural energies in man's constitution to the service of his thought. They are the "seven devils" that had to be cast out of Mary Magdalene (type of the mother or nature again), the seven plagues of Egypt, the seven lean kine that ate the fat kine, the seven lean years, the seven ages of servitude. They were previously our pole stars, but are to be displaced now and cast down by intellect, which should be our pole star or rod of stability henceforth. In their human phase they are the earth elementals under whose dominion Paul asserts that we fall when we woo the carnal mind. *They govern the life of every child until the age of seven, when mind begins to dispossess them and move toward the throne.* And again they are the seven diabolical propensities, the seven deadly sins, which, only too thinly covered over by a veneer of social restraint, gush up now and again in the individual, in the nation, in the world, when vital forces sweep upon them and fan them into expression. Apap is being bound, but he is yet far from being securely tied by the thongs of reason and disciplined mind.

In the *Kabalah* the seven, or first hebdomad, headed by Ildabaoth, say: "Come, let us make man after our image"; and the mother having furnished them with the idea of a man, they formed a giant of immense size. But he could only crawl along the ground until the Father had breathed into him the breath of life, emblem of mentality. From Ildabaoth's sentence in the *Kabalah* it can be seen who it is in the *Genesis* story that propose to make man after their image—not at all Supreme Deity, but the seven lower archangels, one of whom was Jehovah. But Jehovah is used in the Bible myth to represent the entire seven, as are also Sabaoth and Adonai at times.

And in the *Divine Pymander* of Hermes one reads. "This is the mystery that to this day is hidden and kept secret; for *nature being mingled with man* brought forth a wonder most wonderful." There are accounts of previous creations of worlds or systems that fell because they were imperfect. Perfection awaited the generation of man, the advent of the *Christos*. The septenary creation was the formation, principle by principle, of the natural man in the image of the seven Kabiri, Elohim, who could endow their creature with the six (often called seven) elementary constituents, culminating in sensation and emotion, but could not give him the baptism of air and fire, or mind and soul. The twelve-part division came when the pole star passed from Lyra into Hercules, the sign of the Man, whose twelve labors are the achievement of twelve distinct stages of evolutionary development. The music of the spheres ceased—for the time—with the conquest of the seven; and the introduction of free will, coupled at first with primal ignorance, brought the beginning of the world's woe, man's slow attainment of mastery by the sweat of his brow, in a milieu of disorder, misery and struggle, typed by the twelve labors of the solar figure. The struggle of man, the thinker, with the seven maternal forces which he has to surmount is the great Battle of Armageddon, which Paul and Plato make the supreme moral issue of mundane life.

The Druid and other ancient temples were formed of twelve stones set in a circle or oval. A most striking repetition of this duodecal symbol is found when Joshua (Jesus) in crossing the Jordan into the kingdom of peace and plenty is commanded to set up twelve stones in the bed of the river, the waters being dried up. Also it is seen in the Gilgal circle which became the lodging place of the Israelites. The "chosen people" were to be given a Promised Land abounding in milk and honey; but it was already occupied by the Canaanites, Hittites, Amorites, Perizzites, Hivites, Jebusites and Girgashites, the primal seven powers! The Lord kept promising Israel that he would dispossess these seven tribes of the land on behalf of his nation of twelve tribes. *Old Testament* narrative leaves little question as to the mythical nature of this whole story. For it is told later on with what inhuman ruthlessness the Eternal, in campaign after campaign under Joshua, Gideon, Jephthah and other leaders, slew "multitudes in number as the sands of the seashore" on single days. The only salvation of sense and sanity for the narrative is to transfer its meaning from outer history to inner relevance, where it properly belongs. Then one can absolve the Eternal from unthinkable cruelty, in understanding that the solar ray within us, after crossing the boundary between the two kingdoms of our nature, before it can institute its twelve-act regime, must dispossess (by conversion of nature) the countless myriads of natural instincts, animal impulses, carnal desires that previously operated there—the progeny of the seven mother powers.

Seven blasts upon the ram's horn on the seventh day brought the fall of Jericho (seven letters in the name); and seven blasts upon the seven angels' trumpets in *Revelation* announced the new heaven and new earth, founded upon the twelve bases in man's constitution.

Sut, the head of the seven first powers, is said to be bound in chains each morning. "Chains are flung upon thee by the scorpion-goddess and slaughter is dealt out to thee by Maati [Judgment]. Apap is fallen and is in bonds" (Ch. 39). This daily drama was enacted yearly as well. Sut is put in chains, cast into prison, or made to flee with a chain of steel upon him (Ch. 20). Or he is pierced with hooks. Horus is described as "putting an end to the opposition of Sut, the power of darkness" (Ch. 137B). Sut and his minions, the Sebau, are declared to have thrown down the pillars of Osiris on the ground. Horus, the young solar god, came to set them upright. Sut was the master of the legions of devils that Jesus (Horus) had to cast out of the man whom they had obsessed on the Gadarene lake shore in the Gospels. Could anything be more significant than that the dispossessed demons should be made to come out of the man beside a body of *water* and enter animals? And there is the further detail that the herd ran down the "steep into the lake and were choked" (*Luke* 8: 33). The demoniacal powers could not be permitted to rule *man;* their activity appertained only to the animal kingdom, to which the Christ relegates them in the watery milieu of the body. Was this incident original in Gospel literature? In the Egyptian judgment scene, when the person whose life record marked him as evil was condemned and rejected, he was delivered over immediately to the Typhonian beast, crocodile-hippopotamus-pig all in one. And he was, as thus indicated, sent down again into incarnation in the body of the beast! In short, he was not released, but thrust back into animal body for more experience.

Matching the temptation scene in the Gospels, Sut is said to have seized Horus in the desert of Amenta and carried him to the top of the Mount called Hetep, the place of peace, where the two contending powers were reconciled by Shu or Taht, according to the treaty made by Seb.

In the *Gospel of the Infancy* there are two boys, the bad one and the

379

good one. In some of the Apocryphal Gospels the bad boy, who in *Pseudo-Matthew* (29) is called the Son of Satan, runs at Jesus and thrusts at him in a way to injure his shoulder and paralyze his arm. The *Gospel of Thomas* recites the incident. In the Egyptian material Sut has weakened Horus by pinning down his arm, and in this condition Horus is subject to his assailant's might. But at the resurrection Horus frees his arm and strikes down Sut or stabs him to the heart. Sut was designated "the eater of the arm."

Sut thus has a manifold function to fulfill in the typology. He is a versatile adversary. He puts out Horus' eye; he seizes and imprisons him; he ties his arm; he sows the tares amid the grain; he lets loose the locusts and other plagues; he entraps Horus and his company in the ark; he swallows the falling stars and devours the damned (those condemned to earth life). He represents opposition to Horus, the good light, at every point and in every form. So Horus comes to put an end to this opposition. In victory he says to his father Osiris: "I have brought thee the associates of Sut in chains."

When Jesus was seized in the Garden of Gethsemane he acknowledges the (temporary) triumph of the enemy: "This is your hour," he says to his captors, "and the power of darkness" (*Luke* 22:53). In the seizure of Horus by the associates of Sut, they see the double crown on the forehead of Horus and fall to the ground upon their faces (*Rit.*, Ch. 134). The magical efficacy of the double crown of Horus lay in the fact that it signified the god's control over both Lower and Upper "Egypt." When Judas and his associates came to take Jesus he said: "I am" (not "I am he"—Massey). Then "they went backward and fell to the ground." Scene for scene the two are the same.

The seven stars of the Lesser Bear were figured as the followers or reflections of the greater creation, the second creation in the likeness of the first, or the small creation in the image of the cosmic one. The microcosm was formed over the grand lines of the macrocosm. In the center of the great Denderah zodiac there is the hippopotamus (identical with the Bear) and her dog, fox or jackal. The two are Typhon-Sut, or the mother and her child at the center of all. This is nature's ancient stellar picture of the Madonna and her child before it was reduced to the human phase. The dog, fox and jackal, with their instinctive faculty of following a trail in the dark, were limned as the guide of souls in the darkness of incarnation; and the little bear, dog or fox,

380

whose pivotal star was the pole itself, thus became the "cynosure" ("dog's tail") for night-bound mariners in a literal sense, the spiritual meaning being evident to all who are not obtuse. The guide or watch-dog was double-headed, a watcher by day and by night, or guardian of the two segments of our life, the heavenly and the earthly. The great stellar universe served as the model for the formation of the smaller, though higher, universe in man's life, for the great first gods of nature said they would create man "in their own image." The Great and Little Bears type these two creations. And the Little Bear, symbolizing man's divine part, is the only one anchored fast to the very pole of heaven, the pledge of eternal stability. Truly "the heavens are telling."

The fiends of Sut are allegorized as transforming themselves into beasts. The elementary powers naturally became embodied in the forms of life below man, as well as in the animal part of man himself.

Strangely and with amazing fidelity, in spite of intervening centuries of ignorance, social custom preserves the original form, if not the meaning, of symbolic festivals. Horus or Iusa (Jesus) in the "house of a thousand years" was the bringer of the millennium. Sut or Satan was released for a little period, seven days at most ("days" meaning cycles), and the commemoration of this cyclic event was fixed in the world-wide carnival which indicates by its name its derivation from Satan—the Saturnalia. Saturn, the chief of the primary seven powers, was identical with Sevekh, Seb, Set, Sut or Satan. He was, as in *Job, Genesis* and elsewhere, released for the seven periods of a cycle, during which Horus had to do combat with him. Then he was bound for a thousand years, the millennium of peace. It is instructive to see in the Saturnalia, with its license, the far-flung prolongation of the ancient idea of the release from bondage of the elementary powers, both in and out of human nature. The elemental forces, or Saturn or Satan, are unbound when the god comes into incarnation, and, as Paul shows, they bring sin to birth. In astrology Saturn is the power that limits or constricts the native. Horus and Sut alternately bind each other and as often escape the bondage. The lower instincts are given rein to test the god and develop his fiber when he comes to fight them. They do not succumb without a battle. And here at last is the end of the mystification for orthodox Bible students of the disconcerting riddle, as to why God gave Satan free hand to tease and harry a godly man like

381

Job. Thousands in ancient Roman streets, gay throngs in Paris, Naples and New Orleans once a year commemorate the freedom of the elemental nature to play upon the spiritual, by the temporary relaxation of conventional bonds and the venting of sexual suggestiveness.

Horus wounded Apap so severely that he sank in the depths of the sea, and his defeat took place, according to Maspero, Birch and Chabas, at the very moment of the beginning of the new year. In the solar *mythos* this point of time betokened the end of the dark powers' reign and the beginning of the new dispensation. The constellation Corvus, the Crow, reveals the bird (the soul), perched on the body of the dead monster, pecking at its folds, sign of victory.

But while Apap lives, he subsists on "the slaughter of the glorious ones, the gods and the damned in the nether world." He feeds upon those gods who became enamored and infatuated with his clammy seductions, and thus supply him with food and fuel to keep alive his natural hunger. He feeds upon the livers of the princes. The degenerate gods become the damned, on whom the monster lives. The Manes, personating Horus, addresses Apap:

"I see the way toward thee. I gather myself together. I am the man who put a veil upon thy head without being injured. I am the great magician. Thine eyes have been given me and *through them I am glorified . . .* I am he who takes possession of thy strength. I go round the sky; thou art in the valley, as was ordered to thee before."

Here speaks the conqueror, the solar fire, reciting that he has grappled with the elementary serpent, subdued him without being injured in turn, and yet, be it noted, converted his opponent's elemental strength to his own high purposes. "I have repulsed Apap and healed the wounds he made."

As hinted, the far-famed but generally misconceived Battle of Armageddon, supposed ignorantly to refer to some catastrophic world conflict, is this spiritual warfare between the two opposing parties in the great drama of life. With reference to man's life, it is the warfare waged between the spiritual and the material energies on the stage of human consciousness. We are fighting the Battle of Armageddon now. The conscious life of every soul is the battle ground, and individual moral character is the issue. The terrain of this conflict is man's own psycho-physical organism. Misguided Christian interpretation has removed the meaning of every representation as far from the life of the individual as it was possible to take it. The Battle of Armageddon is the Battle of Incarnation. We are deciding its issue by every act of present living. A likely derivation of the word traces it from the Egyptian title of Horus as Lord of the Two Horizons, *Har-Makhu;* to which the Hebrews or Greeks added the Hebrew word for "Lord," *Adon;* making it *Har-Makhu-Adon,* or "Lord God of the Two Horizons." And the *Ritual* gives a significant detail in connection with the battle between Horus (*Har-Makhu*) and the hosts of Sut. It is fought *at midnight* (incarnation) and *on the horizon!* This assuredly clinches its purely symbolical character.

The Sebau or Sami were just "the imps of Satan"—really the word Seb pluralized. They are Paul's "elementals of the earth" and those "that by nature are no gods" (*Galatians:* 4). In the legend they were finally defeated *on the night* of the judgment, when the last adversaries were overthrown. Horus, Un-Nefer, is to triumph over Apap in the presence of Osiris, Lord of Amenta, and of the great sovereign chiefs who are in Annu, on the night of the battle with and overthrow of the Seba-fiend (Seba equals seven).

Horus, the new-born divine child, is immune to serious injury from the evil Apap. "Not men or gods, the glorious ones or the damned, not generations past, present or to come, can inflict an injury on him who cometh forth and proceedeth as the eternal child, the everlasting one" (*Rit.,* Ch. 42). He tells the serpent, here called Abur, that he is the divine babe, the mighty one. One of the representations shows Horus as a cat, cutting off the serpent's head with a knife. The god is a cat because he can see in the dark and his eyes shine in the dark—of incarnation.

Apophis, like Sut, was not originally evil. He was formerly the divine messenger, the earliest Mercury, the character afterwards assigned to the moon-god Taht. He was termed "The Good One, the Star of the Two Worlds."

One of the water forms of the Dragon was Leviathan. In the *Psalms* (74) the soul is addressed: "Thou breakest the heads of leviathan in pieces; thou gavest him to be meat to the people inhabiting the wilderness." This appears to be a reference to the Good Dragon, the gods descending to be food for "the people" in this "wilderness." The breaking in pieces seems a clear allusion to the dismemberment.

This treatment of the entire theme of the Titans, Prometheus, Lucifer, Satan, Sut, Apap, Seb, the Sebau, the two serpents, fiery and watery, the dragon and the crocodile, under all their mythical representations, has made a long and perhaps prolix recital. But it is justified if it will demonstrate the original good character of the Saturnian personage, clarify the reasons that led to his transmogrification into a "personal devil" to frighten humanity, and replace harrowing misconception in the Western mind with sane comprehension, with reference to this lamentable miscarriage of wisdom. The discussion has opened up the cryptic meaning of a score or more of pivotal constructions in the Bible. With keys derived from the *mythoi* we can once more read intelligible meaning into material that by perversion has thrown the human spirit under subjection to motivations the most fiendish and diabolical. Surely the world desperately needs the scholarly perspicacity that will cast this "devil" out of human thought.

Chapter XVI

BAPTISM AT THE CROSSING

THE water symbol yields a series of special scriptural and theological interpretations which will correct much insufferable misconception. It is questionable if today any hierophant of orthodox religion has the most distant idea of the esoteric meaning of the rite of baptism. People receive baptism or impose it on their children with a sanctimonious acquiescence, but with heads guiltless of comprehension. It is vaguely felt to betoken an outpouring of divine grace upon the recipient. This may be conceded to be a part of the meaning. Yet in the form in which it is conceived by the participants, it is not in the faintest degree an image of the hidden truth. It is hardly a quarter of the full import. In consonance with the force of the great Law of the Two Truths, or the doubleness of truth, it is not only the mortal who is baptized by the god; the profoundest understanding flows from the knowledge that it is the god himself who is undergoing a baptism. Indeed, as long as it is a baptism with water, it is not at all the baptism of the human by the god, unless again the water be taken as the higher well-spring of life. It is more truly the baptism of the god by the animal. For John, the pre-solar or natural man, says: "I indeed baptize you with water," while the baptism of the lower by the higher nature was with fire! Jesus, the god, was baptized by John, the mortal, in the waters of the river Jordan. Jesus was there baptized as part of the process of his further divinization. The water baptism was the god's submergence under the waters in the body of man.

What, then, is the basic meaning of the ceremonial? It is simple indeed. Reverting to the four elemental signs, we have the adequate data for interpretation. Bluntly, water is the symbol of bodily life, the body being mainly water in composition. Also water symbols man's second psychological principle, emotion, because it is intimately linked with the body and its humors. The sea, the swamp or Reed Sea, or the mire, is the typical picturization of life in the body. Water types soul in body, or the god in matter. Baptism with water, then, is just the experience of the god in this bodily life. It means what the incarnation means, and nothing more. The ceremonial of sprinkling or immersion is but the dramatic representation of the fact of this life itself. By the application of the Law of the Two Truths it *can* be made to typify the baptism of the lower nature by the celestial water. But this is the obverse of the meaning usually intended in symbolism, and would involve the baptism of water by or in water, which wrecks the typism. It is the god's immersion in the waters of generation that is the theme of most baptismal ritual.

That this statement embodies the correct view is competently attested by the zodiacal signatures used in the typology. The sun in the lower half of the zodiac is symbolically pictured as being immersed in a sea of water; and according to one derivation the word "Galilee" signifies "water-wheel." The Sea of Galilee is the lower material world—in man the watery body itself—through or across which the fiery spark of soul must pass in rounding its cycles of necessity. Heraclitus' statement that "man is a portion of cosmic fire, imprisoned in a body of earth and water" (Plato's "mire") is apt here. And earth and water stand for the physical and emotional aspects of man's life, or sense and feeling, both sub-mental. The soul in its rounds must dip down into a life that is irrational, motivated by elemental impulses that are not amenable to reason. It comes under the sway of the pure instinct of life itself and is overswept by the surging tides of elemental being. This is its baptism, its going into or under the water. It is not by chance that the name Galilee was given to the lake or sea of mortal life in the Jewish adaptation of the uranograph. For on it the savior of mankind had to quell or quiet the raging storm of sensual passion. The storm is a true mythograph of the sweep of the forces at play in the lower segment of man's constitution, for they blow through his life, for the long first cycle of his evolution, in nearly uncontrolled intensity. They rush in upon his spirit, which is as yet unawakened, asleep like Jonah and Jesus in the hold of the ship, and stir up a welter of animal instincts and rapacities in lower man. Proserpine, the soul, was held for half of each year in duress in the underworld of Pluto. Merely put under water symbolism, this is the soul's baptism. It is earthly embodiment.

A profound significance never fully fathomed attaches to Jesus' ringing statement to Nicodemus (*John* 3: 1 ff) :

"Except a man be born of water and the spirit he cannot enter the kingdom of God. That which is born of the flesh is flesh, and that which is born of the spirit is spirit. If I told you earthly things and ye believe them not, how shall ye believe if I tell you heavenly things? And no man hath ascended into heaven but he that hath descended out of heaven, the Son of Man which is in heaven."

The elemental man, child of Mother Nature and her seven powers, can never enter the kingdom of conscious immortality except he be reborn of the spirit. His chance to be so reborn arises only through the great sacrificial oblation of the sun-gods. For they came to share their nature with him, to tabernacle with his flesh, and to suffer that he might be quickened to a new expansion of capacity to know life. Jesus is stating the rudiment of all practical knowledge. Unless a man unite the two fiery elements, the mortal and the imperishable, he can have no access to the kingdom of divine mind. For flesh and blood can not inherit the legacy of spiritual consciousness.

Herein lies the necessity for the twice-born experience of every initiate. Hermes describes the form of the second birth:

"I see in myself an unfeigned sight or spectacle made by the mercy of God: And I am gone out of myself into an immortal body, and I am not now what I was before, but am *begotten in mind.*"

To this may be added Paul's inspiring statement that we can transform ourselves by the *renewing of our mind.* Hermes also says of the physical and spiritual natures:

"He that looketh upon that which is carried upward as fire, that which is carried downward as earth, that which is moist as water, and that which bloweth or is subject to blast as air; how can he sensibly understand that which is neither hard nor moist, nor tangible nor perspicuous, seeing it is only understood in power and operation? But I beseech and pray to the mind; which alone can understand the generation that is in God."

The phrase "born of water" embalms implications that are commonly passed over unnoticed. All birth in the natural world is by or in water. Paleontology discloses that the first protozoan life emanated from the salt water. The human foetus grows in a watery sack. It

387

emerges from water into air. All growing things must have water as a primary condition. The fact was therefore used by the sagacious myth-makers as an index of birth of any kind. Says Massey:

"Birth from the element of water was represented in the Mysteries of Amenta by rebirth of spirit from the water of baptism."[1]

It was out of the primordial "waters" of space that the first forms of cosmic life were generated. From the infinite bosom of watery night flashed out the first rays of that light which was to be the life of all things. So in the rain-storm of summer, fire is born out of the banks or moisture or suspended water. Hence the very deities had to be incubated in bodies of water like the foetus in the watery egg. This accounts for the presence of the god in the lake of the moist human body. Horus is born from the lotus plant in the water, as Venus from the sea-foam. So the souls that come forth to populate earth are born of the Lake of Sa, one of the two lakes of paradise, which contained the "waters of life." One of the meanings of this short word "Sa" is "spirit"; another is "soil or basis." It was a lake or body of primordial life essence, spiritual "matter," from which spirits were drawn, as snowballs from a bank of snow. The word is part of the name for the spiritual body, the Sahu.

The twice-born, then, were those born first of the water of nature and again of the fire of spirit. The upper lake yielded the nuclei of spirit force that were to find a higher birth of divinity from immersion in the water and mire of the earthly lake beneath. The Lake of Sa generated the fiery seeds that were to be brought to lotus growth in the muddy lake of the earth. "Heaven conceived him, the Tuat brought him forth." The one was the Pool of Sa(lt), the other the Pool of Natron (Nature). The upper was the pool of life, the lower the pool of death, which is ever the gateway to new life. The spirits from the Lake of Sa needed further cleansing. The sa(lt) may lose its savor. They came down to bathe in the lake of the world, where, linked to a creature already born of water and earth, they would have the chance to wash away ingrained impurities. The *Ritual* text (Ch. 170) calls to the glorified soul: "Hail, Osiris, thou art born twice!" Again: "Stand up living forever. Thy son Horus reconstituted thee. Arise on thy bed and come forth! Come! Come forth!" They call him to come forth "like a god" "from the mysterious cave." (Cf. the raising of Lazarus and the man who took up his bed and walked.)

This double birth, or birth and rebirth, is no more strange than is its physical counterpart and lower symbol in the life of any mortal. We are born out of nature at physical birth; we are reborn, as a being of dawning mind, again at twelve, when we leave Mother Nature for Father God.

Life advances by periodical and unending regenerations. To live again, the soul must indeed enter again and again into the body of its mother matter and experience repeated new births. This was another esoteric hint beneath Jesus' answer to Nicodemus.

We are conceived in spirit and born to actual power in nature. The natural man is reconstituted by a spiritual birth. We should be reminded here of the wine, born or made of water, but reborn as "spirit" through fermentation. The twice-born were the twice-baptized, first in water, then in fire. Says Irenaeus (Bk. 1, Ch. 21:2): "The two baptisms of the Gnostics were recognized by them as the animal and the spiritual." In olden times children were baptized first with water, later with smoke! One form of the cleansing was by fumigation. In certain places there were administered two baptisms, one a passage through water, the other an ordeal by fire. Already spoken of was the tribal ceremony of having girls after the puberty initiation run naked in the first thunderstorm to receive the blessing of the water and the fire. Every seed cast into the ground for incubation undergoes the baptism by water or moisture, followed by the fiery baptism of the sun's rays.

Horus in his baptism is transformed from the word made flesh to the word made truth. This again delineates the change from natural to spiritual.

Temples and pyramids were generally built over or near a water course, lake or well. In the *Vision of Hermas* it is asked: "Lady, why is the tower built upon the water?" She replies that it is because the soul's life is saved and shall be saved by water. The necessity that forced the gods into this low life was that of purification. In (the Alexandrian version of) *John* (5:2, 4) we read: "An angel of the Lord washed at a certain season."

The Manes in the *Book of the Dead* says: "I purify me in the southern tank, and I rest me at the northern lake" (Ch. 125). After dipping into the ordeal of bodily existence he had to rest in the peaceful fields of the northern Aarru-Hetep. The first chapter of the *Ritual* contains the saying by the priest: "I lustrate with water in Tattu and anoint with oil in Abydos." The sheen of oil replaced the fire typism here.

The ceremonial purity so often insisted on in the texts of the *Ritual* is acquired by the Manes after he

"purifies himself in the Lake of the Country of Reeds. Horus dries his body, Thoth dries his feet, Shu raises him up, and the Heaven-goddess Nut gives him her hand. He appears in the Field of Reeds and purifies himself therein." [The diseased in the Gospels were promised healing if they bathed in the Pool of Siloam.]

On the second day's celebration of the Mystery rites in Greece, the one commemorating the descent of the gods into matter, the cry *"Alade, mustai"* ("to the sea, ye initiated ones!") was the keynote of the ceremony.

"Besides, the sea was an emblem of purity, as is evident from the *Orphic Hymn to the Ocean* in which that deity is called *theon agnisma megiston*, i.e., the greatest purifier of the gods; and Saturn . . . is pure (intuitive) intellect . . . Pythagoras called the sea a tear of Saturn (Meursius)."

Plutarch affirms that the child Jesus fell into the sea and was drowned. Likewise Horus.

In many religions the baptism was apparently a rite held for the dead and again for the living. This confusion was due to the loss of the original connotation of "death" as the life *lived* on earth. Of a surety it was for "the dead"—on earth, who were alive enough to get the instruction. Therefore Paul asserts that we are circumcized "with a circumcision not made with hands, in the putting off the body of flesh in the circumcision of Christ; having been *buried with him in his baptism* . . ." (*Col.* 2:12). This is weighty, for here Paul distinctly figures the burial and the baptism as one and the same. This firmly supports the primary claim of this study, that the incarnation is the one central theme of all scripture. Burial of the soul in the water of the body on earth is all that could ever have been meant by the baptism.

An aspect of the baptism formula was the rite of feet-washing.

Jesus washed the disciples' feet. This act surely was a dramatization of his laying aside his superior dignity, humbling himself to become a servant and pouring out the water of deific potency for the cleansing baptism of the lower nature of man. For he himself poured out the water in a basin. The Speaker says that he comes that he may purify this soul of his in the most high degree. The Teacher in the *Pistis Sophia* says that he *tore himself asunder* to bring unto mankind the "Mysteries of light to purify them . . . otherwise no soul in the whole of mankind would have been saved" (Bk. 2:249, Mead). Here is one of the most explicit references to divine dismemberment anywhere to be found.

In the text of Unas it is said of the Manes: "Horus takes him with his two fingers and purifies him in the Lake of the Jackal." Again: "The followers of Horus purify him. They cleanse him." It is asserted of the purged soul: "He hath been purified in the Lakes of the Tuat, he hath undressed in the Lakes of the Jackals." The unregenerated Manes was always pictured as black or black-haired. But when he kneels before the throne of Osiris his hair has become white. This is the mark of his having been washed pure in the waters. The four sons of Horus are said to wash his face. The *Book of the Dead* says the soul is "censed" or purified with fire, with the Smen incense and the "bet" incense, which are the

"saliva that comes from the mouth of Set, wherewith Horus was purified, whereby the evil which appertained unto him was cast to the earth when Set performed the censing for him; wherewith Set was purified, whereby the evil which appertained to him was cast to the earth, when Horus performed the censing for him. This Pepi is purified thereby, and the evil which appertains to him is cast to the earth."

The symbolism of spittle as a cleansing substance has before been pointed out. But this passage yields most direct corroboration of the idea that has been presented several times—the reversibility or double direction of the application of the meaning of scriptural glyphs. For here Horus and Set mutually purify each other! Soil and plant mutually exalt each other. God and the human reciprocate purification. The god bathes in the southern tank, the animal in the northern lake. Each baptizes the other. The Gospel story is incomplete without an alternate baptism of John by Jesus.

The Great Harlot, or mother of prolific life, whose fornicatory ways the kings of the earth (the descending gods) had followed into a mire of iniquity, when they yielded to her blandishments, was likewise consumed in the purifying fires.

Those who had exchanged their dark robes for the garments of white linen had, it is declared, "washed their raiment in the blood of the Lamb of God until it was white without blemish."

In the *Ritual* the mummied deceased is said to go "purified in the place of birth." This is of importance because the purification is categorically stated to be on earth, the place of birth. "He has been steeped in resin in the place of preservation." Divinity, the immortal preservative, is won on earth. Else why did we leave the empyrean?

A passage later to be noted says that the body-soul which rises from Amenta has to suffer "purgatorial rebirth" before it can become pure spirit.

Apollo, who collected and restored the dismembered Dionysus, is called a deity of purification. Greek philosophy was itself the offspring of Mystery systems designed to effect the purification of the soul from the contaminations of life in the flesh.

A striking picture of the alternate besmirching by earth and purification by water is given in a Zulu tale of transformation. A beautiful girl enters the earth, and it is said of her that her body glistened, for she was like brass in her pristine purity; but she took black earth and smeared her body with it. She was then seen, very dirty and soiled, to enter a pool, from which she emerged with all her radiance restored and body shining.

Among the Yorubas a remarkable ceremony of purification is performed over both mother and child seven days after the latter's birth. The water which is always in the earthen vessels placed before the images of the gods, is brought to the house and thrown upon the thatched roof, and as it drips from the eaves the mother and child pass three times through the falling drops. The performance of the ceremony on the seventh day is meaningful, as final purification in any cycle comes with the crowning seventh round.

The rite of circumcision was generally performed on the eighth day following birth. It types the cutting off of the god from the cycle of generation in the flesh, and was outwardly symbolized by the cutting off of the foreskin of the organ of generation itself. The seventh power

392

released man from bondage to the flesh, and its celebration followed on the next day.

The Manes with satisfaction exclaims:

"I have made an end of my shortcomings and I shall put away my faults. What then is this? It is the cutting off of the corruptible in the body of Osiris, the scribe Ani, the victorious one before all the gods; and all his faults are driven out. What then is this? It is the purification (of Osiris) on the day of his birth. I am purified in the great *double* nest which is in Suten-Khen(en)."

Another text affirms:

"He is conceived in Isis and begotten in Nephthys, and they cut off from him the things which should be cut off."

An important corroboration of the purely figurative value placed on the rite of circumcision (matching the similar elucidation of mummification) is found in a passage from Budge:

"The general trend of the evidence suggests that circumcision was practiced in the Sudan, as well as in Egypt, from time immemorial, that it had nothing to do with considerations of health, that it *had a religious significance,* and that it was originally connected with some kind of phallic worship." [2]

The rite indicates man's cutting himself free from the law of bodily generation, and his readiness to generate by spiritual will. He stands clear of the law which bound him to sexual carnality. A passage from Paul stoutly vindicates this interpretation:

"Circumcised with the circumcision not made with hands, in putting off the body of the sins of the flesh by the circumcision of Christ." (Moffatt trans.: "In him ye have been circumcised with no material circumcision that cuts flesh from the body . . .")

A most curiously involved application of the circumcision typism is seen in *Exodus* (4), wherein, after the Eternal had *tried to kill Moses on his way back to Egypt,* his wife Zipporah took a *flint* knife, cut off the foreskin of her son Gershom (Stranger) and touched his (apparently, Moses') feet with it, crying, "There, you are my bridegroom in blood . . . by this circumcision." Then the Eternal left him alone!

By the curious operation of the Law of the Two Truths, both circumcision and its emblematic organ, the foreskin, may be taken as typing two distinct phases of meaning. The cutting off can have a double signification. The gods in descending suffered a severing of their connection with deity above; and the mutilation of the phallus, organ of their attachment to sexual generation, would directly type this "discerption" from deity in order to be linked with animality. The foreskin was the symbol of the god's bond with, and bondage to, matter. Yet on the other wing of the symbolism, the phallus was a type of male virility, spiritual creative renewing power, generative productiveness, and as such it seems to figure in the Moses incident. Salvation from the menace to the young incarnating soul came through the wife, the material life, by means of the application of the *son's* foreskin to the father's feet. Here again, as in Egypt, it is the power of the son that reconstitutes the father. In a word, the meaning of it all is that earth experience brings the power of the reborn god to bear upon the salvation of the original god seed, buried and disintegrated in matter. The earth (mother) joins the creative power of the god to the animal nature (feet) of man. Horus performs almost identically the same operation on his father Osiris in the latter's reconstitution and renovation.

Foreskins were piled in a heap in the circle of the twelve stones set up at the Eternal's order by the Israelites at Gilgal. The meaning can be taken in any of the three ways suggested: (1), The twelve legions of angels were sacrificing their foreskins as types of their lost divine power; (2), They were coming into generation, typed again by the foreskin; (3), They were, in the exodus, cutting themselves loose from generation, typed by the removal of the foreskins. Herein is demonstrated the advantage of myth over dogma; the former leaves the mind free to make its own application of the truth adumbrated.

The umbilical cord served as a companion symbol with circumcision. Its cutting betoken the severance of the god from his connection with elementary mother nature. It was thus a figure of rebirth, adapted from its part in the function of birth. Weaning was used in much the same fashion.

We, as gods, are sent down to earth to undergo a further bathing in the waters of experience. This experience is nature's available instrumentality for refining untested spiritual quality. Incrustations which are the deposit of earlier ignorance and error have to be dissolved, burnt out, washed away, by the pedagogical agencies of physical contingencies. There is no power in heaven, where the soul is detached from body, to cleanse or purify it. Only earth can provide the requisite conditions of suffering and hardship to burn out the crudities of undevelopment. Nature must have our hard predicaments of bodily life in order to reach and impress our souls, which, apart from body, float in dreamy irresponsibility and unrealized potentiality. Nature casts us here in order to furnish the conditions of realism which alone can wake our slumbering faculty. We can not in the spirit world be linked with an animal by whose tutoring on earth we advance our own progression.

The children of Israel were "tried as silver is tried," "in the refineries of the nether world"; and they were on earth, not in the hazy spirit realm.

Mesheck, or *Meska*, was the Egyptian place of scourging and purifying in Suten-Khen. It is the Kamite purgatory, the place of cleansing, then of rebirth and resurrection, Amenta in fact. This is doubtless identical with the *Meskhen*, the Thigh or Haunch, a term applied to the Great Bear cluster, as the old first mother, Apt or Typhon, from whose thigh emerged all birthing. The purging took place in the lower part of man, the oft-mentioned Suten-Khen, the dwelling place of the Sut powers; *khen* meaning birthplace.

Examining the baptism of Jesus, we find it in itself a complete representation of the incarnational experience. Contrary to most interpretative opinion, it must be said that the pivotal experiences and allegories of the Christ do not mark successive stages in spiritual development according to a fixed pattern, but are sententious glyphs of the entire cycle. It appears to be so with the baptism. Jesus' baptism by John, the antecedent earthly man, in the Jordan River adumbrates the incarnation unquestionably. Next we have John's hitherto utterly misconstrued reluctance to baptize one of a higher order than himself. It was as if the animal man said to the god within him: "My Lord, it is not fitting that *I* should subject *you* to the incarnational ordeal. It is more seemly that *you* should baptize *me* with your divine fire and lift *me* up. This is the wrong order of procedure." And as if the Lord rejoined: "No; to you it may seem so. But a necessity of which you can know little forces me to undergo the incarnation and baptism through your good offices. I must, if only for a cycle, be subject unto you and be further educated to divinity in your watery realm. And thus only can *your* salvation, too, be won." "But Jesus answered him: 'Come now, this is how we should fulfil all our duty to God'" (*Matt.* 3:15). Then the immersion took place. And it was at the conclusion of the rite that the spirit from heaven descended upon him in the symbol of the dove. This bird, sharing the role with the hawk and bennu or phoenix, emblemed primarily the life-giving power of the third element, air (mind). Dove is traced to *"Tef,"* the breathing force. It stands in general for the divine energy of the soul. In the planisphere another star beside Sothis, somewhat farther south, stood in position to announce the coming of the solar year and the sun-god. This was the star Phact, the Dove. The hawk, allied to the dove, was the divine symbol of Horus. When divinized Horus received the hawk, Jesus the dove. Horus rose as the dove as well as the hawk; for he exclaims: "I am the Dove; I am the Dove!" Seven doves, showing the seven-fold nature of all deific emanation, are frequently found. In Didron's *Iconography* (Fig. 124) the child Jesus is represented in the virgin's arms or womb, surrounded by seven doves as symbols of the seven nature powers he was to spiritualize.

The baptism preceded and is followed by the deification. Earthly sojourn was to place man finally on Mt. Olympus.

In this exposition is to be found the reason for the forerunners of the Christs, as John, Anup and Mercury, performing the function of the baptism. The earth-soul is to subject the heaven-soul to its immersion in matter, and must precede and prepare the ground. John says: "After me cometh a man who is come before me." "I make way," says Horus, "by what Anup has done for me." What is obviously implied in John's statement is that the Christ principle, a superior and therefore older evolutionary product than the man of earth, will come to occupy the physical house when nature has made it ready. Earth has but recently fitted a tabernacle to be occupied by a guest who is of venerable age and station in the cosmic family. The house is new, never constructed before; but the coming visitant from celestial spheres is of the family of the Ancient of Days and has been abroad many times before and lived in other houses. John means to say that he is the physical self, a new and late creation, but that the *Christos* had preceded him in manifestation by aeons. Anubis (Anup) is designated as the "preparer of the way of the other world," the power making straight the paths to the upper heaven. Anup was the guide of the sun and the sun-souls in the nether earth. The *Ritual* (Ch. 25) speaks of "the god Anubis, who dwelleth in the city of embalmment," and who gives a heart to the deceased. Sut-Anup, the stellar guide and announcer of the new cosmic cycle, was superseded by Taht-Aan, the lunar Mercury, whose more frequent periodicities made him a more reliable measurer of time cycles.

Anup and Mercury are closely allied. Mercury's character as the swift-winged messenger of the gods is matched by Anup's reputation as the "swift-runner." The planet Mercury was said to be the servant of Sothis, the star announcing the solar birth at the winter solstice. Plutarch suggested that the horizon immediately before the rising and after the setting of the sun was symbolized by Anup (*De Isid. et Osir.*). Says Renouf: "I believe that he represented twilight or dusk immediately following the disappearance of the sun." He was typified by the jackal that came out at night, and was painted with a black head, as the guide through the dark. The planet Mercury, as sometimes evening and again morning star, fulfills the terms of this identity with the functions of Anubis. As a warder of the gate of sunset and dawn, of descent and resurrection, it is written of him: "All the festivals of earth terminate on the hill (or over the hill) of Anup." It is Anup who in the judgment tests the beam of the scales, and if he finds the balance even between the heart and the feather, reports the verdict to Thoth. This he does as watcher on the two horizons or the scales of nature, where spirit and matter are exactly balanced in our constitution. Aan, the scribe, records it.

It is notable that Jesus is not baptized by John until he is thirty years of age. Horus was baptized at thirty by Anup. There are occurrences of thirty in connection with Samson. There is a lacuna in the life history of the sun-gods between the ages of twelve and thirty. Both numbers are purely typical, standing for the completion and perfection of cycles, the end of an age, or stages of transition and transformation.

The study shifts to another aspect of the water symbolism, but one intimately related to the baptism, if it is not but another typing of the same thing. It is one of the most frequent of religious figurations, and demands sufficient attention to settle clearly its function and scope. This is "the crossing of the waters." Best known are the Biblical crossing of the Red (Reed) Sea and the Jordan, the classical ferrying of the souls of the departed over the underworld Styx by Charon in the Greek *mythos,* the crossing of the sea by Ulysses and Aeneas in the *Odyssey* and the *Aeneid,* the crossing of the Euxine Sea by Jason, and others. Baptism by immersion was a simple glyph of the incarnation, but a crossing of some water permitted a more extended play of fancy to elaborate the symbolism. Such a natural phenomenon as the salmon fighting its way from the vast primal ocean up the waters of an individual stream to the sources, there to deposit the spawn of new generation, was indeed a vivid emblem of the soul fighting its way back to source against the downward current of elementary pressure. The soul, like the salmon, comes out of the great original ocean of life, the lake of Sa(lt), works its way into the channel of an individuality, battles its way far up the stream in the face of the current of animal propensity, and there plants the germ or seed of new life, which in the next generation will run down and join the mother sea. It is a nearly complete analogue of man's incarnation history.

The crossing of a stream was a serviceable allegory of the passage of the life spark through and across its span of experience in the watery body. As the crossing involved the use of a boat or ark, the chain of ideas carries the research into the whole mass of material dealing with the crossing, the Passover, the cross, the ark and the flood or deluge. An enormous amount of relevant material must be drastically abridged.

The mummy was ferried over the water to the western mount where Hathor-Isis or the Cow-Goddess awaited the solar god and the crowd of Manes with him. This was in preparation for his burial—fittingly on the west side where the sun sank—and the body was placed in a mausoleum there.

But the journey of the Manes across the sea of this life, over the "waters beneath," was from west to east, from the gate of entry to the underworld on the west to the gate of resurrection on the east. That which dies in the west must rise again in the east. The level stretch of "water" between, over which the voyage is made, is the "sea of life." Across this expanse of stormy water the soul essays to sail in the "boat of Horus," with the young god himself in the pilot house directing the course, and with his twelve (collective) sailors, rowers or companions, who man the craft. Alongside swims the great Apap reptile, eager to devour careless sailors who fall overboard. His figure stretches out closely parallel with the horizon line of the zodiac. The Manes prays to the Conductor of Heaven that Osiris may safely pass the "great one who dwells in the place of the inundation." And the deceased rejoices in that "He had made me a boat to go by." A boat is now the symbol of safety.

In the chapter "of breathing air and of prevailing over the waters in Hades," the Manes have to escape from the devastating flood by means of the Makhu, or ark of plaited corn, with paddles formed of straw. Here is background for the ark of bulrushes that bore Moses.

A phrase several times used symbolically is: "going into the cabin." This might be taken as the equivalent of the soul's going into the "belly" or hold of the ship. Yet as the cabin is the locale of the directing intelligence of a ship, it might again refer to the inmost seat of divine spirit in man's "ship," the holy of holies in the deep center of being, into which he enters as the "captain of his destiny." Release from it in the end seems to bespeak salvation. On the day of the birth of Osiris the utterance is:

"The valves of the door open, the gateway of the god opens. He has unclosed the doors of the ark. He has opened the doors of the cabin. Shu has given him breath, Tefnut has created him; they serve in his service." (Ch. 130)

The Greek imprisonment of soul in body is here seemingly the poet's "cribbed, *cabined,* and confined" life in flesh. Escape comes with final victory over the elements.

The picture of the sun-god swallowed by a great fish is very common. In the "crocodile" chapter of the *Ritual* we read: "I am the crocodile whose soul comes from men . . . I am the Great Fish of Horus." The crocodile was perhaps the earliest form of the Fish-Mother Atergatis, Hathor or Venus, who first produced life from the water. The seizure of the souls of men by a great fish in the sea suggests both capture and safety, as both are implied in incarnation. The astrotype is the constellation of Cetus, the Whale.

The baptism, the crossing a water, the death by drowning, and the transformation from a being water-born to one born of fire, are all closely interwoven in various depictions. Confusion has come to scholars from this admixture. Massey is puzzled a trifle to observe that "in

399

the inscription of Shabaka the baptism occurs without death." He adds:

"Either way, the baptism or death was but figurative of the regeneration or rebirth which was affected in this region; from which the second Horus issued at the age of thirty years as the Adult God, the Sheru or *Homme Fait*. The baptism for the dead was continued by the Christians, although its origin and significance seem to have been unknown to them."

As we have seen, Massey lacked in his exegesis the one key that would have enabled him to unlock the mystery of how baptism can be for the dead, and yet not be attended with ceremony suggestive of the sort of death he is thinking of. It was itself the "death" or experience of incubation of the soul, to achieve a new generation from the seed of its parent. In the cycle of necessity, in which the soul makes the round of all the elements, it must go through those kingdoms in which water is predominantly subsistent.

In the Hottentot fable the sea opened to let the men cross in safety, and the floods closed on the pursuing enemies. The ax, as in the Roman *fasces,* was a symbol of the sun, because in making its transit through the earth and water of fleshly life it was known as the divider or cleaver of the way. It cleft a passage for itself through the lower elements, dried up the water by its fiery potency and crossed on dry land!

Egyptian ingenuity, using the typology suggested by the life habits of certain water animals, represented the god as making his way across the water in more ways than one. He crossed on its surface, through it and even under it. Sebek-Horus, the crocodile-headed god, the child assigned to Neith in Virgo, swam across as a crocodile; the god, as Atum, the Eel, crawled through the mud; Kepher-Ptah, the beetle god, bored through the earth; Horus Behutet rode across on the vulture's back; Horus, deified, flew across as a hawk; and Har-Makhu crossed through the corridor of the Sphinx.

In *Joshua* (1:2), after the death of Moses, the Eternal bade Joshua "arise, go over this Jordan, thou and all this people, unto the land which I do give thee, even to the children of Israel." "All Israel passed over on dry ground."

The eastern shore was the terminus of the voyage. There a plate of *tahn* was given each disembarking sailor, as a type of protection and salvation. This matched the recovered "eye of Horus" and the white stone given to the redeemed in *Revelation*. It may be seen at the place of the vernal equinox, between Aries and Pisces in the zodiac of Denderah. *Tahn* was resin and symboled eternal preservation, and was given to the soul at the completion of its crossing, as a badge of new-won immortality.

The Manes-soul entered or embarked on the sea on the western marge, plunged into the underworld of darkness and emerged on the eastern horizon of light. So he was the evening and the morning star through sheer symbolism. The Gospels keep a slight but unmistakable suggestion of the Egyptian typism in Jesus' entry into the boat to cross the lake "when even was come." "He entered into the boat and his disciples followed him. And behold there arose a great tempest in the sea, insomuch that the boat was covered with waves, but *he was asleep*." "Then he arose and rebuked the winds and the sea and there was a great calm" (*Matt.* 8:24). Of Apap it is said: "Now at the close of day he turneth down his eyes to Ra; for there cometh a standing still in the bark, and a great slumber within the ship." The attack of Apap or Sut and the storm of sensual riot of the carnal passions are made while the deity is asleep in his bodily tomb, the belly of the flesh. Then the god awakes to his task, exercises his sovereignty over nature, and the elemental forces obey him.

Other solar heroes beside Jonah crossed the sea in the belly of a fish. Both Horus and the Greek Hercules crossed inside the fish during the three days at the winter solstice. In some ancient calendars three to five days were intercalated at the winter solstice, additional to the 360 days of the twelve solar months—30 days each—and corresponded to the three dark days of the lunar "solstice," or dark of the moon. They typed the time of the incubation, when there was a calm or balance or *stasis* in the cycle, the solstitial stasis or balance between spirit and matter in evolution.

After these many centuries of zealous study of the Bible in Christian lands it is questionable whether one person in a thousand knows why the number three is basically connected with the baptism. The answer is presumed commonly to lie in the ministrant's phrase accompanying the threefold sprinkling of water on the head or the three immersions under the water: "In the name of the Father, Son and Holy Ghost." The ceremony commemorates man's baptism by and under the three forces of the solar triad, mind-soul-spirit, according to this view. This may be taken as a correct interpretation, if the rite is performed by sprinkling, and if it is regarded as the baptism of John by Jesus. But Christian baptism is alleged to be modeled after the Biblical baptism, which is that of Jesus by John! And if the ceremony is that of the three immersions under the water, as performed by many sects, it can not then signify the downpour of the threefold spiritual nature from above on the recipient. Or it could do so only by reading the submergence of the god under the waters of sense as somehow imparting his threefold divinity to lower man. This is most indirect. One would have to say that the god brings his three aspects of higher selfhood under the water. This is implied, of course; and here as elsewhere the intimations of allegorism and symbolism apply both ways and work from either end. Both man and his god subject each other to a mutual baptism, we have seen, the god pouring his flood of transforming fire upon lower man and lower man drenching the god with water of sense and sin.

But the three immersions in or under the water speak definitely of a cosmic meaning that is little known, but that is one of the cardinal features of the arcane systematism. It is a numeral cosmograph of the death, burial or incubation of life in matter before its germination and resurrection. It is the ideograph of soul-death. Jesus was three days in the tomb. Under water emblemism it was the three-days' sojourn of Jonah in the belly of the fish, though even there it is called "the belly of death." It is primarily expressed in the *New Testament* verse: "As Jonas was three days in the whale's belly, so must the Son of Man be three days in the bowels of the earth." In its broad cosmic reference it outlines the great truth that the soul of life must evolve upward through three earthy kingdoms of nature, the mineral, vegetable and animal, in its pre-mental period of gestation. The fiery spark of consciousness must lie dormant in "death," its conscious functions unawakened, for the three aeons of its involvement in dense matter before it comes to self-awareness in the fourth kingdom. In the lunar cycle of twenty-eight days, the three days of the dark moon, when the sun lights no part of the orb's surface (visible to us) are the emblem.

But Egypt adds a most pertinent and apt phrase to this group of designations in a passage already given in another connection, from an inscription called "The Destruction of Mankind." Atum-Ra decreed that he would punish the rebellious angels who broke in upon his song with raucous shouts by destroying them "in three days of navigation." This carried the meaning that he would commit them to incarnation in lower ranges of being characterized as the sea or realm of "water." They would have to sail across the water of mortal life or become mariners or navigators in the great ocean of what Massey calls "the lower Nun." And that this period of "sailing" was to be three days attests to its identity of meaning with the other glyphs and graphs.

In addition to the cited instances, the three days as glyphs of incubating life are quite numerous all through the Bible and in other scriptures. There are scores of them in varied form. Before the Exodus from Egypt "darkness was over all the land of Egypt for three days; no one could see another, and no one could move about for three days, although the Israelites enjoyed light in their dwellings." In *Exodus* (3) Moses declaims to the people: "Pray let us travel for three days into the desert, then, that we may sacrifice to the Eternal our God." A *Chaldean Oracle* matches this passage remarkably: "And yet three days shall ye sacrifice and no longer." *Revelation* (11:11) says that after the oblation for sin had been made for three days and a portion of a day, the two witnesses of God rose upon their feet to renew their testimony. (The "portion of a day" will receive its very important treatment in its proper place.) The detail given here as to the witnesses rising to their feet to renew their testimony intimates that the old Egyptian dramatism of throwing down the Tat cross with its face to the ground as a sign of the soul's fall into matter and death, to be raised up in the opposite season, was employed in this verse.

The three months from the autumn equinox to the winter solstice, ending with the new birth at Christmas or New Year, were one facet of the same symbolism. Again, the three months from the dead of winter to the spring equinox, ending in the resurrection of the solar god, were kindred types. And in a purely symbolical zodiac the three autumn months were earth signs, and the three winter months were water signs, those of spring being air signs, and those of summer fire.

Amsu, the rejuvenated Horus, rose in a new body of light on the third day. Horus, the child, is crowned in the seat of Osiris at the end of three days. In the lunar typing, Osiris dies at the winter solstice to be reborn again as Horus on the third day in the moon. He then rose from the water in his baptism. The resurrection on the third day must have been vividly motivated by lunar phenomena.

As the Eye (of Horus) was a symbol of light reflected (as the eye reflects all images in it), the moon reflecting solar glory could be called the "Eye of Horus." It is a matter of note that the *Ritual* says: "His eye is at peace . . . at the hour of night; (it is) full *at the fourth hour of the earth* . . ." So odd a phrase as the one italicized could hardly be given relevant meaning except in the sense of the fourth kingdom of life, the human, on the earth. It is to be noted here that since the two phrases, "the hour of night," and "the fourth hour of the earth," are obviously matched in this passage, this must be the Egyptian origin of the Gospel's "fourth watch of the night."

Many of the myths contain a hiding or seeking of refuge for three days or three months. In *Joshua* Rahab the harlot, who sheltered the two Israelite spies, hurried them off with instructions to get away to the hills and "hide themselves there for three days till the pursuers return." A clear intimation of the resurrection on the third day is seen in an Egyptian text which runs: "I will arrange for you to go to the river when you die, and to come to life again on the third day." Here again water types the incarnation and it is also figured as a death. In speaking of the rearising of the dead Pepi, the *Ritual* says: "Pepi is brought forth there in the place where the gods are born. The star cometh on the morrow and on the third day." Mary searches for Jesus for three days as Isis sought the hidden Horus. In *Matthew* (15: 29-32) Jesus takes compassion on the multitude that followed him into the desert "because they continue with me three days and have nothing to eat, and I would not send them away fasting." The three days' fast is emblematic of the three "days" in the bleak underworld without the sustenance of the solar light, the divine bread of life. In the story of the dismembered concubine in *Judges* (19), previously noted, the girl's father detained the husband three days. With the reference to Herod, Jesus enjoined his followers to "Go tell that fox, Behold I cast out devils and I do cures today and tomorrow, and the third day I shall be perfected." Then there is his memorable declaration: "Destroy this temple and in three days I will raise it up. But he spake of the temple of his body," (*John* 2:9)—and obviously of his spiritual body. The thunder and lightning that emanated from the summit of Mount Sinai at the Eternal's appearing to Moses came "on the third day in

404

the morning." The manifestation of the Lord's glory on the mountain was anticipated by Moses, who had been instructed to go to the people and tell them to "consecrate themselves to-day and to-morrow; let them wash their clothes and be ready for the third day, for on the third day the Eternal will descend upon the Mountain of Sinai in the sight of all the people." Joshua told the people to prepare food, for within three days they would cross the Jordan and enter the Promised Land. And they remained three days on the banks before crossing the river. A study of these and the many other occurrences of the three days' period will disclose to any mind the general idea of life being held in bondage or limitation for three cycles or aeons and its release to liberty or to function on the third (properly fourth).

The significance, then, of the Passover festival becomes clear in relation to the only cosmic or anthropological datum to which it could have any reference. In its widest sense it memorialized simply the passing of the soul over the flowing stream of this life. It was the pilgrimage of the Manes across the sea of experience that lay between mortal and immortal life. It must never be lost sight of that the Jordan was a stream that marked the boundary line between the desert and the Promised Land. To migrate from animal existence to godlike stature of being we must cross the boundary line separating the two kingdoms. The soul plunges in this water on the western marge, swims or sails across and reaches the "farther shore" on the eastern boundary where he rises to a new day like the sun. As the final stage and termination of the passing over came at the equinox of spring, this date, the first full moon after the equinox, was invested with the cumulative and culminating significance of the whole pass-over. It was the fourteenth or the fifteenth of the Hebrew month Nisan. But after all it is a question of minor difference whether the term "Passover" is taken to embrace the whole extent and duration and experience of the passing across life's sea, or more specifically the crossing of the final boundary line at the Easter equinox; whether the passage is over the lines at beginning and end of the journey, or over the entire space between them. It may mean the passing into, the passing out of, or the passage across, the realm of bodily life, and has apt significance in any case.

The sun, typing ever the immortal fire in man, dipped down into the sea at evening and underwent his baptism during the night. He crossed the water of the Nun each night and emerged each morning. Also it is to be observed that the boat of Horus makes its journey across the sea on the border of the earth *at night*. Night in the diurnal cycle matches winter in the annual cycle in solar typism. And both figure the incarnation. Our voyage across the water of mortal existence is made when our souls are struggling through the darkness of material night. At any rate this is the symbolical language in which the ancient sages try to delineate our experience. This is "the dark night of the soul," and "the twilight of the gods." The "dead" are described as those who have voyaged in the boat at night, bound for the city of Akhemu at the polar Paradise.

A flood of light is released by the statement of the *Ritual* that the ship of Nnu, described in the "chapter by which one saileth a ship in the nether world," was ordered built with three decks or stories. It was to bear the crowd of Manes in safety across the abyss in which the devourer Apap lurked. The Manes supplicates the god:

"O thou who sailest the ship of Nnu over the void, let me sail the ship. Let me be brought in as a distressed mariner and go to the place which thou knowest."

And again he exclaims:

"O thou who sailest the ship of heaven over the gulf which is void, let me come to see my father Osiris" (Ch. 44; 99).

He is told he has to know each part of the bark by name and to repeat each name before he is admitted on board. From the examination in the judgment hall we learn the nature of the boat and its three stories. The lowest story is Akar (Hagar), which is identical with the Hebrew Achor, and that is the same as the Valley of Sheol (Amenta). Akar means also the hold of a ship, deep within which the god fell asleep while the storm raged without. The god was first intoxicated with lethargy and drowsiness. The ark was built first with one story, then two, then three. The lower was earth. The next was lunar, that is, the emotion body; and the third was the lower mind body; and the spirit lives in each or all of the three according to its focus.

In the "chapter of *bringing home a boat in the underworld*," the several parts of the ship are specified and their correspondences given. The posts at stem and stern are "the two columns of the nether world," or the points of entry and egress, west and east. The ribs are the four sustaining gods, or the four bodies typed by earth, water, air and fire. The boat is said to be brought in over the evil lake of Apepi, and the Manes prays that he may bring the boat along and coil up its ropes "in peace, in peace." Bringing in the boat must be taken to figure the soul's final uplifting of the animal self to the human kingdom, or "landing it." The wood of the right and left sides constitutes the Lord of the Two Lands, master of soul and body. The rudder is the leg of Hapi, one of the four supporters of the world and of man. The towing rope is the hair of Anup. Spiritual guidance is indicated here, as Anup is the keen-scented guide of souls in the dark of incarnation. He also helps to tow the boat, as one of the two "Openers of the Way." The oar-rests are the pillars of the underworld. Earth and water furnish the basic leverage against which one can exert force to push ahead. The mast is described as "he who bringeth back the great lady after she hath gone away." The lower deck is the station of Apuat, protector of the Manes, who sees that they do not fall overboard into the jaws of Apap. The sail is Nut, the original driving power of nature. It is that which engenders moving power by opposing matter to the invisible force of spirit, the wind or breath. The paddles are the fingers of Horus, taking hold and exerting power from within. The planks are the seven constituent elements furnishing the groundbase for all operation. The hull is Mert (Meri?), the womb and sustainer. The keel is the thigh or leg of Isis that Ra cut off with a knife to bring blood into the Sektet boat. The sailor is the traveler, the Manes. The wind "cometh from Tem, to the nostrils of Khenti-Amenti" (Osiris), and is the impelling spiritual power that gives life to the Manes. The river is "that which can be seen," the visible material world, on the bosom of which all flows along. The mooring post is the celestial pole to which the voyaging ship is made fast with the cable of divinity.

The Speaker says: "I stand erect in the bark which the god is piloting." He is the god himself, learning to pilot the boat. "I am the great god in the bark who fought for thee." Ra says to the sailors: "Take your oars, unite yourselves to your stars." And again he assures them: "O my pilots, you shall not perish, gods of the never-setting stars."

A most enlightening name of the boat of Horus on the nether sea is "Collector of Souls for Ra." This name at once takes on meaning against the background of the dismemberment doctrine, and would be otherwise unintelligible. As the overlord fragments himself to nucleate the multitude of souls in the world, the return journey across the sea of this life will operate to reunify the individualized units in the Lord's reconstituted body. The ship of this world will bring the scattered members of that original unitary body together in a new bond of fellowship. As it sails along it will collect again the fragments scattered broadcast in the descent to earth. Whatever unity of spirit and action mankind will achieve will to that extent make life the collectors of souls for Ra. The Horus spirit in man will reunify the dismembered Osiris.

The offices of scholarship have served no better purpose than to have us look through the glass of ancient mythical construction into a world of alleged fantastic conception of primitive naïveté. Our essay is to direct the modern eye through the same glass to see, not a bizarre world of childish fancy and credulity, but a factual world of meaning enhanced for the first time to resplendent illuminating power. Nothing beyond a meaningless Egyptian word has been to scholars and the world the name given to the boat of Horus in which we cross the lower main from west to east—from birth to death: the Semketet boat, or "boat of the setting sun." That there was another boat that made the voyage back again from the eastern morn to the western eve to repeat the cycle, and that it was named the Maatet boat, or "boat of the rising sun," has remained hidden in dry-as-dust Egyptological research as a pretty poetism, but nothing more. Yet these two boats and their two journeys are almost the two facts of prime import for mankind in its life. For the Semketet and Maatet boats are respectively the physical body in which the soul makes its way across the river of life in the flesh, and the spiritual body of solar light in which it ascends to heaven and traverses the sky in its summertime of disembodied being toward the autumn of another descent into matter. The one is Paul's "natural body," the other his "spiritual body." The latter is now being gestated within the other as its womb, and upon its delivery at its Easter morn on the side of the rising sun, the soul will transfer its residence from the old body to the new one. Since flesh and blood can not inherit the kingdom of heaven, the soul prepares for its habitation there a fit vesture that can subsist in the celestial Paradise. All this is told in Egyptian myth in which, when the Semketet boat of the setting sun, after voyaging through the night on the sea, arrives at last on the eastern marge of sunrise, the passengers with Horus, who are the human Manes with their twelve powers perfected, disembark from it and embark anew on the Maatet boat, or glorious ship of Ra, the spiritual Sun. With the redeemed, the elect and the glorified humanity on board, this majestic boat of the sun then sails upward to the zenith of heaven, and on across the sky till the recurring cycle brings it down to the western gate of the Tuat once more. Man at Easter, or at sunrise, steps out of his mortal vesture into his immortal spirit vehicle to live forever in non-physical realms, robed in light as a garment. The night voyage of the fleshly vessel of Horus ends at dawn, and the joyous sailors, now divinized humans, leave the mummy body of flesh and crowd exultingly on the shining ship of spiritual sunlight, to make the ascent to heaven.

In this boat, along with Ra, there sat the gods Khepera and Tem; but these were only the personifications of Ra's own forms as descending and rising god of evening and morning, or of incarnation and resurrection. These two are again known as Hu and Sa, the two gods who had their places in the boat of the sun at creation. They personify the two nodes of being, spirit and matter. It is written in the *Ritual* (Ch. 120) that while Unas sails towards the east side of heaven, his sister, the star Septet, giveth him birth in the Tuat. This is based on the fact that the west-to-east journey through incarnation fits the soul for birth into the vesture of the sun-god. Ra-Harmachis, a later form of the risen Horus, is denominated "the great god within his boat." Another name for the sun-boat was the "bark of Millions of Years."

The lower boat of Horus, the Semketet, is also that place of refuge or retreat in which the Manes find sanctuary from a pressing menace of the great Dragon Law of the wheel of birth and death. In *Numbers* (35:6) it is stated that six cities were appointed for refuge; and six is the number typing the elemental forces that built the physical body. The lower boat is the earthly refuge for spirits fleeing from heaven. The solar heroes were saved in a basket of reeds. The typology depicts the birth of heavenly beings into the human body on earth. There was always conveyed the idea of safety from circumfluent waters in some sort of enclosure, a boat, ark, or nest of reeds, or an island. In the Norse *mythos* it was the ash-tree, called "The Refuge of Thor," that caught and saved the young god when he was being swept away by the overflowing waters of the river Vimur. Osiris is saved in the midst of the bole of the tamarisk tree that floated on the water. The reed that offers an escape from the water to the dragon-fly, whereby it may ascend into its proper sphere of the air, is a type of salvation from the water.

A mound of earth, the papyrus reed or a willow stuck in the moist ground were some of the portrayals of emergence or rescue from water before the boat had furnished a more generally used type. The soul must find a place or means of stability amid the flux of life. The early symbols of wading and swimming shadowed the stage of evolution when the soul was deeply mired in matter. The boat typifies the time when the higher entity was able to cross over dry-shod.

It is an extraordinary confirmation of the theses here presented that the entry into the boat to begin the underworld journey was in all respects identical with the burial of Horus or Osiris in their coffins. This certifies to the identity of the physical body of man with the boat of the lower Nun. The boat and the coffin are the same symbol in effect, both typing the physical body. For the Manes says: "I am *coffined in an ark* like Horus, to whom his cradle is brought." For he is to be reborn in the same body in which he "dies." He transforms his coffin into his new cradle. This cradle is the nest or ark of papyrus reeds, and indicates that the "death" and burial take place in the same realm where a new birth is to occur. The lotus was a type of the boat or ark of safety in the water and of the womb of birth in one. Some of the later ships were lotus-shaped at prow and stern. The cabin was the Hindu Argha-Yoni or the womb of the mother. The constellation Argo Navis, the Pleiades, the Little Bear and Orion were uranographic picturings of the boats of salvation in various relations.

It is evident that the tabernacle which the Eternal ordered Moses to build, in which he might dwell with his children, the Israelites, and eventually be raised up, is but another form of typism for the inner shrine of the sanctuary, the holy of holies in the ark of the covenant. And this in turn is depicted under the water emblemism as the ship of the sun, or boat of Ra. The exchange of passengers from the boat of Horus to the ship of Ra betokened the successful completion of the incarnation cycles. It was the index of their new birth, which was not now that of water. For they had finished the water baptism at that point, and were to enter upon the baptism of fire, which would

410

induct them into the spiritual universe. The solar bark was to pick up the survivors of the mundane sea voyage and transport them across the expanse of a kingdom of air and fire, which required a boat of airy and fiery texture. The happy passengers were carried upward on board the "bark of Hasisadra" "to be like the gods." "Nu saileth round about the heavens and voyageth along with Ra." The material of the ship of Ra is imperishable stuff, formed out of the indestructible essence of solar light. Imprisoned for many incarnations in the tabernacle of the flesh, we finally are released from it, to pass over into another temple of shining glory, our true spirit body. One of the great purposes of our coming into the world is to build this fabric. When it is finished we exchange our house of darkness for this vessel of light. This is most plainly indicated in a sentence on a Chaldean tablet: "O man of Surippak, son of Ubarratutu, destroy the house and build a ship." A house is stationary, bound to a given locale. A ship is mobile. In the glorious vesture of the sun-body the soul of man can traverse all realms and worlds with electric alacrity. When the Osiris obtains command over the upper sea he exclaims: "Collector of souls is the name of my bark. The picture of it is the representation of my glorious journey upon the canal." The canal was probably the Milky Way, which was thought of as the path of souls to reach the empyrean. The solar boat is fastened to the celestial pole by seven ropes. Both boats are drawn by groups of seven or twelve powers, represented by the seven horses of the sun, the seven swans, seven dolphins, and others. The boats were drawn first by the seven nature powers, later by the twelve spirit forces; or the lower boat by the seven and the celestial by twelve. In fact the Egyptians enumerate and name seven boats to suggest the seven principles which carry evolution along. The *Ritual* (Ch. 89) contains an apostrophe of sublime beauty to these basic energies of life:

"Hail, ye gods who tow along the boat of the lord of millions of years, who bring it above the underworld and who make it to travel over the Mount, who *make souls to enter into (their) spiritual bodies*, whose hands are filled with your ropes . . . destroy ye the enemy, thus shall the boat of the Sun be glad and the great God shall set out on his journey in peace. May it (the soul) look upon its material body, may it rest upon its spiritual body, and may its body neither perish nor suffer corruption forever."

411

Chapter 136B is entitled: "of sailing the great boat of Ra to pass over the circle of Bright Flame." And in it the Manes says: "I am the spiritual body (*sah*) of the lord of divine right and truth made by the goddess Uatchet."

A vast flood of light is let in upon Gospel interpretation at one burst if it is understood that the twelve disciples of Jesus symboled the twelve powers of spiritual light energy to be unfolded by man in twelve labors or stages of growth, all imaged by the twelve signs of the zodiac. It should from the first have been seen without cavil that the function of "the Twelve" in the Gospels was far more than that of useful agents of a historical personage to found an earthly ecclesiasticism. For when the Gospel Jesus told them they would sit with him on the twelve celestial thrones and judge the twelve tribes of Israel, the declaration took them at once from the realm of personal history into that of cosmic hierarchism.

Egypt gave them a more definitive naming and function. Accompanying Horus or Ra, the twelve were astronomical powers, rulers or *"saviors of the treasure of light."* As light was the crowning product of all cosmic operation, the saviors of its treasure were the culminating depositories of dynamic agency. They became the twelve great spirit-children of Ra's unimaginable might. With Horus they became the twelve who accompany the god to earth as sowers of the seed and later reapers of the divine harvest reaped on earth for enjoyment in heaven. When the Gnostic Jesus of the *Pistis Sophia* (1:5) rises as the first fruits of them that slept, he becomes the teacher of the twelve on the Mount of Olives (the Mount of the Olive Tree of Dawn, or the resurrection). He suddenly appears in their midst as they sit on the Mount and dazzles them with his glory. It was the function of the *Christos* to gather up and synthesize in himself the potentialities of all lower forces. In the *Ritual* we find this remarkable duplicate of the scene on the Mount of Olives (Ch. 133, Renouf): "Ra maketh his appearance at the Mount of Glory, with the cycle of the *gods* about him." Here is incontestable evidence that the twelve disciples represent twelve deific powers, and not men.

The twelve were also the Gnostic Aeons, who were powers or "saviors" of light. The Gnostic Jesus gives this testimony:

"When I first came into the world I brought with me twelve powers. I took them from the hands of the twelve saviors of the treasure of light."

There is power in these mighty utterances from old Egypt's *Ritual* to dispel the fogs of many centuries of religious superstition.

The first seven powers in physical phenomena had been gathered up, divinized and unified by the coming into evolution of the Christ Avatar. Additional unfoldment raised them to twelve. As the young solar deity passed through the twelve signs of the zodiac, he appropriated to himself and harmonized in the alembic of his own constitution all the natural radiations of deific light put forth by the twelve aeons or emanations. Jesus speaks of them as his ministers and messengers, whom he hath made "a flame of fire." Jesus brought the gift of soul to the natural energies and converted them into agents of cosmic mind. These were the twelve who as kings rowed the solar bark for Ra, with Horus at the prow. These were the twelve knights about the table of King Arthur; they were the twelve sons of Jacob; and the twelve gods with Odin in their midst. And they were the divine powers which were said to be unfolded, one each year, for the first twelve years of the solar god's life, bringing him to the stage of divinest birth at the age of twelve. And this was a sublimated meaning shadowed in the ancient puberty festivals of many tribes. All the solar gods ended their childhood, or subjection to Mother Nature's law, at twelve and entered the period of spiritual maturity, consummating it at the age of thirty.

The twelve were called "the saviors of light" because they upheld the radiance of the spiritual sun. They are described as the emanations of the seven voices and the five supports. The seven voices are the seven primary radiations of tonal vibration that carries the energies of the Elohim or Logoi into manifestation. The five supports are apparently the five basic elements, earth, water, air, fire and aether, that support the edific of the being of man and planets alike. The twelve in Egypt were Sut, Horus, Shu, Hapi, Ap-Uat, Kabhsenuf, Amsta, Anup, Ptah, Atum, Sau and Hu. They accompany Jesus and Horus through the twelve zodiacal signs (*Pistis Sophia*, 339-371), and it is said they "go forth three by three to the four quarters of heaven to preach the gospel of the kingdom." This "preaching" does not sound as if it meant the Sabbath pulpit oratory. The four quarters of heaven is a description of their location on the zodiacal chart.

The Gospel Jesus repeats some of the features of the sea voyage of "the ark of earth" sailing eastward. Horus emerges from the nocturnal storm on the waters into the calm of daybreak. Jesus comes walking over the water to the boat, while the lower soul (Peter) implores his help in saving him from sinking in the lake and is "lifted into the bark" (*Matt.* 14:22) like the rescued Manes in the *Ritual*. Jesus sustains the character of Horus who in the boat is the oar, paddle and rudder of Ra, and who exclaims: "I am the Kheru [ruler, controller] of Ra, who brings the boat to land" (Ch. 63). Jesus becomes master in the ship. It is again noteworthy that the Gospel sun-god appears on the water in the morning watch, the *fourth* watch of the night. The god of intellect rises after "three days" in the tomb of matter and the sea of earth. The Manes prays: "Grant that I, too, may be able to walk on the water as thou walkest on the Nun without making any halt." In another place he cries: "I fail, I sink in the abyss of the flowing that issues from Osiris."

Before the sun-boat can begin its upward journey from the eastern boundary, the giant Apap must be forced to relinquish his hold on the Tree of Life and to "disgorge the waters of Light." This apparent mixing of metaphors would indicate the birth of the sun-god's powers out of the womb of lower nature. In man it would connote the parturition of the solar Christ principle in and from the physical body. If the figure of "disgorging" is not a most impressive suggestion of evolution from within the heart of life outward to the periphery—which modern science has now asseverated—one would be at a loss to think of a more forceful one.

The crossing is not the same as the cross in immediate portrayal of meaning, yet the two lead by a short step into each other's province. In a very direct sense the cross is connected with the flood of water that must be crossed, with the baptism and the lower sea voyage. In its totality, as the allegorical expression of a real experience, racial and individual, all this *was* the cross. This most ancient, perhaps, of all religious symbols (by no means an exclusive instrument of Christian typology) was the most simple and natural ideograph that could be devised to stand as an index of the main basic datum of human life— the fact that in man the two opposite poles of spirit and matter had crossed in union. The cross is but the badge of our incarnation, the axial crossing of soul and body, consciousness and substance, in one organic unity. An animal nature that walked horizontally to the earth, and a divine nature that walked upright crossed their lines of force and consciousness in the same organism. The implications of this situation are all that the great symbol ever connoted. There can be nothing more religiously holy and sacred about the sign than about any other figure of human life. It means just that human life—nothing more. By ecclesiastical psychologization it has come to betoken a range of emotional repercussions, but it still carries no basic meaning other than that of the god immersed in matter. Whatever is sacred in human life is so by virtue of that single fact. However, since all values in life flow from that fundamental ground, the symbol may legitimately be made the talismanic focus of both emotional and intellectual reaction. If it conveys to the mass mind the strong intimation that this life itself is haloed with august significance, is essentially sacred and worthy of being lived with deepest consecration of purpose and effort to its intelligently discerned ends, its symbolic influence would indeed be salutary. If it is taken to be a cross of wood on which a man of flesh was physically nailed some nineteen centuries ago, its effect on thought must be stultifying and deadening.

Plato says that the divine man was "bicussated and was stamped upon the universe in the likeness of a cross." When primal unity of life bifurcated into spirit and matter, the two forces had to be crossed in interplay in order to engender the worlds and all manifestation. The coming of mind in man to rule nature brought the figure of the cross into symbolism because it brought the upright line to cross at right angles the horizontal line denoting the feminine or natural creation. Man was the first to raise the animal from horizontal position to the vertical; yet both natures live in him, considerably at "cross purposes" with each other. At any rate typology figured the mother creation, before mind came with man, by the horizontal line, which is the minus sign. Nature was privation—the Greeks called matter "privation." The union with it, however, of the intellectual principle made it capable of adding and increasing, giving itself *more* life, and so the cross is the plus sign. But great multiplication of living beings could not come until the forces were set in motion; and motion was indicated by a moving of the straight cross one half of a quarter revolution, or out of motionless position; and this gives the multiplication sign, as well as the numeral (Roman) ten, the number that joins male and female signs, I and O, in activity. It was the crossing of spirit with matter that moved and multiplied the worlds. And ten is the number of the completed cycle, and the tenth letter of the Hebrew alphabet is Yod, the name of God. The bread of life had to be vastly multiplied before it could be distributed. The mathematical sign of division is the horizon line, with a dot above and below to signify that when life divided it split into two kingdoms, one above, the other below, a median line. And we shall see that this gives a perfect picture or glyph of man's nature lived on the horizon line between "Upper and Lower Egypt."

The Toltecs called the cross the Tree of Sustenance and the Tree of Life. The tree and cross are identical, and even the staff or rod is a reduced form of the tree-type, for Aaron's rod was fabled to be a stem from the Tree of Life in *Genesis*. The cross is a symbol of life, never of death, except as "death" means incarnation. It was the cross of life on earth because its four arms represented the fourfold foundation of the world, the four basic elements, earth, water, air and fire, of the human temple, and because it was an emblem of the reproduction of new life, and thus an image of continuity, duration, stability, an eternal principle ever renewing itself in death. The whisperings of esoteric fable report that the very tree on which Jesus was hanged was grown from a sprout or seed from the forbidden Tree of Life in *Genesis!* There are many instances of the cross burgeoning into fresh life. The savior is not nailed *on* the tree; he *is* the tree. He unites in himself the horizontal human-animal and the upright divine. And the tree becomes alive; from dead state it flowers out in full leaf. The leaf is the sign of life in a tree. The Egyptians in the autumn threw down the Tat cross, and at the solstice or the equinox of spring, erected it again. The two positions made the cross. The Tat is the backbone of Osiris, the sign of eternal stability. And *Tattu* was the "place of establishing forever."

That the cross betokened the basic idea of the impregnation of elemental matter with divine potency typed as male is evidenced by the fact that Apt, the old first Mother, figured as the hippopotamus and the Great Bear, is depicted with a fourfold phallus on her breast in the form of a cross. Again and again the goddess of primal source is figured with male features or the male member, mutely proclaiming her power as re-begetter of the dead. The Christ in the form of the *Stauros,* or cross, impregnated the Mother Sophia and gave to her who was otherwise formless an ideal form and beauty. Forgetting the ancient Gnostic teaching and calling it "heresy," the early Christians warred over the question of the sex of the Logos. The knowledge that would have saved them all this sad miscarriage of zeal can be summarily stated. The Logos is the product of cosmic male mind and virginal female substance, in union. A virgin is unproductive until embraced by creative power. At bottom the cross indicates sex union, be it on the plane of the cosmos, in the heart of the atom, in the solar systems, or on the nuptial bed. A crossing is consummated or a cross made wherever the positive and negative poles of life cross each other in their interblended affinity. And then the Son, or Logos, is born. And the child becomes a man, and must enter into creative relation with his Mother Nature in his turn. Gnostic literature states that the Christ fertilized the Mother Sophia by making the sign of "Kr" or "Chr" (Greek XP) over her body. This was the cross within the circle, or the male crossed with the female. The symbol then gave rise to the many words beginning with Chr- or Kr-(Cr-), such as *Charis,* Christ, *Kheru,* Cross, Chronos, Course, Circle, *Karast,* Crest; as well as, by the curious process of reversal employed by the ancients, *Rekh,* Ark, *Arche,* Argo, Arch, etc. The letter "A" bears testimony likewise to some ancient philosophy, as it apparently represents the single vertical line of male deity, or god in unity, split apart or in two, as male and female, and then joined by the middle cross stroke, the Ankh-tie. The "O" also proclaims its own meaning as being the boundless infinite, without beginning or end, self-contained, ever returning unto itself, embosoming all things, yet, as the Absolute (that is, released from all finiteness or form), the sign of total negation of Nought. And we are now in position to see something of the significance of the great Gnostic name for the sun-god or Logos, son of Sophia: I A O. It reads under our eyes: "I" am the "A" (Alpha) and the "O" (Omega), the beginning and the end. But, seen with a bit more philosophical penetration it reads again: I, the first emanation of being (typed by the straight vertical line, the No. 1), split into two phases, joined (in the "A") in incarnate and manifest existence, and end in a return to infinite Be-ness, "O." The "Y" near the end of the alphabet is an "A" reversed, and the two separated streams returning into the "I." The "U" and "V" show the original "I" split in two, united at the bottom in incarnation, and the force descending and then returning. The "J" indicates the turning to return of the "I." "S" and "Z" are types of

417

turning and endlessly returning life. Other letters show design in their construction, as they were glyphs of esoteric philosophy.

A tradition that the cross of Calvary was made of four kinds of wood, palm, cedar, olive and cypress, signifies again that it stood for the four segments of the nature of man and the world.

The cross of Calvary of Christian iconography is common on the breasts of Egyptian mummies. It is identical with the Ankh-cross, denoting life and renewal. The cross was placed in the hands of the dead as an emblem both of incarnation and the new life to come. It was carved on the back of the scarab, with the same meaning. The Horus of the resurrection is pictured with the Cross of Life in his hand in the act of raising the dead body from the bier. The sign of the cross was made upon the mummy entering the realm of the dead; it was also given to the soul as it arose out of the body as an emblem of rebirth.

The cross has been appropriated by Christian ecclesiasticism as the unique and distinctive emblem of its faith. Yet in the iconography of the catacombs no figure of a *man* on the cross appears during the first six or seven centuries of the era! Instead there are all forms of the cross except the one which is claimed to be the very basis and origin of the religion itself. The cross of Calvary was *not the initial, but the final* form of the crucifix. The cult that now buttresses its authenticity upon the historic Calvary presents not a single reproduction of its crucified Redeemer in its symbolic art during the first six or seven centuries! According to Massey the earliest known form of the human figure on the cross is the crucifix presented by Pope Gregory the Great to Queen Theodolinde, now in the Church of St. John at Monza; while no image of the crucifix is found in the catacombs at Rome earlier than that of San Siulio belonging to the seventh or eighth century. In the earliest representations of the Trinity made by Christian artists, the Father and the Holy Spirit, the latter being feminine in the form of the Dove, are pictured beside the cross. A Christ, and him crucified, is utterly absent. Not the Crucified, but the cross, is the primary symbol of the Christian faith. Yet that same cross is pre-Christian, is a pagan and heathen symbol. For centuries the cross stood for the Christ, and was addressed as if it were a living thing. Crucifixes have been found in Christian churches antedating the fourth century, with a human figure nailed or bound in the conventional way; but the figure is **not** that of Jesus! It is that of Orpheus! In Christian imagery the Lamb was the usual figure on the cross, when a sacrificial victim was added to the bare cross emblem. But it appears that about the end of the seventh century it began to be felt that the alleged histórical life of the personal Christ was in danger of being lost amid the mass of symbolic representations and the multiplicity of Messianic and sun-god characters which were current in most countries as the heritage of pagan symbolism. In order, then, to focus emphasis upon the uniqueness of the Christian Jesus as the physically crucified one, it was decreed by the Council of Trullo, or the Quinque Sixtum, in the reign of Justinian II, that in future the figure of the real historical Jesus should supersede the astrological sign of Aries "in the image of Christ, our God." "He shall be represented in his human form, instead of the Lamb, as in former times" (Cited by Didron: *Icon. Chret.*, pp. 338-9).

In the eighth century Adrian I, Pontiff of Rome, in a letter to Barasius, the Patriarch of Constantinople, voiced the opinion that the time had come for the Christ to be no longer portrayed as the Lamb:

"Forasmuch as the shadow hath passed away and that Christ is very man, he ought therefore, to be represented in the form of a man."

"The Lamb of God must not be depicted on the cross as a chief object; but there is no hindrance to the painting of a lamb on the reverse or inferior portion of the cross where Christ hath been duly portrayed as a man."

No criticism can be legitimately lodged against the Holy Fathers for desiring to use the human figure as a symbol to carry the vital truth that the Logos had put on the form of a man, and that the new heaven and earth was to be formed "according to the measure of a man." It would indeed have more impressiveness than the more abstract symbol of the astrological Lamb. But the world, and especially those millions of souls whose earthly lives were snuffed out in the name of an alleged gentle Galilean peasant, call out a vigorous challenge to the procedure of turning an innocuous symbol into a veridical historical personage, when the change entailed, as the sequel showed, the transformation of devotional reverence for a spiritual ideal into frenzied zeal and inhuman cruelty, in the name of an actual man. It was not until the long process of mental corrosion had brought to decay the ancient power to discern spiritual truths through outward symbols that the figure of the personal God was thrust into the place of immolation, and the cross as emblem became the cross of wood.

In John's account the crucifixion takes place at the time of the Passover, and for the Paschal Lamb is substituted the victim in human form. The killing of the Lamb of God (the Logos under the sign of Aries, as it had been the Bull in the preceding 2155 years) was the divine sacrifice; and his slaughter, with the sprinkling of the doorposts, or gates of the new life, with his blood, was the sign of the new birth of spiritual life. In one sign humanity was washed in the blood of the Bull, in the next in the blood of the Lamb; and again in the next in the blood of the Christ whom the Greeks named Ichthys, the Fish.

The sprinkled blood of the gods, poured out for humanity on earth, was symboled as fertilizer to nourish the earth. In early times the mother's blood, too, was believed to fertilize the fields for the new sowing. The function of fertilizing the ground is assigned both to Sut and to Judas, the adversaries and betrayers of the sun-god in the Christian and Egyptian myths. Sut was said to fertilize the fields with his blood "on the night of fertilizing the field in Tattu." The coming of divinity to dwell with man was to make the soil of his life productive by enriching the natural self. What more apt symbol, then, than that of fertilizing?

An ancient festival not copied by the Roman Christians was that of the Hiding of the Cross in the Nile, followed in the opposite sign by the ceremony of Finding the Cross. The person traditionally assigned to the finding was Helena, a name which must be taken as derived from *Helios,* the sun, in Greek. It was the boast of Isis that she had given birth to *Helios*. The "Hor" of "Horus" is also *Har, Hal, Hel* (the Egyptian "R" becoming the Hebrew "L"); hence Horus is *Helios* by name, as Jesus is Joshua. Isis lost the fiery cross in the ocean of incarnation and Helena or the sun-spirit recovered it from the river to blaze in renewed glory at the Passover or crossing in March. Nothing more is depicted by these festivals than the incarnation and resurrection of life in matter, or the god in mortal man. As Isis lost her child at the autumn equinox and found him again at the equinox of spring, there is again a clear identification of cross with Christ-child.

Nothing could more definitely point to the meaning of the cross as the fact of incarnation than the name of the ancient Mexican cross itself, which was Tonocaquahuitl, "the tree of our flesh." We are nailed on this tree of flesh, out of whose symbolic wood alone is to be con- structed the only cross on which the god has ever died. This is the only death on the cross known to erudite sages. And every imagined hammer-stroke driving nails through rended flesh on a geographical Golgotha has been a renewed stroke of misguided fanaticism nailing the free spirit of man still more firmly to the cross of ignorance, super- stition and bondage.

Baptized with the god in his death on the cross, we shall happily disburden ourselves of this weight of toil and suffering when we have finished the crossing of the waters and see the golden sun rise at the end of the fourth watch of the night.

Chapter XVII

THE ARK AND THE DELUGE

THE treatment of the symbolism behind the figure of the ark and the deluge in the Christian Bible naturally belongs in the chapter on the baptism and the crossing of the water. But this allegory conveys a recondite message of such luminous beauty and cosmic majesty that it merits a chapter in its own right. It need hardly be announced at the start that the ark was not a wooden structure and the deluge had nothing to do with water. They are ideotypes of the most cogent intellectual suggestiveness. They are cosmographs, or figurative sketches of grand universal truth, sublime in conception and challenging in the sweep of their import.

From one angle of approach the ark symbolism duplicates or parallels that of the two boats analyzed in the previous chapter. For the exegesis here again manifests the dual aspect of the meaning portrayed, and shows two arks pertinent to man's life, one floating on the terrestrial water, the other soaring across the celestial sea of crystal. The one above is the paraphrase for Apollo's glorious chariot of the sun climbing across the sky by day; the one below is the raft, boat or ark in which the "dead" soul makes its passage by night across the Styx of the nether world, with Horus, Charon or Christ for pilot. In short, the upper one is man's body of glowing spiritual light; the lower is his ark or temple of flesh. And the peculiarity of the operation of the great Law of the Two Truths comes to view here in the fact that in the alternate arcs of the cycle each body becomes in turn the ark that houses and preserves the other. In the earth cycle the physical body becomes the ark that contains and treasures the spiritual; conversely, in the discarnate cycle the spiritual body contains and treasures the seeds of the physical. It exemplifies the eternal alternation of spirit and matter, soul and flesh, discarnate and incarnate existence in the universe of life.

The one thing that is definite beyond dispute is that the legend of the ark and flood could never have had reference to a physical vessel bearing living animals and humans on the breast of a world-ocean raised to the mountain tops. For thousands it will be a gratuitous labor to point out the features of impossibility and absurdity in accepting the account as objective or literal history. They are in this case so glaringly preposterous that their brief review for the sake of shaking thousands of stubborn minds loose from literalism appears to be pardonable.

In the first place no vessel of the size described could house the number of living creatures—two of every species of "unclean beasts" and fourteen of every species of "clean beasts"—that Noah was ordered to take with his family into the ark. It would take a well-equipped army of many thousands of men at least a year to go over the earth now and collect the two or fourteen specimens of every living creature. And many types of animal and insect can not live when transported to different climatic habitats. Many insects live only a few hours and so could not possibly be taken a long journey to the ark. Noah and his family were given by the Eternal *just seven days* to make this collection, impossible to begin with! Then, if by some miracle there were space on board for all the animals, birds and insects (not to say fish and reptiles), there certainly could not be found space for the supply of food necessary to tide them over one hundred and fifty days' imprisonment in the ark. And nearly all animals and insects require different kinds of food, impossible to provide, even to know what to secure and where to find it. Carnivorous animals would have to be given other animals to eat. And the imagination can depict the living conditions on such a boat after a few days.

Then as to the rain of forty days and nights, alleged to have raised the ocean over the whole world to the mountain tops! This is allegorism pure and simple, since forty thousand days of rain could not raise the ocean an inch! Rain is moisture that has been taken out of the ocean to begin with, and only returns to it, keeping its level constant. To raise the entire ocean of the globe, water would have to be brought here from the "canals" on Mars or other celestial body. Literally the story is as chimerical as the star of Bethlehem and Jonah's whale.

In addition to all this, an examination of antecedent deluge traditions and accounts will demonstrate that the Biblical version is but one of numberless presentations admittedly allegorical, and its historical authenticity will be seen to effervesce away in the profounder import of the whole cycle of such mythical heritage. Consistent study of Comparative Religion through the centuries would have prevented Christianity from wresting its allegories and spiritual constructions in the scripture so utterly apart from kindred material of the pagan world in frightful distortion of their meaning.

When we transfer the reference from external symbol to subjective reality, the myth is seen to be a somewhat fanciful but lucid pictorialization of the reciprocal relation of the two bodies of man's constitution, physical and spiritual, as well as a formula for the routine of evolutionary growth. In life the material body is the ark in which the soul is carried over the sea of sense and realism; in the heavenly state the ark is the spiritual body that enwombs the seeds of physical creation. From the moment of first entry into incarnation the soul is borne across the waters of earthly existence, from west gate of life to east gate through the dark underworld, in the ark of the physical body. But when the six water signs of the zodiac have been traversed, and the soul comes to the point of emergence from the sea, it then embarks anew on the ark of Ra on the eastern marge and is borne up the ascent of heaven to the Paradise about the Pole, to join the company of the gods and the stars (souls) that never set (incarnate). The ark below matches and reflects the structure of the ark above, but in inverted form. The tabernacle was to be fashioned after the pattern of things in the mount. And the lower and the higher tabernacles were to enwomb each other in turn.

The figure of the womb as matching the ark-type is by no means an impertinent fancy. There is no sense in which the ark symbol can be better understood in its truest reference to cosmology and anthropology than in its character as the womb. Ancient religion tended to take on phallic coloring because all living process *is* a birthing, and life passes from one womb to another. It swings from a gestation in matter to a gestation in spirit. The soul is incubated in the physical body; but the form of the next body is incubated in the deep womb of the soul after death. Mind gestates in body, but body also gestates or is engendered in mind. Intelligence conceives the creation, matter gives it birth. We must be born of water (matter) *and* the spirit. Life has two wombs, and every sun-god had two mothers. All life is conceived in the womb of Nut or Isis and given manifest birth in the body of Nephthys, Egypt told us five millennia ago. The great *Ritual* of that land condenses this mighty truth into a sentence in the discourses to Pepi: "O Ra, the womb of Nut is filled with the seed of the Spirit which is in her." Our word "nut," the fruit of the tree, may be derived from this venerable source. The Hindus had their Argha-Yoni, the feminine or uterine symbol of all creative source. And Argha is cognate in root derivation with "ark." The ark is the inner shrine and most holy sanctuary of life, from which the worlds issue.

Matter has been conspicuously published as being the *Mater* or mother of spiritual manifestation, but the correlative truth that in the opposite swing of the cycles of life and death, spirit likewise in its arc of the round becomes the gestating mother of the next expression in matter, has apparently become too abstruse for popular conception and has been lost out of the theological picture. Spirit goes into the cabin of the boat of the physical body to be gestated to new birth there. In turn, the body, going to dissolution outwardly, sends its principles into the inner shrine, or ark of the covenant, to be incubated there for its new birth in the next generation. Matter and soul eternally reciprocate dominance and leadership in living nature. And the flesh is no more the ark of the soul than the soul is the ark of the flesh. Spirit conserves the gains in matter, to reproduce them in later form, as matter does those of spirit.

As soon as Life bifurcates into its two opposite but complementary nodes, there is set in motion the operation of mutuality and reciprocity, rhythm and balance, between the two. Deep inside the ark was the shrine for Deity; buried in the secret depths of every physical man is Amen-Ra, the hidden Lord. But when the form of material man has vanished off the scene, deep within the heart of the god is the conception of the next organic form to be deployed into the visible world. And it is worth a moment's comment in passing, to assert that a familiarity with the truth of this mutual and alternate birthing of soul and body in the order of life would have saved the western world the degradation of descent into the modern age of materialism now happily passing out. As noted in the first chapter of our study, modern science has now announced that all evolution is but the unfolding from within the geneplasm of qualities that were already implicit in the system of nature. Had vision not been beclouded by crass theological obsessions, and symbolic science not obliterated, these great truths could have been descried in Biblical texts in one or another form. In *Exodus* (25) the Lord's instruction to Moses is given: "Inside the ark you must place the laws I give you." This is not an order to deposit documents in a chest, as childish orthodoxy might suppose. It is the divine decree that bids mankind imprint the laws of life, learned from mundane experience, indelibly upon the inner tablets of the human spirit. Says the Eternal: "I will write my laws upon their hearts, and in their minds will I write them." The lessons of truth must be engraved upon the eternal memory of the seminal divinity within. Thus, when the outer body of life is dissolved, the imperishable soul preserves the fruits of all past living in the unseen world of ideal archetypal forms.

Inside the physical matrix there hides the form of the god. Inside the god (when not embodied) hides the form of the (next) body. Each will give birth to the other in the cycle. To carry the image of birth in and from water, the boat or ark symbol was introduced. And the vastly important identity between the ark of the Biblical flood and the ark of the covenant in the *Old Testament*—the boat on the water and the chest in the temple—has been entirely lost sight of. Egypt kept the intimate relation in view when the chest from the sanctuary was carried on the shoulders of priests in procession in the shape of a boat or inside a boat. The tabernacle was a combined boat and shrine, or ark sanctuary. The fire on the altar or the shrine in the holy of holies was the symbol of divine mind nestling imperturbably in the heart of every material form.

When the *Ritual* expounds that the womb of Nut (nature) is filled with the seed of the spirit to which she is to give birth, the passage gives us the one central clue to full comprehension of the whole structure. It is found in the word "seed." Here is indeed our Ariadne thread by which to reach understanding. The entire scope and full force of the meaning can not be seen without viewing it through the analogy of the function of the seed in relation to its parent tree or plant. The ark *is* the seed of life. The analogy must be drawn in full.

Life, as said, ceaselessly alternates shuttle-like between the two nodes of manifestation and withdrawal, activity in matter and rest in spirit. From the heart of invisible being it issues forth to express its creative pleasure in building the universe. But it operates rhythmically in cyclic rounds, for it is never static; and its periodic activity is focalized in time, and runs its course to an end, at which the forms built up to express its nature are dismantled and vanish away. The Hindu Trinity expresses aspects of truth that the Christian Trinity has never conveyed. There was Brahma, the Creator, and opposite him Shiva, the Destroyer; and between them Vishnu, the Preserver of the eternal balance between them. The vast and vital function of Shiva has not been given due place in theology. Life has power to build forms, but if it did not also have power to destroy them, it would have to remain forever prisoner to its own formations! Nothing would be worse than that it should have to live eternally in the forms it first built. There could be no evolution. Life's power to destroy a present construction and build a "more stately mansion" for its dwelling is its guarantee of advance to more abundant richness.

But provision then had to be made for preserving its gains at the end of each cycle when Shiva's force brought all material forms to decay. Nature's provision for this contingency is of course the *seed*. Every living organism has inherent in it the marvelous capability of nucleating on its outer periphery, just before the end of its career or of each "year" of growth, a miraculous embryonic reproduction of itself, its child in its own image and likeness, which has implicit within it the potentiality of renewing its parent's life in complete stature in the next generation. In a word, every organic being, before death, is able to pack all its essential attributes into a tiny chest—Pandora's box—in which is harbored the possibility of its living organically again in the next cycle, when the present corpus of matter is gone. This is its going into the ark, for the ark is the seed. It is that tiny vessel of sheer potentiality into which the living qualities now expressed in organic body can retire unseen, and be preserved in safety during the period when dissolution sweeps like a deluge over all the "earth" and washes all forms away! Earth here is a type of materiality, as heaven is the type of spiritual consciousness. The astute reader will already have divined that the Flood or Deluge is nothing other than the tide of Shiva's force that, under water typology, sweeps away all living forms and creatures. When that flood has washed away all foothold for soul or life to stand upon in cosmic waters, matter being the resting place for spirit, the indestructible nucleus of consciousness must retire into the invisible worlds and find a locale in structures of spiritual tenuity.

427

The innermost vessel of purely spiritual substantiality in the invisible realms is the ark shrine of man's life, and is at the same time his seed vesicle, for in it are condensed as in a capsule the capability of renewal and reproduction of every character of his present life, to start a fresh expression in due course.

The great Flood, then, is the tide of dissolution of forms at the end of each cycle. Massey comes close enough to the significance of the Deluge legends to assert correctly that the Flood marks the end and the new beginning of a cycle. Life must go on; there must be a next cycle. The ark is the inner shrine or seed body—in the tree visible, in man invisible and spiritual—into which the life principles of any being retire to be tided in security over the period when the waters of dissolution wash away all other foothold on earth. And at the end of the Flood it will emerge from the ark to set foot on or in matter once more, and renew the living creatures on "earth."

The clue and the certification to the correctness of this interpretation lie in the very meaning and origin of the word "ark." The dictionaries give the source of the word as from the Greek *arkein,* "to keep off, ward off, fend, defend, protect in an enclosure," such as a palisade or corral. Moses' ark of bulrushes is a typical mythical usage of the idea. The seed is just that enclosure of safety into which it withdraws when the waters of menace to its continuity are swirling around.

But who shall find authority strong enough to deny that the Greek *arkein* is not a slight variant or modification of the primary stem *arch-?* In this stem at any rate is the source of the basic meaning of the typism underlying the ark symbolism. For *arche* (Greek) means, most significantly, "the beginning"; and the seed is the beginning of the new generation, as it is the end of the preceding growth! When the cycle is ended and life has had its development and withdrawn from the form, it goes into rest for a night, after which it begins another cycle to gain further advance in enrichment. And here life operates according to a methodology that is basic for knowledge of its laws. In every new life period the indwelling and animating principle of soul begins its new career back at the point of the original beginning of all evolution itself. Every minor cycle becomes a miniature and reflection of the whole cycle of life in manifestation. It starts each new round at the point where first life started, or as the first word in the Greek Bible (*Genesis*) has it, *en arche* (Hebrew *B'rashith*), "*in*

428

the beginning" of all creation. Each round starts from the same *arche,* for it has retired into that *arche,* or first primeval state of being, at the end of the preceding cycle, and must issue thence at the beginning of the next. More quickly, however, in each succeeding round it recapitulates its initial stages of growth. It is itself the Ancient of Days, a spark of that Infinite Being which is neither young nor old, but is ageless. Its new physical vehicle in each generation, however, traverses the successive stages of the entire evolution up to the point which the soul had achieved in the last activity, to go on a step farther from there. The immortal principle of soul retires into the primordial abysmal *arche* at the end of each active period, and emerges from it at each new beginning. And while in retirement in this *arche* it is tided safely over the waters of dissolution of form. Life does nothing else endlessly but go in and out of the *arche.* From manifest appearance in the worlds of actuality it retires into just what Plato denominated it, its *arche*typal form in *noumenon.* It comes out of this bosom of primordiality and withdraws into it in endless turn. It shuttles between adult growth in one cycle and embryonic seed beginnings in the next.

What characters, then, should we expect to find going into the ark to ride the flood? The names of Noah and his sons have not been competently etymologized, and much of the sequel is found here. The Greek word for the divine Mind is *Noë,* a feminine form of the universal cosmic Intelligence, the *Nous*—though Massey traces it from the Egyptian Nu or Nnu. The feminine form of the word, Noë, is quite significant, since it is in its feminine form in the Hebrew language that it comes to its form of *No-ah, ah* being a feminine termination. The *no-* is the stem of our own word "know," and of course the basis of such a word as "Gnosis." *Noah* is therefore the name of the divine intellectual principle, which, having projected itself into matter for the period of the active cycle, withdraws into the *arche* at the dissolution of its outward forms, as the spirit of the oak tree retires into the acorn before the storms crash its form to molder away. The French word for "Christmas" derives from the same stem, being *No-el,* which reads "(the birth of) God-Mind." And who are Noah's three sons, who go with him into the ark?

This divine principle of mentality manifests or deploys outward into the cosmic field of creation, not as one ray, but divided into three, which give ancient religions their "solar triads" of mind-soul-spirit, three aspects or modifications of the one single first emanation of cosmic mind. They find Biblical typing in the persons of the three angels who visited Abraham under the oaks of Mamre, the three men in the fiery furnace in *Daniel,* and the three magi who come with the incarnating Messiah to "adore" him. They even find a physiological replica in the threefold segmentation of the spermatozoa of the male creative fluid, which is often the type of creative mind. Noah's three sons, Ham, Shem, and Japheth, must be taken as the three primal segmentations of the first ray of divine consciousness. They are sometimes equated with the first three patriarchs of Israel, Abraham-Isaac-Jacob. Since a twelvefold progeny eventually issued from their cosmic activity, Jacob's parentage of a race of twelve groups of Israelites is in line with the graph of the emanations. So, then, when the conscious principle is called upon to retire into its aboriginal *arche* at the "end of the aeon"—most disastrously translated "the end of the world"—it is quite clear that the intellectual entity could not disappear off the scene without absorbing his three radiations back into himself to disappear with him. Likewise their three *shakti* or materially implementing forces, or "wives," accompanied them into "the ark."

Then they were given "seven days" in which to build their structure of safety and gather the fourteens and twos of all creatures together. To be sure, the period for accomplishment of the work to be consummated in every cycle of life is "seven days." Life could not withdraw from its outward manifestation in matter before the end of the cycle, which is seven "days" of creative activity. Thus the allegory is in utter true conformity with ancient cosmology.

The collection of seven (presumably of each gender) of "clean beasts" and but two of each kind of "unclean beasts" into the ark has been an item of puzzlement to exegetists. This is simple enough. To be "clean," the lower animal nature would have had to be perfected by its development and purification attained at the end of the entire cycle of seven sub-cycles. Those that were figured under the number of the primal duality, which represents the condition in which they begin the cycle, when purgation of evil has but only begun, were the "unclean." The "sevens" were finished and "clean"; the "twos" were still imperfectly developed and "unclean."

The forty days of rain types the period of the "inundation," which is another glyph for the incarnation or incubation in the womb of matter. The grain of Egypt was considered to be forty days in the ground before germination, when planted in the overflowing waters of the inundated Nile. The germ of human life incubates forty weeks in the womb of the mother before birth. The 120 days of durance in the ark seems to represent this typical period of forty, number of incubation, considered as threefold, in conformity with the kindred emblemism of the three days in the tomb, that is, forty taken three times. The basic significance of the three numbers—three, seven and forty—which occur endlessly in Bible symbolism, is uniformly that of the gestation of incarnation. *They all betoken the period life spends in matter before re-arising.* It is buried in the three lower kingdoms, mineral, vegetable and animal; it works in matter through the seven cycles of any period; and it lies latent through the forty days of pre-natal growth.

The dove is the emblem of spiritual fire as in the baptism at the Jordan. As divinity sent out its Son, so likewise it sent out, figuratively, its dove, which could not find a landing to settle on the earth until the waters had ceased raging and the time of the new cycle was at hand. The raven is the type of the first, natural, carnal nature, the animal Adam, and obviously, as Paul says that is first which is natural, the raven was sent forth first as the forerunner and preparer of the way.

And lastly comes the significance of the landing place of the ark when the flood of dissolution had ended and the principles could move out into material organization once more. This is a most important item of the allegory, and that it has been missed utterly bespeaks the *gaucherie* of centuries of Bible elucidation. Again the name reveals the hidden sense. In the case of a human being, the principles at death flee from earth habitat to heaven or higher consciousness. When the time is ready for their next embodiment in flesh, they return from heaven and land again on earth, where alone a body of requisite character is available. There is, then, only one place indicated as appropriate for the ark to land after the flood has subsided, and that is—on earth. And that is precisely what the word "Ararat" means! Life fled into the ark when the earth was obliterated and washed away. If it is to be active again, it must return to earth and let the principles out to begin creation anew at the point and place where they had left off at the end of the previous cycle. Many times in old scriptures, indeed in the Bible, the earth is designated as "the mount of earth"; and at any rate it was typed under the figure of a mound or mount amid the water of space, a landing place amid the waters of the abyss, a station of security or foothold for life based on matter. We have seen it as Mount Sinai, and we shall see it as the "mount of the horizon." It is that Mount of the Lord on which the *Christos* delivers his "sermon" or divine message to humanity. This is no far-fetched alignment, but the downright meaning of the various Biblical mounts. And Ararat is the patent, obvious, direct word "earth" itself. The present Hebrew word for "earth" is *arets*. And one reliable authority states that it was earlier *areth*, or practically the English "earth." Mt. Ararat is just this old earth, on which life had to "land" in order to express itself in its next turn at physical existence. And in the light of this exposition it is to be hoped that the befuddlement of the western mind by bigoted literalism may be washed away in the flood of the dissolution of the incrustations of ignorance by a rain of ideas and symbols that will bring the ark of sanity back again to land on "Mount Ararat."

The ship or ark was also the *navis*, from the Latin stem *na-*, which has already yielded for us the cognate ideas of "to swim" and "to be born,"—the new birth in water. In Egyptian the ark was the *theba*, or *teba*; whence can be seen the origin and implication of the word Thebes, as a city name, carrying this whole segment of meaning in the uranograph. As Abydos and Annu were cities named to portray the death and rebirth of the sun-god, so Thebes was named to convey the idea of the soul's voyaging over the waters in the ark of the body, and finding its new birth therein.

The sacred chests that play a part in many myths of creation find their clue in relation to the ark. In them always are kept the most holy things, as in the ark of the covenant. In the Mysteries of Bacchus a sacred box was carried in procession. There is the legend of Pandora's box containing the *seeds* of all good and evil; the Argo of Jason; the moon-shaped boat in which Isis floated over the waters and gathered together the dismembered limbs of Osiris; and the whole list of coffins and chests out of which the various gods rose from a state of death for the redemption of the world. That the ark was identical with the coffin and mummy-case is attested securely by that remarkable line quoted before, the utterance of the Manes: "I am coffined in an ark like Horus, to whom his cradle is brought." The ark, as the physical form in the lower lake carrying the soul across the sea, is the coffin and tomb, as it is the womb; the tomb of death and the womb of new life all in one. The boats, arks and coffins alike evidently refer to the mystic womb of nature, typed by that of woman, and are symbols of salvation amid the "defluxions" of mortal life, as Plato intimates. The Manes says: "I have not been shipwrecked, I have not been turned back on the horizon, for . . . the Osiris-Nu shall not be shipwrecked in the great Boat."

There is a secondary imputation of meaning in the flood or deluge allegorism that can be delineated briefly. It is possible that the deluge epic can be taken, in a poetic sense at any rate, to adumbrate the release of the higher water (or fire) of spirit and intellectuality by the god upon the animal part of man after incarnation; and conversely, in its opposite phase, the release of the lower water (sensualism) upon the god by the lower animal man. Each flooded the other with their respective higher and lower forces, and this is in some sense an implied connotation of the deluge, as of the baptism. *Revelation* does say expressly that the Dragon loosed a water flood to overwhelm the Woman who fled from heaven to this refuge, and that earth swallowed up the flood and helped the Woman. We have seen that this interchange of influences underlay one meaning of the baptism, god and man reciprocally baptizing each other, the one with water, the other with fire. It could be extended to the deluge symbolism. Likewise god and man intoxicate each other, the one with spiritual, the other with sensual, wine of life. The gods were almost submerged under the mighty tide of sensuality that swept in upon their souls at their entry into animal bodies. A deluge of passion and beastliness broke loose to engulf all humanity and carry the Christ principle down into the "belly" of fleshly instinct.

A mass of legends center about the fact that in the early stages of human history an Eden of happiness was submerged under a deluge that covered the Mount. An initial Paradise was overthrown and buried under waters that flooded the earth. Various peoples even localized this drowned garden under the waters nearest them. The Black Sea, Lake Van in Armenia and Lake Copais in Egypt were a few of the seas on whose bottoms the sunken Eden might be found. A typical deluge myth that preserves the sunken Eden feature is one related by a Miztec tribe of Indians, to the effect that "in the day of

433

obscurity and darkness the gods built a palace that was a masterpiece of skill, and made their abode on the summit of a mountain. The rock was called 'the Place of Heaven.' It was the primary dwelling of the gods. The children of the gods then planted a garden of fruit trees." But the universal fate of such gardens overtakes it: there comes a deluge; the garden of delight is submerged and "many sons and daughters of the gods are swept away" (Bancroft: *Native Races*, Vol. 3, p. 71). Massey says that "inevitably at times our earth gets substituted for the mound (mount), island," or eminence of whatever name that stands for a refuge of stability and security amid chaos. Naturally enough; for the reason that the "mount" *was* the earth. The celestial mount was transferred to earth by and with the arrival of the gods. The gods sank the Eden of spiritual mindedness and semi-Nirvanic blissful dreaminess under the deluge of the carnalism that the Dragon released to overwhelm them as they enter the lower sea of bodily life. There was for a time a Golden Age of angelic delight on the globe itself. But this was in the incipient stages of the descent, when as yet the higher mind hovered over, rather than fully inhabited, the physical constitution. Then it passed away under the encroaching waters of sensualism, as the angels were swept deeper into the coils and toils of incarnation. The gods transferred their focus of consciousness and interest from the heaven world of intellect down into the belly of sense and lust for physical life. They moved from the regions of air and fire down into the morasses of earth and water, all, however, within the frame of man's material existence. Egypt and Plato both remind us that through intellect we are gods in heaven, while through body we are animals on earth. The god may descend from his tower or parlor to live in his stable. The submergence of Eden was the shift from divine mentation to gross carnality. To transfer Paradise from heaven to earth was for the gods merely to undergo the drastic delimitation of their scope of consciousness necessary to achieve incorporation in bodies of lower capacity.

The baptism or deluge from above on life below was well imaged by the Nile inundation in Egypt. The fresh water poured down from heaven in the upper ranges of the hills of source in Central Africa and flooded the land of Lower Egypt. And whether one takes this deluge in an evil or a good sense is only a matter of judging temporary burial of the land against lasting enrichment. Similarly with

434

the human deluge. It flooded lower man, but with the waters of more abundant life. It is as the gentle rain from heaven, that blesses the earth. The deluge was the descent of the *fiery* solar god, through the *air,* in the form of *water* to nourish and make fertile the *earth*. And this is the outward description of the history of the human soul. Likewise it was the central theme of Mystery drama.

The mount of heaven was the original place of bliss and security; later the mount of earth became the refuge of safety. It afforded a firm landing place for souls destined to wrestle with matter's inertia to achieve greater power.

The sunken Eden is not a stranger to Bible pages. It is definitely alluded to by Ezekiel as lying in the nether parts of the earth, typed now as Assyria instead of the usual Egypt:

"To whom art thou thus like in glory and in greatness among the trees of Eden? Yet shalt thou be brought down with the trees of Eden into the nether parts of the earth. Thou shalt be there in the midst of the uncircumcised"—obviously the still animal races.

The Ovaherero, an African tribe, say that the sky was once let down in a deluge by which the greater part of mankind was drowned. This falls into agreement with the general Egyptian conception of the downfall of stellar hosts due to the shifting of the polar axis and the resultant dropping of many stars below the horizon. All this was set forth in Egypt as the superseding of the earlier gods, Nnu, Seb, Shu and Taht by Ra, the supreme god of Intelligence, or their reduction to subserviency under him. Ra rose to hegemony over all the elemental powers when he "resolved to be lifted up in an ark or sanctuary." This was the spiritual inner body of light now being formed within us, as Paul says, in which the principle of Mind could rule the natural creation in and through man.

The deluge from heaven brought down seven great powers to be submerged under the lower waters. The seven great pole stars fell one after the other, as the end of each aeon brought a shift in the axis. At each turn of the cycles one of the seven mountains was submerged, one of the seven provinces inundated, one of the seven rulers dethroned. These seven were imaged under many forms of description, as seven kings, seven heads, seven horns, seven mountains, seven islands, seven lampstands, seven stars, seven eyes, seven pillars and

435

seven angels. The dragon that falls from heaven and goes to perdition is none other than these seven collectively. The fall of the seven as islands sinking in the abyss is stated with surprising clearness in *Revelation* (16:20): "Every island fled away and the mountains were not found." They had gone down to earth. We have seen that the mountain went down into the sea and turned it into blood.

In Wales there is the legend of the destruction of the seven divisions or provinces of Dyfed, when the drunken Seithenkin let in the deluge and drowned the land. The Mangaians recognize the seven islands of the Hervey group as the seven islands of Savaiki (Sevekh!), which they say lie in the underworld, or beneath the waters.

We read of the "deluge that afflicted the intrepid dragon." The seven heads of the Dragon were cut off one by one and thrown down as the seven cycles rolled around. The crowning stroke of creational activity was the dethronement of the last of the elemental seven by the solar god, who slew and succeeded the Dragon, after cutting off its seven heads. The overthrow of the Dragon by the solar god is one of the most ancient traditions of Greece. Apollo overcame the Dragon and took his place as guardian and inspirer of the oracle. In Babylonia Bel became a solar god and conquered the Dragon. Michael conquered him in *Revelation*. In the place of the outcast seven powers, devils, giants, ogres, "the god of the bright crown created mankind." This was the seventh creation, and astronomically it was marked by the the passage of the pole from Lyra, the Harp, into the constellation of Herakles, the man, typing the inception of the reign of intelligence.

One of the labors of the all-conquering sun in his journey through the underworld is to obtain command over the lower water. One of his claims to vindication at the judgment is that he has prevailed over the deluge! In the *Ritual* (Ch. 136A) there is this: "He turneth back the water flood which is over the thigh of the goddess Nut at the staircase of Seb"—or the ascending grades of evolution on earth, in the thigh or womb of matter.

The Nile inundation began in late June (Cancer) and was pouring out the fullness of its waters in July, the sign of the Lion. Hence the universally adopted symbol of the lion, or two lions, from whose mouths gush streams of water in fountains!

Horus, who was born of the water, has given his name to the month in which the waters of the inundation have their birth in Egypt. June

436

in Egyptian nomenclature is *Mesore. Mes* is "to be born," "to be reborn"; *Hor(Har)* is the divine child, Har-Makhu, Har-Tema. *Mes-Hor* or *Mesore* is, then, the godly child born of the June waters. Many hints in old tomes point to the sign of Scorpio (October-November) as the true beginning of the year. This was in congruity with the typology of the Nile flood, as the inundated earth re-emerged from the waters at that time. In sculptures at Karnak the autumn equinox is represented as one of the divinities and the first month of the year; the vernal equinox appearing as the seventh month, when the seven principles of deity were born, or perfected.

From the deluge imagery rises the symbolism of a ladder, mound or tower, tree or rock, that should be built high enough to be beyond the reach of flooding waters. This is but another variant of the Rock of Ages, that eternal principle of divinity in man, which though cast into the midst of the sea of turbulent natural forces, becomes the ark of safety or the rock of stability outlasting all decay and movement. *Bab-El* means "the gate of God," and equates Cancer in the zodiac, the northern gate of heaven. In the cyclic round of incarnations the soul ascends after each dip into matter and resurrection therefrom up to the high gate of heaven to dwell in the bosom of deity. But as the summer turns to fall, it is cast down again to earth, its unitary mentality is dissipated and its divine unity of speech scattered into many various dialects.

A Thlinkeet tradition recounts a deluge from which men saved themselves in a large floating structure. When the waters subsided the building drove on a rock and broke in two by its own weight. There is a detail omitted from the Ararat story in *Genesis*. Again it corroborates the reading of the earth for Mount Ararat, as deity does break into two aspects, male and female, when it lands on earth. This bifurcation is the meaning of the first verse of *Genesis*, "heaven" and "earth" standing for spirit and matter.

An Indian saga says that in the deluge a virgin caught hold of the foot of a bird as it flew above her and was carried up out of the water where all were drowning. As the bird is the universal image of the soul, the implication is that man's lower nature saves itself by catching hold of the foot (heel?) of the soul's power as it sweeps down close to the level of physical life and being lifted up thereby.

But a strange and at first unaccountable element of mystery and

437

oddity enters the many deluge traditions with the frequent mention of the monkey. For instance, the Tlascalans say that after the deluge those who were preserved were changed into monkeys, who later evolved into human beings. In the *Codex Chimalpopoca* the result of the great hurricane was to change men into monkeys (Bancroft). A belief of the Catalans is that after the deluge those who had been previously changed into monkeys were subsequently transformed into men. An Arawak rendering is very curious. It recites that the waters had been confined in the hollow bole of an enormous tree by means of an inverted basket. The mischievous monkey saw the basket and believing it contained something good to eat, he lifted it up, whereupon the deluge burst out from the tree. A Guiana story runs much to the same effect. The waters were pent up in the stem of the tree of life, to be let forth in appropriate measure to fill every lake and stream with water for the fish. But Warika, the mischievous monkey, forced open the magic cover that held back the waters, which then gushed out to sweep away not only the meddling culprit, but all living things besides. The points of similarity of these fables with that of Pandora should be noted. Many other legends charge the monkey with being the villain in the deluge piece.

What is the significance of this connection? In the cosmic sense adumbrated by the astrological mythology, Hapi, the ape, was one of the four (of the seven) elemental powers holding up the four corners of the earth. The Kaf-Ape, Hapi, personated the element of air, and it is from the powers embosomed in the air that an outpouring of water takes form. Hapi is typed as the fury of the air in motion, engendering the hurricane and the deluge. Hurricane, we have seen, is a derivative of the name of the Quiché deity of the storm wind, *Hurakan* (French *ouragan*), he who brought life to man through breath, Shu. The ape was the zoötype of Shu. Hapi, the Ape, is one of the four who are, in Ezekiel's vision, the eagle, bull, lion and man; in *Revelation* the lion, calf, bird and man; and in Egypt Amsta, Hapi, Tuamutef and Kabhsenuf. Amsta was the human, Hapi, the ape, Tuamutef the jackal and Kabhsenuf the hawk. These, so mystifying and so confusedly presented in various forms, must be conceived to represent the four basic supports of man's life, the four elemental essences, earth, water, air and fire, of each of which substances man has a body. These four are placed symbolically at the four corners

438

or cardinal points of the zodiac, the two solstices and equinoxes. Massey locates Hapi, the ape, at the autumn equinox, yet in the tables of the four elementaries he is found at the spring equinox. His position on the horizon at the equinox is vastly appropriate. The horizon is the dividing line between two realms, and the monkey stands there as the type of man because he himself is on the dividing line between the animal and the human kingdom, and thus symbols man, who in his turn is on the dividing line between the human and the divine.

Yet it is possible that still another meaning of momentous import lurks behind the figure of the monkey in deluge mythology. The culpability of the monkey may be seen from the angle of anthropology. In other connections reference has already been made to the "harlotry" so vehemently reprobated by the Lord in the *Old Testament,* and to the miscegenation perpetrated by the early sons of God with some of the higher animals after the descent. The result of this transgression of natural restrictions upon procreation was the generation of the various monkey types. They were the offspring of male humans and female animals, according to much evidence in such old books as *Enoch,* the *Avesta,* the *Gilgamesh Epic,* the *Bundahish* and the *Vedas.* The monkey is by parentage equally man and beast, and can stand as the type of man, who is man and god together. When the legends hint that the result of the deluge was to change men into monkeys, and as in one version to restore men, changed into monkeys, back to human form, it is, in the guise of a Märchen, the statement of a great anthropological datum, for the truth of which science is still groping. The gods were told not "to marry the women of that place" or to "make alliances with the natives of that land." But it seems they did so, and the miscegenation that is marked by the existence of the monkey was apparently used to typify the letting loose the deluge of carnal lust that swept over the world in consequence. The monkey would therefore vividly personify the deluge that swept the gods down to the very depths of sensuous riot. He would stand as the badge of the god's biological sin, that released the flood of the lower waters to enmire the feet of deity, and bring the "destruction" of mankind. Archaic fable reports that early races and continents had to be destroyed as a result of the breach in evolutionary law, for it is stated that there were bred monsters terrible and great. Paul has told us that wickedness changed the image of the incorruptible god into the likeness of loathsome beasts and creeping things. The monkey is the living sign of this degradation.

.   .   .   .

There has been substantially covered the body of arcane · wisdom touching the coming of transcendent celestial power to earth to perform a mighty segment of evolutionary work in this sphere. The god had descended to the bottom of his arc, his evolutionary nadir, and would go no further. He stands at that point poised in the balance with material inertia, gripped in the tentacles of matter, locked in a tense struggle with opposing powers. He is engaged in the great Battle of Armageddon, which is fought, says the *Ritual*, at midnight and on the horizon. To modern thought, for the first time, is to be revealed the momentous significance of the mighty Egyptian symbol of the Horizon.

Chapter XVIII

THE LAKE OF EQUIPOISE

MAN on earth is an epitome of the zodiacal or heavenly man, and the zodiac has depths of meaning for the mind of man that are still unfathomed. The twelve signs, the four quarters, the twenty-four "elders," the thirty regents, the thirty-six rulers, the seventy-two messengers and other numerical divisions have each their special significance in the total of twelve times thirty degrees. And all of these are prominent throughout the Bible to mystify the unenlightened. Of particular illumination to the mind is the study of the four "corners," the points where the four arms of the cross in the circle intersect the circumference, that is, at the two solstices and the two equinoxes. The "story of mankind," collectively and individually, is both concealed and revealed in the recondite significance of these four poles. The story will remain sealed in dark unintelligibility until the four cardinal points of the zodiac are seen to denote four critical epochs in the life of evolving man, namely, his entry into the four planes of consciousness,—sensation, emotion, thought and spiritual intuition, on and over which his life of awareness extends. Any life cycle exhibits these four turning points, so that the zodiacal chart will be seen to be a key to living process universally.

With this fundamentum in mind it will be advantageous to present a group of other cycles or processes in life and nature which manifest the division of wholes into four-part segmentation:

YEAR: .... June 21.	September 21.	December 21.	March 21.
CARDINAL POINTS: .. North.	West.	South.	East.
DAY: .... Noon.	Evening.	Midnight.	Morning.
ZODIAC: .... Cancer.	Libra.	Capricorn.	Aries.
ELEMENTS: ...... Fire.	Earth.	Water.	Air.
MOON CYCLE: .... Full Moon	Last Quarter.	Dark Moon.	First Quarter.
ANIMAL SYMBOL: .. Man.	Beast.	Fish.	Bird.
KINGDOM: .... Human.	Mineral.	Vegetable.	Animal.

FOETAL CYCLE:	Love.	Impregnation.	Quickening.	Birth.
HUMAN LIFE:	Death	Birth.	Puberty.	Adulthood.
THEOLOGY:	Descent.	Incarnation.	Awakening.	Resurrection.
FESTIVALS:	Fire Festival	Michaelmas.	Christmas.	Easter.
MYSTERY FIGURE:	Harlequin.	Pantaloon.	Columbine.	Clown.
EGYPTIAN GOD:	Ra.	Seb.	Uati.	Shu.

This chart may seem to many like the work of sheer analogistic fancy. If so, it is to be remembered that nature, life and mind are constantly playing at this game of correspondences: Mind can discern at every turn the analogies between nature and life, life and truth. All ranges of life are illuminated by the light of the universal parallelism that shows all orders of being to be cognate. The point of value here is that these correspondences are distinctly traceable in the cycles indicated and that they introduce a certain systematism and provide a norm for our perception of times, seasons, periodicities and epochs. By means of what is known of one cycle new meaning may be discerned in another less directly observable. A thorough knowledge of one operation becomes a clue to all others. Taken in relation to the significance of the four cardinal points, the line bisecting the zodiacal circle horizontally from east to west, or Aries to Libra, or March to September, is to be regarded as the "Horizon" of Egyptian symbolism, which will be found to bear the burden of such mighty meaning for mankind.

It will be seen that the June quarter of the circle suggests the point of ideal conception in the noumenal world, when as yet no relation to matter or body has been established. The September point marks the entry of the ideal form into matter in embryo—incarnation, the Word beginning to put on flesh. Here matter and spirit join, or spirit is submerged in matter. December, to our enlightenment, marks the point of the awakening or germination of life after death under matter's power. This is particularly well seen in the foetal cycle in what is called the "quickening" of the child in the womb half way through the gestation period. If Christmas is celebrated in the December solstice, its meaning can not be strictly that of the "birth" of the Christ in humanity, but rather its quickening after torpidity, preparatory to its true birth at Easter. For then delivery from the womb of matter takes place, introducing the Mother's child into a higher world of consciousness. The point of release from earth and body is at the March equinox, not at December. And, strangely enough, roughly for three and a half centuries the early Christian Church celebrated the birth of the Savior on March 25! A decree of Pope Julian in 345 A.D. fixed the date authoritatively for the first time at December 25. The sun, of course, is reborn at the December solstice, but his victory is not won until he conquers darkness finally on the horizon line of March 21. The spring equinox is the point of ultimate triumph of spirit over matter and its return to the kingdom of the Father.

Yet very markedly each of the four cardinal crises represents a "birth" for man. At each "corner" of his evolutionary cycle man was born afresh into a higher world of being. This is especially reflected in the four turns of the foetal cycle. June represents the first "birth" of the child, which really takes place when the husband falls in love with her who is to be his wife. The child is then conceived noumenally. The second "birth" falls at September when the father's seed joins with the ovum and fertilizes it. The third comes with the quickening in the womb, when that which showed no life stirs into activity, at December. And the March date brings the final stage of birth in the child's delivery. The four stages are: the ideal conception in love's mind; the actual junction of spirit with matter; the quickening to life after apparent death; and the final victory in release from matter. Transferred to theology these basic conceptions yield a wealth of new discernment.

The four great early religious festivals are important. Only two of the four original celebrations survive in the Church calendar, prominently. We have only the shadow of the former great autumn equinox solemnization in our Hallowe'en on October 31, removed just forty days from the autumn equinox, this period being the true Lent. It was the primal celebration of the death and burial of the god in body. Then came Christmas at the winter solstice, Easter at the vernal equinox, and in June the great fire festival, revived recently by the return to "pagan" ideals in Germany, and perpetuated down to the present in a few parts of Ireland. The September festival commemorated the birth of spirit or soul *into* flesh; the spring equinox denoted the second birth, or birth *out of* body into a higher world. The upper half of the circle of signs is the home of soul when detached from flesh, and floating free, in bodies of light, in the empyrean; the lower half is its earthy and watery home when immersed in body. Most of

443

the meaning for humanity obviously lies below the line, or at least upon the surface of the water of this life, which surface is marked by the horizon line, which is the boundary between the two realms. Whether advancing clockwise or downward to the left, we enter body on the west; we leave it on the east to join the gods above. "Pepi saileth with Ra to the east of heaven, where the gods are born." The Egyptian statement is that "the Heavenly Man faces South." Having climbed the steep of heaven and passed through the Babel gate in Cancer, he turns to look down upon the world of matter below, and thus faces "south." Yet the north was considered the "hinder part of heaven," and the counterpart cosmically of the physical portion of universal life. It was the womb or navel of the world of life, and for this reason the constellation of the Great Bear(er) was denominated the *Meskhen,* or Thigh of the old genetrix. Life was spiritual (masculine) in the front part of its organism and material (feminine) in the hinder part. And the Eternal told Moses (man) that he dared look only on that hinder part, the glory of deity's face being overpowering. When the Egyptians portrayed life and man as dual under the form of double animal types, such creatures were always male in front and female behind. The Sphinx is so constructed. If the north is the region of matter and the south that of spirit, then conceivably the heavenly man would look away from the former to the latter. The symbolism that for early ages went with the directions and antithesis of north and south later swung about and came under the typology of west and east direction.

The important fact emerging from all this specification is that man is born *au naturel* when he enters incarnate life on the west as a falling star or setting sun; and that he is reborn *au spirituel* when he leaves fleshly life finally on the east with the rising sun of a new epoch. He is born a man on the west, and a god on the east.

If all this seems too finely spun for serious consideration, let the incredulous reader be shocked to hear that it was through losing sight of the analogies connected with this symbolical chart that the Christians actually placed one or more of their most important church festivals on the wrong side of the year! The forty-days' fast of Lent, for instance, has been placed at a season in which it is utterly out of fitting relation to the natural symbolism of the solar year.

Since the number forty alphabetized in symbolic script the period

444

of gestation of soul in matter, it was chosen as the time for fasting and abasement. This fasting is but another glyph for the privation and lack of true spiritual being suffered by the god in the flesh. Forty days of lamentation and grief were set aside to commemorate the death and burial of the sun-god and the shrouding of his light in the tomb of matter. For ten thousand years B.C. it was part of the celebration of the cult of Iusa, the ever-coming or annually-coming solar god, to keep the forty days and nights in which the sun-hero in the underworld fought the battle with Sut and his Sebau "fiends," in the desert of Amenta. Forty days was the period of seclusion after childbirth appointed for the women by Parsee and Levitical law. In the transformation of Apis, when the old bull died, its successor remained forty days shut up on an island in the Nile. The spies sent out returned after forty days. For forty days Goliath came out to fight each day (*I Samuel*: 17). David reigned forty years. Moses was with Jehovah in the Mount forty days and nights. Jesus was forty days on earth after his resurrection. Forty appears in the *Old Testament* some sixty-three times. Forty days was the length of the incubation period of grain in the mud and water before germinating in Egypt; and the human foetus gestates forty weeks. The period of forty days after the planting was a time of scarcity and fasting, which, says Massey, gave a very natural significance to the season of Lent, with its mourning for the dead Osiris, to be followed by rejoicing when the grain germinated. This was transferred to the Hebrew Gospels and became a fast of forty days during which Jesus wrestled with Satan and was hungry.

By every intimation of logic and analogy, Lent should follow, not precede, the burial of the solar god. Only by typing the soul as the seed planted in early spring could it have any natural appropriateness. Christians start in late winter to mourn the death of a god who, according to their own calendar had not yet died, but who, by the calendars of the ancients, had died, under solar symbolism, in the preceding autumn! In spite of the fact that many trace the word "Lent" to the German *Lens*, meaning "spring," the season of bursting new life is utterly inappropriate to the spirit of such a festival. The death which is placed by Christian error just prior to the Easter resurrection, is thus made to fall in the zodiacal season when all nature is approaching the consummation of her effort to release—not to kill and bury—the solar Christ! All is sadly awry here. Nature herself writes the mark of error upon the Christian Lent in the spring. Whatever the word "Lent" may mean, the spirit of the commemoration is that of sorrow and lament for the Christ crucified and buried. This is appropriate to the autumn season, when "the melancholy days have come," and quite out of harmony with the spirit of nature in the spring. In the vernal season all life is being reborn; the intrusion of the idea of death into the midst of nature's happy rejuvenescence is a monstrous anachronism and ineptitude. The ancients celebrated the Lord's death and burial (in the grave of matter only) for forty days following the September equinox, the period ending on October 31, the date of our Hallowe'en. This is the true Lent, no matter how it is taken. The waning sun of autumn is the natural hieroglyph of the Christ's crucifixion and death, and it is a foul blasphemy against the rhythmic soul of life to send the human spirit into the doldrums of misplaced grief and maudlin sympathy with imagined suffering when grass is greening and earth is opening the tomb of winter's death for her annual resurrection. Only if it types the god-soul under the symbol of the grain lying six weeks or forty-two days in the earth before re-arising can it escape reprobation. Its only other point of fitness is that it does end with the glory-burst of the resurrection on Eastern morn.

The Christians took all three of the numbers denoting the imprisonment of life in physical form—three, seven and forty—and placed periods of three, seven and forty days respectively in the spring at such times that the terminal of each of the three periods fell simultaneously on Easter morning. This is the only extenuating feature of the fixture. In mythical import the entire half year from September to March is the period betokening the death of the god in matter or human life. But it would be most unphilosophical for us to give half of each year to gloom even for symbolism. However, by all the intimations of typology the crucifixion should be in the fall and the resurrection at Easter. And so it was with the ancients.

With his own symbol, the sun, the sun-god plunged into death with the sunset and the autumn waning. The Tuat, the gate of entry to Amenta, was approached at eventide or in autumn on the western side. A commonplace expression for death found in the *Ritual* and other scriptures of old is "going west." Abraham went west from Ur, to descend into Egypt. The setting sun or expiring day is the universal poetry for death, which our study discloses to be not extinction but incarnation, or life in the actual. The Hallowe'en, or All Souls' Night, was the primeval commemoration of this event, and became in the course of blunted perception and obscuration of pristine motifs, a motley blending of mummery, buffoonery, witchery and dark magic. The keynote of the celebration was struck in the masking behind animal features! This was the plainest kind of language saying that the gods had taken residence in animal bodies! They were down here on earth disguised as animals! They had clothed themselves in "coats of skin," more bluntly, the hides of animals. They had hid themselves behind a false face. And with their true nature almost obliterated by the animal covering, they could but make ridiculous grimaces and awkward gestures through the coarse vestments of flesh. Distorted by the animal nature, "marred in his visage, deformed out of the semblance of a man" (*Isaiah*), the god was little better than a clown cavorting ludicrously on earth behind the beastly exterior. All his efforts to express his more lordly selfhood came forth in weird and uncouth jargon. The Hallowe'en buffoonery is all too realistically a depiction of the soul's antics and gambols when first incorporated in body.

Likewise the suits of divided color worn at the occasion tell clearer than words the dual nature of the human, when, on this night, god and animal became tenants of the same household, and shared each a half of man's nature.

That there was confusion in Christian counsels as to the appropriate date of the annual festivals is indicated by the following passage from Massey:

"But there was a diversity of opinion amongst the Christian Fathers as to whether Jesus the Christ was born in the winter solstice or in the vernal equinox. It was held by some that the twenty-fifth of March was the natal day. Others maintained that this was the day of the incarnation. According to Clement of Alexandria the birth of Jesus took place on the twenty-fifth of March. But in Rome the festival of Lady Day was celebrated on the twenty-fifth of March in commemoration of the miraculous conception in the womb of the virgin, which virgin gave birth to a child at Christmas, nine months afterwards. According to the *Gospel of James* (Ch. 18) it was in the equinox, and consequently not at Christmas, that the virgin birth took place." [1]

447

The early Fathers commemorated the death of the sun-god in a seven-days' ceremonial called the *Fetes de Tenebres,* or festival of darkness and gloom, which, according to the eminent Egyptologist Brugsch, commemorated the "seven days which he passed in the womb of his mother, Nut," or the seven elementary kingdoms so often mentioned. Perhaps this was the remote origin of the "Ember Days," when the light of the god glowed nearly extinguished, a mere ember.

We come at last to grips with the colossal significance of the horizon symbol. Here there is offered by ancient Egypt a feast of enlightenment rich beyond expectation. The horizon and the equinox! In these zodiacal and seasonal positions, symbolizing both the same inner data, man will find the delineation of his nature and mission with clearer specification than in elaborate treatises on the subject. The horizon and equinox lines tell of man's definite place in evolution and in nature, and announce most distinctly the terms of his progress. The horizon symbol becomes the open sesame to the clarification of more religious doctrinism than perhaps any other natural feature. There is concealed under it the key to whole segments of the Egyptian texts, the true apprehension of whose meaning has not yet been achieved by modern exegesis. Indeed, the proper elucidation of the meaning of the sun standing on the two horizons, or at the two equinoxes, may be said to be the first actual unlocking of the mysteries of ancient scripture and secret teachings. The very heart of the mystery is enwrapped in the translation of the import of this natural datum and the texts dealing with it. The whole status of man's life on earth is interblended with the oft-repeated reference to "Horus of the Two Horizons." The release of this hidden truth to modern knowledge will necessitate the revision of much misguided theological dogmatism and will sweep away errors of ghastly consequence in history. Perhaps the opening of this closed mine of priceless intelligence may even awaken the age to a new consciousness of humanity's mission and a new inspiration to achieve it.

The prologue to the discussion of the location of Amenta in an earlier chapter emphasized the truth that religion had been instituted by its sagacious founders to focus man's efforts upon the energization of his life here on earth. It was pointed out that earth was the critical of human destiny. The location of Amenta on this earth, instead true heavens, was held to be the most vital determination in

448

the field of religion since the third century. What was there fundamentally posited on strong supports receives its final and unimpeachable confirmation in the implications of the horizon and equinox symbology. The single word "horizon" is perhaps fraught with more cogent meaning than any other term in religious usage.

The solution of the mystery behind this symbol may be advantageously approached through the interpretation of some arithmetic cryptically presented in the *Books of Daniel, Ezekiel* and *Revelation*. Particularly in the eleventh and twelfth chapters of the last-named there are given three numbers, the recondite import of which hints at the horizon meaning. The three numbers are twelve hundred and sixty, forty-two and three and one-half. The first is connected with days, the second with months and the third with days and years. To the casual reader the three numbers as they occur in the verses of the text seem hopelessly mystifying. They seem to refer to a period of duress, captivity or suspension of activity, or exile. It all seems like some mathematical legerdemain that is insoluble. But a little speculation quickly reveals that the three numbers are a numerical periphrasis for the basic one which carries the meaning, namely, three and a half. Twelve hundred and sixty days is found to be forty-two months (of 30 days each), and that in turn is three and a half years. One of the presentations of three and a half is in the famous "for a time, and times, and half a time," which can at least mean one, plus two, plus one-half; and nothing else certainly. But, if all the numbers given resolve into three and a half, what is *its* great significance?

Here some details of ancient cosmological systematism are necessary to find a positive clue. But the whole mystery breaks clear in the light of the fact that three and a half is one half of seven! A simple fact is this, yet it is the great key to our understanding the real meaning of scriptures. If, as is subtly intimated in these texts, man's position is at a place cryptically marked by the number three and a half in a seven-cycle series, then it is clear that the esoteric information purveyed to the astute is that man stands at a point which is half way through his entire cycle. His position is just half way between the two ends of the scale or gamut of being. And precisely this is what is conveyed by both the numerical and the horizontal suggestions. Three and a half is at the half way point between the upper and lower termini of a seven series. And the horizon is half way between heaven and earth, typing, as always, spirit and matter, the two ends of being. The momentous information, then, which is vouchsafed to man in this recondite fashion is that he, as a creature in a stupendous cyclical evolution, stands at the point exactly midway between the beginning and the end of the complete area to be traversed. Man is half way through his evolution and stands at its midmost point.

Several deductions at once flow from this datum. The first is that the line marking off three and a half stages in seven would equate the horizon line in the zodiacal chart, and that this fateful line would at the same time mark the boundary between the two natures in man's constitution, the earthly and the heavenly. It would indicate the border line where the two natures, separated by life's aboriginal act of bifurcation into spirit and matter, remain contiguous to each other. It would be the fence between the two kingdoms, from the opposite sides of which they face each other. If there is warfare between the two, this would be the battle line, the front of the Battle of Armageddon. And amazingly does the *Ritual* say that this aeonial conflict is fought on the horizon! At last weird speculation as to the meaning and location of a pertinent Biblical symbol is settled by, and as, a bit of Egyptian imagery.

The implication is clearly, then, that man was taught that he stands on his evolutionary boundary line between the immortal nature of spirit and the mortal nature of material body. He stands directly on the line between the two great kingdoms into which life split itself in the *arche*. And the further deduction is that he stands in two worlds at once. Put differently, it can be said that the two worlds are in him, the world of spirit localized or functioning in the upper half of his body, and that of matter's powers centered in the lower half. So that now it becomes possible to read greater cogency into the many Egyptian statements that man lives in heaven by virtue of his soul faculties, and on earth by virtue of his bodily senses. His soul is in heaven with Ra, and his body on earth in the form of an animal, asserts the text. Man stands with both feet in the "grave," but his soul is in heaven. And to crown this knowledge with inspiring impressiveness, it is intimated that he is the only creature in existence that stands at this pivotal and strategic place in all evolution! For he is the only being in whose constitution spirit and matter meet to affect each other in exactly equal measure. Even the angels are said to envy man from their seats, for man's experience will put him ahead of them. "Know ye not," says St. Paul, "that we are to manage angels, let alone mundane affairs?" And "he hath made man *for a little while* lower than the angels" (Moffatt trans.), to crown him eventually with greater glory and honor than theirs.

It follows likewise from the terms of the situation that the horizon line is precisely the point at which the two elements of soul and flesh are in exact equilibration with each other. If man stands at the middle point in his journey from matter back to spirit, then he is also at the point where the two nodes of his being, spirit and matter, exactly counterbalance each other in efficacious influence. And this at once opens the way for the introduction of the whole range of symbolic values connected with the sign of Libra, the Scales of the Balance, and the Scales of the Judgment. And precisely at the horizon's western terminus stands the Libra sign! The Judgment is a corollary aspect of the horizon typism and will be treated in a following chapter.

The sun standing on the horizon line at evening and morning, autumn and spring, is the graphic symbol of man's position in the universe of flowing life. For the horizon marks the dividing line between heaven and earth, so that man stands directly on the line between the heaven of spiritual consciousness and the earth of physical being. He bestrides this evolutionary horizon line and finds his living activity and expression equally measured between the two kingdoms. No more lively utterance of this fact could be had than the statement of the *Book of the Dead* that man "cultivates the crops on both sides of the horizon." This advises us that we are farmers of both a spiritual and a physico-sensual domain. And we reap the harvests both in Amenta and in the Aarru-Hetep or fields or peace. Man's sovereignty extends across both sides of life's total area. He occupies the Two Lands, or Upper and Lower Egypt. And after long cycles it will be his prerogative to settle the aeonial warfare between these two provinces of his nature, reconcile them in harmony, and finally unify them under his single spiritual lordship. Straight and clear is Egypt's proclamation of this sterling truth: "He cultivates the Two Lands; he pacifies the Two Lands; he unites the Two Lands." Man is "the god of the two mysterious horizons," and the glowing pronouncement of his final evolutionary triumph is given in the words: "Thou illuminest the Two Lands like the Disk at daybreak."

451

Ancient scripts set forth repeatedly that in the middle of the "fourth watch of the night" of every sevenfold cycle in evolution's recurrent rounds of manifestation, the hidden and latent power of spiritual mind comes, as it were, walking out on the surface of the sea of life, to quiet its chaotic tempest and harmonize its contending forces and elements. The fourth watch in the night of incarnate evolution would be the human kingdom, following the mineral, vegetable and animal. Every creative life wave building a globe and an evolution of life and consciousness on it does its work in seven successive releases or impulses of its power. It works through six creations before it can crown its effort with the establishment of mind as king and conscious ruler of all lower energies, in the seventh and last round. But the first six of these efforts work for the creation of material substance and organic forms built from it, the last and highest of which forms is to be brought to capability of embodying the kingly mind. And the first three formative impulses work with matter in its sub-atomic states, which are in the invisible world. The first stirs up inchoate formless root-substance; the second separates, as the white and yolk of an egg, the two basic elements into opposite sides of polarity; the third granulates the substantial essence of the material half. It is not until the forth wave strikes that matter is brought out onto the stage of visible substantiality, in the elements of the mineral kingdom on earth. The fifth wave raises mineral elements to organic structure of the vegetable type, and the sixth lifts these up to the forms of animal bodies. Only in the seventh comes man, whose physical vehicle is to be the cradle of the Christ child of divine Intelligence. Man stands therefore at the summit of the material creation. He is the Egyptian Iu-em-Hetep, the deity that comes *seventh* to make *peace,* and rule the six (or seven) lower elements. But the seventh wave comes midway in the fourth kingdom, or at the point of three and one half.

But the summit of the material creation is just under the foot, or *heel,* of the spiritual kingdom. And man is the union of the highest physical potency with the lowest divine consciousness, and he therefore stands on the horizon line dividing spirit and matter, and so bears the title: "Lord of the Two Halves of Egypt."

The three activities of life energy taking root-matter through its three primary formative stages in the invisible world prepare finally the mineral kingdom on a globe—Earth—which represents the nadir of descent of life energization in dense matter. Life has descended to its deepest death in matter in the mineral state. Its involution ends there, and its evolution through form begins. The mineral kingdom, therefore, is the lowest plane of created matter. We count upward from it. The vegetable is the second, the animal the third, and the human is the fourth evolutionary kingdom, though it brings man on the crest of the seventh wave of life force. And it is in the middle of the human kingdom—certainly not at its beginning—that the Christ divinity comes out on the surface of conscious existence and takes responsible control of the processes thenceforth. Arcane texts state that humanity itself has subsisted through three great cycles of development from rudimentary state as human, and is now in the middle of the fourth round. We stand exactly at the line marking three and one-half stages of the entire life cycle on earth, or succinctly at the middle of the fourth human energization, which in turn is in the middle of the fourth natural kingdom of life expression on this globe. And never a Christian priest in sixteen centuries has told his flock why the number three and a half occurs in the middle of the *Book of Revelation*. It may be helpful to attempt a diagram that will, crudely enough, delineate the rationale of the seven and the three and a half in the scheme of evolution.

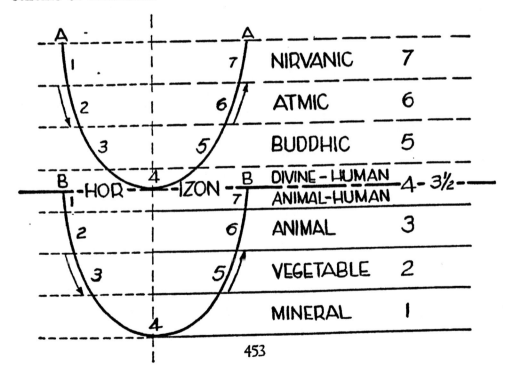

The curved line B B represents the dip of the wave of purely matter-building energy, unconscious and controlled by higher agents of the hierarchy, into the heart of matter. It goes as low as the bottom of the mineral kingdom, and there turns to return—its Mount Sinai. A A represents the dip of the unit of divine self-consciousness into matter. Since it can not be embodied in a form less complex and responsive than the human body, it reaches its nadir of descent in the human body at its mid point of development, and so goes into its Mount Sinai exactly on the horizon line. And there it begins its aeonial "warfare" to regenerate the animal. As the chart will reveal, there are three and a half stages of purely spiritual evolution to be accomplished from our present station. We are on the horizon, where animal dominance ends and spiritual governance begins.

It will be found extremely enlightening to juxtapose Paul's statement (*Ephesians* 2) that a "middle wall of partition between us"—between our two natures—will in the end be broken down, permitting the Two Lands to unite under one sovereignty, beside Jesus' anthropological declaration to his disciples, "I am from above; ye are from beneath." The Christ here announces that he is the god above the horizon, while the natural man, disciple or learner, is the creature below it. Man is created when the life force has evolved organic fleshly structure up to the point of capability of becoming a fit living dynamo for spiritual forces. Then, with affinities established, the Christ principle can descend and tabernacle with flesh. Man then occupies the most strategic point in evolution. For he can pit the two nodes of life in equilibration and mutuality against each other, and effectuate that balance and intercourse between them which is the prime prerequisite for the birthing of the next generation of ongoing life. The balance, the warfare, the friction, the alternate bruising of head and heel, is the condition basic for the new propagation. This situation outlines a whole vast portion of the theological field and covers wide ranges of salient meaning.

Theology has gone on blindly for centuries, never dreaming that the zodiacal sign of Libra was all the while the cryptic sign and seal of the great doctrine of the Judgment, and that man was being weighed in the scales of the living balance between spirit and matter in the life in body. Emerson writes that "man stands midway betwixt the inner spirit and the outer matter." The name for the Norse region of life where man dwelt was Midgard, or the middle ground. Man's life *is* the Libra Scales. Through him as a gate, unseen spirit steps forth for the first time in evolution onto the plane of open conscious being in a world constituted of matter. It comes out of the depths onto the surface, from submergence in earth and water into the light of the air and the sun, and walks on the water. It is only in man that soul wakes from dreamy semi-consciousness to exert its creative powers upon and through matter in world structure, in co-operation with God. Man is the channel through which every portion of spiritual intelligence must pass to be transformed from sheer potentiality to actual dynamism. The kingdom of the human is the only breeding ground in which the ungerminated seed of munificent divine being can be incubated, hatched and grown to maturity of self-conscious rulership in the cosmic field. All higher ranks of angels, gods, thrones and dominions have once been men on some former planetary stage, and we present men shall rise in time to grandeur, while the dull brutes below us will tread the ascending path in our wake.

One aspect of the typology touches the opposition of light and darkness. The sun on the horizon is midway between the kingdom of light and that of darkness, as it appears to man's view. It therefore stands in the twilight. Human life is similarly environed. It stands halfway between full spiritual light and complete material darkness. We are the gods in the twilight. We are neither in gross darkness nor in undimmed splendor. Oddly enough the Talmud preserved the statement that the tabernacle which man was ordered by deity to build was to be erected "half in light and half in shade." The equal arms of the cross likewise carry the same idea of balance between dark and light. And the cross was set up on a hill, the hill of the horizon. The Scales on the horizon were the cross on the hill. Horus and horizon both spell *hor*, which is the same as *hel*, and means "light." *Izon* is in all probability the Greek *ison*, meaning "equal." So then we have the horizon as the place of equal light and darkness, as in the day period on September 21 and March 21.

Salvation is won on the cross because the place of preservation, in the *Ritual*, is stated to be where "the body and soul are *united to be saved.*" Death on the cross of matter, as we have clarified previously, is at the same time the preservation of the soul's integrity. It was earth, the region of twilight, that opened its gates and cities of refuge to the mother fleeing with her sun-child from the Dragon of Necessity. A quotation from Massey will prove timely:

"The opening of the mount is in the equinox, and it is there the pursued ones attain safety by entering the earth to escape from Apap, the devouring dragon. Seb is the Egyptian Joseph, as the consort of Isis, the earth mother, and foster-father of the child; and at this point in the western equinox where Horus enters the earth or earth-life, Seb, as god of earth, takes charge of the child and mother to convey them on the way to the lower Egypt of Amenta."

Seb, however, does not convey them to any other realm than his own, but fosters them there.

The horizon line is to be seen as the equivalent Egyptian symbol for the values depicted under a different typology in the Hebrew Bible. It matches the great "cleft in the rock" imagery of the *Old Testament*. And this figment of theological fancy only finds its concealed sense when examined side by side with its cognate Egyptian glyph. The Eternal Being of God was by the mythicists typed by that which is most enduring and stable of all earthly things—the rock. But that everlasting Rock split itself into two at the beginning of creation. The line of cleavage runs midway through the center of its being, dividing the upper millstone of spirit from the lower one of matter. And right into that aperture between the two nodes of being deity placed man. Graphically is this depicted in the *Old Testament*. The Eternal says to Moses (man) that he will *hide* him *in the cleft of the rock* and will place his hand over his eyes, so that as his glory passes by man will not look full in the face of his overpowering effulgence; but when he shall have passed, and his hand is removed, man may then look safely upon his hinder part. Matter is this hand of God over mortal eyes, and it is the veil that deity has suspended between his mighty glory of spirit and our feeble powers of sight. We see God only through the veil which he has flung over our face. So man, standing on the horizon, gazes upon deity with its light dimmed to twilight by its admixture with the powers of darkness. God veils his face, or veils our power of vision, as Moses put on a veil every time he went into the Mount (of the horizon) to commune with deity. But it is in the Cleft of the Rock of Eternal Being, or on the horizon line between heaven and

456

earth, that we are hidden by deity. That Rock was cleft in twain for man, and though we have sung

> "Rock of Ages, *cleft for me,*
> Let me *hide* myself in thee."

with pious unction, no one has ever told us that God has thrust our life into the fissure made by the cleaving asunder of the two aspects of divine life, or that this cleft is in the human body of man itself. The rock cleft of Hebrew imagery is expressly called in Egypt the "rock of the horizon." Humanity is born in this rock cleft, and primitive necessity used the cave or rock recess as the place of birth actually. It is by name the Tser Hill, and it is where the dead body of Osiris was laid for its repose when buried in Annu. When the mummied Osiris rises to come forth like Lazarus from the sarcophagus or cave of the body on the other side of the horizon, he passes through "the gate of the rock, to approach the land of spirits." It is at this rock-gate that Shu stands when he uplifts the heavens (Ch. 17). This god is the uplifter of buried divinity, raiser of the grave rock, or opener of the sepulcher and the bringer of breath to the long-inert soul now awakened.

Shu's counterpart is Anhur, identical with Moses, and he is hyphenated with Shu as Shu-Anhur. He is represented as being the medium of communication between God and mortals. "His substance is identical with the substance of Ra," which is the truth about humanity likewise. He makes divine law known to men, as did Moses, when he brought the twelve tables of the law from the Mount. As the breathing force of deity he is pictured as the panting lion on the Mount of Dawn. He was, like the morning star, absorbed into the blazing fires of Ra, with whom he reunites after his separation on the western mount. His transubstantiation is said to have taken place during a nine days' tempest, which may be assumed to figure the disappearance of the god in his cycle of earth life, itself typed by the nine months of gestation, at the end of which his apotheosis into the being of Ra occurred as "he ascended alive into heaven."

This intermediary office of Anhur in the earlier cults is afterwards borne by Horus who, after stating that he disrobes himself to reveal his nature "when he presents himself to earth," says: "I am the babe born as the *connecting link between earth and heaven,* and as the one who does not die the second death" (Ch. 42). He then escapes Apap and the slaughter of the Innocents and goes on to conquer death in Suten-Khen. Shu-Anhur is equated in another cult with Atum-Iu, who as the opener and closer of the gates in and out of Amenta, holds the keys of death and of hell.

Horus' succession to the functions and titles of Shu-Anhur, guardian of Amenta's west and east gates of entry and exit, yields further exegesis and edification. The title of Horus as the god of the two horizons, west and east, is Har-Makhu. *Har* is "light, sun or sun-god." *Khu* is the divine spiritual body or entity in man. *Ma* must be taken as the root of *Ma,* "mother, matter." The title then subsumes in it the meaning of "the divine sun-god of spirit and matter." Therefore he stands on the horizon. Now Shu was the "lion-god," and Horus, as his successor, inherited Leo signatures. Atum-Ra-Har-Makhu was portrayed in the form of a lion-god upon the Mount of the horizon as the "lion of the double force" of spirit and matter. "I am the twin lions," he says. He rose or stood between the two lions which image the double force of being, betokened by the fore and hind parts of the lion, or the sphinx. The male lion is spirit, the female hinder part is the material power requisite to implement spiritual conceptions. Science has dealt with "matter and force" as the two exclusive factors in the living world, but omitted the invincible king of all, spirit. The spiritual or fore part directs, but must use the material hinder part, its *shakti,* as the fulcrum against which to exert power.

The two lions are much in evidence as representatives of the two natures that are balanced on the horizon line. The two leonine figures that are still placed as the guardians of doorways, driveways, steps and portals, may now have their arcane riddle unraveled for an oblivious world. They are survivals through many millennia from the time when Leo was at the point of the autumn equinox in the reckoning. Instead of the scales, the two lion-gods stood, one on either horizon, to guard the entry and exit gates of Amenta. And these two lion figures type something more than fanciful guardianship. They dramatize god-man himself in his two characters of deity gone to its death in the flesh, and deity re-arisen. The lion on the west border is the figure of dying divinity; the lion east is the figure of divinity born anew, conqueror of darkness and death, opener of graves, lifter-up of humanity. The two are Horus the Elder, decrepit, wizened, disfigured, ready to die and give place to his seed; and Horus the Younger, radiant, blooming, triumphant. Dying lion and the "lion's whelp" of the *Old Testament,* they were the two phases of godhead at the two opposite sides of the eternal cycle of death and rebirth. At once a large segment of disguised purport in theology is opened to enlightened view when we examine the Egyptian name for these two antique lion figures. It is *kherufu.* This is at once seen to be the Hebrew *cherub* and its plural *cherubim,* the angelic powers that support the ark of the covenant at its two ends. And further thrilling revelation accrues from this connection through a passage in *Exodus* (25:22), in which it is stated that Moses (Man) was bidden to commune with deity "from between the two cherubim"! The best that literalism could do for us in this matter was to leave us with a picture of Moses ensconced atop the ark of testimony crouched under the two overarching wings of the cherubim trying to meditate! Now we can see the portrayal redeemed from nonsense to positive and gripping meaning for us. Naturally all communication must come across at the point where the two natures, human and divine, can effect a contact, and this is on the horizon line, in the body of man. Where mind and body meet is our holy mount. Our life stretches from the western gate of physical birth across the dark nocturnal sea of earthly experience to the eastern horizon of bursting light. *The space between the two cherubim is the span of mortal life.* In this life alone we have our chance to commune with deity. Our elaborate study is worth all its labor if it brought us this one gleaming light of realization alone. Man stands or travels between the two divine lions of dual force, the dying lion on the west and the panting lion of the resurrection dawn. The tree of life is often pictured between two lions, or two goats (Capricorn), or two cherubs, or two rams (Aries). Seraphim is a companion figure with the cherubim, for they designate the same two phases of deity under the zodiacal form of Taurus. *Ser* is Osir(is), or Lord, Sire; and *Apis* is the Bull, Taurus. Serapis yields in Hebrew "seraph" and "seraphim." Cherubim and seraphim, like Urim and Thummin, at last are seen to be the two alternating powers of divine life, entering and leaving earthly embodiment. The solar disk is often drawn between two animals. Earth is the place between two trees, two lions, bulls, pillars, gates, mounts, altars, lampstands, doorposts, or the two horizons. In this life we are on the mount of the horizon, the hill of the Lord, our Mount Sinai, whereon with veiled face we may approach close enough to deity to hear his voice, his uttered manifested Word of Truth, though we can not face his full glory.

In the vignette to chapter 138 of the *Ritual*—the "chapter of entering into Abtu"—there are drawn the forms of the two lion-gods on the horizon, one of whom is called "Yesterday" and the other "Tomorrow." Nothing could be more instructive than these titles, for, of the two natures of man, the lower has been built up as the result of past experience now consigned to the realm of the "subconscious," being our habitual or natural tendencies; and the higher, the "super-conscious," is to be the development of "tomorrow." Conscious man of the present would be "Today."

A variant of the typology set the dragon of spirit, or serpent of fire, upon the horizon in such a position that his upper half projected above the skyline and his lower portion was below the rim of the earth. This is a perfect typograph of the situation in the human body, where, with the diaphragm for horizon, all spirito-intellectual elements function above the line and all physico-genetic ones below it.

The dualism of man was commonly typed in Egypt by the sphinx-figure of the lion, with fore and hind parts in various forms. Also the giraffe became an eloquent biograph of this meaning, because of the unusual feature of his eyes protruding so far on each side of his head that he can see both fore and aft without turning his head.

Another zootype of the same import was the crocodile, which was placed in the sign of Scorpio. The Scorpion represented breath and dryness, the crocodile typed water. Hence the one at the station of the other suggested the god and animal in union in one organism—man. The crocodile at the place of the equinox limned the idea of equal balance of the air and water. The ape, half man and half animal by descent through miscegenation, stood as a most apt embodiment of the horizon idea. The various chimerical animals conceived by mythological fancy to typify mankind were often half brute, half human, such as the centaurs, harpies, satyrs, mermaids, sphinxes, gryphons and others.

Greek philosophy places man in a midway position in the scale of being. Proclus states: "We, however, being of a middle nature . . ."[2] Again: "Hence that which is in our power, neither pertains to the first, nor to the last of things [pure spirit and matter], but to the medium between both." And many another Proclean passage voices the Greek statement that man stands at the line where the "summits of inferior natures" touch the bases of the superior orders.

The mystic seer Swedenborg writes that "while man is in the world, he is in the midst between heaven and hell; and then he is kept in freedom to turn himself either to hell or to heaven." [3] In *Jeremiah* (21:8) we find: "Thus saith the Lord, Behold, I set before you the way of life and the way of death." And *Deuteronomy* (30:19) iterates: "I call heaven and earth to record this day against you; that I have set before you life and death, blessing and cursing."

The Roman god Janus (whence the first month January, from *janua*, "a doorway") was also a type of the lower nature facing the higher, enabling man to see both before and behind. The same implication attaches to the two brothers Prometheus and Epimetheus, forethought and afterthought; likewise to the two dogs of Orion, Cyon and Procyon. The occult philosophers summarized their doctrine by saying that man was the hinge point of the universe. On him as pivot rested the crossbeam of the balance, with the natural constituting the one end and the supernatural the other. As intimated in other connections, the Hebrew Sinai plays a most prominent part in this exegesis. After the passage of the Red (Reed) Sea in the *Exodus,* the children of Israel arrive at the "Wilderness of Sin, which is between Elim and Sinai." Elim, the plural form of *El,* Hebrew "God," would mean "deity," and Sinai the opposite station from it. The Egyptian *Sheni* denotes an orbit, circle or circuit, a place of turning face about, as in a transformation. It is the mount of the equinox, whereon man pivots as he stands poised between his downward descent and his return to spirit. Another name for the two lions was *Sheni* (Massey).

Standing on the dividing line, *homo sapiens* surveys the lands on both sides. In the *Ritual* Isis addresses the rising Horus: "Thou risest on us; thou illuminest the Two Lands. The horizon is covered with the tracks of thy passings. The faces of gods and men are turned to thee." The statement that the horizon is covered with the tracks of the god's passings can mean nothing but that the soul has passed over the west and east horizon lines time after time in his descents and ascents, in his pilgrimages from heaven to earth, from earth to heaven. That the faces of gods and men are turned upon us as we cross the line confirms our position on the boundary. It is declared to the soul: "The

461

Light-God rolleth over thy body. Thou art the Lord of the two halves of Egypt." And these are the two kingdoms which every noted Egyptologist and historian has mistaken for two geographical divisions of the country, in spite of the obvious impossibility of a separation and reuniting having taken place in the reigns of ruler after ruler, as the record appears to show. Spiritual and not political history is being recorded.

Horus leaves us in no doubt as to his position: "I make my appearance on the seat of Ra and I sit upon my seat which is upon the horizon." And in all sacred literature there is hardly to be found a passage of more natural strength of meaning than that from the *Ritual* which says: "His mother suckleth him and she giveth to him her breast on the horizon." Mother Nature feeds man's spirit in that world where alone soul and flesh can interchange reciprocal influence.

When water symbolism is resorted to, the Two Lands are the Two Lakes. On approaching the two lakes, the Speaker says:

"Lo, I come that I may purify this soul of mine in the most high degree. Let me be purified in the lake of propitiation and *equipoise*. Let me plunge into the divine pool beneath the two divine sycamores *of heaven and earth*." (Ch. 97, Renouf)

Revelation states that the two witnesses "are the two olive trees." It also states that the tree of life is rooted on either side of the river of water.

Already noted is the statement that the soul "makes to flourish the crops on both sides of the horizon." It cultivates either mundane or celestial interests. "He is the Bull of the Gods, with the *twofold* light in his Eye . . . he unites the heavens, he has dominion in the lands of the South and North. He rules the night." The south is the front, male or spirit; the north the back, female or matter. By ruling the night he is lord of the lower or darker half. The climactic utterance is that he "pacifies the Two Lands, he unites the Two Lands." As he closes the gate of heaven on the west, he opens it on the east. "Thou openest the gate of heaven leading to the horizon and the hearts of the gods rejoice at meeting thee." "The doors are opened and the gates are thrown wide open to Ra as he cometh forth from the horizon." In the "chapter of making the transformation into a swallow," Nu says: "I am a swallow. I am the Scorpion, the daughter of Ra. Hail, thou

462

flame which cometh forth from the horizon . . . in the Pool of the Double Fire. I am pure at the place of the passage of souls"—which is the horizon. Ra is apostrophized:

"Thou art the lord of heaven; thou art the lord of earth; thou art the creator of those who dwell in the heights and of those who dwell in the depths. Worshipped be thou whom the goddess Maat embraceth at noon and at eve."

At "noon" Ra is at the height of the spiritual empyrean, with the celestials; at "eve" he is descending to glorify mortals. He then crosses the underworld by night from the west, "the place that thou lovest." And the chapter ends with the gripping statement that "This thou doest in one little moment of time." This follows the recital of his journey "over untold spaces requiring millions of years to pass over," and is a reminder to world citizens that in the consciousness of higher "dimensions" a thousand years are as an instant. The grand simplicity of Isaac Watts' hymn should not be slighted:

"A thousand ages in Thy sight
Are like an evening gone;
Short as the watch that ends the night
Before the rising sun."

To Pepi (the soul) it is said: "Thou takest thy seat in the two halls of the horizon. . . . Thou art Ra appearing at the horizon. Ra is born every day and Pepi is born every day like Ra." In the *Book of Unas* we read: "He sails in the horizon like Ra and Heru-Khuti . . . he sails to the east of heaven . . . where the gods are born."

Unmistakably the situation of man between the two natures is implied in the following:

"The water of life cometh into heaven, the water of life cometh on the earth. The sky catcheth fire before thee, the earth quaketh before thee, at the hands of the children of God. The two mountains are cleft, the god appeareth, and the god hath the mastery over his own body."

The *Ritual* prayer for Pepi asks:

"Make him to embrace the two horizons of the sky; this Pepi saileth therein with Ra to the horizon. Make Ra to embrace the two horizons of the sky."

463

To embrace the two horizons would be to unify the two natures in one identity. Of Osiris-Ani (the soul) the *Ritual* states: "He cometh into his city . . . the horizon of his father Tem." Tem means "total" and intimates the union of the forces of the two horizons. "The divine power hath risen and shineth in the horizon." Adoration is paid to the risen sun-god: "Homage to thee, O thou that shinest from thy disk, thou living soul that cometh forth from the horizon."

Anubis was a double-headed deity, one of the twelve guardians of the Light. One head could watch by day, the other by night; or the two could watch the opposite sides of the line.

Pepi, the *Ritual* states, "makes the two regions of heaven to embrace . . . so that Ra may sail over them with Heru-Khuti to the horizon. This Pepi cometh forth on the east side of heaven where the gods are born, and he is born there with Horus and the Khuti." The Khuti are those who have evolved the Khu, or shining body of imperishable flame.

Reconciliation between the two hostile natures is indicated in the *Litany of Ra:*

"He made the two Rheti goddesses, the Two Sisters of the Two Lands, to be at peace before thee. He did away with the hostility that was in their hearts, and each became reconciled to the other."

Here is the doctrine of the Atonement. In the *Hymn to Osiris* we find:

"Thou rollest up into the horizon, thou hast set light over the darkness, thou sendest forth air from thy plumes, and thou floodest the Two Lands like the Disk at daybreak."

In *Zechariah* (14) there stands the following:

"When the very *cleft* shall open into a deep valley, the living waters shall go out from Jerusalem; half of them toward the southern sea (in front or before) and half of them toward the hinder sea."

The valley is used many times in the Bible to indicate this sphere of existence, our earth, into which the cleft opens out. It is the space between the two mountains which open and close, giving man his interval of opportunity to dash in and fill his chalice before being caught. The *Zechariah* passage uses the symbolism of two waters

464

dividing. What more could possibly be connoted by the *Exodus* typology of the waters of the Red Sea dividing to let the children of God pass, and closing to catch those coming behind in hostile pursuit?

The great philosophical debate as to the Monistic or Dualistic view of life is largely gratuitous. All ancient systems of philosophy rise out of a basic initial proposition stating that a primal Oneness opened out to become a duality. The shell bursts asunder to release the seed; the seed splits in two to release the ideal pattern of form within. The first beginning was from the bosom of the Absolute, which opened to generate the twins, Light and Darkness, Day and Night, Manifestation and Reabsorption. The two Dioscuri or heavenly twins were pictured with half of the severed egg on each of their heads as a cap or helmet. One of the earliest of all symbols was the circle divided horizontally.

Now, wherever out of the void of primal space and darkness came visible substance into concrete status, as a world, there was a "hill" or "mount," a station in the abyss, an "island" in the firmamental waters. The exegesis of the mount or hill scripturally used is of great value, for the words have never had careful and explicit definition. When a globe appeared, born out of the formless abyss, it was a resting place or foothold of stable life for finite beings, who could have no local habitation in the vast areas of nothingness otherwise. The hill and mount were glyphs for the earth itself.

A work attributed to Simon the Samaritan called *The Great Announcement* teaches that the root of all things branched into two powers. Of these, one appears above and is the Great Father, the mind of the universe, directing all things; the other appears below, producing all things, female. The Great Mother divided into the two heavens, or heaven and earth, giving rise to the Two Women, the Mothers of all life. These two women, who brought forth the twin brothers of light and darkness, *were placed in the zodiac six months apart*. They stand at the same stations as the two lion gods. This makes the one the mother of incarnating deity in his first half, or the natural man, the other the mother of resurrected deity, the spiritualized man. The one, Virgo, was the virgin mother of the god-seed buried in body and undeveloped; the other, in Pisces, was the mother, no longer virgin, but impregnated by spiritual mind, so that her offspring was not merely born, but also begotten of the Father. This double motherhood and double birth of twin saviors is duplicated in *Luke*. Elizabeth, who is described as barren (virgin) when she is six months gone with the child John, bears her child six months earlier than Mary (*Luke* 1: 36). "Of the vivifying Goddesses," says Proclus, "they call the one older but the other younger" (*Timaeus:* B. III).

The figure of Aquarius, the Waterman standing in the zodiac at the January station and pouring out the two streams of the water of life from the "Ur-n," pictures the division of life at the very start. The name of the great primal God Tem means "total," and it was Tem's seed or seminal life-blood falling upon earth that begat the two personifications of spirit and matter, Shu and Tefnut, or Hu and Sa. Massey says that "there is no god that is not a biune being, a twin form of the 'double primitive essence' like Ptah." "Manifested existences are in his hand; unmanifested existences are in *his* womb," runs the *Ritual*. Many gods were represented with female marks, many goddesses with male ones. Deity was epicene, in token either of its original unity or of its later return to androgyne state. The first Horus was most significantly pictured with the locks of girlhood. Even the mummy was dual in sex, another proof incidentally that it typified living man, since only in Amenta does the soul split into the two halves of sex. There is the Jesus with the female paps in *Revelation*, matching Bacchus and Serapis. Horus is shown with the cteis, Venus with the beard, and Christ as Charis and Jesus as St. Sophia. Astarte wore on her head a bull's horns (Philo). A bull-headed goddess is found on Egyptian monuments; Neith and the vulture, her emblem, were both depicted with the male member erect in front of them. Aphrodite is sometimes written Aphroditos, the masculine form. And men sought to parody the androgyne condition of divine perfection by making themselves eunuchs for the kingdom of heaven's sake. Even Jehovah was half feminine gender (Hovah) and was called Jehovah-genetrix. The sun-gods in incarnation went into their feminine phase.

Life was Father-Mother in one at first, and only in long slow development did it become Father *and* Mother. The human race, which represents a miniature *eidolon* of cosmic creation, reflects the same process. Humans were androgyne or male-female for aeons before, in the third root race, they bifurcated into separate sexes. A single life portrays again the same stages. For the human child, matching early humanity as a whole, is of dual or epicene gender until puberty unfolds true differentiation of sex. This is why Horus, the mummy and the child Jesus of the catacombs, were represented with legs bound together. The two legs are the signs of bifurcation, the one typing spirit, the other matter, and free to move in counterbalance with each other. The human child represents the pre-Adamic races, the pre-manifestation deity, who was androgyne. The human race had its time of puberty. Man bifurcated in the image and example of primordial God. The impubescent stage was made the general type of life or deity undifferentiated.

Massey's summary of the dual nature of Horus or the Christ, so long lost and so sorely needed to bring clear ideas into religion, is valuable:

"In the west he is Horus in matter, feeble and dwindling; on the east he is Horus in spirit. In the one he is the child of twelve years, in the other he is the adult of thirty years. The first is the founder, the second is the fulfiller. The first was Horus of the incarnation, the second is Horus of the Resurrection . . . In both phases of character this is Horus of the double force, the double crown, the double feather, the double Uraei, the double life, or other types of duplication, including the *double equinox*." [4]

He is addressed: "Fearsome one, thou who art over the two earths . . . to whom the double crown is given" at his second coming (*Rit.,* Ch. 17). And here it becomes imperative to dissolve in the clear light of understanding a false apparition of doctrinal accretion: the second coming of a god in bodily form to earth historically. Every god figure, typing *the* god in all mankind, comes twice; first as purely man, secondly as man become god. The presentment is only figurative, though the mighty truth it adumbrates is actual. Horus rises on the east to avenge the wrongs inflicted on his father on the west; to raise his father's paralyzed arm, to reconstitute his dismembered, mutilated body. This redemptive work wins for him the second crown.

In the *Epistle to the Hebrews* (5:7) is a brief sketch of the twofold Horus, who suffered as Horus the mortal and overcame as Horus the immortal spirit. He "learned obedience through the things which he suffered; and having been made perfect he became unto all them that obey him the author of eternal salvation." The *spirit* of God came upon him in his adulthood, when he was divinized as the hawk; and he who had been dumb and meek as the lamb or bull led to the slaughter, became Horus Ma-Kheru, the utterer of very truth. The change of the boy's voice from feminine tone to masculine at twelve is a most astonishing natural parallel with arcane truth. The feminine or child voice is a falsetto; the false word must become the Word made Truth.

The Horus of the western horizon, taking the plunge into matter, is, somewhat confusedly to many, typed as both the decaying Osiris, the dying old man, and the infant, speechless, impubescent child Horus. Har-Ur, or "old-child is his name." As a portion of the "Ur" or aboriginal essence of conscious being, he is infinitely old, the Ancient of Days. But in his present incarnation he starts embodied life afresh, as a child. He is old in timeless being, but young in the present life cycle. He says: "I die, and I am born again, and I renew myself and I grow young each day." The sea of earth life lying between the two cherubim guarding the gates of west and east is verily the fountain of eternal youth, whose waters impart to the bathers the potent elixir that restores a vigor agelessly fresh. The disappearing old man merges insensibly into the helpless infant at the winter solstice and again transforms into the radiant new divinity at the vernal equinox. Horus says: "I am the twin lions, the heir of Ra" (Ch. 38). As he passes across the space between the two horizons he blends the powers of his two forces into one, carrying over the first natural potencies into the spiritual realm exalted and glorified.

The word "child" in a number of languages, notably Spanish, is a derivative of the original Nu, firmamental water of first life, which was life in a form unexpressed and unproductive. The child was of Nu(neu)ter gender. He was the negation, or privation, as yet, of true life. So the Nu, Nnu, Nun, and eventually the ninny and in Spanish the *niño* (child).

Some tribal legends retain descriptions of primeval ancestors of humanity who were *half male and half female,* and were unaware of their unlikeness and innocent of sexual desire until a god created a longing to eat of the earth. Tasting earth's fruit, they lost the power to fly back to heaven. One Arunta legend tells of ancestors who were double-sexed when they first *started on their journey,* but before they had proceeded very far, their organs were modified and their mothers "became as other women are." The races emerging from Paradise were hermaphrodite.

A long narrative from the *Pymander* discourses of Egypt recounts how God, or the creator gods, becoming exceedingly enamored of their own forms, brought forth man in their likeness. But man, seeing the beauty of creative workmanship, must needs fall also to work, and so he separated himself from the Father and descended into the sphere of generation. He stooped down to break through the harmony and strength of the Circles, and manifested the "downward-borne nature." And seeing in the "water" of earth the fair reflection of his own beauty, he loved it and would cohabit with it. (Here is probably the genesis of the Greek fable of Narcissus.) In his love for it he wrapped himself about it and became married unto it. And for this cause man above all creatures is double; mortal because of his body, and immortal because of his celestial part. Immortal and having power over all things, he yet suffers mortal experience and is subject to Fate and Destiny. Being hermaphroditic, he is governed by powers both male and female. Air and water, the account runs, drew down from Fire and Aether their subtle powers, and so nature produced bodies in the shape of men. Thereupon the bond of all things was loosed by the will of God, and the males were cut apart from the females. And straightway God ordered the creatures to increase and multiply, and bade them know themselves to be immortal, the cause of death being the too ardent love of body. He that knew himself to be a mixture of high spirit with lowly body advanced to "superstantial good." But he that through erroneous love was enamored of body, abode wandering in darkness, sensibly suffering the things of death.

Manifestation can not arise without the breaking apart of primal unity into duality. But the soul that "makes the journey through Amenta in the two halves of sex" must reunify its two halves before it can return to the Father. Bisexuality is for the journey in time, not for all eternity. That which has been put asunder by God must be remarried for the return to the invisible world. "This soul, divided in the two halves of sex, must be united again in establishing an eternal soul." Manifestation is the result of bifurcation; retirement must be accompanied by reunion. Here is the rationale of the Atonement doctrine; the two halves, spirit and matter, god and man, must return to antecedent oneness. Man began as androgyne, and as androgyne he must end the cycle. Spirit and matter must marry in the body of man. Shu and Tefnut "are *blended in Tattu*." And this statement is of critical moment to the race, for it asserts that the blending of the two natures is done in Tattu, our earth. We are sent to bathe in the Pool of Siloam so that the two halves of our nature may be made into the original whole. Earthly human wedlock is but an emblem of the greater marriage of the two elements of matter and consciousness in one organism. "The Manes could only enter the kingdom of heaven as a being of both sexes or of none," writes Massey lucidly. In the light of which we venture to suggest an entirely new and undreamed-of meaning in Jesus' statement that man, to be regenerate, must become as a little child. The child is of neither sex, functionally; and the man returned to deity is of neither sex. The redeemed must return to the sexless state of the child. Orthodox ignorance has read into Jesus' utterance only a return to "the simple faith and purity of childhood." But there is in this no lift to the plane of cosmic and racial significance where alone the esoteric interpretation of ancient books is to be made. The Gospels are not dealing with everyday homiletics. They expound the occult laws of evolution. Jesus was telling the race that it must return to angelic epicene state, spiritually. We must reunite the two divided sexes in us. Paul endorses the necessity when he says that the wall of partition between us must be broken down, and the two made one new creature. And the Gnostic Jesus tells Salome that his kingdom will come when there shall be neither male nor female, but when both shall be one. Paul again supports the thesis when he says: "There is neither Jew nor Gentile, there is neither bond nor free, there is *neither male nor female,* for ye are all one in Christ Jesus," the biune being, the Alpha and Omega of any cycle. And no one can forget that impressive assurance of the Master himself that "when they shall arise from the dead they neither marry nor are given in marriage; but are as the angels which are in heaven" (*Mark* 12:25). Sex is an appurtenance of the body only. This is the meaning of the statement in *Revelation* that "the dragon shall rise up and slay" the two witnesses, the two thieves between whose opposite tensions the Christ has been crucified. Unification slays duality. This is outlined in the "mystery of Tattu,"

"where the body-soul in matter (Osiris) is blended with the holy spirit of Ra; the female with the male (Tefnut with Shu), or Horus, the child under twelve years, with Horus, the adult of thirty years. The transaction of blending occurs on the day that was termed 'Come thou to me'" (*Rit.*, Ch. 17).[5]

The primal cleft and bifurcation is the genesis of the horizon situation. There could be no horizon line in man's life but for the primal bicussating that Plato tells of. The duality of our nature is a trite religious truth. Yet its consideration from the angle of the horizon typology has yielded new disclosures of piercing meaning.

Jerome, the Church Father, states that the crucifixion was not signalized by the rending of the veil of the temple, but by the breaking in twain of an enormous beam. The beam was the cross bar of the balance. But we also catch a new and stirring significance of "the veil." The rent veil is indeed another framing of the horizon and cleft rock symbolism. The veil was the curtain of invisibility that shrouded unmanifest deity in its primal oneness. As seen, life can not come to view until it is broken into the two nodes of spirit and matter, to provide a subject-consciousness which can become aware of object-matter. The celestial rending of the veil was then the division of the All-life into its positive and negative phases, and through the rent thus made, archetypal life emerged to view. The rent veil is again the bifurcation, the cleft rock. Through the rent life emerges to view on the hill of the horizon. It was specifically rent *in twain*. The rending of the veil of the Absolute broke the primal homogeneity and brought life to manifestation. For visible life only exists where the two opposing forces engage in the neutralization of their contrary tensions. The ancients did their best to expound these abstrusities under appropriate and striking representations; but we have been blind.

The horizon symbol brings further grist to the interpretative mill in another direction. It puts us in position to see at last the meaning of the "rib" figure in the creation story. The rib that has been a bone of contention and mystification for centuries yields readily to mythic art. The form of the myth must have been mangled to some extent, for the hidden sense is not readily evident in the *Genesis* statement. Since it is the account of the split into sexual duality, which is, or is the emblem of, the bifurcation in the beginning of creation, it must mean both these things. Therefore the rib mentioned is to be taken in the sense of "midrib"! God ran a midrib through the center of his one unitary nature, and thus separated off spirit and matter, male and female. All the root significance of the stem *"rib, rif,"* which yields "rift," "riven," supports this interpretation. Riven is "cleft." The hymn speaks of "the blood, from thy *riven* side which flowed." Deity muti-

471

lated, cleft its body in twain by a mid-rift (mid-rib is written "mid-rif" in Shakespeare), and from the life blood which flowed forth mankind was nourished.

Reconciliation is attested in the following: "Pepi is the uniter of the Two Lands." And by this again: "The heart of Osiris rejoiceth and the heart of Horus; and therefore are the northern and southern parts of heaven at peace." Even Keb (Seb), earth-god, is dualized in the following: "Behold, one arm of Keb is to heaven, and the other is to the earth, and he taketh Pepi along to Ra." In *The Crown of Triumph* (*Rit.*, Ch. 19) the announcement is made to Horus: "Thy father Seb hath decreed that thou shouldst be his heir. He hath decreed for thee the *two earths,* absolutely and without condition." The two earths are heaven and earth. Hor-Apollo narrates that the Egyptians signified the course of the sun in the winter solstice (the underworld) by two feet or legs walking, a miracle, for the legs walked without a body or a head. The god in matter was indeed regarded as having lost his head. The sun-god in the underworld, Af-Ra, was without a head. It is said that Osiris goes into Tattu and finds there the soul of the sun or Ra. There the one god embraces the other, and divine souls spring into being.

It seems certain that Michael is the *Revelation* character on the horizon under the title of Makhu-El, the god of the dividing line. And, true to type, Michaelmas was placed at the autumn equinox on the western horizon! And Gnostic literature names the western hill Mount Bakhu, while the eastern one is the Mount of Olives, or Mount Manu.

A prayer is made that the Osiris may be saved from the attack made against him "at the crossing." (Ch. 135.) This indicates that assault on his young divinity is made as soon as he crosses the line on the west in his descent. He is then "the youngling in the egg" and subject to the Herut attack. Here the dragon lay in wait to devour the young child.

Direct corroboration of our interpretation of Satan as just the god on earth is seen in this forthright statement: "Unas standeth up and is Horus! Unas sitteth down and is Set! Ra receiveth him, soul in heaven and body on earth!" This shows the incarnation itself to be the root of "evil"; the resurrection overcomes it. The gender differentiation of the two aspects, as female on the west, male on the east, is carried out remarkably in a passage from a Babylonian tablet: "Venus is a male at sunrise; Venus is a female at sunset" (Sayce: *T.S.B.A.*, Vol. 3, p. 196).

In the *Ritual* the soul must open thirty-six gates (the twelve decans each of three zodiacal signs?) by as many transformations of character. Chapter 145 is devoted to the opening of twenty-one of these gates. The sun-god is the King of Glory for and by whom these gates are opened. Taht, the Egyptian Psalmist, says:

"Opened be the gates of heaven! Opened be the gates of earth! Opened be the gates of the west! Opened be the gates of the northern and southern sanctuaries! Opened be the gates and thrown wide open be the portals as Ra ariseth from the mount of glory! Glory be to thee, O Ra, lord of the Mount of Glory! . . . He is the King of Glory; these are the gates of glory that were opened on the mount of glory 'at the beautiful coming forth of his powers.' "

The *Book of Enoch* designates the west wind under the "name of diminution," because "it is there that all the luminaries are diminished and descend."

"Pepi takes possession of the Two Lands, like a king of his gods." He seizes first the west or natural kingdom, then the spiritual east, after making the crossing via the solstice of winter. To Pepi in his resurrection the joyful announcement is made:

"Hail, Pepi, heaven has conceived thee with the star Seh (Orion), the Tuat has brought thee forth with the star Seh—Life, Life, by the command of the gods, thou livest. Thou comest forth (risest) with the star Seh in the eastern part of heaven; thou settest with the star Seh in the western part of heaven."

Again:

"This Pepi appears in the eastern part of the sky. Thou art renewed in thy season; thou becomest young again at thine appointed time. Nut brings forth this Pepi with the constellation of Orion."

Though traveling through the earth of Amenta, "he belongs not to the earth, he belongs to heaven. . . . He pounces upon heaven like the ahau bird, he kisses heaven like the hawk." As he emerges in his splendor in the east side, he "makes the hearts of the dwellers in the east to expand with joy." "He strides over Akar, he stands up in the eastern part of heaven."

The glory of the Lord in Ezekiel's vision "went up and stood upon the mountain which is *on the east side* of the city." The four fishers in the *Ritual* pull the dragnet through the water in the act of fishing for Horus. These are they who are described as fishers for "the great prince who sits at the east of the sky" (*Rit.*, Ch. 153B). Jesus was accompanied by four fishermen.

The legend of the stone in the temple of Memnon which sang at sunrise is a poetic dramatism of the joy that greets the rising god on the eastern horizon.

"The gods or spirits that mount with the great god to the eastern horizon . . ." are spoken of. "In our mysteries," says Jerome (cited by Bingham: *Christian Antiquities*, Vol. I, 517—and evidencing, too, a thing often denied: that the Christians had *their* mysteries along with the pagans) "we first renounce him that is in the west, who dies to us with our sin; and then turning about *to the east*, we make a covenant with the Sun of Righteousness and promise to be his servants." Christian exegesis has not always done so well in the transmission of ancient teaching! The *Ritual* (Ch. 44) reiterates: "I am the sun; very glorious, seeing mysteries—*hating him who dwells in· the west*, telling his name." As Horus (Osiris) when he sank in the west became Set, the theological basis for the mythic hatred here expressed is easily discerned.

We have seen that in *Luke* Jesus delivered the sermon, not on the mount, but on the plain. Nothing but our interpretative diagram will reconcile the apparent contradiction, since by its aid we see that the horizon may be either a hill or the open plain. Two variant aspects of a symbol chanced to cross or appear in conflict in this case. The theologians are saved the annoyance of having to explain a seeming contradiction. But—the point of utmost moment in the matter is that the "sermon" was not uttered by fleshly lips on either hill or meadow; it is the living utterance of the Christ who stands on the hill of the horizon between the two natures in man.

Before Horus came to the underworld, the sky had to be held up by Seb, the earth-god. And Horus' coming to relieve Seb of his burden recalls the relief of Atlas by another sun-god, Hercules. The Greeks also assert that Hercules separated two mountains to form the two columns or pillars—fabled to be geographically at Gibraltar. And this again repeats Egyptian dramatization in the erection of the two pillars of Tat, tokens of dual stability. The meaning is that the god in man could enter the opening made by the cleaving apart of heaven and earth. Man is the Atlas who stands with feet (body) on earth and head (soul) in the sky, supporting the two realms by the power of his two equal arms. So the patriarch's two arms had to be held up till the battle was won, in *Old Testament* copying of Egypt's deepest lore. The sun-god came to relieve Atlas of his burden until he could go and get the three golden apples from the garden of Paradise; which three golden apples, be it known at last, were the solar triad of mind-soul-spirit.

The two equinoctial points of September and March in our zodiacal chart have yielded a rich meed of interpretative insight. Do the solstices speak as voluble a message?

The June solstice has rather little to offer for mundane instruction, because it is the index of divine soul entirely out of relation to the earthly scene in highest heavens. Its intimations point to the life of spirit in the empyrean, which is of little direct concern for man below. The sun-spirit of evolution stands at its high *noon*, which is seen as cognate with the *Nun* or non-manifest state. His interests lie on or below the horizon line. Antiquity celebrated the great Festival of Fire at the June solstice to do homage to the principle of Fire or spirit in the universe and in man. Maintained in a few scattered districts over the world, it has entirely disappeared from Christian notice.

But the December solstice yields a harvest as bountiful as that of the equinox and the horizon. It shows soul at the nadir of its dip into matter, and all its implications bear immediately and weightily upon the human situation. In the large general view the winter solstice significance is a reinforcement of that of the horizon. The suggestion of balance between spirit and carnality is accentuated again in the fixed relation between light and darkness at the turn of the year. At the equinoxes light and dark are equal in quantity and sovereignty. But at the solstice the two powers are *stabilized* for the period, albeit in unequal relation. The balance, in the special sense of fixity and stability, is the ground for further striking disclosures of cryptic meaning and symbolic beauty fully matching those based on the horizon. As a flood of rich meanings gushed up from consideration of man's position on the evolutionary horizon, so another stream of cogent revelation wells forth from examination of his position at the evolutionary solstice. For under a shift of the hieroglyph, man stands also at the winter solstice of his entire evolutionary cycle. He stands at the point where his soul has made its deepest descent into matter, having taken actual residence in a body of animal flesh. The soul has emanated from the bosom of the Father and gone forth under primal impulse into the heart of matter. But with the exhaustion of its projecting force, it comes to a dead stop in the arms of matter's inertia. The material force that was able to bring it to a stop must be exactly equal to its own power at that point. For an aeon—a section of the entire evolutionary round—it stands motionless, locked in the arms of matter. Here, at the nadir of descent, is its evolutionary solstice. And that solstice covers the period of human evolution.

As sheer metaphor it can be seen in a flash that the interlocking of male and female principles in each other's arms is the condition precedent and necessary to a birth. The Logos, and below him the Christ, are both the products of wedlock and intercourse between spirit and matter, and must therefore be born at the solstice. And so the Christ birth (*mes, mas,* in Egyptian) fell at the winter solstice.

All values are born out of the struggle between the opposing nodes of consciousness and material inertia. The exertion necessary for latent consciousness to awaken its energies to greater awareness and function alone brings it to its birth. Heraclitus' declaration that "war is the father of all things" is a great philosophical truth that applies here most forcefully. All birth arises out of the stabilized wedlock between spirit and matter, and their frictional interplay. The two parents must cohabit to produce their child of divine consciousness. And they are married at the solstice. Heraclitus adds a most pertinent observation: "The harmonious structure of the world depends upon opposite tension, like that of the bow and the lyre." Stability is gained only by the mutual annulment of two opposite forces. The planets swing in fixed orbits because of the exact counterbalance of centrifugal and centripetal energies.

The significance of the solstice (the word meaning "sun standing still") lies in the fact that for the time both light and darkness *stand still* in relation to each other. The basic feature is motionlessness. Neither is losing or gaining. They are stabilized. In the parallel situation in human evolution, soul and body stand in precisely the same relation. Soul has come down in involution and come to a stop in exact equilibration with matter, which on its side had come up from below. The spirit is from above, the body from below, as Jesus has told us. The first man is from the earth, the second is the Lord from heaven, is Paul's corroboration. The one ascending, the other descending, the two meet, are thrown into stable equilibrium with each other, enter wedlock and birth the Christ. Each brings the other, by the exact equilibration of forces, to a standstill. Again flashes into thought the brilliance of the Egyptian phrase-name for this life: *the Lake of Equipoise!* We are in the pool of balanced, stabilized forces. The term "pool" has great significance here because the water in a pool is stagnant, not in stream. At the angle made by the turn in direction of the line of involution into that of evolution—*"the angle of the Pool of Fire"*—the water of life is stagnant, as in a bay, cove or "bight of Amenta." The moving forces coming from above and below meet and hold each other still in the Pool of the Solstice. It is the lake or pool of human life, the Pool of Siloam.

The animal evolution, up from below, came to the meeting point with soul and was stabled or stabilized with it. Soul, coming down from above, met the animal and was stabled or stabilized with it. Copulation and birth took place in this stable relation. Now a stable is a building erected by man for animals, a station where they may come to stand (*sta-* is the root of the Latin word meaning "to stand") *for the night* or *in winter*—both symbols of incarnation, be it noted. Evolution was *stalled* for the night in a "stable." Animal life came to a stand in a stable place, to stay or stand still in a stall or static state or station, along with soul. Along and together with the divine, animal evolution was stabled for the night. Soul came to lift up the animal, and to do so he had to build a stable for him and enter it with him. So the Christ was born in a stable.

The features of motionlessness, stillness and midnight quietude are played upon in much allegorical material that could be adduced to support the reading. Hymns and legends emphasize these aspects:

> "The world in solemn stillness lay
> To hear the angels sing."

.   .   .   .

> "O little town of Bethlehem,
> How still we see thee lie;"

And perhaps no single chant has ever so powerfully inclined the shallow and boisterous western mind to a moment of real reverence and devotion as the lines of Franz Grueber's *Silent Night, Holy Night*, sung at midnight of December 24. For the Christ mind was born in the midnight stillness—of evolution.

This dead stoppage of all motion in evolution received a dramatization in one of the Apocryphal Gospels in so graphic a form and so laden with significant implications for all religion that we are constrained to reprint it here. It is an entire chapter from *The Protevangelium* or *Gospel of James*. It reveals that the Nativity scene was so obviously a drama that one speculates whether this fact does not supply an all-sufficient reason for its being kept out of the official canon of *New Testament* books. The recondite meaning of the solstice pause and motionlessness had somehow to be represented in the stage play. It was depicted thus:

1. And leaving her [Mary] and his sons in the cave, Joseph went forth to seek a Hebrew midwife in the village of Bethlehem.

2. But as I was going (said Joseph) I looked up into the air and I saw clouds astonished, and the fowls of the air stopping in the midst of their flight.

3. And I looked down toward the earth and I saw a table spread, and working people sitting around it, but their hands were upon the table and they did not move to eat.

4. They who had meat in their mouths did not eat.

5. They who had lifted their hands up to their heads did not draw them back.

6. And they who lifted them up to their mouths did not put anything in.

7. But all their faces were fixed upwards.

8. And I beheld the sheep dispersed, and yet the sheep stood still.

9. And the shepherd lifted up his hand to smite them, and his hand continued up.

10. And I looked into a river and saw the kids with their mouths close to the water, and touching it, but they did not drink.

Here is represented the sudden stoppage of all motion in the field of nature and human life. The sons of men, typed as crude working people, below; the birds of the air, symbol as ever of the divine soul, above; and both suddenly motionless. The sheep and their shepherd,

478

repeating the same classification—and all caught by the *stasis,* or stand-still of evolution! It is drama.

The *New Testament* parable of the wise and foolish virgins contains a most direct reference to the midnight pause: *"At midnight* arose the cry, The Bridegroom cometh."

And another clear intimation of the solstice purport hides in the story of Hannah and the relief of her barren condition through the birth of God's prophet Samuel: *"At the turn of the year* she bore a son."As Hannah equates Anna, the mother of the mother of the Christ in the Gospels, we have an identity of reference with the Christ story.

And light is available at last to enable us to read rational sense and meaning into the otherwise impossible riddle of Joshua at Ajalon commanding the sun and moon to stand still, until the battle was won. It is a variant of the solstice symbolism. The sun types soul always, the moon, body. The battle of evolution could not be won unless these two forces were brought to a standstill to birth the Christ. And this again is a variant typing of the holding up of the two arms to insure the victory.

The ox and the ass are present at the divine birth as zoötypes of prophetic meaning. Both these animals represent, along with other subtle typology, the end of purely animal procreation in human history with the coming of the *Christos*—much the same as circumcision. They stand at the birth of the Christ as indices of the beginning of humanity's return from male and female progenation to androgyneity through spiritual evolution. The ox is sterile through castration, and the ass through cross breeding. And man is to become a eunuch for the kingdom of heaven's sake.

The dramatic ritual also arranged that the new-born Christ should be laid in the manger, where the animal eats, since his own explicit command to all mortals who would win immortal life was that they should eat his very body. God and man conjoined were reciprocally to nourish each other. An old script reports Adam as asking: "Am I and my ass to eat out of the same manger?"

Now indeed is the winter of our discontent in evolution; but our faces are set toward the lengthening light and the sun-glory of the vernal equinox, where we shall rise as gods.

Chapter XIX

WEIGHED IN THE BALANCE

THE implications and corollaries of the horizon and solstice symbolism will be found to be little short of revolutionary to the highest degree and disruptive of many a solid bulwark of orthodox theology. For one thing they announce the total error of the entire system of eschatological doctrine in Christian preachment for centuries. They will make necessary nothing less than a complete reformulation of the whole of that phase of ecclesiastical dogmatism.

It has been found essential, on the postulates of the archaic teaching, to transplant hell from some vague place of mystery under the earth or "beyond the grave" to the surface of the globe on which we live. It was necessary to define the mummy as the living human, the grave as his body of flesh, and the "dead" of old scriptures as living mortals—ourselves. It devolved upon us to re-locate Amenta, bringing it from its indefinable place somewhere above or below the earth to the open light of our own world. Along with it we were obliged to shift the locale of purgatory from the somber shadows of some unknown Sheol to the present field of our actual existence. But none of these modifications of conventional theology, drastic as they have been, will prove so shattering of commonly accepted ideas as the next transfer of a region of theological fiction from the spirit world back to our good earth. This other mislocated domain is the Hall of Judgment of Osiris in Amenta!

Orthodox religionism and popular belief must receive with what composure they can the forthright declaration that the judgment scene is enacted on this earth, not in the life of spirit following our sojourn here! *We are in the scales of the Judgment now!* For we are also in Hades, Sheol, Amenta, now. The Egyptian trial of the soul and the weighing of the heart in the Hall of Osiris are located by the old books in Amenta, and this Amenta, according to our now corrected knowledge, is the life we are now living. As argued in an earlier chapter, the Spiritual Guides of humanity gave the race a code of religious instruction that was meant to apply to the world in which it was given, not to a succeeding one. The seers were not concerned with teaching mankind about the supervening consciousness of the discarnate life. They taught humanity how to live in the world in which the teaching was imparted, well assured that philosophic behavior of life here would put them in favorable condition to meet the exigencies of the life of rest following the day on earth. They were vastly concerned to instruct mortals in what it behooved them to learn here, as this was the only realm in which progress could be made,—unless it be contended that one makes greater progress in sleep at night than in one's waking life by day.

We were led to the discovery that the judgment takes place on earth from the figures, phrases, statements and identities found in the *Book of the Dead*. When these were noted, related, and studied, it seemed impossible that the plain and obvious truth of the primal doctrine of the judgment could have been so fatuously misconceived as has been the case. The statements are clear and their purport is indubitable. An incredulous world will demand the evidence in hot haste. It is given with what clarity and cogency are at our command. It could not be advanced with any expectation of intelligent reception until the long exposition of the significance of the horizon was prefaced. The brief summary of the position and relevance of the zodiacal sign of Libra is the link between the horizon and the judgment. The cross on the horizon hill is the primary emblem of theological philosophy; but it is not until one transforms the cross into the Scales or Balance that there is introduced the idea of moral quality and judgment pronounced. It is not until the two arms of the cross are made mobile to register any failure of the equilibrium that moral culpability enters the theological situation. Neither above man with the angels, nor below him with the beasts, does moral responsibility reside. It inheres solely in the kingdom of man, who is poised, the only creature in evolution so placed, on the two arms of the balance between mind and matter. Man on the horizon is not only nailed on the cross of matter; he is being weighed in the scales of the balance, to see if his heart is so spiritualized as to be light as a feather! Man's heart against a feather, and his fate hanging thereon!

The first broad consideration that led the mind to the truth about the judgment was the reflection that if Amenta was this earth, then the judgment trial must necessarily take place in this life. If the argument for the identification of earth with Amenta was sound, the matter was established conclusively by the data presented in that relation. But the position is strengthened by the force of other material drawn from ancient tests. Nothing contravenes it; all the data confirm it.

Thoth, who is the "Attorney" at the trial in Amenta, is entitled "Lord of the Balance." Thoth, or Taht, embodies the power symbolized by the *Tat* cross of Egypt, which was the emblem of eternal stability, and the power that raised up life which had fallen under the sway of matter. He therefore presides at the horizontal balance where soul and matter are in their conflict. In other words, he is the divinity within us. And this is confirmed by the *Ritual* passage which says that "Pepi is Thoth, the strength of all the gods." And Pepi, Teta, Unas, Ani and others are kingly puppet figures acting the role of the human soul. Thoth is the divinity that lifts us up when fallen under the seductions of sense. Thoth is he who, "when the eye (of Ra) is sick, and when it weepeth for its fellow eye; then Thoth standeth up to cleanse it." He is the god who comes between Horus and Sut "through the judgment of him that dwelleth in Sekhem." Of the seven cakes to be brought in by the soul, four were to be offered to Horus, the upper three to Thoth. The three upper spiritual principles were to be rendered pure from matter's stain. Thoth is the god who healed the mutilations of dismemberment. But he was also the god of knowledge. What more direct hint does the mind need, to be assured that the ills of mortal flesh are to be healed by knowledge? Like Jesus, Thoth dries the disciples' feet. He is said to present to Pepi "his life which was not to him." At the trial he is represented by the ape, which has been shown to be *par excellence* the symbol of the god who stands at the point of balance between the animal and the human kingdoms. He is described as standing at the door of the pure chamber to recite his formula which shall give life to the soul each day. The ape is the scribe or secretary or recorder for the gods because he typifies man, who combines flesh with spirit and who is thus the only being in evolution who is able to write or record the thoughts of his heart and the deeds of his hand in the form and substance of the material world—his own

482

body. Man's body registers the record of his life. Thoth is the power that imprints the record of living experience upon the subtle ethers of man's inner spiritual vehicles. As regards the individual human, then, Thoth is the god within, who binds up our broken hearts, our mutilated intelligence, reconstitutes the dismembered corpus of spirit, and raises us up again. And he is Lord of the Balance, the god of the judgment scales.

A second powerful hint that the judgment is staged on earth comes with the declaration of the texts that Thoth, when he found Sut had stirred up the gods to resist the entrance of Osiris (the soul) into their company, decided that the matter should be tried in the Hall of Seb, the *earth-god*. It was later believed that the trial took place in the city of An. In whatever "city" held, the trial would be typical of the temptation that was universal to mankind, *taking place continuously*. In the solar myths there was a judgment annually. But such local or temporal judgments were either mythical or memorial, a drama to depict a deeper and constant reality.

A further intimation was seen in the statement that the Egyptian Judgment Hall was at times denominated the Hall of the Two Truths. This name enforces the conclusion that all the weight of the material concerning the horizon as the place of the two truths of life must then bear heavily on the proposition that the earth is the Hall of Judgment. This is additionally supported by the passage from the *Ritual* which states that the Tree of the Two Truths stands in the place of the Judgment Hall. And on a tablet of Tahtmes, a Memphite functionary of the 18th Dynasty, a reference is made to the judgment under the Tree. The text states that on the thirtieth day of the month Tibi (Dec. 16 of the Sacred Year), the "day of filling the eye in Annu" (the birthplace), "the great Inspectors (or Judges) came out at the end of the Dais under the trees of Life and Perseas." This was the place of the Judgment. Then comes an important item. "Having been questioned, thou answerest in Rusta on the third of the month Epiphi," or on the 17th of June, six months afterwards; the two dates, the one of questioning and the other of answering, corresponding to the two opposite sides of the zodiac of life, the Hall of the Two Truths, and the Tree of Heaven and Earth. Shu, who upholds the heaven with his two arms, like his Hebrew antitype, Moses on the Mount, was represented by the two lawgivers of astrology, the two stars of the solstices, north and south, Kepheus and Cor Leonis. The character of these personifications as lawgivers connects them with the Judgment. The Judgment Hall, then, was the space between the two horizons, or the north and south (east and west, spiritual and material) nodes of our life, a fact which is forever irrefutably established by the inscription here quoted, to the effect that the question or problem of destiny which is put to the Manes on the horizon of September is to be answered in the court six months later on the horizon of March, at the conclusion of the life experience, or in the large, at the end of the whole human cycle. The trial then began at the entrance to Amenta, where the evolutionary problem was propounded to the soul, to which it was to render answer at the culmination of its sojourn on the earth, the Hall of Judgment. The horizon line between the two cherubim is the place of the Great Balance. The two Horus forms or lion gods are the two pillars of justice, and *the judgment is the long series of decisions which the man himself renders as he journeys across.* At the completion of his journey over the intervening terrain, the man hears Thoth pronounce to the gods: "Hear ye this judgment. The heart of Osiris hath in truth been weighed and his soul hath stood as witness for him; it hath been found true by trial in the Great Balance."

The heart that is weighed in the scales could not be physical. It was the second or spiritual heart. The Manes appeals to this second heart, as to a person detached from himself, not to bear testimony against him in the presence of the god who is at the balance. This second heart was that which was *fashioned anew according to the life lived in the body.* "The conscience or heart (Ab) of a man is his own god," says the *Ritual,* and it also is his only judge. The divine words spoken by the soul, the soul's projection of its highest conception of truth, were to be given flesh and made concrete truth in the life lived on earth. This recording of its own inner nature upon the body of flesh was the writing of its own book of life. And that which was written upon the outward form would in the repercussion stamp its lineaments back again upon inner spirit vestments, or deposit them in the ark. And this book of life, the record inscribed at the end upon the imperishable soul itself, was opened anew *at the beginning, not at the end,* of each fresh incarnation of the soul. The facing of the record of the past began afresh for each individual every time he plunged into earth life. *We meet the book of life at birth, not at death!* For we bring with us our own past record, written upon our inner ethereal vestures in letters of character. *In life, not in death,* we must face the issues raised by former good or ill. By our active deeds we must break the bondage of the past. Never will moral problems be envisaged aright until it is seen that their issues must be met and settled by conduct in the daylight of life, not in the dark night of death. This knowledge can transform human society.

Revelation (20) records the vision of the seer:

"I saw the dead, small and great, stand before God; and the books were opened, and the dead were judged out of those things which were written in the books, *according to their works.* The sea gave up the dead which were in it; and death and hell delivered up the dead which were in them; and they were judged every man according to his works."

With the *esoteric* reading of the words "sea," "death," and "hell," there is no passage in ancient writing that more explicitly sets forth the meaning of the Judgment than this. Categorically it is declared that it is the "works" wrought in this present domain of life that determine the fate and status of the soul. The truth which is thus overwhelmingly established is that "the dead" come to their judgment in this life. It is, of course, possible to abstract from the phraseology of such passages as this apparent support for the idea that *after this life is over* (a thousand years after, it is expressly claimed by numerous cults) the dead will be summoned out of earthly graves and arraigned in ghostly lines before some august spiritual court, by which the record of the deeds done in the life will be weighed against some standard of abstract justice, and the righteous ones rewarded with a crown of eternal life, while the evil ones are parted off for eternal torment. But such a reading is a sorry distortion of the mythical sense, and was never the true intent of the framers of the allegory. This life is, as we now see, the realm of the "dead." *In* it, not *after* it, is the trial of the soul's qualities, as every common sense conception of the value of earthly life testifies. We are summoned into this Amenta of the body life after life, and in each we are being put to the trial of our character in a varied series of experiences. This is an incontrovertible fact of common knowledge. This world is the high mount into which the dark power, Satan, led the Jesus spirit for its trial and temptation. Given a moment's sane reflection, any soul will know that this life is the period of its trial and testing. The soul is drawn here to exercise her undeveloped powers, as Plotinus has so well told us. Without such a testing she would remain forever ignorant of her own latent capacity, or would never bring it to expression. Here is where she is thrown into the scales of the balance, in Libra on the horizon, and here is where she is being weighed. How does she measure up under the test of earth? In no other realm of her evolutionary experience is she so situated that her acts become decisive for good or ill. The human life is the only stage on which every act is an act of destiny. Standing on the equally balanced bars of the scales, or arms of the cross, with spirit on one side, matter on the other, her every motivation, word or deed inclines the arms up or down, and thus she frames her destiny. Man is the only creature whose inner spirit writes the record of its character on outer flesh, and receives the rebound or echo of this uttered word on its inner bodies in turn. For every fleshly experience sends an impression inward and makes a record on soul, which holds it. A man writes his book of life on the body, temporarily, and upon the tablets of immortal spirit-essence, eternally. The body he inherits in his successive incorporations is the outer expression on the visible plane of all his previous activities in the cycle. Whatever is hidden within will be revealed, and, cleansed and purified by suffering, returned within. A man's soul *will* speak out through his body. For the soul enforms the body, and after its own pattern: "For soul *is* form, and doth the body make," as the *Faerie Queen* states.

The earth is the Court of Judgment and Justice because it is the only place in which the consequences of past living and thinking come to light in a living embodiment. The kind of body, mind and emotional nature a person brings with him into incarnation is the book of record of all his past deeds done in the flesh, only now republished in the newest and latest edition. Not a court in a spooky spirit-Amenta, but earth life judges a man, because it subjects the nature and character he brings as his book of life to the test of further experience. And his good, bad or indifferent success in undergoing that test is again recorded in his personal character for further testing and reformation in the next life. "The opening of the books" in the trial in *Revelation* is just the bringing *out* of what is *in* one. Earthly life is expressly designed to do this. How else could nature make a record of the individual's career save in the permanent nucleus of his soul, which

486

from life to life brings its hidden qualities, its beauty or its deformities, forth to view in the lineaments of both outer body and inner impulse! When the laws of righteousness and good are at last written upon character, then will the body reflect fully the inner glory. Only that can be brought out which is resident within, a fact which has become an accepted principle of modern biology after seventy years of research since Darwin's day.

Someone may offer as evidence against our conclusions the verse from *Hebrews* (9:27): "It is appointed unto every man once to die, but after this the judgment." One knows not whether this is a corruption of some original statement of text by partisan or factional zeal, or a true version of what the philosopher wrote. But even if correctly rendered, it is readily interpretable in full consonance with the philosophy here expounded. For it is in line with the ancient wisdom which declares that it is appointed, by the Cycle of Necessity, the Great Dragon, that man should go once through human evolution, subdivided of course into many single lives, and have once the experience of embodiment in all the elements of nature. This study has revealed that the allegories in scripture practically all refer to the complete cycle of embodied or incarnate life, and not to single stages or steps. Here again, then, the "once" covers the entire human round. And to enter life in matter is, as shown, "to die." Then "after this" is as well rendered "in this" or "throughout this," since the judgment begins after, or from, the very beginning of the "death." To be sure, all judgment holds for after-time, but it is immediately concomitant with the acts judged. There is a rounding out, finishing and perfecting of judgment in the last stages of the entire round, naturally, and it may be legitimate to think of these last denouements as the final judgment at the end. *Hebrews* (9:26) does expressly say: "Nay, once for all, at the end of the world, he has appeared, with his self-sacrifice to abolish sin." The havoc wrought upon millions of morbid minds by the mistranslation of *teleuten aion* as "the end of the world" instead of, properly, "the end of the aeon or cycle," has already been emphasized. But the passage indicates that as the whole cycle rounds out to its conclusion, the registry of the record will reach its beautiful consummation. The writing will then be in final form—until the next great cycle begins. At the end of the aeon nature must reckon with her child and pronounce the verdict on the aeon's activities and accomplishments.

Nevertheless it is during the run of the cycle that the soul is being weighed in the scales of the balance, for that is the only time when the two elements of being, spirit and matter, are poised in solstitial balance against each other.

That the whole question has perplexed scholars is revealed from the following by Budge:

"The question naturally arises here:—When did the judgment in the hall of Osiris take place? To this *no definite answer can be given,* for the reason that no text supplies the information needed. There are no grounds, so far as I see, for assuming that the Egyptians believed in a great general day of judgment, when all the world should be judged, and the wicked shall be punished, and the righteous shall be rewarded, or for thinking, as some have done, that the mummified bodies were laid in the tomb to await a general resurrection. On the contrary, all the evidence seems to point to the conclusion that the judgment of each individual was thought to take place *immediately after death,* and if this was the belief, it follows that punishment or reward was allotted to the dead at once. The evil heart or heart which had failed to balance the feather, symbolic of the law, was given to the monster Am-mit to devour; this punishment consisted of instant annihilation, unless we imagine that the destruction of the heart was extended over an indefinite period." [1]

Budge barely escapes committing himself to childish literalism at the end of this speculation. And his assertion that no text "supplies information" is but a confession of scholastic inability to read the hieroglyphs and symbols. The whole *Book of the Dead* and other texts are definite attempts to transmit or preserve knowledge about the judgment. The pity is that modern scholarship has not yet learned to interpret the fathomless wisdom of those texts. But Budge lends authoritative corroboration to the claim that the ancient religions envisaged no such universal "Judgment Day" as exoteric Christianity has plagued the conscience of people with for centuries. It is at any rate inconsequential when a final judgment is pronounced upon life; for the ingredients of that sentence are being compounded by the individual at all moments, in the ever-present Now. Every passing act helps determine the nature of "final" decision. Budge again speculates on the subject:

". . . there exist definite proofs that the Egyptians believed in a judgment which was to be held in the domain of Osiris" [it should be recalled that

488

Osiris was "Lord of Amenta"—earth!] "and we should hardly expect the spiritual body to begin its career until after the trial of the heart in the balance, and until the verdict of the gods at this judgment was favorable to the deceased."

But the noted scholar confesses his confusion and want of definite knowledge in the sentences immediately following the above:

"The whole question is full of difficulty, chiefly because the Egyptians themselves did not, I imagine, *form definite ideas on such subjects,* or if they did, they did not put them in writing. It is, however, perfectly certain that they believed that Osiris had power to make men to be born after death into a new life, and that such life was everlasting."

In uncertainty over the cryptic and baffling texts, Budge, like others, took the easy way of foisting his own failure on the Egyptians themselves. If we can not make sense out of their texts, they could not themselves have had very clear ideas, is the conclusion. But this work refutes that verdict. In the face of the evidence presented herein the claim that the ancients were unable to form definite ideas, and true ones, upon the profoundest questions of being, can no longer be supported.

It seems never to have been seen that the idea of a universal Day of Judgment commits its holders to the absurd premises that the law of cause and effect, or action and reaction, is inactive or in abeyance throughout all the time of our present energetic life in human society! All consequences of action are somehow being absorbed in Infinite Mind and held suspended in a *pralaya,* or motionless state, from the time of their causation until the great climactic "Day." This predicament puts the exoteric doctrine out of court where intelligence presides. Moreover, the absurd delusion has so far worked *its* natural consequences in immediate precipitation that it has impaled the general consciousness of the masses on the idea that somehow one can do as one likes in this world, and escape the Eye of the Law and of Retribution. It has promoted in large measure the present age of lawlessness.

The *Ritual* speaks of the secret knowledge of the periodicities and cycles of incarnation as requisite to render safe the passage through all the trial scenes in the Judgment Hall. The salvation of the deceased depended on his having the facts treasured up in his memory. As the soul walked through the valley of the shadow of death, his security depended upon his knowledge that he was a divinity threading his way through the dark underground labyrinth of matter. His memory of his intrinsically deific nature would be his safeguard; and this memory was his book of life and character, for it was his own self, come hither to purify itself of dross.

Massey affirms that the Rabbins have preserved a tradition that the dead are summoned before the divine tribunal to be judged upon the day of doom, which occurs each New Year's Day! The theological dogmatist will scowl at this as a survival of heathen sun-worship. But he is not probably aware that the unknown writer of the *Epistle to the Hebrews* has discussed at some length this identical matter, and stated succinctly that the annual festivals were but a typical ritual, merely a reminder of spiritual realities! In the ninth chapter we read:

"For Christ has not entered a holy place which human hands have made (a mere type of the reality!)"—[parenthesis *not* ours]—"nor was it to offer himself repeatedly, like the high priest entering the holy place *every year*, with blood that was not his own:—for in that case he would have had to suffer repeatedly, ever since the world was founded. Nay, once for all, at the end of the world, he has appeared with his self-sacrifice to abolish sin . . . For as the law has a mere shadow of the bliss that is to be, instead of representing the reality of that bliss, it can never perfect those who draw near with the same *annual sacrifices* that are perpetually offered . . . As it is, they are an *annual reminder* of sins . . ."

The writer of the Epistle was finding it necessary to warn devotees not to fall into the error of assuming that the annual commemorations of spiritual transactions would automatically bestow divine grace and unction upon them by and through their mere performance. It was a caution against literalizing a ritual. For so, says the writer, Jesus would have to come and be crucified over again each year, if the rituals were anything more than "reminders." Even at that time it had become necessary to caution votaries that the religious festivals and myths were only symbols of an inner mystery. How much more is the same caution necessary now! If the Day of Doom came once each year on New Year's Day, it was set only as an annual commemoration of a fact which was perpetual, constant, persistent throughout life.

Thoth (or Horus in his capacity), the scribe of fate, makes the final summary of the case and presents it to the jury. He introduces Ani (the soul) to Osiris, saying:

"I have come to thee, O Un-nefer, and I have brought unto thee the Osiris-Ani. His heart is right; it hath come forth guiltless from the scales . . . Taht hath weighed it according to the decree pronounced unto him by the company of the gods; it is most right and true. Grant that he may appear in the presence of Osiris; and let him be like unto the followers of Horus for ever and ever."

To come forth guiltless from the scales may now be seen to convey the deep significance of the soul's emergence from earth life between the two horizons, washed clean and gloriously spiritualized. If the judgment had been adverse, the soul would have been cast to the monster Am-mit, which only means, however, return to animal incarnation until final purification.

We have descanted sufficiently upon the seven elementary powers, which, being mindless, chaotic, had to be cast down. It was an age-old legend that there were seven watchers who were tried in the judgment, found not faithful, and overthrown. Now in the *Ritual* there appear the seven mortal sins "that lie in wait *at the balance where all hearts are weighed,* to arrest the further progress of the soul" (Ch. 71). These seven natural instincts of the mortal self constituted the seven-headed serpent that lay in wait at the "bight of Amenta," to devour the infant and innocent god-soul. The present exegesis receives striking corroboration in the statement of the *Ritual* that this place of ambuscade is "at the balance where all hearts are weighed." For assuredly it is in the incarnate state only that the soul could meet the seven enemies whose very existence is in the animal body and the carnal nature. The seven early mindless rulers were to be displaced by the twelve archons seated on the twelve thrones of judgment. Massey writes in enlightening fashion:

"The seat of justice in the solar mythos was shifted to the point of the equinox, and the balance was erected on the later mount of glory in the zodiac. This is the *mountain* of Amenta in the eschatology. It is described in the Ritual (Ch. 149) as the exceeding high mountain of the nether world, the top of which touches the sky . . . This was the mountain, as judgment seat." [2]

It is an exceeding high mountain, but it is not in Massey's ghost-Amenta, but in our world here. Its top touches the sky, which is just the heaven side of the horizon line in our own natures. It is important to note that the scholar definitely places the judgment mount on the horizon. The Scales figured, he says elsewhere, at the equinoctial level and marked the division, at the same time being the link between the two "heavens," and Libra was the express emblem of the Two Truths of Life and Death.

The main Egyptian symbol of spiritual being in humanity's trial was the feather. The appropriateness of this emblem consists likely in the fact that, held in certain angles of light, the two sides divided by the midriff reflect, the one a glossy, the other a somber dull appearance. It was a sign, at any rate, of light and shade, and the two halves represent the deities Ma and Shu. And Ma and Shu were unified and pluralized in the name Mati. This introduces us to the Egyptian personification or goddess of Justice, who was Maat. To express her functions we can do no better than to repeat Massey's characterization:

"The Balance is a symbol of *maat* and its oneness in duality. The *equilibrium* of the universe was expressed by *maat*, which represented the natural, immutable and eternal law. *It was erected as a figure at the equinox* . . . *Makha* is a name for the scales and to weigh. The scales were erected *at the place of poise and weighing in the equinox* . . . The sphinx was a figure of this duality in oneness at the equinox. The feather of Shu (or Ma) was another type of the same duality of light and shade, which meet and mingle as one at twilight." [3]

It was against this feather that the heart of the Manes was weighed in the judgment trial. It was either a symbol of mere balance and equilibration, or its lightness was to test the purity of man's spirit. A reduplication of the same balance between light and shade as symbol of justice was later brought into use in the form of the black and white ermine worn by judges. The two lion *kherufu* (cherubim) at the two gates were likewise symbolical of the idea. Chapter 136B of the *Ritual* recites: "I am come," says the Speaker, "so that I may see the process of Maat and the lion-forms." The soul comes here to have the experience of weighing ephemeral values against eternal ones, good against evil, and seeing how the balance works for evolution. The Manes waiting to enter the mount is summoned: "Come, come, for the father is uttering the judgment of Maat." In the papyri of Ani and Nunefer the judges or assessors in the trial appear as twelve in number, instead of the twenty-four or the forty-two. They are thus a prototype of the twelve thrones in *Revelation* and the twelve judges of Israel.

Budge's description of the hall of the two horizons is worthy of notice:

"The Hall of the two Maat Goddesses, the two Goddesses of Truth, shows one goddess presiding over Upper and the other over Lower Egypt. One guards the soul, the other the body."

Here is the clearest authentication of our analysis and characterization of the two Lands spoken of in the ancient texts, the one as soul, the other as body. Yet in spite of this clear statement of the esoteric significance of the terms, the great scholar has joined the company of those who constantly take Upper and Lower Egypt to refer to two geographical divisions of the Egypt on the map. How long indeed will it take them to learn that very ancient scriptures dealt with the eternal interests of the human soul, and not with the tawdry facts of geography and history?

The two goddesses are also called the "Two Daughters Merti, Eyes of Maat (Truth)." Then comes a detail that must be seen to be of central moment for theology. The hall is in the form of an elongated funerary coffer! In other words, the judgment hall is the coffin, tomb or grave, the place of "death," which we have conclusively shown to be the body of man.

The hands of the god seated at the head are extended over the Two Pools, each of which contains an Eye of Horus. An ape (Thoth) is seated before a pair of scales. Thirteen feathers of Maat and thirteen Uraei or elementary serpent-powers are arranged alternately. The two Maat goddesses are seated beside one of the double doors, each holding a scepter of "serenity" in her right hand and one of "life" in her left. On the head and scepter of each is the feather, symbol of truth. Everything suggests the dual nature of an even balance, and herein the Manes is tried.

A remarkably suggestive statement is made in the 47th chapter of the *Ritual,* intimating that the judgment came as a result of the splitting of primal biunity into duality. It is the "chapter of not entering in unto the block":

"I have joined up my head and neck, in heaven and on earth . . . the goddess Nut hath joined together the bones of my neck and back, and I beheld them as they were in the time that is past when as yet I had not seen Maat and when the gods were not born in visible forms."

How clearly this says to us that after the unifying of our two natures here the soul beholds itself restored to its primal unity! It sees itself whole, as it was before it came out into the duality of sex polarization; and the identification of this splitting with "seeing Maat" or the judgment on the two horizons, is most direct testimony to the correctness of our resolution of hidden meanings.

We have considered the significance of the term *Makhu* in the name of Horus or Har-Makhu. Another correlative name of Horus is Har-Tema, which signifies "he who makes justice visible." Har-Tema was lord of the double earth, wherein justice was wrought out in the form of real existence in the life on earth. The *Ritual* says ('Ch. 79): "I am Tem . . . the creator of things which are, who cometh forth from the earth, who maketh to come into being the seed which is sown." He is the power which brings the hidden things of God to light in matter.

Hints have already conveyed the general relevance of the great old scriptural term, the Battle of Armageddon, and we have traced its origin from the Egyptian *Har-Makhu,* with the addition of the Hebrew word *adon,* meaning "lord," at the end. The name signifies "the sun (spirit) power, lord of the balance between spirit and matter, standing on the horizon." The term has overcast the consciousness of deluded Christians with fearsome speculation and solicitude for so many centuries that its sane clarification at last in the glow of Egyptian symbolism is quite worth an additional paragraph. Again has the mythical shadow of a great natural truth been turned by Christian ignorance into the substance of a catastrophic historical denouement. But, like purgatory, hell and the judgment, this dreaded battle is taking place now, and is indeed partly over. For it is fought "at night" and "on the horizon." These terms of description settle the question, if there is any, whether it is symbolism or factuality. It is just that perennial struggle fought between the two opposing powers of life, on the dividing line between their areas of influence at the place of the balance, where the *Makhu,* or scales of justice, were erected to weigh the past and present character of the Manes. The scales were said to be erected on the night of the great battle between Horus and

494

Sut, when the Sebau were defeated and the adversaries overpowered. The great contest is nothing but the whole of the battle of life that we are now waging; the war between Horus, the spiritual light, and the seven-headed dragon of darkness. Great military conflicts on the continental plains may be a phase of the struggle in one of its manifestations, but the term refers to the entire aeonial battle. It is notable, however, that in *Revelation* this battle is fought after the pouring out of the contents of the seventh bowl of divine essence. As it was the coming of this seventh principle which brought the triadic unity of solar deity into the body formed by the six elementary forces, it is precisely the time when the great battle between the god and the six lower powers, the Sebau, could begin. The battle could not start, surely, until the god arrived on the scene. The battle is *preceded* by the emptying of the great bowl and the sound of a great voice which proclaimed: "It is done!" The struggle only begins when the seven natures had been conjoined in the physical body on the horizon line. With the coming of the solar triad of mind the battle was on between it and the six (seven) evil spirits which had to be made subservient, or "cast down." "Slaughter" was to be "dealt out to Apap" by Maati! The battle of Armageddon was begun as the "war in heaven" and continued on earth between the sun-god incubated in the body and the six demoniac forces of the natural "first man." We have long been fighting the Battle of Har-Makhu-Adon.

One account of this battle (translated by Goodwin) records that the twins, Sut and Horus, transformed themselves into wild beasts and remained in that state during three days! This is not arrant nonsense, inasmuch as the single unified deity, after splitting into twin powers as matter and spirit, did come into the bodies of beasts before the human stage, typed as the three days of incubation in the kingdoms below the human.

Man has entered the Götterdämmerung; he stands within the twilight. He stands on the mounts both of crucifixion and transfiguration, with the shadow of the two beams of the cross or the scales falling athwart his body. Every act, word and thought of his causes those arms of the scales to move up or down, according as he gives an impulse to spiritual or to sensuous expression. In their motion they write the scroll of his book of life, alternately upon outward feature and inner character. Every movement of the bars is a decree of judgment for him. Taht-Aan, the scribe and recorder, is filling the pages of his book. Who shall estimate the difference in world history since the third century if this knowledge of the sages of Egypt that man is now undergoing trial in the Hall of Judgment on this mount of the double equinox, on the morning and evening horizons of evolution, had not been lost to western humanity through the fatal triumph of ignorance and bigotry over chaste wisdom? Christendom has been taught that the individual can perpetrate what heinousness he will in this life, and wait a millennium before being brought to reckoning. The certitude of the instant judgment of the two Maat goddesses has been obscured or denied. Western man has been deprived of the definite knowledge that the consequences of his acts are in immediate reaction upon him. The shadow of the law has been deludedly removed from his mind and conscience, with the result that human life has proceeded largely without consideration of the certainty of justice. And with this sense of immunity bolstered by the concomitant doctrines of a vicarious atonement and the forgiveness of sins, the misguided mind of Occidental man has indulged in such revelries of license and heedlessness as history has not recorded at another period. The assurance that the world is under law, that acts carve the shape of destiny, is scarcely to be found in Western areas. The habitual philosophy of the "average" mind of modern civilized nations consists of the hazy notion that the Eyes of Maati are mostly asleep, and that the theological Day of Judgment, if it is to come at all, is a long way off.

All the while the arms of that Balance on the hill of the horizon in the twilight are moving, and they are the pen of Taht-Aan inscribing the record.

Chapter XX

SUNS OF INTELLECT

As the human eye recoils before the overpowering splendor of the solar disk in the sky, so the human mind strives in vain to realize the marvel of sublime grandeur in the ancient religious myth of the sun-gods. This was no curious faith of a diminutive Parsee sect; it was the universal form and dress of religion. The sun-myth was the heart's core of all religion and philosophy everywhere before the Dark Ages obscured the vision of truth. And world religion will not fulfill its original function of dispelling from the soul of mankind the dark earth-born vapors that envelop it until the mind once again is irradiated with the light of that transcendent knowledge. Christianity forsook its high station on the mount illuminated by solar radiance when it submerged the Christly sun-glory under the limitations of a fleshly personage and dismissed solar religion as "pagan." In converting the typical man into a man of history, it forswore its early privilege of basking in the rays of the great solar doctrine. Light, fire, the sun, spiritual glory—all went out in eclipse under the clouds of mental fog that arose when the direct radiance of the solar myth had been blanketed. Christianity passed forthwith out of the light into the dreadful shadows of the Dark Ages. And that dismal period will not end until the bright glow of the solar wisdom is released once more to enlighten benighted modernity. Ajax crying for the light is still the appropriate heraldic figure on the modern shield, and until the myth of the sun-gods is restored to its place in knowledge, there will be no response to the cry but the echo.

Near the end of November, 1932, the public press reported the announcement of Dr. George W. Crile, noted scientist of the Cleveland laboratories, that he had discovered in the heart of every cell of protoplasm tiny centers or foci of energy which he called "hot points" or "radiogens," with estimated temperatures of from 3,000 to 6,000 degrees of heat. Protoplasm emitted radiations of various wave lengths, "some as powerful as those emitted by the sun." "The sun 'shines' in the protoplasm of animals and plants, and therefore animals and plants can confer on atoms chemical affinities such as are conferred by the sun."

"Who would think that there are 'hot points' in man and animals on the order of the temperature of the surface of the sun? . . . If one could look into protoplasm with an eye capable of infinite magnification, one might expect to see the radiogens spaced like stars as suns in infinite miniature . . . Without exaggeration the concept may be taken to mean . . . that within the very flesh of man burns the fierce fire of the sun, and that within man's body glow infinitely small counterparts of the stars." [1]

This report, which fell more or less unheeded upon millions of minds racked with economic fear, at last marks the discovery of the direct point of contact between "science and religion," of which the world has so long stood in such desperate need. It provides that common ground of a mutual datum on which both can meet with perfect accord at last. For this discovery of modern science posits, after sixteen or more centuries of obscuration, the fundamental authenticity of the solar myth, out of which all religions took their rise. Science has now restored to religion its basic principle, of which it had been bereft by nearly two millennia of ignorance. Religion now returns to its place in the sun, because the sun returns to its place in religion. Sunlight builds all things that are the subjects of scientific scrutiny; sunlight is also the Christly excellence in man's life and body. Science and religion meet at last in the happy glow of sunlight. The Christ in man is a god of solar energy.

One is permitted to wonder what would be the amazement of Dr. Crile and his fellow-moderns if it was shown to them that in an old book on the Rosicrucians published about 1872 the following brief sentence has stood in the silence of scientific scorn for nearly seventy years:

"Every man has a little spark of the sun in his own bosom . . . A spark of the original light is supposed to remain deep down in the interior of every atom." [2]

The secret purpose of the "Fire Philosophers," whom modern savants still like to class with imbeciles and children, was to release that spark of solar flame from its trammels of the flesh and unite it once again with the radix or point of emanation in "heaven." This was the mysterious aim of the alchemical science, whose "gold" was that Lux or Light of the Ineffable Source, into which all baser forms of conscious manifestation had to be transmuted. The sun was typed as gold and the moon as silver, a poetization to which nature has been a party in the coloring of the two orbs. For the gold was the radiant energy of the sun embosomed in man's interior being. It was his spiritual fire, that true light that lighteth every man that cometh into the world; while the silvery moon typed the feminine or bodily nature which was to be raised by the alchemy of spiritual vibration into the golden glow.

A spark of the sun in the inner heart of every human! That is the center of light about which all religion and philosophy can again rally their disconcerted forces of interpretation. That is the point of gravity toward which all meanings can be seen to tend with perfect constancy. This is the radiant gleam of mental light, by which mankind may again see to read aright the ancient books of wisdom. And this is the torch that will in our day illumine the darkened portals of the temple of religion, so that the menacing hordes of materialistic devastators will see its beauty in time to stay their impious hands. It is only because a benighted ecclesiasticism permitted religion to be divorced from its basic principle which roots it in science, that the partisans of a modern "scientific" interpretation of life have been able to see no beauty or utility in it. To them religion has seemed a delusion of fancy, a hallucination thrown over feebler minds. To them it is not basically or structurally related to nature. On the whole their repugnance to the system was legitimate, for religion had been distorted into the unnatural thing it has come to be. But with the restoration of religion and philosophy to their ancient bases in true science, and the god seen as the solar fire within man's bosom, resentment against it can no longer find apology. For science now finds itself on bended knee before this tiny glint of solar light at the heart of every atom; and when religion finds that it, too, worships the counterpart of the same fire in man's heart, the two estranged brothers, science and religion, will find themselves kneeling side by side at the same altar at last.

Not only is there a spark of solar fire in every particle of matter, but every higher organism partakes of the empyreal largesse in proportion

499

to its grade of being. Thus every man harbors a solar god or fiery spirit within him! Above man, the planets are cosmic beings with resplendent souls of unimaginable glory. The suns are the glowing hearts of the bodies of gods!

The sun was the center of religious ideology because it was the center of all life. Religion was once organically constructed about a nucleus of profound teaching directly related to the phenomena of life. It was no detached scheme of emotionalism. It was an alignment of devotion and conduct in relation to knowledge of the elements and facts of life itself. The central fact was the presence of a solar fragment, a spark of deity, in the inner soul of every being, unintelligent below man, intelligent for the first time in Atum, the Man. The immortal soul was a beam from the eternal Sun, a spark of divine fire, an irradiation of the essence of God's own being. This spark of cosmic intelligence was, as shown, the seventh emanation crowning the elementary six, and summing their powers all in itself. Man, in whom this spark was for the first time made local in nature, was the crown and summation of all precedent expression. All lower kingdoms are in him, the three sub-mineral, the mineral, vegetable, animal and human thus far evolved. They are comprehended in him in the constituency of his four lower vehicles, which make him the composite being he is. His physical form is from the earth, his emotion body from the moon, his mind from the race evolved on Venus, and his spiritual soul from the sun. The sun-spark was then the guiding intelligence, the king, within him. By his body and his senses he was linked with the earth, with nature; by his mind and soul he was tied to the stars of heaven. Head in heaven, body on the earth, said Egypt. "I am a child of earth and the starry skies, but my race is of heaven alone," seconded the Orphic philosophy. By virtue of the two lower creatures within him he is a mortal being, doomed to temporal extinction; by the higher two he is constituted an immortal entity, facing a future of endless glorification. The lower rose from the earth by the force of the expansion of powers elemental in the atom of matter, and was a product of "natural" evolution. The higher was "the Lord from heaven," as Paul names it. And the union of the two in one organism gave to humanity a local habitation and a name, a form, a character and a cosmic stage for its activities.

But the ancients knew that the history of each fragment of solar light impounded in a corral of flesh on earth was a reflected miniature of that of the great solar orb itself. And the growth and progress of the tiny spark that had got individualized in each man was studied in the light of its parental analogue in the heavens. Hence the basis of religion was the course of the sun through the solar year, which course again reflected the round of the sun through the 25,868 years of the Great Year of precession, and both were marked by the orb's passage through the twelve stages of zodiacal meaning. He who will interpret the zodiac with full intelligibility will depict the life of man in all its reaches. The knowledge of this stellar script, this book with seven, then twelve great seals, was imparted in full or in part in the sacred Mysteries of old. It is gravely doubtful if anyone now living knows the import of the entire wheel. We catch fragmentary glimpses of its meaning, but the deeper connotation of the structure eludes the mind. Its profundity is next to fathomless. We can but follow the hints given us by the archaic sages in their writings.

It is clear, in outline, that the solar year is a marvelously precise reflection in outer nature of the spiritual life of man the individual and man the race. It is particularly a vivid typograph of the history of the soul in and out of incarnation. The two groups of upper signs, three air and three fire (symbolically), represent the life of the soul when out of body in the empyrean. The six lower signs, dubbed the six "water" signs, cover the life of the soul in the watery physical body. The lower six are a reflection or image of the upper six, as water reflects what is above it in the air and the light! That is to say that the life of man below is a reflected counterpart of his life in spirit above. And the soul's journey round the wheel through the alternate realms of incarnate and discarnate life comprises its cyclical history in this aeon. As nature sets the norm in her life-method by her alternations of day and night in the physical and astronomical domains, these are seen to be typical of the experience undergone by the soul in its successive sojourns in the realms of spiritual "day" and material "night." The systole and diastole of the heart's action, the inhalation and exhalation of breath, are but the common evidence and confirmation of the universal modus of living procedure. The conscious immortal spirit in man swings endlessly through the two phases of the zodiac, upper and lower, of which circulation the daily and annual phenomenon of the sun's movements is an exact miniature copy. Solar religion was based solidly on the ground fact that the sun was not only the type, but the essential essence of the divine soul of man, and that its annual course was graphically pictorial of the soul's cyclical history. The sun's annual round is typical, first, of a single life history; secondly, of the entire series of single lives making up the complete experience of the human cycle. Like the stars, the galaxies and the super-galaxies now seen by astronomy, many individual life cycles constitute a larger cycle, and many of those a still larger one. It is futile for the little mind of man to quarrel with the limitless expansiveness of the Universe of Life. Such quarrel has already cost us the loss of our clearest understanding of cosmic processes, which by reflection open our minds to the meaning of the lesser processes of our life here. Life is vast, and its vastness would crush our thinking if philosophy did not fortify us with the consideration that the little repeats the immense and is identical with it. *Each man is a solar universe, a planetary system, comprised of infinite cells or minor systems, and the spiritual light glowing at the center of his being is the central sun of his system.* And if he learns to control *this* universe, he will be put in charge of larger spheres. "My mind to me a kingdom is," and if one be found faithful in the governance of that world of self, one will be made ruler over many things. "The Framer made the creations six in number and for the seventh he threw into the midst the fire of the sun," is ancient truth. Likewise the seventh outgush of creative force threw the sun of intellect into the midst of the six lower natural energies, to become their head and ruler. This was the work of the divine Father implanting the seminal seed of his fiery spiritual consciousness into the body of Mother Nature, and so closing her unfruitful womb and stopping her wastage to make her pregnant with Christ child. Hence the antipathy, detected in ancient texts, between the menstruating woman and the sun or fire. A verse in the *Shayast La-Shayast* (Ch. 2:29) runs:

"A fiend so violent is that fiend of menstruation" that "where another fiend does not smite anything with a look (*akhsh*) it smites with a look," so that "the sun and other luminaries are not to be looked at by her, and conversation with a righteous man is not to be held by her. She must not look on fire, and a fire must not be kindled in the same house that she is in."

Wilson in his *Parsee Religion* (p. 224) writes:

"The flow was looked upon as the Azi-damp by which the devil desired to extinguish the fire that Zarathustra brought from heaven."

This is in the realm of symbolism, of course, intimating the general significance of the divine soul, as fire, being extinguished by the water of the body. It may not be utterly fantastic to suggest that the fire of spirit that dries up the "red sea" of the menstrual flow in the allegory may be the subtle meaning behind the *Exodus* story of the drying up of the Red Sea, alleged to be on the map. As we have seen, however, modern translation has made it the "Reed Sea."

Leprosy was spoken of as the result of an offense against the sun. Amenta, the realm of the six elementary powers, both in nature and in the human body, was a land of chaos and darkness until lighted up by the nocturnal sun, or the spirit buried in the flesh. Hor-Apollo observes that the star which bears the name of Seb signifies, amongst other things, the soul of the male or virile adult. "This is the star of soul," they said; "let us keep it pure and bright and shining star-like."

"This is the sun within us, the seminal source of life; do not dim its lustre or cause it to suffer eclipse. Save your soul (seminal) and do not sin against the sun of light."

And it is said of Osiris in the *Ritual*:

"Give ye glory as to the Sun; he is the chief, the only one ever coming from the body, the head of those who belong to the race of the Sun."

In the *Clementine Gospel* the Christ is portrayed in the character of the sun-god. This eastern Christ says:

"I must work the works of him that sent me while it is day; the night cometh when no man can work. When I am in the world I am the light of the world."

The world was represented as being created from the drops of bloody Gethsemanic sweat, or male seminal essence which fell from the phallus of Ra, Tem, Atum or Khepera onto the earth. The male creative fluid became the type of spiritual creative power. It is the concentrated essence of the blood, which in turn is highly charged with the electric soul of spiritual energy. It was the seed of the gods'

503

creative essence. It was therefore held to be a condensation of solar energy. It is said that the holy emanation which proceeds from Osiris vivifies gods, men, cattle and creeping things, and that in his season he flows forth from his cavern in order to "pour out the *seed of his soul* which produces offerings in abundance for his Ka, and vivifies both gods and men." The expulsion of the seeds of deity into lower realms of matter was a part of the dismemberment or mutilation. In the case of Bata, the younger brother of Anup, in the tale of the Two Brothers, the phallus is torn away and thrown into the water and devoured by a fish. The "masturbating deity" matched on the male side the virgin mother and the immaculate conception on the female side. He was Khepera, and his symbol was the male beetle, which produced new life from his own body without conjunction with the female.

"To denote an Only Begotten," says Hor-Apollo, "the Egyptians delineate a Scarabaeus, because the Scarabaeus is a creature self-produced, being unconceived by a female. The Scarabaeus also symbolizes generation and a father, because it is engendered by the father solely." Massey adds: "Khepr, the beetle, buried himself, with his seed, in the earth; there he transformed, and the father issued forth as the son."

The sun was the type of the male creative power in the universe, but he was portrayed with feminine attributes to indicate his subjection under matter when involving his energies in creation. He was a kind of male-mother. His growing weak in the autumn was likened to the feminine weakness in menstruation. "When the sun becomes weak, he lets fall the sweat of his members and this changes to a liquid; he bleeds much." Then he was called the sun bound in linen, and wrapped as a woman. He was known as Osiris Tesh-Tesh, in his bloody sweat in Smen. The male as sole reproducer was spoken of in female terms. He is god the mother. Num, Egyptian deity, was the Mother of Mothers as well as the Father of Fathers. "In like manner Jove is designated by Orpheus 'the mother of the gods.' He was Ju-mater, or Jupiter creatress." Proclus in *Timaeus* says: "All things are contained in the womb of Jupiter." Brahm is likewise feminized. "The great Brahm is the womb of all those forms which are conceived in every natural womb." "The great Brahm," says Krishna, "is my womb and in it I place my foetus and from it is the procreation of all nature"

(Moor's *Pantheon:* Krishna, p. 211). Baal and Astarte exchange genders in the Assyrian books. Nu was the original mother-heaven, the feminine celestial firmament. Yet she is masculinized: "It is the water or Nu who is the father of the gods. I am the great God creating himself." Creative power was conceived as feminine during the first creations. But when the sun, Helios, came to govern planetary revolutions, the gender was conceived as male. Life was androgyne before the bifurcation. The only quarrel in ancient religions was over the question whether deity was male or female in its first manifestations. Deity frequently had to carry the functions of both sexes.

The hidden purport back of the Egyptian symbolism of the beetle and the self-begetting god was that which was really the nub of the dispute in the early Christian Church over the creedal rendering of the Greek term *monogenes* (Latin: *unigenitus*), translated "only-begotten" in the Bible. It led to the great Arius-Athanasius controversy which rent the early Church into factions, which have not yet united. Had Egyptian symbolism been envisaged understandingly, that grievous dispute could have been avoided. The god who poured out and mixed his life blood with earth, and the beetle that goes underground to come forth renewed, are two vivid symbols of bright angelic spirit incarnating in human life. Life buried itself to be born anew. It is quite possible that Onan's sin was a reference to the first group of five legions of angels who, as it were, poured out their spiritual substance in the direction of incarnation, but who nevertheless failed to plant their seed fully in the soil of mortal flesh. Their effort proved abortive. The old books recite the story.

It is possible to see that the monogenetic theory was current in early Christian times and could have been comprehended by Christian exegetists if they had not already begun to look with scorn upon all things pagan. Irenaeus alludes to the belief in an excerpt from his book *Against Heresies* (I, Ch. 2:1, 4, Ante-Nicene Library): "It was also taught by the Egyptian Valentinus that the father produced in his own image without conjuction with the female." Had a little analogical penetration been displayed by the somber Fathers of the Church, there might have been intelligence enough extant to save the translators from perpetrating the damaging rendering of *monogenes* as "only-begotten." The term meant, of course, simply born of the father or male principle alone, without birthing in the womb of matter. Yet it was at the same time the story of the father or spirit incarnating in matter and reissuing on the opposite horizon as his transformed son. The fatality of the incorrect translation can not be seen until it is realized that the term "only-begotten," misapplied to a single man in history, has operated to dispossess every mortal in Christendom of the consciousness of his own inborn divinity, the one inestimable boon that religion was designed to extend to all the race.

The famous *Litany of Ra* describes Atum as the supreme sun-god in man. In his descent into Amenta, which is *at sunset*, "his form is that of an old man," while later in his resurrection it is that of a lion. He sets as Ra; he rises again as Horus. Atum in Amenta is the hidden soul of spiritual life, imaged by the nocturnal sun, buried in darkness. He suffers dethronement and exile in material darkness in order that he may "cause the principles to arise." He brings the new generation of solar power to birth, as in dying he is reborn from himself.

There is involved herein the secret of one of the most inexplicable and, at first sight, most irrational customs, the explanation of which has baffled anthropologists without end. This was the *couvade*. When the student or casual reader encounters the historical evidence establishing the fact that many tribes in different parts of the world in archaic times observed the strange custom of sending the father, instead of the parturient mother, to the bed of confinement at childbirth, the impression is that human mental processes had gone sadly awry. But it is only necessary to keep ever in mind that the sages and formulators of conventional practice were before all else typologists, to see that the eccentric custom was only an outward ritual of a very high spiritual commemoration indeed. The practice was only a symbolic act to dramatize the fact that in the birth of a son or daughter the father had injected his seminal spirit into the bosom of matter, had buried his seed in incarnation in the body of the babe, or had himself gone into confinement or "under cover" of flesh in the new babe! It only adumbrated the eternal fact of the incarnation. The sun went into retirement each evening, to be reborn on the morrow. *Couvade* means "going under cover."

The *Litany of Ra* contains an apostrophe to the great sun-god:

"Homage to thee, Ra, the beetle (Khepr), that folds his wings, that rests in the Empyrean, that is born as his own son!"

506

Khepr is designated "the Scarabaeus which enters life as its own son." Ptah, who was an embodiment of Khepr-Ra, is thus addressed:

"O God, architect of the world, thou art without a father, begotten by thine own becoming; thou art without a mother, being born through repetition of thyself."

In another text we read:

"O divine Substance, created from itself! O God, who hath made the substance which is in him. O God, who hast made his own father and impregnated his own mother." [3]

Some accompaniments of the *couvade* are of great interest. In the custom, as carried out by some Carib tribes, the father ate neither fish nor fowl for six months. Here we have a direct reference to the god, or father, as being deprived of water and air, or any higher element than that of earth, during its incubation period.

Hor-Apollo interestingly observes again: "They say also that the beetle lives six months underground and six above." If he does, nature surely has cast him in the role of Proserpina, not to say that of the human soul, figuratively. The six lower signs typify incarnate life.

But the beetle has further instruction for us. Hor-Apollo describes the Scarabaeus as a lunar typologist also. He observes that the beetle deposits its ball of eggs rolled in dung in the earth for the space of twenty-eight days—a lunar cycle—during which the moon passes through its smaller round of the twelve zodiacal signs. But on the twenty-ninth day, the day of the resurrection according to lunar markings, there occurs the baptism of the beetle. The Scarabaeus then casts his ball into the water. It opens to give birth to the young beetle. This immersion and baptism leads to renewal and regeneration. So Taht, the lunar god, was always declared to be self-created, never born.

The egg, as a primitive type of birth and rebirth, finds intriguing relation to this exegesis. As the *couvade* figured the return of the father's powers in the embryo of his child, incarnation betokened the return of the soul to its egg state. "Oh! Sun in his egg!" is an exclamation in the *Ritual*. The image used represented the return of "the sun or the dead" (Massey) to the egg-state in the underworld for the rehatching, or the *couvade*. And this furnishes the answer to Nicodemus' question: the soul must return again and again to the egg-state, to be rehatched—which is what has again been intimated in the ark symbolism. Man—the god in man—is as it were a grub worm hatched in the earth, and, expanding his wings of spirit as he emerges like the chrysalis, flies away with body glistening in the golden light of morning. The sun-god arising is thus addressed: "Adoration to thee, who arisest out of the golden and givest light to the earth!" The sun was emblemed as the winged scarab. And the beetle follows the sun, keeping in the angle of its direct rays, from morning till evening. The Christ is the "sun of righteousness."

In Gnostic iconography the child Horus reappears as the mummy-babe wearing the solar disk. The sun is again typified by the hawk, with a disk encircled by an uraeus on its head. Seven apes stand, four in front and three behind, denoting that the sun has put under or behind him three of the elementary powers, but faces the conquest of the other four in man.

The "Ur" from which Abraham, the first emanation from the Father, came forth, means the original sea of elemental fire. And when the emanation has gone to its death and rebirth in matter, it has become a new creature and is given a new name. The injection of the solar principle into material creation lends to mythology or primitive theology its most striking analogies and types. This is confirmed by Max Müller, who writes (*Selected Essays,* Vol. I, 604): "As soon as *Suryas* or Helios appears as a masculine form, we are in the very thick of mythology." *Suryas* or Helios is the sun. Mythology deals with the presence of this kingly force in life, its fight for sovereignty and its dominance over the lower powers. It is the central personage in all earthly myth and drama. The phoenix, dying and being reborn from its own ashes, depicts the death of the sun power in mortality and its renaissance from the grave.

The Egypto-Gnostics affirmed: "Seven powers glorify the Word." These were the seven nature spirits, which out of gratitude to the Propator, had each contributed of his best gift to the production of the most perfect being, the Christ aeon. Like the golden bough and the star atop the Christmas tree, he became the beauteous flower at the summit of creation, comprehending and synthesizing all lower elements in himself. He was thus the King of Glory.

After this consummation the heaven of seven divisions is described as rolling up like a scroll and passing away. Then the new heaven and the new earth are inaugurated. When the contents of the seventh bowl are poured out, the book of life is sealed with the seven seals, and the angel announces: "Behold I make all things new." A zodiac of twelve signs was then requisite to portray the life experience of the god in man. In the *Book of Exodus* we see the one God Ihuh superseding all the other gods, El-Shadai and the Elohim, when he assumes the suzerainty and orders that a sanctuary be built in which he shall be lifted up. This shrine or tabernacle was to be the hitherto unknown body of solar glory, or body of the resurrection, that temple not to be built with hands, eternal in the heavens of consciousness. "He subdues the dwellers in the darkness and there is none who can resist his power in the horizon." "He shineth like a new king in the East." "The great god who is there is Ra himself . . . the water of Maati is the road by which Atum-Ra goes to traverse the fields of divine harvest."

The *Book of the Dead* is primarily a sketch of the journey of the solar spark through the underworld across the Pool of Pant, or Lake of Maati, by night. The soul follows the track of the all-conquering sun, who is the cleaver of the way or opener of roads through the tangled thickets of sense life. He builds a dwelling of light for those who dwell in the darkness. The "Egyptians" are in gloom, but the "Israelites have light in their dwellings." The home of light for the glorified is Ammah, the place of no more night. When we realize that the Israelites were not an earth race, but a host of sun-fragments of intellect in incarnation, we can catch the sublime imputations in these figurative details of scripture.

The six (later seven) supplanted powers that come under the sway of the central sun of mind become the "attendants" or "companions" or "associates" of the sun-god. They are depicted as seven doves that hover around Jesus *in utero*, the seven solar rays that flash about his head, the seven lambs or rams with him in the mount, the seven as stars with Jesus in their midst, the seven as fishers in his boat, and finally the seven who as communicants solemnized the Eucharist with the loaves and fishes in the mortuary meal of the Roman catacombs.

The *Pistis Sophia*, furnishing much valuable material deleted from the Gospels, describes Jesus, after superseding the seven foundation pillars of the world, as passing through the twelve signs of the zodiac, mentioning each by name, and gathering a portion of the light from

509

each to incorporate in his own person. He says that he took the twelve saviors of the treasure of light and bound them into the bodies of your mothers. This is to say that he circumscribed the operation of the twelve deific powers in bodies of mortal flesh. He was thus to judge the twelve "tribes of Israel," or twelve segmentations of divine intelligence; those rays of cosmic mind which figure as the twelve tribes, sons, stars, brothers, kings, reapers, rowers, fishermen, sowers, and twelve voices and teachers. All these had begun as powers of light in the physical domain, and were in the end endowed with spiritual status with Jesus in the Father's kingdom. The Christ became the rose in the center of twelve knights. And, says Paul, the whole creation groaneth and travaileth to bring forth these twelve Sons of God, or powers of spiritual light.

The *Rig-Veda* asks:

"Who has seen the primordial at the time of his being born? What is that endowed with substance, which the unsubstantial sustains? From the earth are the breath and blood, but where is the soul? What is that one alone who has upheld these six spheres in the shape of the unborn?"

And the answer is given by Egypt in the person of the solar deity who was at last made the base and support of the six spheres. When the fire that enlightens supplanted the powers of Seb and Sut, there was present a new type of power as soul or Sol. This unborn power was personalized as Ptah, in the form of an embryo that transformed like the beetle to reproduce itself. It is the sun-god performing his *couvade* to raise up both the six spheres and himself. He is the hidden light, Amen-Ra, the unborn god, the support and rock of the whole creation. He is the unsubstantial, that nevertheless sustains substance.

Massey well expounds that "the Savior who came by spirit was the soul of the sun." "This suffering deity was the god in matter." When plunged into matter and ensouling creation, he became Osiris. In this phase he was the stricken one, the dead, lying inert in his mummy-case. He is figured as the "little old child," with finger at mouth, wizened, impotent, decadent, as the sun-god losing his power. He is the Jack of nursery legends, the Scottish Assiepet, the Danish Askepot, the German Aschenpüttel, who pokes in the ashes and blows up the fire, the solar fire which he has to rekindle from dying embers. He is the male Cinderella, the ash or ember maiden.

Before descending below the horizon of incarnation these souls are denominated in Egypt the Hamemmet Beings. They originated as the germs of souls emanating from the sun, whence Scipio saw them abstracted in his vision. "Hamemmet" signifies "that which is un-embodied," not yet incorporated in material bodies. This matches the "virgins" and the "Innocents" of Biblical terminology. They are the embryonic souls of future beings, children of the sun or Ra. They were the "children of Israel." If the monster Apap or Herut could slay them "in the egg" he would avert his later doom of having his head crushed under their heel. At enmity with the sun, the dragon of darkness seeks to devour the new-born sons of the light-god who are destined to overthrow his rule in nature. So he lies in wait at the bight of Amenta until the woman clothed with the sun shall give birth to them. They are called, in addition to other names already given, "the issue of Horus." Their slaughter is to be prevented, as is indicated by the title of Chapter 42 of the *Ritual*: "Chapter by which one hindreth the slaughter which is in Suten-Khen," the birthplace. The Manes at this stage is the child-Horus himself, and he says four times over: "I am the babe." As the child of the incorruptible sun, no power can harm him, and so "he steppeth onward through eternity," gathering up all the manifold powers of ineffable Light. "Not to be seen is my nest. Not to be broken is my egg." "I have made my nest in the confines of heaven" (*Rit.*, Ch. 85).

Lower Egypt was called "the desert in which the flocks of Ra were shepherded and fed." Horus says to them:

"Protection for you, flocks of Ra, born of the great one who is in the heavens. Breath to your nostrils, overthrowal of your coffins" (*Book of Hades,* 5th Div., Legend D).

Horus indicates how he steps onward through eternity in the statement: "I live in Tattu and I repeat daily my life after death, like the sun."

It need hardly be repeated that the *Christos* was represented under a different title and character during each 2155 years of a cycle of precession. In Leo he was the lion of the house of Judah (Iu-dah), and his whelp; in Cancer he was the "Good Scarabaeus," ever renewing himself, the crab emerging from the water onto the land; in

Gemini he was the twins, the two opposite phases of life contending in the womb of being for supremacy; in Taurus, the shining bull and golden calf; in Aries, the ram, the lamb of God and the golden fleece; in Pisces the great whale and the little fish with the gold in its mouth, the fisher of souls, the food in the water; in Aquarius the emanator of the water of life in two streams; in Capicorn the dual god again, half goat or land animal, half fish or sea animal, duplicating the sign of Cancer opposite, only that the crab is emerging from the water and the goat is in the water; in Sagittarius again double as the Centaur, half man and half horse, the archer aiming at the eye of Horus to put it out on the downward course of the autumnal sun, when deity is going blind; in Scorpio, double again as the scorpion that stings divine power to "death" and the eagle that soars aloft again; in Libra as the god of the two horizons holding the scales of the balance between spirit and matter in exact equilibrium; in Virgo double as the divine child of the mother and the wheat for the bread of Christ, as well as the branch of the true vine that was constellated in Virgo.

The *Ritual* states that Horus "is united at sunset with his Father Ra, who goeth round the heavens" in the zodiacal cycles. Perhaps the Gospels retain a parallel to this in the life of Jesus in his retirement each night *to the mountain* to commune with his Father. Horus says: "I see my father, the *lord of the gloaming,* and I breathe." Horus again is called "the Lord of the Staircase, at the top of which his father sat enthroned." He is lord of the evolutionary ladder, the planes by which the soul mounts up to godhead. Again he says: "I seek my father at sunset in silence and I feed on life." Be it noted that he *feeds on life* after his descent into embodiment, or in this world. And once more the *Ritual* dispenses wisdom of transcendent importance in the statement: "Thou settest as a living being within the dark portal; . . . thou *becomest a divine being in the earth. Thou wakest as thou settest* . . ."

The declarations of ancient wisdom that we are divinized on earth and that the soul awakes as it sets, or incarnates, are mighty items of knowledge for benighted mortals. But it has been set forth that the descent is a swoon and a going into oblivion, the very sleep of "death." Now it is pictured as an awakening. Here again is exemplified the doubleness of esoteric methodology in picturing the two aspects and movements of being. But the paradox in all these reversals of imagery

512

is readily resolvable. The soul does fall under a spell of Lethe when enshrouded in dense body; nevertheless it finds in that very state the beginning of its true awakening to a higher sense of reality than ever before. This world is "the place of establishing forever," of bringing purely latent capacity to dynamic realization. There is involved here the ultimate mystery of life, which is the necessity of the soul's "death" in matter to gain a new birth.

The Egyptians, observes Plutarch, offer incense to the sun three times a day: resin at its rising; myrrh when it is at midheaven; and kyphi about the time of its setting. Here is the "gold, frankincense and myrrh" of the later Hebrew myth, brought by the solar triad of Atma-Buddhi-Manas, the three Magi or knowledge-principles. The trident of Neptune was a Greek symbol of the three-forked spiritual sun-power. The sun at mid-day zenith is Ra; at the evening horizon is Tum (Atum); at rising on the morrow he is Khepr, renewing himself.

The three most celebrated emblems used in the Greek Mysteries were the Phallus (I), the Egg (O) and the Serpent, symboled by the Greek letter Phi, being the O bisected by the I. These are the male symbol, the female and the two united. The union of the two yields the great "serpent power" or the driving force of life itself. It was this serpent power that the Ophite sect of early Christianity elevated to dominant place in their system, paying homage thus to the creative energy and power of endless renewal, the serpent in this conception being by no means the malefic principle "with the vulgar downward literal meaning that we ascribe to it." Ra tells Seb to "be the guardian of the serpents which are in thee," referring to the swirling elementary life principles enwombed in the earth and matter.

The sun's might as Jupiter was triform: Jupiter in the heaven, Neptune in the sea, and Pluto in the underworld. Sunlight itself has three primary colors, before it breaks into the seven. The gods are male, but the three regions are made female, holding the *shakti* powers that implemented their activity. The great Hindu Mother Mahadevi divides into three colors, black, red and white, to become Sarasvati, the *shakti* of Brahma; Lacksmi, that of Vishnu; and Parvati, the consort of Siva. There is the Hecate triad in Greece. The three Parcae or Fates of Greece are matched by the Egyptian Neith, spinner of the web (net), and her two sisters, Isis and Nephthys, and by the three Norns of the

513

Norse pantheon. Of the three Fates Atropos conferred the solar power of generation; Clotho was lodged in the moon, as she who joins, mingles and unites the light with the dark, spirit with flesh; Lachesis is on the earth supervising the flow of mortal events, "and with her does fortune very much participate."

The ancients conjoined the twin male and female triads and from the union produced the interlaced triangles, or Solomon's Seal, the six-rayed star which is a perfect numerical typograph of the linking of the three spiritual with the three physical principles, the apices pointing in opposite directions. Their inextricable interlinking bespeaks the incarnation or entanglement of soul with body.

The *Clementine Homilies* set forth that the body of man consists of three parts and derives its origin from the female; the spirit consists of three parts and derives its origin from the male. The sperm-cell of the male creative fluid is three-ply. The union of the two triads in man makes him the sextuple being he is. His life has six facets and manifests in a world where any object has six faces, as a cube. The seventh principle is that which subsumes the six of the cube in a higher synthesis, which is achieved, however, on the plane of the dimension above it. The seventh principle always lifts a creation up to the next plane above it. It resolves the formation of the six into soul and meaning. Its day is the Sun-day, crowning the natural or secular operations with their apotheosis into spiritual being. The mystic AUM is a concealed glyph of the trinity, we are told. Our word "triumph," seen particularly well in its French form, *triomphe,* is composed of the root tri, "three"; *om,* the shortened AUM, the triple Logos; and *phe,* from the Greek, meaning "spoken." Our cry of triumph will then be our ability to unify again the "thrice-spoken word," or bring the three primary rays of divine mind back to unity.

The two sexes are not only marked in man by the division into male and female persons; there is another segmentation into sex which is one of the great keys in theology. The division of humanity into male and female is only an outward mark of an inner sacrament which is the main theme of religion. The most important sex division is that which inheres in man's individual life, whereby everyone is male on the spiritual side, and female on the physical. The diaphragm is the horizon line in man physiologically, for the individual is male above it and female below it. The marriage of the Bride and the Lamb is to

514

take place between these two parties. The dividing wall is to be broken down and the two united. The great Sphinx of Egypt depicts this duality in man, proclaiming under the zodiacal sign of the Lion that each human is spirit-male and matter-female in himself, facing the evolutionary duty of wedding the two. The three psychic centers below the diaphragm are concerned with the reproduction of body; the three above deal with spiritual destiny, and the crowning one in the head will unify all seven. Mythology teems with half-man, half-animal creatures, male in front and female behind. And says the Hebrew Psalmist (*Ps.* 139:5): "Thou hast fashioned me Behind and Before." This must be translated to say that we are humans in our upper half and beast in the lower. This is the incontestable reading of the symbology. The female is assigned the creation of the animal body of man. The female's interests are infinitely more directly centered in the body than are the male's. Man is, in the large, the intellectual creator; woman the physical.

The ancients in their stellar configurations represented the great Divine Man as facing the south, his back to the north. Hence the south was male, the north female. The constellation of the Great Bear was the lower, hinder part, the thigh or womb, of nature. The gods of the four quarters, the bases of the human pyramid, the four "Sons of Horus," "are they who are behind the thigh in the northern sky." They are the hind quarter of the heavenly man and are the four lower elements in man's constitution. The haunch of the lion that is carried on the head of Anhur is a sign of natural fecundity. The fore part, the face and head of the lion, denotes the glory of solar radiance. "The Lord God is a sun and shield," says the *Psalm;* and man is made in his image. The rear material part shields mortal eye from the too great effulgence of solar glory. But Samson sets fire to the *tails* of 300 foxes, as a suggestion that the fire of soul must light up and transform the rear or lower half of our nature.

In the *Ritual* chapter "of making the transformation into the god that giveth light in the darkness," the Manes says he is the robe of light that dispels the darkness, "which uniteth the two fighting deities that dwell in my body through the mighty spell of the words of my mouth." Two fighting deities in our bodies! The robe alluded to is called elsewhere "the garment without a seam," since the marriage obliterates the seam or dividing line. The unification of these two warring elements is each individual's specific task, the main reason for his incarnate existence and a pursuit worth all its hardship.

In one of the hymns to Osiris the god is greeted:

"Hail to thee, Osiris, Lord of Eternity! When thou art in heaven thou appearest as the sun, and *thou renewest thyself in the moon.*"

The soul of life, we have seen, renews itself by eternal rebirth following cyclical death in matter. The moon is ancient symbol for the physical half of human nature, since the two lower elements and man's two lower bodies, the physical and emotional, were the products of a precedent evolution on the moon. And sun and moon, in their interaction each lunar month, enact the whole drama of human evolution with such graphic fidelity that the delineation of it becomes a perpetual marvel. No graphology of mythicism has excelled nature herself in vivid portrayal of the dual history of the human being upon the very face of the moon, where the story, endlessly repeated, has been enacted before the eyes of successive generations of mortals, but never read since the days of ancient Egypt. In the various phases and aspects of the registration of the sun's light upon its body, the moon stages the entire symbolic drama of the blended physico-spiritual life of mortal man with a precision so astonishing that a mind which once follows' the analogies can hardly escape the conclusion that Intelligence presided at the ordering of the movements of the three bodies, sun, moon and earth, in their interrelation. As seen from the earth, the sun and moon together depict in the heavens each month the record of man's typical life so fully that it becomes a prime enigma to account for the loss of the wisdom to interpret this sky-book after it had once been known. The rejection of paganism by Roman Christianity cost the world the forfeiture of its ability to read this elementary textbook and its story written in characters of light and darkness.

As spirit was reborn periodically in matter, so the sun was reborn monthly in the moon, matter's planetary symbol. Both Horus and Khunsu, two characters representing the renewed solar deity, as well as Taht, were depicted in the disk of the full moon. The planisphere of Denderah shows the two in this position. Khunsu's father is Amen, the hidden god, the youthful Khunsu being his visible representative reborn in the new moon. Horus was the renewed Ra, Osiris or Atum. That divine self which in solar symbolism was reborn in the vernal equinox or the eastern rim of morning, was re-dramatized in lunar symbolism as finding its rebirth in the young crescent moon. Osiris, Atum or Ra, sinking to feebleness and death in the cycle of waning moon, came to their renaissance between the two horns of the crescent in the west at nightfall. The moon repeated thirteen times the death and resurrection story while the sun traced it once. Ages of intelligence have gazed upon this monthly drama without once descrying its tacit narrative. Yet the Egyptians discoursed about the meaning of this phenomenon in chapter after chapter. Must we conclude, therefore, that ancient eyes penetrated deeper into nature's secrets than modern? The evidence is before us. This datum may become again the bulwark of religion, rendering it impregnable to materialistic or agnostic assault. For while sacred Bibles may be brushed aside with scorn, the chart of man's spiritual constitution, written ineradicably on the open sheet of the nightly sky, can not be gainsaid. Here is an indelible scripture whose ever-turning pages the atheist must read alike with the theist. Here is a book which no mind dare flout. Here are the heavens themselves preaching a sermon and reciting a gospel narrative that no mortal can contemn.

The story is by no means easy in the telling. It must be lived with and be given time to mellow in the mind, ere it will bestir the profoundest psychic intuitions. Only the groundwork for the structure of beautiful meaning can be given in a series of facts, relations and phenomena. Each one must in the end be his own poet.

We have seen the sun-god pictured as passing through the dark underworld at night. His voyage is made amid spiritual darkness. The body is the soul's dark prison, grave and tomb. The god is then the sun in the dark underworld. Therefore it is a light in the darkness. His mission is to bring light into this dark region. Come to earth, his light ceased shining in heaven, as the Chinese said, and shone only in the underworld for the benighted inhabitants thereof. Jesus is the light of the world by night.

Yet it is by no means his true full splendor that shines on our darkness. It is a sadly diminished light that he shows, his full radiance being dimmed by the veil of matter which is thrown between it and our eyes. It is therefore a light, which, itself hidden from sight, *shines through an intermediary body,* or shines by reflection or indirect transmission. Now in the first chapter of *John's* Gospel there is that noteworthy statement that there was a man sent of God to bear witness to that "light that shineth in the darkness." *"He was not that Light, but was sent to bear witness of that Light."* He was himself not the full or true light, but only the harbinger of it. This was John the Baptizer, or leader of souls into the waters of generation in the dark lower half of evolution. He was typed as Anup, and again as Taht-Aan, the dark phase of the moon, or the moon itself as the sun's witness when it is not itself shining on us. So the Christ-light within us is that secondary or transmitted radiance which shines into our prisons when the full glory of divinity is cut off from us and out of our sight. If God is the full ineffable Sun of Divinity, then the *Christos* is, as it were, the reflected radiance from that Sun coming second-hand to us from the surface of bodies of matter.

In the interpretation, this intermediary is the physical human body, with its emotion apparatus. In the realm of astronomy it is the moon. The lighted moon, then, is the symbol, representative, vice-regent, of the sun when that orb is buried in darkness. It holds the proxy of its power. It is the transmitter of solar light when that itself is out of sight. It is the only witness and evidence of the sun's light when that luminary is unable to shine on the world. It is the sun's lower or secondary self. The moon is the sun by night. So the *Christos* is that reduced and reflected ray of the Father's infinite glory. When the sun is in full panoply in the heavens of day, the moon is eclipsed. It is man's "noon." But she comes into her glory in the night. The moon stands between man and total darkness, yet she has no light to give of herself. She but transmits the brightness of one higher than herself. So the body stands between man and his god and transmits what can not be received directly.

Here, then, we have the two great characters in the drama, with man the spectator and interpreter, and as he finally realizes to his amazement, the ultimate actor. Meaning begins to rise as soon as we have fixed the two chief *dramatis personae* and their roles. The sun and moon play the parts of man's soul and his body respectively, and their interaction will be found to depict in detail the connected history of the two on earth in the world of the body.

These determinations lead to the second great fact, which opens wide the door into a world of new meaning. If the sun represents spirit and the soul body, the deduction is that the sun is male and the moon female. The stage is then set to register the play of the two great interacting forces of life, the positive and negative poles. The evolutionary conflict between the two, the battle between Sut and Horus, the twins, which is reproduced everywhere in nature, is transferred now to the lunar surface and re-enacted there for man's eternal behoof. As the moon encircles her lord in monthly course, she traces a stream of significant interrelations. From dark to full moon, it is the story of man's deification and glorification, his en-light-enment, through repeated life in body; the nightly increase of the area of light is the sealed promise of our ultimate divinization. By analogy, the increase night by night endorses the postulate of the soul's reincarnations. It is the cycle of evolution. From full moon to total obscuration it writes the record of involution, or the spirit's descent into matter. The following tabulation is suggested for the readier tracing of the analogies:

Sun	Moon
Spirit-soul-mind.	Body.
Consciousness.	Flesh.
Intellect.	Sensation.
Male.	Female.
Light-giving.	Light-receiving.
Upper body.	Lower body.
Fire.	Water.
The god.	The animal.

In its complete cycle the moon analogizes the conception, birth, growth, perfection, decline, death and rebirth of the sun-god in his incarnating cycle. The moon records the progress of the rebegettal or divinization. Hence the principal moon-deity of Egypt, Taht-Aan, is known as the recorder or scribe for Horus. He keeps the record of the advance or decline of spiritual light. And the moon's function of bearing witness to the sun when the latter was out of sight, constitutes Taht-Aan and Anup the "two witnesses" for the hidden Christ. In the court of life the body holds the record and bears witness of the character of the deity who is buried out of sight within us!

The Greeks regarded the moon as "the self-revealing emblem of nature." As bringer of the hidden sun to light the moon was named the goddess Diana, who, says Proclus, "presides over the whole of generation into natural existence, leads forth into light all natural reasons, and extends a prolific power from on high even to the subterranean realms." [4] And we are told that "the sexual parts of this god are denominated by theologists, Diana," for no more subtle reason apparently than that it is sex which brings all things to outward birth. The moon is Diana because the orb brings all to light, as the woman who reflects, regenerates and reproduces the hidden germ of life. Spirit would be inchoate and lost to view if some matrix did not give it birth as concrete form. That the moon is in affinity with the natural creation rather than with the spiritual world is also attested by the *Chaldean Oracles*, one of which recites that "the moon rides on every thing generated, and all these terrestrial natures are manifestly governed by her, as the Oracle says." She is the nature power, the woman, who becomes clothed with the sun of intelligence, which lights up her *head* finally with twelve facets of divine radiance.

The moon, then, is the register of solar or spiritual history, and the fact of crowning pertinence for us is that the nightly increase of light area on her dark surface is nature's cosmic hieroglyph recording our growth toward full divinization. It marks to what extent divine light has spread over and through the physical body. From total darkness the sun-god begins to impregnate the lunar body with his bright power, until finally her whole body becomes irradiated with his glory. So the sun-deity of mind meets the physical man, first Adam, at the dawn of racial history, and finds no spiritual light in him. He then implants his tiny seed, and life after life he adds to the growth until at the end of the aeon the whole being of physical man is irradiated with intellectual light. He lights the darkened prison from within with that shining power that Jesus said his disciples had in themselves. Each night of incarnation increases the area of light. And the material body, like the moon, records the measure of the god's occupancy of the vehicle. Even in ordinary social judgment, that countenance is most beautiful through or upon which the most of soul shines forth.

The nightly spectacle of the waxing moon should impress every mortal that nature bears incontestable evidence of the gradual divinization of humanity. "If thine eye be single, thy whole body shall be full of light," is the Biblical assurance to this effect. The supreme message of lunar symbology to man is that divine light is measurably spreading over our whole being. At the fullness of his perfection the Manes cries: "There is no part of me that is without a god. I am the god entire."

520

In phallic terms it would be said that the moon, female, being impregnated by the active germ of solar, masculine, light, registers the growth of the babe of the sun in her womb by the swelling of the gestating foetus night by night, till its birth at the full moon. Then the child is delivered, and the mother returns to normal condition.

A most striking series of analogies extends further this parallelism between the moon and the mother, body, nature. The bodily world of incarnation, is, as has been demonstrated by the table of the four elements, typed by the two planes of earth and water, which two are often generalized under the one, water. The body is chiefly water, and this is the first unassailable confirmation of the legitimacy of the symbol. Its life of sensation and emotion is most aptly pictured by the shifty, ceaseless mobility of water. All bodily processes are in constant flux. Therefore if the sun is typified by fire, the moon is just as fitly emblemed by water. Is it by "coincidence" then, or by an amazing natural endorsement of the meet character of the symbol, that there is found to be that mysterious affinity between the moon and the water of earth? For it is the moon that draws the seas of earth toward it in the daily tides!

But even that remarkable vindication of the analogies involved is dwarfed by the magnitude of another natural relationship,—that between the moon and the female. It need hardly be elaborated that it is the physiological function of the female, and not that of the male, that is rendered periodic by the cycle of the moon! Does it need any smart juggling of poetic fancies to relate the woman to the moon, when the very periodicity of her bodily functions is fixed by the twenty-eight days' cycle of the orb? And the function energized by the moon has everything to do with body and procreation, nothing directly with the woman's mind or higher nature. The moon affects the woman, not the man; and her body, not her spirit.

Together moon and woman repeat each month in identical manner the story of descent, incarnation and rebirth of the soul. From the night of the full moon the light of the sun-god visible on its face begins to wane, going down again into darkness. Its movement is downward across the sphere, as the direction of its increase is from the under surface to the upper. At the lowest ebb of the cycle the light is totally hidden for three days! While in this dark underworld which lies below the horizon, the virgin moon is met by the sun, who has

521

entered the underworld with it at early evening, or the time of his descent! Let this fact be noted carefully, since it is of great import. The sun and moon meet and are conjoined in wedlock while both are buried out of sight *in the west* below the horizon, or in the dark of night. Transposing this situation to the kingdom of man, we find that nature has reproduced the story of incarnation and its collateral values once more. For here again nature records that it is in the dark underworld of this nether earth that the only conjunction of spirit (soul) and matter (body) takes place. This world is that place of darkness wherein alone the sun of spirit and the moon of matter can meet and copulate for reproduction. Says Massey: "It is only in the darkness of Amenta that the two ever meet." Sun and moon meet and embrace just at the end of her dark period, and while both are in the nether earth. Man's soul and his body meet in the same dark period in the lower world of earth. Immediately the mother, impregnated, begins to swell until she delivers the sun's child on the fifteenth day.

The Egyptians said that Osiris copulated with the dead body of Isis and impregnated it and that the touch of his sperm revived it—all in the dark, out of sight. Another version is that Isis drew the seed from Osiris' dead body and impregnated herself, giving birth to Horus. The Egyptians were not evil-minded pagans, but beautifully pictured truth and need not be defended against the charge of a revolting sacrilege. Nor do we need to ascribe posthumous sexual rapacity to their favorite god and goddess. Isis, typed by the dark moon, was nature unspiritualized, unfructified, barren, dead. It required the touch of the sun-god's vivifying rays, the implantation of the germinal light of spirit in her inert body, to awaken her to fruitfulness. The other version reads that Isis was fecundated by the god dead and buried in matter. He fructifies her when he has gone to his "death" in matter.

With incredible exactness human biology matches this procedure of sun and moon. Each month during the "dark" period of the female cycle, when nature runs to waste unchecked by male fecundation, there *descends* from the "upper room" of the Fallopian tubes the ovum, or foetal nucleus, which falls, as does the unfertilized earth soul, into the belly of darkness in the lower body, the prison, cave, tomb or womb. What then happens? Hither, also *descending* into the dark cavern, but *from outside,* is projected the seed of the male, the seminal essence, typical ever of the solar light, threefold like the solar triad; and once again in nature's economy "sun" and "moon" copulate in the dark cave of the underworld to engender a new birth.

The seed is placed in the ground, its underworld, and lies there inert until the sun penetrates into that hidden womb and warms it to life.

The tale of the Sleeping Beauty is but a form of this tropology. The beautiful maiden is the moon-goddess, waiting in a state of negativity until awakened to reproductive life by the lover's kiss—the sun's rays.

Tracing analogies further, we find that the new moon is born in the west, and, like the "Innocents" which it types, it is immediately threatened with extinction by the power of darkness. Each night it becomes more able to combat and outlive the assaults of the enemy. The west is the place of entry into lower life, and the soul was endangered at the beginning of its immersion in the body. But what about the fully-divinized sun-child at full moon? Where is he born as the finished mortal made immortal? Surely at a place where danger lurks no more for him. Majestically he rises *in the east!* No longer now is he subject to the attack of darkness, for he rides in full glory across the sky by night. He is not plunged into the earth, but is the "sky-runner," the ancient term for a god. Born as man on the west, he is now born anew as god on the east, "where the gods are born," and reincarnation is over.

Some of the legends poetize the moon as seducing the sun in the darkness of night to be impregnated with his light. Some say the sun was in love with the moon. A kiss in mythical language was a euphemism for copulation. Judas betrayed his Lord with a kiss, which is the Gospel's continuation of former Egyptian imagery by which the betrayer, seducer—matter—the woman, lured the sun or soul into her darkened realm to give her the seed of light. The allegory was later applied to the resurrection, in which the slumbering soul was awakened by the kiss of Horus. The Prince awakens Snow-White with a kiss.

The great Egyptian symbol, the Eye, stands for the solar light. But, who swallows it at evening, restores it at morning. Nature, earth, the mother, all of whom absorb the sunlight, are made to reproduce it again in new beauty! Says Massey:

"Thus the lunar orb was the consort of the sun; his Eye by night as the reproducer of his light when he was in the underworld; and in reproducing the light she was the mother bringing forth her child"—*his* child, he might have said.[5]

The "Cow-Goddess" Hathor is portrayed with the solar disk between her horns, the imagery denoting the mother-moon as bearer of the sun, or rebegetter of his light. The eye reproduces objects by reflection; the moon reproduces the sun. Here indeed is the woman *clothed with the sun,* bathed in its splendor, and periodically bringing forth her man-child, with the great dragon of darkness ready to devour him, re-enacting endlessly the type of that Christ-birth that occurs to man once. For three days the father's dwindling light disappeared in the belly of the great fish. Jonah issues from the great fish, constellated in Pisces, in the form of the Christ, who stills the storm on the sea of carnality. As the moon retired out of sight of men in her dark period to copulate with the sun, so woman, the moon's human counterpart, was made by early religious usage to retire from the sight of men during her period. Nor was she to come into the presence of the sun or fire, a restriction perpetuated in some quarters to this day.

The Egyptians, it will have been noticed, manifested an uncanny penchant for discerning in the characteristic traits of animals many striking analogies with spiritual or creational verities. If their work was restored to religion, it would revitalize the latter by establishing a knowledge of the *fundamental affinity between man and his environing universe.* In no one respect, perhaps, have they revealed a more astonishing correspondence between animal trait and cosmical philosophy than in the case of the cynocephalus or dog-headed ape. This animal, be it recalled, is the zoötype of the moon-god Taht-Aan. To avoid faulty presentation of this parallel it is desirable to quote the datum from its ancient source in the writing of Hor-Apollo, as cited by Massey:

"Hor-Apollo says of the cynocephalus, the personified speaker, singer and later writer, that the Egyptians symbolized the moon by it on account of a kind of sympathy which the ape had with it *at the time of its conjunction with the god.* 'For at the exact instant of the conjunction of the moon with the sun, when the moon became unillumined, then the male cynocephalus neither sees nor eats, but is bowed down to the earth with grief, as if lamenting the ravishment of the moon. The female also, in addition to its being unable to see, and being afflicted in the same manner as the male, *ex genitalibus sanguinem emittit;* [6] hence even to this day Cynocephali are brought up in the temples, in order that from them may be ascertained the exact instant of the conjunction of the sun and moon. And when they would denote the renovation of the moon, they again portray a cenocephalus in the posture of standing upright, and raising its hands to heaven, with a diadem on its head.' " [7]

Any attempt to add point to this natural fact seems inadvisable. It speaks volumes of rebuke for those who blatantly decry the suggestion of astrological influences upon our earth and its citizenry. Plutarch, it will be remembered, stated that the "astral" or emotion body of man came from the moon, as the spiritual one came from the sun. These counterparts in man retain an affinity with their source, as they are of kindred essence with their progenitors. Hence powerful currents from the parent bodies must vitally affect their offspring even down here. Distance imposes little obstacle to such forces as cosmic rays.

The ape sets mankind another singular example of harmony with nature which we will be amazed to ponder. There is a widespread ancient tradition that certain species of apes assemble at the time of sunrise on an elevation or river bank facing the east, and with cries, prostrations and "clicking" salute the lord of day as he appears above the horizon. Biologically the ape heralded the *coming of the man with the sun of intellect,* and with ability to express the motions of thought *by speech.* How astonishing that nature has dramatized this event in the matutinal hailing by the apes of the physical symbol and embodiment of that intellect! The advent of divinity gave man speech; the rise of the solar lord sets the apes to clicking!

The ibis, sacred to Taht, the moon-god, emblemed the dark and light aspects of the moon in its two colors of white and black. The dark of the moon types the unspiritualized state of the first Adam, the Gentile. Sut, Anup, Krishna and the little Bambino or Italian Christchild, were depicted as black.

The Biblical narrative of Samson and his consort Delilah seems quite definitely to be a growth from lunar typology. With the sun (in Hebrew) for his name, Samson is the sun-god; Delilah is traced (by Massey) to mean the feeble, waning, drooping aspect of lunar light, or the dark of the moon, its obscuration, and the menstruation. Conjunction with the woman during the dark period meant negation,

525

abortion, waste of virile power, as in Onan's case. Delilah represented the wretched sun-god in his reduced and fallen state of incarnation. As with Horus, Samson's eyes are put out, his light is lost. Delilah causes his ruin, as her allurements lead to his being bound and shorn of his hair (a general type for solar rays). Ishtar is also the ruin of her solar lovers, and is charged with being an enchantress, a poisoner, a destroyer of male potency. Izdubar, the sun-god, reproaches her with witchcraft and seductive murderous lust, and saves himself by refusing to be her lover. The havoc wrought by Aholah and Aholibah, the two unholy sisters in harlotry portrayed in *Ezekiel* (23), upon the mighty sun-men of "Egypt" and "Babylon," is depicted without restraint of language. They, like Delilah, lure young men to their "destruction," that is, to union with matter and descent into it.

In old texts the date on which Osiris is affirmed to descend into the underworld is given as the seventeenth of the month Athor or Athyr. This was to match the date of the autumn equinox. Zodiacally it was the time of his entering the six lower signs for the "three days of navigation." Significantly the ark in which he was to be borne across the waters was a boat in the shape of the crescent moon. Then on the nineteenth of the same month, or after two (i.e., three) days, the priests proclaimed that he was re-found, or that his bark had come to view after being lost sight of.

The lunar phase of the meaning back of the term "Bull of his Mother," applied to Horus, is readily glimpsed. As the growing light of the new sun-child spreads over the body of the moon, his mother, he is said to impregnate her and fill her body with his virility. The old light re-begets itself on its own mother. The horn is a type of male power, as witness the rhinoceros (nose-horn) and the unicorn. The "horned moon" represented the virile young sun-god exercising his function of begetting light on his mother. Horus impregnated his mother Isis.

The context makes it appropriate to introduce here the figure of another animal used by the ancients in symbolism—the ass. His mythical usage has brought much of his own reputed quality, asininity, into the interpretations. Much, if not all, of his typical significance can be seen in relation to lunar imagery. Anup, the god of the dark moon, was figured by the ass, as well as by the jackal. As the lunar orb becomes illuminated with light, the mythicists framed the allegory of

526

the sun-god's riding into full glory on the back of the dark moon, Anup, the ass, or ass-headed god, as he is depicted on the tomb of Rameses Sixth. Hence Jesus' triumphal entry into Jerusalem, the city of heavenly glory, is only a fabulous construction of the mythicist to portray the final triumph of the sun-god or soul in man over his lower world. The climactic act in mundane life is the departure from mortal flesh and the entry into the kingdom of spirit, the Aarru-Salem or Fields of Peace. And nothing so decisively betrays the befuddlement into which exoteric literalism has thrown Christian practice than the Church's placing the triumphal entry of Jesus chronologically ahead of the crucifixion, death and burial. The victorious entry into spirit, to join the glorious company of the gods, ends all earthly crucifixion. By no jugglery of sense can the triumph precede the crucifixion, in the same cycle.

The god rides into glory on the back of the lower animal self. The *Ritual* has told us that Horus would be set on Sut's back, to be upborne safely by him. The spiritual world rests upon the physical, which fact let idealists never forget. Without being carried patiently by these ascetically despised bodies of ours we could never reach the gates of the celestial city.

That the ass-riding legend *is* purely a mythical drama past all contradiction on the basis of the Biblical context is evident from the fact that the Gospels state Jesus would be found "sitting on an ass and a colt, the foal of an ass." Impossibilities that can pass as myth prove ruinous when myth is turned into history. Picture Jesus physically astride the two animals at once! And this is a fair sample of the ludicrousness which the entire theology has taken on in modern presentation from the sheer despoiling of the mighty allegories of past wisdom. Nothing but the derided pagan mythology can eradicate the buffoonery of this scene and restore it to dignity. Theology has gone far to reduce the mind of Western humanity to imbecility; let mythology be called upon to restore it to sanity.

In this connection the linking of the symbol of the palm branch with the triumphal entry also indicates the luni-solar path to meaning. For, says Massey, the palm branch was an ancient type of time and periodicity. And Hor-Apollo avers that it was adopted as a symbol of a month or "moonth," because it alone reproduces an additional branch at each renovation of the moon. One might call a lunar month the

527

period of a palm branch. In the degree of subtlety and refinement to which the sages carried the art of natural portrayal of truth, they seem to have far overshot the capacity of later, even modern, mind to evaluate their constructions.

We have Balaam riding the ass, and Samson slaying the Philistines with the jaw-bone of an ass. The jaw is the lower and moveable part of the head, working up and down against a stable unmoved counterpart. In this bit of anatomy nature has typed again our duality and the deep truth that over against a stable and unmoved eternal nature within, an activity in the lower levels of life moves out and back, to and fro, to nourish and express life's inner attributes. Only by the activity of this lower part can the inner soul slay its adversaries.

Another revelation of hidden Bible typology comes to light through lunar representation. The jackal of Anup and the cynocephalus of Taht-Aan, which figured as types of the dark lunation, were conceived as having stolen the light from the bright moon. As the dark period before and that after the illumination, they stood on either side of the Christ light on the moon. They were dubbed "thieves of the light," in contrast to the twelve solar characters who were guardians of the treasure of light. Hermes, cognate with Anup, was in Greek mythology the thief. In the zodiac of Denderah just where Horus is shown on the cross or at the crossing of the vernal equinox, these two thieves Anup and Aan are drawn on either side of the sun-god. Here would appear to be the authentic pre-Christian prototype of the Gospel crucifixion between two thieves. Incarnation steals away the divine light—only to add to its brightness.

Orion, the mighty hunter, type of the sun-god, is represented as pursuing the moon which leaps ahead one hour's jump each night, like a hare. In his chase of the hare he is accompanied by his two dogs, constellated as the stars Cyon (Greek *kuon* (*cyon*), "dog") and Procyon. On emerging from the darkness of Amenta Osiris says: "I come forth as a Bennu (the Phoenix-type of the Dog-star Sirius) at dawn. I urge on the dogs of Horus." These again may be Anup and Aan, the dog and the dog-headed ape, symbols of man in his early evolutionary state as animal, then as half animal and half man, the ape, before becoming full man. The god in man urges on in his evolution the animal part of himself.

We are now in position to understand a detail of Sut's dismemberment of Osiris passed over before. The dark power cut the god's body into fourteen pieces! The meaning is under our eye in the lunar symbolism. To reduce full moon to dark moon, the Sut power must cut off the light in fourteen separate pieces, one each night! The lunar phenomena likewise dramatize the companion idea of the disrobing of the soul at each step of her descent into matter, as she loses a portion of her robe of light at each of fourteen steps.

The moon phases and periods furnish the actual origin of ancient and some modern festivals in a manner known to few. If not entirely a growth out of lunar periodicities, our Sabbath on the seventh day and the Jewish one on the sixth day, are traceable to origins in identical ancient festivals commemorating the sixth and seventh days of the lunar month. The early civilizations marked off three dates in the lunar cycle as worthy of celebration, the first, the sixth (or seventh) and the fifteenth. These were apparently all festivals in honor of Ra (or Osiris), though in conjunction with Luna. The feasts on the first and fifteenth were lunar festivals corresponding to the solar Christmas and the solar Easter, or the sun-god's birth and resurrection. The new moon might be thought of as born on the first day. He completed his conquest of darkness in full light on the fifteenth (fourteenth). But there was a feast day set for the sixth and seventh days of the lunar month. This was the *Feast of the Tenait*. The word denotes a measure of time, a division, week or fortnight. It was primarily associated with the seventh day of the month. The *Ritual* recites (Ch. 1): "I am with Horus on the day when the Festivals of Osiris are celebrated, and when offerings are made on the sixth day of the month, and on the Feast of the Tenait in Heliopolis" (city of the sun). The significant basic datum here is that, according to the old texts, "*Osiris entered the moon on the sixth day of the month.*"

Now a great quantity of material could be adduced to support the contention that the sixth day was named as the date of the god's entrance into the moon, picturing his entry into earthly body, because the implantation of the seed in the material womb could not be made until the day after the completion of the five days of menstruation! A lunar dark period was three days, but the reckoning was made on the basis of the woman's actual period of five days. This five-day period of female non-productivity looms large in primitive number types of meaning. Indeed some African creation legends set a secular creation of five days with a Sabbath on the sixth. The five days signifying negation, it is curiously found that the Egyptian Nun, the abyss of nothingness, is written with five successive N's. We have seen how ancient law insisted on woman's playing the part of negation, disappearance, retirement, during the five days. In Parsee law even a woman who became clean in three days was not to be washed until the fifth day. On this account five became considered the evil or untoward number, and the five intercalary days injected into the year at the end to make the difference between the 360 days of twelve solar months (of 30 days) and the 365 (364) of the thirteen lunar months of 28 days each, were charactered as the unlucky days of ill and darkness. They came at the winter solstice, the era of yearly darkness.

Hence it was that the sixth day, the first succeeding the five days of taboo, was the time of a new impregnation, connoting new birth and renewal. It was marked by the rising of the Pleiades, a figure of six always. Hence the first five days of the moon cycle were made memorial of the preliminary natural cycles of life in the kingdoms of darkness before the advent of the mind principle, solar intelligence, in the world. The sixth was considered to have deified the early five as later the seventh deified the first six. At any rate this was the figure of representation when the female period was the norm of typing and measurement. Thus Osiris, the seminal seed of divinity, entered the womb of matter to fecundate life on the first day after the dark period, which is incidentally the most fertile period of the month's cycle. And this is indeed notable, for it is undoubtedly the origin of the Jewish Sabbath, which begins at eventide of Friday and ends the following eve. The commencement of the Sabbath at sunset is attributable to the symbolism of the setting sun, which figuratively marked the time of the god's descent into the underworld for the night—of incarnation. This gave a Sabbath beginning on the evening of the fifth day, but covering mainly the sixth day, Saturday. This was the true Sun-day under lunar typism, because it marked the birth of the new sun in the moon.

But the festival of the full moon came on the fifteenth, bringing another Sun-day eight days later,—if on the fourteenth, then seven days later. But if the seventh was a solar day, the sixth was dedicated to Saturn, and on the night of it the love-feast or Agapae began at six o'clock to commemorate the conjunction of the sun and moon, or

Horus with Hathor-Isis. This day was a phallic festival celebrated in symbolic appropriateness by the conjunction of male and female, the basis of the Saturnalia. Merely typical significance was given concrete dramatization in the actual union of males and females; for it is said that "couplings did abound." It was Saturn's day to conjoin with his mother. From being held once a month, the two-day soli-lunar celebration was later repeated *every* seven days, or weekly.

Annu was the Egyptian city where festivals were held in honor of Osiris. One of these was kept on the sixth day of the month. The Speaker in the *Ritual* says that he is with Horus on the festival of Osiris on the sixth day of the month. As Annu became Beth-Annu (Bethany), it is instructive to compare with this the following from the Gospels (*John* 12): "Jesus, therefore, six days before the Passover came to Bethany, where Lazarus was, whom Jesus raised from the dead. So they made him a supper there," at which were present the two women, Mary and Martha, as the two Meri's or Merti (Mertae) were present at Beth-Anu in Egypt. This was the mortuary meal at Annu, corresponding to the supper at Bethany.

The festival of the sixth day is clearly the one known as the *Hakera* (as well as the Tenait), that was solemnized on the sixth night of the Ten Mysteries. At this great festival was commemorated the resurrection of Osiris. This one of the Ten Mysteries was celebrated "before the great circle of the gods in Abydos [city of death and rebirth] on the night of the Hakera when the glorious ones are rightly judged; when the evil dead are parted off and 'joy goeth its rounds in Thinis'" (Ch. 18, Renouf). This was the festival of "Come thou to me," or the resurrection. On this day the solar healer and deliverer of the Manes in Amenta rides in glory as the "divine one that dwelleth in heaven and who sitteth on the *eastern side of heaven*" (*Rit.*, Ch. 25).

The goddess-mother Ishtar (the Hebrew Esther!) of Akkad was, like Venus and Hathor, designated "the *Goddess Fifteen*": being named from the date of the full moon or her productive heyday. The Egyptian goddess exclaims (Ch. 80): "I have made the eye of Horus when it was not coming on the festival of the fifteenth day." This is perhaps a reminder that at an early day the moon revolution was more definitely known than the solar cycle, and the fourteenth was counted as the date of the full moon. Ishtar is described as ascending and descending the steps of the moon, fifteen up and down in consonance with her title of *Goddess Fifteen*. In *Pseudo-Matthew* (Ch. 4) we learn that when the Virgin was an infant, just weaned, she ran up the fifteen steps of the temple at full speed without once looking back. In the *History of Joseph the Carpenter* Jesus says that Mary gave him birth in the fifteenth year of her age, by a mystery that no creature can understand except the Trinity. And Mary is the Egyptian Meri, who was Hathor, the *Goddess Fifteen*.

The *Pistis Sophia* dates the Transfiguration of Jesus on the fifteenth day of the month Tybi, the day of the full moon. The resurrection, or new birth, was always reckoned in Egypt on the full moon of this month, and as it came close after the winter solstice, about December 27 (Massey), it points to the Christmas nativity as being either ignorantly confused or knowingly identified with both the Transfiguration and the Resurrection. An address to Isis in the *Ritual* runs:

"I have come to see thee and thy beauties within the Utcha in thy name of Heb-enti-ses (i.e., the sixth-day festival). Thou hast conquered heaven by the greatness of thy majesty in thy name of 'Prince of the festival of the fifteenth day!' . . . Gods and men live at sight of thee. Thou risest to us . . ."

In the *Ritual* the Mother is she who "gives thee water on every first and every fifteenth day of the month."

A considerable amount of mythic construction has grown up around the poetic conception of the crescent moon as shaped like a tortoise shell, across which seven strings were drawn to form a lyre or harp. Many gods and goddesses play upon a harp of seven strings, Orpheus notably. Man must learn to draw consummate music from his evolutionary instrument of seven keys.

The moon is the source of much numerology, especially that dealing with the quantity: four times seven equals twenty-eight. The circuit of twenty-eight days found a natural division into four weeks of seven days each, the basis of a thirteen-month lunar year, or 364 days. Here was the meat for a veritable feast of mythological and numerological revelry. Man is founded, we have seen, on a natural basic structure composed of the four elements, each of which provides the substrate for one of his four bodies. His upper three principles rest on these four. Man is a spiritual triangle resting on a natural quadrilateral—the Pyramid. Each one of the four elemental strata is itself subdivided into seven sub-planes. Hence man's foundation is numerically a four-fold seven, or four times seven, or twenty-eight. In Hindu literature one finds this distinctly confirmed in a statement which says "the last of the Buddhas advanced by 28 steps, seven toward each of the four quarters." Man has thus far established himself on four of the total seven platforms of the mount, with seven sub-steps to each.

But when the solar reckoning had supplanted the lunar there was a new basis of division. Thirty days were taken to the month and these were divided into three decads, or $3 \times 10 = 30$. This was in conformity with the new constitution of man, presided over, as he now was, by the solar light as a trinity or triad. The sun of intellect added its three crowning rays to the seven lower forces, making the tenfold man, the perfect type. A week on this basis would be composed of ten days, and three would make the month. Spiritual light is amenable to the same decomposition as is sunlight in passing through a three-sided medium, and it goes into seven divisions, which, united with the three primal ones, make the ten.

The study yields a sudden and unexpected return on effort expended by revealing to the world at last the true origin of the superstition of ill luck or sinister influence attaching to the number thirteen. It was the number of *lunar* months in the solar year. This was the year as founded on lunar or feminine determination. When the father's part in parenthood came to be known, and the moon's light was discovered to come from the hidden father of lights, the great differentiation between the two sexual hemispheres of humanity became established, with the ascription of every high and favorable, right and propitious influence to the spiritual male side, and the ominous, unfavorable, sinister and left-handed (Latin: *sinister* means "left-handed") to the material or female. Hence a thirteen-month year, a lunar or "left-handed" year, was ill-omened; while the number twelve, as the final numerical basis of the new heaven in man's constitution, was the accepted sign of everything desirable. Thirteen is sinister, then, because it was governed by luni-feminine influence, always redolent to the mythicist of the baser elements of the human frame. "Left" in Latin is "*sinister*," in French it is "*gauche*," which works into *gaucherie*, awkwardness.

The moon sent the hare to tell mankind that as the lunar god died and rose again, so should mortals also be renewed and rise again. So

533

runs a tribal tradition of the Khoi-Khoi. They regarded the moon as the deity that promises man immortality. We would do well to keep a hold on that Khoi-Khoi suggestion. As with obvious design and precise calculation of times and cycles, the silvery orb is set in the sky as a perpetual object-lesson to the human race, a reminder to man that in the darkness of the night of his earthly burial, the solar light of divinity is still shining gloriously upon him, and shining more brightly unto the day of perfection. So comprehensive is that allegory that twenty pages have scarcely sufficed to outline the main facts involved. When the history written in soli-lunar language on the sky of night is read once again, a race distracted by loss of fontal wisdom may gain a foothold for peace and sanity on the ground of the knowledge there revealed.

The light of the sun on the moon shows spirit transfiguring body. And this nocturnal stage-play is far from being merely allegorical. The final word of crowning moment in the whole presentation of solar symbolism has not yet been spoken. At the heart of every living organism is a nucleus of solar light and energy. That is the sublime beginning of knowledge. Half of the task of liberating the modern mind from its hangover of medieval darkness will be achieved by the propagation anew of that fountain truth. But the still unuttered word that will complete the enfranchisement of thought from its present shackles has been hidden away amid the neglected pages of Neo-Platonic literature. From that grave of oblivion we drag it forth and set it beside the other luminous fact so that the two may be seen as the twin lights of the modern renaissance of wisdom. The light of the sun has been proclaimed as the essence of the deity within us. The sunlight on the moon has been heralded as the symbol of our growing godhood. How infinitely more it is than essence and symbol, and how much closer sun-worship has been to truth than modern superciliousness has ever dreamed, is disclosed in the short but mighty sentence of Proclus:

"The light of the sun is the pure energy of intellect." [8]

Here is the vital link of knowledge, long missing, that has been needed to join matter with spirit, nature with God, science with religion, and mind with the universe. For if, then, there is a nucleus of radiant light at the core of every life, the long puzzle as to how

534

mind became introduced into body is indeed solved. That unquench-able spark of intense light glowing at the center of all life is itself the pure energy of intellect! The body does not generate intellect; intellect is the force that generates the body! The *Faerie Queen* has intimated that soul shapes the body's form over its own inner model. Matter and mind are never found disjoined, for mind is the primal energy and builds a body to be its instrument in this arena of life. The substance, or body, of any organic unit is only an accretion of matter about a fiery nucleus, itself non-physical, which is mind itself. Mind is the energy of solar light; or solar light is the effect of mental energy. Can we imagine the stupendous power of that thinking energy of cosmic Mind which engenders a light like that of the sun! Mind is the core and cornerstone of every creature. Its light is blinded in lower orders, but shines forth in men and gods. Here is the beginning of wisdom and the re-beginning of religion. Could Christians have been persuaded to understand and accept their own Bible, this matter would have been established long ago. For the *Psalms* (84) stated this truth to an un-comprehending world centuries ago: "The Lord God is a sun. . . ." Nor less has the *New Testament* given witness to the same truth, for it has proclaimed that the son of the Father of Lights is the "*sun* of righteousness, risen with healing in his wings." The face of Jesus did "shine as the sun" in his transfiguration; and the ultimate promise given to sincere mortals is that at the end of earthly struggle, with victory won,—"then shall the righteous shine *like the sun* in the king-dom of their Father."

Chapter XXI

AT THE EAST OF HEAVEN

THE human drama ends with the sunrise of Easter. The voyage across the underworld sea by night terminates on the rim of the eastern horizon at break of Easter light. The somber cross turns into the garlanded maypole of Merry Mount. The ark shrine of Horus reaches at last that other shore, and its enthralled crew disembarks, to take passage anew on that other boat, the majestic ship of Ra, beginning its voyage across the crystal sea. The door of the cabin is flung wide open to let the King of Glory emerge. He advances amid the joyous acclaim of gods and men as they hail him who has arisen victorious over the underworld.

To limn the reality of that experience is beyond the power of language. This fact explains indeed why the ancients did not attempt to describe it. They strove to present it under forms of typology that would impress the mind through subtle powers of suggestion not open to language. All religious ceremonial grew out of typal operations which wrought their influence through the hidden potencies of sound and rhythm. And long contemplation of zoötypes and living natural symbols of truth produced repercussions in psychic awakening and vivid realization that may well be regarded as magical. The continued consideration of any living embodiment of truth will achieve a transformation into a new birth of spiritual vision and a liberation of currents of power not dreamed of before. If we are to effectuate some measure of this release of latent efficacy, we must revive the ancient figurative typology. *We must align truth once again with natural processes,* so as to view it under the forms of its endorsement by outward reality. The human psyche, tortured too long under the strain of sheer unsupported faith, will leap forward in gladness if again it can find the proffered truths of religion cast in harmony with living veracity. The outer world is itself living mind come to view in its own formations, which must then be the veridical images of truth. In conformity with this axiom the effort must now be made to portray the later phases of the arc of the human cycle, in which the soul undergoes processes that find vivid analogues in the realm of lower nature.

The soul or god in man has been represented as in actuality the foetus of a great divine being in the womb of earthly nature and individually in the body of each human, awaiting delivery. The task of evolution in the human round is to bring this embryo to the consummation of its pre-natal period, and to give it birth at last into the kingdom of the celestials. Birth is delivery from some womb. Matter is the mother of the gods and the body of physical man is the womb of the god who is struggling to come to being in it. It groans and travails in pain until the Christ is formed within it. All nature is in labor to generate the mind principle. Paul says that "even we ourselves groan within ourselves," waiting for our redemption through the new birth. The Apostle adds that the body is the temple of the living God, and emphasizes that "the temple of God is holy, which temple ye are" (*I Cor.* 3:17). With all this direct force of literal statement to empower his utterance, a stupid world has never yet seemed to grasp that Paul was delineating an actual *physiological* fact. He fairly shrieks at our dullness with the cry: "Know ye not your own selves, how that Jesus Christ is within you?"

One of the variety of natural symbols under which the sages pictured the generation of the embryo god was that of "germination." We have seen how pointedly the seed in the ground was employed to type this new birth. Germination was a vivid mirror of an inner experience.

Budge, in his introductory treatise to the *Book of the Dead,* writes that the Egyptians conceived the *sahu,* or spiritual body, the *ka,* or double, the *ba,* or soul, the *ab,* or heart, the *khu,* or shining spirit, the *sekhem,* or vital force, the *ren,* or name, and the *khabit,* or shade, all as coming forth into existence *after death.* With no better conception of what was meant by "death" than the scholastics have had, it would be assumed on the basis of this interpretation that man has none but his physical organism while living, and that the various higher bodies come into being after his demise. But these inner bodies are vital to the very existence of the physical, and must subsist with it. Man is on earth to bring these subtle bodies into development, for they can not evolve without the solar essence resident in the core of the bodily cells

537

to furnish them their texture of light. They readily interpenetrate the coarser bodies and subsist on them. What is to be understood as the coming forth of these bodies after death, as formulated by Budge, is the fact that at the consummation of the long series of lives—which are themselves the "death" spoken of, these bodies, having been born, formed and matured within the womb of the outer body, then step forth through the rent in the veil, the opened tomb door, and float free of their old mother-womb, or "bird-cage of the soul." The ones below the body of immortal essence, disintegrate in turn, to be nucleated again about the new physical body of the next generation. The higher ones persist intact through the "Flood" of dissolution and return to embodiment. But these bodies are not fully formed and perfected until after many "deaths," and it is their final liberation at the termination of the climactic life in flesh that the seers of old are commenting upon. Budge concludes his statement by saying that "it seems that the various ethereal bodies which we have enumerated together made up the spiritual body, *which 'germinated' in the khat, or material body.*"

The *Ritual* (Ch. 56) gives this utterance of the Manes: "I keep watch over the egg of Kenken-Ur (the Great Cackler); I germinate as it germinateth; I live as it liveth, and my breath is its breath." And in Chapter 64 he says:

"I hide with the god Ala-aaiu, who will walk behind me, and my members shall germinate and my khu shall be as an amulet for my body and as one who watcheth to protect my soul and to defend it and to converse therewith; . . ."

In chapter 129, the book of making perfect the Khu, it is stated that "the goddess Menqet shall make plants to germinate upon his body; . . ." And in chapter 165, called significantly the "chapter of arriving in port," the text to be recited is designed to "make the body germinate, and to drink water and not disappear." The prayer to be recited pleads as follows: "Grant thou that all his members may repose in Neter-khertet (the underworld) . . . *let his whole body become like that of a god.*" The sequence of the phrases indicates that the sprouting of the seed of divinity in the body was integrally a part of the process of becoming like a god.

In the "chapter of making the transformation into the bennu bird," Nu saith:

538

"I am come into being from unformed matter. I come into existence like the god Khepera; I have germinated like things which germinate (i.e., plants) and I have dressed myself like the tortoise. I am the germs of every god . . . I have come by day and I have risen in the footsteps of the gods."

The doctrine of the "virgin birth" as from "unformed matter" is concisely stated in the first sentence, and the germination of every god is clearly asserted. The roots of the profoundest of all Christian doctrines can be discerned in these Egyptian discourses.

Germination parallels closely the other symbol of "quickening" touched on earlier. Sent to die in matter, the latent power of the seed bestirs itself in the tomb, and sends out its first tendrils to take hold of the soil below, and others to woo the air above. It begins at once to "cultivate the crops on both sides of the horizon," the upper and lower worlds, simultaneously. This is indeed a graphic picture of how life reaches both upwards and downwards, linking two kingdoms. It must root itself in the lower in order to get a firm hold to aspire upward. Without its rootage in the soil below it could not evolve the organism by which it reaches aloft to air and sun. Out of the cruder elements of the underworld it absorbs the material which the magic power of the sun is able to transmute into finer body, crowning the whole with the soul of beauty and glory in the flower at the summit. Germination is the analogue of man's life in every general aspect and in many minor particulars. Our souls must germinate in the khat or physical body, and the transaction is one of the larger regenerations undergone by the incarnate Ego, as described by the students of the past.

Germination is a step antecedent and preparatory to emergence from the buried state of any seed, earthly or celestial. It is introductory to the resurrection, to a more realistic appreciation of which one can best be led through the gate of the mighty Kamite wisdom. The sacred books of Egypt deal mainly with the two segments of the arc of life, embodiment in flesh and resurrection therefrom. The first chapter of the *Book of the Dead* deals with the resurrection, and the title of this great antique script is itself but a term for the resurrection: *The Coming Forth by Day*. The title obviously refers to the coming of a living entity out of some state of darkness and imprisonment into the light of day and freedom. It is the book of the resurrection of the "dead."

It is the book for the living "dead" on earth. It has little reference to the experiences or conditions beyond the grave. It concerns the birth, burial, incubation, baptism, purgation, circumcision, temptation, crucifixion; the bleeding, the shame, the nakedness, the suffering; and then the quickening, germination, rebirth, reconstitution and final transfiguration and resurrection of the divine-human psyche *in this life*.

Lewis Spence very justly, amid his complete misconception of Egyptian mythology, states:

"It is probable that the name had a significance for the Egyptians which is incapable of being rendered in any modern language, and this is borne out by another of its (sub)-titles—'The chapter of making perfect the Khu' (or spirit). Osiris had now become the god of the dead *par excellence,* and his dogma taught that from the preserved corpse would spring a beautiful astral body, the future home of the spirit of the deceased."

The only real difficulty in rendering the name in other languages, however, has been the complete ignorance of the reversed meaning of the word "death." Naturally enough the translation and the sense would seem to be complicated with difficulties when nothing of the cosmic history of the soul, the evolutionary states from and into which it is to be resurrected, and other basic data, are known. Difficulty vanishes when these fundamenta are taken into account.

The name—"Coming forth by day"—demands a moment's scrutiny. The question arises as to just what the Egyptians mean by "day." Is it the "day" of our life here in body or the brighter "day" that follows this life? Is the coming forth to be reckoned as from the darkness of non-existence *into* this life, or as from the darkness of earth into the bright "day" of celestial being? With all its bright sunshine and vivid sense of reality, this life is still the dark night of the soul, the twilight of the gods, the burial in death and hell. The coming forth by day then must refer to the final transfer of the imprisoned soul from this darkness to the Elysian meadows of supernal delight. This interpretation is inherent in every implication of the great mass of typology.

A statement from Massey is interpolated here because it repeats so faithfully the typical language of Egyptian texts:

"Resurrection in the Ritual is the coming forth to day (*Peri-em-heru*) whether *from* the life on earth, or *to* the life attainable in the heaven of eternity. [Why not both?—we ask.] The first resurrection is, as it were, an ascension from the tomb in the nether earth by means of the secret door-way. But this coming forth is *in,* not *from,* Amenta, after the burial in the upper earth. He issues from the valley of darkness and the shadow of death." [1]

The reader will doubtless share our own inability to assign definite location to Massey's "nether earth" and "upper earth." They were terms hit upon by him to enable him to go on talking without committing himself to anything definitely meaningful. As locations they are perfectly pointless and fictional, in his usage. Nether and upper earth are the two realms of man's nature, and surely in his resurrection he rises out of or *from* the lower and ascends *into* the upper. If Amenta is this life and not some semi-ghostly existence after demise, then the resurrection must be *from* Amenta *into* heaven. But if a prisoner is released *from* a cell his release at least starts *in* the cell. So our resurrection is both *in* and *from* Amenta, and *to* a kingdom above. It must be described as in and from this life to a higher. Yet in reality it is an apotheosis in consciousness which plays havoc with the strict sense of in, from and to. Three dimensional directions become synthesized in a new direction on the plane above this type of consciousness. Our arising then is from lower to higher state of being.

We call the *Ritual* itself to witness the correctness of the exegesis. In the Rubric to chapter 18 directions are given: "Now if this chapter be recited over him, he shall come forth *upon earth* and shall escape from every fire." What could be more explicit? Not less decisive is the chapter 64 title: "The chapter of coming forth by day in the underworld." The soul is itself hailed as "Lord of the shrine that standeth in the middle of the earth." And again definiteness is seen in the title to chapter 188: "Chapter of the coming in of the soul to build an abode and to come forth by day *in human form.*" This might at first glance seem to be a denial of the resurrection in a spiritual body; yet it is not. Massey himself understood this clearly. He writes:

"But the individual is shown to persist [after demise] in human form. He comes forth by day and is living after death in the figure, but not as the mummy, that he wore on earth."

"Also the ka-image of man the immortal is portrayed in the likeness of man the mortal. The human form is never lost to view through all the phantasmagoria of transformation." [2]

541

Though a spirit and no longer a mortal, Jesus came forth from the grave in human form. As Massey well says, the resurrected Manes appears in the figure of, but not as, the mummy or earth body. The soul steps forth in a garment that has the form but not the substance of physical man. Why? Because the outer physical form was in the first place shaped over the mold of that inner invisible body. When the latter has divested itself of the former, it appears in its original and characteristic shape.

The Manes asserts that he rises as "a god amongst men," which must be on earth. The resurrecting entity was styled "he who cometh forth from the dusk and whose birth is in the house of death"—which is the physical body. Chapter 65 bears further succinct testimony: "Behold me, I am born and I come forth in the form of a living Khu, and the human beings who are upon the earth ascribe praise unto me." He must be where human beings can perceive him to render him this praise.

It may fall with disconcerting effect upon religionists who so sharply differentiate between *Old* and *New Testaments* to be told that the *Old Testament* exodus is identical in meaning with the *New Testament* resurrection! To be sure, it is set forth under vastly different forms of typology in the two versions. The Hebrew representation perhaps also depicts the entire scope of the cycle rather than just the concluding or climactic stage of it. Massey's words will make this clear:

"Thus the origin of the exodus, as Egyptian, was in the coming forth of the heavenly bodies *from below the horizon* as the mythical representation. This was followed by the coming forth of the Manes from dark to day, from death to life, from bondage to liberty, from Lower Egypt to Upper Egypt in the eschatology." [3]

The exodus, he says, is the experience of the Manes in making their journey through, and their exit from, Amenta.

Luke's "multitude of the heavenly host praising God" fills also the *Book of the Dead* with celestial chorus: "They rejoice at his beautiful coming forth from the womb of Nut," or, as it might be rendered, the womb of Meri (Mary), for Meri is another name for the Mother-heaven. And as the glory appeared to the shepherds in such effulgence that they were sore afraid, so "the coming forth to day is attended by a great flood of light that emanated from the solar glory and enveloped him entirely." When Horus has revived his dead father, he says: "I am Horus on this fair day at the beautiful coming forth of thy powers, who lifteth thee up with himself on this fair day as thine associate god." Chapters 2 and 3 provide that the deceased may come forth *in* the underworld and "live after he hath died, even as doth Ra day by day." And chapter 72 says that he may "come forth by day in all the forms which he pleaseth to take." "He sails over heaven . . . he arrives at the high place of heaven . . . the storm winds of heaven bear him along and present him to Ra." The Manes is told: "Thy soul flieth up on high to meet the soul of the gods . . . " The famous *Hymn to Ra* is sung "when he [Ani] riseth in the eastern part of heaven."

It is likely that the "two men in white apparel" in the *Acts* (1:10) who say to the disciples, "Ye men of Galilee, why stand ye gazing into heaven?" are the Gospel counterparts of the two sons of Atum, Hu and Sa, who attend their father in his resurrection in the Egyptian scene.

In *Job* (25:14) it is asked: "How can man be clean that is born of a woman?" The resurrection followed the cleansing from earthly dross. The Manes prays that the solar glory should shine upon him and that *"no pollution of my mother be upon me."* He hopes to fare across the miry lake with no stains of base defilement clinging to him. The Speaker in the *Ritual* is desirous of making his transformation into the glorious body of light which is at the opposite pole of manifestation from that earthy body that was engendered by the blood of the mother. At the apex of his triumph he must have sloughed off every last vestige of earthly taint if his radiance is to shine undimmed.

The coming forth implicates certain theological considerations that must be scanned. It is not the same as the "coming" which is involved in the Messianic advent. The Egyptian Amen seems to be derived from *Amenu,* "to come." He was that aspect of Ra whose emergence upon earth brought the deific fire to man. This was the coming of divinity to earth, yet hardly its coming forth upon earth. They are an inceptive and a concluding phase, however, of the same large movement. The one begins, the other ends, the cycle of mortal life. The seed comes into the soil and then comes forth from it. A human comes on the day of his birth, yet he only comes in his adulthood when a man. And in a larger sense the whole of his life is his coming to whatever he is to be. So with the theological "coming"; it is not completed until its final act is consummated. The god has not fully come until his resurrection. The coming Son is not only the Messiah whose advent is celebrated at Christmas, but is as well the buried lord re-arising at Easter.

For many thousands of years before Christ, the prototype of all coming saviors was the Egyptian Iusa. The name is from *Iu* (*Ia, Ie, Io* or *Ja, Je, Jo, Ju*), the original name of biune divinity, combined with the Egyptian suffix *sa* (or *se, si, su,* or *saf, sef, sif, suf*), meaning, with the grammatical masculine "*f*," the male heir, son, successor, or prince. Iusa then means the son of the divine father *Iu* (Ju-piter, "father god"), or the son of Ihuh (Jehovah). He was *Iu,* coming as the *su,* or son. His mother in the Atum cult was Iusaas. He was God the son, the prince, the heir. He was the original of all Jesus figures, of whom there are some twenty or more *by the name* of Jesus (Joshua, Jesse, Joses, Hosea, Isaiah, Isaac, Esau, Josiah, Joash, Jehoaz, Jehoahaz, Job, Jonah, Joel and others) both in the *Old Testament* and outside of it. Samson, Saul and Solomon are prior types of Jesus, all bearing the solar character in their name. Iusa, Solomon and Jesus were all temple builders. Iusa was the divine modeler of the spiritual temple, and an inscription says that the temple of Edfu was "restored as it is in the book of the model composed by Prince Iusa, eldest son of Ptah." He was Iu-em-hetep (Imhotep, Imothes) of a later cult. He was that seventh principle that came to bring peace (*Hetep*) by fusing and reducing to harmony the lower six powers which were anarchic until the advent of the Prince of Peace to subjugate them. The seventh principle is the savior and redeemer of creation. The Manes says: "I am one of those to whom it is said, Come, come, in peace, by those who look upon him"—that is, the company of the gods. He says again in Chapter 25, the "chapter of giving a heart to Osiris in the underworld:" "My soul shall not be fettered to my body at the gates of the underworld; but I shall enter in peace and I shall come forth in peace." These and similar phrases of promise are to be fulfilled on that great day, the name of which is itself significant—the day of "Come thou to me," or "the day of 'Come unto us,'" or "Come thou hither." This was to be the opening day of the resplendent new creation. *Revelation* speaks of the same grand inaugural: "The spirit and the bride say

'Come'!" (Ch. 20:11). Spirit and matter, calling from the horizon, bid us come to the crowning.

The natural man, first Adam, the race's ancient half-animal progenitors, prepared the way and saluted and announced the coming one. The Manes cries: "Let the fathers and their apes make way for me, that I may enter the Mount of Glory, where the great ones are" (Ch. 136B). The ape typed the pre-solar morning star that announced the coming of the human sun, and the morning star is one of the seven rewards promised to him that overcometh. The morning star (at one time) was Sothis, the watch-dog that barked to announce the coming of the Day-Star from on high, as the ape clicked at the rising sun.

In the beginning of the cycle, "the god comes to his body"; in the end Horus exclaims: "I have come to an end for the lord of heaven, I rest at the table of my father Osiris." This immediately precedes his piercing the veil of the tabernacle and coming forth as the divine hawk or soul.

A quite instructive statement stands at the end of the "chapter by which the soul of Osiris is perfected in the bosom of Ra":

"By this book the soul of the deceased shall make its exodus with the living and prevail amongst, or as, the gods. By this book he shall know the secrets of that which happened in the beginning. No one else has ever known this mystical book or any part of it. It has not been spoken by men. No eye hath deciphered it. No ear hath heard of it. It must only be seen by thee and the man who unfolded its secrets to thee. Do not add to its chapters or make commentaries on it from the imagination or from memory. *Carry it out in the judgment hall.* This is a true Mystery unknown anywhere to those who are uninitiated." (Rubric to Chapter 149, Birch).

It is singular that Paul (*Ephesians* 3:3 ff) speaks in quite similar terms of a mystery made known to him "which in other ages was not made known unto the sons of men; as it is now revealed unto his holy apostles and prophets by the spirit"—that the Gentiles should be fellow-heirs and partakers of the promise of Christhood. It would seem, then, that the great aeonial mystery of this portion of the universe was the coming of the solar deities to link with the animal races and lift them up. This is the theme of our book. It is for man the greatest of all mysteries, since it is the mystery of his own being. We, unspiritualized, are the Gentiles.

As the heir of Seb, Horus says that he was suckled at the breast of Isis, the spouse of Seb, "who gave him his theophanies," or manifestations (*Rit.*, Ch. 82). "Horus on earth lies down to embrace the old man who keeps the light of earth, and who is Seb, the earth-father" (Ch. 84). It is notable here that it is Seb, earth-power, that gives to undeveloped solar intelligence, its "theophanies" or actualization in concrete worlds.

The Messianic Son came ever as the manifester and witness for the father, who had sunk his life in matter to reproduce himself in his next generation. According to Herodotus (2:43) the Egyptian Jesus with the title of Iu-em-hetep was one of the eight great gods who were in the papyri twenty thousand years ago! He bore a different name according to the cult. To the sages of old time the coming was a constantly recurring and only typical event. The ancient Messiah was a representative figure coming from age to age, cycle to cycle. He came "each day" in the *Ritual;* he came periodically; he came "regularly and continuously." He came once through the cycle; but his solar and lunar and natural *types* came cyclically and in eternal renewal. *The Egyptian Messiah was one whose historical coming was not expected at any date, at any epoch.* The type of his coming was manifest in some phenomenon repeated as often as the day, the year, or the lunation came around. The constant repetition of type was the assurance of its unfailing fulfillment. For the ancients, the idea of a fulfillment "once for all" would have been to accept the possibility of stopping dead the march of the universe. And for one to be saved in a final sense for *all* eternity, would have been to drop out of step with the rhythmic pulse of life. To them salvation meant to consummate the present step or cycle and keep marching on with nature. Viciously the corrupt notion has undermined the wholesome spirit of natural progress, that one may attain final bliss and drop out of the movement of life into eternal rest. It is a fatuity, and it has partly paralyzed the instinctive sympathy between man and his world of nature. We have torn our life asunder from its basic symphonic relation to the seasons and the elements, and lost thereby our sensitiveness to currents of subtle force that were designed to carry us onward.

The coming was taking place in the life of every man at all times. Each man had his evolutionary solstice, his Christmas; and he would have his Easter. The symbols were annuals; the actual events they typed in mankind's history were perennials. In nature every process is but typical and repetitive. But it is typical of all other process and of life in its entirety.

Horus, a form of Iu-em-hetep, was not an individual historical person. For he says: "I am Horus, the Prince of Eternity." Jesus was with the Father before the foundation of the worlds. Horus calls himself "the persistent traveler on the highways of heaven," and "the everlasting one." "I am Horus who steppeth onward through eternity." Here is wisdom to nourish the mind and lead it out of its infantile stage into maturity of view. Horus declares himself forever above the character of a time-bound personage, an indestructible spirit that advances onward through one embodiment after another to endless days. He is the Ancient of Days, who eternally renews himself in cycle after cycle. Let moderns ponder his other mighty pronouncement: "I am a soul, and my soul is divine. It is the self-originating force." It can perpetually renew itself, entering the womb of its mother, wife, sister, Isis, mother-nature, to be born again and again.

His career in any life cycle was typified by the ancients under the phases of the rolling year. Being himself the sun-god, his life was analogous to the sun's movements round its cycle. He was born or baptized in the water signs below and rebaptized in the air and fire signs above the horizon. His typical reign was the period of one year! This was "the acceptable year of the Lord." Tradition has carried the legend of a one-year ministry. The Gnostics Ptolemaeus and Herakleon, as well as the two great Christian philosophers Clement and Origen, held the view of a reign of Jesus that lasted one year.

The ancients used other cycles than the solar year to represent the comings of the perennial traveler. One was the Great Year of 25,868 years, during which the sun traversed the entire twelve signs of the zodiac in the precession of the equinoxes. A lesser one was a twelfth of this year, or the cycle of one sign, 2155 years. Another was the "house of a thousand years," which was calculated to mean fourteen average lifetimes of 71 years each, 994 years. A surprising reference to the division or cycle of fourteen generations is found in *Matthew* (1:17), where those who may dispute the significance of the number fourteen will find themselves forced to reckon with it again:

"So all the generations from Abraham to David are fourteen generations; and from David until the carrying away into Babylon are fourteen generations; and from the carrying away into Babylon unto Christ are fourteen generations."

Even if this statement matched no facts of veridical history, it marks a specific cycle of fourteen generations, and once more the Bible is found to hold to "pagan" usages. The Magi, the Zoroastrians, Chaldeans, Jews, Gnostics, Essenes and others kept the reckonings of the great religious cycles that were astronomical from the first. There were the Phoenix Cycle of 500 years and the great Cycle of Neros of 600; also the Egyptian Sothiac Cycle of 1461 years. The 1260 "days" of *Revelation* became the basis of another measurement.

Horus, Iusa, Iu-em-hetep and the Jesus of the "Infancy" Gospels all wrought miracles of resurrection in their childhood. At *three* years of age Iusa performed the wonder of making a dead *fish* (Pisces, the house of the birth of Christs) come to life (*Latin Gospel of Thomas,* Bk. 3, Ch. I). At five years of age he takes clay and molds twelve sparrows, which he commanded to fly, and not in vain. Here is a beautiful little allegory of bringing the dead divinity to life in twelve aspects of evolving intelligence. Papias emphatically declares that the Gospels originated in the *Logia,* or Sayings of Mu, or Ma. *Mythoi* were also *Ma-ti* (*-ti* being an Egyptian plural ending). Mati, the goddess of the Hall of the Two Truths or the equipoise of truth, would be the deity who uttered the true sayings or *Logia.* Research discloses that all the salient features of the life and character of Jesus were anticipated in the person of Horus, including the virgin motherhood, the divine sonship, the miracles, the self-immolation, the compassion, the discourses, the resurrection and a host of minor particulars. Egypt was the cradle of the Jesus figure, and in that cradle lay Iusa and Iu-em-hetep, Khunsu and Horus, Amsu, Khepr and Aten, all resurrected sons of dead fathers. In a sense both humorously and ironically unsuspected, the proclamation of the God of Christendom has been true: "Out of Egypt have I called my son." God sent his sons into this "Egypt" of the flesh-pots to gain what such an experience alone could yield; but in the turn of the cycle he called them home to him.

The coming of the ancient Christs was not historical. They did not come as persons, but as principles. Being spiritual light, their coming is in the form of an intenser glowing, as man feeds their flame with truth and love. They are the fire that burns with unquenchable persistence and gradually transforms the body itself into more ethereal substance. They come to transubstantiate the body that is host to them. These processes were embodied in several theological doctrines, which have become misread, misconceived and disastrously misapplied, through their ascription to the lone experience of one man.

There was the basic doctrine of transubstantiation. In the performance of the Mystery ritual an actual transformation might take place in more or less ample measure. Always there was the release of a psychic force through the powerfully suggestive nature of the rites and symbols. Symbolic ceremony need not stop at the portals of the mind, but might, through repetition, penetrate to the seat of the deeper consciousness and effect a liberation of latent power. Sincere performance of the ceremony might bring surprising repercussions in the organism. Continued cultivation of the presence and power of the god would gradually transmute baser elements into spiritual gold, and end by elevating one to the rank and number of the gods.

The god himself, fallen into carnal mire, buried and inert, had to be raised and restored to sound condition. As he awakened his faculties and sloughed off the imprisoning vesture of decay, it was as if every member of his body was resuscitated and made over. He is to come forth as a god in the form of a man. It is the mystery of life that he was to realize his latent divinity in the lower manger of the mortal body. It is said of him: "The secret dwelling is in darkness in order that the transformation of this god may take place." The seed must germinate in the dark earth. Not only the beetle, but the tadpole, the moth, the serpent, the human foetus, the boy at puberty, all were images of the great transformation which should at some late day metamorphose the man into the god. This work is gradual and is accomplished piecemeal. The god finds his glorification coming day by day, feature by feature; he is reconstituted limb by limb, member by member, until he says there is no part of him that remains mortal. He is given the hair of Nu or heaven (solar rays); the eyes of Hathor; the ears of Apuat; the nose of Khenti-Kas; the lips of Anup; the teeth of Serkh; the neck of Isis; the hands of the mighty lord of Tattu; the shoulders of Neith; the back of Sut; the phallus of Osiris; the legs and thighs of Nut; the feet of Ptah; and the nails and bones of the living Uraei "until there is not a limb of him that is without a god." "My leg-bones are the leg-bones of the living gods. There is no member of my body that is not a member of some god. I am Yester-day, and Seer of Millions of Years is my name." Here is notice to man that he must traverse every kingdom in order that he may absorb and embody in himself every aspect of nature's power, the efficacy of every god. Mighty truth is this.

In the Gospels this reconstitution is hinted at in the passage in which the acceptable year of the Lord is announced, when the Messiah shall preach recovery of sight to "the blind" and bind up the "broken-hearted." Horus goes "wherever there lieth a wreck in the field of eternity." This redeemer is announced with joy:

"Hail, Osiris! Horus makes thee to be joined to the gods. . . . He brings to thee the gods in a body. None among them escapes from his hand. Horus loves thee more than his own offspring, he unites thee to those of his own body. Horus makes his Ka to be in thee. . . . He makes a spirit to be in thee."

And the Manes again is hailed:

"Ho, Ho! thou art raised up! Thou hast received thy head, thou hast embraced thy bones, thou hast collected thy flesh, thou hast searched the earth for thy body."

Here is strong assertion again that man is to summarize in himself the qualities of the whole scale of being, denominated gods. All their powers and virtue have to be embodied in man's organic wholeness to make him, like the resuscitated Osiris, "Neb-er-ter; the god entire." Every member of the old Atum, deceased and defunct, had to be fashioned anew in a fresh creation. Like a person recovering from amnesia, he had to recollect his former knowledge, reassemble the component elements of his dismembered integrity. He was so long the lifeless mummy he had forgotten how to walk; so long mute he had forgotten how to speak. "Let me," he says, "come forth to day and walk upon my legs. Let me have the feet of the glorified." He says again: "I have come myself and delivered the god from great pain and suffering that were in trunk and shoulder and leg. I have come and healed the trunk and fastened the shoulder and made firm the leg." He remembers his name. A new heart is given him. His jaws are parted, his eyes reopened. Power is given to his arms, the con-stricting bandages being removed by Horus-Amsu, the freer of the arm. He is no longer bound to the khat at the gate of Amenta. Clad in bright new vesture, his Easter morning finery, he prepares to take passage on board the boat of the sun. "Behold me," he exclaims; "I have come to you and have carried off and put together my forms." Perfected in his unified septenary nature, he is ready to ascend to the Father in his original glory. For he has prayed that the Father may give unto him that glory which he had with him from the creation of the world. He has been told that he may behold his Ka. This was that soul that came forth from the hand of God at the beginning of his individual career, was in attendance on him all life through as a genius or daemon, and reabsorbed the lower personality to itself at the dissolution of the various elements. When honors were paid to a Pharaoh, offerings were made to his Ka, not to his mortal self, which could not be permanent.

In the *Seventh Book of Hermes,* which is entitled "His secret *sermon in the Mount* of regeneration and the profession of silence," Hermes instructs Taht in the nature of the "tabernacle of the zodiacal circle." There is often more enlightenment in an Egyptian phrase or name than in whole works on theology. Peter wished, we are told, to build three tabernacles on the Mount, one for Jesus, one for Moses and one for Elias. These must be taken for the three spiritual aspects of the solar triad. But Hermes then defines the transfiguration in terms of a philosophy of superior wisdom. "This is regeneration, O son, that we should not any longer fix our imagination upon the body, subject to the three dimensions."

To Horus it is said: "Thou dost renew thy youth"; and his rising to life is declared to make men and women alive. "I went in as a hawk," he sings; "I came out as a phoenix"—that is, transformed. Says *Job:* "I shall die in my nest, and I shall multiply my days like the phoenix." "My transformations are those of the double god, Horus-Set" (Ch. 180). He became "the lord of both parts," with the atonement made. Jesus in matter and the Christ in spirit are identical with the two Horus phases. In the Gnostic writings the two meet in Tattu and blend in the mystery of a divine union. They unite in one divine soul "which dwelleth in the place of establishing a soul that is to live forever" (Ch. 17). The scene of this transformation, as in the case of the Buddha, is beneath the tree; the tree of dawn; the tamarisk, persea, olive or sycamore-fig. Horus reborn as the sun of morning says: "I am the babe. I am the god within the tamarisk tree" (Ch. 42). Chapter 84 of the *Ritual* is that "of making the transformation into a heron":

"I have gotten dominion over the beasts that are brought for sacrifice. . . . I have set the gods upon their paths . . . the light is beyond your knowledge and ye cannot fetter it; the times and seasons are in my body."

To know of a certainty that with all our stupidity we can not fetter the light, is a truth that should be republished and pondered by an age intent only upon outward accomplishment and heedless of the light within.

The soul is rescued from animal incarnation when it consummates its Easter. We are indeed blind if we fail to catch the significance of the animal typology of the zodiac. Massey informs us that it was not more than three or four centuries since in England the zodiac was called "the Bestiary." The sun was represented as passing through a series of animal forms. This is of Egyptian origin. Horus in the Pool of Persea made his transformations into the cat, the lion, the hawk and the phoenix, the heron and the swallow, each a type of a stage of progression—for deeply recondite reasons. The soul transforms into the various animals, fishes, birds; and his emphatic words are to the effect that he becomes these animals. He crawls as a serpent, burrows as a mole, sees in the dark of death as a cat or owl or hare, swims the water as a fish, hibernates as a bear, follows the lost spiritual scent in the night as a dog, fox or jackal (Anup), divides his nature like the ape, floats on the water of life like a swan, undergoes transformations like a beetle and breaks his eggshell like a chick. The passage of the sun through the bestial signs was depicted as a series of transformations denoted by the signs. The Manes says: "I establish myself forever in my transformations that I choose." As he was to sum and unify the total powers of the living kingdoms, he was to gather up in his journey through earth the typical qualities and nature of every animal, and transform them into their spiritual form. He was thus to become king over nature, and the angels from their seats would envy him. In John's and Ezekiel's visions he was to rule the gods of the four corners of life's temple, the lion, eagle, bull and animal man. He was to convert animality into divinity.

The misty specter of an unsolved problem in anthropology arises here to twit us with our ignorance. Totemism is the most perplexing riddle of archaeology, and in want of a single decisive datum to elucidate it we have ascribed it to "primitive superstition," our most convenient limbo into which to consign a thing we can not solve. By this resort we do but pit modern superstition against ancient knowledge. So far as can be discerned, there has been hardly a single word uttered by learned anthropolgists or sociologists that betrays the slightest hint of an approach to solid ground as to the rationale of Totemism. An institution that was world-wide in prevalence and profound in relation to social life, is set down as due to nothing more germane to actual life than caprice of primitive imagination.

But no student can bring his mind to grips with the implications of Egyptian religion without confronting the steady insistence of an inference from the old data which, however incredible it may appear, at least furnishes the first rational or plausible ground for an understanding of Totemism. Even through the corruption of originally pure conception can be traced the outline of the profoundest intimation of evolutionary truth.

Many ancient texts advance the suggestion that early man and the animals were practically kindred. Perhaps the central fact of archaic anthropology is the declaration that the sons of God took incarnation in the bodies of animals. *Genesis* (6: 4) assures that they had intercourse, in contravention of their demiurgic commission, with the females of the animal races. Whole groups of the sense-blinded gods may have taken residence in the bodies of particular species, thus making their blood cognate with that of the animal in each case. Groups seized upon different species, and the various animal natures thus became distributed amongst the incoming humans. The particular animal would be reverenced as the progenitor of the tribe, the present members of the species would be regarded as brothers, and except at the sacrificial Eucharist, when the beast's virtues were to be incorporated by eating its flesh, its body would be sacrosanct. Oriental ideas of the inviolability of animal life may spring from such an early conception of kinship and sanctity. It is certain that the line of division between animal and human was at the start quite inappreciable. There are legends of interminglings and cross-breedings without end. As life distributed its manifold qualities out amid its multiplicity of creatures, and man was to gather them all up and unify them again under intelligent rule, it is no wild conception to assume that the sages spread some knowledge amongst early races that different tribes were manifesting the qualities of this or the other animal, which they would transmute to grander expression when mind wrought its miracle upon them. Whether Totemism commemorated the incorporation of raw animal quality-germs in man by actual incarnation in animal forms or by typal representation only, is a matter to be specifically determined. That the higher aspect of the allegorical rituals may have been known to but few, or lost entirely for long stretches, does not impugn the validity of the original meaning. The sharp line of distinction between that which is purely representative in symbolic act and its esoteric true meaning is easily transgressed when perception flags and insight grows dull; and idolatry and superstition are the result when confusion thickens. But man, who exhibits the results of his incorporation in the animal orders in his tigerish ferocity, his foxy cunning, his leonine courage, his eel-like slipperiness, his serpent-wise slyness, his scorpion sting of anger, his sheepish meekness, his dogged pertinacity, his wolfish rapacity, his cat-like stealth, his beaver persistency, his dove-like dreams of sweet purity, or his phoenix-like aspiration to soar aloft at·times—with his obvious embodiment of the attributes of lower orders within himself—man may not rationally repudiate the theory of his sometime kinship with those grades of life. Man is weaving a pattern composed of the commingled strands of every species of experience, which must be consciously had to be appropriated. If there never was at any primordial time a living link with these animal creatures, then there is a problem of explaining how the obvious parallelism between human and animal characteristic traits arose. The *Ritual* of Egypt states that the "seven Uraeus divinities are my body." This is to say that man's physical nature is a compound of the seven natural powers that formulated the material creation. It must be summed up, then, that man's composite life is an epitome and codification, as it were, of all the precedent powers of creation, including the animal traits, but now sublimated by the mystic and magic operation of the superior solar intelligence which glows in his brain alone on earth. Totemism would have a very real foundation.

It seems that the final and climactic episode in the transformation of man into god was considered in isolation and named the Transfiguration. This majestic initiation is a harbinger of the resurrection, if not indeed a part of that epochal experience itself. It is no less splendid.

554

Much instruction is gained in reading the account of this great mystery as given in the Gnostic *Pistis Sophia*. It is in the first place of tremendous importance to note that the Transfiguration here *follows,* not *precedes,* the resurrection. For in this and other Apocryphal Gospels it is given that when Jesus had risen from the dead in his first advent, he passed eleven (or twelve) years speaking with the disciples and instructing them up to the stage of the first statutes only (the Lesser Mysteries):

"It came to pass, therefore, that the disciples were sitting together on the Mount of Olives speaking of these things, rejoicing with great joy and being exceedingly glad, and saying one to another, 'Blessed are we before all men who are on earth, for the Savior hath revealed this unto us, and we have received all fulness and all perfection' "—as these had been received likewise upon Mt. Bakhu, the Egyptian Mount of Olives, in the ascent of Horus from Amenta.

"And while they were saying these things the one to the other, Jesus sat a little apart from them. It came to pass, therefore, on the fifteenth day of the month Tybi, the day of the full moon, on that day when the sun had risen in its going, that there came forth a great stream of light shining exceedingly. It came forth from the light of lights. And this stream of light poured over Jesus and surrounded him. He was seated apart from his disciples and was shining exceedingly. But the disciples saw not Jesus because of the great light in which he sat, for their eyes were blinded by the great light." (Mead's Translation, p. 4, 5.)

The calendar position of the Transfiguration on the full moon of Tybi (about December 27 in the Christian calendar) aligns the event with the Christmas Nativity. This only indicates that the imagery of an outburst of sun-glory had been intertwined with the suggestion of "quickening" at the winter solstice. We have seen that the early Christians celebrated the "birth" on March 25. The full moon can type nothing but the completion of a process of divinization. This may be associated with the quickening from inert death at Christmas or with the birth of full glory at Easter. Let it be established beyond cavil that the varied imagery of ancient representation comprises many forms of depicting that which is but one grand event, any critical epoch of which is typal in a measure of the whole experience. The statement of the disciples that they had "received the fulness of all perfection" would point to the consummative nature of the events

555

comprising the climactic transition from mortal to divine. The fact that the Transfiguration took place on the Mount of Olives on the east would indicate the culminative value of it. The eastern mount was the point of departure from earth, all values won.

The *Ritual* of Egypt speaks of the same illuminative power of solar deity: "Horus gives thee the gods, he makes them come to thee, they illumine thy face." On the Mount of Transfiguration in the Gospels Jesus' "face did shine as the sun and his garments became white as the light." When the deceased mortal climbs out of matter and approaches the verge of the Paradisiacal Aarru, or Hetep, "his members become like those of the gods. He goeth forth pure spirit."

It is to be noted that this great transaction is described as instantaneous. When in the *Ritual* it is stated to Ra that "thy rays are upon all faces," and the transition into spirit is described, the conclusion is given as follows: "This thou doest in one little moment of time." Says Evans-Wentz in elucidating the *Tibetan Book of the Dead* (p. 168): "In a moment of time a marked differentiation is created; in a moment of time perfect enlightenment is obtained." When the mummy comes forth and assumes the likeness of Ra, the statement in the *Ritual* is that Osiris "is renewed in an instant." It is the consummation of his second birth, when "he raises his soul and hides his body." We have Paul's similar statement that we are changed in a moment, in the twinkling of an eye. These statements either are descriptive of the flooding luminosity of the very last moment of our deification, or the "little moment of time" may be in terms of fourth-dimensional consciousness.

The misconstruction of the resurrection by Christian theology has been most lamentably serious and fatal. The imagery of the rent veil, the discarded swathings, the rolled stone and the opened tomb were converted into occurrence and attached to a personal life. As the figure of the *Christos* was nailed on a wooden cross, so was his body consigned to a rocky tomb. And what may be asserted to have been gained in gruesome realism by the maneuver has been more than overbalanced by the loss of the universality of the experience and of its ineffable beauty as a spiritual mystery. There was neither reason, justification nor need for the literalization of the crucifixion and the resurrection. People who were children in intellect took the grand parables and allegories of arcane science and fed them to other infantile minds as veritable history. The Logos was declared to have come as the man Jesus, born as a babe in Judea, and walking the lanes, lake strands and hills as any peasant. It is the good fortune of humanity, however, that enough of the material embodying the ancient intellectual achievement has survived the bigotry of that movement to enable us to rekindle the lamp that once burned so luminously. While the blinded worshipers of the carnalized Logos were obliterating in frenzied zeal all traces of a more spiritual philosophy, there lay securely buried from their devastating hands the great Egyptian wisdom, safe from their predatory fury by reason of their own inability to decipher the writings, as well as by their sorry misjudgment of the value of that "pagan rubbish." Now the discovery of a slab of stone by one of Napoleon's soldiers has arisen to confound their design after centuries. And Christianity can now be seen as a sad travesty of original knowledge. Only the restoration of its esoteric meaning by the keys of that despised paganism can save it.

Osiris rose on the third day under lunar or cosmical typology. The germinal seed of divine consciousness, buried for three aeons or kingdoms in lower matter, rose in the middle of the fourth day. Aeons of anthropological history were dramatized by the three dark days of the lunar month. The seed of seminal light spent three "days" in the bowels of earth and matter, and rose in the fourth round, or "watch of the night." As history the resurrection after three literal days in the tomb falls into absurdity; but as ritual symbolism it stands in such grandeur as the mind can only vainly struggle to conceive.

Much Biblical reference to the period of three days has been quoted, but there is a remarkable forecast of resurrection imagery in Hosea (6:1-3):

"Come let us return unto the Lord [who is described in the preceding chapter as the double lion!] for he hath torn and he shall heal us; he hath smitten and he will bind us up. After two days will he revive us; *on the third day* he will *raise us up;* and we shall live for him. . . . His going forth is sure as the morning; . . ."

The essential truth of the resurrection is the central Egyptian conception of the one life force, the one soul of being, the self-generating, self-sustaining power, *ever renewing itself in phenomena.* The grossest error of conventional religionism is the prevalent idea of a static eternity for man's spirit after departure from earth. This is one of those dreary delusions with which the despoiling of esotericism has afflicted the mass of humanity. Immortality we have, but it is not static. The placid "at peace" and "at rest" on gravestones is but a temporary interlude between active lives. Life is immortal, but its immortality is won by the effort of an endless succession of cycles of birth and death, manifestation and retirement. Immortality is through repetition of cycle; and that is why the cycles of nature that are endlessly repeated before our eyes are set as the symbols of our life. The imperishable spark of life that goes into and out of matter was typed as the breath of God, the spirit of the Father, the mind of the Logos, the pillar of earth, the salt of the earth, the ark of heaven, the elixir of life, the fount of youth, the backbone of the universe, the water of life, the oil of anointing, the spark of eternal fire, the bread of life, the river of blessing and the resurrecting soul. Each rhythmic renewal of itself in matter was called its own son. It forever bred itself anew as its own child.

That the festival of the resurrection was an astronomical event used as a type of spiritual truth is attested by the date set for it. In the Gospel account it was by one calculation on the fourteenth of the month Nisan, on the eve of the vernal Passover. This was the date of the full moon in a lunar month of 28 days. Yet by another reckoning the feast of the Passover preceded the morn of resurrection and fell on the fifteenth of the month Nisan. The fifteenth brings the full moon of a solar month. The resurrection being the result of the union of male and female principles, both a feminine (lunar) and a masculine (solar) dating had to be combined in fixing it. Therefore it falls on the first Sun-day following the first full-moon-day after the vernal equinox.

The ancient type of resurrection and rebirth was the tree. The tamarisk, persea, sycamore-fig, olive, oak, pine, ash, palm, acacia, cypress, banyan, juniper and others were made emblems of the eternal renewal. The vernal rebirth of the tree could hardly be surpassed for beauty in its miracle of annual resurrection of "dead" life. Massey's statement as to the purely typical character of the doctrine is clear:

"There is no possible question of a corporeal resurrection. The mummy of the god in matter or mortality rises from the tomb *transubstantiated into spirit*. The Egyptians had no doctrine of a physical resurrection of the dead."

Obviously not, when we see, as Massey did not, that they spoke not at all of the dead as the defunct mortal. Budge lends corroboration:

"The educated Egyptian never believed that the material body would rise again and take up a new life, for he well understood that flesh and blood could not inherit immortality." [4]

The truth is, alleges Massey again, that the Christian religion is the only one in religious history that is based on the resuscitated corpse instead of a spiritual transformation. In no other religion is continuity in spirit made dependent on the resurrection of the earthly body. The spirit rose from the corpse, not in it. It was the soul emerging radiant from its grave in matter. All religion must rest for ultimate values on the resurrection, as Paul says; but the rising again is not that of the cadaver. Paul himself says that man re-arises in spirit body.

The deceased prays that he may emerge from the world of the dead and revisit the earth. This has been taken by many to mean a return of the spirit to earth in the ghostly sense. It hardly seems to mean this, though it may not be necessarily excluded. It seems rather to point directly to its return in future embodiments in the cycles. The living soul on earth and not the wraith in its celestial rest is the chief and central concern of religion. Misguided pietism has tended to contemn earth and glorify heaven. Egypt answers this false discrimination decisively when the Manes says (Ch. 30A, Renouf): "Although he is buried in the deep, deep grave, and bowed down with the reign of annihilation, he is glorified [even] there."

After his 40 days in the desert of Amenta, tried under Satanic power, the Manes prays: "Let me reach the land of ages, let me gain the land of eternity, for thou, my Lord, hast destined them for me" (Ch. 13). Osiris passed into Amenta as the Lord of Transformations, and he was therefore to emerge transformed in the resurrection. He was the power of renewal, able to overcome death and bring life and immortality to light. As the Lord of Transformations he carried the magic wand, symbol of divine power, by which he could effect the chrysalis-like alterations of his followers' nature, as he opened one door of initiation after another. He became the magician of folk-tales.

The term Sekhem, the name of the place in which magical operations were performed upon the Manes, denotes the power of erectile force. It was therefore the region in which all that had been thrown down in incarnation was re-erected in new birth. In Sekhem the weak mortal nature was quickened and established firmly. It is not difficult to see the application here of one of the common phallic emblems, the erection of the male member to become creative. All phallism was originally purely symbolic. Massey's statement is appropriate here:

"The self-erecting member was the type of the resurrection, as the image of Khem-Horus, the re-arising sun, and of Khepr-Ra, the re-erector of the dead." [5]

The power to raise up fallen divinity and unspiritualized nature was supplied only by the Sekhem or virile force. Without it the Manes could not have stood upon his feet, as Paul was told to stand on his feet after being thrown down on the way to Damascus. Horus was called the Prince of Sekhem. The *Ritual* contains two chapters, one concerning the arranging of the funeral couch, the other concerning its being made to stand up. This ritual is made into a miracle in the Gospels, when the dead are raised and the paralytic takes up his bed and walks. Chapter 170 says to the Manes: "Horus causes thee to stand up at the risings." "Thou art raised up, thou art not dead," exults the *Papyrus of Teta*. "Thy (spiritual) body to heaven, the *empty case* of Horus to the earth," indicates the release of the immortal soul from the now empty shell of the corpse. "Thou shalt not be imprisoned by those . . . who shut up the shades of the dead. It is heaven alone that shall hold thee" (Ch. 92). Imprisonment was over; the liberty of the sons of God was won at last.

Tedium in quotation is risked for the sake of the majestic nobility of such a verse as this from the *Ritual:* "I am the bright one in glory, whom Atum-Ra hath called into being, and my origin is from the apple of his eye. Verily *before Isis was* I grew up and waxed old and was honored before those who were with me in glory" (*Rit.*, Ch. 78, Renouf). Again it is the voice of the cosmic Aeon and not that of a man of flesh. And here is the affirmation that Horus existed before his mother! "The soul is more ancient than the body," is the parallel dictum of Greek philosophy. The womb of nature that the soul enters is a new formation; but the entering soul is a spark of primordial fire that existed from beyond time itself.

> "The soul that rises with us, our life star,
> Hath had elsewhere its setting,
> And cometh from afar."

The riddle offers no greater complexity than to understand that an aged man may be much older than the house he lives in, having lived elsewhere before.

In one of the scenes in the *Ritual* Horus is enjoined to perform his eastern task. He is addressed: "Rise up, Horus, son of Isis, and restore thy father Osiris," the mummy. Then he bids his father: "Rise up, then, Osiris. I have stricken down thine enemies for thee; I have delivered thee from them." He opens his father's two eyes and raises him to stand among the living. All this is outward allegorism, outlining the truth that the son brings the inert powers of his father to new life in his youthful splendor. Then it is that the Hebrew Horus, that is, Jesus, concludes his address to his Father—Horus had given forty addresses to Osiris—with "Now I come to thee." "Father, the hour is come; glorify thy son that thy son may glorify thee."

"I glorified thee *on earth,* having accomplished the work which thou hast given me to do. And now, O Father, glorify thou me with thine own self with the glory which I had with thee before the world was. I manifested thy name unto the men whom thou gavest me out of the world. I am no more in the world. But now I come to thee. I kept them in thy name, which thou hast given me. I guided them and not one of them perished, but the son of perdition" (*John* 17: 5-12).

Could purblind Christian theology have rightly divined the cosmogenetic and anthropogenetic truth so plainly expressed in this passage, it need not have left its following to grope in darkness for futile centuries. It is a clear statement of the coming and return of the solar ray of the Logos, who was from all time in the bosom of the universal Father, Ra, and suffered death in matter to glorify a race of men whom the Father gave him to uplift in nature. The work accomplished, this son of Ra asks that he may again be restored to his pristine effulgence, nay, that he may be raised to a superior station above the angels who had not descended to courageous adventure in lower worlds. The soul, by incarnation, becomes mightier than the virgin deities that have never been wedded to matter. In the texts of Unas there is described the terror of the gods when they see Teta (the soul) arriving triumphant. They discover that he is mightier than they. Likewise Pepi, fresh from his conquest of the Two Lands,

"comes forth to heaven. He finds Ra; *standing up* he meets him. He sits upon his shoulders. Ra permits him not to rest upon the ground, (for) he knows that Pepi is greater than he. Pepi is more a Spirit than the Spirits, more Perfect than the Perfect Ones, more stable than the stable ones. Pepi takes possession of the Two Lands like a king of his gods.".

Again the returning soul is beautifully apostrophized:

"The Comer! The Comer! This Pepi cometh! The Lady of Tep is agitated and the heart of the goddess dwelling in Nekheb fluttereth on this day when Pepi cometh in the place of Ra. Pepi hath carried away for himself thy light under his feet."

The part that old earth has played in this mighty consummation is shown in these passages:

"Behold, Keb taketh Pepi by the hand and he guideth him in through the doors of heaven like a god into his place; beautiful is the god in his place . . . he cometh to the gods of heaven . . . he goeth to the gods of earth."
"Pepi is raised up and passes into his spirit."
"This Pepi is the Eye of Horus, which is stronger than men and mightier than the gods."
"Horus hath taken his Eye, he hath given it to this Pepi."
"Heaven saluteth him joyfully; the earth trembleth before him."

This is part of the word picture of the first-born Horus divinized and upraised in his second birth, when human suffering has brought its guerdon of glory. And when he rises up, like Jesus he lifts up all men with him. He says: "I have raised up the exalted ones who dwell in their shrines," who slumber in their mummy bodies unawakened. Three or four of our main theses find corroboration in the following short excerpt:

"Each day right and truth come into my eyebrows. At *night* taketh place the festival of those that are *dead;* the *Aged One* who is in *ward* in the *earth.*"

Chapters 96 and 97 are entitled: "of being nigh unto Thoth and of giving glory unto a man in the underworld." Says the soul:

562

"I have made myself clean in the Lake of Making to be at peace and in the Lake of *weighing in the balance,* and I have bathed myself in Netert-utchat, which is under the holy sycamore tree of heaven. Behold, I am bathed. . . ."

"Now is Christ risen from the *dead* and become the first fruits of *them that slept.*" Likewise Horus, "the Lord of Resurrections" from the house of death, is the first of them that slept in darkness to wake as a "soul most mighty."

Chapter 92 of the *Ritual* is entitled: "of opening the tomb to the soul and to the shade of Osiris . . . so that he may come forth by day and have dominion over his feet," or lower self. The vignettes represent the deceased as having opened the tomb door, *with his soul by his side,* or as standing before the open door with hand stretch out to embrace his soul. The chapter reads: "That which was shut hath been opened, that is to say, he that lay down in death hath been awakened." The Manes has prayed that his soul "may not be kept captive, but that a way may be opened for its release."

In the fragment of an Egypto-Gnostic gospel assigned to Peter, one of many such discovered in the East, the resurrection scene pictures two men descending and entering the tomb, and three coming forth. Two powers united and brought forth a third.

"They beheld three men coming out of the tomb, and two of them were supporting a third, and a cross was following them; and the heads of the two men reached to heaven, but the head of him that was being led along by them was higher than heaven."

And they heard a voice from heaven which said: "Hast thou preached to them that are asleep?" And the response of "Yea" was heard from the cross. This scene is a version of the rising of Osiris or Ptah with the Tat cross, coming forth supported by his two sons, Hu and Sa. The critical question put to the god when leaving earth was whether he had preached to the souls imprisoned in the underworld and awakened them. For this was that commission which he had taken an oath to perform with diligence and despatch.

Hosea (13: 14) sings of the release of the captive soul from mundane thralldom:

"I will ransom them from the power of the grave; I will redeem them from death: O Death, I will be thy plagues; O Grave, I will be thy destruction."

This brings to mind Paul's rapturous refrain in his resurrection chapter in *Corinthians*. Another triumphant resurrection shout rises from the divine scribe in *Revelation* (1:18): "I am he that liveth and was dead; and behold I am alive for evermore." The Prodigal Son "was dead, and is alive again; he was lost and is found," like the Tat cross. "I am the resurrection and the life," announces Jesus; "he that believeth on me, though he were dead, yet shall he live"; "I will raise him up at the last day."

An expressive symbol of the release of the captives was the unwrapping of the burial bandages. Horus frees the sleeping mummies from their cerements, which he rends asunder. "Thou hast loosed my sackcloth and girded me with gladness," rejoices the soul. This speaks of the divestiture of the soul's various physical sheaths or "coats of skin" preparatory to his return clothed in imperishable light. In the Kamite rite the bandages of burial were cast aside so that the mummy might be invested with a lighter and brighter robe. Horus burst the funeral bonds and rent asunder the coffin in his awakening. He freed himself from every bond and strode forth on uncramped legs, the most triumphant figure in "history." The dead were "the bandaged ones." Jesus, the child, was wrapped meanly in swaddling bands. The rising Egyptian savior exclaims: "O my father! my sister! my mother Isis! I am freed from my bandages! I can see! I am one of those who are freed from their bandages to see Seb" (Ch. 158). *Matthew* states that with the rent veil and loosened rocks and quaking earth, the graves were opened and "many bodies of the saints that had fallen asleep were raised." This is more truly the *fact* of the resurrection, of which Jesus' rising is but a *symbol;* but all is figurative.

When the left arm of Horus is freed, the fan, typical of the mind (air), or of the Khu spirit, is held in its grasp. This is "the arm of the Lord" which hath gotten him the victory. It is the arm of which it is asked, while inert in death: "Is his arm foreshortened that it cannot save?"

Jesus is born in Bethlehem, "the house of bread" by name; Horus comes forth in (Beth)-Annu, "the place of multiplying bread!" The

Gnostic Jesus says he comes now not as when they crucified him. He comes now in spirit; he has passed from the afflicted one to "the active one of Heliopolis," the city of the sun!

The two-aspected Horus, or the infant and the adult Horus, furnish for all symbolic religion the enigma of the two births. Pagan zodiacal dramatism placed the birth of the god in matter, the first Adam, at the autumn equinox; Christianity placed it at the winter solstice, where the inert god was quickened (but not strictly born) in the womb of death. The three-months' period of hiding the child parallels the "sixth to the ninth hour" of darkness over the earth preceding the rending of the tomb-bars. Six months or three, the meaning was the same. The Jews rejected the babe born at the winter solstice because their traditions committed them to the mysteries of Harmachis, Horus of the double horizon.

Egyptian genius described the resurrection as the "dawn upon the coffin of Osiris," the mummy. He rose a spirit, spreading the light of divine radiance like dawn over the scene of his burial. In the *Litany of Ra* (34) adoration is paid to the sun-deity: "Homage to thee, Ra! Supreme power, the ray of light in the sarcophagus!"

Just previous to his asking the Father to glorify him Jesus had said to his disciples: "I know whence I came and whither I go." "I go unto the Father." So Horus declared: "It is I, even I. I am Horus in glory. I am the Lord of Light, and I advance to the goal of heaven" (Ch. 78). "I raise myself, I renew myself. I grow young again." And this is the most compact statement of the resurrection that could be made. Again he says: "I am the victorious one . . . There hath been assigned to me eternity without end. Lo, I am the heir of endless time and my attribute is eternity . . . I, even I, am he that knoweth the paths of heaven. Its breezes blow upon me."

The study now brings us face to face with a denouement in the realm of comparative religion which must be seen as fraught with the most momentous, perhaps catastrophic, consequences for the unique claims of the Christian faith and theology. This items concerns the raising of Lazaraus at Bethany, which is pointed to as perhaps the highest demonstration of Jesus' possession of divine power, his sublimest and most convincing miracle. Yet, in a word, the examination of Egyptian material reveals conclusively that it was not and could not have been, a historical occurrence! It is nothing but a dramatic etching of the resurrection. The identical transaction, with locale and actors the same in name, had been depicted or enacted in Egyptian ceremonial for perhaps ten thousand years before Christ. The story even in the Gospels stands as but another cinematograph of the resurrection. There is the same rocky tomb, the same cerements, the same lapse of time—three (four) days—in the hall of death, the same women watchers, and other similar items of the old symbology. The correlations have been outlined in the Prologue, but there are supplementary features that should not be slighted.

Origen in the second century reports that he was unable to find any trace of a "Bethany beyond Jordan" in his day.[6] If the Hebrews had taken the name from inherited Egypto-Gnostic literature or from the spiritual uranograph and given it to a village alleged to be near Jerusalem, it was but another instance of their adaptation of purely representative names to places and features of their local geography. But whether there was a Bethany beyond Jordan or not, the practical identity of the miraculous event alleged to have occurred there with an Egyptian dramatization of a purely spiritual initiation that had been portrayed in Kamite ritual for some millennia prior to the time of the Christian Jesus, seems to preclude with finality the possibility of its having been the scene of the episode narrated in the Gospels as history. The name Bethany points to a distinctly Egyptian origin, as we have seen. It is proximately identical in significance with Bethlehem, sharing the latter's meaning of "house of bread." Both towns were scripturally the place where the divine bread was given out and "multiplied" in the persons of the Saviors, Horus and Jesus, "born" there. We cite Massey's competent scholarship to support our claims as to the status of Anu:

"The tomb of Osiris was localized in Annu, the solar birthplace. Osiris, under one of his titles, is the great one in Annu. Annu is the place of his repose. 'I go to rest in Annu, my dwelling,' says Osiris. . . . Jesus goes to rest in Bethany. It was in Annu that the soul was united to its spiritual body. Annu is termed 'where thousands reunite themselves,' soul and body. . . . Annu is the abode of 'those who have found their faces.' The house or *beth* of Osiris, then, was in Annu. . . . The house of Osiris in Annu was . . . the abode of Horus when he came *to raise Osiris from the tomb*."[7]

566

Similar are the two proceedings, the Egyptian ritual and the Gospel "miracle," in that both Horus and Jesus first declared the mummy to be not dead, but only sleeping. Similar also are they in the reference to the already corrupt state of the corpse. Martha reminded Jesus in *John's* account that "by this time he stinketh: for he hath been dead four days." In the *Ritual*, when Horus comes to those who are in their cells, he utters the words of Ra to enliven them and says (Budge): "I am the herald of his (Ra's) words to him whose throat stinketh"; meaning, to the soul suffering corruption in the tomb of the body (Ch. 38B). Paul, the *Psalms, Isaiah* and other sources contribute replicas of this feature of the sleeping, not dead, entity.

Similar also are the two narratives in the manner of the calling forth. All such enactments of the resurrection episode repeat the basic Egyptian summons to the mummy to awake, come to life and rise, symbolically. It is the glorious coming forth to day, the theme of the great *Book of the Dead*. Jesus cries at the mouth of the tomb with a loud voice: "Lazarus, come forth! and he that was dead came forth bound hand and foot with grave bands." Horus, previously, had entered the dark grave, opened the Tuat door, recited to his father what he had done to reconstitute his shattered divinity, and bade him come forth to the sunlight and to victory. "Rise up, thou Teta! Thou art not a dead thing," he exhorts the mummy. The inert one was called the sleeping divinity, the breathless one, Urt-Hat, the god of the non-beating heart, the silent Sekari. The sleeping god is vigorously appealed to awake and rise up. "Arise, O God, and awake for me" (*Ps.* 7:6). "Awake; why sleepest thou, O Lord? Rise up for an help" (*Ps.* 44:23). "Then the Lord awaked as one out of a sleep and he smote his adversaries backward" (*Ps.* 78:65). Jesus said: "This sickness is not unto death." And Lazarus, as pointed out, is Osiris.

From an obscure corner it was our hap to unearth a bit of evidence bearing upon these conclusions which adds a strong sidelight to reinforce the identification. In the scholarly work of G. R. S. Mead, *Did Jesus Live 100 Years B.C.?*, there is the following footnote to page 377:

"It is somewhat strange to find Tertullian (*De Corona*, VIII; Oehler I: 436) referring to the 'linen cloth' with which Jesus girt himself, mentioned in *John* 13: 4, 5, as the *'proper garment of Osiris.'* Tertullian thus appears to have picked up a phrase which he did not quite understand and used it inappropriately."

Mead's surmise as to Tertullian's lack of understanding of the phrase is a likely enough one, but that the Church Father used it inappropriately is not so evident. In fact this remarkable reference of Tertullian must be taken as a most direct clue of connection between Christian Bible material and Egyptian sources of the same. Justin Martyr and other second-century Fathers not only did not so suddenly conceal the traces of relationship between Christian and earlier pagan literature, but at times pressed the evidences of derivation and identity. At all events, that we are able to discover some bit of *Christian* support for linking together Jesus and Osiris in the resurrection ritual must be conceded to strengthen the case materially.

And as to the two women, the two sisters of Lazarus, Mary and Martha?

When Horus declaims the forty discourses to his father, in recounting the blessings he has brought him, he says: "I have given thee thy victory, I have given thee thy two eyes (*Mertae*), and I have given thee Isis and Nephthys." Here we have the Egyptian prototypes of the two Maries of Gospel legend, or the sisters Mary and Martha. The much-mooted question of the identity of the "two women" of both *Old* and *New Testaments* is settled by Egyptian lore at last. They are the traditional replicas of the two great divine mothers of the sun-god, Isis and Nephthys, the Apt and Hathor of an earlier cult. They are the two protectors of the hidden babe, the two eternal watchers of his growth. They are also his two sisters who weep for him in his suffering state. In Egypt Anu was also "Rem-Rem, the place of weeping" for the buried lord of life. In the *Litany of Ra* Horus says: "I tread the dwelling of the god Rem-Rem," who is elsewhere denominated "Remi the Weeper." It was at Bethany that Jesus wept! Isis lay watching in tears over her brother Osiris when he had been cut to pieces and destroyed. The two goddesses also both watch and weep over the dead body. They call him in weeping, addressing to him long supplications. Isis bewails:

> "Come to thine abode! Come to thine abode!
> God An, come to thine abode!
> Look at me; I am thy sister that loveth thee.
> Do not stay from me, O beautiful youth;
> Come to thine abode, with haste, with haste.
> Mine eyes seek thee;

I seek thee to behold thee.
Will it be long ere I see thee?
Beholding thee is happiness.[8]

Isis and Nephthys, Jesus and Horus, Mary and Martha, all wept over the inert lord, El-Asar-us, at Bethany!

Then the two goddesses sing the song of the resurrection as a magical means of raising their beloved from the dead. A form of this song is to be found in the evocations addressed to the dead Osiris by the two sisters, who say:

"Thy two sisters are near thee, protecting thy funeral bed, calling thee in weeping, thou who art prostrate on thy funeral bed" (*Records of the Past*, Vol. 2, pp. 121-126).

Horus, the deliverer of his bound father, it is written, reaches him in the train of Hathor, another name of whom is Meri. He follows Meri to the place where Asar lies buried in the sepulcher, as Jesus follows Mary who had come forth to meet him on the way to Bethany. Jesus reaches the tomb in the train of Mary and Martha.

In the resurrection scene it is the two women who first see and announce the rising and the empty tomb. The risen Horus says: "The goddesses and the women proclaim me when they see me." Everywhere in sacred scripts of old it is the world of nature that hails deity rising from its bosom. The supporters and nourishers of solar deity in matter would be the first to witness the apotheosis in their domain. But all the while the lord of life is inert in their realm they are the ones solicitous about his rebirth. They lead the way to the cave where he lies and urge his quick resuscitation. Volumes of instruction are condensed in the words they address the god slumbering in humanity:

"Thy two sisters Isis and Nephthys come to thee: they fill thee with life, health, strength and all the joy that they possess. They gather for thee all kinds of good things within their reach."

And this proclaims the function of nature and earth in the life of spirit.

The two Eyes of Ra (or Horus) called "Mertae," who are the two Maries, or Mary and Martha, symbolized the cosmic and the individualized divine powers of spirit-soul. Spiritual intelligence can find no focus to open its inner vision on worlds of reality save through material instrumentality. Sight must have its organ, the eye. The organ is a material construction. The cosmic and the substantial forms of matter become then the two eyes of the spirit of Ra. As eyes they are watchers, and as the two women they are likewise watchers. In their service they stand, one at the head, the other at the feet, of the body on the bier. This is where they would be assigned to stand in any dramatization of the meaning, the one functioning in heaven or at the head, the other on earth, or at the foot. They figure as mourners, also anointers and embalmers. Mary anointed Jesus for his burial. *Luke's* account states that the woman who stood behind at the feet of Jesus, weeping, began to wet his feet with her tears and wiped them with her hair. Here again is the contacting of the head of the lower or feminine order with the feet of the Christ nature. Nephthys bears another mark of identification with Martha, as she is styled "the mistress of the house"; she carries the small replica of a house on her head, and is designated also "the benevolent saving sister." Martha was the home economist, always represented as concerned with household affairs.

More than two women act a part as ministrants to Jesus in the Gospels. There are the three Maries and Martha and others who might be enumerated to a possible seven (Massey does so enumerate them), matching the seven Hathors, or elementary powers, that, from being at one time equal with Jesus, later become subordinate and ancillary to his exalted position when he becomes lord of the new sanctuary. The seven Maries, like the seven Hathors, were superseded in their primal sovereignty in evolution; and so the Gospels, instead of saying directly that the seven Maries were cast out, has it that the seven devils were cast out of the one Mary (Magdalene).

A matter of theological consequence is that the four "sons of Horus," who also were placed in position at the bier of Osiris to aid in the resurrection, were constellated in the four stars of the body of the Great Bear to form the astral bier or coffin of Osiris, according to Arabian astronomers.[9] The Arabs called the three tail or handle stars the "Daughters of the Bier." In the *Papyrus of Teta* it is given that "Isis was in front of him, Nephthys behind him." The four sons of Horus stand facing Osiris and praise him thus:

"Glory to thee, Osiris Un-Nefer, the great god within Abydos, king of eternity, lord of everlastingness, who passeth through millions of years in his existence. Praise be unto thee ... whose forms are manifold and whose attributes are majestic."

These four gods were four of the seven elementaries, whose powers Horus had brought under control and raised up. They are changed from brothers among the primal seven to sons of the chief power, when he rose up as their king. An Egyptian vignette shows four fishermen drawing a net. These were the four cardinal gods, assistants to him who came under Piscean signature as the Divine Fish to feed mankind, and to make them "fishers of men."

Many chapter titles of the Egyptian Bible deal with the resurrection. Chapter 46 is entitled: "of not perishing and of becoming alive in the underworld." Says the Manes in it: "Like the Hamemmet beings may I arise, even as Osiris doth arise and fare forth." Chapter 45 is headed: "A chapter of not suffering corruption in the underworld."

The one consummate symbol of the resurrection, nature's own resplendent heliograph of man's moment of apotheosis, is the rise of the sun at dawn or the ascending of the sun above the line of the vernal equinox. The breaking of the morning light and the bursting from winter's captivity of the soul of life in verdant nature are the kindred operations in the phenomenal world which were given as constant reminders to man of that unimaginable transformation into a being of light which awaits him at the summit of the mount of mundane existence. Insensible any longer to the subtle power of ancient symbolical philosophy, deadened and unreceptive to the moving efficacy of commonplace natural glories, modern life neither heeds nor exults at the rising of the sun, and only feebly twitters a note or two of garish poetry on the arrival of the singing birds and bursting buds of springtime. But so potent is nature's sheer force of symbolism for the mind that has grasped the reality back of the outer show, that the daily or the annual solar, or monthly lunar, typology may work such minor transformations in the soul as the ancient Mysteries were designed to effectuate. Sunrise expresses the spirit of man's most climactic experience, his closest rapport with the ecstatic joyousness of life. The daily or annual rising, endlessly repeated for the race's instruction, is the type of that one consummative event of ecstasy past all transcription, which it will be the rapturous privilege of every grown son of God to undergo when the soul bursts like the morning rays from darkness

571

into ineffable glory. Nature recapitulates without end the physical type of that transfiguration which man has experienced in ever-recurring cycles, but which on the grand scale is destined to occur once for each individual at the climax of his earthly career. At the end of each life there supervenes a momentary opening of higher vision, giving the soul a vivid if fleeting glimpse of cosmic reality, and a review of its own progress in its last adventure. This is itself a typical resurrection as the soul rises out of its seventy-years' tomb. But this is only the faint adumbration of the final resurrection, which comes for the Manes at the summit stage of a long series of earth lives, when the soul has gathered its powers and stabilized itself in the shining immortal body. Then in one transporting thrill of expanding life it breaks loose from the (living) physical body and rises on wings of ecstasy, a phoenix, to its radiant home among the gods.

The ancient mythic poets strove right royally to signalize the potency of the rising sun symbol of the resurrection. They strove to impart some measure of the dynamic significance of nature's gorgeous ritualism in poetry, odes to the deities and hymns to the Sun. These are majestic, and capable of wielding transforming power over the human psyche. Liberty is taken to insert Thomas Taylor's effort to convey something of the grandeur of the coming of the lord of day.

"But you will ask, what has the rising of the sun through the Ocean from the boundaries of earth and night to do with the adventures of Bacchus? I answer, that it is impossible to devise a symbol more beautifully accommodated to the purpose: for, in the first place, is not the ocean a proper emblem of our earthly nature, whirling and stormy, and perpetually rolling without any periods of repose? And is not the sun emerging from its boisterous deeps a perspicuous symbol of the higher spiritual nature, apparently rising from the dark and fluctuating material receptacle, and conferring form and beauty on the sensible universe through its light? . . . This description, therefore, of the rising sun is a most beautiful symbol of the new birth of Bacchus, which, as we have already observed, implies nothing more than the rising of *intellectual light,* and its consequent manifestation to subordinate orders of existence."

Chapter XXII

SKYLARK AT HEAVEN'S GATE .

PAUL asks (*I Corinthians* 15:35) a question which, had it been envisaged in the light of the succinct answer which he himself immediately gave to it, would have left world religion in far better case than its present position.

"But some man will say," he argues, "How are the dead raised up? And with what body do they come?" Paul's first word of answer is a rebuke to the stupidity of such a question. He says: "Foolish man!" And by a quirk of ironic fate the rebuke administered to such ignorance of basic Greek philosophy (in which Paul was steeped) as the question implied, now falls upon the very institution which exalts him as its original propagandist and builder. By one of the most arrant perversions of clear philosophy ever to be perpetrated in world history, the Church he founded has put itself in the very place of the "some man" asking the absurd question—whether the dead rise up in their corpses or in some other form. And this in spite of the fact that the great Apostle addressed himself, in the remainder of his chapter, to as lucid an exposition of the spiritual resurrection as is to be found anywhere in sacred literature. This 15th chapter of *I Corinthians* marks the high point of spiritual sublimity reached in the *New Testament*. Its oracular grandeur should have lifted the body of Christian theology far above the mists of controversy that overhang it over the question of the corporeal resurrection. But the later formulators of orthodox theology looked askance at Paul and classed him as a heretic. They would have ousted his Epistles from the canon if they had dared. For he had grown in disfavor among them. His studies were not in line with the policy of the literalizers of religious drama; he was the exponent of that Orphic-Platonic wisdom from the Chaldean and Egyptian springs that they had come to revile. He indited more than one of the grandest chapters of their Bible; yet they frowned upon him because his writing was not in accord with their cult-Christianity. His was cosmic Christianity. It was embodied in terms of Platonic Gnosticism, the flower of Greek rational mysticism. Orphic paganism glows throughout that 15th chapter of *Corinthians*. The sublimest chapter in the Christian Bible is clearly pagan philosophy.

Let us follow Paul in his exposition and see how completely he is in accord with pagan teaching. First he announces the great law of incubation, as the prelude to any understanding of the resurrection in spirit: "What you sow never comes to life unless it dies." Then he clarifies a moot point: "And what you sow is not the body that is to be; it is a mere grain of wheat . . . or of some other seed." But "God gives it a body . . . gives each kind of seed a body of its own. Flesh is not all the same; there is human flesh, there is flesh of beasts, flesh of birds and flesh of fish." Has it ever been noticed that Paul here enumerates precisely the four kingdoms on which man's life rests at its corners, matching the four figures in Egyptology, and in Ezekiel's and John's celestial visions? Man, animal, bird, fish. Amsta, Hapi, Tuamutef and Kabhsenuf, the four sons of Horus; the man, lion, eagle and fish (crocodile); the four quarters of the zodiac; the four bases of man's life. Paul's vital statement is that God plants "bare grain" (Authorized Version), that is, souls of pure spirit untried by matter in incarnation, our Hamemmet Beings, Innocents, younglings, Kumaras, Asuras, virgin souls; and he later gives to these tender spirits garments of solar glory.

Then Paul tells us that "there are heavenly bodies and also earthly bodies," but the splendor of the one is greater than that of the other.

"There is a splendor of the sun and a splendor of the moon and a splendor of the stars—for one star differeth from another in splendor. So with the resurrection of the dead:

> what is sown is mortal,
> what rises is immortal;
>   sown inglorious,
>   it rises in glory;
>   sown in weakness,
>   it rises in power;
>   sown an animate body,
>   it rises a spiritual body.

574

As there is an animate body, so there is a spiritual body. Thus it is written:

'The first man, Adam, became an animate being,
the last Adam a life-giving spirit;'

.   .   .   .   .   .

Man the first is from the earth, material;
Man the second is from heaven.
Thus as we have borne the likeness of the material Man,
so we are to bear the likeness of the heavenly Man.

I tell you this, my brothers, flesh and blood cannot inherit the Realm of God, nor can the perishing inherit the imperishable . . . the dead will rise imperishable, and we shall be changed. For this perishable body must be invested with the imperishable, and this mortal body invested with immortality; . . . then . . .

Death is swallowed up in victory."

How in the face of this lucidity of statement the Church perpetrated its frightful dogmatic travesty of "the resurrection of the body," it is hard indeed to understand. And now we can see also that the first and second Adam of Paul were the Egyptian Horus of the two horizons, the "lions of the double force" of soul and body, Horus the younger, and Horus the elder.

The seed is sown in and as the natural material body, but unless that dies, and in dying transmits its essential strength over to a finer vehicle that will be built out of its disintegrating elements, it will not live again. The old material seed will never rise again; and the physical corpus of man will not rise from the grave. But the germinal essence will come forth from decay shining in new life. That which is sown in the earth will die; but out of its death will rise the stem that bears the new generation of beauty aloft to sun and air. Well did Paul say, "Foolish man!" to ask such a question. And well may the world say "Foolish Church!" to have missed and confounded the simple clear meaning of the resurrection.

The putting on of the robe of immortality has not been adequately translated into rational comprehension. It hovers in the background of the Christian consciousness as a beautiful haze of indefinite meaning. A clearer grasp of its significance may accrue from inspection of some of the ancient material touching it.

The deceased says to Osiris:

"Do thou embalm these my members; for I would not perish and come to an end, (but be) like unto my divine father Khepera, who is the divine type of him that never saw corruption. . . . Let not my body become worms, but deliver me as thou didst deliver thyself. . . . Homage to thee, Osiris; thou didst not decay, thou didst not become worms, thou didst not waste away, thou didst not become corruption, thou didst not putrefy. . . . I am the god Khepera and my members shall have an everlasting existence. I shall not decay, I shall not rot, I shall not putrefy . . . and I shall not see corruption beneath the eye of the god Shu. I shall have my being . . . I shall live . . . I shall germinate . . . I shall wake up in peace . . . I shall not suffer from any defect; mine eye shall not decay; the form of my visage shall not disappear; mine ear shall not become deaf; my head shall not be separated from my neck; my tongue shall not be carried away; my hair shall not be cut off; . . . and no baleful injury shall come to me."

In spite of death the Manes cries: "I am, I am; I live, I live; I grow, I grow; and when I awake I shall awake, I shall awake in peace, I shall not see corruption . . . I shall not perish in the earth forever" (Ch. 154, Naville). The immortality that was previously potential in the first Adam-Horus became established at last in Tattu and secured by the resurrection of the illumined soul from the pit of Akar (*Rit.*, Ch. 30A). At the consummation of the Manes' victory over earthly forces it is declared to him: "Thy father Tum hath prepared for thee this beautiful crown of triumph, the living diadem which the gods love, that thou mayest live forever" (Ch. 19). The Manes says (Ch. 85):

"I am the first-born god of primeval matter, that is to say, the divine Soul, even the Soul of the god of everlastingness, and my body is eternity. My form is everlastingness, and is the lord of years and the prince of eternity."

The soul is assured in the text: "Thou shalt never perish, thy Ka shall never perish, a Ka established." The flow of events in time is connected with the temporal and impermanent vestures in which the seed-spark of divinity has embodied itself to travel through Amenta. Decay does not touch the core of being itself, the Ka.

But what specifically is this robe of immortality that the mortal must put on if he is to live forever? It is Paul's "spiritual body" as contrasted with the natural or "animate body." But what is a spiritual body, the world has been asking for these hundreds of years, and "science" has also asked contemptuously. The answer is to be found in an early chapter, in the theses that modern science itself has now reified or hypostasized matter of various grades of ethereal fineness, sublimated essence, capable of being organized into material structures in the world invisible to man. The Egyptians predicated a total of seven such successively finer bodies in man's constitution, of which the lower or coarser four have been so far developed to function. Besides his obvious physical body, man possesses inner bodies of what a scientist called "immaterial matter."

That sublimated vesture, then, which seems to be the "spiritual body" in which the dead specifically rise, is the Sahu, though the next higher one, the Khu, is frequently mentioned in the experience. The Khu is so high in its structure that of it is said: "Thou shalt not be imprisoned . . . it is heaven alone that shall hold thee." Also it is written that the Khus, or glorified ones, "live on the shades of the motionless, or the souls of the dead." This means that the highest bodies absorb and transmute into their own subtler essence the substances of the ones below, as a candle flame absorbs the tallow below it. The Khu was thus figuratively conceived of as a "ghoul" or "feeder on the shades" of the Manes in the nether worlds. It is constellated as the "Ghoul," the star Beta in the Perseus group.

The Ka always accompanies the soul through its incarnations and returns. "Thou hast come and thy Ka with thee" is the welcome greeting on the soul's return. The Manes passes from the state of a shade to that of a Ka when he is said to have completed his investiture. Then as a Sahu he is reincorporated in a spiritual body, and as a Khu he is invested with the robe of light and glory. No healthy child was believed to be born without this Ka, the soul of animate life; and in their pictures of it they made it resemble the physical body. They looked upon it as the "double" of the body. It did not die with the body.

In open contradiction to other reasons he had assigned elsewhere, Budge gives a motive for mummification:

"It has been urged by some that the custom of mummifying the dead, which obtained throughout Egypt for so many thousands of years, was maintained because the Egyptians believed in the resurrection of the material body, but *it is not so*. They mummified their dead simply because they believed that spiritual bodies would 'germinate' in them."

This passage is a remarkable demonstration of how a scholar can state the surface facts in a particular matter and yet tell nothing true about it. Yes, the Egyptians believed that spiritual bodies would germinate from or in the physical Khat, but while it was a living body, not the long-preserved cadaver! Germination of finer spiritual bodies would come in the living man, and in the mummy only as the ritual symbol of the body of this death.

Budge gives both "Ba" and "Sahu" as meaning "something like" "noble" or "sublime," "chief," "free." The Ba, he says, was free to travel over all heaven and mix with souls there and to take any form it pleased; for such statements are found. Far more free were the higher bodies to do the same. The learned Egyptologist writes again:

"Concerning the form in which Osiris rises from the dead the texts are silent, and nothing is said as to the nature of his body in the underworld; that he dwelt in the [same] material body which was his upon earth there is no reason whatever to suppose, for there are indications in the texts which point to a definite belief in the resurrection of a spiritual body, both in the case of the god and of man." [1]

When the reader has noted with us even the limited and haphazard collection of passages from these same texts describing the bodies in which Osiris lives and rises, he will be able to determine for himself whether "the texts are silent, and nothing is said as to the nature of" the body of Osiris in the underworld; also how futile seems to have been the reading of these venerable texts by such savants as Budge and others. In the present matter Spence has read somewhat more intelligently:

"The soul, ba, and the spirit, Khu, which were usually represented as a hawk and a heron in the hieroglyphics, partook of heavenly food and became one with the gods, and in time became united with the glorified body or heavenly frame, so that the soul, spirit, power, shade, double, and name of the deceased were all collected in the one heavenly body, known as the Sahu, which may be described as the spiritual body. It was considered to grow out of the dead body, and its existence became possible through the magic ceremonies performed and the words of power spoken by the priests during the burial service." [2]

Budge endorses this general view in saying:

578

"When the material body had been brought to the tomb for burial . . . it acquired the power of sending forth from itself a body called the Sahu, which was able to ascend to heaven and dwell with the gods there. The only suitable rendering for the word 'Sahu' is 'spiritual body,' and the meaning fits very well into the translation of the texts where the word is found."

This is in the broad sense true, but thrown out of due symmetry by the scholar's ignorance of the cardinal meaning of "death" and "the dead" in symbolic usage. The name unquestionably means "spiritual body" and "free, noble, chief" might be applicable to it. But the derivation would seem to be closer at hand than Budge presumes. The two divine sons of the great first god Tem, or Tum (meaning "total"), were the gods Sa and Hu. These two short names seem either broadly or in some particular reference to connote "spirit" and "matter," the opposite nodes of primal energy. Souls were said to be composed of the essence of Sa, drawn in the beginning from the great "Lake of Sa" in the southern heavens. "Sa" also meant the son, or spirit born of matter. Hu was the basis of Ihuh, or Atum-Huhi (Adam-Jehovah), the spark of flame in matter. As the spiritual body was built up of spirit and matter in combination, the two basic god-names seem to have been combined to designate it. Massey says that the word "Sahu" means "to incorporate." It is the incorporated spirit or its product. Chapter 47 of the *Ritual* reads: "I am a spiritual body (sah), therefore let me rise among those who follow the great god." As Osiris-Sekari, the god was the coffined one; as Osiris-Sahu, he rose again in a spiritual body. *"I am the spiritual body of the god,"* cries the Manes on fleeing the grave (Ch. 99). In chapter 128 Osiris exclaims: "Horus hath made for me a spiritual body through his own soul, to take possession of that which belongeth to Osiris in the Tuat." In the text of Unas we read: "Behold, he cometh forth this day in the real form of a living spirit." The *Chaldean Oracles* say: "The powers build up the body of the holy man."

In the *Hymn to Osiris* the risen soul is praised: "Thou art a shining Spirit-Body, the Governor of Spirit-Bodies."

Luke (24: 39) represents Jesus after the resurrection as calling attention to his very members: "See my hands and my feet, that it is I myself." This is clarified by the knowledge that, the resurrection once consummated, the soul has power to assume what form it will and to materialize for the moment its old physical semblance. Did not Jesus pass through closed doors and appear to his disciples, so that Thomas put his hands in the wounds in the flesh to resolve his doubts? Of spiritual essence, he could yet become palpable to sense.

Budge's assertion that the texts are silent with respect to the nature of the vesture in which the soul arose might have been modified had he seen the following from the *Papyrus of Pepi:* "They draw thee unto heaven in thy soul, and thou art endowed with soul among them. Thou appearest in the sky as Horus from the womb of the sky in this thy form which came forth from the mouth of Ra, as Horus, the Chief of the Spirits." And again from the same text: "When Osiris ascended the ladder, he was covered with the coverings of Horus, he wore the apparel of Thoth." In chapter 180 the soul says: "I stretch myself at my desire, I run forward with my strides in my spiritual form of hidden qualities." And how striking is the following from the text of Teta: "He receives bones of a marvelous nature and a complete and imperishable body is bestowed upon him in the womb of his mother Nut!"

The Egyptians regarded the physical body as being powerless and lifeless save for the more magnetically powerful inner bodies. Of itself it could never have arisen. It could not rise as flesh and blood; it could ascend only after being transformed, like water converted into vapor, by more potent spirit. It was only the presence in it of the Ba, the Sekhem, the Khu that gave it erectile force. As says *James* (2:26): "the body without the spirit is dead." So much more vital was the spirit than the body, so much "more ancient" and established, that even the destruction of the latter would not annihilate it. For well the Egyptians knew, before Paul, that "if our earthly house of this tabernacle is dissolved, we have a building of God, a house not made with hands, eternal in the heavens." When the deity descended to earth he put on the mask of a crocodile, an ibis, a lion, or other zootype of the primary powers. But when rising into spirit, he divested himself of these "filthy rags" and stood forth clothed in the majesty of solar light. He personates in turn each of the gods and appropriates their strength and qualities.

"Their magical powers are in his body, the Sahu do not retreat from his hands. He *eats* the wisdom of every god, his period of life is eternity, his limit is everlastingness in this form(sah) of his."

"I am come," says Horus, "as a sahu in the spiritual body, glorious and well-equipped; and that is given to me which *lives on amidst all overthrow.*"

Here at last is that element which all philosophy, all religion, all moral feeling has been seeking for ages as the indubitable foundation of both faith and knowledge. All rationalism and mysticism alike are the search for the enduring real, that which abides amid the flux. Here it is, says Horus. Here is the ages' Rock of Certitude.

The soul was released from the khat or physical body when the latter had been itself sublimated to such tenuity that it quickly vanished away. Horus, coming out of Sekhem, left his earthly body behind in the sepulcher, and was greeted as pure spirit by those who had forerun him in the glorification. They rejoiced to see him walking upright and ready to stride onward through eternity. He who had earned these salutations was the re-establisher of time "for millions of years." He came in raiment like the dawn, as the true light of the world newly kindled in the night of death. He says he comes forth equipped with Ra's words of power. In the *Book of Teta* the risen soul is greeted: "Hail, thou hast received thy robe of honor, thou hast arrayed thyself in the Hata garment. Thou art clothed with the Eye of Horus . . . which giveth thee thy apparel before the gods." "Let love for him," proceeds the text, "be in the body of every god who shall see him. This is the swathing which Horus made for his father Osiris," "the proper garment of Osiris" mentioned by Tertullian. "Thou art provided with thy form, O dweller among the spirits." "Thy movement is like that of a star. No ruin falls to thee . . . Thou art complete in thy members of crystal." "Thou hast thy state of glory . . . thou hast thy faculty of *knowledge.*" "Thou art pure with the purity of the gods, who journey unceasingly." Chapter 171 is captioned: "Of trying on the garment of purity." In the Pepi test it is stated that as he rises he puts on the *sheth* garment of Horus and the apparel of Thoth. The coming forth of Jesus as a spirit, or as the *Christos,* is called his investiture. He says: "The times are fulfilled for me to put on my vesture. Lo, I have put on my vesture, and all power hath been given to me by the first mystery" (*Pistis Sophia* 1:10).

In his first advent as the Virgin's son he was the "bare grain," the word made flesh but not yet made truth. In his second advent he revealed the glory of the Father through that body which God gave him. He now regains the glory he had with the Father before he laid it aside to put on the sackcloth of earth. The *Ritual* details how the ransomed spirits, redeemed from the mummy condition and all the ills of the corruptible flesh, put on the pure white robe of righteousness, called the vesture of truth. This is given them by the god Taht for their entrance into the boat of the sun. Earth's apron is removed, and he receives a bandage of the finest linen "in place of the old garb of shame." In chapter 64 there is this explicit statement: "I have made the dress which Ptah has woven out of his clay." Spirit must draw its light from the very womb of matter. Ptah was the divine Potter, as Jesus was the Carpenter and Hiram the Mason.

When the deceased has been resuscitated he says (Ch. 85): "The seven Uraeus divinities are my body. . . . My image is eternal." The lower elements form his material body; his spirit body is imperishable. But the soul synthesized the seven and raised them aloft to share its everlastingness. Ptah tells Rameses II that he has refashioned his flesh in vermilion. The texts speak of the dead bones being refleshed with a coating of red earth. These are references to the renewal through the soul's bath in the pool of the body's blood.

The Manes were of two classes, the clothed and the naked. Those were clothed who had passed the judgment trial and received their investiture of the robe of righteousness. "I hasten to the land (of Aarru) and I fasten my stole upon me," says the Manes, "that I may come forth and take possession of the wealth assigned to me" (Ch. 110). "I range within the garden of Hetep (Aarru); I fasten my stole upon me." "I am the glorified one coming forth in triumph." Paul has said that we "groan, earnestly desiring to be clothed upon with our house which is from heaven," "clothed upon that mortality might be swallowed up of life." "I was naked and ye clothed me," says the Gospel Jesus himself. *Isaiah* (61:10) sings: "I will greatly rejoice in the Lord . . . for he hath clothed me with the garment of salvation, he hath covered me with the robe of righteousness." Hermes says: *"I am gone out of myself into an immortal body,* and am not what I was before, but am begotten in mind." How well this describes what the Greek philosophers call the *"ekstasis,"* or transport of release from the physical body-tomb! *Ekstasis* means literally "a standing out" of the soul from the body, so that one is in truth "beside oneself" with "ecstasy."

In Iamblichus' great work on the *Mysteries of the Egyptians* (p. 55) he unfolds the doctrine thus:

"The Gods, being benevolent and propitious, impart their light to theurgists in unenvying abundance, calling upon their souls, procuring them a union with themselves, and accustoming them, *while they are yet in body,* to be separated from bodies, to be led around to their intelligible principle."

Thus they, too, were "begotten in mind." Hermes tells Ptah he "would that thou also wert gone out of thyself, like them that dream in their sleep." This is the ecstasy and transport when the soul passes from the boat of Horus to the ship of the sun, from mortal flesh to radiant spiritual glory.

In chapter 19 of the *Ritual* is the whole detailed struggle of the powers of intellectual light to gain the victory for Horus over his enemies "on the day of making his triumph over Set and his fiends." For a purpose of very great importance we quote some of this chapter at length. The great final conquest is achieved by Horus—

"on the night of the battle and overthrow of the Seba-fiend in Abtu; on the night of Osiris' triumph over his enemies; on the day of the festival of Haker (on the fifteenth of the month); on the night of setting up the Tat in Tattu in the presence of the great sovereign princes; on the night of the judgment of those who shall be annihilated in Sekhem; on the night of laying the things on the altars in Sekhem; on the night of the establishing of the inheritance by Horus of the things of the father Osiris, at the great festival of plowing and turning up the earth in Tattu or in Abtu (Abydos); on the night of the weighing of words or a weighing of looks; on the night when Isis lieth down to watch and make lamentation for her brother in Re-stau; on the night of making Osiris to triumph."

The design in making this strange quotation is to call attention to the multiplicity of *symbolic* occurrences that are thrown into the period of the night preceding the Passover of the vernal equinox, which is just the "dark night of the soul" in incarnation, ending with the passing of the soul across the boundary at Easter. All processes of transformation, purifying, perfecting, glorifying, reach their consummation on the last marge of the "night" period, as it breaks into the dawn of Easter's spiritual Sun. In the yearly calendar this would be the night of the Passover of spring. Hence Egyptian drama placed the crowning

583

of every process on this eventful "night." Being purely symbolical, there would be no difficulty in allocating to this date *any number* of representations of the various aspects of the soul's experience as it concluded its earthly history. The Christ's trial, his bloody sweat, his battle with the fiends, his mockery and suffering, his crucifixion in its last stages, his last supper, his bearing the cross, and every other phase of his "death" and "burial" in matter could be "staged" on this night. But it would not and could not be "history." What then would happen if at a later time symbolic events in such number were turned into alleged history? Here indeed is a point for "higher criticism," if not for downright common sense.

It seems to be incontestable that the many events of the last night of Jesus' life as narrated in the Gospels are a somewhat attenuated copy of this momentous nineteenth chapter of Egypt's *Ritual!* Perhaps the material was not taken directly from it, but was drawn from the dramas and Mystery plays that had been based on it and worked out in consonance with it. *Obviously* so blind was fanatical zealotry in hurrying to crush paganism and to change spiritual allegory into history that it did not pause to reckon with the difficulty of crowding a long series of varied events into the course of a single night of clock time. So Jesus was given a busy night to close his sad career! The literalizers of drama did not scruple to ask zealotry to believe that there could actually have occurred in the brief space of one night the Last Supper with the disciples, the walk to the Mount of Olives, the long watch in the garden of Gethsemane, the incidents of the disciples falling asleep when Jesus upbraided them for not being able to watch with him one little hour, the arrest, the severed and healed ear cut off by Peter, then *three* separate and distinct judicial trials involving the summoning of judges, juries, attendants, officers, the populace *in the dead of night* (a thing impossible if considered in realism), then the mockery of the soldiers, the parting of Jesus' garments, the forcing on him of the crown of thorns, then the march to the hill of Golgotha ("the place of the skull"), and the harrowing "crucifixion" running into the next morning. There is an obvious very meager limit to what can occur in the temporal span of one short night. The Gospels here stand helplessly exposed to the attack of plain reason in view of the patent conditions of the problem raised. The Gospels are the old manuscripts of the dramatized ritual of the incarnation and resurrection of the sun-god, which was first Egyptian, later Gnostic and Hellenic, then Hebrew and finally adopted ignorantly by the Christian movement and transferred to the arena of history. They were not history until in Christian hands the esoteric meaning had been obscured and the wisdom needed to interpret them non-historically was wanting.

An important link is the identification of the Sahu body with the sun. The *Kabalah* intimates that the soul in each solar system spends six aeons on planets and the seventh in the sun of the system. In the seventh or human kingdom, then, life would be preparing for the soul a body of solar essence. And solar energy is the expression of deific intellect, according to Proclus. The soul of humanity is to clothe itself in an indestructible armor of solar light, eternally self-luminous and self-perpetuating. The Bible's statement that "the Lord God is a sun" is echoed in Egypt: *"I am the lord of light,* and that which is an abomination unto me is death; let me not go into the chamber of torture which is in the Tuat." A hundred texts exalt the principle of light, and here its rebellion against being overwhelmed by the darkness of matter in incarnation is registered.

Here was the whole gist of theology outlined in terms whose significance for human life could not have been missed save by minds hopelessly warped by previous obsession of fantastic conceptions. For "death" is here distinctly defined as residence in a world where the intellectual light of deity would be sadly darkened. But we have seen how the failure properly to locate "the underworld" blocked the way to all true comprehension of intrinsic wisdom for centuries. The appearance of the angel who descended from heaven to roll away the stone from the grave was "as lightning, and his raiment was white as snow" (*Matt.* 28:2). *"He has come forth like the sun,"* says the Osirian in his eulogy of the soul. "He comes in raiment like the dawn," sings the sacred writer. Osiris is said to give life "to the ministers of the sun," the sun-gods. Says Horus: "I have come like the sun through the gate . . . and have passed pure" (*Rit.,* Ch. 148, Birch): Jesus insisted that each man had light within himself, and with its increase by spiritual cultivation, it would even supplant the sun and moon as light-givers. In man all previous powers of creative light were to be synthesized in the glory of a new order of radiant being.

We read in the *Litany of Ra* (Ch. 2:7): "Thou commandest the Osirified deceased to be like Khuti, the brilliant triangle which appears

585

in the shining place." This was the solar trinity of mind, soul, spirit. Horus is seated in the decans of the Ram, the whip of rule in his left hand and the starry "Triangula" in his right. Thus the dead god rose on the horizon of the resurrection like the sun in the vernal equinox when that sun was in Aries, bearing the triangle as symbol of the tri-unity of man's spirit. "He shineth like a new being in the east," is a tribute to the risen glory of the soul. In chapter 129 of the *Ritual*—the book of making perfect the Khu—we have: "And the majesty of the god Thoth lovingly shall make light to rest upon his corruptible body." The very gods "withdraw themselves when they see thee arrayed in the awful majesty of Ra." .

In *Exodus* we read that the vestments worn by the children of Israel were to be woven of violet, purple and scarlet yarn. These three vivid colors likely typify the higher triad in the scale of seven colors, or the coat of many colors. Macrobius, commenting on the *Orphic Hymns,* speaks of the sacred dress in which those initiated into the Dionysiac Mysteries were invested, preparatory to their enthronement:

> "He who desires in pomp of sacred dress
> The sun's resplendent body to express,
> Should first a veil assume of purple bright,
> Like fair white beams combined with fiery light."

"I shine forth from the egg which is in the unseen world" (Ch. 22).

The mummy-swath was, like the *shenti,* a linen tunic, made from *shena,* and this was the garment woven without a seam. The "young man" who left his garment and fled naked from the resurrection scene was the figure of the rising soul that had shed its mummy-cloth and made its transformation into spirit that no longer needed earthly covering. The seam was obliterated when the two halves of man were made into one whole and new man.

Spence states that the spirits of heaven "lived upon the rays of light which fell from the eyes of Horus; that is, they were nourished upon sunlight, so that in time their bodies became wholly composed of light." [3] This is true. They emaned their own light and there was no need of external light, "for the glory of the Lord did lighten it." The Talmud says: "There is a light which is never eclipsed or obscured, derived from the upper light, by which the first man could view the world from one end to the other" (*Avodath Hakodesh*). This is presumably that light of the poets which never was on land or sea; the gleam, of Tennyson's conception. "I live by reason of my splendor," chants the emancipated soul.

The souls having attained the resurrected state in shining raiment were called the Khus or the glorified. Jesus asked the Father to glorify him with primeval radiance; Horus pleads in the same way (Ch. 175): "But let the state of the shining ones be given unto me instead of water and air. . . ." The elect "arriveth at the Aged One, on the confines of the Mount of Glory, where the crown awaiteth him" (Ch. 131).

Mt. Olympus of the Greeks was identical with Mount Hetep of the Egyptians. Hence the Kimmerians of Homer may possibly be identified with the Egyptian Khemi, or Akhemu, the dwellers in the northern heaven, as never-setting stars or spirits of the glorified, the Khus or Khuti.

The whole course of evolution on earth is designed to perfect the individualized humans, who are the crown of animal development. This perfection comes through the spiritualization of the gross animal nature by the impacting upon it of currents of intellectual and spiritual forces which gradually refine the lower self. When a certain degree of sublimation has been achieved the lower bodies become capable of affording free course to the influx of the higher influences, which then so transform the lower that a practical identity between the two is established. Greek mythology called it the union of Cupid and Psyche; in Egypt it was the embrace of Horus and Osiris; in Churchly language it was the marriage of the Bride and the Lamb. It was that welding at last in blissful harmony of the mortal and immortal elements. Of this ultimate union of male and female components, the body-soul with the spirit-soul, all marriage and sexual intercourse is only the outward sign and symbol. For its attainment the male and female natures in the individual must be "married"; the centers below and those above the diaphragm must merge in interchange of activity. The wedding or welding of these two groups of energies will divinize human nature. For it will return man to his original androgyne state which obtained before the "fall" into physical generation, when he assumed the garb of the animal nature and put on the mask of personality.

Massey concisely sums up this basic datum of theology:

587

"The marriage of Cupid and Psyche is a fable that was founded on this union of the two souls which we have traced in the Ritual as the soul in matter, or as the human, and the soul in spirit." [4]

Evolution's work in the moral sphere was to unite a soul inherent in matter with a higher soul that was divine. This operation takes place in the body and consciousness of mankind. The divine soul was a unit of sublimated intellectual essence from beyond the skies, but temporarily united with the lower body to engraft upon it its own higher potencies. Physical evolution was impotent to pass a certain point, the boundary between sense and soul, until the germ of conscious selfhood linked with it from above. Life languished on earth until the heaven spirit descended like a dove to free it. "As soon as thou enterest the Utchau and unitest thyself thereto, the beings on earth flourish."

A strong and moving assertion of the influence of the union of lower life with higher is seen in the following from the *Book of the Dead:*

"Thou joinest thyself unto the Eye of Horus and thou hidest thyself within its secret place; it destroyeth for thee all the convulsions of thy face, it maketh thee strong with life, and thou livest . . . thou joinest thyself unto the upper heaven, O luminary."

The soul is addressed here as the luminous person of the sun, and most challenging is the statement that the force of the solar intellect released in the personal life will destroy the convulsions of the face, caused by the painful constraint of the soul under the bondage of matter. Like lovers' kiss, the embrace between the spiritual soul and the psychic entity in the body brought harmony and expanded life. A complementary and salutary interchange of health and strength flashed between spirit and matter in the embrace, when the two meet in Amenta.

Budge says that the conjunction of the lower ba, or animal soul, with its Ka, or spiritual soul, took place in Heliopolis, the city of the sun, Annu. This would correspond with the revival of Osiris, or Lazarus, at Beth-Any. The ba comes forth upon earth to do the will of its Ka. This is important, matching Jesus' declaration that he comes to do the will of his Father.

The work of the exiled god on earth being now consummated, his effort having prevailed to overcome the flesh and transform the soul of the body into the likeness of the glorious sun-soul, the risen deity stands on the eastern threshold of heaven, ready to complete the last stages of the twelve-months' journey, and with the waxing sun of spring to climb the steep ascent of heaven from March to June. This is the final arc of the return to the Father who stands at the apex of heaven at the gate of Cancer. The summit of the mount of the zodiac was the place of reunion and reconciliation; the paradise of perennial plenty and everlasting peace, the land where there was no more sea and no more night, where beings carried their own light eternally within them. Hither the twelve companions of Horus bring the sheaves of golden grain which they have reaped in the harvest fields of Amenta. Horus tells Osiris at the festival of the Harvest Home that he has cultivated his corn for him and reaped the golden crop in the Aarru Fields of Peace, or Hetep.

Exodus (3:12) reports the Eternal as saying to Moses: "When thou hast brought the people out of Egypt, ye shall serve God upon this mountain." It was there called Mt. Horeb, and the first syllable, *Hor-,* can be equated with the *Hor-,* of Hor-us, the sun. The injunction to Moses precedes:

"Thou shalt bring them in and plant them in the mountain of their inheritance, the place, O Lord, which thou hast made for them to dwell in, the sanctuary, O Lord, which thy hands have established."

Here "the Lord shall reign for ever and ever." This was the Mount of Jerusalem, the Aarru-Salem, or Aarru-Hetep, the mount of eternal peace. In escaping from Egypt or Amenta, the goal of refuge is the Mount of Peace, as every religion on earth has attested. As spirits, not human marching columns, the children of Israel, after crossing the swampy Reed Sea of this life, are led to the celestial land flowing with milk and honey. Here the Eridanus emptied its stream of purifying water. This heavenly home was located and dramatized as the circumpolar paradise, the Homeland of exiles and captives. "I am master there," says the beatified spirit who has attained this mansion in the skies and built his homestead there. "I am in glory there; I eat there; I plant and I reap there; I plough there; I take my fill of love." "I net ducks and I eat dainties." "I am united there to the god Hetep"—the *seven* powers completely exalted, unified and at *peace.*

There the risen spirit becomes one of the glorious stars that nevermore shall set in ocean's or in earth's depths. "A divine domain hath been constructed for me: I know the name of it; the name of it is the garden of Aarru" (Ch. 109, Renouf).

Instead of being damned eternally for eating of the fruit of the tree of life and knowledge, the Manes is part by part divinized as he transmutes the substance of its food into higher essence. In the Rubric at the end of chapter 99 of the *Ritual* we read: "This chapter being known, the deceased appears in the fields of Aarru. He receives food there, the produce of its fields." The cakes, corn, bread and wine which he shall partake of there are described. "And he shall come forth in Sekhet-Aarru in any form whatsoever he pleaseth, and he shall appear regularly and continually." Chapter 110 tells of the soul's going in and out of Sekhet-Hetep, of the coming forth by day, of becoming a glorified Khu there; of reaping, eating, drinking, making love there and "doing everything even as a man doeth upon earth." The soul exults: "And I have sailed into the divine city of Hetep . . . I array myself in apparel and I gird myself with the *sa* garment of Ra." To have attained this blessed home the soul must have undergone the earthly baptism:

"I have gone into the city of An-Aarret-f (the place where nothing groweth) and I covered my nakedness with the garments which are there."

In the midst of Sekhet-Aarru was a door, with a sycamore of turquoise on each side of it, through which the sun-god Ra appeared every day. The outgoing and return of the celestial glory was thus depicted for the blessed each day, as it is for mortals on earth.

The soul's reward for leaving its celestial home and spending the long toilsome cycle of necessity in dreary exile on earth is the evolutionary gain therefrom, which is vast and permanent, as is attested by the ecstasy that accompanies the return. The pitiful nostalgia which has oppressed it throughout its long sojourn among "the wild beasts" is blithesomely appeased by its nearing vision of the Father's portals and the sunny meads and shady bowers of the Homeland. Death is indeed swallowed up in victory and the night of gloom and the Götterdämmerung are followed by the fresh sweetness of supernal dawn.

Iamblichus presents beautifully the philosophy of our escape from the iron fetters of fate and return to the liberty of the sons of God:

"But neither are all things comprehended in the nature of fate, but there is another principle of the soul, which is superior to all nature and generation, and through which we are capable of being united to the Gods, of transcending the mundane order and of participating eternal life and the energy of the super-celestial gods. Through this principle, therefore, we are able to liberate ourselves from fate. For when the more excellent parts of us energize, and the soul is elevated to natures better than itself, then it is entirely separated from things which detain it in generation, departs from subordinate natures, exchanges the present for another life and gives itself to another order of things, entirely abandoning the former order with which it was connected." [5]

Iamblichus says elsewhere that there is found no other dissolution of the fetters of fate and necessity than the knowledge of the gods. For to know the godly powers is felicity. Oblivion of them while in terrestrial body is the greatest source of evil to a deific nature. Knowledge of the gods preserves the true life of the soul and leads it back to the Father, the Noetic principle. For fate ties the soul to natures that are inferior, that are perpetually unstable, flowing from one impermanency to another, and prevents it at every turn from obtaining a vision of immutable good. Intellectual union with the gods alone will anchor the soul to the support of its true felicity.

Proclus is as luminously clear on the same point:

"The one salvation of the soul herself, which is extended by the Demiurgus and which liberates her from the circle of generation, from abundant wanderings and an inefficacious life, is her return to the intellectual form, and a flight from every thing which naturally adheres to us from generation." [6]

For the soul, he continues, having been hurled *like seed* into the realms of generation, should cast aside the stubble and bark, as it were, which she accumulates about herself from contact with the fluctuations in these realms, and preserve her pristine purity. Purging herself from everything she touches, she should become the intellectual flower and fruit, delighting in the stable circles of sameness, rather than in the revolutions of difference. Having fallen from celestial harmony into the jangling diffusion of divine energies, she had, as Proclus says, become something belonging to an individual instead of to the universe. Departing from her connection with the lower irrational nature, and steering her course by reason, she will be led happily from her wanderings about the realms of sense, and from the passions which adhere to us from generation, back to the blissful contemplation of the one universal Life.

In a cosmic upper chamber the "old ones" and "the ones gone before" gather to welcome the return of the exiled souls. There are reception hosts who assemble to "welcome the pilgrims of the *night.*" The text of the *Ritual* gives some faint picture of the joy that thrills through the heavenly arches when the solar sons return triumphant from their long expatriation:

"The divine power hath risen and shineth in the horizon. . . . The Khus shine in heaven . . . for there is among them a form which is like unto themselves; and there are shouts and cries of gladness within the shrine, and the sounds of those who rejoice go round about through the underworld . . . and his majesty shineth as he shone in the primeval time, when the Utchat was first upon his head."

The script of Teta reads:

"Thou standest at the doors. . . . Khent-Ament-f comes forth to thee; he grasps thy hand and leads thee to heaven before thy father Keb [Seb], who rejoices to meet thee and gives thee his two hands. He kisses thee, he fondles thee, he pushes thee forward at the head of the indestructible spirits . . . thou keepest the festivals of the first day of the month and the festivals of the fifteenth day of the month, according to the decree which thy father Keb made for thee."

When Osiris, reborn as Horus, triumphs, "Joy goeth the rounds in Thinis," the celestial city; and even earth catches the repercussion of the jubilee in the heavens. The *Book of Enoch* relates that the same heavenly host that met to anoint the collective angelry that was preparing to come to earth to do evolution's work assembled again to welcome the returning victors, and that the reaches of farthest space were filled with angelic halleluiahs, as heaven and nature sang in unison.

Yet the paeans of heaven are hardly more intriguing than the more restrained pronouncements of Greek philosophy. Says Proclus:

There is "the race of men, who through a more excellent power and with piercing eyes, acutely perceive supernal light, to the vision of which they raise themselves above the clouds and darkness, as it were, of this lower world; and there abiding, despise every thing in those regions of sense; being no otherwise delighted with the place which is truly and properly their own, than he who, after many wanderings, is at length restored to his lawful country." [7]

The *night* of earthly sorrow breaks into the morn of heavenly rejoicing, for "joy cometh in the morning."

"The great and mighty gods cry out: 'He hath gotten the victory.'"

. . . .

> Earthly dust from off thee shaken,
> Soul immortal thou shalt waken,
> With thy last dim journey taken,—
> All through the *night*.

NOTES

CHAPTER I

None.

CHAPTER II

1. Quoted in the *Tibetan Book of the Dead,* by W. Y. Evans-Wentz, in a note to p. 234, from Origen's *Contra Celsum,* Book I, Ch. VIII.

CHAPTER III

1. For corroboration see such works as *The Six Books of Proclus on the Theology of Plato,* Iamblichus' *The Mysteries of the Egyptians, Chaldeans and Assyrians,* and Thomas Taylor's *Eleusinian and Bacchic Mysteries.*
2. Vide *From Orpheus to Paul,* by Vittorio D. Macchioro, a recognized world authority on Orphism.
3. See such a work as Lothrop Stoddard's *The Revolt Against Civilization.*
4. See Bouck White's *The Call of the Carpenter,* which builds an entire economic interpretation of the Gospels on such specious material in the texts.
5. Quoted by Edward Carpenter, *Pagan and Christian Creeds,* p. 22. Also in Glover's *Conflict of Religions in the Early Roman Empire.*
6. *Pagan and Christian Creeds,* p. 221.
7. Quoted in *Pagan and Christian Creeds,* p. 206.
8. *Pagan and Christian Creeds,* p. 130.
9. See Tertullian's *Apologia,* C. 16.
10. *Pagan and Christian Creeds,* p. 263.

CHAPTER IV

1. From *Hibbert Lectures,* p. 217.
2. Quoted in Preface to *Lectures on Ancient Philosophy,* by Manly P. Hall.
3. *Phaedrus,* p. 64.
4. Emile Baumann, *Saint Paul,* p. 275.
5. Quoted by Gerald Massey, *Ancient Egypt, the Light of the World,* p. 543.
6. E. A. Wallis Budge, *Osiris and the Egyptian Resurrection,* II, p. 30.
7. *Ancient Egypt, the Light of the World,* p. 33. As Massey is an authority frequently to be cited in this work, it is well to state that he was an English literary figure of some prominence in the latter half of the nineteenth century and the first years of the twentieth. He studied the Egyptian hieroglyphics for

forty years and had a force of transcribers employed in his later years of investigation to assemble the material from the monuments, tombs and papyri. His interpretation of Egyptian writings has been all too largely ignored by savants, yet he has the merit of having approached the task with a mind free from scholastic, theological or conventional biases, which have so utterly blinded the discernment and vitiated the conclusions of orthodox authorities. It is permissible for us to state that it was his works that opened our eyes to the hidden meaning under the material, when the works of more accredited specialists in the field had left us without a single enlightening hint. Massey is the only scholar in whose hands the recondite Egyptian material begins to take on rational significance. All the others leave it resembling unintelligible nonsense. Several important misconceptions in his interpretation are dealt with in the course of our work. Indeed we have used one or two of these as the most direct approach to a correction of the profound misconstructions which have vitiated the work of scholars in this field up to the present.

8. *Lecture on Luniolatry,* p. 2, by Gerald Massey.
9. Introduction to the *Book of the Dead,* p. xlvi.
10. *Osiris and the Egyptian Resurrection,* I, p. 101.
11. *Osiris and the Egyptian Resurrection,* I, p. 334.
12. *Osiris and the Egyptian Resurrection,* I, p. 370.
13. *Osiris and the Egyptian Resurrection,* I, p. 280.
14. Massey: *The Natural Genesis,* I, p. 431.
15. *Ancient Egypt, the Light of the World,* p. 29.
16. *Ancient Egypt, the Light of the World,* p. 30.
17. *Osiris and the Egyptian Resurrection,* II, p. 201.
18. *Myths and Legends: Egypt,* p. 271.
19. *Myths and Legends: Egypt,* p. 283.

CHAPTER V

1. Massey: *The Natural Genesis,* I, p. 168.
2. *The Mythical Interpretation of the Gospels,* T. J. Thorburn, p. 108.
3. Massey: *Ancient Egypt, the Light of the World,* p. 539.
4. *The Mythical Interpretation of the Gospels,* p. 109.

CHAPTER VI

None.

CHAPTER VII

1. *Eleusinian and Bacchic Mysteries,* p. 4.
2. *Eleusinian and Bacchic Mysteries,* p. 120.
3. The superior intellect of man is indeed the "god" spoken of. "Man's genius is a deity," said Heraclitus.
4. *Pagan and Christian Creeds,* p. 239.
5. See later explication of all lunar typology in the present work.

6. *The Six Books of Proclus on the Theology of Plato*, II, 275.

7. *Mysteries of the Egyptians, Chaldeans and Assyrians*, p. 93.

8. *Mysteries of the Egyptians, Chaldeans and Assyrians*, p. 312.

9. T. J. Thorburn: *The Mythical Interpretation of the Gospels*, p. 80 ff.

10. See Proclus: *The Six Books of Proclus on the Theology of Plato*, 2 Vols., wherein the two hundred and eleven principles of Greek theology are listed and expounded.

11. See later exposition of the Law of the Two Truths, *passim*.

12. *The Natural Genesis*, I, p. 332.

13. It should be understood that the Egyptians often used the names of kings for the character of the *Christos*, or the sun-god.

14. *Book of Hades*, First Division.

15. Detailed by Massey: *Ancient Egypt, the Light of the World*, p. 556.

16. See: *The Book of Job as a Greek Tragedy*, Horace M. Kallen.

17. *Ancient Egypt, the Light of the World*, p. 559.

18. This spiritual edict has often been sadly misconstrued by mystical devotees. It does not, to be sure, imply the stern negation of all carnal impulses, far less their total annihilation. The animal nature is not to be ruthlessly slain, but transformed into the likeness of the spiritual man.

19. *Greek Philosophy*.

CHAPTER VIII

1. Hindu, Tibetan, Platonic and other ancient systems are at one as to the accuracy of this item, difficult as it appears to us in our ignorance of cosmology and occult science.

2. Known also as Gandharvas, Suryas, Kumaras, Rudras, Adityas, Manasaputras, Agniswatha Pitris, and by some dozen or more other names.

3. *The Natural Genesis*, I, p. 315.

4. Hargrave Jennings: *The Rosicrucians*.

5. Quoted by Iamblichus: *The Mysteries of the Egyptians, Chaldeans and Assyrians*, p. 364.

6. *The Six Books of Proclus on the Theology of Plato*, II, p. 355.

7. Quoted by the editor in Iamblichus' *The Mysteries of the Egyptians, Chaldeans and Assyrians*, p. 345.

8. Article by Thomas Taylor in *Classical Journal*, Vol. 16, p. 338.

9. *Pagan and Christian Creeds*, p. 132.

10. Tylor: *Primitive Culture*, I, p. 469. (Edn. 1903.)

11. An approach to this viewpoint is notable in a recent study of great importance by the English scholar, Lord Raglan, in his book, *The Hero* (Oxford University Press). The work presents evidence that the masks worn in olden celebrations were those of animals.

12. Massey: *The Natural Genesis*, I, p. 74.

13. Massey: *The Natural Genesis*, I, p. 74.

14. A fuller elucidation of this theme will be given at a later place when the profounder significance of mummification is dealt with.

15. Massey: *Ancient Egypt, the Light of the World*, p. 231.

16. Massey: *Ancient Egypt, the Light of the World*, p. 211.

17. *Mysteries of the Egyptians, Chaldeans and Assyrians*, p. 355.

18. That part swayed by mere sense intimation and superficial impression.

19. *The Six Books of Proclus on the Theology of Plato*, II, p. 475.

20. *Mysteries of the Egyptians, Chaldeans and Assyrians*, p. 179.

21. *The Enneads*, I, Bk. VI.

22. Rather the impulse of sense uncensored by critical thought.

23. *Eleusinian and Bacchic Mysteries*, p. 103.

24. *The Six Books of Proclus on the Theology of Plato*, II, p. 456.

25. In Alexander Wilder's Introduction to the *Eleusinian and Bacchic Mysteries*, of Thomas Taylor, p. vxiii.

26. Be it noted, the use of the term "Gentiles" here bears out the interpretation (as the not fully humanized animal souls) given in a former place.

27. *Ancient Egypt, the Light of the World*, p. 479.

28. Given in verse in *The Book of Job as a Greek Tragedy*, Horace M. Kallen, p. 165 ff.

29. *Ancient Egypt, the Light of the World*, p. 508.

30. *Incantation Records*, Vol. II, p. 131.

31. *Eleusinian and Bacchic Mysteries*, p. 104.

32. Sekari, the god suffering diminution as he passed through incarnation.

CHAPTER IX

1. Mistaken for the defunct human, but really the descending god.

2. *Ancient Egypt, the Light of the World*, p. 846.

3. *Eleusinian and Bacchic Mysteries*, p. 7.

4. *Ancient Egypt, the Light of the World*, p. 152.

5. *Osiris and the Egyptian Resurrection*, II, p. 306.

6. Question mark is Budge's—showing how much the scholar has been confused by his failure to apprehend the technical theological use of the term by the Egyptians. Passage from the *Book of the Dead* cited by Budge.

7. Quoted by Thomas Taylor, *Eleusinian and Bacchic Mysteries*, p. 91 ff.

8. *Ancient Egypt, the Light of the World*, p. 706.

9. *Ancient Egypt, the Light of the World*, p. 868.

10. Quoted by Budge: *Osiris and the Egyptian Resurrection*, II, p. 8.

11. *Osiris and the Egyptian Resurrection*, II, p. 67.

12. *Osiris and the Egyptian Resurrection*, II, p. 69.

13. Cf. the raising of Lazarus.

14. *Myths and Legends: Egypt*, p. 121.

15. Later equated by Massey with Achor, the valley of Sheol, the Hebrew Hades.

16. *Ancient Egypt, the Light of the World*, p. 415.

17. *Ancient Egypt, the Light of the World*, p. 643-4.

18. Here would seem to be authentic rebuttal of the major premises of so

much Oriental philosophy which builds on the general thesis that the whole of life on earth is evil, "a calamity to be avoided at all costs." (Radhakrishnan: *Indian Philosophy*, Vol. I.)

CHAPTER X

1. *Ancient Egypt, the Light of the World*, p. 416.
2. Massey: *Ancient Egypt, the Light of the World*, p. 644.
3. *Ancient Egypt, the Light of the World*, p. 198.
4. Massey: *Ancient Egypt, the Light of the World*, p. 211.
5. Massey: *Ancient Egypt, the Light of the World*, p. 416.
6. *Ancient Egypt, the Light of the World*, p. 648.
7. Iu, a name of the Egyptian Messiah, equivalent to Jesus or Horus.
8. As we saw, equals the "cave" of the body.
9. Upper Egypt, by the uranographic transfer, denotes the spiritual man and his spiritual body, while Lower Egypt denotes the carnal man and his body of flesh.
10. Sheol may be taken as identical with the Egyptian Amenta.
11. So named because of the golden hues of the chrysalis.
12. *Ancient Egypt, the Light of the World*, p. 219.
13. *Ancient Egypt, the Light of the World*, p. 213.
14. *Ancient Egypt, the Light of the World*, p. 883.
15. *Ritual*, Ch. 173 (Renouf and Naville).
16. The specific significance of this term will appear in the chapter on Dismemberment.
17. *Ancient Egypt, the Light of the World*, p. 190.
18. Mead's Translation, p. 394.
19. *Ancient Egypt, the Light of the World*, p. 210.
20. *Ancient Egypt, the Light of the World*, p. 374.
21. *Ancient Egypt, the Light of the World*, p. 415.
22. *Ancient Egypt, the Light of the World*, p. 455.
23. Taylor: *Eleusinian and Bacchic Mysteries*, p. 105.
24. *Ancient Egypt, the Light of the World*, p. 709.
25. Budge: Introduction to the *Book of the Dead*, p. xc.
26. *Osiris and the Egyptian Resurrection*, II, p. 144.
27. Italics are Budge's.
28. *The Natural Genesis*, I, p. 525.

CHAPTER XI

1. Introduction to the *Book of the Dead*, p. lxxx.
2. Massey: *The Natural Genesis*, I, p. 108 ff
3. Massey: *Ancient Egypt, the Light of the World*, p. 154.
4. Massey: *Ancient Egypt, the Light of the World*, p. 479.
5. Taylor: *Eleusinian and Bacchic Mysteries*, p. 134.
6. *Eleusinian and Bacchic Mysteries*, p. 152.

7. Massey: *Ancient Egypt, the Light of the World*, p. 814.

8. Massey: *Ancient Egypt, the Light of the World*, p. 815.

9. Quoted by Edward Carpenter: *Pagan and Christian Creeds*, p. 239.

10. *Pagan and Christian Creeds*, p. 28 (note).

11. *Osiris and the Egyptian Resurrection*, I, p. 352.

12. *Ancient Egypt, the Light of the World*, p. 525.

13. Talbot: *The Legends of Ishtar; Records of the Past* (Vol. I).

14. *Ancient Egypt, the Light of the World*, p. 877.

15. *Ancient Egypt, the Light of the World*, p. 466.

CHAPTER XII

1. *I Corinthians* 10: 14 ff.

2. It is impossible to pass these verses by without a remark upon what is commented upon them by Sweitzer, one of the most popular European writers of the day on religious themes, in a recent work. He follows his quotation of John's verses with the statement that it is not the purpose of John's discourse to be understood; that its aim is solely to direct attention to the miracle which is to happen in connection with the bread in the future; and that it does not matter, therefore, that it should offend the multitude.

One is indeed permitted to ask: What is the poverty of modern spiritual discernment when it is frankly stated by a leading religious publicist that John's immortal verses are not meant to be understood? But, after all, is it to be wondered at that there should be complete befogging of vision when all but a few Docetic wings of Christian thought have been bent on taking the eating of the flesh and the drinking of the blood of the Son of Man in a physical sense? There has not seemed to be present the matured capacity to assimilate the entirely spiritual purport of the transaction.

3. *Ancient Egypt, the Light of the World*, p. 900.

4. *Osiris and the Egyptian Resurrection*, II, p. 32.

5. *Osiris and the Egyptian Resurrection*, I, p. 264.

6. Massey: *Ancient Egypt, the Light of the World*, p. 64.

7. Reclus: *Primitive Folk*, pp. 311-315.

8. Budge: Introduction to the *Book of the Dead*, p. xcix.

9. Proceedings: *Biblical Archaeology*, Dec. 2, 1884, p. 45.

10. *Ancient Egypt, the Light of the World*, p. 465.

11. *Ancient Egypt, the Light of the World*, p. 3.

12. *Eleusinian and Bacchic Mysteries*, p. 142.

13. *Ancient Egypt, the Light of the World*, p. 729.

14. *Ancient Egypt, the Light of the World*, p. 561.

15. *Mysteries of the Egyptians, Chaldeans and Assyrians*, p. 133.

16. In Iamblichus' *Mysteries of the Egyptians, Chaldeans and Assyrians*, p. 7.

17. *Lectures*, Vol. I, p. 383. Ed. 1862.

CHAPTER XIII

1. Massey: *The Natural Genesis*, I, p. 344.
2. *The Natural Genesis*, I, p. 529.
3. Massey: *The Natural Genesis*, I, p. 147.

CHAPTER XIV

1. Thomas Taylor: *Eleusinian and Bacchic Mysteries*, p. 126.
2. See R. H. Matthews: *The Wiradthuri Tribes*, Journal of Anthropology Inst., Vol. XXV, 1896.
3. If this term is the same as the Sanskrit *Atma*, it means the high spiritual essence, the soul of the soul of man.
4. *Ancient Egypt, the Light of the World*, p. 359.
5. *Pagan and Christian Creeds*, p. 129.
6. *Osiris and the Egyptian Resurrection*, II, p. 175.
7. *Mysteries of the Egyptians, Chaldeans and Assyrians*, p. 272.
8. *Pagan and Christian Creeds*, p. 129.
9. Taylor: *Eleusinian and Bacchic Mysteries*, p. 139.
10. *The Natural Genesis*, II, p. 78.
11. *Book of Hades*, Fifth Division, D.

CHAPTER XV

1. Westrop and Wake: *Phallism in Ancient Religions*, p. 47.
2. *The Natural Genesis*, I, p. 324.
3. *Osiris and the Egyptian Resurrection*, II, p. 236.

CHAPTER XVI

1. *Ancient Egypt, the Light of the World*, p. 131.
2. *Osiris and the Egyptian Resurrection*, II, p. 222.

CHAPTER XVII

None.

CHAPTER XVIII

1. *Ancient Egypt, the Light of the World*, p. 745.
2. *The Six Books of Proclus on the Theology of Plato*, II, p. 482.
3. *Foundation Truths of the Christian Religion*.
4. *Ancient Egypt, the Light of the World*, p. 335.
5. Massey: *Ancient Egypt, the Light of the World*, p. 771.

CHAPTER XIX

1. Introduction to the *Book of the Dead*, p. cvii.
2. *Ancient Egypt, the Light of the World*, p. 703.
3. *Ancient Egypt, the Light of the World*, p. 679.

CHAPTER XX

1. From an article in the *New York Times* of Nov. 25, 1932.
2. *The Rosicrucians: Their Rites and Mysteries;* Hargrave Jennings, p. 211.
3. From a papyrus rendered by M. Chabas.
4. Thomas Taylor: *Eleusinian and Bacchic Mysteries,* p. 145.
5. *Lecture on Luniolatry,* p. 14.
6. Latin: "Emits blood from the genitals."
7. *The Natural Genesis,* I, p. 44.
8. *The Six Books of Proclus on the Theology of Plato,* II, p. 148.

CHAPTER XXI

1. *Ancient Egypt, the Light of the World,* p. 210.
2. *Ancient Egypt, the Light of the World,* p. 210.
3. *Ancient Egypt, the Light of the World,* p. 639.
4. Introduction to the *Book of the Dead,* p. lxxxv.
5. *The Natural Genesis,* I, p. 127.
6. T. J. Thorburn: *The Mythical Interpretation of the Gospels,* p. 131. As Thorburn is antagonistic to the mythical interpretation, his data are therefore all the more valuable.
7. *Ancient Egypt, the Light of the World,* p. 844.
8. Plato mentions this as one of the hymns of Isis that were ten thousand years old.
9. The story of the rich man and Lazarus, the beggar, repeated in the Gospel of *Luke* (Ch. 16: 19), is told at length in the second tale of Kamuas, as Egyptian.

CHAPTER XXII

1. Introduction to the *Book of the Dead,* p. lxxxv.
2. *Myths and Legends: Egypt,* p. 126.
3. *Myths and Legends: Egypt,* p. 127.
4. *Ancient Egypt, the Light of the World,* p. 223.
5. *Mysteries of the Egyptians, Chaldeans and Assyrians,* p. 312.
6. *The Timaeus,* Lib. V, p. 33.
7. *The Six Books of Proclus on the Theology of Plato,* II, p. 272.

INDEX

A

Printed in the United States
53450LVS00002B/7-16

9 781564 591777